This book is concerned with the changes in religious thought and institutions from the late eleventh century to the third quarter of the twelfth. It concentrates on monks and nuns, but also takes into consideration hermits, recluses, wandering preachers, crusaders, penitents, and other less organized forms of religious life. In particular it studies the variety of reform movements, the relation of the reformers to each other and the outside world, and their spirituality and motivation as reflected in their writings and activities.

The work stands in close relation to the author's *Three Studies in Medieval Religious and Social Thought* (1995), which took what may be called a horizontal approach, studying three topics over the entire Middle Ages. The present work takes a vertical approach, looking at many aspects of reform during a comparatively short period. Together the two works show the relatively rapid change in religious life and sentiments in the twelfth century.

THE REFORMATION OF THE TWELFTH CENTURY

THE TREVELYAN LECTURES GIVEN AT
THE UNIVERSITY OF CAMBRIDGE, 1985

THE REFORMATION
OF THE
TWELFTH CENTURY

GILES CONSTABLE

Institute for Advanced Study, Princeton

CAMBRIDGE
UNIVERSITY PRESS

Published by the Press Syndicate of the University of Cambridge
The Pitt Building, Trumpington Street, Cambridge CB2 1RP
40 West 20th Street, New York NY 10011-4211, USA
10 Stamford Road, Oakleigh, Melbourne 3166, Australia

© Cambridge University Press 1996

First published 1996

Printed by Bell and Bain Ltd., Glasgow

A catalogue record for this book is available from the British Library

Library of Congress cataloguing in publication data

Constable, Giles
The reformation of the twelfth century/Giles Constable.
p.   cm.
Includes bibliographical references and index.
ISBN 0 521 30514 4
1. Monasticism and religious orders–Europe–History–Middle Ages, 600–1500.
2. Europe–Church history–600–1500.
3. Twelfth century.
I. Title.
BX2590.C66   1996
282'.4'09021–dc20   96–13516 CIP

ISBN 0 521 30514 4 hardback

WV

To
the memory of
three exemplars of
monastic scholarship

David Knowles
Kassius Hallinger
Jean Leclercq

CONTENTS

ILLUSTRATIONS

Between pp. 140-1

PREFACE

THE origins of this book go back to the edition of the letters of Peter the Venerable, upon which I started work in the autumn of 1952 and which was published in 1967. The letters touch on many of the subjects discussed here, and the reader should not be surprised that they are cited more frequently than any other source, except for the works of Bernard of Clairvaux. My first effort to bring together my ideas on the changes in religious life and spirituality in the twelfth century was in a lecture entitled 'The Monastic Crisis of the Twelfth Century' given at the State University of Iowa (now the University of Iowa) in the spring of 1957. Since then they have been developed in a number of publications, which are mentioned (perhaps too frequently) in the notes. This book is therefore the summation of many years of research, and in going back over my old notes I have been keenly aware of how my ideas have changed since I began working on the subject. They took their present form in the series of Trevelyan lectures given at Cambridge University in the spring of 1985. I am indebted not only to the committee that invited me but also to the audiences that heard (and occasionally commented on) the lectures and to Clare Hall, which extended its hospitality to my wife and myself during the tenure of the lectureship.

This work stands in a particularly close relation to my recently published *Three Studies in Medieval Religious and Social Thought*, which are concerned respectively with the interpretation of the story of Mary and Martha, the development of the ideal of the imitation of Christ, and the conceptual divisions of society in the Middle Ages. Each of these studies covers a long period, from late Antiquity to early modern times, but they concentrate on the eleventh and twelfth centuries, when there were some fundamental changes in the way men and women saw themselves and God. The present book deals with a broader spectrum of developments, including institutions as well as ideas, over a shorter period of time, extending approximately from the third quarter of the eleventh to the third quarter of the twelfth century. Whereas the *Three Studies* took a horizontal approach, as it were, looking at three specific topics over a long period, this book takes a vertical approach, looking at many aspects of religious life and thought during a century. The *Three*

Studies was intended to serve as a control for the *Reformation*, which runs the risk of exaggerating the extent of change in a comparatively brief period.

Since each chapter was planned as a lecture that could be understood by itself, there is some repetition, not all of which could be eliminated in the course of revision. The notes to each chapter are also self-contained, and, unless there is a specific citation to another chapter, the cross-references are to notes in the same chapter. The primary sources are identified in the notes. References to secondary works, which are listed in the bibliography, are given in chronological order (normally of their original publication) unless they relate to more than one passage in the text. It is inevitable in a work prepared over many years that some new editions of original texts and relevant secondary works have been missed. At the time I started only a few volumes of the *Sources chrétiennes* and none of the *Corpus Christianorum* had appeared. I have cited new editions when they have come to my attention, occasionally in conjunction with an older (sometimes more accessible) edition. I have tried to avoid technical terms that came into use after the twelfth century, such as chapter-general and laybrothers as a single word, though by late twelfth century *conversus* probably had a technical meaning in some houses. I have likewise not used the term Benedictine, which was unknown at the time and came into use only long afterwards. For most monks and nuns in the eleventh and twelfth centuries, however, *regularis* meant 'according to the rule of Benedict'.

The titles of primary sources are cited in the text in English (except for a few well-known terms like *Decretum* and *Summa*) and in the notes in Latin, but *Liber*, *Expositio*, and *Commentarium*, and the like, have been omitted for the sake of brevity.[1] References to the bible are to the Vulgate and to the Douai translation. The translations of Latin passages tend to be literal and use the same word in English for a repeated word in Latin, but 'and' has sometimes been silently added between phrases and before the last term in a series. Latin nouns and adjectives cited in the text have usually, though not invariably, been transposed into the nominative. Modern place-names have been used unless there are established English forms, like Brussels and Venice. Personal names are in Latin or in English but not in other modern vernacular languages. Henry is used rather than Henri, Enrico, or Heinrich; and Albinus, Benignus, and Saturninus are called by their Latin names, as are the churches and monasteries named for them, like the abbeys of St Albinus (St Aubin) at Angers in France and St Albans in England. Sometimes it is hard to tell, as with Geoffrey *Grossus* (Fat) and Ralph *Viridis* (Green), whether a second name is a family name or a personal nickname. Traditional spellings like Abelard, Gerhoh, and Hildebrand have been used owing to their familiarity, even when they were spelled differently at the time. Many people mentioned here are known by more than one name or from several places with which they were

---

[1] This and the following paragraphs resemble in wording the corresponding sections in the introduction to the *Three Studies*, which cover similar material.

associated during their lifetimes, like Ulrich of Regensburg, Cluny, and Zell; Hildebert of Lavardin, Le Mans, and Tours; Norbert of Xanten, Prémontré, and Magdeburg; Hugh of Amiens, Reading, and Rouen; Stephen of Muret and Grandmont; and Nigel of Canterbury, who is also known as Wireker and Longchamp(s). When in doubt I have preferred the birth-place (Lavardin and Xanten) unless another association is standard, as for Bernard of Clairvaux. Honorius *Augustodunensis* poses a special problem, since he appears to have deliberately concealed his identity. There is reason to believe that he was associated with Regensburg rather than Augsburg, but for the time being it seems wisest to continue to call him *Augustodunensis*. Orders named both for their founders and mother-house, like the Gilbertines (of Sempringham) and Norbertines (of Prémontré), are named here from the mother-house.

It is impossible even to begin to list the countless colleagues, students, and friends who have helped with this work. Over the years I have gathered information from many sources, and I regret that I failed to keep a list of everyone who helped in one way or another. The contributions of some of them are recognized in the notes, and the names of the others (as was said in medieval 'Books of Life') are known to God. I should say a word, however, about the three friends to whose memory this book is dedicated, each of whom made a particular contribution to its development. I started work on my edition of Peter the Venerable's letters at the suggestion and with the help of David Knowles, who was also the editor of the series in which my first book was published. Kassius Hallinger, who was a pioneer in the study of the comparative history of medieval monasticism, introduced me to the study of monastic customaries and invited me to contribute a volume to his *Corpus consuetudinum monasticarum*. The many publications of Jean Leclercq, a friend and mentor for over forty years, have thrown light on almost every aspect of the history of religious life in the Middle Ages and have guided me in much of my work. Finally, special thanks are owing to Frans van Liere and Hubertus Lutterbach, who helped to find books and check references; to Penny Perna, who typed successive versions of the text; and to Evhy and Pat, without whose help and support this book would never have been finished.

ABBREVIATIONS

Works cited with dates are listed in the Bibliography

AASS	*Acta sanctorum*, 3rd edn (Paris, Rome, and Brussels 1863–70)
AASS OSB	*Acta sanctorum ordinis s. Benedicti*, ed. Jean Mabillon, 2nd edn (Venice 1733–40)
Ampl. coll.	*Veterum scriptorum ... amplissima collectio*, ed. Edmond Martène and Ursin Durand (Paris 1724–33)
Anal. boll.	*Analecta bollandiana*
Anal. mon.	*Analecta monastica* (*Studia Anselmiana* 20, 31, 37, 41, 43, and 50; Rome 1948–62)
Anselm, ed. Schmitt	*S. Anselmi ... opera omnia*, ed. Franciscus Salesius Schmitt (Edinburgh 1946–61)
Baluze, *Miscellanea*	*Miscellaneorum libri VII*, ed. Etienne Baluze, 1st edn (Paris 1678–1715), and 2nd edn, ed. Giovanni Domenico Mansi (Lucca 1761–4) (2nd edn cited except when specified)
Bernard, ed. Leclercq	*Sancti Bernardi opera*, ed. Jean Leclercq, Charles H. Talbot, and Henri-Marie Rochais (Rome 1957–77)
Bernard, ed. Mabillon	*Sancti Bernardi ... opera omnia*, ed. Jean Mabillon (Paris 1839)
BHL	*Bibliotheca hagiographica latina* (Subsidia hagiographica 6; Brussels 1898–1901) and *Novum supplementum* (Subsidia hagiographica 70; Brussels 1986)
Bibl. Clun.	*Bibliotheca Cluniacensis*, ed. Martin Marrier and André Duchesne (Paris 1614)
BRG	Bibliotheca rerum germanicarum, ed. Philipp Jaffé (Berlin 1864–73)
Caesarius, *Dialogus*, ed. Strange	Caesarius of Heisterbach, *Dialogus miraculorum*, ed. Josef Strange (Cologne, Bonn, and Brussels 1851)

xv

Canivez, *Statuta*	*Statuta capitulorum generalium ordinis Cisterciensis*, I. *Ab anno 1116 ad annum 1220*, ed. Joseph-Marie Canivez (Bibliothèque de la Revue d'histoire ecclésiastique 9; Louvain 1933)
CC	*Corpus christianorum. Series latina* (Turnhout 1953ff)
CC:CM	*Corpus christianorum. Continuatio mediaevalis* (Turnhout 1966ff)
CCM	*Corpus consuetudinum monasticarum* (Siegburg 1963ff)
Chartes de Cluny	*Recueil des chartes de l'abbaye de Cluny*, ed. Auguste Bernard and Alexandre Bruel (Collection de documents inédits sur l'histoire de France; Paris 1876–1903)
CHFMA	Classiques de l'histoire de France au moyen âge (Paris 1923ff)
Clm	Codex latinus monacensis
Conc. oec. decreta	*Conciliorum oecumenicorum decreta*, ed. Giuseppe Alberigo a.o., 3rd edn (Bologna 1973)
Corpus, ed. Friedberg	*Corpus iuris canonici*, ed. Emil Friedberg (Leipzig 1879)
CSEL	*Corpus scriptorum ecclesiasticorum latinorum* (Vienna 1866ff)
CTSEEH	Collection de textes pour servir à l'étude et à l'enseignement de l'histoire (Paris 1886–1929)
DHGE	*Dictionnaire d'histoire et de géographie ecclésiastiques* (Paris 1912ff)
Duchesne	*Historiae Francorum scriptores*, ed. André Duchesne (Paris 1636–49)
Dugdale, *Monasticon*	William Dugdale, *Monasticon anglicanum*, ed. John Caley, Henry Ellis, and Bulkeley Bandinel (London 1817–30; repr. 1846)
Elizabeth of Schönau, ed. Roth	*Die Visionen der hl. Elisabeth und die Schriften der Aebte Ekbert und Emecho von Schönau*, ed. Friedrich W.E. Roth (Brünn 1884)
España sagrada	*España sagrada*, ed. Henrique Florez a.o. (Madrid 1747–1886)
FSI	Fonti per la storia d'Italia
GC	*Gallia christiana* (Paris 1715–1865)
Geoffrey of St Thierry	*Sermones* in MSS Reims, Bibl. mun., 581 and Paris, Bibl. nat., Lat. 13586, cited from the unpublished Harvard dissertation of Robert Sullivan
Guibert, *De vita sua*, ed. Bourgin	Guibert of Nogent, *Histoire de sa vie (1053–1124)*, ed. Georges Bourgin (CTSEEH 40; Paris 1907)

Herrgott, *Disciplina*	*Vetus disciplina monastica*, ed. Marquard Herrgott (Paris 1726)
Hist. litt.	*Histoire littéraire de la France* (Paris 1733ff)
Hugh of Kirkstall, *Narratio*, ed. Walbran	Hugh of Kirkstall, *Narratio de fundatione Fontanis monasterii*, in *Memorials of the Abbey of St Mary of Fountains*, ed. John R. Walbran a.o. (Surtees Society 42, 67, and 130; Durham, London, and Edinburgh 1863–1918), I, 1–128
Idungus, ed. Huygens	Robert B.C. Huygens, *Le moine Idung et ses deux ouvrages 'Argumentum super quatuor quaestionibus' et 'Dialogus duorum monachorum'* (Biblioteca degli 'Studi medievali' 11; Spoleto 1980) = *Studi medievali*, 3 S. 12 (1972), pp. 291–470
JK, JL, JE	Philipp Jaffé, *Regesta pontificum Romanorum*, 2nd edn (under the direction of Wilhelm Wattenbach) Ferdinand Kaltenbrunner (JK: to 590), Paul Ewald (JE: 590–882), and Samuel Löwenfeld (JL: 882–1198) (Leipzig 1885–8)
Libellus, ed. Constable	*Libellus de diversis ordinibus et professionibus qui sunt in aecclesia*, ed. Giles Constable and Bernard Smith (OMT; Oxford 1972)
Mansi	*Sacrorum conciliorum nova et amplissima collectio*, ed. Giovanni Domenico Mansi (Florence and Venice 1759–98; repr. 1901–27)
Max. bibl.	*Maxima bibliotheca veterum patrum*, ed. Marguerin de la Bigne (Lyons 1677)
MC	[Nelson's] Medieval Classics (London and Edinburgh 1949ff; cont. as MT and OMT)
Medieval Monasticism	Giles Constable, *Medieval Monasticism: A Select Bibliography* (Toronto Medieval Bibliographies 6; Toronto and Buffalo 1976)
MGH	*Monumenta Germaniae historica*
	Briefe *Die Briefe der deutschen Kaiserzeit* (Weimar 1949ff)
	Dipl. *Diplomata regum et imperatorum Germaniae* (Hanover, Berlin, and Weimar 1879ff)
	Epp. *Epistolae* in quarto (Berlin 1887ff)
	Libelli *Libelli de lite imperatorum et pontificum saeculis XI et XII conscripti* (Hanover 1891–7)
	SS *Scriptores* in folio (Hanover 1826ff)

	SS rerum Merov. Scriptores rerum Merovingicarum (Hanover 1884ff)
	SSRG *Scriptores rerum Germanicarum in usum scholarum separatim editi* (Hanover and Berlin 1871ff)
Miraeus–Foppens	A. Miraeus (Aubert le Mire), *Opera diplomatica et historica*, ed. J.F. Foppens, 2nd edn (Louvain and Brussels 1723–48)
Monuments, ed. Guignard	*Les monuments primitifs de la régle cistercienne*, ed. Philippe Guignard (Dijon 1878)
MT	[Nelson's] Medieval Texts (cont. of MC)
Nova bibl.	*Nova bibliotheca manuscriptorum librorum*, ed. Philippe Labbe (Paris 1657)
OMT	Oxford Medieval Texts (cont. of MC and MT)
Ordericus Vitalis, *Historia ecclesiastica*, ed. Chibnall	*The Ecclesiastical History of Ordericus Vitalis*, ed. Marjorie Chibnall (OMT; Oxford 1969–80)
Papsturkunden	*Papsturkunden* volumes in the *Nachrichten der Gesellschaft der Wissenschaften zu Göttingen*
Peregrinus, *Historia*, ed. Salmon	Peregrinus of Fontaines-les-Blanches, *Historia monasterii beatae Mariae de Fontanis Albis*, in *Recueil de chroniques de Touraine*, ed. André Salmon (Societé archéologique de Touraine: Collection de documents sur l'histoire de Touraine 1; Tours 1854), pp. 257–91
Peter the Venerable, ed. Constable	*The Letters of Peter the Venerable*, ed. Giles Constable (Harvard Historical Studies 78; Cambridge, Mass., 1967)
Pez, *Thesaurus*	*Thesaurus anecdotorum novissimus*, ed. Bernhard Pez (Augsburg and Graz 1721–9)
PG	*Patrologia graeca*, ed. Jacques Paul Migne (Paris 1857–76)
Pitra, *Anal. nov.*	Jean Baptiste Pitra, *Analecta novissima spicilegii Solesmensis* (Paris 1885–8)
PL	*Patrologia latina*, ed. Jacques Paul Migne (Paris 1841–64)
PL Suppl.	*Patrologiae cursus completus: Supplementum*, ed. Adalbert G. Hamman (Paris 1958–74)
Reg. Ben.	*Regula Benedicti*
Reginald of Durham, *Vita Godrici*, ed. Stevenson	Reginald of Durham, *Libellus de vita et miraculis s. Godrici, heremitae de Finchale* [ed. Joseph Stevenson] (Surtees Society 20; London and Edinburgh 1847) (*BHL* 3599)

Renaissance and Renewal	*Renaissance and Renewal in the Twelfth Century*, ed. Robert L. Benson and Giles Constable with Carol D. Lanham (Cambridge, Mass., 1982)
Repertorium	*Repertorium fontium historiae medii aevi* (Rome 1962ff)
Reprehensio, ed. Wilmart	André Wilmart, 'Une riposte de l'ancien monachisme au manifeste de saint Bernard', *Rev. bén.* 36 (1934), pp. 296–344
Rescriptum, ed. Leclercq	Jean Leclercq, 'Nouvelle réponse de l'ancien monachisme aux critiques des Cisterciens', *Rev. bén.* 67 (1957), pp. 77–94
Rev. bén.	*Revue bénédictine*
RHGF	*Recueil des historiens des Gaules et de la France* (Paris 1738–1904)
Rouleaux des morts	*Rouleaux des morts du IXe au XVe siècle*, ed. Léopold Delisle (Société de l'histoire de France; Paris 1866)
RS	Rolls Series (= Chronicles and Memorials of Great Britain and Ireland during the Middle Ages; London 1858–96)
SA	Studia Anselmiana (Rome 1933ff)
SC	Sources chrétiennes (Paris 1941ff)
Stegmüller	Friedrich Stegmüller, *Repertorium biblicum medii aevi* (Madrid 1950–80)
Stephen of Tournai, ed. Desilve	*Lettres d'Etienne de Tournai*, ed. Jules Desilve (Valenciennes and Paris 1893)
Textes de Cîteaux	*Les plus anciens textes de Cîteaux*, ed. Jean de la Croix Bouton and Jean Baptiste Van Damme (Cîteaux-Commentarii Cistercienses: Studia et documenta 2; Achel 1974)
Thes. nov.	*Thesaurus novus anecdotorum*, ed. Edmond Martène and Ursin Durand (Paris 1717)
Vies des saints	*Vies des saints et des bienheureux* (Paris 1935–59)
Vita Gileberti Sempinghamensis, ed. Foreville and Keir	*The Book of St Gilbert*, ed. Raymonde Foreville and Gillian Keir (OMT; Oxford 1987) (*BHL* 3530)
Vita Stephani Obazinensis, ed. Aubrun	*Vie de Saint Etienne d'Obazine*, ed. and tr. Michel Aubrun (Faculté des lettres et sciences humaines de l'Université de Clermont-Ferrand: Publications de l'Institut d'études du Massif Central 6; Clermont-Ferrand 1970) (*BHL* 7916)

William of St Thierry, William of St Thierry, *Un traité de la vie solitaire,*
Ep. ad fratres de ed. Marie-Madeleine Davy (Etudes de philoso-
Monte Dei, ed. Davy phie médiévale 29; Paris 1940)
Zimmermann Alfons Zimmermann, *Kalendarium benedictinum*
(Metten 1933–8)

1

INTRODUCTION

'THE title of this work,' said Sir Walter Scott at the beginning of *Waverley*, 'has not been chosen without the grave and solid deliberation which matters of importance demand of the prudent.' He went on to examine, with elaborate sarcasm, the impression made on a potential reader by the title and, even more, the subtitle of a book, which was 'a matter of much more difficult election', he said, because it pledged the author 'to some special mode of laying his scene, drawing his characters, and managing his adventures'.[1] Scott was referring to a work of fiction, but his words are equally applicable to historical writings, of which the titles both reflect the views of the writers and shape the expectations of readers. The Roman Empire is inseparable from its decline and fall owing to Gibbon, and the civilization of fifteenth-century Italy from the Renaissance owing to Burckhardt. Haskins's *Renaissance of the Twelfth Century* was part of what has been called the revolt of the medievalists, who resented the implicit aspersions cast on the Middle Ages by the application of the term renaissance exclusively to a later age, and who continue to find other renaissances all over medieval Europe.[2] The same is to some extent true of the title of the present work, which applies to the twelfth century a term commonly associated with the sixteenth.

The first version of this book, which was presented as a lecture almost forty years ago, was entitled 'The Monastic Crisis of the Twelfth Century'. 'Crisis' is a fashionable term in current scholarly writing and has been used in the titles of countless works on history, sociology, and current events.[3] It comes from the Greek term for division or separation and entered historical usage from medicine, where it implies a turning point or decisive moment. Germain Morin used the term in the subtitle to his article on the hermit Rainald and Ivo of Chartres, published in 1928, and since then many scholars have referred to a crisis of monasticism or monastic crisis in the twelfth century, expanding

---

[1] Walter Scott, *Waverley; or, 'Tis Sixty Years Since*, was first published at Edinburgh in 1814. The passages cited are found in the Introductory to chapter 1 (Harmondsworth 1985, p. 33).
[2] Ferguson (1948) and the introduction, especially p. xxvii, to *Renaissance and Renewal* (1982).
[3] Starn (1971), p. 15, said that in the twentieth century the term crisis became 'a ready-made catchword for the dramatic historical pressure points and processes that have been increasingly on the mind of the historian and his public'.

Morin's use of cenobitism to cover all forms of monastic life.[4] It is a vivid but not, in its strict sense, an appropriate term, since it implies that monasticism was suffering from a fundamental illness from which it had to recover. It was rarely used in the Middle Ages and never, so far as is known, to describe an historical situation.

A sense of division and disorder in the church, however, was expressed by various writers of the late eleventh and twelfth centuries. Pope Urban II, speaking of the foundation of Cîteaux, expressed his fear of 'a dreadful schism in the house of God', and abbot Richard of Ely wrote to Herbert of Losinga in the early twelfth century that the devil had aroused 'schisms [and] dissensions in the holy church . . . as if in conflict with our army', that is, of monks.[5] Peter the Venerable called it a monastic schism (*schisma monastica*), and the terms schism and *scissura* were used by Rupert of Deutz, Reimbald of Liège, Potho of Prüm, and in the treatise *On the various orders and professions that are in the church*.[6] Others were conscious of a sense of confusion. The author of the *Antigraphum Petri* cited Bernard's description of the state of the church in *On consideration* soon after it was written, saying 'Behold what he felt and said about this, not as you say "order", but as he himself says, and is indeed true, this "confusion".'[7] The prelates gathered at the Fourth Lateran Council in 1215 prohibited new types of religious life 'lest an excessive diversity of religions should introduce serious confusion into the church of God'.[8] Schism would be a better term than crisis in the title of this work because it refers to a split rather than a turning point, but for modern readers it smacks of the division between the Latin and Greek churches and of the ecclesiastical quarrels of the late Middle Ages.

---

[4] Morin (1928). Cf. Dereine (1948a); Leclercq (1958a); Cantor (1960–1); Châtillon (1977), pp. 5–8; Van Engen (1986b), pp. 269–72, who questioned the use of the term crisis; Resnick (1988b), p. 118, who interpreted 'crisis' as 'a changed and diminished valuation of Benedictine life'; and Morris (1989), p. 71, calling the term 'monastic crisis' misleading 'if it is understood as describing a failure of traditional monasticism'. Tellenbach (1993), pp. 341–7, included a section entitled 'A crisis in western monasticism'.

[5] Ordericus Vitalis, *Historia ecclesiastica*, VIII, 26, ed. Chibnall, IV, 322, and Herbert of Losinga, *Ep.* 59, ed. R. Anstruther (Caxton Society; Brussels and London 1846), p. 103, and tr. in Goulburn and Symonds (1878), I, 262.

[6] Rupert of Deutz, *In regulam s. Benedicti*, IV, 1, in *PL*, CLXX, 525D ('Nonne hujusmodi contentiones habere schismata facere est?'); Reimbald, *Ep. de schismate Anacletiano*, in *CC:CM*, IV, 118–21; Potho of Prüm, *De statu domus Dei*, 3, in *Max. bibl.*, XXI, 500E ('Scissura mentium assiduo illorum unanimitatem et quietem rumpere uidentur'); *Libellus*, II, 18, ed. Constable, p. 36; Peter the Venerable, *Ep.* 28, ed. Constable, I, 290 ('si inquam scismatis monastici haec sola et tota erat occasio . . . in cordium uestrorum iam uetus scissura unietur?'). On the terms *schisma*, *scissura*, and *dissensio*, see Petré (1936), pp. 320–5.

[7] Bernard, *De consideratione*, V, 20, ed. Leclercq, III, 447–8, and *Antigraphum Petri*, ed. Arnold Fayen, in *Compte rendu des séances de la Commission royale d'histoire [de Belgique] ou recueil de ses bulletins* 68 (5 S. 9) (1899), pp. 299–300. See Goossens (1983), pp. 105–6.

[8] IV Lateran (1215), 13, in *Conc. oec. decreta*, p. 242. This decree has been seen as an attack on the new mendicant orders.

The terms most frequently used for religious change in the eleventh and twelfth centuries were *reformare* and *reformatio*.[9] These, like reform today, were multi-purpose words and could refer either to restoration and revival, in a backwards-looking sense, or to rebirth and re-formation, as a forwards-looking change.[10] In its traditional Christian sense, as Paul used it in Romans 12.2, *reformatio* described the ideal of personal renewal, but in the eleventh and twelfth centuries it was also applied to institutions, including the church, the empire, and society as a whole. It is a less exclusively cultural and secular term than renaissance, as it is used today, and is thus a reminder that the movement of renewal included religious life and institutions as well as intellectual and artistic developments. It involved Gregory VII and Bernard of Clairvaux as well as Bernard of Chartres, John of Salisbury, and poets like Marbod of Rennes, Baldric of Dol, and Hildebert of Lavardin, all of whom were churchmen as well as poets and took an active interest in religious life. There was no clear-cut distinction in the twelfth century between a secular renaissance and a religious reformation, or, in their attitudes towards reform, between the clergy and the laity, among whom were found some of the strongest supporters of reform. 'Unreformed' has a sinister ring, but not all institutions needed reform, and in some parts of Europe the work of reformers, and especially their insistence on the separation of ecclesiastical and secular authority, may have done less good than harm.[11]

The choice of the term 'reformation' for the title of this work is intended to convey this contemporary sense of change rather than to challenge the concepts of either the twelfth-century renaissance or of the sixteenth-century Reformation, with a capital R. It can indeed be argued that the developments in religious life and sentiment in the twelfth century were as important as those in secular thought and culture, and that in many respects they prepared the way for the history of the church in the late Middle Ages and early modern period, but the questions here are not (as Christopher Brooke put it) 'whether the Reformation really took place in the twelfth or the sixteenth century', or what exactly is meant by 'reformation' in an historical context.[12] The point is, rather, that the changes in religious attitudes and institutions in the twelfth century justify using the term reformation beside and almost

---

[9] See the articles by Gerhart Ladner and Giles Constable, in *Renaissance and Renewal* (1982), pp. 1–67, and Borst (1992), p. 86, who said, referring to the twelfth-century effort to revitalize a model past, that 'Then it was called a reform, later it was to be called a Renaissance: changing the present state of affairs to regain that which is always valid.' Morris (1989), p. 179, said that the term Renaissance 'was not used at the time'.

[10] Peter the Venerable, for instance, used the term *reformare* in both senses in his *Stat.* 2 and 29, in *CCM*, VI, 43 and 65.

[11] The mixture of lay and ecclesiastical authority that characterized Carolingian society was only subsequently seen as an abuse: see Miccoli (1966a), pp. 3–4, and especially Magnou-Nortier (1974), pp. 533–8, who stressed the damage done by the so-called reform movement.

[12] Brooke (1968), p. 129.

as part of renaissance. This book is not designed as a contribution to the seductive game of precursorism, which involves a selective search in the past for anticipations of what happened later, but will look at the twelfth century in itself and, as much as possible, in its own terms. Though there are occasional looks both backwards and forwards along the spectrum of history, these are in order to illuminate the period itself and not to assert its importance as the culmination of what went before or as the harbinger of what came later in the near or the distant future.

The eleventh and twelfth centuries, and especially the years between about 1040 and 1160, were a period of intense, rapid, and to a high degree self-conscious change in almost all aspects of human thought and activity. Two long lifetimes, like those of Hugh of Cluny, who lived from 1024 to 1109, and Gilbert of Sempringham, who died in 1189 at a reputed age of over a hundred, covered the entire period, and if Gilbert as a young man had talked with Hugh before his death, he could have told much of the story. In recent years, scholars have tended to see this time as a single period of reform divided into four subperiods, each lasting about thirty years and representing a distinct phase of thought and action.[13] The first, from about 1040 to 1070, was concerned with the moral reform of the clergy, especially simony and celibacy; the second, from 1070 to 1100, is associated particularly with popes Gregory VII and Urban II and concentrated on the freedom of the church from lay control and on the supremacy of the pope within the church;[14] the third, from 1100 to 1130, was transitional in character and saw both the last phase of the controversy over investiture and a growing emphasis on monasticism, which developed in the fourth and final period, from 1130 to 1160, into an intense concern with the nature of religious life and personal reform of all Christians.[15] To put it this way is a gross simplification, since the four phases or generations overlapped at many points. People living at different times and in different parts of Europe had their own concerns, which did not always coincide with those of their contemporaries. But at the centre of each period there was a

---

[13] Joachim of Fiore applied the concept of generations to all history in his *Concordia novi ac veteris testamenti*, III, 1, 1, and IV, 1, 1–46, ed. E. Randolph Daniel, in *Transactions of the American Philosophical Society* 73.8 (1983), pp. 209–14 and 312–404. See Peter Classen, in *Renaissance and Renewal* (1982), pp. 412–13; Jean Leclercq, ibid., p. 70, for the history of theology in the eleventh and twelfth centuries; pp. 38–9 below on Cistercian history, art, and architecture, and pp. 299–300 below for other works on the idea of generations. For shifts of interest in propagandistic writings, see Constable (1983), pp. 189–91.

[14] The terms Investiture Controversy and Gregorian Reform are less used now than in the past, but they were not unknown at the time. Suger, *Vita Ludovici Grossi regis*, 29, ed. and tr. Henry Waquet (CHFMA 11; Paris 1929), p. 215, said that the Lateran Council of 1123 was for 'compositioni pacis de querela inuestiturarum'. On the importance of the autonomy of the church, see Fornasari (1986).

[15] According to White (1960), p. 321, 'the Bernardine epoch', which came between the Gregorian period and the 'era of papal monarchialism', marked 'an interruption of or deviation from the line of development inaugurated by the Gregorian Reform'. On the concept of generations, see pp. 299–300 below.

concentration on particular issues, which can be seen in the activities and writings of both the reformers and their opponents, and which seems to set it off from the preceding and following periods. It would be foolish to insist on this point of generational change, but it is a helpful way of looking at the period of reform as a whole. Seen through the eyes of Hugh of Cluny and Gilbert of Sempringham, Hugh saw the first two generations, when the primary emphasis was on the church and on clerical reform; and Gilbert the second two, which emphasized religious life and personal reform, though he lived on into a fifth generation, at the end of the twelfth century, and saw many compromises in the initiatives of his youth, including his own order of Sempringham, and many new developments as the attitudes on all sides hardened.

The second half of the eleventh century and first half of the twelfth was one of the most significant periods in what may be called the social history of Christianity, when traditional institutions and attitudes were stretched to the maximum and made to accommodate new forms of life and new sentiments. It was marked by what Lucien Febvre, referring to France in the sixteenth century, called 'a profound revolution in religious sentiment', which must be studied not simply in terms of the church, theology, or politics but in a broad context of historical change and as part of the search by people at that time for a religion suited to new spiritual needs and social conditions.[16] It was an age of experiment, enterprise, flexibility, and tolerance for both new ventures and new ideas. It is easy for historians to remember only its successes – the great religious orders and profound spiritual writings – and to forget the failures, of which many vanished without leaving a trace. The reform movement included some strange characters and curious institutions, which challenged and sometimes flouted the accepted standards of society and behaviour and yet which were on the whole tolerated and even admired. A few of the reformers touched on sensitive issues of doctrine and discipline and got into trouble with the ecclesiastical authorities, and many of them encountered the hostility of individual bishops and monasteries, but only a few individuals or small groups either questioned the sacraments or openly defied the authority of the church.

Heresy lay for the most part on the borders of the religious movements that will be studied here, and fear of heresy did not become a major concern until the second half of the twelfth century.[17] For most churchmen orthodoxy and heresy formed a continuum of religious belief and practice, and the line between them became clear only when established interests were threatened, as at Antwerp, where the Premonstratensian house of St Michael was established in 1124 specifically to combat the heresy of Tanchelm, whose poisoned

[16] Febvre (1957), pp. 26 and 69.
[17] Grundmann (1961), pp. 531 and 537; Moore (1970), esp. p. 35; Suttor (1985); and Lambert (1992), p. 55, who said that heresy as a 'fully international movement' appeared in the 1140s.

words, according to the foundation charter, 'turned many people away from the faith and from the sacraments of the church'.[18] A century earlier, in 1025, some heretics who were summoned before a council at Arras declared:

> Our law and discipline which we receive from our master seem at variance, if considered with care, with neither the evangelical decrees nor the apostolic sanctions. For it consists of this: to leave the world, to keep the flesh from its desires, to provide food by the labour of the hands, to seek harm to no one, and to show love to all whom the zeal of this our intention holds.

These are unexceptional sentiments, aside from a hint of exclusiveness (which was also not unknown in orthodox circles), and the accused would have got into no trouble had they not gone on to deny the validity and need of baptism and to draw other conclusions that were clearly unacceptable to the authorities.[19] They were exceptional in doing so, however, and most reformers would have agreed with the first part of their programme. Dualism was always a danger, and a few preachers, like Peter of Bruys, may have come under dualist influence from the east, but the Cathars, Albigensians, and other dualist heretics did not appear in force until the end of the twelfth century. It is hard to classify even some of Peter's followers, such as Henry of Lausanne, who in spite of dualist elements in his teachings resembled many orthodox reformers and wandering preachers. Arnold of Brescia was likewise primarily a reformer, who got into difficulties with the church owing to his political views.

There was a common concern at that time, and especially in the period from about 1100 to 1160, with the nature of religious life and the ideal of personal perfection. A set of values as well as a way of life, embodied in various institutions, was at the heart of the movement of reform, which can be seen as an effort to monasticize first the clergy, by imposing on them a standard of life previously reserved for monks, and then the entire world.[20] The influence of monasticism permeated society. Many of the popes and cardinals were monks,[21] and monastic values and institutions were carried into every corner of Europe by hermits, pilgrims, and wandering preachers, for whom the Alps, the Apennines, and the Pyrenees were points of attraction, rather than barriers, and for whom any road or river offered an opportunity to pen-

---

[18] Miraeus–Foppens, I, 85. On Tanchelm, see Wakefield and Evans (1969), pp. 97–101, and Lambert (1992), pp. 50–2, who said that Tanchelm, like Arnold of Brescia, showed 'how the ferment of reform ideals in the post-Gregorian age could lead to heresy'.

[19] Mansi, XIX, 425D, and (better) Fredericq (1889–1906), I, 4, and tr. in Wakefield and Evans (1969), p. 84. See Lambert (1992), pp. 22–5.

[20] See, for instance, Bonizo of Sutri, *De vita christiana*, ed. Ernst Perels (Texte zur Geschichte des römischen und kanonischen Rechts im Mittelalter 1; Berlin 1930) and, among secondary works, Genicot (1983), p. 149, and Laudage (1984), p. 113, on the Gregorian efforts to 'monasticize' the church, and Gryson (1980), esp. p. 176, and Gaudemet (1982) on the 'crusade' for clerical celibacy.

[21] Hofmeister (1961b).

etrate further into new lands. A nobleman like Leofric in eleventh-century England led an almost monastic life, drinking little, praying in secret places when others slept, and hearing two or more masses a day.[22] Later the practice of systematic prayer was spread among the laity by books of hours. 'No one can finally be saved', wrote Gilbert Crispin, 'unless he follows the life of a monk as much as he can'; the Cistercian Everard of Ypres said to an imaginary stranger who had no knowledge of monasticism that 'You are a true monk by virtue of your mind, although not by the profession of your habit'; and the great churchman and preacher James of Vitry declared in the early thirteenth century that not only those who renounced the world and led a religious life should be called regulars but also 'all the faithful of Christ serving the Lord under the rule of the Gospel and ordained under the one highest and supreme abbot', that is, God.[23] The application of monastic life to all people, and the interiorization of monastic values and spirituality, eventually led to monasticizing everyone and destroying the special position held by monks in the early Middle Ages.

Monasticism in the Middle Ages was more loosely defined than it is today. As a term, indeed, like most of the modern -isms, it did not exist, and the closest equivalents were the monastic *institutio*, *nomen*, *professio*, or *propositum*, which has been called 'a general commitment to the monastic life'.[24] *Monachatus* was sometimes used for the state of being a monk, and *monachare* for becoming a monk, but the commonest term was *religio*, which was equivalent to monastic observance and which Aquinas defined as the obligation by which people bound themselves to serve God.[25] Religion was a way of life, a *conversatio* or *ordo*, not a system of belief, and a *religiosus* was a man who led a religious life and who might also be a *regularis* and a *claustralis* if he followed a known rule, in particular that of Benedict, and lived in a monastery.[26] The canon lawyer Henry of Susa (Hostiensis) distinguished between regular and religious in a narrow and a broad sense (*largo modo*). A regular religious (either a monk

---

[22] *Visio Leofrici*, ed. Arthur S. Napier, in *Transactions of the Philological Society*, 1907–10 (1910), pp. 182–5.

[23] Leclercq (1983), p. 121; Häring (1953), p. 247, and (1955); and James of Vitry, *Historia occidentalis*, 34, ed. John F. Hinnebusch (Spicilegium Friburgense 17; Fribourg 1972), p. 165. See pp. 268–9 below. See also *De vita vere apostolica* (which has been attributed to both Rupert of Deutz and Honorius *Augustodunesis*), 4, in *Ampl. coll.*, IX, 1012.

[24] Yeo (1982), p. 85. For Waddell (1987), p. 82, the *propositum* was 'ascetism as a way of life and rule of conduct'. On the terms monasticism, of which the earliest use recorded in the *Oxford English Dictionary* is 1795, and monachology, which refers to the personal as contrasted with the institutional side of monastic life, see Antin (1964).

[25] Thomas Aquinas, *Contra impugnantes Dei cultum et religionem*, 1, in *Opera omnia*, XLI A (Rome 1970), p. 53, and tr. John Procter (London 1902), p. 51. In the early church *religio* was used, together with *sanctitas*, *studium*, and other terms, to translate the Greek *ascesis*, according to Mohrmann (1962), pp. 185–6; but in the Middle Ages it was equivalent to monastic observance: see Grégoire (1970) and Waddell (1987), pp. 80–2. According to Bieler (1985), p. 363, it began to be used for a system of faith and worship in the late twelfth and thirteenth centuries.

[26] Grégoire (1970), p. 417 ('Le *religiosus* sera celui qui vit ou possède une *religio*'); Hourlier (1974), p. 11; and Van Engen (1986a), p. 546 and n. 93. In effect it was a synonym for monk.

or canon), as distinct from a cleric or lay man, he said, 'was subjected to the authority of a superior by the expression (*emissio*) of profession or by paternal devotion', that is, by being given to a religious house as a child, 'and was bound to live regularly', that is, according to a rule. 'Someone who lives in a holy and religious way in his own house, although not professed, is also called a religious in a broad sense', Hostiensis continued. This included a lay man who promised to live chastely with his wife (and not to remarry if she died), renounced his property, and promised obedience, but not a peasant who simply changed his clothing, received some sign (*certum signum*), and exercised hospitality, but who remained married and owned property.[27]

The origin and precise meaning of the term *monachus* is a subject of uncertainty among scholars.[28] It was called 'a term of mystery' in the eleventh-century *On preserving the unity of the church*, and its etymology was much discussed in the twelfth century.[29] Most writers agreed that the first part (*mona-*) meant 'one' in the sense of alone, single, or, more rarely, united, but they were less certain about the second part (*-chus*), which they thought might come from *cor* or *oculus*, since monks were supposed to have one heart, like the apostles in Acts 4.32, and a single eye, as in the Gospels, which saw no evil and was directed toward heaven. The oneness or singularity of the monk might be of habitation, spirit, or way of life, like celibacy, and *monachus* sometimes meant almost the same as *sanctus* or holy in its root meaning of separated. Ratherius of Verona in the tenth century said that an abbot should be 'of all monks . . . the most like a monk (*monachissimus*)'.[30] *Claustralis* was a more specific term and was sometimes contrasted with *obedientialis*, which referred to a monk who held an office in the monastery or who lived in a cell or priory, which was called an *obedientia*. *Frater*, on the other hand, which was later adopted by the mendicants, was a broader term and applied in the eleventh and twelfth centuries to members not only of religious communities but also of the many types of associations known as *fraternitates*, *confraternitates*, and other names.[31] The usual term for women in religious life was *sanctimonialis*, which derived from *sanctimonium*, meaning piety, but *monacha*, *soror*, *nonna*, and later *dame* were also used.[32]

---

[27] Henry of Susa (Hostiensis), *Summa aurea*, III, 1–3 (Venice 1586), coll. 1107–8.

[28] Adam (1953–4); Leclercq (1961b), pp. 7–38; Morard (1973); and Judge (1977), citing a document of 324 as the earliest use of *monachos* for monk.

[29] *De unitate ecclesiae conservanda*, II, 42, in MGH, *Libelli*, II, 277. See Van Haeften (1644), pp. 265–7, and Lunardi (1970), pp. 66–8.

[30] Ratherius of Verona, *Praeloquia*, V, 32, in *CC:CM*, XLVIA, 167. See Adam (1927), p. 174.

[31] Other terms for collective life were *amicitia*, *caritas*, *collegium*, *compagnia*, *gilda*, *pax*, *schola*, *societas*, and *sodalitas*: see Michaud-Quantin (1970a), pp. 179–98 and, for the early Middle Ages, Wielers (1959), esp. pp. 4–26 on *pax*, 81–98 on *amicitia*, and 98–118 on *fraternitas*. See also Chenu (1973) on *fraternitas*.

[32] Parisse (1983), p. 126. Philip of Harvengt, *De institutione clericorum*, 4: *De continentia clericorum*, 110, in *PL*, CCIII, 817A, said that in the works of the fathers he found them called *sanctimoniales*, *nonnas*, and *monachas*.

Monasterium was likewise a broad term and referred to almost any type of religious community, not only a house of monks. According to the *Bridlington dialogue*, it derived from *monos* meaning *solus* and *sterio* meaning *statio* and therefore technically meant a solitary place or hermitage, whereas *coenobium* meant a house of several monks, but the author admitted that in practice the two terms were interchangeable.[33] Parish churches were sometimes called *monasteria*, which is related to the Old English *mynster* and German *Münster*, and also *coenobia*, perhaps because they belonged to monasteries.[34] *Conventus* and *congregatio* could refer to almost any type of religious community, and *claustrum* as a rule to the cloister and the surrounding buildings, which is now called the enclosure.[35] The term *abbatia* became common in the west only after the ninth century, when the view of the abbot shifted from a personal superior to the head of an institution, to which he gave his name. It was used for any house, male or female, of which the head was an abbot or abbess, and in the twelfth century it became the official term for Cistercian houses in order to distinguish them from dependent priories headed by a prior.[36] In the twelfth century, however, the term prior also applied to the superiors of some independent houses, which were likewise called priories. The varied uses of rector, provost, prelate, dean, minister, and master gave rise to controversy even at the time and seem to be indistinguishable now.[37]

The technical vocabulary of medieval religious life is complicated and elusive,[38] but a brief examination will help to clarify the way it is used here and also serve as an introduction to some of the problems lying ahead. *Clericus*, for instance, which meant 'chosen' or 'from the part (or portion) of the Lord', commonly referred to anyone who was ordained, as distinct from *laicus*, which was associated with the word for stone.[39] Already in the twelfth century, how-

---

[33] Robert of Bridlington (attr.), *Bridlington Dialogue*, 8 and 11 (London 1960), pp. 102 and 118. See Colker (1962), pp. 181–99, on the sources and author of this text, which may date from the third quarter of the twelfth century.

[34] See Schaefer (1903), pp. 4 n. 1, and 5 n. 2, on the terms *monasterium* and *coenobium*; Stenton (1920), p. lxxiii n.; Michaud-Quantin (1970a), pp. 104–9; and *English Episcopal Acta*, II: *Canterbury, 1162–1190*, ed. Christopher R. Cheney and Bridgett E.A. Jones (London 1986), p. 51, no. 72.

[35] According to Siegwart (1965), pp. 48–9, *monasterium* referred to the church building, *conventus* to the whole monastery, and *claustrum* to the cloister and surrounding buildings. The use in English of the term convent for houses of female religious is modern.

[36] Blume (1914), p. 53. In some regions the term *abbatia* applied to the area under the control of an abbot, but not to the monastic buildings, which were called the *monasterium*.

[37] Constable and Somerville (1992), p. 848. Gilbert of Sempringham was referred to as *magister*, *prior*, and *summus prior*.

[38] The best guides are the works of Leclercq (1961b) and (1963a). The antiquarian terms found in the nineteenth-century historical works have largely been abandoned. Even 'chapter-general', which is still widely used, is better avoided, for the twelfth century, in favour of the less specific general chapter.

[39] According to Leclercq, Vandenbroucke, and Bouyer (1961), p. 129, Peter Damiani was the first to derive *clericus* from the part or portion of God, which involved the renunciation of private property.

ever, *clericus* began to mean someone who had studied and was literate, and *laicus*, like *simplex*, *idiota*, and *rusticus*, was used for someone who was illiterate. A priest of Pescia named Rusticus who died in 1132/3 was described on his tombstone as rustic without the fact of rusticity.[40] A monk, according to Rupert of Deutz, could be either literate and clerical or illiterate and lay, in the sense of unordained,[41] but as more lay men learned to read, and many clerics were badly educated, the situation arose where a literate lay man might be a better cleric than an unlettered priest. Philip of Harvengt said that a monk would call himself a *clericus* if he was literate and a *conversus laicus* if he was illiterate, and the same was true of lay men and even women. 'I wonder why, when clerical learning is declared (*praedicetur*) in a woman, she is called not a *bona clerica* but *bonus clericus*, since it would seem more suitable that *clerica* should be named from *clericus* just as a *monacha* from *monachus*.'[42]

The various usages thus overlapped. The hermit Godric of Finchale was described in his *Life* as *laicus et pene ineruditus litteris* and as *laicus et illiteratus*, presumably because he was not ordained, although he knew how to read the psalter, was called a monk, and was subject to the rule of the prior of Durham.[43] The Cistercian Christian of L'Aumône, who was a monk and not a lay brother, was also described as an *idiota* and *laicus*.[44] The meaning of *conversus* likewise varied with the context. It was used primarily for adults who entered religious life, but later it became the standard term for lay brother and also applied to various types of lay people who associated themselves in one way or another with a religious house.[45] *Heremita* was usually equated with *solitarius* or *anachoreta*. These sometimes meant almost the same as monk or *religiosus*, but they were also distinguished in ways that are not entirely clear.[46] Hermits often owned property and exercised a greater freedom than monks, who were distinguished by obedience and lack of possessions.[47] *Inclusus* and *reclusus* also appear to have been synonyms, though their use may have varied regionally. The same person was entered in two different necrologies once as *inclusa* and once as *conversa*, which probably meant that she entered

---

[40] Constable (1988), p. 103, line 2.
[41] Rupert of Deutz, *Quaestio utrum monachis liceat praedicare*, in Endres (1906), p. 146.
[42] Philip of Harvengt, *De institutione clericorum*, 4: *De continentia clericorum*, 110, in *PL*, CCIII, 816B–17B.
[43] Reginald of Durham, *Vita Godrici*, XI, 30, XXXVIII, 84, and XLVII, 103, ed. Stevenson, pp. 45, 94, and 110.
[44] The two parts of the *Vita Christiani de Eleemosyna* were edited by Bruno Griesser, in *Cistercienser-Chronik* 57 (1950), pp. 21–32, and by Jean Leclercq, in *Anal. boll.* 71 (1953), pp. 30–52 (*BHL* 1735ab). For the relevant references see Griesser's edn, p. 23, and Leclercq's edn, p. 30.
[45] Hallinger (1959) listed nine uses of the term *conversus*. See pp. 77–9 below.
[46] See Jean Leclercq, in *Eremitismo* (1965), pp. 27–44, on the terms *eremus* and *eremita*.
[47] Oudart (1988), p. 378.

the religious life as an adult and became a recluse.[48] 'The old monasteries', wrote Dubois, 'accepted in their orbit a crowd of people who served God in their own way and who, not having wished while they were living to enter into any definite category, cannot be put into one now they are dead.'[49]

One of the most confusing terms is 'canon', for which Siegwart found eight distinct meanings in the early Middle Ages, ranging from the clergy and an ecclesiastical rule or law to various specialized liturgical and economic uses.[50] *Canonicus* usually meant a cleric who performed liturgical services, often as a member of a group in a large church, and who was supported from its revenues. Such churches might be called a *canonica*, for which there is no good translation into English, like the German *Stift* or French *collégiale*. 'Collegiate church' or 'chapter' will sometimes do, but these suggest more organization than was found in many of the churches served by canons in the Middle Ages. They will be referred to here, as they were at that time, mostly as monasteries, convents, communities, and houses. From time to time rules were written for canons in an effort to make them live more in the manner of monks, and those who practised celibacy and common life and who renounced private property began in the eleventh century – and more frequently in the twelfth – to be called regular canons, in order to distinguish them from secular canons who still lived in the world like clerics. Geoffrey of St Victor in the *Fountain of philosophy* praised the life of

> those who are called regular canons, [who are] trained in the saving ways of the holy rule, equal in life, vows, habit, and manner (*gestu*), and have everything in common and nothing in private. Now they are free for the clerical office; now they proceed to manual labour; now, returning to the vessels of the father, they drink as they please some spiritual refreshment.[51]

Some writers objected to the term regular canon as a neologism or as a tautology, since one of the meanings of 'canon' was rule and a regular canon was thus a regular regular, but it was increasingly accepted, and as time went on 'regular' came to be used, as by James of Vitry, for anyone who followed a rule. At the same time, 'secular' was used for anyone living in the world and

---

[48] Wollasch (1973a), p. 84.
[49] Dubois (1968a), p. 47.
[50] Siegwart (1967), pp. 195–226.
[51] Geoffrey of St Victor, *Fons philosophiae*, lines 745–52, ed. Pierre Michaud-Quantin (Analecta mediaevalia Namurcensia 8; Namur, Louvain, and Lille 1956), p. 61, and tr. Edward Synan (Toronto 1972), p. 66. The term regular canon became common about 1130, according to Dereine (1952), p. 28. For examples of criticism of the terms 'regular' and 'secular' canon, see Idungus, *Dialogus*, ed. Huygens, p. 427; Adam of Dryburgh, *Liber de ordine, habitu et professione canonicorum*, III, 2, in *PL*, CXCVIII, 462AC; and Adam of Eynsham, *Magna vita Hugonis*, I, 11, ed. Decima Douie and David Hugh Farmer (OMT; Oxford 1985), I, 80 (*BHL* 4018): 'secularis, ut uulgus loquitur, . . . canonicus'. Reginald of Durham, *Libellus de admirandis beati Cuthberti virtutibus*, 16, ed. James Raine (Surtees Society 1; Durham 1835), p. 29, referred to the manner of canons 'qui nunc dicuntur secularium'.

occasionally, in a pejorative sense, for monks who followed no rule, who were also called *semilaici* or pseudo-monks.[52] Communities of regular canons were often indistinguishable from houses of monks, especially when the superior was called an abbot, as was customary in some regions, rather than the more usual provost, and when the house was referred to as a *monasterium* or *abbatia*.[53] Contemporaries sometimes confused regular clerics and canons with monks. Alcuin wrote to Arn of Salzburg in 802 about the need to study what pertained to canons, to monks, and to a third grade, 'which varies between these two, standing on a higher grade than canons and lower than monks'.[54] During the tenth and eleventh centuries the differences between them were increasingly blurred as more monks were ordained and as more canons adopted rules resembling those of monks. In the *Dialogue of two monks* written by Idungus of Regensburg in 1154/5, the Cistercian monk said that 'Everyone who has professed that rule [that is, the Augustinian rule of canons] is a monk, whether they like it or not. For they are either monks, or they are of no order.'[55] The regular canons of Arnstein were said to observe the monastic religion, and the introductory letter to Hildegard of Bingen's commentary on the rule of Benedict shows that the canons of Ravengiersburg, which was the third oldest house of regular canons in Germany, were confused with monks and may indeed have regarded themselves as monks. The Augustinian canonesses of Clerkenwell were referred to as nuns even in papal bulls.[56] In theory, however, and sometimes in practice, the distinctions between monks and canons and between regular and secular

---

[52] Edgar in his privilege for New Minster Winchester in 966/84 expelled the canons and installed 'regulares monachi non seculares': *Councils and Synods with Other Documents relating to the English Church, I: A.D. 871–1204*, ed. Dorothy Whitelock, Martin Brett, and C.N.L. Brooke (Oxford 1981), pp. 125 and 127. There are references to secular monks in the *Libellus*, ed. Constable, pp. 54–6; the treatise (perhaps by Abelard) entitled *Adtendite a falsis prophetis*, in Engels (1975), p. 226; and Herman of Tournai, *De restauratione monasterii sancti Martini Tornacensis*, 68, in *MGH, SS*, XIV, 306, who referred to monks living next to a town 'quos populares siue seculares quidam nominant'. According to John of Salisbury, *Policraticus*, VII, 23, ed. C.C.J. Webb (Oxford 1909), II, 208, seculars were those 'whom a dark costume does not distinguish from the others'. For *semilaicus* as a term of abuse for monks, see p. 74 n. 142 below, and on *pseudomonachus*, Lampert of Hersfeld, *Annales*, s.a. 1071, ed. O. Holder-Egger (*MGH, SSRG*; Hanover and Leipzig 1894), pp. 127 and 132.

[53] Wibald of Corvey wrote to pope Eugene III in 1152 that in the region of Liège regular canons called their superior 'provost' rather than 'abbot': Miraeus–Foppens, III, 341.

[54] Alcuin, *Ep.* 258, in *MGH, Epp.*, IV, 416. See Oexle (1978), pp. 124 and 131, and Felten (1980), pp. 237–41, who concluded that Alcuin himself, whose status has been debated by scholars, became a monk at the end of his life.

[55] Idungus, *Dialogus*, 2, ed. Huygens, p. 422; see p. 425, where he said that the Premonstratensians and 'all those having a common life' were monks.

[56] *Vita Ludovici de Arnstein*, ed. S. Widmann, in *Annalen des Vereins für nassauische Altertumskunde und Geschichtsforschung* 17 (1882), pp. 258–9 (*BHL* 5033); Hildegard of Bingen, *Explanatio regulae s. Benedicti*, in *PL*, CXCVII, 1053–4, on which see Wirges (1928), pp. 153–4; and *Cartulary of St Mary Clerkenwell*, ed. W.O. Hassall (Camden 3 S. 71; London 1949), p. viii n. 3. Some houses of canons, such as Goldbach, Andlau, and Etival, were founded by and depended on houses of monks: see Dubled (1952), pp. 305–7.

canons were maintained and even enforced. The customs of the canons of Springiersbach forbade them to receive professed monks owing to the equality, and hence incompatibility, of the two orders,[57] and Alexander III in 1167 rejected the nomination of a regular canon to a chapter of secular canons, saying that he had never read or heard 'that someone was ever made a secular out of a regular canon'. He was reported to have said of this case, citing Deuteronomy 22.10, that 'Those shalt not plough with an ox and ass together, that is, psalmody shalt not be sung in the same choir in a different habit and profession.'[58]

The broad use of 'monk' and 'nun' was paralleled in the twelfth century by the use of 'Cluniac' for all black monks, even though it properly applied only to members of Cluny and its dependencies, all of whom were supposed to make their profession to the abbot of Cluny. The successive movements of reform created various groups and orders, which cannot be classified as either 'old black' or 'Cluniac', like the so-called *Jungkluniazenser* or neo-Cluniacs, who took various elements from the Cluniac customs without being formally affiliated with Cluny. For reasons that are not entirely clear, however, 'Cluniac' came to be used for all monks who observed the rule of Benedict and wore black habits and who were later called black Benedictines in order to distinguish them from members of newer orders who followed different rules and wore undyed and lighter-coloured habits.[59] In the second half of the twelfth century Gerald of Wales, who knew that Cluny and its members constituted a distinct congregation or order, nonetheless referred to almost all black monks as 'Cluniacs'.[60] Similarly, some monks and nuns who followed the *Charter of love* and other Cistercian rules and regulations were called, and called themselves, Cistercian, although they were not strictly speaking members of the order. These inconsistencies seem on the whole to have disturbed contemporaries less than they do scholars, who try to understand and impose order on the developments at that time and to classify the religious movements as old and new, black and white, and conservative and reformed.

Reformer is a loose term, and in a personal sense every Christian is, or should be, a reformer. It is used here primarily for institutional reformers: the founders or members of new communities who sought a different type of life from that in the old houses, whether they looked back to an established

---

[57] Dereine (1948b), pp. 428 and 430.

[58] *PL*, CC, 528B, and *Papsturkunden in Frankreich*, N.F. VII, 394–5, nos. 124–5 (JL 11485–6). See Falkenstein (1993), pp. 129–31.

[59] Hallinger (1950–1), pp. 4, 182–4 n. 14, and 517–18; Wollasch (1973a), pp. 182–4, and (1973b), pp. 288–9 (criticizing Hallinger); and Jäschke (1970), esp. p. 23 on neo-Cluniac and neo-Gorzian houses in the eleventh and twelfth centuries. Though the papal chancery used *ordo s. Benedicti* in the thirteenth century, the term Benedictine dates from the seventeenth century: see Leclercq (1964b), p. 30.

[60] As in the *Gemma ecclesiastica*, II, 26, and *Speculum ecclesiae*, II, 1, 6 and 29, and III, 19 and 21, ed. John S. Brewer a.o. (RS 21; London 1861–91), II, 289, and IV, 29–37, 45, 93, 244, and 246.

model from which the existing monasteries had departed or whether they looked towards a new ideal, like the military orders or, in many respects, the regular canons. It is the opposite less of unreformed than of conservative, another loose term that refers not to a body of doctrine but a temper of mind and personality and to a dislike for change and innovation, an attitude technically known as misoneism. One reason that it is difficult to see what was going on beneath the surface of expressed feelings and policies is because many contemporaries found it hard to accept that their established and admired ways of life might no longer meet the religious needs of the Christian community, and they therefore hid the changes under traditional names. Whereas the reformers, including someone like Bernard of Clairvaux, characteristically preferred truth to custom and the better to the good, the old black monks held that 'Le mieux est l'ennemi du bien' and that changes were rarely for the better.[61] Not all black monks were conservative in this sense, however, and many of them took the lead in adopting and supporting reforms. Generally, but only generally, the new houses or orders can be equated with the reformers, who often wore white robes. Since almost every community had both old and new features, one can speak of new 'old' houses of black monks of the established types and old 'new' houses of black monks who resembled the reformers.[62] Indeed, some reformers were so extreme that they left, between themselves and the old types of monasticism, a gap that was filled by moderates from both sides.

Before leaving the vocabulary of religious life, something should be said about the language of spirituality, which is also a hard word to define. As used today, it refers not just to piety and devotion but to the point where faith and action intersect: how a faith is lived and what people do about their religious beliefs. For Christians, according to Post, it covers

> the attitude of the faithful to God and to Christ, . . . not in the domain of dogma or morals, but in that of adoration, recognition, love, the desire for union, the striving after virtue, the avoidance of sin, the ways to achieve this, the exercises suitable for this end (*ascesis*), the paths which lead to a union with God and with Christ (mysticism), prayer, meditation, religious fervour, worship.[63]

---

[61] See, for instance, the reply of the monks of Molesme to the proposed reforms of abbot Robert, in Ordericus Vitalis, *Historia ecclesiastica*, VIII, 26, ed. Chibnall, IV, 316. Stephen of Tournai, on the other hand, in his *Ep.* 1, ed. Desilve, p. 9, concerning some Grandmontines who had transferred to the Cistercian house of Pontigny, cited Gregory the Great to prove that a greater must be preferred to a lesser good.

[62] Monte Cassino and Canterbury can thus be described as old old houses (i.e. ancient houses of the old type), Cluny and Gorze as new old houses, the *Jungkluniacenser* and *Junggorzer* as new new old houses, and so on.

[63] Tentler (1983); Post (1968), p. 314. In the Middle Ages *spiritualitas* meant spiritual as opposed to bodily, carnal, material, and mortal and took on its modern meaning principally in the twentieth century: see (among many other works) Leclercq (1962a); Vauchez (1975), pp. 6–7; Principe (1983); Tentler (1983); and the essays in *Spiritualità* (1987).

Spirituality in this sense cuts across the distinction between written and oral and between learned (or elite) and popular and includes attitudes and practices that were shared by most Christians at the time. It expressed the commitment of the individual to God and started, for monks and nuns, with their *conversio* and *conversatio morum*, as it was called in the rule of Benedict, to a life of religion. There is a large and growing literature on these two terms. *Conversio* meant a turning around, in the sense of turning from one type of religious belief to another, but it was also used as the equivalent of *paenitentia* and as a translation for the Greek *metanoia*. *Conversatio*, on the other hand, especially when it was joined with *morum*, meant something more like moral conduct or behaviour, or even simply way of life.[64] Hildebert of Lavardin wrote a letter to William of Champeaux after he retired from teaching in 1108 saying that he rejoiced *de conversatione et conversione tua*, which presumably referred to his changed way of life and his conversion to religion.[65]

The substance of conversion was called the *propositum*, which is usually translated here as 'undertaking' or 'way of life', and which carried, like *arbitrium*, an implication of purpose and determination. It involved a turning away from the world and its values towards a life of religious *quies*, *vacatio*, and *otium*, which was contrasted with the vice of *otiositas*. *Otium* usually meant peace and quiet in a good sense, whereas *otiosus* was lazy, bored, and afflicted with *taedium* or, worse still, *acedia*, a sense of spiritual and physical weariness that was equated with *tristitia*, *tepiditas*, and *torpor*.[66] Meditation, on the other hand, according to Hugh of St Victor, was *valde subtilis et simul iucunda*.[67] The stages of *lectio*, *meditatio*, *oratio*, and *contemplatio* were distinguished in technical treatises on monastic spirituality, as by Guigo of La Chartreuse, who compared them to the rungs on the ladder of humility, but they tended to overlap and flow one into the other.[68] Monks and nuns were professional contemplatives, and in the twelfth century their way of life was increasingly

---

[64] See the differing views, with references to previous works, in Winandy (1960); Lottin (1961); and Hoppenbrouwers (1964); and the survey in Wathen (1975). G.G. Meersseman, in *Eremitismo* (1965), pp. 267–8, stressed the parallel of *conversio* and *conversatio* with *metanoia* and *paenitentia* in the sense of an aversion to sin and a turning to God.

[65] Hildebert of Lavardin, *Ep.* 1, in *PL*, CLXXI, 141A. See Jaeger (1993), pp. 72–3.

[66] Richard of St Victor, *De questionibus regule s. Augustini solutis*, 14, ed. Marvin Colker, in *Traditio* 18 (1962), pp. 215–16, gave three meanings for *otium*, two praiseworthy and one bad. The author of *De professionibus monachorum*, in Martène (1736–8), II, 486–7 (see n. 80), said that the stable monk should avoid *otium*, which leads to restlessness, and according to the *Vita Mironis*, in *España sagrada*, XXVIII, 309 (*BHL* 5971), 'Qui in otio est, contemptor diuinorum bonorum est.' *Otium* is one of the spokes in the fifth section (laziness) of the wheel of the hypocrite in plate 4. On *acedia*, see Wenzel (1966) and (1967) and on *otium*, Leclercq (1963a), pp. 27–41 and 71 n. 10, where he said that 'l'otium est bon ou mauvais selon l'usage qu'on en fait; mais en lui-même, à la différence de l'otiositas, il est un bien', and J. Biarne and M. Harl, in *Temps* (1984), pp. 103 and 240.

[67] Hugh of St Victor, *Didascalicon*, VI, 13, ed. Charles Henry Buttimer (Catholic University of America: Studies in Medieval and Renaissance Latin 10; Washington, DC 1939), p. 130. See Chenu (1957), p. 344 n. 1.

[68] Guigo, *Scala claustralium*, 1, in *PL*, CLXXXIV, 475C. See Lodolo (1977), pp. 272–4.

contrasted with the active life led by the clergy and laity.[69] Contemplation was often equated with private prayer, but it could also refer to public worship or simply to a secluded life.[70]

Authenticus meant not only original, as when a tenth-century notary said that he had seen and copied the *authenticum* of a charter,[71] but also true, as in the contrast of truth with custom. Bernard of Clairvaux contrasted *authentica et antiqua* with *novella vel levia* in his letter to the monks of Montiéramey about the liturgy, and Matthew of Vendôme in his *Art of versification* distinguished *exempla authentica* derived from other writers from *exempla domestica* invented by the writer himself.[72] The twelfth-century reformers laid great emphasis on authenticity and return to the original sources, which has been described as a movement of *resourcement*. *Affectus* covered a range of meanings from feeling and disposition to intention, as it was used in the maxim, which was attributed to Ambrose, that 'Your *affectus* gives a name to the deed.'[73] *Conscientia* developed from its basic meaning of 'knowledge' and 'awareness' to 'consciousness', which it retains in most modern European languages, and, further, towards the special inner sense of right and wrong, based on knowledge of oneself, to which the term 'conscience' now refers in English.[74]

Since entry to religion in the eleventh and twelfth centuries implied a way of life more than a legal status, it was not entirely clear how someone became a monk or nun. Ivo of Chartres in a letter written to abbot Geoffrey of Vendôme in 1094 maintained that 'contempt of the world and complete love of God' made a monk and that profession and benediction (by either a monk or an abbot) were not sacraments or consecrations but guarantees against backsliding, 'since all stability in religion, unless it is strictly bound and conserved, flourishes when it is new and unusual [and] grows old and worthless when it

---

[69] On the growing identification of monastic life with contemplation and definition of monks and nuns as contemplatives, see Leclercq (1965c); Lunardi (1970), pp. 57 and 72; and Constable (1995a), pp. 72–86.

[70] For Guigo, *Scala claustralium*, I, in *PL*, CLXXXIV, 476B, contemplation was 'mentis in deum suspensae eleuatio, aeternae dulcedinis gaudia degustans', as distinct from meditation, 'studiosa mentis actio, occultae ueritatis notitiam ductu propriae rationis inuestigans'. See Berlière (1927a), pp. 186–8 and 194, on the conpenetration of these terms, and Schroll (1941), pp. 165–6.

[71] *Libro croce* [of S. Zeno at Pistoia], ed. Quinto Santoli (Regesta chartarum Italiae 26; Rome 1939), p. 35, no. 8; cf. *Liber potheris communis civitatis Brixiae* (Historiae patriae monumenta 19; Turin 1899), p. 15. On the concept of authenticity, see Chenu (1957), pp. 351–65, and Sokolowski (1978–9), pp. 655–7, who described it (656) as 'a philosophical construct' that should be understood as 'the historical result of the development of certain philosophical ideas'.

[72] Bernard, *Ep.* 398, ed. Leclercq, VIII, 378, and Faral (1924), pp. 156–7.

[73] Odo of Ourscamp, *Quaestiones*, II, 307, in Pitra, *Anal. nov.*, II, 128–9, defined *affectus* as *motus mentis* and said that a deed was defined not by *affectus* alone but *affectus informatus*; Simon of Tournai, *Disputationes*, XIX, 1, ed. Joseph Warichez (Spicilegium sacrum Lovaniense 12; Louvain 1932), p. 66; and Alan of Lille, *Summa*, cited from MS London, British Library, Royal 9 E. XII, fols. 82ʳ and 207ʳ, by Lottin (1942–60), IV.1, 321 and 337. See Chenu (1969), pp. 28–9.

[74] See Lewis (1967), pp. 181–213; Chenu (1969); and Potts (1980).

is aged and popular'.[75] Anselm of Canterbury wrote at about the same time to king Harold's daughter Gunnilda urging her to resume the monastic habit which she had abandoned.

For although you were not consecrated by a bishop and did not read a profession in his presence, the fact that you wore publicly and privately the habit of the holy way of life (*propositum*), by which you affirmed to all who saw you that you were dedicated to God no less than by reading a profession, is itself a manifest and undeniable profession. For before the profession and consecration of the monastic way of life that are now usual were made, many thousands of people of both sexes professed by their habit alone that they were of this way of life and attained its height and crown. And whoever cast off this habit that had been taken without this profession and consecration, were adjudged apostates.[76]

Anselm's reference to *ista nunc usitata monachici propositi professio et sacratio* shows that he regarded the practice of profession and consecration as relatively recent and not essential to making a monk or nun. Among other spiritual writers who adhered to this point of view was the anonymous author of the treatise *On the truly apostolic life*, who said that Paul and the apostles were monks because they renounced the world, were single in sanctity, and followed Christ. 'This is what it is to be a monk,' he said, 'wherefore, since every man wishes to be like Him, every man therefore wishes to be a monk.'[77]

The practice of profession grew steadily in the course of the twelfth century, however.[78] A monk named Boso in Anselm's own monastery of Le Bec wrote a letter probably early in the century stressing the need for profession, by which a monk gave himself and his property to God and lived, he said, 'under the rule (*imperium*) and obedience of an abbot'.[79] Somewhat later another monk of Le Bec wrote a treatise *On the professions of monks* in which he argued that, in spite of various views on the subject, benediction and consecration, though not found in any rule, were necessary 'because there is no sacred order in the holy church which does not have its own benediction';[80] and Idungus of

---

[75] Ivo of Chartres, *Ep.* 41, ed. Jean Leclercq (CHFMA 22; Paris 1949), pp. 164–6; see also *Ep.* 73, in *PL*, CLXII, 93D–4A.

[76] Anselm, *Ep.* 168, ed. Schmitt, IV, 44–5. A century later a nun of Ankerwyke who claimed never to have been a nun was excommunicated for abandoning her habit and leaving her monastery: *English Episcopal Acta*, III: *Canterbury 1193–1205*, ed. Christopher R. Cheney and Eric John (London 1986), p. 3.

[77] *De vita vere apostolica*, 4, in *Ampl. coll.*, IX, 1012A.

[78] Yeo (1982), esp. pp. 75–85 on the structure of monastic profession in the *Decretum* of Gratian, and Constable (1987a), pp. 808–34, on the increasingly formal character of entry to religious life in the eleventh and twelfth centuries.

[79] Boso of Le Bec, *Ep.*, ed. Henri Rochais, in *Revue Mabillon* 43 (1953), p. 45. He went on to say, like Ivo, that profession made commitment more permanent and more worthy than self-donation without profession. Boso became a monk in 1088 and was abbot of Le Bec from 1124 to 1136.

[80] *De professionibus monachorum*, in Martène (1736–8), II, 474B; see also 457, where he stressed the irrevocable character of benediction, and 481, where he said, like Ivo and Boso, that the *subscriptio* made at the time of profession did not make a monk but bound him, especially to

Regensburg said that 'Nothing makes a monk except a lawful profession.'[81] Writing about a woman who said that she had been forced to become a nun, Peter of Blois said that entry to a life of religion should not be urged 'violently' and that a monk or nun was made by 'one's own profession or paternal devotion'. He compared it to marriage, which had to be free according to both secular and canon law, and commented that 'If carnal marriage rejoices in a liberty that has been granted, spiritual marriage is privileged with a fuller grace of liberty, for where the spirit is, there is liberty.'[82]

Peter was a lawyer, and although his comparison of entry to religious life with marriage showed the need for voluntary profession, it did not follow from his stress on liberty that an involuntary entry was invalid. For the commitment to a religious life, once entered, was normally considered inviolable, irrevocable, and overriding, since it subsumed such lesser obligations as going on a pilgrimage or a crusade.[83] This created particular problems when a monk wanted to transfer from one religious house or order to another, and the view developed that entry to what was regarded as a higher or stricter form of life was irreversible. Even a promise made in ignorance by a child was binding according to a text attributed to pope Urban II concerning the obligation of all members of a community, whether or not they had taken a vow of poverty, to lead a common life, like that of the apostles.

> But someone may say that 'I did not promise the apostolic life, but to live according to the new customs of that monastery and according to the traditions of those fathers.' Behold you have heard [the words of the Lord in Jeremiah 3.5], since you were not able to do this. But you may say: 'I did not understand thus, for I was a boy.' If you did not understand, the vow was nonetheless made. . . Search the Scriptures, search your rule, and see what you promised [John 7.52].

Urban cited the parallel of a man who as an adult has to discharge the obligations promised for him at baptism.[84] Entry to religious life was often compared to a second baptism, from which a new man emerged, reborn into a new and better life.[85]

---

stability. On this work, see Wilmart (1932b), who dated it in the second quarter of the twelfth century and corrected the title given by Martène from *De professione monachorum* to *De professionibus monachorum*.

[81] Idungus, *Dialogus*, 2, ed. Huygens, p. 412.

[82] Peter of Blois, *Ep*. 54, ed. J.A. Giles (Bibliotheca patrum ecclesiae Anglicanae 5; Oxford 1847), I, 162. See the view of Hostiensis cited pp. 7–8 above.

[83] Peter the Venerable, *Ep*. 51, ed. Constable, I, 152, and Bernard, *Epp*. 57 and 64, ed. Leclercq, VII, 149 and 157, cited in Constable (1976b), p. 136.

[84] Fuhrmann (1984), pp. 43–4.

[85] In addition to Rupert of Deutz, *De sancta trinitate*, 41: *De operibus spiritus*, VIII, 8, in *CC:CM*, XXIV, 2082–3, and Geoffrey of Vendôme, *Ep*. IV, 12, in *PL*, CLVII, 158A, see Giovanni Miccoli, in *Théologie* (1961), pp. 469–72, on Peter Damiani, and other texts and secondary works cited in Constable (1987a), pp. 779–80, 795, and 799, to which should be added Longère (1982),

The question of whether a second monastic profession and benediction could be made was also debated. Ivo admitted in the letter cited above that if the benediction was indeed a consecration, it could not be repeated, and Anselm's use of the words *sacrata* and *sacratio* rather than *benedicta* and *benedictio* shows that he regarded it as a consecration, though not as essential to making a monk or nun. Among the Cistercian charges against the Cluniacs, to which Peter the Venerable replied, was that monks who had professed stability, *conversatio morum*, and obedience in one place were allowed to swear them again in another. Peter replied that there was no harm in repeating a vow that was neither contrary to nor less than a previous vow and cited the permission given in the rule of Benedict for wandering monks to profess stability (which Peter presumed to be a second profession) in a monastery.[86] In practice, second professions and benedictions were probably not rare, especially in cases of transfer from one monastery to another and of deathbed entry to religious life, known as *ad succurrendum*. The fact that Abelard, who was a monk before he came to Cluny, took 'a superior grade' among the Cluniacs and participated in their processions, as Peter the Venerable wrote to Heloise after Abelard's death, suggests that he made a second profession at Cluny.[87] Idungus admitted in his *Dialogue of two monks* that while he was still at Prüfening, before becoming a Cistercian, he had made two professions, one *ad succurrendum* in the infirmary, when he was thought to be dying, and another four months later, before the altar, after he recovered. Since both professions were made within less than a year of his entry to the monastery, Idungus regarded them as irregular, because the rule required a year of novitiate, and he may have made yet another profession, though he did not say so, when he became a Cistercian.[88] Such situations were anomalous if not rare, and in the course of the twelfth century the principle of a single profession and benediction (or consecration) became established, together with a vow that bound a monk both to his monastery and to his abbot, like a vassal to his lord.[89] What had in the early Middle Ages been primarily a commitment to a way of life and a promise to God thus became an entry into a consecrated

---

pp. 438, 442, and 458–9, and Vuillaume (1991), on the modern theological aspects of the question.

[86] Peter the Venerable, *Ep.* 28, ed. Constable, I, 55 and 76–8.

[87] Idem, *Ep.* 115, ed. Constable, I, 306.

[88] Idungus, *Dialogus*, 2, ed. Huygens, pp. 412–15. When he was challenged about the double profession at Prüfening (which he called Cluniac), Idungus attributed it to the personal policy of the abbot.

[89] Capelle (1959), pp. 243–4, and Hourlier (1974), p. 190. Lefèvre (1932) and (1957), p. 157, stressed the parallel between entry to monastic and strict canonical (Premonstratensian) life. The author of the *De professionibus monachorum*, in Martène (1736–8), II, 490AD, opposed the vow, saying that a monk made his profession to God and the church, not to the abbot, who was only a witness and should not speak of 'my monk' and 'my professed': see Wilmart (1932b), p. 33. His protest shows the way the wind was blowing in the twelfth century.

status bound by obligations to men. Knights and monks both tended to close ranks against the variety and mobility of society in the twelfth century. Just as knights amalgamated into an order with vows and ceremonies of entry, so the outer forms of monasticism were institutionalized, while the inner life of monks increasingly stressed a direct relationship between the individual and God.

The concept of monastic life as a consecrated status, entered by a sacrament equivalent to baptism or marriage, underlies the ecclesiological view of monasticism and the idea, which is close to the hearts of some modern monastic theorists, that monks constitute a church in miniature and that there is a parallel, like that between the microcosm and the macrocosm, between the individual monk and monastery and the entire church, *peregrinans et militans*.[90] A follower of Anselm named Ralph said that since *monachus* came from *monos-corde* and all monks had a single heart, 'Not only one monk but also all monks are in this way one monk, that is, altogether having one heart and one spirit.'[91] Gilbert of Sempringham wanted 'to remove [the nuns] from their land and family and paternal home so that in the manner of the church, indeed made into a church (*immo ecclesia facte*). . . they might make the highest King desire their beauty',[92] and Joachim of Fiore in his treatise *On the four evangelists* said that Mary stood not for the universal church nor for 'the crowd of the monastic profession generally but for that special church of the same monastic profession to which the Lord has more specially given to choose and to love a celibate life'.[93] The terms *congregatio spiritualis* and *homo spiritualis* were used for monasteries and monks long before Joachim gave them a technical significance as special marks of the work of the Holy Spirit on earth.[94] The application to monasteries of images that were used for the church as a whole may also have fostered a view of each community as an *ecclesia minor*. On one occasion a monk of Göttweig had a vision of both his own abbey and also Siegburg transplanted into paradise, and Caesarius of Heisterbach told of a vision of the crucifix by a priest who interpreted the *corpus Christi* to be the congregation of his abbey and the cross to be 'the strictness of the order'.[95] A few writers in the eleventh and twelfth centuries argued that, in view of the growing number of monks who celebrated mass alone and had to accommodate 'the plural salutation', a congregation was

[90] De Lubac (1959–64), I, 576–86, discussed the application to monasteries of texts traditionally applied to the whole church. See Giovanni Miccoli, in *Théologie* (1961), pp. 466–7, and Fornasari (1981) on the monastic ecclesiology of Peter Damiani.

[91] Ed. Jean Leclercq, in *Anal. mon.*, III, 165.

[92] *Vita Gileberti Sempinghamensis*, 9, ed. Foreville and Keir, p. 34. The precise meaning of this passage is obscure.

[93] Joachim of Fiore, *Super quatuor evangelia*, 1, ed. Ernesto Buonaiuti (FSI 67; Rome 1930), p. 32.

[94] See Faust (1964), pp. 303–4 and 307, for these terms in the works of Godfrey of Admont.

[95] Smalley (1966), pp. 658–9, who said that this was the only vision of this type known to her, and Caesarius, *Dialogus*, IV, 18, ed. Strange, I, 190.

mystically present and that a single monk thus represented the entire church. Odo of Cambrai in his commentary on the words *et omnium circumstantium* wrote that

> Although originally masses were not made without a group, later the custom grew in the church to make solitary masses, especially in monasteries. And since they had no group to salute in the plural, and they could not change the plural salutations, they turned to the church, saying that they saluted the church in the church and addressed the whole body in [one] body.[96]

Ivo of Chartres referred to some wandering preachers who maintained that the church belonged to only a few solitaries,[97] but he evidently disapproved of the view of monks as the true church or as a sort of anti-church based on a protest against existing institutions or on a radical distinction between the church and the monk or sect type.[98] The idea that the true church consists of those who remain after others have fallen away (which is known technically as remnant ecclesiology) emerged in the thirteenth century among the radical Franciscans and Joachimites, who had a strong sense of their own identity, but it was not prevalent among monks and nuns in the previous century, who normally regarded themselves not as distinct from the church or as an *ecclesia minor*, but as an essential part of the entire church as the body of Christ and of Christian society as an organic whole.[99] Even an accused heretic like Lambert le Bègue associated himself with the structure and values of the church as a whole when he said that his followers were not *sectatores* but only a few priests and some lay people who saw in him 'humility of habit, moderation in food, contempt for glory and wealth, and a disposition for the purity and care of the divine cult'.[100]

Some scholars have seen monasticism in terms of the anthropological concept of liminality, which describes the ceremonial transfer from one stage of life to another in tribal societies. It is marked by a period of withdrawal to the margin or *limes* of society, during which people live in physical separation and according to standards of community, equality, poverty, and simplicity

---

[96] Odo of Cambrai, *Expositio in canonem missae*, in *PL*, CLX, 1057B. Cf. Stephen of Baugé, *De sacramento altaris*, 13, in *PL*, CLXXII, 1289B, who followed Odo and added that after monks secular priests also celebrated private masses. On this work, see Van den Eynde (1950), who questioned the attribution to Stephen of Baugé.

[97] Ivo of Chartres, *Ep.* 192, in *PL*, CLII, 201C.

[98] See Blazovich (1954), pp. 112–14, citing the works of Troeltsch and Von Martin; Hill (1971); and Séguy (1971).

[99] Monks and clerics were compared to stars of different brightness in the sky by Lampert of Hersfeld, *Annales*, s.a. 1075, ed. Holder-Egger (n. 52), p. 204. Marbod of Rennes, *Laus vitae monasticae*, in *PL*, CLXXI, 1657C–8A, compared monks to angels, ants, and bees (a frequent metaphor) as well as to the stars. Monks were called the stomach of the church (*venter ecclesiae*) in a Bernardine text published from MS Lincoln 201 in Rochais and Binont (1964), p. 88, no. Lc 18.

[100] Fredericq (1895), p. 1002.

that are uncharacteristic of normal society.[101] This concept may help to understand some of the temporary types of medieval religious life, such as pilgrimages, crusades, and periods of eremitical retreat, though these were not rites of
passage in the anthropological sense, but it cannot be applied to the permanent
experience of monastic life, which was seen as part of society as a whole and
as representing its highest values. Monks were the true seekers after theology,
philosophy, and theory in the sense of wisdom and contemplation.[102] Their
life was reasonable, *aequalis*, secure, and safe; it resembled that of the angels
in paradise, Adam in the Garden of Eden, and the apostles in the primitive
church. They were soldiers serving in the army of God and Christ; their
models were the prophets of the Old Testament, John the Baptist, the early
saints and martyrs, and the desert fathers. Bernard of Tiron was said to have
suffered a bloodless martyrdom in the form of his chastity in youth, abstinence
in plenty, and generosity in poverty.[103] Religious life was one of struggle,
flight, exile, pilgrimage, and homelessness, in a spiritual as well as physical
sense, and religious houses were compared to paradise and the Garden of
Eden, and also to cities, schools, armies, training-grounds, and ships. The
monastery was a safe port of refuge from the storm of the worldly life, a
furnace of spiritual refinement, a prison and a place of punishment before the
final liberation, and a tomb for those who were dead to the world while still
living in the flesh.[104] A life of this sort was especially pleasing to God, and
both the example and the prayers of those who led it helped to win salvation
for themselves and for society as a whole.

---

[101] The concept of liminality, which was first developed by Arnold Van Gennep in his *Rites de
passage*, was applied to monasticism particularly in Turner (1972), pp. 392–3 and 398, where
he defined liminality as 'the mid-point of transition in a status-sequence between two positions', and (1974a), pp. 47, where he called liminality 'any condition outside or on the periph-
eries of everyday life', 166–7, and 196. See also Turner and Turner (1978), of which the first
chapter is entitled 'Pilgrimage as a Liminoid Phenomenon'. For a critique of these views, see
Bynum (1984), who defined liminality (pp. 106–7) as 'a moment of suspension of normal rules
and roles'.

[102] See Leclercq (1961b), pp. 39–69 (philosophy), 70–9 (theology), and 80–121 (theory).

[103] Geoffrey *Grossus*, *Vita Bernardi Tironiensis*, XI (92), in *PL*, CLXXII, 1422B (*BHL* 1251). On this
Life see von Walter (1903–6), II, 15–16, who distinguished two sources (A and B) put together
by a later redactor (R) and attributed this chapter to B.

[104] See Penco (1960). According to the *De professionibus monachorum*, in Martène (1736–8), II,
486A, a monk who promised stability placed himself 'in a great prison' for the sake of God,
who made it a paradise for some and unbearable for others. On the civil death of monks, who
were considered dead and to be without legal rights, see Durtelle de Saint-Sauveur (1910).
The author of the *De vita vere apostolica*, 3, in *Ampl. coll.*, IX, 999, held that monks (like the
saints) were dead to the carnal life but alive to the spiritual life of pastoral activities. Hugh
of Rouen, *Dialogi*, VI, 2, in *Thes. nov.*, V, 970CE, distinguished between bodily and spiritual
death and in spiritual death between those who were dead to the faith through crime and
those who were dead to crime through faith. Richard of St Victor, *Serm.* 42, in *PL*, CLXXVII,
1011B, compared the monastery to a furnace in which the monks are refined. These sermons
were long attributed to Hugh of St Victor, but Châtillon (1948), esp. pp. 343–66, concluded
that they were all composed by Richard of St Victor between 1147 and 1163, though Van
den Eynde (1960), pp. 33–4, maintained that a few were by Hugh.

'Taking refuge in monasteries', according to William James, 'was as much an idol of the tribe in the middle ages, as bearing a hand in the world's work is today.'[105] In the eleventh and twelfth centuries monasticism was not on the defensive, as it became in the later Middle Ages, and it was not considered, as it often is now, an escape from the real world. It was on the contrary a call to a more difficult and demanding life, and one that excited almost universal admiration. Carlo Cipolla said that, judged by the economic criteria that goods and services have only the utility attributed to them by consumers, the medieval clergy, including monks and nuns, were 'part of the economically active population' because they produced a service for which there was a demand, which, like other producers, they did their best to stimulate. Even hermits, Cipolla said, had 'every right to be included in the category of producers' to the extent that they interceded 'with God, by means of their prayers, for the remissions of the sins of the world, and to the extent that people were ready to pay for the service'.[106]

The amount of material support and the number of recruits are two of the key indications of the place of organized religious life in society and of the value attached to it by people who are not themselves members of religious houses. Any change in religious or social values affecting this flow will inevitably also affect religious institutions, and in studying the movement of reform in the eleventh and twelfth centuries attention must be given not only to what the reformers criticized in the existing institutions but also to what they and their contemporaries felt was lacking. It is sometimes said that the standard of religious perfection, being based on the bible, never changed, but the history of hagiography shows that the perception of sanctity varied from time to time and from place to place and that contemporaries were sometimes aware of these changes. Even the lists of virtues attributed to saints, while fundamentally stable, like most hagiographical topoi, show some significant shifts in terminology and emphasis, such as the use of *meditatio* and *contemplatio* in place of *oratio*, and the appearance of negative virtues like *non tristis in adversis*.[107] Hamo of Savigny, who died in 1179, was said to have shown himself 'not astonished, not stupid, a sane head, a pious light, an accustomed word (*verbum solitum*), not sighing, not tearful, not openly groaning, not contemplative, not singular, not judging others, not preferring himself to others, but always social and without complaint and following a known way of life'.[108] This remarkable list clearly sets Hamo off not only from the type of ascetic miracle-worker of the early Middle Ages but also from many of the most admired figures of his own age.[109] The author of Hamo's *Life* wanted

---

[105] James (1902), p. 371.
[106] Cipolla (1976), p. 81.
[107] Hertling (1933), p. 264.
[108] *Vita Hamonis*, 3, ed. E.P. Sauvage, in *Anal. boll.* 2 (1883), p. 507 (*BHL* 3752). See Zimmermann, II, 33–5.
[109] See Schmeidler (1927) and Constable (1992b).

to identify him with an ideal of unpretentious and inconspicuous simplicity that was a particular, though not exclusive, characteristic of Cistercian saints in the twelfth and early thirteenth centuries.[110] A lay brother 'of singular grace and piety' at Fountains in the late twelfth century was described as an *homo simplex et illiteratus*; and Caesarius of Heisterbach told of a Cistercian monk who, when questioned by his abbot about his miraculous powers, denied that he in any way led a stricter life than the other monks and attributed his calmness of spirit to his love of God, saying that he had committed himself totally to God. 'And the abbot recognized that the cause of such great virtue was the love of God and contempt for worldly things.'[111] In this man, but not apparently in Hamo, the quality was accompanied by special powers and mystical insights, which became more prominent in the thirteenth century and represented a highly inward ideal, in which visible deeds and worldly position were almost entirely eclipsed by personal piety and simplicity.[112]

A clear statement of awareness of change in the standard of sanctity is found in the *Life* of abbot Robert of La Chaise-Dieu, which was written at the end of the eleventh century, about a generation after Robert's death, by Marbod, the future bishop of Rennes, who was a shrewd observer of the contemporary religious scene as well as a famous poet.

> This new saint turned around the old order of sanctity for us. For although all the others, who with love faithfully raise up their spirits to the heights, are disposed to 'ascend by steps' [Psalm 83.6] in their heart, and undertake higher things always by way of lower ones, this man alone when he had formerly placed his foot on the height, immediately afterwards came down to lower things. He had begun far from worldly and laborious tumults, rising above the clouds with his lofty head, to look upon only divine and celestial things with the tranquil vision of his mind, and behold by degrees he came down to active labour and human affairs, and finally to the work of a stonemason.[113]

In this passage Marbod not only contrasted the *novus sanctus* with the *antiquus ordo sanctitatis* but also saw the essence of the new ideal, as in the 'mixed' life

---

[110] This ideal was frequently expressed by the biblical maxim 'si oculus tuus fuerit simplex, totum corpus tuum lucidum erit' (Matthew 6.22 and Luke 11.34), which was cited by Peter the Venerable in *Ep.* 28 to Bernard of Clairvaux and other letters, ed. Constable, I, 60, 66, and 281. See Nelson (1992), p. 257, on the name Charles the Simple, where *simplex* meant straightforward, with further references, and, on the spirit of simplicity in the Cistercian order, [Chautard] (1948), which was published anonymously with other relevant texts on simplicity, and Lewis (1967), p. 171.

[111] Hugh of Kirkstall, *Narratio*, ed. Walbran, p. 118, and Caesarius, *Dialogus*, X, 6, ed. Strange, II, 221–2. On Hugh's *Narratio*, see Bethell (1966) and Baker (1969a and b).

[112] See Roisin (1943) and (1947) and, more generally, Wolpers (1964), pp. 157–69.

[113] Marbod of Rennes, *Miracula Roberti Casae-Dei*, in *Nova bibl.*, II, 652 (*BHL* 7262). See Zimmermann, II, 60. I am indebted to John Callahan for help with the translation and sources of this passage. According to Jaeger (1994), p. 90, 'Marbod had a conception of individual identity, at least of identity shaped by some gift-bestowing force.'

praised by later writers, in the tension between the upwards and downwards movements of the spirit, which probably derived ultimately from Neoplatonism through Augustine, and between action and contemplation. Many reformers at the time Marbod was writing were moved by a desire for a life of this sort. The religious thought of the twelfth century was imbued by the biblical concepts of the *novus homo* and *sancta novitas*. Abelard in the *History of his calamities*, which was written in 1132/3, referred to 'the new apostles, in whom the world put great credit and of whom one gloried that he had resuscitated the life of regular canons, and the other [the life] of monks'.[114] Norbert of Xanten was praised in his *Life* for 'leading a new type of life on the earth and having nothing and seeking nothing from the earth',[115] and Bernard of Clairvaux gave a well-known expression to the conflict between the old and new ideals when he said that 'My monstrous life, my miserable conscience cry out to you. For I am a sort of chimera of my age, neither a cleric nor a lay man. For I long ago shed the way of life [but] not the habit of a monk.'[116] The chimera in this passage has commonly been taken to mean a monster, but it also represented a sort of non-existence, and the real source of Bernard's anguish was probably his feeling that he was neither one thing nor another. When Bernard behaved in a way that seems high-handed and self-righteous, it should be remembered that his influence was almost entirely personal and that in spite of his faults he was held in almost universal esteem by his contemporaries, who saw in him precisely the combination that they admired of an intense inner life with outward concern.[117]

Bernard as an ascetic practised severe physical austerities, as did some of the other most influential reformers of the period. Bernard of Tiron was described by his biographer as 'hairy, bearded, and covered with cheap and shaggy clothes, according to the eremitical custom' at the time he returned to the abbey of St Cyprian, where he was shaved and clothed in the monastic

[114] Abelard, *Historia calamitatum*, ed. J.T. Muckle, in *Mediaeval Studies* 12 (1950), p. 202. Heloise, *Ep.* 1, ed. J.T. Muckle, in *Mediaeval Studies* 15 (1953), p. 68, referred to the 'detractationes ... grauissimas duorum illorum pseudo-apostolorum'. These two 'new apostles' or 'pseudo-apostles' have commonly been identified as Norbert and Bernard: see Muckle, in *Mediaeval Studies* 12 (1950), pp. 212–13; Miethke (1972), pp. 167–9; Silvestre (1985), pp. 180–2, with references to previous works; and the unpublished paper by Chryogonus Waddell, 'The Trial of Peter Abailard, Bruxelles (1985)', pp. 69–79, who proposed Norbert and Hugh of Fosses.
[115] *Vita* [B] *Norberti*, V, 28, in *PL*, CLXX, 1276D (*BHL* 6249).
[116] Bernard, *Ep.* 250.4, ed. Leclercq, VIII, 147. On the interpretation of this famous passage, see Bredero (1966), pp. 26–8 and 36, and (1980), p. 64, and, on the meaning of chimera, Norman Kretzmann, in *Renaissance and Renewal* (1982), pp. 502–3 and 505–6.
[117] For examples of contemporary admiration and praise of Bernard, see William of St Thierry, *Vita prima Bernardi*, I, 3, 15, ed. Mabillon, II(6), 2102D, and *PL*, CLXXXV.1, 235CD (*BHL* 1211), and Gilbert Foliot, *Ep.* 108, ed. Adrian Morey and C.N.L. Brooke (Cambridge 1967), pp. 148–9, who referred to Bernard as *sui temporis sol*. The description *doctor mellifluus*, according to de Lubac (1959–64), I, 599–620, referred to Bernard's ability to extract the inner sweetness of doctrine more than to the honeyed quality of his preaching. On Luther's regard for Bernard, see Constable (1971), pp. 38–9, and p. 326 below.

habit.[118] Stephen of Grandmont had a curved nose from hitting his face on the ground and callouses like a camel's on his hands and knees from his prostrations while praying.[119] Robert of Arbrissel lacked only a stick to look like a lunatic, according to Marbod of Rennes, who described his ragged clothing, uncovered legs, bare feet, full beard, and unusual haircut. Marbod particularly warned Robert not to rely excessively on his own holiness (*de tua sanctitate*) in his relations with women and not to expiate 'the pollution of ancient iniquity by the example of a new religion'. 'The wise man will not disturb public morals', Marbod wrote, 'nor convert people to himself by novelty.'[120]

Men like this did not fit easily into established ecclesiastical institutions, and many of them either lived as hermits or founded new religious houses, where they could live according to their own ideals and practices. When Robert of Knaresborough went from his hermitage to the monastery of Headley, the monks found that 'It is difficult for us to see this singular man, since he is contrary to our activities and altogether unlike us in clothing and in food.'[121] These differences gave rise to the disputes that fill contemporary polemical writings and that often shed more light on the views of their authors than on the substance of the controversy, which lay underneath the surface of quarrels over personalities and relatively minor matters of monastic discipline and observance. The significance of the controversy as a whole should not be judged, as it is in many modern works, primarily on the basis of the polemical literature.

An interesting impression of the way of life in old black monasteries in the third quarter of the eleventh century, as remembered by a moderate black abbot, who was no reformer, is found in the *Memoirs* of Guibert of Nogent, which were written in 1115:

> Thus in our times the oldest monasteries, in spite of overflowing material supplies given in ancient times, were reduced in numbers and satisfied with small congregations, in which very few could be found who had rejected the world out of scorn of sin. Rather, the churches were principally occupied by those who were delivered by the devotion of their parents and raised in them from the earliest age. The less these men were afraid for their own evils, of which they thought they had none, the more they lived within the walls of their monas-

---

[118] Geoffrey *Grossus*, *Vita Bernardi Tironiensis*, V, 42, in *PL*, CLXXII, 1393BC, and (on his weeping) XI, 101–3, ibid., 1427C–8B (*BHL* 1251).

[119] Stephen of Lecey, *Vita Stephani Muretensis*, 19, in *CC:CM*, VIII, 115 (*BHL* 7907).

[120] Marbod of Rennes, *Ep.* 6, in *PL*, CLXXI, 1481–3 (quotes on 1481C and 1483B) and (with many differences) in von Walter (1903–6), I, 182–6 (quotes on 182 and 185). See also Baldric of Dol, *Vita Roberti de Arbrisello*, II, 11–12, in *PL*, CLXII, 1049C–50B (*BHL* 7259), on Robert's appearance and popularity, and Geoffrey of Vendôme, *Ep.* IV, 47, in *PL*, CLVII, 182A, showing that Robert practised the ancient type of chaste cohabitation with women known as syneisactism (see p. 68 below). In spite of his eccentricities, he was deeply admired and influenced highly placed women like Ermengard of Brittany and Raingard of Montboissier.

[121] *Vita* [A] *Roberti Knaresburgensis*, ed. Paul Grosjean, in *Anal. boll.* 57 (1939), p. 372 (*BHL* 7270d).

teries with slacker zeal (*remissiore studio*). When they were assigned administrative positions or exterior offices either for the need or at the pleasure of their abbots, inasmuch as they were eager to follow their own will and inexperienced in exterior freedoms, they had many opportunities to waste ecclesiastical revenues, which they dispersed as expenses or as free gifts. And as religious life, which was of little concern to them, became rarer, the monks themselves became scarcer.[122]

Two particular points to be noticed in this passage are Guibert's criticism of the system of oblation, to which he attributed the monks' complacence, lack of zeal, and incompetence, and his reference to very old monasteries (*monasteria vetustissima*), which was probably intended to exclude from his strictures more recent foundations like Cluny and his own abbey. Some old black houses, including some very old ones like Marmoutier, enjoyed a relatively high reputation, of which Guibert was certainly aware, in spite of his general feeling that the world around him was declining and man sinking into sin.

Among the prestigious older monasteries, pride of place belonged to Cluny, of which the very prominence, and the tendency to call all old black monks Cluniacs, made it a target of attack especially by the Cistercians, whose writings sometimes give the impression that Cluny was in greater need of reform, or was more opposed to reform, than other old black houses. Criticism tended to concentrate on Cluny precisely because it was the most eminent representative of the old type of monasticism, and many of the criticisms of Cluny sound like those later brought against the new monks. It counted among its admirers not only Peter Damiani, who praised its 'vigorous mortification and regular severity', and Anselm, who remarked on 'the severity of the order' there, but also new monks like Robert of Arbrissel, who said that no one in their right mind would dare to disparage Cluny, 'where by the grace of God there is so great a benefit every day'.[123] The Cistercian Amedeus of Hauterives, who left Cluny because he disliked its rich vestments and 'sweet songs', nonetheless acknowledged that its monks 'shone forth in holy ways and in the highest religion'.[124] Even satirists like Nigel of Canterbury and Guiot of Provins, who had little good to say of monks, commented on the discipline and silence at Cluny.[125] Cluny's prestige and growth during the period of monastic reform

---

[122] Guibert, *De vita sua*, I, 8, ed. Bourgin, pp. 23–4, and tr. John Benton (Harper Torchbooks; New York 1970), p. 54.

[123] Peter Damiani, *De gallica profectione*, 12, in *PL*, CXLV, 873D; see also *Epp*. VI, 3 and 5, in *PL*, CXLIV, 373C and 380A, and Hamilton (1975), p. 197; Eadmer, *Vita Anselmi*, I, 5, ed. Richard W. Southern (MT; London and Edinburgh 1962), p. 9 (*BHL* 526a); and Andrew of Fontevrault, *Vita Roberti de Arbrissello*, VI, 31, in *PL*, CLXII, 1073C (*BHL* 7260).

[124] *Vita Amedaei Altae Ripae*, 5, ed. M.-Anselme Dimier, in *Studia monastica* 5 (1963), p. 288 (*BHL* 385b). For references to Cluny as an asylum, refuge, and safe port in the second half of the eleventh century, see Cowdrey (1970), pp. 128–30.

[125] Nigel of Canterbury (Longchamps), *Speculum stultorum*, lines 2077–110, ed. John Mozley and Robert Raymo (Berkeley and Los Angeles 1960), pp. 77–8, and Guiot of Provins, *Bible*, lines 1670–6, ed. John Orr (Publications of the University of Manchester: French Series 1; Man-

show that it should be seen more as a rival than as an opponent of the reformers, whose attacks were inspired as much by feelings of competition as by a sense of its laxness.

The most serious charge against Cluny, aside from the specific points raised by the Cistercians, which will be examined later, was not slackness in the observance of the rule but its ambition to expand and dominate, to which its record of growth in the eleventh and twelfth centuries gives some colour. During the abbacy of Hugh and his immediate successor Pontius, the mother-house grew from between sixty and eighty to over three hundred monks and established dependencies for the first time in the Ile-de-France, Normandy, England, Germany, Italy, Spain, Portugal, the Low Countries, and perhaps also Byzantium and the Holy Land.[126] Already in the early eleventh century bishop Adalbero of Laon called abbot Odilo the *rex* and *princeps* of a new *militia* of Cluniac monks, the *bellicus ordo monachorum*; a parish priest in Germany who opposed the establishment of a Cluniac house by Ulrich of Zell said to his congregation that 'These monks coming from the monastery of Cluny into these parts are full of deceit, avarice, and envy and are entirely contrary to your salvation'; and when Bernard of Tiron was abbot of St Cyprian he accused Hugh of Cluny of trying to control him 'like an archabbot by proud tyranny'.[127] A grant to Font-Just in 1138 allowed the monks to submit 'to the Cistercian order or to some other church living in a similar manner and law' but not 'to the Cluniac order or to any monastery ordered by a similar custom', and the abbot appointed at Fleury by the Cluniac cardinal Alberic of Ostia in 1141 had to promise not to introduce 'the order of Cluny there'.[128] This resistance was motivated less by hostility to Cluniac monasticism in itself than by a desire for independence and an adherence to established customs. Similar criticisms were made of other old black houses with many dependencies, and of the old monks generally, for their desire, as a Cistercian critic put it, to be called 'not monks but lords'.[129] The custom of referring to monks and regular canons as *dominus* began in the twelfth

---

chester 1915), p. 62. On Nigel's name, see his *Passion of St Lawrence, Epigrams and Marginal Poems*, ed. Jan Ziolkowski (Mittellateinische Studien und Texte 14; Leiden 1994), pp. 6–11.

[126] On the growing number of monks at Cluny, see Peter the Venerable, *Stat.* 55, in *CCM*, VI, 85, and the note there, and on the expansion of the order in Germany, Wollasch (1992); in the Low Countries, Constable (1977a), pp. 216–23; and in Lombardy, Violante (1979–81), pp. 658–9.

[127] Adalbero of Laon, *Carmen ad Rotbertum regem*, lines 115 and 155–6, ed. Claude Carozzi (CHFMA 32; Paris 1979), pp. 8 and 12; *Vita Udalrici Cellensis*, 48, in *AASS*, 10 July III, 154 (*BHL* 8370); and Geoffrey *Grossus, Vita Bernardi Tironiensis*, VII, 58, in *PL*, CLXXII, 1401D (*BHL* 1251). Von Walter (1903–6), II, 15–16, assigned this chapter to source B.

[128] *GC*, II, *instr.*, p. 61, and Thomas of Morigny, *Ep.* to Bernard of Clairvaux, in *PL*, CLXXXII, 683B. See *Chronicon Mauriniacense*, ed. Léon Mirot, 2nd edn (CTSEEH 41; Paris 1912), pp. xiii and 77 n. 4; *Hist. litt.*, XII, 220–2; and Hampe (1898), p. 395. On 'clauses of return' in case the original purpose changed or the site abandoned, see Dubois (1968a), p. 46.

[129] Rochais and Binont (1964), p. 162, no. Lc 57. On the use of *dominus* and *frater*, with references to the Cluniac customaries, see the customs of Marbach, 34, no. 74, in Siegwart (1965), p. 141, and the notes by André Duchesne in *Bibl. Clun.*, coll. 148–9.

century and persists in the practice of calling Benedictine monks 'Dom', against which there is a reaction in some modern monastic circles. Institutional wealth was not often cited as a fault in the early years of the reform movement, though personal property and avarice were strictly forbidden. A monk who has left the world and made himself a prisoner, 'for whom the world is crucified and he to the world', said Ratherius of Verona, should not possess an atom, and Peter Damiani objected to receiving even gifts for his monastery.[130] Prosperity in itself was not condemned, aside from a fear of luxury and slackness that it might bring, but in the course of the twelfth century there was a growing sense of the dangers of money and wealth, especially among the reformers. In their respective mortuary rolls Andrew of Chezal-Benoît (d. 1112) was praised for begging and Vitalis of Savigny (d. 1122) was twice called a beggar.[131] The letter concerning the abbey of St Mary at York attributed to archbishop Thurstan of York in 1132, but in fact written some ten or fifteen years later on the basis of a lost original, said that 'With riches the virtues flourish less and remain firm more rarely.'[132] Bernard of Tiron forced a companion to dispose of some money, saying 'Either you will not be my companion or you will cease to carry those coins,' and Aybert of Crépin and Berthold of Garsten, who died in 1141 and 1142 respectively, were said to have refused to touch or carry money.[133] This may have been owing to monastic rigour or fear of venality, but it suggests a growing dislike of money even in relatively conservative circles. Towards the end of the century Robert of Torigny, who was abbot of Mont-St-Michel, specifically attributed the decline of the old monasteries to their wealth.[134] And a frequently cited passage in the *Life* of Robert of Molesme, the founder of Cîteaux, written in connection with his canonization in 1221, said that 'Since a plenitude of possessions brings a paucity of morals [the monks of Molesme] began to be empty of spiritual things when they began to abound in temporal things.'[135]

---

[130] Ratherius of Verona, *Exemplar*, in *Miscellanea Cassinense*, 1 (1897), 11, 3: *Monastica*, p. 18, and Peter Damiani, *Opusc.* 53 *De patientia in insectatione improborum*, 4, in *PL*, CXLV, 793D–6B, on which see Little (1978), p. 73. See also Damiani's remarks on the involvement of monks in worldly affairs in his *Ep.* 96, ed. Kurt Reindel, in *MGH, Briefe*, IV.3, 50–1.

[131] *Rouleaux des morts*, pp. 170, 307, and 308.

[132] Hugh of Kirkstall, *Narratio*, ed. Walbran, p. 11. On this letter, of which the surviving text is probably a revised version of a lost original, see Bethell (1966), p. 16, and Baker (1969a), pp. 17 and 40, and esp. (1969b), pp. 33–5.

[133] Geoffrey *Grossus*, *Vita Bernardi Tironiensis*, IV, 26, in *PL*, CLXXII, 1384AB (*BHL* 1251); Robert of Ostrevand, *Vita Ayberti*, II, 15, in *AASS*, 7 Apr. I, 674 (*BHL* 180); and *Vita Bertholdi Garstensis*, 5, ed. Josef Lenzenweger (Forschungen zur Geschichte Oberösterreichs 5; Graz and Cologne 1958), pp. 232–3 (*BHL* 1274–82). On Aybert, see Trelcat (1924), pp. 63–9, and pp. 313–15 below. There is an interesting reference in the *Translatio* of Romanus of Rouen in 1090, in MS Rouen, Bibl. mun., 1406, fol. 48ᵛ, cited in Lifshitz (1988), to the condemnation of people who refused legal money and accepted only goods in kind, 'which greatly oppressed the people', but who they were is uncertain.

[134] Robert of Torigny, *De immutatione ordinis monachorum*, 7, in *PL*, CCII, 1313C.

[135] *Vita Roberti Molismensis*, 9, ed. Kolumban Spahr (Fribourg 1944), p. 13 (*BHL* 7265). On this frequently cited passage see [Ducourneau] (1932–3), pp. 236–8, and Salmon (1954), p. 276.

This reflects the attitude towards wealth in the early thirteenth century, however, after the beginnings of the mendicant movement.

In the eleventh or twelfth centuries, material prosperity was generally considered a blessing for a religious community, and decline was more often attributed to poverty than to wealth. Guibert of Nogent, after remarking on how 'the love of holy life grew cold' in his times, went on to associate the paucity of recruits to religious life with the growing poverty of various churches, where manual labour was also despised.[136] Reformers occasionally refused to found or take over a house owing to lack of resources. Bishop William of Durham in the late eleventh century received permission to combine the ancient monasteries of Wearmouth and Jarrow 'because the smallness of the diocese is not sufficient for three communities of monks', and at Baumberg it was decided to combine two endowments because it was thought wiser to establish 'one church with abundance than two churches with scarcity'.[137] In 1090 the abbot of St Jean d'Angély said that he had endeavoured to improve (*in melius reformare*) and enlarge the abbey's chamber (that is, the department concerned with material supplies) 'so that bodily necessity may not, by any chance, God forbid, afflict the monks who are fighting for God in this house under the rule and that for this reason (*per hoc*) the spiritual discipline of the holy master may not grow cool in them'; and abbot Philip of L'Aumône sent to other monasteries some recruits whom he was unable to receive owing to lack of resources (*prae inopia*).[138] Many similar passages in monastic charters and histories and in the *Lives* of monastic saints stressed the advantages of a sufficiency of material goods and the dangers of poverty, and they connected material with spiritual (or external and internal, as they were often called) well-being in a religious community.[139]

Misuse or display of wealth was another matter and was often associated with neglect of the rule and especially with the little luxuries in food and clothing, and with comfort in travelling, which formed the stock-in-trade of

[136] Guibert, *De vita sua*, I, 8, ed. Bourgin, p. 23.

[137] *Liber vitae ecclesiae Dunelmensis*, ed. Joseph Stevenson (Surtees Society 13; Durham 1841), p. 74, and *Fundatio monasterii Baumburgensis*, in *MGH, SS*, XV.2, 1063, playing on the words *copia* and *inopia*.

[138] *Cartulaire de Saint-Jean d'Angély*, ed. Georges Musset (Archives historiques de la Saintonge et de l'Aunis 30 and 33; Paris and Saintes 1901–3), I, 30, no. 20. See Bruhat (1907), p. 137, and Philip of L'Aumône, *Ep.* 22, in *Bibliotheca patrum Cisterciensium*, ed. Bertrand Tissier (Bonnefontaine and Paris 1660–9), III, 252.

[139] The author of the *Libellus*, 4, ed. Constable, pp. 54–6, attributed the number of secular monks to the negligence of their superiors and abundance or (he added) lack of material possessions. See *Vita Gosuini Aquicinctini*, I, 16, ed. Richard Gibbons (Douai 1620), p. 66 (*BHL* 3625); *Vita Joachimi abbatis*, in Grundmann (1977), p. 346 (*BHL* 4284); and *Vita* [B] *Norberti*, X, 55, in *PL*, CLXX, 1295C (*BHL* 6249), where the early Premonstratensians feared that their poverty and austerity would undermine their stability and repel rather than attract recruits. See also de Moreau (1909), p. 135, and *Les chartes de l'abbaye de Waulsort*, I: *(946–1199)* ed. Georges Despy (Académie royale de Belgique: Commission royale d'histoire, Publications in-quarto; Brussels 1957), p. 24.

anti-monastic satires, and of some serious works, in the twelfth century.[140] The topos of the proud abbot riding a horse rather than a mule or donkey, or better yet travelling on foot, went back at least to the *Life* of Martin by Sulpicius Severus and is found in countless later *Lives*, often in the form of a simple reference to travelling on foot or on a mule or donkey.[141] The terms secular monk and *semilaicus* were applied to monks who lived too openly in the world and enjoyed its pleasures too freely. Abuses of this sort were not found only in old black monasteries, however, and as the twelfth century advanced members of the new reformed orders came in for increasingly hard knocks. Charges of sexual improprieties, for example, were less commonly brought against the members of strictly cloistered old monasteries than against the reformers who welcomed women not only into their communities but also into their beds, as a form of ascetic discipline and test. The Cistercians in particular were the butt of many unsavoury jokes on account of their refusal to wear trousers under their robes, which was attributed to lasciviousness.[142]

Even the greatest reformers ran into criticism. Bernard himself seems to have been comparatively immune, but not entirely, since Wulfric of Hazelbury accused him of wanting to usurp a knowledge of the secrets of God.[143] Norbert's change from a wandering preacher and reformer into the archbishop of Magdeburg was seen by some critics as apostasy. According to the Cluniac in the *Dialogue of two monks*, which was written some twenty years after Norbert's death, 'From a barefooted rider on a donkey, he became a well-shod and well-dressed [rider] of a caparisoned horse; from a hermit, a courtier in the court of the emperor Lothar; from common bread and cheap foods, to royal and splendid feasts; from a great scorner of the world, a great performer in the cases of the world.'[144] These are hard words, though no harder than those used by the reformers (including Bernard in his *Apology*) about the old black monks, and their inclusion in a work written by a Cistercian, with no effort to refute them, is noteworthy.

[140] See the sins mentioned in the *Visio monachi de Aineshamma*, 31, in *Eynsham Cartulary*, ed. H.E. Salter (Oxford Historical Society 49 and 51; Oxford 1907–8), II, 337–8, and the list of twelve abuses in Hugh of Fouilloy, *De claustro animae*, II, 11, in *PL*, CLXXVI, 1058C, which includes precious clothing, exquisite food, the *monachus curialis*, and the *monachus causidicus* in addition to misbehaviour and negligence and standard failings like disobedience, laziness, and obstinacy. On this work see Grégoire (1962), who attributed it to an Augustinian canon, and Fonseca (1973), who defended the authorship of Hugh of Fouilloy. On anti-monastic satire in popular and vernacular literature, see Walther (1920), pp. 163–5, and Schneider (1928), pp. 14–43.

[141] Sulpicius Severus, *Dialogi*, I, 21, 4, in *CSEL*, I, 173, and the note in the edition of G. de Prato (Verona 1741–54), I, 104. Martin's example was cited in Thomas of Reuil, *Vita Petri Monoculi*, 28, in *PL*, CCIX, 1030B (*BHL* 6730). See Gougaud (1922) and (1923) on ascetic forms of travel.

[142] See pp. 192–3 below.

[143] John of Ford, *Vita Wulfrici Haselbergiae*, 54, ed. Maurice Bell (Somerset Record Society 47; n.p. 1933), p. 79 (*BHL* 8743–4). This criticism carries more weight because the author of Wulfric's *Vita* was a Cistercian.

[144] Idungus, *Dialogus*, 2, ed. Huygens, p. 426.

By the middle of the twelfth century it was more or less open season for all religious orders. Even the Carthusians, who were often considered (among others, by themselves) as above reproach, were charged with litigiousness and other failings by Berengar of Poitiers and with phariseeism in the *Life* of Hugh of Lincoln, who was himself a Carthusian.[145] Stephen of Tournai in the same sermon criticized the Cluniacs for hypocrisy and dissimulation and the Cistercians for cupidity and robbery, and wrote to the archbishop of Reims in 1177/ 84 that 'I know that the Cistercians are among those who storm heaven with violence, but I have yet to read that they are allowed to seize lands with violence.'[146] These words throw some doubt on the sincerity of the views he expressed in a letter written about the same time to the prior of Pontigny, in which he praised the observance of the rule by the Cistercians, 'so that they seem to omit not one iota of it', and their charity and self-sufficiency: 'If you counted how many benefits flow from them onto the people, they confer more on the whole (*universitas*) than the whole [confers] on them.'[147] Brunellus the Ass in Nigel of Canterbury's *Mirror of fools*, which was written in 1179–80, examined all the orders in order to put together his own out of the most lenient features of each. He took horses from the Templars, permission to travel from the Hospitallers, eating fat on Saturdays from the Cluniacs, wearing no trousers from the Cistercians, freedom to speak from the Grandmontines, only one mass a month from the Carthusians, soft and full robes from the Premonstratensians, and a companion from the nuns. He took nothing only from the Gilbertines, who were new and, so far as he knew, good. Some of this was relatively innocent fun, but earlier in the poem Nigel attacked the Cistercians more particularly for their lack of hospitality, refusal to pay tithes or to wear trousers, and above all for their wealth.[148] When Richard I of England was accused in a well-known *exemplum* of the sins of pride, luxury, and avarice, which were called his three daughters, he replied that he had married pride to the Templars, luxury to the black monks, and avarice to the Cistercians.[149] The tables were fully turned, and many of the charges previously brought against the old monks were by this time levelled at the reformers.

[145] Klibansky (1946) corrected the text published in *PL*, CLXXVIII, 1875–6, and Adam of Eynsham, *Magna vita Hugonis*, II, 17, ed. Douie and Farmer (n. 51), I, 81. The accuser was Alexander of Lewes, who later became a Cluniac.

[146] Stephen of Tournai, *Ep.* 70, ed. Desilve, p. 84; Bourgain (1879), pp. 222–3; and Warichez (1937), pp. 111–12.

[147] Stephen of Tournai, *Ep.* 1, ed. Desilve, pp. 5–6.

[148] Nigel of Canterbury, *Speculum stultorum*, lines 891–4, 957–62, and 2413–64, ed. Mozley and Raymo (n. 125), pp. 51–2 and 83–4; see generally lines 2051–412, pp. 76–84, where he discussed the good and bad points of these orders.

[149] Gerald of Wales, *Speculum ecclesiae*, II, 12, and *Itinerarium Kambriae*, I, 3, ed. Brewer (n. 60), IV, 54–5, and VI, 44, and Ward and Herbert (1883–1910), III, 74, no. 168. See Odo of Cheriton, *Parabola* 153, in Léopold Hervieux, *Les fabulistes latins depuis le siècle d'Auguste jusqu'à la fin du moyen âge*, IV: *Eudes de Cheriton et ses dérivés* (Paris 1896), p. 325. On the Cistercian reputation for greed, see Peter of Blois, *Ep.* 82, in *English Episcopal Acta* (n. 34), II, 84–5, no. 106.

Criticism of the Cistercians began in the 1130s and became a cause of serious concern, to themselves as well as to others, by 1150. The most frequent and serious charge against them during the first half of the twelfth century was self-righteousness and their apparent assumption that their order was the safest, and sometimes the only sure, way to heaven. 'O the new breed of pharisees that has come again to the world', wrote Peter the Venerable at the beginning of his reply to the Cistercian criticisms of Cluny in his Letter 28, 'who separate themselves from others, prefer [themselves] to others, and say that the prophet predicted that they would be called, "Do not touch me" [John 20.17] because I am clean [Job 33.9]'.[150] Bernard of Clairvaux was reputed to have said that Judas himself could be saved 'if he sat in this school of Christ and were incorporated in this order'.[151] Although in speaking to his own monks Bernard freely admitted the presence of weaker brethren among them, in works addressed to outsiders he confidently compared Clairvaux to the heavenly Jerusalem as the port of salvation.[152] The insistence of the Cistercians on strict observance of the rule, and their selective citation of sources, led the Cluniac in the Dialogue of two monks to say that 'Since you Cistercians judaize, following the killing letter of the rule, you therefore diligently study the authorities pertaining to the pure letter in order to defend your judaizing through them.'[153]

Avarice closely followed self-righteousness among the charges brought against the Cistercians in the second half of the twelfth century, when the statutes of the general chapters show an increasing concern at the involvement of the order in secular affairs.[154] Pope Alexander III in the early 1160s took the Cistercians to task for deserting their early economic principles and threatened to revoke their privileges if they did not mend their ways.[155] The right not to pay tithes made sense when they were poor and worked new and uncultivated lands, from which no tithes had previously been paid, but as they acquired more and other lands, it cut into the revenues of monasteries and churches that were poorer than themselves. The practice of expelling the inhabitants from the lands they acquired, in order to make 'deserts' to be

[150] Peter the Venerable, Ep. 28, ed. Constable, I, 57; see also 94.
[151] Exordium magnum Cisterciense, II, 5, ed. Bruno Griesser (Series scriptorum s. ordinis Cisterciensis 2; Rome 1961), p. 101. See McGuire (1983b), p. 43.
[152] Bernard, Ep. 64.1–2, ed. Leclercq, VII, 157–8, comparing Clairvaux to Jerusalem, and Serm. 3 in ascensione, 6–7, ed. Leclercq, V, 134–5, on differences among the monks. See also Nicholas of Montiéramey, Ep. 36, in PL, CXCVI, 1631D–2A.
[153] Idungus, Dialogus, III, 15 ed. Huygens, p. 444.
[154] See the Cistercian statutes published under the years 1152 and 1180 in Canivez, Statuta, pp. 45–8 and 86–7, and Waddell (1994), pp. 32–4, who said (p. 32) that 'Despite the obvious fact that Cistercians were very much involved with feudal society at large, the General Chapter statutes make it clear that they also intended, and sincerely intended, to keep a certain distance from the kind of involvements we find in page after page of the Molesme cartularies.' Buczek (1971) dated the beginning of criticism of the Cistercians from Innocent II's bull of 1132.
[155] Leclercq (1952) and (1954). See also Reuter (1976), pp. 331–2 and 336, and pp. 34–5, 118–19, and 225–6 below on tithes and the expulsion of inhabitants from settled lands.

worked by themselves, likewise gave rise to many criticisms. The concern among the Cistercians themselves is reflected in the story told by Caesarius of Heisterbach about an abbot who hesitated to accept lands from which the inhabitants had been expelled and who was reassured by a vision.[156] Among the many critics of the Cistercians in the second half of the twelfth century, in addition to those already mentioned, were Peter the Chanter, cardinal Odo of Tusculum (who was a former Cistercian abbot), the hermit Wulfric of Hazelbury, Joachim of Fiore, and above all Walter Map, who never lost a chance to mention the failings of the Cistercians.[157]

It is hard to say what truth, if any, lay in these charges and counter-charges, which were probably a sign more of the times and the mood of ecclesiastical rivalries and politics than of the real circumstances of religious life. Monks could never fully live up to the lofty ideals set by themselves or by society, and there were inevitable discrepancies between the ideal and the reality. It may be that the ability to make fun of institutions was a mark of their strength rather than their weakness. The wide-ranging nature of criticisms, however, and above all the growing emphasis on hypocrisy as a characteristic of all monks, was an indication of the changing position of monasticism in society, which no longer looked for the same qualities in monks as it had in the past. A feeling that monks, both old and new, were wolves in sheep's clothing and not what they claimed to be ran through the criticisms and was taken seriously at the time. In a letter written in 1109 to the countess Ermengard of Brittany, who wanted to become a nun, Robert of Arbrissel said that 'Many clerics are hypocrites, and monks and hermits simulate long prayers in order to please men and be well regarded by them.' He went on to say, 'Short prayer is useful; prayer from the heart, not from the lips, is pleasing to God. God pays attention not to the words but to the heart of the person who prays. All the good work of a just person is prayer.' Robert was a characteristic and influential religious leader, and these words from his only surviving written work give an idea not only of his message to lay people but also of what he and other reformers felt was lacking in the existing forms of religious life, which stressed long liturgical prayer and had close ties with secular society. 'Love voluntary poverty', Robert told Ermengard. 'Amid dignities and honours, amid riches and silks, amid your husband and beloved boys, and rich relations,

---

[156] Caesarius, *Dialogus*, IV, 63, ed. Strange, I, 232. See pp. 118–19 and 218 below.
[157] Peter the Chanter, *Verbum abbreviatum*, 86, in *PL*, CCV, 257CD; Odo of Ourscamp, *Ep.* 8, ed. Jean Leclercq, in *Anal. mon.*, III, p. 157, and *Papsturkunden in Frankreich*, N.F. VII, 418–19, no. 141; Joachim of Fiore, *Concordia novi ac veteris testamenti*, V, 49 (Venice 1519), fol. 84ᵛ, and Leclercq (1954), p. 81 n. 2; and Walter Map, *De nugis curialium*, ed. and tr. Montague R. James, rev. C.N.L. Brooke and R.A.B. Mynors (OMT; Oxford 1983), pp. xliii–iv; Griesser (1924); and Deug-Su (1992). See also The *Latin Poems Commonly Attributed to Walter Mapes*, ed. Thomas Wright (Camden Society 16; London 1841), p. 169, and McGuire (1983a), pp. 249–50.

say, sighing with the prophet: I am a beggar and a poor woman, may the Lord take care of me.'[158]

This passage, like Marbod's new saint, Bernard's monstrous life, and Norbert's new type of life, helps to lift a corner of the curtain dividing the substance of the reform from the externals that figure so largely in the polemical literature. The difficulty of understanding the real nature of the movement is increased, on the one hand, by the reformers' attachment to the old ways and ideals, and their consequent difficulty in expressing clearly their own deepest needs and desires, and, on the other hand, by three specific problems in interpreting the sources, with which the final section of this chapter is concerned. The first is that they were written by clerics and religious, almost all of them men, who were involved in the movement and committed to one position or another and whose works, aside from a few translations and vernacular versions of saints' *Lives* and sermons, are in Latin. The views of lay people and especially lay women have to be deduced either from their actions or from the works of religious writers who wanted to promote a particular view or interest. What Anselm wrote to Gunnilda and Robert of Arbrissel to Ermengard is known, but not how those two women, both from the highest rank of society, received their words, except that one apparently wanted to be a nun and the other (who already was one) did not. The personal involvement of writers showed itself in the reappearance, after many centuries, of autobiographical works, like those of Otloh of St Emmeram, Abelard, and Guibert, in which the writer spoke about himself and his experiences, and also in various types of writing, which will be discussed later, such as dialogues and letters, which allowed for the expression of personal views.[159] Sermons, works of spiritual advice and exhortation, commentaries on religious rules, and customaries were all addressed to special audiences, which knew what to look for and usually found what they wanted in these works. Accounts of visions, dreams, and miracles were also highly personal and often served as a way of giving assurance or guidance and of resolving doubts and problems that an individual was unable to handle alone.[160]

The second difficulty is of a different, and in some ways opposite, nature and lies in the unchanging character of spiritual writings and their reliance over the centuries on the same themes and topoi, behind which it is hard to perceive the currents of change. Of all types of literature, spiritual writings

---

[158] Robert of Arbrissel, *Sermo ad comitissam Britanniae*, ed. J. de Petigny, in *Bibliothèque de l'Ecole des chartes* 15 (3 S. 5) (1854), pp. 232–3.

[159] See, for the eleventh century, Pivec (1939), pp. 45–6, and for letters of monastic vocation, Leclercq (1955).

[160] See Bogdanos (1977), p. 34, on the pattern of allegorical dream visions; Dinzelbacher (1981), esp. pp. 210–22, on the functions of visions; and Wittmer-Butsch (1990), esp. pp. 115–26 on the new value put on dreams in the twelfth century and 190–368 on dreams as personal experiences.

are perhaps the least obviously bound to the time they were written. Many works written in the twelfth century masqueraded, and some may still masquerade, under the names of Augustine and other fathers of the church, and late medieval works were often attributed to Anselm, Bernard, and other eminent spiritual writers of that time. There is hardly a word in the *Imitation of Christ* by Thomas à Kempis that could not have been (and a few scholars still maintain was) written in the late twelfth or early thirteenth century.[161] Some of these works, like forgeries made up of authentic fragments, defy critical analysis and expose the scholar to the constant risk of making false judgements. The only way to determine basic changes in spirituality is by balance, context, and emphasis, rather than by the actual words used in individual instances. When William James was accused of relying in the *Varieties of religious experience* on narratives that represented ideal types rather than literal truth, he replied that 'In a general account of religious experience I think these inaccuracies of detail of no great moment; for ideals all are *pointed to* by experience (*and reached* in some cases).'[162]

It is equally difficult to assess the influence of contemporary spiritual currents and intellectual schools. Much has been written, for instance, about the school of Chartres and about Cistercian spirituality, but aside from some general tendencies, it is unknown what views their influence covered, how it was transmitted, or whom it included.[163] Spiritual writers are rarely completely original, but it is hard to assess the relation of their ideas to those of their predecessors and contemporaries.[164] Writers shared rather than borrowed ideas, and they participated in general tendencies rather than belonging to particular schools of thought or spirituality. Geoffrey of St Thierry, for instance, whose unpublished sermons are cited here from time to time, brought together elements found in the works of many other writers, and the so-called Cistercian school, which is sometimes called Bernardine after Bernard of Clairvaux, includes writers who were not Cistercians for much of their lives, like William of St Thierry, and omits others who were long-time members of the order, like Otto of Freising.[165] Joachim of Fiore was a Cistercian before establishing his own religious order, but he is not commonly considered part of the Cistercian school. Some types of writing, including histories and saints' *Lives*, clearly show regional interests and concerns, but regional schools are harder to detect in theological and spiritual works. Rupert of Deutz, Honorius *Augustodunensis*, Gerhoh of Reichersberg, and in certain

---

[161] Constable (1995a), pp. 239–40.

[162] Perry (1935), II, 338.

[163] On the debate over the school of Chartres, see Richard Southern, in *Renaissance and Renewal* (1982), pp. 113–37, and (1995), pp. 58–101.

[164] Kristeller (1993), p. 20: 'The alleged originality of a thinker often reflects the ignorance of his readers and interpreters.'

[165] Chenu (1957), pp. 49–50, argued that William was not characteristically Cistercian, and Javelet (1967), I, xvii, called him 'autant le maître que le disciple de l'abbé de Clairvaux'.

respects Anselm of Havelberg and Otto of Freising, are sometimes grouped together as a conservative German school in contrast to the more rationalistic and forward-looking writers in France.[166] Their view of history can hardly be characterized as conservative, however, nor can Rupert's sense of his own talent or his tender and emotional devotion to Christ and the Virgin, which resembled that which is often associated with the Cistercians. Nations and institutions today often claim as their own writers and artists who were associated with them for only a brief period of their lives. At a time when national and institutional structures were comparatively weak, and personal influences strong, and when both people and ideas crossed boundaries with comparative ease, it is wise to avoid classifications of this sort and to recognize frankly the difficulty of determining the source of any particular idea or spiritual attitude.

The third problem is that many of the sources were composed, or revised, after the events they describe in order to show how things might or should have been, in the opinion of the writer, rather than how they actually took place. These works include both intentional forgeries, which are a useful indication of people's hopes and fears, and, more especially, charters, histories, and saints' *Lives* written in the light of later events. Circumstances that did not fit the purposes of the writer were passed over in silence, and rhetorical phrases like *sicut audivi* were inserted in the interests of verisimilitude. Foundation charters of religious houses often recorded, in the present tense, events stretching over many years, and scholars have sometimes called them forgeries on account of anachronisms that were well known to contemporaries. As legal documents, they record the gifts and rights (if any) of the original donors, who were usually lay men or women, rather than the purposes of the spiritual founders, whose roles were emphasized in other types of sources.[167] The histories of monastic foundations in particular tend to fit institutions into an accepted series of topoi, starting with the wildness or deserted state of the original site (for a new house) or with the evil character of the previous occupants (for a change of order, as from canons to monks or from one type of monk to another). Some accounts conceal altogether the earlier history of a house.[168] Many *Lives* of saints were written long after the deaths of their heroes and heroines, and reflect, like the *Life* of Stephen of Grandmont, the needs

---

[166] See Peter Classen, in *Renaissance and Renewal* (1982), p. 404. Hugh of St Victor is sometimes associated with this group on the basis of his alleged birth in Saxony, but Dereine (1960a), p. 908 n. 2, suggested he came from Ypres to Paris by way of Hammersleben.

[167] See Galbraith (1934); Dereine (1952), pp. 89–90, and (1959), pp. 43–5; Milis (1979), pp. 45–6, on the different dating of narrative and non-narrative sources; and Despy (1983) on the relation of the early charters of Afflighem to the annals and chronicle, which he called 'écrits de propagande *pro domo*'.

[168] Kastner (1974) and Ruyffelaere (1986) studied the distinction of oral and written sources in foundation histories. Both the Cluniacs and the Cistercians tended to suppress or distort the previous histories of houses they took over, often making them out more corrupt than they actually were: see Moyse (1973), p. 433, on the Cluniacs, and Epperlein (1967) on Cistercian 'foundation myths'.

or standards of the time they were written rather than those of the saint's own period.[169] The *Life* of Robert of Molesme is an interesting case in point owing to the uncertain nature of his departure from Molesme and subsequent return, which almost certainly delayed his canonization and may have influenced the accounts of the foundation and early history of Cîteaux, some of which play down Robert's role or blacken his reputation.[170] The date and reliability of the earliest known Cistercian documents are the subject of debate, but they certainly evolved over a period of time and reflected changes in the constitution of the order in matters like exemption, lay brothers, the general chapters, and the position of the abbot of Cîteaux.[171] Scholars now look at the history of the Cistercian order, including its liturgy, art, and architecture, in terms of successive generations, each of which adjusted the past to meet its

---

[169] Wilkinson (1990) and esp. (1991) argued that this *Vita* is a paradigm of the history of the order seen in the light of the papal reforms of 1186.

[170] In addition to the *Vita* (n. 135), see Lenssen (1936–7), who defended Robert and asserted his claim to be the founder of Cîteaux, and Lefèvre (1956).

[171] The early Cistercian documents are cited here from the *Textes de Cîteaux*, except for the *Carta caritatis posterior* (*Monuments*, ed. Guignard, pp. 79–84, and Canivez, *Statuta*, I, xxvi–xxxi), *Exordium magnum Cisterciense* (n. 151), *Ecclesiastica officia* or *Liber usuum* (*Monuments*, ed. Guignard, pp. 87–245, and Choisselet and Vernet (1989)), *Usus conversorum* (*Monuments*, ed. Guignard, pp. 276–87), and the liturgical texts and statutes of the general chapters, on which see Turk (1948) and Waddell (1971), (1978), (1993), and (1994), esp. pp. 27–9. The dates and versions of these texts are the subject of extensive scholarly dispute, into which it is impossible to enter here. There are bibliographies in *Repertorium*, III, 636–9, and IV, 406–8; de Waha (1978); de Place (1984); and Elm (1994), p. 18 n. 49; see also Auberger (1986). The three principal versions of the *Carta caritatis* (in addition to a conjectural lost first version) are (1) *Summa cartae caritatis* (pp. 117–21) found with the *Exordium Cistercii* and *Capitula* and probably dating from c. 1136; (2) *Carta caritatis prior* (pp. 89–102), which is now commonly dated 1152 but may be earlier; and (3) *Carta caritatis posterior*, which dates from the later twelfth century and became the standard text. Comparisons of the *Carta caritatis prior* and *posterior* are given in Turk (1948), pp. 109–14, and *Textes de Cîteaux*, pp. 132–42. There are three distinct texts traditionally entitled 'Exordium', in addition to a possible lost early text: (1) the *Exordium Cistercii* or *Summa exordii* (pp. 111–16) found with the *Summa cartae caritatis* and *Capitula* is a highly abridged account of the foundation of Cîteaux and the early growth of the order and is dated 1134/50 by Hallinger (1983), 1123/4 by Auberger (1986), p. 26, and about 1123 by Bredero (1993), pp. 313–14, who dated the *Summa cartae caritatis* about 1130; (2) the *Exordium parvum* or *Exordium Cisterciensis cenobii* (pp. 54–86), a more detailed account of the origin of Cîteaux (including several official acts and related documents), was added to and revised shortly before 1147, and is dated after 1134 by de Waha (1978), 1134–51/74 by Hallinger (1983), and 1140/50 by Auberger (1986), p. 59; and (3) the *Exordium magnum* (attributed to Conrad of Eberbach) is a compilation (including almost the entire *Exordium parvum*), completed probably after 1206, and is made up chiefly of edifying stories about the early history of the order and its members. The *Instituta monachorum Cisterciensium de Molismo venientium* (pp.77–8), which forms chapter 15 of the *Exordium Cisterciensis cenobii*, consists of a description of decisions made by the founders of the order. The *Capitula* (pp. 121–5) found with the *Exordium Cistercii* and *Summa cartae caritatis* is an abridgement and thematic arrangement of statutes of the early general chapters, of which the last dates from about 1136. I am indebted to Chrysogonus Waddell for assisting me with this summary.

own requirements.[172] The *Charter of love* and *Little beginning* are no longer considered reliable guides to the early history of Cîteaux, which is more safely reconstructed from other accounts and by comparison with similar contemporary houses than from the records of the Cistercians themselves.

The difficulties of interpreting written works enhance the value of the non-verbal sources, like works of art, architecture, and music. The layouts of the third church at Cluny, of a characteristic Cistercian abbey, and of a hermit's rock-cut tomb or chapel, if they are rightly read, express the spirituality of those who lived in and used them.[173] The repair and redecoration of churches at the turn of the millennium, as Ralph Glaber pointed out at the time, paralleled the renewal and regrowth of Christian society, which was symbolically displayed in the luxuriant vegetation shown in the painting and sculpture of the twelfth century.[174] Music established its autonomy from mathematics at this time and was recognized as a voice of its own, attuned to the religious needs of mankind. Even the songs of birds were recognized as a call to the religious life by Miro of Ripoll.[175] Art increasingly spoke to the hearts of men both from the walls of churches and from smaller paintings and sculptures that could be kept in oratories and cells and also in private homes. The bronze-casters and enamellers of Limoges kept Europe supplied with crucifixes and other works that fostered private devotions and personal piety. Bishop Gerard of Angoulême sent Geoffrey of Chalard a pyx that was described in his *Life* as decorated with pictures of Jesus, Mary, angels, and apostles; and Aelred of Rievaulx advised recluses to have 'an image of the Saviour hanging on the cross which presents to you His passion that you imitate, invites [you] with extended arms to His embraces in which you delight, and pours out to you from His bare breasts the milk of sweetness in which you find consolation'.[176] A new note of tenderness and pity also appeared in the representations of Christ as a child and on the cross, where the main stress had traditionally been on His power and glory and on the rewards of the faithful and the

---

[172] See Auberger (1986), pp. 124–7; Fergusson (1983), p. 82; and, on art and architecture, Stratford (1981), p. 227; Norton and Park (1986) on the three generations *c.* 1130–60 (pp. 5 and 286), *c.* 1160–1200 (pp. 60 and 257), and beginning *c.* 1200 (pp. 8, 38, 135, 236, 266, and 303); and Rudolph (1990), pp. 187 and 198, who (like Stratford) argued that the second generation, inspired by Bernard, was more extreme and ascetic than the first.

[173] Conant (1968), p. 50, for instance, suggested that the chapels and crypts in the monastic enclosure at Cluny may have been used for ascetic retreats. The presence or absence of an oratory in a hermitage is an indication of the liturgical inclinations of the inhabitant. According to Gervers (1967), p. 11, 18 per cent of known hermits in France lived in caves or among rocks.

[174] Ladner (1983c).

[175] *Vita Mironis*, in *España sagrada*, XXVIII, 306 and 310 (*BHL* 5971). See generally Guy Beaujouan, in *Renaissance and Renewal* (1982), p. 466, citing John of Afflighem.

[176] *Vita Gaufridi Castaliensis*, II, 11, ed. A. Bosvieux, in *Mémoires de la Société des sciences naturelles et archéologiques de la Creuse* 3 (1862), p. 111 (*BHL* 3283), and Aelred of Rievaulx, *De institutione inclusarum*, 26, ed. Charles Dumont (SC 76; Paris 1961), p. 104.

punishments of the sinners.[177] The growing interest in works of mercy and charity can be seen on the late twelfth- or early thirteenth-century portal of St Gall of the cathedral at Basel, which shows six works of charity in conjunction with the Last Judgement, and in scenes of St Martin and the beggar, where the charitable act of dividing the cloak was given greater prominence than Martin's subsequent vision of Christ wearing the cloak.[178]

Manuscripts are of interest not only for the texts they contain but also in themselves, as evidence of when and where they were made and of their later movements. The copying of a customary, or the neglect of a necrology, are signs of changes in religious life and attitudes, quite apart from what the texts say. Manuscript 101 in the University Library at Münster contains among other works an eleventh-century copy of the rule for canons compiled at Aachen in 816, a contemporary or slightly later copy of the so-called *Praeceptum* of Augustine in the margin, and an account of the consecration of the church at Xanten by archbishop Norbert of Magdeburg in 1128.[179] Norbert himself may indeed have seen and studied this manuscript, in which the two main sources for the life of regular canons are associated with the founder of Premonstratensians.

Changes in the popularity of holy personages and saints are shown by the dedications of churches, representations in art, and the liturgy.[180] The devotion to the Virgin is reflected in countless prayers, hymns, and exempla, as well as in art and church dedications. There was a growing interest in the Trinity, as the Trinitarian order shows, and especially in the Holy Spirit, who bore for many thinkers in the twelfth century the special responsibility for God's ongoing work of renewal and reform in the world.[181] The dedication of Heloise's monastery to the Paraclete was unusual at the time and has been seen as a sign of the primacy of the Holy Spirit in the new contemplative life.[182] Mary Magdalene, whose cult reached its height in the twelfth century, was

---

[177] Constable (1995a), pp. 194–217, esp. 210–12.

[178] On the Galluspforte, see Moullet (1938), esp. pp. 62–3 on the works of mercy; Homburger (1939), who dated it to the late twelfth century; and Yvonne Labande-Mailfert, in *Laici* (1968), pp. 504–5. On the iconography of the miracles of St Martin, see Sauvel (1956), esp. pp. 170–2, and Otto Pächt, in Pächt, Dodwell, and Wormald (1960), pp. 94–5. See plate 2 for depictions of works of mercy.

[179] Two folios from this manuscript are reproduced in Elm (1984), pp. 185 and 294. See Fonseca (1970), pp. 186–7, on other manuscripts concerning the rule of regular canons.

[180] Van Gennep (1935–6), pp. 557–9, and (1939) stressed the difficulty of establishing the dates of foundations and dedications and the distinction between liturgical, monastic, and popular cults, which do not necessarily coincide. See also Genicot (1984c), p. 383, and Zimmermann (1958–9), esp. pp. 5–124, distinguishing between reform patrons, knightly patrons, and popular saints.

[181] Rupert of Deutz, *De sancta trinitate*, 34: *De operibus spiritus sancti*, I, 3, in *CC:CM*, XXIV, 1824–5. See Van Engen (1983), p. 91, and, on the importance of the Trinity in vernacular literature, Zorzi (1954) and Delaruelle (1962), pp. 152–4. The Trinity also played a special role in the works of Joachim of Fiore.

[182] Kantorowicz (1965), pp. 341–2.

associated with hermits,[183] and the apostles, who began to be honoured in the eleventh century, with pilgrimage and wandering preaching. James was one of the patrons of pilgrimage, and John the Evangelist of the developing cult of the Sacred Heart, particularly among the Premonstratensians in the twelfth century.[184] The popularity of St Alexius is of interest because he was a lay man as well as a devotee of voluntary poverty and of pilgrimage.[185] Dedications to four new saints, each associated with a characteristic feature of eleventh-century spirituality, appeared in the diocese of Toul during the episcopate of Pibo, which lasted from 1069 to 1109: Nicholas from the east, James the apostle and pilgrim, Theobald the hermit, and pope Leo IX.[186] Nicholas showed the growing interest in earlier saints, and James the interest in the apostles and pilgrimage. Theobald was a noble from Champagne who became a hermit in Germany, where he performed 'the meanest and hardest work of peasants, such as carrying stones, harvesting grain from the fields, caring for stables, and above all . . . making charcoal for the work of blacksmiths', and who towards the end of his life went on a pilgrimage to Compostela and then spent nine years as a hermit in Italy, where he died in 1066 and was buried at Vicenza.[187] Leo IX had been bishop of Toul before he became pope in 1048. His cult is explained both by his connections with the diocese and by his prestige as a reformer.[188] There was a rising interest in the cults and relics of contemporary saints in the twelfth century, which has been called the *saeculum reliquiarum*,[189] and the bodies of well-known holy men were the objects of competition. There is a vivid picture in the *Life* of Stephen of Obazine, who died at Bonaigue in 1159, of the efforts to obtain relics and even his body, which his followers, who were taking it back to Obazine, refused to leave for a night in a church of countess Margaret of Comborn for fear she would keep it.[190]

The popularity of saints also influenced the naming of children, which reflected changes in spirituality as well as in family groupings and local

---

[183] See Saxer (1959), II, 355, and Constable (1995a), pp. 122–3.

[184] Delaruelle (1962), pp. 144–6, and Schreiber (1940), (1940–1), pp. 5–13, (1941), and (1942), p. 82.

[185] Manteuffel (1970), p. 13; Gieysztor (1967–8); and Gnädinger (1972), p. 57.

[186] Choux (1952), pp. 89–94 and 97. The cell dedicated to St James, for which Pibo granted a charter in 1097, was founded by Ursus of Benevento, showing that there were links with southern Italy: ibid., p. 151, and *GC*, XIII, *instr.*, 477–9. See Jones (1978), p. 168, on the cult of St Nicholas.

[187] Peter of Vangadizza, *Vita Theobaldi eremitae*, 4 and 6, in *AASS OSB*, VI.2, 160–1 (*BHL* 8031). On charcoal-burning, see p. 61 below.

[188] Jakobs (1968), pp. 234–5, and Erkens (1987), pp. 7–26.

[189] Guth (1970), p. 131. See Schwarz (1957) on canonization dossiers in the twelfth century, and generally Angenendt (1994), esp. pp. 149–82.

[190] *Vita Stephani Obazinensis*, III, 5, ed. Aubrun, p. 203. See the old French translation of the lost final section of the *Vita Roberti de Arbrissello*, 57–64, in Dalarun (1985), pp. 291–4, on which see ibid., pp. 27, 36–8, and 154–76, and *Vita Gileberti Sempinghamensis*, 51, ed. Foreville and Keir, p. 120.

allegiances. Before the eleventh century, most personal names in northern Europe were Germanic and individual. Repeated names appear primarily in royal and noble families, and biblical names were probably given only to children who were destined for the church or a monastery.[191] The introduction of Christian names has been thoroughly analysed for only a few regions, but they amounted to 16.5 per cent of the names in Lorraine between 1000 and 1200, 12 per cent in the county of Vendôme in the twelfth century (rising to 24 per cent in the thirteenth), 34.8 per cent in Normandy, and 43.2 per cent in Picardy in the thirteenth century.[192] It appears, as might be expected, that the use of Christian names spread from south to north and from west to east, but whether this represented a triumph of religion over barbarism or of social conformity over early medieval tribalism and variety is hard to say in the present state of research.

The greatest difficulty in studying the changes in religious life and sentiments is to look behind the uncertainties and inconsistencies of people at the time in order to distinguish the ideal from the reality and the old from the new, or, harder yet, what looked like or might be called old, but was really new, from what looked new but was really old. Both individuals and institutions must be studied, bearing in mind that each shaped the other, and the nature and extent of the changes involved in the movement of religious reform and their relation to other changes must be assessed. In doing so, three contradictory tendencies, almost paradoxes, should be kept in mind. The first was the tension between the reformers' emphasis on withdrawal from the world and their desire, fired by their own religious personalities, to take an active role in secular society. This was paralleled in institutional life by a tendency towards exclusiveness on one hand and openness on the other and in spirituality by a simultaneous emphasis on inwardness, which at times almost approached quietism, and on the outer battle against the forces of spiritual and material evil. The second contradictory tendency was the conflict between the desire of the reformers to break out of the established forms of religious life and to find new ones suited to their spiritual needs and their continued adherence to and confidence in existing institutions. The new and relatively formless communities felt a pressure to institutionalize both from their own need to survive and from the ecclesiastical and secular authorities, who wanted to fit them into a recognized and controllable framework. Communities that started as almost spontaneous groupings around a charismatic and individualistic leader therefore tended to become more like other religious houses and

---

[191] The pioneer work on this subject, still of value, is Depoin (1914). See also John Benton and Norman Kretzmann, in *Renaissance and Renewal* (1982), pp. 277–82 and 494; Littger (1975) on the new names in the Rhineland in the twelfth century; Genicot (1984c), pp. 382–3; Fine (1987); Clark (1992), pp. 561–2, who discussed, with further references, 'the rising popularity of "Christian" forms'; Bartlett (1993), p. 278; and Geary (1994), p. 75.

[192] Jacobsson (1955), pp. 28–9; Barthélemy (1993), pp. 623–6; Le Pesant (1950); and Morlet (1967), p. 23.

to adopt established solutions to practical problems, even when they were at variance with their original character.[193] The third tension, more seeming than real, was between the backward-looking ideals based on models from the past, in accord with which the reformers tried to reshape existing institutions, and the forward-looking vision that opened the way to real innovations and to changes that now seem more significant than the type of issues that predominate in the polemical writings. The contemporary criticisms of institutions often look petty, but they dealt with matters that were important to people at the time, for whom the difficulty of change was all the greater because they valued their traditional routines and ways of life.

[193] On the loss of distinctiveness of the 'new' in relation to the 'old' monasticism in the late twelfth and early thirteenth centuries, see Violante (1977), p. 785.

2

THE VARIETY OF REFORMERS

A MONG the most dramatic aspects of the movement of reform in the elev-enth and twelfth centuries was the sheer number of new religious com-munities and forms of life and of men and women from all over Europe who were attracted to them. Ralph Glaber, writing in the 1040s, wrote in a famous passage about 'the shining costume' of new and restored churches put on by the world after the turn of the millennium,[1] and the biographer of William of Hirsau, who died in 1091, said:

> By the effort of this holy father the monastic religion, which among those who had assumed the religious habit had almost grown cold in the Teutonic regions, began to grow warm again (*recalescere*) and to recover (*recuperari*). Not only did the monastic institution advance by emulating him, but every grade of the ecclesiastical order was also taught by his examples. For he instructed monks by his humility, love, fervour, and religion; he moved bishops, priests, and all clerics forward in doctrine and authority; he trained lay men in how to live (*conversione*) and subjection; he moulded virgins, widows, and women in clean-ness and chastity; he exhorted by words and deeds the poor of Christ and pil-grims to be content with little and to have the world and all its glory under their feet. All the faithful of Christ took refuge in him as in the bosom of a mother, and through him they advanced greatly in God.[2]

In spite of the many conventional images in this passage, it gives a vivid picture of the work of a reformer seen through the eyes of one of his admirers. It is especially remarkable for its wealth of instructional language (*docere, eru-dire, informare, instruere, proficere, promovere*, and *suadere*) and for its classifi-cation of the types of people who benefited from William's teaching and example.

---

[1] Glaber, *Historia*, III, 4, ed. Maurice Prou (CTSEEH 1; Paris 1886), p. 62, and ed. and tr. John France (OMT; Oxford 1989), p. 116. On this passage, see Aubrun (1986), p. 95, who suggested that it referred to restoration and maintenance rather than new buildings.

[2] Haimo of Hirsau, *Vita Willelmi Hirsaugiensis*, 21, in *PL*, CL, 913AB, and *MGH, SS*, XII, 218 (*BHL* 8920–1). There are other accounts of the growth of monasticism in Germany, equally full of topoi, in Sigeboto, *Vita Paulinae*, 29, in *MGH, SS*, XXX.2, 923 (*BHL* 6551), and Wolfger of Prüfening, *Vita Theogeri s. Georgii*, I, 11, in *MGH, SS*, XII, 452 (*BHL* 8109), where the reflowering of religion was attributed to the search for solitude of those seeking to avoid the excommunicates during the struggle between Gregory VII and Henry IV. See also the passage from Bernold of St Blaise cited p. 80 below.

Herbord of Michaelsberg in his *Dialogue* on bishop Otto of Bamberg, who died in 1139, put into Otto's mouth a speech explaining why in the course of his long episcopate he had founded fifteen monasteries, in seven different dioceses, and five cells:

> At the beginning of the world, when there were few men, the propagation of men was necessary, and therefore they were not continent, but everyone married and gave in marriage. Now, however, he said, at the end of the world, when men have multiplied beyond measure, is the time of continence, [when] whosoever can must be continent and free for God. But continence and other works of holiness can be better observed inside than outside monasteries. This is my reason, he said, this was my purpose, in multiplying monasteries.[3]

There are also many commonplaces in this passage, especially the idea that the world was aging and approaching its end and that its population had grown and needed to be controlled, which went back to the writings of the fathers, but they were now given a special application as the reasons for founding monasteries and leading a celibate life. Andrew of St Victor, writing about 1145, said in his commentary on Elcana's two wives in 1 Kings 1.2 that 'Among the ancients it was permitted to have two wives at the same time owing to the multiplication of children that was then needed owing to the paucity of men. Now, since the human species has grown many times, it is enough to have one wife; it is enough to have none.'[4]

Many writers in the twelfth century saw the spread of monasticism as a revival and renewal after a period of death, cold, and darkness.[5] 'After the long winter of simony, the vine of the Lord reflowered when the vernal sweetness blew', wrote Gerhoh of Reichersberg in his commentary on the Psalms, 'religious houses and hospices were established, and new songs of praise spread abroad'.[6] Peter the Venerable wrote to his friend Matthew of Albano in the early 1130s: 'O how innumerable a crowd of monks has by divine grace multiplied above all in our days; it has covered almost the entire countryside of Gaul and filled the towns, castles, and fortresses.' And in his Statute 22 Peter stressed that his Cluniac monks should be no less religious than those 'through whom religious life, which was withered for many years, has reflourished in

---

[3] Herbord, *De Ottone episcopo Bambergensi*, I, 18, in *Monumenta Bambergensia*, ed. Philipp Jaffé (BRG 5; Berlin 1869), p. 717 (also ed. G.H. Pertz (*MGH, SSRG*; Hanover 1868), p. 16). This work was written in 1158/9. On the monasteries established by bishop Bartholomew of Laon, see Herman of Tournai, *De miraculis s. Mariae Laudunensis*, III, 17, in *PL*, CLVI, 1001C–2B.

[4] Andrew of St Victor, *In librum regum*, 1.2, in *CC:CM*, LIIIA, 7. I owe this reference to Frans van Liere. For the fathers, see Tertullian, *De anima*, 30, ed. J.H. Waszink (Amsterdam 1947), pp. 40–1 and commentary on 370–7, and Jerome, *Ep*. 22.21, ed. Jérôme Labourt, I (Collection Budé; Paris 1949), pp. 131–2, and, on the topos of the aging world, Herlihy (1985), pp. 25–6, and below pp. 162–3.

[5] See the passage by Guibert of Nogent cited pp. 26–7 and 36 above and the works of Philip of Harvengt, Adam of Dryburgh, and others cited by Giles Constable, in *Renaissance and Renewal* (1982), pp. 42–4.

[6] Gerhoh of Reichersberg, *In psalmos*, 4 *ad* 39.4, in *PL*, CXCIII, 1435D–6A.

Gaul, Germany, England, Spain, Italy, and almost all of Europe, and, with divine grace preceding and accompanying, the long-established coolness has again grown warm'.[7] Geoffrey *Grossus* in his *Life* of Bernard of Tiron said that

> Within the confines of the region of Maine and Brittany there were vast solitudes which at that time flourished like another Egypt with the multitude of hermits, living in various cells, holy men and famous for the excellence of their religion, among whom were the leaders (*principes*) and masters Robert of Arbrissel, Vitalis of Mortain, and Ralph of La Fustaie, who were later founders of many and great congregations.

Geoffrey later remarked on the wisdom of these three men in establishing their houses in different provinces, 'since each of them built so many and such great monasteries that one region could not hold them and one province did not suffice for the congregations brought together by them'.[8] Colonies of hermits were established not only in these regions but also in north-eastern France and the Low Countries, in central and southern Italy, and in the Holy Land, where hermits from Europe concentrated on Mt Tabor and on the Black Mountain near Antioch.[9] In the early 1190s the Cistercian Geoffrey of Auxerre attributed the invention of claustral solitude, as he called it, to the fact that 'The human race has so multiplied that solitary places can be found in almost no regions, and those who want, or seem to want, to withdraw either take [with them] or attract to them a larger crowd by frequent visits.'[10]

This perception of population pressure and scarcity of space in the twelfth century may raise a smile now (just as future generations may smile at similar concerns today), but it appears to have influenced the foundation of religious houses and the number of people who entered religious life. No precise figures are available, but it would be interesting to compile some general statistics for the numbers of new religious houses and compare them to the regional figures that already exist and to the estimates for population growth in this period. The total number of religious houses in England grew from sixty-one at the time of the Conquest to four hundred by 1154; about thirty houses were founded in Belgium between 1050 and 1125; twenty new houses were added to the existing fifteen in the diocese of Toul during the episcopate of Pibo,

[7] Peter the Venerable, *Ep.* 47, ed. Constable, I, 145 (see also *Ep.* 38 to archbishop Peter of Lyon, ibid., I, 130), and *Stat.* 22, in *CCM*, VI, 60.

[8] Geoffrey *Grossus*, *Vita Bernardi Tironiensis*, III, 20, and IX, 82, in *PL*, CLXXII, 1380D–1A and 1416B (*BHL* 1251). According to von Walter (1903–6), pp. 15–16, these two passages derived respectively from source B and from source A, but they are similar in content.

[9] Dereine (1983a), p. 172, argued that there were as many apostolic preachers in north-eastern as in western France. See Grundmann (1963) on Germany, where there were numerous independent hermits and recluses but relatively few wandering preachers and no eremitical orders, and Kedar (1983) and Jotischky (1995) on the Holy Land.

[10] Geoffrey of Auxerre, *In Cantica Canticorum*, 5, ed. Ferruccio Gastaldelli (Temi e testi 19–20; Rome 1974), II, 460; see also 390, where he said that 'The earth already full of men does not allow solitaries.'

from 1069 to 1107; most of the forty-two houses in the Hirsau group were founded between 1080 and 1120; and forty houses of regular canons were founded in the diocese of Salzburg alone.[11] Comparable figures from other regions suggest, with variations depending upon the number of existing monasteries, that between the mid-eleventh and mid-twelfth centuries there was an overall growth in the number of religious houses amounting, in some areas, to a factor of ten to one, and the same is probably true of the number of monks, nuns, canons, and canonesses. Although they still amounted to only a tiny percentage of the entire population, their presence was felt throughout society.[12]

The contemporary awareness of growth was paralleled by a recognition and increasing acceptance of a variety of forms of religious life. Before the eleventh century, the sense of unity and superiority of the monastic order, in spite of great differences between individual houses, was so strong that other forms of religious life, including canons and even hermits, were often looked down upon. The appearance of the new monastic orders and regular canons, however, created a 'schism in the house of God', as Urban II and others called it, and forced people at first to consider and then to accept diversity.[13] The principle of diverse but not adverse was recognized even by some of the strongest defenders of particular types of religious life, including Peter the Venerable and Bernard of Clairvaux. Among those who went further and asserted the validity and even desirability of diversity, one of the first and most interesting was the author of the *Libellus* or treatise *On the various orders and professions that are in the church*, written in the second quarter of the twelfth century, probably in the diocese of Liège. He was a pioneer in the comparative history of religious life and classified both monks and canons into three categories based on whether they lived far from men, like the Cistercians and Premonstratensians; close to men, like the Cluniacs and Victorines; or among men, like the secular monks (whom he considered no monks at all) and canons. He also had a section on hermits, who lived 'alone or with a few others', and he mentioned a lost or unwritten section on recluses, 'devotees

---

[11] See Knowles and Hadcock (1971), p. 494, and Knowles (1963b), p. 711 (with somewhat different figures), on England; de Moreau (1946–52), II, 135–6, on Belgium; Choux (1952), p. 121, on the diocese of Toul; Jakobs (1961), pp. 36–57, on Hirsau (including subgroups the total was 136, of which only fifteen were west of the Rhine); Mois (1953), p. 1, and Dereine (1960a) on the diocese of Salzburg. See also the figures in Schlesinger (1962), II, 165, on Saxony, where the number of monasteries and collegiate churches grew to about eighty between 1100 and 1300; Tüchle (1950–4), II, 344, on Swabia; Bauerreiss (1949–70), III, 3–56 and 103, on Bavaria; and Bligny (1960), p. 163, who estimated that in the eleventh and twelfth centuries there was a total of between 1,500 and 1,700 religious houses in the kingdom of Burgundy, of which about 25 per cent were houses of canons (p. 200), 65 per cent followed the rule of Benedict (p. 224), and the remainder were Carthusians (thirty-nine houses by 1200), Hospitallers, Templars, and others.

[12] See pp. 88–92 below for some estimates of the total number of men and women in religious life and the size of religious communities.

[13] See p. 2 above and Constable (1985a), where some of the same sources are cited.

of God', *licoisi*, or 'guardians of the law', as he called them, and on female
hermits and nuns, 'those who receive the sweet yoke of Christ with holy men
and under holy men', recluses, and 'devotees of God', *licoisae*, or *nichoisae*.
This section, had it existed, would have thrown invaluable light on the less
institutionalized types of religious life, especially of women, about whom less
is known than about men. The author of this work was remarkable not only
for his breadth of vision but also for his approval of each form of religious
life (except the secular monks), for which he found precedents both in the
Old Testament and in the life of Christ.[14]

A few years later Anselm of Havelberg in the first book of his *Dialogues*,
which was probably written in 1149, went further and saw the emergence of
new and different orders as part of God's unfolding plan for the renewal of
the church, 'which is one in faith, one in hope, one in love', Anselm wrote,
but 'multiform in the variety of diverse statuses'. He addressed himself particularly to readers who were scandalized by these novelties and by the appearance of people who lived and dressed as they wished. 'They devise for themselves a new [way] of psalmody; they establish new ways of abstinence and
measures of food; and they follow neither the monks who fight under the rule
of the blessed Benedict nor imitate the canons who lead an apostolic life under
the rule of the blessed Augustine . . . They are a law unto themselves; they
are an authority unto themselves; and under the pretext of a new religion they
gather what they can into their society.'[15] After discussing several of the new
orders of monks, including Camaldoli, Vallombrosa, and Cîteaux, and of
canons, such as the followers of Arberius of St Rufus and Norbert of Xanten,
and also the military orders, Anselm concluded that, in spite of their innovations and differences, they were all good and part of God's plan. The preface
to the chronicle of Petershausen, which goes to the year 1156, includes sections
on monks, canons, bishops, priests, holy virgins, solitaries, recluses who
'enclose themselves for Christ', pilgrims 'who journey for the sake of God',
and beggars who model themselves on Lazarus and will be gathered, like him,
into the bosom of Abraham. The chronicler criticized some of these but basically justified them all, denying that they were

> something new made up by modern people, since they all take their origins
> from the Lord Himself or from His apostles . . . For although there are differing
> professions and customs, whatever a single catholic faith adorns is made entirely
> pleasing to God, to whom nothing without faith is pleasing. All things that are
> founded in faith, raised in hope, and offered to God in love are considered

[14] See the table in the introduction to the *Libellus*, ed. Constable, p. xxiv. Thus the hermits were
prefigured by Abel in Genesis and Christ's withdrawal into the mountain in John 6.15, which
was also cited by the hermit Rainald in Morin (1928), p. 102.
[15] Anselm of Havelberg, *Dialogi*, I, 1 and 13, in *PL*, CLXXXVIII, 1142C–3A and 1159AB, and ed.
Gaston Salet (SC 118; Paris 1966), pp. 36 and 114.

approved in the Holy Spirit, cherished and raised to the heavenly heights by the one God Himself and our lord Jesus Christ.[16]

The variety of orders and canons was likewise stressed in the accounts of religious life found in histories, chronicles, and didactic works written in the middle and later part of the twelfth century. A well-known example is at the end of the seventh book of Otto of Freising's *History of the two cities*, where he briefly described the monks, anchorites, and solitaries who interceded for the sins of the world and where he distinguished, like the author of the *Libellus*, between monks who lived near to and far from men, 'in the hidden parts of forests and secret places', and between hermits who were associated with communities and subject to a superior and those who lived in cells and caves. Religious people were more numerous in France and Germany now, he said, than they had previously been in Egypt, since religion, like power and wisdom, had been translated from the east to the west. Otto praised them all for leading pure and holy lives and for living together in monasteries and churches with one heart and one soul. Glowing inside with the splendours of various virtues and wearing outside clothing of different colours, they fulfilled the description in the Psalms of the glorious princess 'clothed round about with varieties'.[17] John of Salisbury in the *Policraticus* mentioned the Carthusians, Cistercians, Cluniacs, and Grandmontines among monks and also the canons, hermits, and military orders, though he warned that they included evil and hypocritical men.[18] All of these except the military orders appear in Sermon 72 of Richard of St Victor, who compared them to 'the beautiful places of the wilderness' in Psalm 64.13,[19] and in the *Mirror of the church* by Gerald of Wales, who said that the Cistercians were perfect at first, the Grandmontines more perfect, and the Carthusians most perfect.[20] There are references in the chronicle of Prémontré under the year 1131 to Premonstratensians, Cistercians, Cluniacs, Carthusians, Templars, Hospitallers, and 'nuns and women devoted to God of diverse habit and profession'.[21] Adam of Dryburgh mentioned the regular canons of Limoges, Prémontré, Arrouaise, and Beauvais and, among monks, the Carthusians, Cistercians, Cluniacs, and

---

[16] *Casus monasterii Petrishusensis, praef.*, 24, ed. and tr. Otto Feger (Schwäbische Chroniken der Stauferzeit 3; Lindau and Constance 1956), p. 36.

[17] Otto of Freising, *Historia de duobus civitatibus*, VII, 35, ed. Adolf Hofmeister, 2nd edn (*MGH, SSRG*; Hanover and Leipzig 1912), pp. 369–73 (quotes on 369 and 371).

[18] John of Salisbury, *Policraticus*, VII, 21 and 23, ed. C.C.J. Webb (Oxford 1909), II, 191–3, 199–200, and 204–7.

[19] Published among the works of Hugh of St Victor, *Serm.* 72, in PL, CLXXVII, 1127BC. On the authorship, see p. 22 n. 104 above.

[20] Gerald of Wales, *Speculum ecclesiae*, III, 21, ed. John S. Brewer a.o. (RS 21; London 1861–91), IV, 259.

[21] *Sigeberti continuatio Praemonstratensis*, s.a. 1131, in *MGH, SS*, VI, 450. This continuation of Sigebert's chronicle was written not earlier than 1146 and goes to 1155.

Tironians, and said that each of them had a home in heaven.[22] Geoffrey of Vigeois wrote in his chronicle that 'When the love of earlier cenobites grew cold, at that time the adherents of diverse dogmas arose, such as the Templars, Hospitallers, Grandmontines, Carthusians, Cistercians, the hospices of the poor, the convents of the nuns, the gatherings of lepers, and the congregation of various new canons.'[23]

The most ambitious effort of this type, though still quite brief, was the treatise *On the change of the monastic order* by Robert of Torigny, who died in 1186. It has thirty-four chapters giving brief histories of one or more religious orders or houses, most of them in Normandy but including the Cistercians and Carthusians and the canons of St Victor, Arrouaise, and Prémontré. He attributed the origin of these new orders to the 'dissolute' state of the old monasteries, of which the members,

> covered with shame and either voluntarily or against their wills forced by kings and bishops, summoned monks from the most ordered monasteries, such as Cluny, Marmoutier, Le Bec, and others that strove equally to live in religion and to conform the life of their subjects to the example of these men. Many abbots were taken from these monasteries, which seemed to excel the others in religion, for the rule of less religious abbeys.[24]

Three significant points emerge from these accounts. The first is the diversity of orders and ways of life, which in addition to the generally recognized types of monks, nuns, canons, military orders, hermits, and recluses included various less formal categories, such as the 'devotees of God' in the *Libellus*, the pilgrims and beggars in the Petershausen chronicle, and the hospices and leprosaries mentioned by Geoffrey of Vigeois. The second point is the general acceptance and justification of these differences. Peter of Blois wrote, 'I venerate with the entire affection of my heart the life of religious people, of whom there are diverse types, for it is the "coat of diverse colours" of Joseph [Genesis 37.3] and the bride of Christ "clothed round about with varieties" [Psalm 44.15].'[25] The third point is the general absence of a clear distinction between the old and new reformers. The Cluniacs were included with the Cistercians, Carthusians, and other reformers not only by secular clerics like John of Salisbury and Gerald of Wales but also by regular canons like the chronicler of Prémontré, Richard of St Victor, and Adam of Dryburgh, who later became a Carthusian. That Robert of Torigny saw the entire movement of reform as inspired and directed from strict old black monasteries shows that there was no single locus or type of reform and no simple distinction between 'old' unreformed and 'new' reformed houses. Some of the strictest and most prestigious monasteries in Europe were of great antiquity, and some of the new

---

[22] Adam of Dryburgh, *De tripartito tabernaculo*, II, 19, in *PL*, CXCVIII, 740AB.
[23] Geoffrey of Vigeois, *Chronica*, I, 21, in *Nova bibl.*, II, 296.
[24] Robert of Torigny, *De immutatione ordinis monachorum*, 7, in *PL*, CCII, 1313C.
[25] Peter of Blois, *Invectiva in depravatorem operum Blesensis*, in *PL*, CCVII, 1116A.

and less rigidly organized communities were lax by contemporary standards. In a letter concerning the papal schism written to the bishops of Aquitaine in 1131/2, Bernard of Clairvaux listed among the supporters of Innocent II 'the Camaldolesi, Vallombrosians, Carthusians, Cluniacs, the monks of Marmoutier, also my own Cistercians, the monks of Caen, Tiron, and Savigny, and finally the university and unanimity of brothers both of clerics and of monks of regular life and proven behaviour, following the bishops'.[26] Bernard's purpose here was political rather than historical or spiritual, but the order of the list suggests that he drew no distinction between the old and new monks. A sharp differentiation between reformed and unreformed houses is found more in polemical writings than in general works, where each order or monastery was judged on its own merits. The close ties of sympathy and friendship between the Cluniacs and Carthusians are a reminder of the cross-currents within the reform movement and a warning to scholars not to distinguish too sharply between the various orders. Even the strictest reformer could have found no fault with the statement of Peter the Venerable, in a letter to Bernard, that monks should avoid secular occupations and were required 'to remain assiduously in the cloister and to devote themselves most intently to silence, prayer, reading, and meditation and to other precepts of the rule and ecclesiastical ministries'.[27]

The distinctive character of Cluny derived from its long liturgy and its role of mediation both for individuals and for society as a whole. The work of intercessory prayer promoted the salvation of everyone, and particularly of benefactors and others who were in some way associated with the monastery. Peter the Venerable wrote in about 1140 to bishop Milo of Thérouanne that 'I see the substance of Cluny (*res Cluniacenses*) as the treasury of the entire Christian republic, from which everyone drinks, which they hardly empty, into which a few people put a few things, from which many people receive many things.'[28] This statement helps to explain some of the special characteristics of Cluniac monasticism, including its combination of strict seclusion with close ties to secular society and its reluctance, frequently criticized, to turn away recruits, which was motivated by a desire to save souls and enrol soldiers into the army of God. Odo of Cluny admitted without delay a robber who said that he would be damned if he were rejected.[29] This, far more than slackness in the observance of the rule or purely worldly considerations, as is sometimes alleged, was the reason for shortening the period of probation at

---

[26] Bernard, *Ep.* 126, ed. Leclercq, VII, 317.
[27] Peter the Venerable, *Ep.* 28, ed. Constable, I, 85. On the relations between the Cluniacs and Carthusians, see Constable (1975b).
[28] Peter the Venerable, *Ep.* 102, ed. Constable, I, 264; cf. *Epp.* 131 and 162 to king Roger of Sicily (ibid., I, 332 and 394), where Peter stressed the prayers, masses, and alms at Cluny in memory of its friends and benefactors. Cantarella (1993), p. 159, said that salvation was 'the guarantee of Cluny'.
[29] John of Salerno, *Vita Odonis*, 3, in *Bibl. Clun.*, col. 49D (*BHL* 6295).

Cluny. The leaders of the order were not unaware of the consequences of this policy. Ulrich of Zell in a well-known passage in the preface to his customary, which probably dates from the mid-1080s, complained at the number of physically and mentally unfit monks who were received into Cluniac houses and urged that only voluntary monks of mature years should be received, and Peter the Venerable attempted to lengthen the novitiate and raise the age of profession in order to get a more suitable type of monk,[30] but the habit was deeply ingrained and reflected a fundamental attitude among the Cluniacs. William of Hirsau, according to his biographer, 'roused nobles and non-nobles, rich men and poor men, men and women' to leave the world and love the heavenly life,[31] and the author of the treatise *On the professions of monks*, who was probably a monk of Bec, praised the rule of Benedict because 'strong and weak, healthy and infirm, literate and illiterate, nobles and non-nobles, boys, young men, and old men can live under it and save their souls'.[32] The future cardinal Matthew of Albano persuaded the prior of St-Martin-des-Champs to receive him without any novitiate,[33] and at the monastery of Garsten, which followed Cluniac customs without being dependent on Cluny, 'The multitude of those serving God was increased without cease, because it was the custom of the man of God [abbot Berthold] to admit everyone who out of a desire for Christ wished to throw down the burden of the world and to receive the sweet yoke of conversion.' On one occasion Berthold ordered that a knight who sought admission 'should be quickly tonsured and . . . received into the congregation so that he should escape his merited damnation'.[34]

Some reformers shared this view, and many contemporaries commented on the broad appeal of the new religious communities. Bernard of Tiron, for instance, saying ' "I shall not throw out he who comes to me", wished to exclude no one, [and] he satisfied by word and by example.'[35] But most of the reformers took a view of monasticism that laid less emphasis on the saving power of the monastic habit and the value of intercessory prayer, and its accompanying obligations, than on the opportunity for salvation monastic life offered to individuals and on the personal commitment and suitability of the monks. Bernard in his *Sermon to clerics on conversion* urged them to flee from Babylon to the *urbes refugii* where they could perform penance for past sins, obtain present grace, and confidently await future glory.[36] The reformers

---

[30] Ulrich of Zell, *Consuetudines Cluniacenses*, *Ep. nunc.*, in *PL*, CXLIX, 636A–7A, and Peter the Venerable, *Stat.* 36–7, in *CCM*, VI, 70–1. On Ulrich, see Garand (1988) and Fuhrmann (1988).
[31] *Vita Willelmi Hirsaugiensis*, 6, in *PL*, CL, 905A, and *MGH*, *SS*, XII, 213 (*BHL* 8920–1). See also the passage cited p. 80 below.
[32] *De professionibus monachorum*, in Martène (1736–8), II, 473C.
[33] Peter the Venerable, *De miraculis*, II, 7, in *CC:CM*, LXXXIII, 108.
[34] *Vita Bertholdi Garstensis*, 3 and 10, ed. Josef Lenzenweger (Forschungen zur Geschichte Oberösterreichs 5; Graz and Cologne 1958), pp. 230 and 237 (*BHL* 1274–82). Berthold was abbot of Garsten from at least 1111 until 1142, and this *Vita* was written in 1173/82 (ibid., p. 172).
[35] Geoffrey Grossus, *Vita Bernardi Tironiensis*, 74, in *PL*, CLXXII, 1411C (*BHL* 1251).
[36] Bernard, *Sermo ad clericos de conversione*, XXI, 37, ed. Leclercq, IV, 113.

therefore objected to the practice of receiving oblates and shortening the novitiate and tended to raise the age of admission and to insist upon a novitiate of at least a year, as prescribed in the rule of Benedict. They likewise objected to the long liturgy at Cluny and wanted a life with more opportunity for private prayer and devotions and for manual labour. The Cluniac in the *Dialogue of the two monks* said to the Cistercian that 'Just as your order is active, because with Martha it chooses righteous labour for itself, so our order is contemplative because with Mary it has chosen holy leisure for itself.' The Cistercian replied on the contrary, that because the Cluniacs lived in towns and villages, unlike the Cistercians, 'We can in comparison with you properly be called solitaries and contemplatives.'[37] This text illustrates the difference both in the self-images of the two orders and in the use of the terms solitary, contemplative, and active. To the Cluniac, contemplation was worshipping God and action was working with the hands, whereas for the Cistercian, action was being in touch with the secular world and contemplation, like solitude, involved being cut off from other people and devoted to a mixed life of work and prayer.

An illuminating account of the foundation of an individual reformed house is found in the history of Fountains abbey written by Hugh of Kirkstall in the early thirteenth century. It was allegedly based on contemporary documents and eye-witness accounts of the events, which took place in the early 1130s, but the evidence was probably revised in the middle of the twelfth century to take account of later developments, including the entrance of Fountains to the Cistercian order. The description of the conditions at St Mary's abbey in York, from where the founders came, for instance, is characteristically harsh, and the standard of monastic life there, and also of learning, was probably no lower than that in other contemporary old black houses. Bernard of Clairvaux himself in a letter written before 1135 to abbot Richard of Fountains, who had been prior of St Mary's, said that he and his followers, who 'flourished in a new sanctity', had left the good for the better, not the bad for the good, though he also said that it was necessary to rise above mediocrity and to leave tepidity.[38] Reading between the lines of Hugh of Kirkstall's history, the problem at St Mary's was that it adhered to the traditional standard of an extensive liturgy and was heavily dependent on surrounding society for its economic support. For prior Richard and some of the monks, the Gospel seemed to live again in the monks of Savigny and Cîteaux, and they said to abbot Geoffrey that 'It is more useful to imitate them than to recite the Gospel.' When Geoffrey objected to the novelty of this undertaking, Richard

---

[37] Idungus, *Dialogus*, 1 and 3, ed. Huygens, pp. 378 and 452; see also 2, pp. 408–9, where the Cistercian criticized the prostrations at Cluny and said that Cistercian life involved a mixture of work and prayer. Ulrich, on the other hand, in the *Consuetudines Cluniacenses*, I, 52, in *PL*, CXCIX, 697C, called the Cluniac life active owing to its strenuousness.

[38] Bernard, *Ep.* 96, ed. Leclercq, VII, 246.

replied that 'The rule of the blessed Benedict sets forth the entire Gospel not so much by allegorical exposition as by simple practice (*experimento*) and the visible display of work', whereas at St Mary's it was difficult to observe the rule and life was full of controversies. The dissidents declared to the archbishop of York that they wished to follow 'the poor Christ in voluntary poverty, to carry the cross of Christ on their body, and to keep the evangelical peace and observe fully the rule of the blessed father Benedict'.[39] Whether or not these were their actual words, which may be doubted, it probably represented their feelings, since it agrees with the independent testimony of Gervase, who was one of their number and later became abbot of Louth Park and died in about 1150. In his testament, while expressing his objections to the secular involvements at St Mary's, including the obligations of charity and hospitality, he said that his reason for leaving was to contemplate God and to find 'a stricter life . . . where he could live more securely'.[40]

The emphasis of these documents, even of those that were later revised, is on the desire of the founders of Fountains for a new and different type of life, with less liturgy – the recitation of the Gospel – and fewer secular involvements and with more opportunity for a life based on the Gospel and the rule of Benedict, as they read it, and for peace, solitude, poverty, and work. The terms used by the reformers to describe their observance of the rule, and the scholarly debate over the use and meaning of *ad litteram*, will be discussed later, but it is clear that the founders of Fountains had in mind not literalism in the modern sense but rather a rejection of customs, like those that were observed at Cluny, and a stress on purity, integrity, and simplicity. In this they resembled other reformers who sought not only to break away from the consequences of what they saw as monastic decline but also from the stifling environment of strict black monasticism, with its long liturgy and close ties to the secular world. The movement can be observed in Italy in the first half of the eleventh century, when the general movement of reform in the church was taking place, but it manifested itself all over Europe in a wide variety of new forms of religious life, of which a community of the type represented by Fountains was only one, and far from the most extreme.

A more novel, and in the long run probably more significant, development was the appearance of regular canons, who from this time on paralleled and to some extent rivalled the monastic orders. The confusion surrounding the term *canonicus* and the lack of a suitable English term for a house of canons were mentioned above, together with the emergence in the eleventh century of canons who were called regular because they followed a rule and who resembled, and were often confused with, monks. One of the most perceptive

[39] Hugh of Kirkstall, *Narratio*, ed. Walbran, pp. 15, 20, and 23–4. See p. 24 n. 111 above and, on the term *experimentum*, p. 277 n. 99 below.
[40] Gervase of Louth Park, *Testament*, ed. Charles H. Talbot, in *Analecta sacri ordinis Cisterciensis* 7 (1951), p. 40.

insights in the *Libellus* was the parallel between the monks and canons who lived far from men, of whom the author gave the Cistercians and Premonstratensians as examples, and who resembled each other more than they did the members of their own orders who lived close to or among men, such as the Cluniacs or Victorines. Peter of Celle in his treatise *On the discipline of the cloister* also stressed the parallelism of the two orders, praising both Benedict and Augustine. 'The one an abbot and monk, the other a bishop and canon', he said, 'each one holy, each one a teacher and outstanding leader of the Lord's flock. Our claustral discipline and yours agree on certain points and differ on others.'[41] For in spite of the similarities, there was an awareness of the difference between the orders, and sometimes of rivalry, which was sharpened by the disputes over the respective superiority of monks and clerics and over the right to exercise pastoral functions and own pastoral revenues. Some of the strongest critics of monasticism in the twelfth century came from the ranks of the regular canons.

Of the various rules for canons, the two most important were the decrees of the council of Aachen in 816, which were revised in the mid-eleventh century in order to impose greater austerity and forbid private property, and the so-called rule of Augustine, of which the several versions that circulated in the eleventh and twelfth centuries were distinguished principally by their degree of strictness.[42] In time there emerged two broad types of regular canons: the more moderate *ordo antiquus* based on the revised rule of Aachen and the stricter *ordo novus*, which followed the Augustinian rule, with many modifications borrowed from monasticism, especially from the Cistercians. These corresponded approximately to the two types of canons described in the *Libellus* as living near to and far from men, but in practice there were almost as many different types of canons, both regular and secular, as there were of monks, and each order and house had to some extent its own way of life. Two charters of bishop Bartholomew of Laon in 1124 and 1126 referred to the Premonstratensians as living 'the eremitical life under the canonical profession' or 'the clerical habit', leaving it unclear whether he regarded them as hermits, canons, or clerics, or, as is probable, as all three at the same time.[43] In about 1145 the abbot of the regular canons of St Evurtius at Orléans wrote that their predecessors, who were secular canons, had decided not to enlarge their church out of fear that if they found the body of St Evurtius they would be expelled and replaced by monks or regular canons 'who would devote a more devout cult to so great a father'.[44]

---

[41] Peter of Celle, *De disciplina claustrali*, 2, in *PL*, CCII, 1103D–4A. He went on to discuss some of the differences, divided into *accidentalia* and *substantialia* and including silence, confession, prayer, and *meditatio mortis*.

[42] See esp. Dereine (1951) and Verheijen (1967). The Aachen decrees and the rule of Augustine are found together in the Münster manuscript mentioned on p. 40 above.

[43] Hugo (1734–6), I.1, xliii and cccc.

[44] Roger of St Evurtius, *Revelatio*, in *PL*, CXCIX, 1126A.

In this text monks and regular canons were apparently regarded as interchangeable, and both as superior to secular canons, who lived in the world like clerics. All three were praised in the foundation charter of St Leo at Toul, which was given to the holy men of Chaumouzey by dean Luctulf of Toul in 1091

> in order to lead the apostolic life . . . under the rule and writing of St Augustine in our monastery as [they had] before on their mountain. For it seemed a salutary and suitable symbol that one city should contain the three more perfect members of the Christian religion, that is, canons who hold their own possessions, black monks in woollen robes under the rule of Benedict, and white Nazarenes who lead the apostolic life, so that anyone who wished to convert to the Lord would have in this one town whatever type of stricter life pleased him.[45]

This document suggests that, while all three forms of religious life were considered good, that of the regular canons was the best. The reverse was true a few years later at Tournai, where the biographer of Odo, the founder of the new house of St Martin, said that he and his companions at first followed the canonical rather than the monastic order 'because canons lead a more tolerable manner of life than monks both in ecclesiastical offices and in daily food and clothing'. After a young recruit was reclaimed by his father, however, they were advised to become monks, because the black monastic habit was so hated by the clergy that they would never recall a monk and also because 'the life of clerics, even those who live regularly, was softer and slacker' than that of the 'more rigid' order of monks.[46]

Another aspect of the contemporary view of the relation between monks and canons is illustrated by the *Life* of Miro of Ripoll, who set out in search of 'an eremitical or cenobitical life' and of 'deserted and uncultivated places'. He came to a lonely house of Augustinian canons, who, according to the porter, had bid farewell to the world and 'led a monastic life in this monastery . . . [and] a solitary life in this hermitage', thus combining the qualities of canons, monks, and hermits. According to Miro, monks who spent their entire lives reciting the psalms offered only their lips in praise to God and achieved neither good nor evil unless they learned to avoid *otium* outside the choir. 'He who has not known how to labour outside the choir has not known how to direct his feelings (*affectus*) to God within it.' Miro then gave an interesting defence of a mixed life of action and contemplation and of a clerical vocation devoted to the support of others:

---

[45] *GC*, XIII, *instr.*, 474AB. See Seher, *Primordia Calmosiacensia*, 1, ed. L. Duhamel, in *Documents rares ou inédits de l'histoire de Vosges*, II (Paris 1869), p. 10, and Choux (1952), pp. 33, 163, and 216–17.

[46] Herman of Tournai, *De restauratione monasterii s. Martini Tornacensis*, 6 and 38, in *MGH, SS*, XIV, 277 and 290. He specified that canons, unlike monks, wore linen, ate meat, and had a shorter liturgy. On Odo, see Resnick (1988b), pp. 121–40.

When our fathers stretched upwards desiring the apostolic life, they raised the clerical status to a higher level, seeking in it the monastic life, so that when a monk is separated from the choir and outside it, God continues to be magnified, and he [the monk] does not cease from the active life when the contemplative life is not being enjoyed. In this way he [Miro] ordained the brothers for the active life at one time and the contemplative at another, and from his discipline that church was an exercise in virtue and a school of piety.[47]

Miro evidently shared many of the feelings of the founders of Fountains, but unlike them he did not want to cut himself off from pastoral or charitable work.[48] According to his view, regular canons led a monastic life within the clerical status and so had the best of both worlds, since they had a secluded life in their communities but could preach and perform pastoral and missionary work if they wished. One of the distinguishing marks of canons, according to Caroline Bynum, was their sense of obligation to set an example by their words and deeds.[49]

The preference for canons over monks shown by some founders, both ecclesiastics and lay men, may be explained by this outward-looking attitude, in addition to the down-to-earth reasons that houses of canons were often cheaper to found than houses of monks and that they tended to be more amenable to the wishes of the founders and more submissive to the authority of bishops. The fact that the Cistercian Otto of Freising founded only houses of canons in his diocese was very likely owing to its need for pastoral work, and Gilbert of Sempringham prescribed the rule of Benedict for the nuns living in his houses and the rule of Augustine for the clerics presumably because they were expected to perform pastoral duties.[50] Ordained monks could also serve in churches, however, whereas some strict regular canons refused to do so, and it is impossible to draw any clear distinction between monks and canons on this basis. Among the most pressing needs in the history of medieval monasticism is a study of the regional differences between religious houses following the same rule and belonging to the same order and the development of systematic procedures to study the relations between individual houses and their environment in terms of such questions as the

---

[47] *Vita Mironis*, in *España sagrada*, XXVIII, 307–10 (*BHL* 5971). The passage is filled with topoi and is hard to translate idiomatically. Miro died in 1181.

[48] When Miro arrived at the monastery, he expressed a particular admiration for the infirmary (ibid., p. 308) and later devoted himself both to the *salus animarum* of those who came to the monastery (p. 310) and to the care of the poor (p. 312).

[49] See Bynum (1979), esp. pp. 21 and 87, and (1982a), esp. pp. 36–40. For examples of the reformers' concern for word and example see the *Lives* of William of Hirsau and Bernard of Tiron, cited pp. 78 below and 52 above, and Hugh of Silvanès, *De conversione Pontii de Larazio*, 3, in Baluze, *Miscellanea*, I, 180.

[50] See, on Otto, Mois (1953), p. 150; Krausen (1958), p. 43; Busley (1958), p. 52; and Southern (1995), p. 210, who mentioned Otto's support of three Cistercian houses in the diocese of Passau; and on Gilbert, *Vita Gileberti Sempinghamensis*, 17, ed. Foreville and Keir, p. 48.

performance of pastoral work, the rights of patrons, the position of the advocate, and personal and familial relationships.[51]

The reformers themselves were only vaguely aware of these differences and frequently hesitated over what form of life to adopt. Many of the new houses and orders resisted being fitted into existing niches, in spite of pressure from ecclesiastical authorities to observe a recognized rule. Stephen of Obazine and his followers at first 'followed the canonical rule in the offices and the eremitical way of life (*propositum*)'. When they decided to adopt the statutes of some order, Stephen consulted the prior of La Chartreuse (probably Guigo), who advised him that in view of their numbers and quantity of possessions they should become monks and join the Cistercian order, of which 'the statutes can suffice for all perfection', rather than become hermits with the Carthusians, who imposed limits on the size and property of their houses. The cenobitic profession, he said, 'is open equally to many or to few, since it is judged not by number but by religion, by virtue not by possessions'. They continued to hesitate, however, some preferring the canonical and others the monastic rule, until at last they put themselves under Dalon, which was at that time the only regular monastery in the area, and so 'became monks out of hermits', and later joined the Cistercians in the line of Cîteaux.[52]

The followers of Stephen of Grandmont were even more hesitant. It is said that Stephen himself, when he was asked by two visiting cardinals whether he was a canon, a monk, or a hermit, replied in the words of John 8.54 that if he would glorify himself, his glory was nothing. While this story may be apocryphal, it showed his reluctance to be classified and a sense of distinctiveness that was shared by his order.[53] According to Stephen of Tournai, writing in 1178/80, most of the Grandmontines were illiterate lay men who did not want to be called canons. 'If you ask them of which order they are, they answer, "We are sinners"; if [you ask] others, they say that [they] are good men (*boni homines*); for also in the province from which they originate, where their head and seat is, their cells are called Bonummie.' The clerics

---

[51] In the diocese of Arras, according to Delmaire (1994), pp. 193–203, where there were fourteen houses of canons and seven monasteries (five male and two female) in 1093, the twelfth century was 'le siècle des chanoines réguliers', especially the orders of Arrouaise, Prémontré, and St Victor. See also, on Upper Lorraine, Erkens (1987), and, on England, Mortimer (1978); Brooke (1985), esp. pp. 113 and 121; Herbert (1985), who proposed that the rule of Augustine provided a less detailed framework for hermitages than the rule of Benedict; and Postles (1993), who said (p. 2) that 'The involvement of the Austin canons in English boroughs and towns was an integral part of the original objectives of the Order.'

[52] *Vita Stephani Obazinensis*, I, 7 and 26, and II, 7, ed. Aubrun, pp. 54, 82, and 106. On Obazine, see Barrière (1977), esp. pp. 43–52 on the early period of eremitism, up to joining the Cistercians in 1147. Cf. Hugh of Silvanès, *De conversione Pontii de Larazio*, 20, in Baluze, *Miscellanea*, I, 183, where the prior of La Chartreuse gave similar advice to the followers of Pontius de Léras.

[53] Stephen of Lecey, *Vita Stephani Muretensis*, 32, in *CC:CM*, VIII, 121 (*BHL* 7906–8). See Becquet (1957), pp. 403–4, dating this episode 1124, and (1960), p. 298 n. 55, saying that it was a late twelfth-century addition.

among them might be called canons, Stephen said, and the lay men hermits, but since they followed the life of their master Stephen and had no recognized rule, they should be called, from their way of life (*vita*), *clerici seu laici vitales*.[54] In spite of this anomalous status, the Grandmontines enjoyed a high repute in the twelfth century and were considered by some observers to be no less holy than the Carthusians and Cistercians.

The precise status of the Carthusians is also a matter of uncertainty.[55] Although there is some evidence that they followed the rule of Benedict in the twelfth century, the prior of La Chartreuse's reply to Stephen of Obazine shows that they considered themselves to be hermits and not monks. In a letter probably by Anthelm he referred to himself as 'the useless servant of the Carthusian poor of Christ'.[56] They were not mentioned in the *Libellus*, and their way of life, like that of the Grandmontines, cut across the established categories of religious life. They were like hermits in their emphasis on solitude and in living in cells, which were unknown in communities of monks at that time, but they had some elements of community life and came together at regular intervals for the holy offices. The Carthusian Hugh of Lincoln was said to have cherished 'the Cluniacs and others of this habit' most highly, after his own order, 'among the multiple and mystical variety' of monks because they spiritually cultivated the silences of the cloister in active leisure (*otium negotiosum*).[57] Bernard of Portes wrote to the recluse Rainald that 'It is better to resort from time to time to some manual labour than to insist upon reading by sleeping and to incur boredom (*taedium*) by reading too much, so that when you have done some work you can rise with greater fervour to prayer and reading by a pleasant alternation.'[58] This ideal closely resembled that of Peter the Venerable in his letter to the hermit Gilbert of Senlis, except that it shared with the reformers a stress on manual labour and an explicit recognition of the spiritual advantages of an alternating or mixed life.

[54] Stephen of Tournai, *Ep.* 1, ed. Desilve, p. 14.
[55] Van Haeften (1644), p. 172, excluded the Carthusians from his account of the monks who followed the rule of Benedict, though they took elements from it; Wilmart (1933b), p. 339 n. 6, said that the Carthusians followed the Benedictine rule; Hocquard (1948), pp. 5–6 and 17 n.4, and (1951), esp. pp. 326–7, argued (against Wilmart) that they were never Benedictines; and [Laporte] (1960–7), II, 107–63, cited many texts to prove that they did not follow the rule of Benedict. The profession formula of Guigo published by Edmond Martène in his commentary on the rule of Benedict, in *PL*, LVI, 820B–1A, did not include 'according to the rule of Benedict', but Dubois (1968a), pp. 36–7, cited twelfth-century papal bulls showing that the Carthusians admitted adhering to the rule.
[56] Leclercq (1951a), p. 6.
[57] Adam of Eynsham, *Magna vita Hugonis*, IV, 9, ed. Decima Douie and David Farmer (OMT; Oxford 1985), II, 43 (*BHL* 4018). On the concept of *otium negotiosum*, see Hocquard (1951), pp. 324–5, and on the sympathy between the Cluniacs and Carthusians, Constable (1975b).
[58] Bernard of Portes, *Ep.* 3, in *PL*, CLIII, 893C. Cf. Peter the Venerable, *Ep* 20, ed. Constable, I, 27–41, to the hermit Gilbert of Senlis (p. 213 below), and Stephen of Tournai, *Ep.* 188, ed. Desilve, p. 234, to a former canon of St Evurtius who had become a hermit, stressing the need for variety in eremitical life.

There was considerable uncertainty about hermits, recluses, anchorites, and solitaries.[59] Some of them were independent, but those who had been monks or clerics before leaving the world or being enclosed in their cells normally retained their status. It was not rare for monks to spend some or all of their time living as hermits. According to the chronicle of Cluny, some four hundred monks lived in the woods around Cluny during the abbacy of Peter the Venerable, who visited them from time to time and occasionally himself made eremitical retreats.[60] Many monasteries had dependent hermitages that were occupied either by their own monks or by independent hermits, and small priories served as residences for periods of eremitical life as well as centres of economic exploitation.[61] In the early twelfth century Gerard of St Albinus spent ten years at Bressay eating and working with the peasants, according to his *Life*, 'like a hermit'.[62]

Hermits as such, however, were considered to be either lay people or of their own order, not members of the monastic order. Damiani insisted on the distinction and forbade his hermits to choose a prior 'from the monastic order'.[63] Hermits were listed separately in the witness-lists to some charters, and they were treated apart from both monks and canons in the *Libellus*.

> No one should be disturbed if a certain diversity is found in this order, and if each [hermit] arranges his own life differently, some living alone, some with two or three or more, living a life that is easier for some and harder for others, with a diversity such as we find among the hermits of old, and if each uses the power of his choice in order that he may attempt as much as he wishes or as much as his strength allows, and he will not be condemned by the Lord for it.[64]

Various writers commented, usually with disapproval, on the freedom and voluntary nature – the *arbitrii sue potestas* as it was called in the *Libellus* – of hermits, and on their lack of stability and obedience, living as they did, according to the *Life* of William of Malavale, 'without dependence on the will of

---

[59] In addition to the works listed in *Medieval Monasticism*, nos. 306–13, especially *Eremitismo* (1965), see the two regional studies by Penco (1985) and Dereine (1987).
[60] *Bibl. Clun.*, col. 600BC. See Leclercq (1956a); Peter the Venerable, ed. Constable, II, 182; and Giles Constable, in *Istituzioni* (1980), pp. 255–6 and 261.
[61] Dubois (1967), p. 657. See Barthélemy (1993), pp. 383–6 and 409–10, on the priories of Marmoutier and the Trinity at Vendôme. The four priories of Marmoutier were called *potestas*, *obedientia*, *cella*, and *loca*. Two served as centres of exploitation and two as sanctuaries. The relation between a monastery and a hermitage is well illustrated by Chaumes in the diocese of Bourges, on which see the charter in *Essai de reconstitution du cartulaire A de Saint-Sulpice de Bourges*, ed. Louis de Kersers (Mémoires de la Société des antiquaires du Centre 35; Bourges 1913), pp. 198–200, nos. 106–7.
[62] *Vita Girardi monachi*, in *Chroniques des églises d'Anjou*, ed. Paul Marchegay and Emile Mabille (Société de l'histoire de France; Paris 1869), pp. 99–100 (*BHL* 3548). See Zimmermann, III, 258–60.
[63] Peter Damiani, *Opusc.* 15 *de suae congregationis institutis*, 28, in *PL*, CXLV, 360BC.
[64] *Libellus*, ed. Constable, pp. 14–16.

another'.[65] They were also criticized for owning property, since what they had belonged to themselves, unlike monks, who could be without possessions because the institution owned everything.[66] The Grandmontines, who refused to accept into the order anyone with property, would not receive a solitary 'with his own cell', though they were prepared to accept a solitary without his cell or a cell without the solitary.[67] Hermits were supported either by offerings, which involved contacts with other people, or by their own labour. Some of them made charcoal, and charcoal making, like cutting stone and cleaning out stables, was a topos of humility. The noble hermit Simon of Crépy was said in a twelfth-century vernacular poem to have belonged to the order of charcoal makers.[68] Not all hermits were humble and hard-working, however, and in about 1130 a canon of Chartres named Pagan Bolotinus wrote a poem against false hermits, accusing them of avarice, hypocrisy, gluttony, and vagabondage. Though they criticized the clergy, whose way of life they contrasted with their own austerity, Pagan said, they in fact frequented towns and courts and were the new pharisees predicted by Christ. This suggests that Pagan had in mind wandering preachers, like Robert of Arbrissel, of whom many were hermits, and who aroused the opposition of the authorities by their success as preachers as much as by their outlandish dress and behaviour and by their outspoken criticism of the clergy.[69]

Individual hermits were sometimes given a formal approval or *licentia habitandi* by popes and bishops, but in practice almost anyone could become a hermit and live more or less as they pleased.[70] Hermits were a well-established feature on the early medieval religious scene, but their numbers in the eleventh and twelfth centuries grew, especially in western France, central Italy, and England, and they played a disproportionately large role, relative to their num-

---

[65] Albert, *Vita Willelmi*, ed. Guillaume de Waha (Liège 1693), p. 401 (*BHL* 8922). See Elm (1962), p. 26; Giles Constable, in *Istituzioni* (1980), p. 249, and (1985b), p. 105. On the liberty of hermits, solitaries, and recluses, citing the wild ass set free in Job 39.5, see Goscelin of St Bertin, *Liber confortatorius*, 3, ed. Charles H. Talbot, in *Anal. mon.*, III, 89; Abelard, *Sermo* 33 *de s. Joanne baptista*, in *PL*, CLXXVIII, 586B; and James of Vitry, *Sermones vulgares* 33, in Pitra, *Anal. nov.*, II, 397. See also plate 8, showing Francis of Assisi with a wild ass.

[66] See the examples cited in Giles Constable, in *Istituzioni* (1980), pp. 245–6.

[67] *Regula Stephani Muretensis*, 43 ('De solitario cum propria cella non recipiendo'), in *CC:CM*, VIII, 88.

[68] *Les vers de Thibaud de Marly*, line 212, ed. Herbert K. Stone (Paris 1932), p. 107 (see pp. 78–80 on Simon of Crépy), and Louis (1946–7), III, 99–100. On charcoal-burning, see p. 41 above and Helinand of Froidmont, *De cognitione sua*, 13, in *PL*, CCXII, 734A, for a vision of a former *familiarius* of the count of Nevers who became a charcoal-burner, 'pauper in seculo sed dives in Deo, religiosus et timens Deum'.

[69] Leclercq (1958b), pp. 77–84. See Oury (1975), p. 297, for a treatise against 'false' hermits written about 1135 by Geoffrey Babion of Angers (perhaps the future archbishop of Bordeaux Geoffrey of Le Loroux).

[70] Grundmann (1962), pp. 542–3, said that the written permission given by pope Hadrian IV to the hermit Gerlach (*c.* 1100 – *c.* 1164/5) to live as a hermit on his own lands without becoming a monk was unusual.

bers, both in the life of the church and in popular religious culture, as reflected in literature, where they figured as arbitrators, spiritual advisers, and dispensers of hospitality to travellers, and also as wild men with magical powers.[71] A hermit named Mark, for instance, came to consult pope Alexander III about a woman who had taken a vow of continence.[72] They served as confidants of bishops and abbots, like Christina of Markyate for Geoffrey of St Albans, and as advisers to kings and great nobles. Henry III of Germany consulted the hermit Gunther, and William of Monte Vergine advised Roger II of Sicily.[73] King John visited Robert of Knaresborough, and his brother Richard the Lion-Hearted consulted Joachim of Fiore.[74] Whether their advice was followed by these kings is another matter, but the fact it was sought, or said to be sought, is a sign of the position of hermits in society. Adelelmus of La Chaise-Dieu went to Spain at the request of the king and queen in about 1080 and rode on a donkey in advance of the Christian army advancing against the Moslems across the river Tagus, and Peter the Hermit is better known as one of the movers of the First Crusade than as the founder of the house of regular canons of Neufmoustier at Huy.[75] To leave one's homeland permanently or to make a pilgrimage were considered types of eremitism, as was wandering preaching in the eleventh and twelfth centuries. Bruno of Querfurt in his *Life of the five brothers* said that evangelical work, in addition to monastic life and 'golden solitude', was one of the three treasures of those seeking God,[76] and many hermits engaged in preaching. Robert of Arbrissel covered the entire west of France from Brittany to Toulouse on his preaching tours.[77] He also visited the Auvergne, where he met Raingard, the mother of Peter the Venerable, who after her death wrote that Robert had inspired her with a desire to become a nun at Fontevrault, though she in fact went to Marcigny.[78]

The reaction to such men and their activities ranged from extravagant admiration through suspicion and distrust to outright hostility, like that of Pagan Bolotinus. A bearded hermit appears at the top of the ladder of virtues

[71] There are references to the hermit Ogrin in Béroul, *Tristan*, lines 1362, 2291, and 2357, ed. Janet Caulkins and Guy Mermier (Paris 1967), pp. 63, 102, and 105, and to several hermits in the works of Chrétien de Troyes. See Gougaud (1928), pp. 36–41; Rousset (1961), pp. 42–5; Anna Maria Finoli, in *Eremitismo* (1965), pp. 581–91; Mayr-Harting (1975); Leyser (1984); Moore (1986), p. 53; Leyser (1987); and Dereine (1987), p. 310 n. 117, on hermits in *chansons de geste* and epic legends.

[72] *Decretales*, IV, 6, 5, in *Corpus*, ed. Friedberg, II, 686.

[73] See (on Christina) Elkins (1988), pp. 35–8; (on Gunther) Grundmann (1963), pp. 73–7; and (on William) Joannes a Nusco, *Vita Guillelmi*, VII, 57, in *AASS*, 25 June VII, 113 (*BHC* 8924).

[74] *Vita* [B] *Roberti Knaresburgensis*, 20, ed. Paul Grosjean, in *Anal. boll.* 57 (1939), pp. 393–4 (*BHL* 7270ef); and (on Joachim) Roger of Hoveden, *Chronica*, s.a. 1190, ed. William Stubbs (RS 51; London 1868–71), III, 75–9, and *Gesta regis Ricardi*, s.a. 1191, ed. William Stubbs (RS 49; London 1867), II, 151–5.

[75] *Vita Adelelmi Casae Dei*, 13–15, in *España sagrada*, XXVII, 839–40 (*BHL* 72), and, on Peter the Hermit, Dereine (1952), pp. 137–65 and (1953).

[76] Bruno of Querfurt, *Vita quinque fratrum*, 2, in *MGH, SS*, XV.2, 719.

[77] Von Walter (1903–6), I, 136–44.

[78] Peter the Venerable, *Ep.* 53, ed. Constable, I, 158–9 and 161; see II, 134.

in Herrad of Hohenbourg's *Book of delights*, above the recluse, monk, cleric, lay woman, and knight. He is distracted from prayer and contemplation by his garden, of which there is a little picture, towards which he is falling (plate 1). Bernard of Clairvaux, who knew the dangers of ascetic exhibitionism, took a special interest in a hermit named Schetzelo or Gezzelin, who lived in the woods near Luxembourg and who had 'the heavens for a roof, the air for clothing, and the support of pigs [acorns] for human food'. He tried to avoid Bernard's emissaries, who, when they finally tracked him down, found him 'not like an earthly man but like a heavenly angel, whose way of life was entirely in heaven and from heaven'.[79] When it came to allowing his own monks to live in solitude, however, Bernard was cautious, since he was well aware of the opportunities for sin and self-will offered by a solitary life, without the control of a superior and community. Ivo of Chartres expressed this view in his letter to the monks of Coulombs concerning some wandering preachers who had urged them to leave their monastery for the stricter life of hermits. After refuting the criticisms and telling the monks to remain in the house of their profession, Ivo wrote that

> In saying this I do not condemn the life of hermits, that is of those who after they have been instructed in the regular disciplines in monasteries leave in an orderly way [by which he presumably meant with the permission of their abbot] for a deserted place, for whom solitude is paradise, and a town a prison, in order to lead an active life, living by the labour of their hands, or to restore their mind by the sweetness of a contemplative life, and to thirst after the fountain of life with the mouth of the heart, and, forgetting those things that are behind, not to look back at them anymore.

They must not wander about or criticize others, as if the church consisted only of solitaries. 'For the hidden places of forests and the peaks of mountains do not make a man holy', Ivo said, 'unless he has with him solitude of mind, peace of heart, tranquillity of conscience, and soarings in his heart without which depression (*mentis accidia*), curiosity, vainglory, and dangerous onset of temptations accompany all solitude.'[80]

The emphasis in this and other contemporary works is on the need for careful spiritual preparation, preferably in a monastery, and orderly entry to the eremitical life. The same was true of recluses, though the danger of unauthorized entry was less because they inevitably depended for food upon the surrounding community, which was often a religious house, and they were usually enclosed in their cells by a formal ceremony supervised by the bishop. A well-behaved and holy recluse was considered an asset to a town or monastery. An inscription on the tomb of Emma, who died at St Amand (Nord) in

---

[79] Herbert, *De miraculis Cisterciensium monachorum*, I, 6, printed as part of the *Vita prima Bernardi*, VII, in Bernard, ed. Mabillon, II(6), 2384AD, and *PL*, CLXXXV, 455D–61A (*BHL* 1231). See Zimmermann, II, 544, who dated his death *c.* 1138.

[80] Ivo of Chartres, *Ep.* 192, in *PL*, CLXII, 201B–2A.

1124, after thirty-six years as a recluse, read: 'Here lies the recluse Emma, a nun of the church of St Amand of Rouen who happily moved from there to here owing to the presence of the same saint.'[81] The converted Jew Herman in the book *On his conversion* described two sisters who were recluses at Cologne in the 1120s and 'whose holy way of life diffused a most sweet odour of good opinion throughout the whole neighbourhood of that city'.[82] Some recluses clearly found the life difficult, however, and their misbehaviour was frequently remarked on. According to the chronicler of Petershausen,

> Many of them are found blameworthy in our time, because as soon as they are enclosed, they wish to be doctors and prophets; they predict the future falsely; they attract crowds to themselves; they rarely apply themselves to prayer or to silence; they want to know everything that is done among secular people; they talk all day long with one person or another.

He went on to compare them to clerics and monks who, he said, 'although they sometimes transgress what is just, are however continually restrained by the discipline of a master, but solitaries and recluses, since they use free choice, think that whatever they do is holy and fall into error. For their intention is holy and good, but it is vitiated by freedom.' Later he said of the five recluses at Petershausen (of whom two were lay brothers and one each a monk, a nun, and a religious woman) that 'Almost all these men were of such troublesome spirit (*importuni animi*) that they could not easily remain in the congregation', which throws an interesting light on how some houses used their cells for recluses and why they did not always behave.[83] There are references in other sources, including Aelred of Rievaulx's *On the institution of recluses*, to their laziness and bad reputation and especially to the misuse of the windows to their cells.[84] The temptation of the recluse on the ladder in the *Garden of delights* is his bed, 'on which he rests as he desires' (plate 1). A recluse at Le Bec in the first half of the twelfth century, named Guerric, clearly kept in close touch with the world around him, in spite of his physical enclosure, and sent letters all around 'containing just criticism for those placed above himself and pious exhortation for those below'.[85] Precisely who was considered to be above or below a recluse at that time is uncertain, but his advice may not have been resented, since recluses were generally admired, and their assistance was often sought in material as well as in spiritual affairs.

---

[81] Serbat (1912), p. 197.
[82] Herman, *De conversione sua*, 12, ed. Gerlinde Niemeyer (*MGH*, Quellen zur Geistesgeschichte des Mittelalters 4; Weimar 1963), p. 107. See Ehlers (1973), p. 38; Saltman (1988), who argued that the work was 'a fictionalized autobiography' composed at Cappenberg in the late twelfth century and belonging to 'a genre of conversion narratives, possibly fictitious' (pp. 43–4); and Morrison (1992a), pp. 51–7 and 205 n. 52, and (1992b), pp. 39–113, esp. 40–1 and nn. 6–8.
[83] *Casus mon. Petrishusensis, praef.*, 21, and v, 37, ed. Feger (n. 16), pp. 34 and 230. He criticized solitaries in similar terms in *praef.*, 20, p. 34.
[84] Aelred of Rievaulx, *De institutione inclusarum*, 2, ed. Charles Dumont (SC 76; Paris 1961), pp. 44–7.
[85] Ed. Jean Leclercq, in *Anal. mon.*, II, 170.

The status of a hermit or recluse, perhaps owing to its relative freedom and informality, was particularly attractive to women, who played an important part in the reform movement of the eleventh and twelfth centuries.[86] Reference has already been made to some individual women, such as Christina of Markyate, Emma of St Amand, Ermengard of Brittany, Heloise, Herrad of Hohenbourg, Hildegard of Bingen, and Peter the Venerable's mother Raingard, five of whose sons entered the church, four as monks, and who herself became a nun of Marcigny. The presence of women in contemporary religious life, and especially its less formal types, was mentioned in the lost (or unwritten) section of the *Libellus*, in the chronicle of Petershausen, and in other sources. The reasons for their prominence in religious life, and society generally, at this time are still not clear and may have been demographic and socio-economic as well as religious in nature.[87] More perhaps than at any other time in Christian history (not excluding the present), male religious leaders in the eleventh and twelfth centuries were responsive to the needs of women and welcomed their presence and influence in religious institutions. It has been estimated that the number of houses for, or including, women in Germany alone rose from about 70 in 900 to 150 in 1100 and to 500, containing a total of between 25,000 and 30,000 nuns, in 1250.[88] Religious women were accorded high prestige. Occasionally, as at Ligueux in 1115, nuns replaced monks;[89] many, and in some regions perhaps most, of the recluses were women.[90] Any number of churches had women, probably lay women, associated with them as *familiares, conversae, devotae*, or, as they were called in the *Libellus, mulieres deicolae* or *licoisae*.[91] The hermits, wandering preachers, and early heretics also attracted female followers.[92] The proportion of female saints

---

[86] The classic work on the *Frauenbewegung* or *Frauenfrage* (or *Mulieres religosae* movement, as it is sometimes called) is Grundmann (1961). See also the works cited in n. 92 and McDonnell (1954), esp. pp. 81–96 on the social background; Bernards (1971) on the eleventh century; Bolton (1973); and Roisin (1943) and de Ganck (1984) on the association of women with the Cistercians, principally in the thirteenth century.

[87] For differing opinions on whether there was a plurality of women over men in the high Middle Ages, see Genicot (1984c), p. 315, and Herlihy (1985), p. 102.

[88] Hilpisch (1928), pp. 60–1; Bernards (1955), p. 1; Uhl (1972), p. 110*, citing Hilpisch; and Parisse (1991), p. 22, on the numbers of nuns in houses in Saxony.

[89] Lemaître (1984), p. 66.

[90] See (for the Low Countries) Demaret (1886); Serbat (1912); and Stiennon (1951), pp. 449–51, no. 11; (for France) Ledru (1899); (for Germany) Schelb (1941), pp. 189–90, and Fuhrmann (1988), pp. 369–71; and (for England) Warren (1985), pp. 18–29, who concluded that 'In the twelfth century there is a ratio of about five women to three men; in the thirteenth century, about four to one' (p. 19), and Elkins (1988), pp. 19–42. The *Meditations* of Godwin of Salisbury were addressed to an otherwise unknown recluse named Rainild (see n. 96 below).

[91] The term *pinzochera* was later applied in Italy to religious women living at home rather than in a community.

[92] Grundmann (1961), pp. 46–50, and Iogna-Prat (1977). See also (for a Marxist point of view) Koch (1962) and Werner (1955), who concentrated on Robert of Arbrissel, on whom see also Dalarun (1985). Lambert (1978), p. 50, remarked on the high status of women among the Cathars. Vitalis of Savigny promoted the marriage of prostitutes (*Rouleaux des morts*, pp. 283–4), and Berthold of Garsten forced a nobleman to marry one of his twelve concubines, according to his *Vita*, 34, ed. Lenzenweger (n. 34), p. 257.

rose from less than 1 per cent in the eleventh century to 18 per cent of all saints, and 45 per cent of lay saints, in the twelfth.[93] The earliest version of the rule of Augustine was commonly thought to have been written for women,[94] and among the rules written for women in the twelfth and in the early thirteenth centuries were those of Abelard for nuns, of Aelred of Rievaulx for recluses, and the *Ancrene riwle (wisse)*, which may have been addressed to Augustinian canonesses.[95] The only surviving work of Robert of Arbrissel was addressed to a woman, as were many letters, poems, and works of spiritual advice like the *Book of encouragement* by Goscelin of St Bertin and the unpublished *Meditations* of Godwin of Salisbury.[96] The *Mirror of virgins*, which was written soon after 1140, is entirely concerned with the spiritual life of women.[97] While it is hard to say whether there was anything approaching a distinctive female ministry or spirituality in the twelfth century, Abelard referred to the ministrations of women in the bible 'not by the office of superiority (*praelationis*) but by the merit of devotion', and Gerhoh of Reichersberg commented in 1148 on the new religious songs sung in the vernacular by *sanctae mulieres* in monasteries and by married women whose husbands and sons were away fighting the pagans.[98]

This openness to women showed itself both in an emphasis on the spiritual equality of women with men and in a genuine admiration for qualities that were regarded as distinctively feminine, such as piety, mercy, and tenderness. Abelard wrote in his rule for religious women that 'You are so joined to us in name and the profession of continence that almost all our institutions are also suited to you.'[99] Rupert of Deutz said, 'The substance of a woman differs from the substance of a man in nothing except sex', and went on to stress that women were neither less rational than men nor less entitled to aspire 'to the resemblance of the Creator'. Rupert was particularly devoted to the Virgin,

---

[93] Delooz (1969), pp. 260 and 343. According to Aston (1970), p. xli, a quarter of the saints whose lives were written in French between *c.* 1150 and 1300 were women.

[94] Verheijen (1967), II, 19–21.

[95] On Abelard's rule, which was edited by T.P. McLaughlin, in *Mediaeval Studies* 18 (1956), pp. 242–92, see Luscombe (1988), pp. 273–7, and (1991), pp. 6–9, who stressed Cistercian influence at the Paraclete; for Aelred, n. 84 above; and for the *Ancrene riwle* (now commonly called the *Ancrene wisse*), Dobson (1976), who dated it probably 1217/20 (pp. 15 and 316) and discussed the title (pp. 51–3), and whose conclusions were accepted by Robert W. Ackerman and Roger Dahood in their *Ancrene riwle: Introduction and Part I* (Medieval and Renaissance Texts and Studies 31; Binghamton 1984), p. 4 (see also 85 n. 1 on the title), but were questioned by Wada (1994), pp. lxxi and lxxxix, who proposed a Dominican author writing between 1221 and *c.* 1250.

[96] *Meditationes Godwini cantoris Salesberie ad Rainildam reclusam*, in MS Oxford, Bodleian Library, Digby 96, fols. 8ʳ–68ʳ. On Godwin, see Edwards (1967), pp. 4 and 183 n. 1. There is no reference to Rainild in Warren (1985).

[97] See *Speculum virginum*, in *CC:CM*, V, 32*–7*, on the date, and, more generally, Bernards (1955).

[98] Abelard, *Ep.* 6, ed. J.T. Muckle, in *Mediaeval Studies* 17 (1955), p. 255, and Gerhoh of Reichersberg, *In Psalmos*, 4 *ad* 39.4, in *PL*, CXCIII, 1436AB. See Bynum (1987), p. 21, on the clerical functions exercised by women from the tenth to twelfth centuries.

[99] Ed. McLaughlin (n. 95), p. 243.

whose example should be contemplated 'with the eyes of the heart'.[100] His praise of her tender qualities may have inspired the so-called Madonna of Dom Rupert, which dates from about 1150 and shows Mary feeding the infant Jesus at her breast. Her special role for Anselm was the remaking of all created things, and she appeared in countless visions to both men and women who needed her help. The Virgin was a mother, a wife, and a sister to men, and a model and exemplar to women,[101] and especially religious women, for whom Christ was a husband, lover, and champion.[102] The warm, tender, loving qualities associated with Mary, and with mothers generally, were admired in men no less than in women. The works of Cabassut, McLaughlin, and Bynum have shown the importance of the devotion to Christ our mother,[103] but much research remains to be done on the broader use of maternal and feminine imagery and on the spread of the concepts of mother-church and mother-tongue, which were current already in the early twelfth century. Anselm of Besati referred to the church of Milan as 'my mother'; Suger expressed his desire to honour the church of St Denis 'which had with maternal affection given him milk when [he was] a boy'; and prior Fulco of St-Martin-des-Champs wrote that 'Our mother the church of Cluny nourished us like little ones with the milk of her breasts.'[104] Bishops and abbots were also described as mothers. 'Who will restore to you your mother?', said Herbord in a funeral oration for Otto of Bamberg attributed to bishop Embrico of Würzburg. 'Where will you now seek those maternal breasts, those maternal feelings?'[105] Guibert of Nogent and Peter the Venerable wrote at length about their mothers,[106] and the orphan Albinus said that his uncle, who was a monk, filled

---

[100] Rupert of Deutz, *De sancta trinitate: In Genesim*, II, 32, in *CC:CM*, XXI, 226, and *In Cantica Canticorum*, 5 *ad* 5.2–8, in *CC:CM*, XXVI, 106. See Bernards (1960), p. 415; Silvestre (1968), p. 69; and Stiennon (1968), on Rupert's view of the spiritual maternity of the Virgin; and Van Engen (1983), pp. 86–7, for his view of marriage. On the equality of men and women in spiritual matters, marriage, and certain aspects of the law, see Javelet (1967), I, 236–45; Bernards (1971), pp. 93–100; and Brundage (1980), pp. 380–1.

[101] Roisin (1947), pp. 110–17, and Javelet (1967), I, 366–7, who said that the Virgin was sometimes called the sister of Christ and the angels.

[102] Christ was called the husband of the nuns in the regulations written by abbot Fulgentius of Afflighem for the nunnery of Forest-les-Bruxelles in about 1110, in Miraeus–Foppens, I, 79, and the love of canonesses for Christ was vividly described in the *Ancrene riwle*, ed. and tr. James Morton (Camden Society 57; London 1853), pp. 34–5 and 136–7. See n. 94 above.

[103] Cabassut (1949); McLaughlin (1975); and Bynum (1982a), pp. 110–69.

[104] Anselm of Besati, *Rhetorimachia*, 7, ed. Karl Manitius (*MGH*, Quellen zur Geistesgeschichte des Mittelalters 2; Weimar 1958), p. 116; Suger, *De rebus in administratione sua gestis*, 28, ed. A. Lecoy de la Marche (Société de l'histoire de France; Paris 1867), p. 190; and *Chartes de Cluny*, V, 831, no. 4457.

[105] Herbord, *De Ottone ep. Bambergensi*, I, 42, ed. Jaffé (n. 3), p. 741. Prior Warengarius, who administered Abingdon for a few years after the death of abbot Faritius in about 1117, was described as ruling *uelut benignissima mater* in the *Chronicon monasterii de Abingdon*, ed. Joseph Stevenson (RS 2; London 1858), II, 159.

[106] Some eleventh-century examples are cited in Bernards (1971), pp. 88–93. In 1147 Theobald of Gisors prevented his nephew Ingelramnus from attending his mother's funeral 'ne de matris suae decessu indiscrete dolens abundantiore tristitia gravaretur': *Cartulaire de l'abbaye de Saint-*

the office of both parents, showing him both the severity of a father and the piety of a mother.[107]

Through these attitudes towards women and female qualities there ran at the same time a keen, at times almost erotic, awareness of the differences between the sexes and a failure and even a refusal to recognize a distinction between them, which went back both to the sexlessness of the angels in paradise and of Adam and Eve before the fall and to Paul's injunction in Galatians 3.28, 'There is neither male nor female. For you are all one in Jesus Christ.' Especially in religious communities, which were the image not only of paradise and the Garden of Eden but also of the primitive church, there should be no distinction between the sexes.[108] While this attitude was less marked in the twelfth century than in the early days of monasticism, when women sometimes lived as men in male communities, it may be reflected in the story told by Caesarius of Heisterbach of a woman who remained concealed in a Cistercian abbey.[109] It may also have influenced the reappearance in England and northern France of the ancient practice of syneisactism or *conhospitio* by which a male and female hermit lived together, and sometimes slept in the same bed, in a chaste and spiritual marriage that was considered both a test of chastity and, perhaps more important, a surmounting and denial of sexuality.[110] Such in all probability was the relationship between Robert of Arbrissel and his female companions, upon which Geoffrey of Vendôme and Marbod remarked, and between Christina of Markyate and several male hermits, and also, more strikingly, between the recluses Harvey and Eve, to whom Goscelin of St Bertin addressed his *Book of encouragement* in 1082–3. They both came from England but lived together for many years near Anjou, exciting general admiration not entirely unmixed with concern. According to a poem written in honour of Eve between her death in 1113 and Harvey's in 1119,

Martin de Pontoise, ed. J. Depoin (Publications de la Société historique du Vexin; Pontoise 1895–1904), pp. 80–1, no. 102.

[107] Albinus, *Digesta, praef.* (*Gesta pauperis scolaris Albini*), in *Liber censuum romanae ecclesiae*, ed. Paul Fabre and Louis Duchesne (Bibliothèque des Ecoles françaises d'Athènes et de Rome 2 S.; Paris 1910–52), II, 87.

[108] See Günter (1954), pp. 266–71; Nagel (1966), p. 53, who stressed the eschatological aspects of the denial of sex distinctions; Anson (1974), who said that transvestism 'signalized and effected a transformation of self'; Iogna-Prat (1977), pp. 51–2; and, for a modern psychoanalytical view, Kubie (1974).

[109] Caesarius, *Dialogus*, I, 40, ed. Strange, I, 47–53. See McGuire (1979), pp. 247–54.

[110] See Gougaud (1921), esp. pp. 148–51 on the twelfth century; Werner (1955) on Robert of Arbrissel; Reynolds (1968), esp. pp. 563–4, who saw the practice as a battle against sin and a search for martyrdom and proto-paradisiacal perfection; Bugge (1975), pp. 74–6; Iogna-Prat (1977), pp. 54–63; Smith (1978), arguing that Robert of Arbrissel's concern for women has been exaggerated; and Smith (1985), pp. 54–5, who said (54 n. 7) that in this respect Robert was 'characteristic of his age, when experiments with syneisactism were again common'. See also p. 26 n. 120 above.

There long lived Eve with Harvey her companion
Let you who hear fear not my revelation
Do not mistrust or flee from this suspicion
Not in the world but Christ was their delectation.[111]

Women were prominent in the reform movement as founders, members, and supporters of new religious houses. Paulina, the founder of Paulinzelle, particularly admired Hirsau, from where she got an abbot for her new house. While still in lay life, she visited Rome three times and devoted herself so zealously to the six works of mercy of the active life 'that in these not many of the conjugal order were superior, even if a few were equal'. After her husband's death, she took the veil, living in a chapel in the woods, mortifying her flesh, and devoting herself to manual labour and prayer.[112] St Blaise, Muri, Göttweig, Admont, Zwiefalten, St George in the Black Forest, and Zell all had female members in the eleventh century, although the exact date of their introduction is not always certain, and in the twelfth century the presence of women was almost a mark of neo-Cluniac monasticism in Germany.[113] Abbot Theoger of St George, who later became bishop of Metz and established several houses for women, said, according to his biographer Wolfger of Prüfening, that 'I shall not exclude nuns from the title of this honour, for its highest perfection is found in women.'[114] Not much is known about how they lived except at Admont, where abbot Wolvold (1115–37) gathered the women who had previously lived as recluses into a single building, where they were under the control of a *magistra* and followed the same strict regime as the monks. It had one gate, which was opened only to admit a new nun or for the burial of a dead one, and on one occasion when there was a fire, and the keys could not be found, the locks had to be broken.[115] According to the chronicle of Zwiefalten under the year 1138, 'The common agreement of the monks established the nuns, who had previously lived in a cell next to the parish church, in the area east of the monastery, next to the courses of the waters, surrounded

---

[111] Chamard (1863), II, 563, and 102–19 and 531–41 generally on Harvey and Eve, on whom see also Wilmart (1934 and 1938); Häring (1973), pp. 1089–90, for Harvey's letter to Hilary of Orléans; and Elkins (1988), pp. 21–7, who also discussed (pp. 27–42) Christina and other eremitic women and their male companions.

[112] Sigeboto, *Vita Paulinae*, 7 and 19–21, in *MGH, SS*, XXX.2, 914 and 918–19 (*BHL* 6551). On the performance of charitable acts by women, see pp. 237–8 below.

[113] Hallinger (1950–1), pp. 258 and 490–1. On specific houses, in addition to those cited below, see Jakobs (1968), pp. 41, 51, and 118, and the *Acta fundationis* [of Muri], 11 and 20, in Kiem (1883), pp. 35 and 60–1.

[114] Wolfger of Prüfening, *Vita Theogeri s. Georgii*, I, 25, in *MGH, SS*, XII, 459 (*BHL* 8109).

[115] *Vita cuiusdam magistrae monialium Admuntensium*, in *Anal. boll.* 12 (1893), pp. 362–3; the customs published in Wichner (1874–80), II, 186–7, which probably date from the abbacy of Isenrik (1178–89), refer to the burials of brothers and sisters; and Irimbert of Admont, *De incendio monasterii sui ac de vita et moribus virginum*, in *Bibliotheca ascetica antiquo-nova*, ed. Bernhard Pez (Regensburg 1723–40), VIII, 455–64, which is an excerpt from his unpublished commentary on Kings (*ad* IV, 14.7) written in 1151–2 (Stegmüller 5152). A full publication for the *CC:CM* is in preparation.

by a wall.'[116] These houses were in effect, if not in name, double monasteries, with parallel communities of men and women, like the new orders founded by Robert of Arbrissel at Fontevrault and by Gilbert at Sempringham, though in these the role of the women was more important than that of the men, who were there primarily to perform liturgical offices and work the nuns could not do for themselves.[117]

Many of the reformers were concerned for the religious needs of women and admitted them into their communities. Most of the eremitical foundations of indeterminate status included women on an informal basis, at least in their early years.[118] Springiersbach originated as a group around a solitary widow named Benigna, whose son Richard became the first provost of what developed into an important house of regular canons.[119] The founder and first prior of Aureil, Gaucherius, according to his *Life*, 'knew that neither sex is excluded from the kingdom of God and therefore, striving to build the heavenly Jerusalem with both walls, that is of men and of women, he constructed the habitation of women a stone's throw from his own cell, distributing his poverty both to men and to women'.[120] A follower of another characteristic reformer, Geoffrey of Chalard, named Arnold, on one occasion consulted Gaucherius: 'To this man flocked the men and no less the women of this region, both nobles and non-nobles, because he was made for all men, in the word of the Apostle, in order that he might gain many souls for Christ.'[121] Stephen of Obazine was likewise said to have admitted 'nobles and non-nobles, men as well as women' to his community, where the women 'lived not far from the brothers, separated in their dwellings but joined in religion'.[122] Norbert of Xanten received both men and women, wrote Herman of Tournai, 'so that

---

[116] Berthold of Zwiefalten, *Chronicon Zwiveldensis*, 38, ed. Luitpold Wallach, in *Traditio* 13 (1957), p. 219; see also 18 and 50, pp. 207 and 230 and p. 244 on Zwiefalten as a double monastery. This text is also edited with Ortlieb's chronicle in the series 'Schwäbische Chroniken der Stauferzeit' 2 (Stuttgart 1941, repr. 1978).

[117] 'Double monastery' is a loose term, covering a variety of arrangements by which men and women were members of a single religious community: see the references in *Medieval Monasticism*, nos. 347–53, to which should be added Johnson (1991), p. 7, who rejected the term, and the articles in Elm and Parisse (1992). According to Thompson (1919), pp. 158 and 163–4, the purpose was not to coordinate the sexes but to provide a staff of male clerics to serve the nuns. On Fontevrault, which was headed by an abbess, see de Fontette (1967), pp. 65–80; Dalarun (1985), p. 290; and Michel Parisse, in Elm and Parisse (1992), pp. 135–48, who argued that it evolved after the death of Robert of Arbrissel from 'un monastère double à l'image des creations antiques' (p. 138), where the women and men were equal, into a predominantly female house. In the neo-Cluniac houses mentioned above, the men were clearly in charge.

[118] On their concern for the social condition of women, especially prostitutes and concubines, see the references in n. 92 above.

[119] Dereine (1948b), esp. pp. 422–3; Pauly (1962), pp. 25–8; and Erkens (1987), pp. 3–40. In 1128 the women moved to Andernach.

[120] *Vita Gaucherii*, in *Nova bibl.*, ii, 562 (*BHL* 3272).

[121] *Vita Gaufridi Castaliensis*, i, 6, ed. A. Bosvieux, in *Mémoires de la Société des sciences naturelles et archéologiques de la Creuse* 3 (1862), p. 100 (*BHL* 3283).

[122] *Vita Stephani Obazinensis*, i, 29, ed. Aubrun, p. 86.

in his monasteries we see that there is a more severe and strict way of life of women than of men', since they never left their enclosure and never spoke to a man except in the presence of two men and two women. In spite of this strictness, 'We see every day not so much rustic and poor women but rather very noble and very rich women, both widows and youthful and also girls . . . hastening to the monasteries of this institution . . . so that we believe more than ten thousand women are contained in them today.'[123] Many of the new houses of regular canons made provision for female members, sometimes including the wife of the founder, as at Frankenthal and Arnstein, which joined the Premonstratensian order. A document of 1130 concerning the regular canons of St John at Brescia mentioned six sisters 'who were established under the obedience of the brothers of the above-mentioned church'.[124]

The reformed orders of monks and the strictly enclosed orders tended to be less receptive to women, perhaps because the demand for a fully enclosed life was met by independent houses of nuns and canonesses. The first Cluniac nunnery was established at Marcigny in the middle of the eleventh century, mainly for widows and the wives of men who entered Cluny as *conversi*, and Peter the Venerable in the twelfth century decreed that nuns and *conversae* must live at least two leagues away from the houses of monks.[125] The Grandmontines never admitted women, and there is only one recorded Carthusian nunnery in the twelfth century.[126] The Cistercians refused to admit women to their houses or to include nunneries in the order. The early statutes established that 'The cohabitation of women in our order is forbidden', and the general chapter forbade the reception of women.[127] Bernard of Clairvaux, in spite of his personal concern for the spiritual life of women, strongly opposed their living together with men, and in a letter written in 1124/35 to the abbot

---

[123] Herman of Tournai, *De miraculis s. Mariae Laudunensis*, 7, in *PL*, CLVI, 996D–7A, and *MGH, SS*, XII, 659. On Premonstratensian nuns, see McDonnell (1954), pp. 101–4; de Fontette (1967), pp. 13–25; Parisse (1983), pp. 21–2; and de Ganck (1984), p. 239.

[124] Violante (1963), p. 1069. See Wirges (1928), p. 2, on Ravengiersburg; Dereine (1952), pp. 204–6, on Rolduc; Mois (1953), pp. 217–22, on Rottenbuch; Semmler (1956), pp. 106–7, on Frankenthal; Milis (1969), pp. 502–17, on Arrouaise, Rolduc, St Victor, and Afflighem; and on Arnstein, *Vita Ludovici de Arnstein*, ed. S. Widmann, in *Annalen des Vereins für nassauische Altertumskunde und Geschichtsforschung* 17 (1882), p. 255 (*BHL* 5033). Louis later moved the house of nuns to Enkenbach (p. 259).

[125] Wischermann (1986) and Joachim Wollasch, in Elm and Parisse (1992), pp. 110–11, and Peter the Venerable, *Stat.* 47, in *CCM*, VI, 78.

[126] *Regula Stephani Muretensis*, 39, in *CC:CM*, VIII, 86–7, and Krenig (1954), pp. 81–8.

[127] *Exordium Cistercii, Summa cartae caritatis et capitula*, 17, in *Textes de Cîteaux*, p. 123. On Cistercian nuns, see in addition to the works cited in *Medieval Monasticism*, nos. 327–32, J.-M. Canivez, in *DHGE*, XII, 951–2; McDonnell (1954), pp. 105–19; Despy (1974–5), pp. 66–72; Thompson (1978), who studied the contrast between the initial hostility and subsequent receptivity to women in the order; Parisse (1983), pp. 33–4; de Ganck (1984); and Elm (1994), pp. 23–4 (with bibliography, chiefly of regional studies, in 23 n. 60), who said that the growing number of Cistercian nunneries 'svela un difetto di organizzazione sintomatico'. According to Krening (1954), p. 12, 'Die Hochblüte der Zisterzienserinnenklöster setzte zu Beginn des 13. Jahrhunderts ein.'

of the Premonstratensian house of Cuissy, he said that women should be excluded from a mill that was under the charge of some lay brothers.[128] A few nunneries, however, beginning with Tart probably in the 1120s, were admitted to the order in the twelfth century, and some nuns entered Cistercian houses by the back door, as at Obazine, which when it joined the order was allowed to keep the nuns who had lived there under the guidance of the founder Stephen.[129] Others entered almost through ignorance or inadvertence, since there was no way of preventing a house of nuns from following the Cistercian statutes and calling themselves Cistercians.[130] The nuns in the convent established by Bartholomew of Laon, for instance, led a very strict life and imitated the Cistercian monks *per omnia*, according to Herman of Tournai; and Conrad III in his charter of 1147 confirming the foundation of Ichtershausen, which was composed by Wibald of Corvey on the basis of Henry V's charter for Paulinzelle, added *et ordine Cisterciensium* after *sub regula*. He specified, however, that a discreet and God-fearing man should be chosen 'from the order of regular canons' to serve as spiritual father and rector of the souls and of the material affairs of the abbess, sisters, brothers, and *familia*, and there is no evidence that the abbey was ever accepted into the Cistercian order.[131] In about 1185 pope Alexander III commissioned the abbot of Garandon and the prior of Kenilworth to determine whether or not the nunnery of Langley was Cistercian.[132]

Such communities were sometimes dependent upon and under the patronage of local houses of male Cistercians and Premonstratensians, among whom there was both a sympathy for the spiritual aspirations and insights of women and a belief in the possibility, as McGuire put it, of 'fruitful contacts of a spiritual nature' between men and women in the religious life.[133] In a revealing letter to abbot Hugh of Prémontré, in 1156/61, the Cistercian abbot Philip of L'Aumône wrote that his niece had experienced a spiritual conversion during a visit to *Montem-cultum* 'for the sake of prayer' and that she had put on religious clothing, cut her hair, and dedicated herself to Christ with a vow of virginity. Philip acknowledged that this was contrary to the institutions of the Premonstratensian order, the rules of the elders, and the authentic decrees, but wrote

[128] Bernard, *Ep.* 79, ed. Leclercq, VII, 211–12. On Bernard and women, see Edith Russell, in *Bernard de Clairvaux* (1953), pp. 411–25; Angiolillo (1959); and Leclercq (1983).

[129] *Vita Stephani Obazinensis*, II, 12, ed. Aubrun, pp. 112–14. When Obazine joined the Cistercians abbot Rainald of Cîteaux gave his permission that, although their order absolutely forbade (*omnino uetabat*) the rule of women, there would be no sudden changes at Obazine 'ita duntaxat ut sancte ille femine semper in ordine permanerent'.

[130] De Ganck (1984), pp. 244–5, agreed with Roisin that there was no order of Cistercian nuns but 'a feminine branch of and within the Cistercian order'.

[131] Herman of Tournai, *De miraculis s. Mariae Laudunensis*, III, 17, in *PL*, CLVI, 1002A, and Conrad II, no. 188, in *MGH, Dipl.*, IX, 340–1. There is no reference to the Cistercians in Frederick I, no. 176, ibid., X.1, 298–9. Cf. Parisse (1991), p. 42.

[132] Dugdale, *Monasticon*, IV, 221–2 (JL 13528).

[133] McGuire (1983a), p. 238, and (1983b), pp. 58–9, where he remarked on Cistercian concern 'for women and their experiences within the spiritual life'.

that 'She did what she should but not as she should, [and] she obtained an entry to a vowed change (*votiuae mutationis ingressum*). It was just that her offering was received in an orderly way by the hand of the abbot and of the monks living together.' Philip therefore asked Hugh to give his permission, presumably for the woman to live as a canoness in a female community at *Montem-cultum*.[134]

The attitude of the Cistercians and other strict monastic reformers shows that the openness of the reform movement to women should not be exaggerated and must be seen against a background of general suspicion and distrust. King Cnut abandoned his plan to build a house for women next to the house for men at Ramsey because, according to the abbey chronicle, 'the closeness of the sexes' could lead to harm as well as good.[135] The attitude, even of those who were sympathetic to women and received them into their communities, seems to have changed in the second quarter of the twelfth century, when Admont built a prison-like nunnery and Zwiefalten surrounded its nuns with walls. The Premonstratensians suppressed double monasteries and required women to live in houses at least two leagues away from those of men, and other houses imposed similar restrictions.[136] A striking example of this shift is found at Obazine, where the women, who had at first lived 'not far' from the men, were removed to a greater distance and, later, after the subjection to Dalon in 1142, were enclosed in a building with double doors, of which one was always kept closed.[137] There is no discernible reason for this change of policy, any more than for the previous openness to women. It may have been part of a generational shift, as the initial fervour and confidence of the reformers waned and traditional attitudes reasserted themselves. Idungus in his *Argument on four questions*, written in 1132/45, before he became a Cistercian, discussed the question of women in religious life and stressed that 'The feminine sex, since it is fragile, requires more care and stricter claustration.'[138] Rumours of scandalous behaviour in withdrawn and idealistic communities are almost endemic,[139] and the poem about Eve and the letter from Marbod to Robert of Arbrissel show that suspicions were roused in the twelfth century about any association between men and women that was freer than that found

---

[134] Philip of L'Aumône, *Ep.* 27 (of the Clairvaux collection), in *Bibliotheca patrum Cisterciensium*, ed. Bertrand Tissier (Bonnefontaine and Paris 1660–8), III, 249. Philip was abbot from 1156 to 1171 and Hugh from 1128 to 1161, which dates this letter 1156/61. I have been unable to identify *Montem-cultum*.

[135] *Chronicon abbatiae Rameseiensis*, 81, ed. William Dunn Macray (RS 83; London 1886), p. 126.

[136] Dereine (1952), pp. 204–5; McDonnell (1954), p. 103; de Fontette (1967), p. 15; Milis (1969), pp. 516–17; and de Ganck (1984), p. 237. According to Lawrence (1984), p. 181, 'From 1140 onwards the new orders increasingly adopted a policy of apartheid towards their female branches.'

[137] *Vita Stephen Obazinensis*, II, 3–6, ed. Aubrun, pp. 98–106.

[138] Idungus, *Argumentum*, ed. Huygens, p. 356, who went on to say that women had four enemies, two internal (concupiscence and curiosity) and two external (male libido and the devil's envy).

[139] See Perry (1935), II, 35–8, for the suspicions concerning the Fourierites and Brooke Farm.

in normal society. These were very likely reinforced by a few genuine problems, of which that in the Gilbertine house of Watton is perhaps the best known. The relatively easy access between the sexes that seems to have existed in Gilbertine houses at their origins was replaced in the late twelfth century by draconian measures to ensure their strict separation.[140] For whatever reason, attitudes continued to harden, and by the end of the century women were no longer received in many houses and orders where they had previously been welcome, and they increasingly tended to move outside the formal structures of religious life. The *Life* of Mary of Oignies by James of Vitry gives a vivid picture of the various types of religious life of women in the diocese of Liège in the early thirteenth century, which formed the background of the movement of beguines.[141]

The attitudes towards women in the late eleventh and early twelfth centuries were paralleled by those towards other people who might previously have found it hard, even if not impossible, to enter the older types of religious institutions. Those reformers who wanted to assert the boundaries between the various orders of society more firmly and to stress the distinctive character of monks tended, by lengthening the novitiate and raising the age of entry, to be more exclusive than many of the old houses, which admitted all comers and encouraged many types of associations with lay people. But at the same time they opened some doors (or failed to close others) that allowed lay people to participate to some degree in the benefits as well as the hardships of religious life. In part this arose from the reluctance of many of the reformers to be categorized and the loose use of the term *laicus*. When Stephen of Grandmont refused to be called a canon, monk, or hermit, he implicitly declared that he was a lay man; and the Grandmontines, following his example, remained for some time a primarily lay order. Hermits, if they were not considered a distinct order in themselves, were also often lay men, and illiterate or unordained members of twelfth-century religious houses were occasionally called lay in a pejorative sense, like the secular monks in the *Libellus* or the semi-lay monks (*semilaici*) mentioned by Wibald of Corvey.[142] Some of the informal eremitical communities seem in their early years to have taken almost anyone, but how true this was in practice, and how long it lasted, is hard to say. The two most interesting ways in which the reform movement opened the possibility of a consecrated life for lay men were the military orders and the lay brothers.

The question of whether the members of the military orders were primarily soldiers who led a religious life or monks who engaged in military activities

---

[140] Constable (1978).

[141] James of Vitry, *Vita Mariae Ogniacensis*, in *AASS*, 23 June V, 547–72 (*BHL* 5516), esp. the prologue. See Greven (1912), pp. 53–110; Lauwers (1989); and, on the early beguines, McDonnell (1954) and Simons (1989).

[142] *Libellus*, 4, ed. Constable, pp. 54–6, and Wibald, *Ep.* 230, in *Monumenta Corbeiensia*, ed. Philipp Jaffé (BRG 1; Berlin 1864), p. 349. Robert of Torigny, *Chronica*, s.a. 1157, ed. Richard Howlett (RS 82.4; London 1889), p. 192, applied the term *semilaicus* to abbot Robert of Cluny.

was debated since their origins. Bernard of Clairvaux said of the Templars in his *In praise of the new army* that 'I should be in doubt whether to call them monks or soldiers were it not suitable to call by both these names those men in whom neither the mildness of the monk nor the fortitude of the soldier is lacking.'[143] Although they to some extent developed from a lay to a monastic status, they never entirely lost the characteristics of both.[144] Otto of Freising described the military orders as 'a new type of army made up of men who went to Jerusalem to fight the enemy of the cross, so that, carrying the mortification of the cross continually on their bodies, they seem in life and manner [to be] not soldiers but monks'.[145] It was precisely the genius of the military orders that they combined two types of life that had previously been regarded as incompatible into a single, new type that was neither one nor the other, but both. In practice, however, it seems that the military side predominated over the monastic. 'To go to the Temple', said Amedeus of Hauterives to his followers when they became Cistercians at Bonnevaux, 'is not to give up [worldly] pleasures but simply to change the colour of your clothes'; and later in the century another Cistercian, Isaac of L'Etoile, without specifically naming the military orders, attacked the so-called Order of the Fifth Gospel that made converts by force, killed and despoiled non-Christians, and called its dead members martyrs.[146] All the Templars and Hospitallers whose origins are known came from lay rather than from monastic life, and although they followed a rule and claimed the privileges of monks and canons, they often behaved more like soldiers than monks. Joachim of Fiore, writing about the sixth age of history in his *Book of the concord of the Old and New Testaments*, said that God 'created in the order of lay men new types of religion, such as the brothers of the Temple and the Hospitallers, and some others in Spain, and the lay brothers (*conversi*) of the Cistercian order and those like them, who were all created for the assistance of clerics and monks'.[147] While he recognized that the military orders were a new type of religious life, therefore, Joachim said that they arose from the order of lay men and for the assistance of clerics and monks.

The ethos of the military orders seen from this perspective was the culmination of a tendency, going back to at least the tenth century, to consecrate fighting in support of the church and Christian social values. This is the central theme of Erdmann's book on the origins of crusading thought, which

---

[143] Bernard, *De laude novae militiae*, I, 4, 8, ed. Leclercq, III, 221. This work was written before 1136.

[144] Hiestand (1988), pp. 322–3.

[145] Otto of Freising, *Historia*, VII, 9, ed. Hofmeister (n. 17), p. 320. Anselm of Havelberg, *Dialogi*, I, 10 , in *PL*, CLXXXVIII, 1156B, and ed. Salet (n. 15), pp. 98–100, also called the military orders *nova religionis institutio*.

[146] *Vita Amedaei Altae Ripae*, 4, ed. M.-Anselme Dimier, in *Studia monastica* 5 (1963), p. 282 (*BHL* 385b), and Isaac of L'Etoile, *Serm.* 48, in *PL*, CXCIV, 1854BC.

[147] Joachim of Fiore, *Liber concordie novi ac veteris testamenti*, V, 18 (Venice 1519, repr. 1964), fol. 69ᵛ.

in spite of its age has lost none of its freshness and which examines the emergence of the idea of holy war and the sacralization of the status of the *miles*, who developed at this time from a simple fighting man into a knight, and the new cults of military saints and saintly knights, some of which came from the east.[148] Guibert of Nogent said that 'In our time God has instituted holy warfare so that the knightly order and erring common people . . . might find a new way of deserving salvation.'[149] Hugh of Lacerta when he was a young knight in the early twelfth century went to Jerusalem 'in order to fight for Christ and never to return from there to his own possessions'. While he was there, according to his *Life*, 'the man of God was sometimes a knight and sometimes a pilgrim', which suggests that he both fought the pagans and visited the holy places. He then reluctantly returned to the west and later became a Grandmontine.[150] Stephen of Obazine urged his followers to go against the Saracens 'if perhaps they could convert some of them by preaching or themselves be killed for Christ by the unbelievers'.[151] The parallel of religious and secular warfare is strikingly shown in the account of a knight who gave his chain-mail to the hermit Wulfric of Hazelbury 'as to a stronger soldier', who wore it until it slipped from his shoulders in old age.[152] Abelard in his rule for women said that a convent was an army in which the superior was the emperor, the officials dukes, the nuns knights, and the lay sisters foot-soldiers,[153] and Hugh of St Victor in the prologue to *On the sacraments* described the vast and diverse army of God 'serving the one king and following the one banner' in the war against the devil.[154] The military orders represented one effort to institutionalize this ethos, as did, on a broader scale, the crusades, which opened an almost automatic path to heaven for those who took the cross humbly and penitently and who died fighting the enemies of Christianity. In the crusader the ancient consecrated status of the pilgrim and the penitent came together with that of the Christian knight.[155] To go on a crusade was widely recognized in the twelfth century as equivalent, though inferior, to

[148] Erdmann (1935), esp. pp. 66–82. John of Salisbury stressed the sacred calling of soldiers in *Policraticus*, VI, 8, ed. Webb (n. 18), II, 21–2, and the parallel between soldiers and monks was brought out in a sermon in Rochais (1962), pp. 145–6.

[149] Guibert of Nogent, *Gesta Dei per Francos*, I, 1, in *Recueil des historiens des croisades. Historiens occidentaux* (Paris 1844–95), IV, 124. Guibert gave examples of the promises made to those who fought for the church, in his *De vita sua*, III, 14, ed. Bourgin, pp. 203–4.

[150] William Dandina of St Savin, *Vita Hugonis de Lacerta*, 2–14, in *Ampl. coll.*, VI, 1145–51 (quotes on 1146D and 1147A) (*BHL* 4017).

[151] *Vita Stepheni Obazinensis*, I, 10, ed. Aubrun, p. 60.

[152] John of Ford, *Vita Wulfrici Haselbergiae*, 5, ed. Maurice Bell (Somerset Record Society 47; n.p. 1933), p. 19; see 9–10, 72, and 92, pp. 22–4, 100, and 124 on the *lorica* and the notes on pp. 143–6 (*BHL* 8743–4).

[153] Abelard, *Ep.* 7, ed. McLaughlin (n. 95), p. 252.

[154] Hugh of St Victor, *De sacramentis, prol.*, 2, in *PL*, CLXXVI, 183BC, and tr. Roy J. Deferrari (Mediaeval Academy of America Publ. 58; Cambridge, Mass., 1951), pp. 3–4.

[155] An increasing number of travellers and wanderers left home for non-economic reasons in the twelfth century. See Etienne Delaruelle, in *Eremitismo* (1965), pp. 225–6, on the difficulty of distinguishing pilgrims, penitents, crusaders, hermits, and wandering preachers and, more generally, Vexliard (1956), pp. 16–19, on the types of vagabonds.

entering a religious house, whose members were also *milites* fighting for the Lord.[156]

The new lay brothers and lay sisters also fought for the Lord and occupied a position parallel to that of the military orders, as Joachim of Fiore perceived, by assisting clerics and monks with occupations they could not perform themselves.[157] Joachim called them *conversi*, which by the time he was writing normally meant lay brothers (and *conversae*, lay sisters), but the use of these terms in the eleventh and twelfth centuries is confusing. A *conversus* in traditional usage was a monk who had entered religious life as an adult and who (unless he was a cleric) was normally illiterate and not in holy orders. He was a full member of the community, however, participated in the holy offices, and was not barred from ordination and promotion. *Conversi* of this type were contrasted with *oblati* or *nutriti* who had been given to a monastery as boys and raised in the community. Some of the best-known monks of the Middle Ages were *conversi*, and there is evidence that they were preferred to *oblati* as monastic officials precisely because they had more experience of the outside world.[158]

In the late eleventh and twelfth centuries, however, the term *conversus* was increasingly applied to members of religious communities who had a fixed status from which promotion was impossible, lived apart from the ordained (or choir) monks, did not participate in the offices, and performed distinct functions, often of a menial nature. The origin of this new type of *conversi*, or lay brothers, as they were called, is obscure but was associated with the movement of monastic reform in the eleventh century and seems to lie in the eremitical houses in central Italy, though similar groups were found in the neo-Cluniac houses in south Germany. Peter Damiani in his *Life* of Romuald said that the servants (*famuli*) of the monks at Vallombrosa, and the very swineherds, 'fast, keep silence, and by turns practice disciplines [by which he probably meant flagellation] among themselves and punish by beating a few idle words'.[159] These were clearly servants who led some sort of religious life

---

[156] The parallel of entering a monastery and going on a pilgrimage or crusade, and the superiority of the former, was brought out in Bernard, *Ep.* 64, ed. Leclercq, VII, 157–8; Adam of Eynsham, *Magna vita Hugonis*, IV, 12, ed. Douie and Farmer (n. 57), II, 57; and Caesarius, *Dialogus*, I, 6, ed. Strange, I, 12.

[157] On *conversi* and lay brothers and lay sisters, see the works cited in *Medieval Monasticism*, nos. 768–75, and Elm (1994), pp. 14–16, esp. the articles by Jean Leclercq and Cosimo Damiano Fonseca, in *Laici* (1968); Constable (1973); Hallinger (1983), pp. 229–30, and other works cited below.

[158] Honorius *Augustodunensis*, *De apostatis*, 20–1, in *MGH*, *Libelli*, III, 62, had separate chapters 'De oblatis' and 'De sponte conversis', which referred to 'quis . . . sui arbitrii compos ad conversionem uenerit et, secundum regulae institutum per annum probatus, professionem fecerit'. Guibert of Nogent expressed a low opinion of *oblati* in the passage cited pp. 26–7 above. See also Peter the Venerable, *Stat.* 66, in *CCM*, VI, 97, and the accompanying note. On oblates, see p. 100 below.

[159] Peter Damiani, *Vita Romualdi*, 64, ed. Giovanni Tabacco (FSI 94; Rome 1957), p. 105 (*BHL* 7324).

modelled on that of the monks. According to the *Life* of William of Hirsau, written soon after his death in 1091,

> The lovable father, burning with a zeal for souls, first established that the monks would use the faithful ministry of lay converts (*laicorum conversorum*) in administering exterior affairs and that, vice versa, the same lay men would get from the monks what pertains to the cure of souls and would imitate their claustral discipline as much as they could outside the cloister, in correcting their behaviour.

It then gives an account of the life and activities of these lay converts, ending with the 'suitable habitation' that William built at Hirsau 'for the observance of this spiritual life'.[160] There is no need to assume any connection between the *famuli* of Vallombrosa and the *conversi* of Hirsau, both of whom seem to have filled the needs of the respective houses while themselves leading some sort of religious life. References to what appear to be similar groups are found in various sources, especially in monasteries in southern Germany, where they were known as *laici* or *forinseci*, in contrast to the *claustrales* or *interiores*, or as *conversi barbati*, *fratres barbati*, or simply *barbati* from the beards they wore to distinguish them from the shaven ordained monks.[161] In time they appeared in many houses of reformed monks and regular canons who wanted to avoid using dependent agricultural labourers or hired secular servants and yet were unable to perform by themselves all that needed doing. The spread of the institution was uneven, however. They first appeared in Cistercian houses in about 1120 and did not become numerous until the second half of the twelfth century.[162] They were also found in some old black houses, but it is not always easy to tell the precise status of the *conversi* and *conversae* to whom there are references in the sources. Some of them owned property and occupied responsible positions, such as the priest Ermenricus who witnessed among the *fratres conversi* on a charter of Floreffe in 1130, the *conversi* of Mont-St-Martin who held some lands from Homblières in 1145, the two *conversae* who made grants in a charter of Bartholomew of Laon in 1149, *Andreas conversus heremita cocus* who appeared on a charter of the Cluniac house of Domène in about 1165, and the *conversi* and *conversae* at the nunneries of Rosano and Pratovecchio in the late twelfth century.[163]

---

[160] Haimo of Hirsau, *Vita Willelmi Hirsaugiensis*, 23, in *PL*, CL, 914C–15B, and *MGH*, *SS*, XII, 219–20 (*BHL* 8920–1). See Jakobs (1961), pp. 23–6.

[161] *Barbati* were not necessarily lay brothers, since the term was also used for bearded *conversi* of the old type and, generally, for monks who were old enough to grow a beard. See the introduction to Burchard of Bellevaux, *Apologia de barbis*, in *CC:CM*, LXII, 124–7.

[162] Jacques Dubois, in *Laici* (1968), pp. 189–90, and de Waha (1978), pp. 173–6.

[163] Barbier (1892), II, 7–8, no. 10; *Cartulary and Charters of Notre-Dame of Homblières*, ed. Theodore Evergates (Medieval Academy Books 97; Cambridge, Mass., 1990), pp. 117 and 131, nos. 53 (JL 8779) and 61; *Cartulare monasterii . . . de Domina*, ed. C. de Monteynard (Lyons 1859), p. 92, no. 104; and Passerini (1876–7), pp. 214, 386, 394, and 396–7.

The status and occupations of *conversi* differed from order to order and house to house, and the only sure sign that they were lay brothers of the new type is when they were forbidden to become monks. As a rule they were neither considered to be nor treated like monks. In the *Life* of William of Hirsau they were clearly distinguished from monks, though their life was described as spiritual. The author of the *Life* of Berthold of Garsten distinguished the *fratres barbati* from both the *monachi illiterati*, who performed some of the same functions and were probably *conversi* of the old type, and the *literati*, who were ordained and served the altar.[164] Idungus, who was familiar with conditions in both neo-Cluniac and Cistercian houses in Germany, likewise distinguished between lay brothers and tonsured *fratres* who were monks and, in the broad sense, clerics.[165] The Cistercians strictly forbade a lay brother to become a monk, requiring him to remain 'in that vocation to which he was called',[166] and popes Innocent II and Lucius II referred to 'your *conversi* who are not monks' in their bulls for Cîteaux and Pontigny, and also in a forged bull for Savigny.[167] The superior of an Augustinian house wrote in 1156/78 to a Cistercian abbot proposing an exchange of fugitives, of whom the Cistercian was a lay brother.

> If he had professed your rule, clad in the habit prescribed by the rule of St Benedict, there would be no access for him to the company of our profession. But since as a wise precaution you keep outside the profession of the rule the bearded brothers, to whom you are accustomed to give permission or allow to remain in other places from time to time, we ask you to let us know in writing how you would release this brother.[168]

The lay brothers were not monks, therefore, though they wore a religious habit and were considered members of the community. They may sometimes have been to a certain extent integrated with the monks and shared their liturgical life, but in the stricter orders they constituted a separate community beside that of the monks or lived apart or in small groups in granges. They were occupied principally with agricultural work, and both their status and the nature of their duties made them inferior to the choir monks who celebrated the holy offices. It is not therefore surprising that they were often discontented and occasionally rebelled. During the second half of the twelfth century most of the orders that had lay brothers experienced some sort of

---

[164] *Vita Bertholdi Garstensis*, 6, ed. Lenzenweger (n. 34), p. 233.
[165] Idungus, *Dialogus*, 3, ed. Huygens, p. 463.
[166] *Exordium cistercii*, 22, in *Textes de Cîteaux*, p. 124.
[167] *PL*, CLXXIX, 123AB (JL 7537) and 615B (JL 8259), and Swietek and Deneen (1983), p. 24. There were at Savigny, according to the *Vita Hamonis Saviniacensis*, 7, ed. E.P. Sauvage, in *Anal. boll.* 2 (1883), p. 511 (*BHL* 3752), not only monks but also lay men *quos conuersos nuncupant* and who served God *sub habitu religionis*.
[168] Ebrach Collection, *Ep.* 12, ed. Werner Ohnsorge, in *Quellen und Forschungen aus italienischen Archiven und Bibliotheken* 20 (1928–9), pp. 38–9. See Wilmart (1933a), pp. 327–8, on the possible author and recipient.

difficulty with them.[169] Hildegard of Bingen said that the Cistercians attracted to their houses, in addition to monks and clerics, 'another type of men whom they call *conversi*, of whom many do not convert themselves to God in their way of life, since they love contrariety more than rectitude'.[170]

It is impossible to say whether the institution of lay brothers at its origins corresponded to the needs of monks or to the desires of lay men who wanted to serve in religious communities. Both factors may have contributed. Damiani suggested that the servants at Vallombrosa chose to lead a semi-monastic life, whereas William of Hirsau's initiative is stressed in his *Life*. There may have also been popular pressure in southern Germany, for there is a description in the chronicle of Bernold of St Blaise, under the year 1083, of lay men, including many nobles, who went to St Blaise, Hirsau, and Schaffhausen and performed menial tasks – the nobler the men, the more menial the tasks. 'There both the swineherds and the ploughmen are the same as monks aside from the habit.' In a famous passage under the year 1091, Bernold wrote that

> The common life flourished at this time in many places in the kingdom of the Germans, not only among clerics and monks living in a very religious way but also among lay men who devoutly offered themselves and their property for the same common life and who, although they were neither clerics nor monks in their habit, were considered in no way unequal to them in merits. For they made themselves their servants for the sake of the Lord, imitating Him Who came 'not to be ministered unto but to minister' [Matthew 20.28] and Who taught His followers to come to greatness by serving. So these men renounced the world and devoutly offered themselves and their property to communities of both clerics and monks leading regular lives, so that under their obedience they might deserve to live communally and to serve them.[171]

These men sound like lay brothers, but they may have resembled the semi-independent lay religious communities that developed south of the Alps in the eleventh and twelfth centuries. Most of these were short-lived and left no records, and little is known about them. The earliest surviving statutes date from the eleventh century and are of the confraternity of St Appiano in Valdelsa, which included men and women grouped under an *abbas* for mutual religious, social, and economic support.[172] By the middle of the twelfth century there were various such communities in north Italy. Some developed into

[169] See *Exordium magnum Cisterciense*, IV, 15, and V, 10, ed. Bruno Griesser (Series scriptorum s. Ordinis Cisterciensis 2: Rome 1961), pp. 240 and 292–8 (on Schönau); Donnelly (1949); and McGuire (1983b), p. 56, on the Cistercians; and on other orders, Knowles (1935); Becquet (1960), p. 299; Milis (1992), pp. 33–4 and 178, who said there were about twenty revolts between 1168 and 1200; and Constable (1995b) on the lay brothers and lay sisters of Sempringham.

[170] Hildegard of Bingen, *Ep.* 51, in *PL*, CXCVII, 263D. See Batany (1969) on the disrepute into which the lay brothers fell in the twelfth and thirteenth centuries.

[171] Bernold of St Blaise, *Chronicon*, s.a. 1083 and 1091, in *MGH, SS*, V, 439 and 452–3.

[172] Monti (1927), II, 139–42, and Meersseman (1952), pp. 19–22, who dated the community from the tenth century and the statutes from the eleventh.

monasteries, like St Michael of Guamo, which was originally run by a fraternity and was later taken over by monks.[173] Others consisted of lay penitents, mostly of peasant origin, leading a common life and allowed to leave only for the 'better life' of a monastery. They were served either by their own priest or by the local parish priest and seem to have been entirely orthodox, unlike some of the comparable communities that developed in southern France at the same time and somewhat later.

There are innumerable references in the sources to obscure confraternities, societies, companies, friendships, and other associations that usually served religious as well as other needs. An inscription on an altar of 1096 in Toulouse refers to the *confratres* of St Saturninus who were organized *ad salutem animarum suarum*, perhaps to support the building or to assist pilgrims and *pauperes*.[174] In an agreement with the abbey of St Peter at Chartres in about 1108, the priest and parishioners of Mainvillers gave up an annual measure of wine from the abbey and received a vineyard 'for making a house where the priest may live and where their fraternity may be established'.[175] A council at Narbonne in 1128 organized a confraternity of clergy and lay men to help the church in Tarragona against the Saracens. Each *confrater* had to contribute at least twelve pennies, if he could, and 'each year he should render his vow to God, like a head tax for his soul', and in return his property was taken under the protection of St Peter and a mass was sung for him at his death.[176] The origin of the Cistercian abbey of Silvanès lay in 'an inseparable society' formed by Pontius of Léras with six of his friends, who placed their right hands in his and embarked on a life of penance and pilgrimage before they settled down as a religious community.[177]

Pontius was a wealthy knight with a strong castle who repented his early life 'and turned entirely to penance and wept rivers of tears day and night in order to obliterate the stains of his crimes'. He put his wife and children into religious houses, sold his property and made restitution to those he had robbed, and publicly confessed his sins, 'naked and unshod', before he set out barefoot with his companions.[178] He is a good example of the type of secular lord who converted, often suddenly and unexpectedly, to the religious life in the twelfth century.[179] They included some great nobles, like William II of Nevers, who after many years of worldly activity, including a long and bitter

---

[173] Osheim (1989), p. 65.
[174] Delaruelle (1966), p. 385. In Toulouse at this time, according to Mundy (1966), p. 267, 'The lines dividing an order, a confraternity or a religious brotherhood or business (*societas*) with its *ius fraternitatis*, were somewhat blurred.'
[175] *Cartulaire de l'abbaye de Saint-Père de Chartres*, ed. Benjamin Guérard (Collection de documents inédits sur l'histoire de France; Paris 1840), II, 281. See Chédeville (1973), p. 219, and Aubrun (1986), pp. 150–1.
[176] *España sagrada*, XXVIII, 303–4.
[177] Hugh of Silvanès, *De conversione Pontii de Larazio*, 3, in Baluze, *Miscellanea*, I, 180.
[178] Ibid., 2–9, pp. 180–1. See Baker (1978), pp. 39–42.
[179] Some examples are cited by Evans (1978), pp. 27–9.

controversy with the abbey of Vézelay, retired in about 1147 to La Chartreuse, where his son later found him wearing a poor habit and occupied with pastoral work. He was described by the biographer of Hugh of Lincoln (an admittedly prejudiced source, since Hugh was a Carthusian) as a model of humility, gravity, and wisdom, in whose presence even the king of France was afraid to joke in word or deed.[180] Such conversions were not always inspired by purely religious feelings. When bishop Roger of Worcester accused Henry II in 1170 of ingratitude to Robert of Gloucester and his brothers, he said: 'You kept my other younger brother Robert, a vigorous soldier, it is said, in such a poor and unworthy state that out of poverty he left the secular army and life and gave himself to serve the hospital at Jerusalem in perpetuity and received the form (*schema*) and habit.'[181]

Both lay men and secular clerics entered religious houses when they were dying, or thought to be, in order to take the monastic habit *ad succurrendum*, as it was called, and to enjoy the spiritual benefits of dying as monks, like last-minute baptism in the early church.[182] An awkward situation could arise when monks of this type did not die, and opinions varied over whether or not they could return to secular life.[183] Trehan of St-Broladre, who became a monk at Mont-St-Michel in 1075, when he thought he was dying, and made various gifts to the abbey, gave back the habit after he recovered, but he made further gifts on condition that he could enter the monastery when he wished.[184] A man who became a monk at Marmoutier when suffering from a grave illness later decided to go to Jerusalem rather than receive the monastic habit (*monachatus*).[185] The reformers as a rule refused to accept monks *ad succurren-*

---

[180] Adam of Eynsham, *Magna vita Hugonis*, IV, 12 (calling him Gerard), ed. Douie and Farmer (n. 57), II, 55–8; Hugh of Poitiers, *Chronicon Vizeliacensis*, 2, in *CC:CM*, XLII, 419 and 423. See A.A. Chérest, ibid., 33–7 and 67–8. Walter Map, *De nugis curialium*, I, 24, ed. and tr. Montague R. James, rev. C.N.L. Brooke and R.A.B. Mynors (OMT; Oxford 1983), p. 80, calling him Walter, told a story of Bernard's praying at his tomb. The count of Nevers in the vision-story cited n. 68 above was probably William.

[181] William Fitz-Stephen, *Vita Thomae*, 102, in *Materials for the History of Thomas Becket*, ed. James C. Robertson and Joseph B. Sheppard (RS 67; London 1875–85), III, 105 (*BHL* 8176). On this episode see Warren (1973), p. 216, and Cheney (1980), pp. 47–8. 'R' in this passage is probably an error for 'P', that is, earl Robert of Gloucester's son Philip, on whose role in the struggle between Henry and Stephen and participation in the Second Crusade and subsequent disappearance from history, see Davis (1969), pp. 89 and 91–2. If the R is correct, however, it may stand either for earl Robert's son Robert or for an otherwise unknown illegitimate son. I am indebted for help on this point to Robert Patterson.

[182] In addition to the works cited in *Medieval Monasticism*, nos. 776–9, see Lynch (1976), pp. 27–36, and Bull (1993), pp. 143–6. Monks also occasionally transferred to stricter houses when they were near death.

[183] Figueras (1958), pp. 397–400, maintained Yes, and Dubois (1981), p. 53, said No.

[184] See the charters cited in Morice (1742–6), I, 441, and in *Pouillé historique de l'archévêché de Rennes*, ed. Amédée Guillotin de Corson (Rennes and Paris 1880–6), II, 527–36, and Dubois (1967), p. 644.

[185] *Cartulaire de Marmoutier pour le Dunois*, ed. Emile Mabille (Paris and Châteaudun 1874), p. 123, no. 133.

dum because their vocations could not be properly tested.[186] They were admitted by the Premonstratensians, however, and a number of old monks and bishops, including both Cistercians and non-Cistercians, entered Clairvaux in order to die and be buried there.[187] In about 1176 the Cistercians at Sallay in Yorkshire granted fraternity to a man and his wife in return for giving up their claims to some land and agreed to bury him in their cemetery, to receive him *ad conversionem* when and if he wanted to come, and to let him lie among them in secular habit, if he was ill, and to return home, if he wished, after he recovered.[188]

The right to be buried in a monastic cemetery was highly prized in the Middle Ages and is mentioned in many agreements concerning entry to a religious house and associations between lay people and religious. It was also a source of abundant controversy between ecclesiastical institutions over the revenues associated with burials.[189] During the tenth and eleventh centuries between 10 per cent and 20 per cent of all the gifts to Cluny were made *ad sepulturam*.[190] At the Cluniac priory of St Lupus at Esserent the 'society of benefits', as it was called, was principally a matter of burial and was sometimes given even to women, as in 1134/8 when a married woman who was dying

> summoned her husband Gerard and implored him with what words she could that he would render her to God through the hand of the prior Rainald. Since he was in great bitterness of soul, seeing that he was presently to be deprived of such a loving and lawful companionship, and being unwilling to grieve her, he finally agreed willingly and, as she requested, rendered her into the hands of the said prior.[191]

The canons of Rodez and the monks of St Victor at Marseilles agreed in 1140 that the canons might bury anyone from the parish of St Amantius at Rodez who became a canon 'at the end of life' or 'in illness' provided that a chaplain or cleric from the parish church, which belonged to the monks, was summoned to make sure that it received its *debitum beneficium* from the sick and dying.[192]

---

[186] Figueras (1958), pp. 362–3. *Regula Stephani Muretensis*, 44, in *CC:CM*, VIII, 88, forbade the acceptance of a 'homo infirmus, nisi equitando aut pedibus ambulando uenire possit'.

[187] Dimier (1955c) and Valvekens (1961).

[188] *Cartulary of the Cistercian Abbey of Sallay in Craven*, ed. Joseph McNulty (Yorkshire Archaeological Society: Record Series 87 and 90; n.p. 1933–4), I, 36, no. 54.

[189] Schreiber (1910), II, 105–37, and Lesne (1910–43), III, 129–35.

[190] See Poeck (1981), pp. 92, 101, 122, and 152.

[191] *Le prieuré de Saint-Leu d'Esserent: Cartulaire (1080–1538)*, ed. Eugène Müller (Pontoise 1901), p. 35, no. 31; cf. pp. 10 and 21, nos. 6 and 17.

[192] Baluze, *Miscellanea*, III, 70, confirmed by Lucius II in 1144, ibid., and *PL*, CLXXIX, 843 (JL 8550). The monastery of St Amantius had been given to St Victor at Marseilles in 1079: *Cartulaire de l'abbaye de Saint-Victor de Marseille*, ed. Benjamin Guérard (Paris 1857), II, 203–4, no. 837. In about 1161 cardinal Peter of St Chrysogonus settled a burial dispute between the nuns of Fontevrault and the canons of Candes: A. Giry, 'Chartes angevines des onzième et douzième siècles', *Bibliothèque de l'Ecole des chartes* 36 (1875), pp. 436–7, no. 35.

There were many agreements between lay people and religious houses concerning support in food and clothing (*victus et vestitus*) and sometimes also housing, *stipendia, prebenda, provenda*, and what are collectively known as corrodies.[193] Such arrangements were far from new in the twelfth century, and they were often condemned, but they were an important source of social insurance for lay people and were hard to eradicate. In the early twelfth century a woman was allowed to join St Peter at Chartres and to receive food and clothing there, and at Baigne a priest 'said that he had the right to live (*convivium*) together with the monks on account of his chaplaincy', but he gave up his claim when his predecessor denied it.[194] When Robert of Torpel in 1147 gave himself and some property to God, St Peter, and the abbey of Peterborough, 'It was agreed that in his lifetime he should receive a monk's corrody, and four of his servants knights' corrodies, and on his death he should assume the monk's habit.'[195] Relationships of this type were easily abused, but difficult to avoid, even in reformed houses, which rejected them in theory. In the late twelfth century the abbot of the Cistercian abbey of Casanova received a widow who 'gave herself and her property to God and the said monastery' as a *conversa* and *devota* and agreed to provide her with food and clothing 'as to their other *devotae*, that is the lady Mathilda and the lady Belana'.[196]

The records of twelfth-century monasteries, especially the charters and obituaries, are filled with references to familiars, co-brothers and co-sisters, devotees, friends, adult oblates, and all sorts of people who in some way or another had attached themselves to a religious institution. Very little is known about such relationships, but they were presumably considered mutually beneficial, like those between religious, educational, and cultural institutions today and their benefactors, patrons, and friends – the same old terms – who in return for donations receive prestige, invitations to dinners and receptions, and secular immortality on a bronze plaque, bench, or bookplate or, if they give enough, a building. Medieval monasteries likewise received property and other types of help from benefactors, whose names were entered in necrologies and obituaries and who were given spiritual and sometimes also material support of various kinds.[197] Stephen of Grandmont referred to 'the feasts (*comessationes*) that people call confraternities',[198] and Walter Map considered that the monks exploited knights whom they made 'brothers in the chapter

---

[193] Lesne (1927); Mundy (1966), pp. 258–65; and, on corrodies in England, Stuckert (1923).

[194] *Saint-Père de Chartres* (n. 175), II, 325, no. 1, 81, and *Cartulaire de l'abbaye de Saint-Etienne de Baigne*, ed. P.-F.-E. Cholet (Niort 1868), p. 182, no. 449. See Bruhat (1907), p. 232.

[195] King (1973), p. 28, who translated this charter from MS Peterborough, Dean and Chapter, 5, fol. 27ʳᵛ; see p. 25 for knights' corrodies in the *Descriptio* of *c.* 1130.

[196] *Cartario della abazia di Casanova fino all'anno 1313*, ed. Armando Tallone (Biblioteca della Società storico subalpina 14; Pinerolo 1903), pp. 105–6, no. 115.

[197] See generally Lemaître (1980–92), I, 17–20, and among recent regional studies Barthélemy (1993), pp. 425–38, on the *societas beneficii* in the county of Vendôme, and Bull (1993), p. 160, on the Limousin and Gascony.

[198] *Regula Stephani Muretensis*, 20, in *CC:CM*, VIII, 80 (see n. 205).

and participants in prayers'.[199] But it was presumably a matter of opinion who got the best of the bargain. In the agreement cited above the canons of Rodez were allowed to bury 'the *conversos* who came to them after they had given up their property and likewise the women devoted to God after promising obedience and leaving behind their property'.[200] Who these men and women were, and why they left their property and promised obedience, is unknown, but they clearly got something they wanted. Some people even gave up their freedom in order to obtain the protection and security of dependence on a monastery and its patron saint.[201] At this distance in time these people are almost indistinguishable within the confused mass of dependent agricultural labourers in the Middle Ages, but their names, and the record of their donations, were often entered in the *liber vitae* or obituary lists of the monastery, so that they were remembered in the liturgy together with the other benefactors who had associated themselves with the community, and their servitude, like that of the monks who voluntarily entered the service of God, was seen as a type of freedom.[202]

The precise nature of such arrangements is often obscure. In 1123 the senior monks (*seniores*) or council of the Cluniac house at Sauxillanges (where Peter the Venerable had been an oblate and where his brother Armannus was later prior) received Bernard of *Rippa* in return for a grant 'into their society and familiarity' and gave him a prebend (presumably an allowance of food) in all their dependencies. Bernard on his part, in his own words,

> gave myself to God and to the holy monks living in that place under the patronage of the holy apostles so that when God will inspire [me] I may become a monk in that monastery, and that I may not go to another monastery nor even on a journey to Jerusalem without their permission, and they will receive me as a monk in return for the offering that I have made to them.

From this time on, therefore, Bernard had a sort of proto-monastic status, as a *familiaris* with a right to support and to future entry as a monk.[203] Even stranger, by modern standards, was the arrangement made with the abbey of St James at Liège by Maurice of Glons when he took the cross and left for Jerusalem in 1146. In return for the fief that he surrendered, the monks made provision for his mother and gave him the money he needed for the crusade,

[199] Map, *De nugis curialium*, I, 25, ed. James (n. 180), p. 84.
[200] Baluze, *Miscellanea*, III, 70 (n. 192).
[201] They were called *donati* or *oblati* (who should not be confused with oblates given to monasteries as boys) and also as *censuales*, from the small rent or *census* paid in recognition of their dependence, and as *sainteurs* from the saint upon whom they depended.
[202] See Constable (1972), p. 273, for the stress on the firmness and security of the status of the *censuales* or *servientes* in the *Liber memorialis* of Remiremont.
[203] *Cartulaire de Sauxillanges*, ed. Henry Doniol, in *Mémoires de l'Académie des sciences, belles-lettres et arts de Clermont-Ferrand* 34 (N.S. 3; 1861), pp. 1072–3, no. 905. The restrictions were probably owing to Bernard's other property, which the monks hoped to receive and which they might lose if he entered another monastery or went to Jerusalem.

and he agreed that if he returned, 'He would give himself to serve in obedience either in the habit of a servant (*famulus*) or in the habit of a monk.' His willingness to enter the monastery may be explained by the fact that he had given up his property and had nothing else to live off, but it is surprising that he was prepared to be either a monk or an unfree servant.[204]

The reformers for the most part tried to avoid such arrangements. The Grandmontines refused confraternities as disturbing the spiritual peace, and others cut at the root of the system by forbidding anniversaries for benefactors and intercessory prayers and masses.[205] While it is easy to see the dangers of such associations, it is also easy to overlook their value, since they not only performed an important social service but also acted as a link between monastic and secular society. They may in the long run have done as much to monasticize the lay order as to secularize monasticism. The humble *famuli* at Vallombrosa, the lay religious communities in Germany, Italy, and south France, and the masses of lay pilgrims, hermits, and crusaders were paralleled by great nobles who accepted humiliating penances, such as Boniface of Tuscany, who was condemned by the abbot of Pomposa to be beaten naked before the altar of the Virgin, and Conrad of Meissen, who was required by the patriarch of Jerusalem in 1145 to feed five poor men daily and to fast in Advent and on all Thursdays, Saturdays, and Sundays.[206]

The relative informality and obscurity of many of these arrangements have led scholars to underestimate their importance. They were the tentacles that stretched out from religious institutions into the secular world and bound them to society as a whole. In looking at twelfth-century religious life, and the movement of reform, it is customary to put in the centre the highly institutionalized types of forms, above all the monks and canons, who led a strict community life, and to see the hermits, recluses, lay brothers, and members of the military orders as peripheral, with pilgrims, penitents, wandering preachers, and crusaders on the margins and all the various other types, if they are considered at all, in a shadowy penumbra. It may be closer to the realities of medieval religious life to think in terms of a different model, putting the individual religious experience in the centre, surrounded by various forms of religious life, of which each was no less important for those involved in them than the more highly organized communities were for their members. A pilgrimage or a crusade, a period of eremitical retreat, listening to a wander-

---

[204] Stiennon (1951), pp. 442–3, no. 6; see pp. 449–51, no. 11, for another elaborate agreement concerning a pension to be divided between a canon (who went on a crusade) and the daughter of a recluse, who was to receive the canon's share if he died first.

[205] *Regula Stephani Muretensis*, 20, in *CC:CM*, VIII, 80, and Gerard Itier, *Conclusio vitae Stephani Muretensis*, 9, ibid., pp. 324–5; *Consuetudines Cartusiae*, 41, 3, in [Laporte] (1960–7), IV, 154–6. See Meersseman (1952), pp. 82–3, on this and other prohibitions of confraternities, and p. 304 below, on the Cistercians.

[206] Donizo, *Vita Mathildis*, I, 16, in *MGH, SS*, XII, 373, and *Urkunden der Markgrafen von Meissen und Landgrafen von Thüringen 1100–1195*, ed. Otto Posse (Codex diplomaticus Saxoniae regiae I, 2; Leipzig 1889), pp. 132–3, no. 189.

ing preacher, or even a simple association of prayers might fill as profound a need in some people as a lifetime reciting the psalms or enclosed in a cell did for others. An awakening to the variety of individual religious needs and temperaments and an acceptance of a diversity of forms of religious life – diverse, but not adverse – lay at the heart of the twelfth-century movement of religious reform.

3

THE CIRCUMSTANCES AND TYPES OF REFORM

THE number of new monasteries and forms of religious life, and of the people who entered them, were seen in the twelfth century as an aspect of spiritual reform and revival and also as the result of the increasing population and approaching end of the world. This chapter is concerned with the realities that lay behind these generalizations and in particular with how the reformers went about their task, the problems they encountered, and the variations between different regions, orders, and individual houses, which were affected by the movement of reform in different ways. The relative growth was certainly greater in newly settled areas and in regions where monasticism had suffered either from the Norse and Magyar raids or from civil disruptions than in the more stable parts of Europe, where monasteries were well established.[1] At the time the abbey of Selby in Yorkshire was founded, in 1069, according to its history, 'Neither a monk nor any house of monks could be easily discovered in the entire Syria of York, except for the congregation of Durham',[2] and if the figures given in the biographies of bishop Otto of Bamberg for Michaelsberg, which grew from twenty to seventy monks during his episcopate and then to 100 by 1158, were the same in the fifteen monasteries he founded, they must have represented a substantial addition to the monastic population in eastern Germany.[3] It has been estimated that just over half a per cent of the population in Portugal in the twelfth century was in monasteries and just under half a per cent in Flanders,[4] and that in England in the century following the Norman Conquest the total number of monks, nuns, and canons grew from less than 1,000 to between 10,000 and 15,000, or between

---

[1] See the figures for the number of new religious houses in pp. 46–7 above.
[2] *Historia monasterii Selebiensis*, 12, in *The Coucher Book of Selby*, ed. Joseph T. Fowler, 1 (Yorkshire Archaeological and Topographical Association: Record Series 10; York 1891), p. [14]. This work was written in 1174 and reflects the attitudes of the second half of the twelfth century. The term *Siria* may have been used to stress the emptiness and the parallel with the home of the early monks. See Nicholl (1964), p. 204, on 'the renaissance of monasticism' in the diocese of York in the second quarter of the twelfth century.
[3] Ebo, *Vita Ottonis*, I, 20, in *Monumenta Bambergensia*, ed. Philipp Jaffé (BRG 5; Berlin 1869), p. 610 (*BHL* 6395), and Herbord, *De Ottone ep. Bambergensi*, ibid., pp. 706–7 (*BHL* 6397).
[4] Mattoso (1968), pp. 160–2, and Milis (1992), pp. 7 and 79.

1 and 2 per cent of the adult male population.[5] Even in a period of overall population growth, this represents an increase in percentage as well as in absolute numbers, but the figures on which it is based are estimates and not entirely reliable.

Over sixty years ago Ursmer Berlière published the results of a lifetime of collecting figures for individual houses, and his lists have subsequently been supplemented by other scholars,[6] although there are still no satisfactory overall statistics. From these it is clear that many of the great old monasteries had shrunk by the eleventh century and occasionally recovered in the twelfth. St-Germain-des-Prés at Paris, for example, which had over 200 monks in the early ninth century, had 21 in 1070 and 24 in 1080/1108; Corbie went down from between 300 and 400 to 26 in 1014, 29 in 1137, 38 in 1149, and 10 in 1210; and St Bertin, which had 83 monks in about 820, 60 in 877, and 47 in 961, had only 8 in 1030 but then rose to 120 in 1095/1123 and 150 in the mid-twelfth century. At Monte Cassino the numbers grew from about 100 to 200 during the first three-quarters of the eleventh century.[7] This was probably exceptional, however, and the result of its special circumstances. The chronicler of St Trond remarked on the reduced number of recruits about 1100 and on the consequent need to accept monks, who often proved unsuitable, from other monasteries.[8]

A different picture is presented by the abbey of St Albinus at Angers, which maintained a relatively high level of monastic life, in part owing to the interest taken in it by the counts of Anjou, and which has an exceptionally complete series of lists of the monks who subscribed to abbatial elections. It grew steadily from 11 monks in 970 (of whom 3 were priests, 2 deacons, and 2 clerics) to 15 in 977, 57 in 1038, 78 in 1060, and 105 in 1080.[9] This corresponds approximately to the figures for some of the reformed houses, which enjoyed great prestige in the eleventh century. Cluny grew from between 60 and 80

---

[5] Russell (1944), pp. 185–6, suggested that in England the numbers grew from less than 1,000 at the time of the Conquest to about 5,000 monks and nuns and 3,000 canons by the early fourteenth century, when the numbers were probably lower than in the twelfth century; Knowles (1963b), pp. 425–6, 679, and 713–14, estimated the number of monks and canons in England in the second half of the twelfth century at about 15,000; Brooke (1964), p. 54; Knowles and Hadcock (1971), p. 494, gave the totals as 1,094 in c. 1066 and 12,711 in 1216. Guillemain (1953), pp. 348–9, regarded the numbers of new monks and friars in the twelfth and thirteenth centuries as evidence of demographic expansion, though in other respects he questioned the value of statistics for medieval ecclesiastical history.

[6] Berlière (1929–30) and Dubois (1969). The figures given below, when not otherwise specified, are taken from these works. See also Morris (1989), pp. 58 and 245, citing Lekai's estimate that there were 11,000 Cistercian monks and lay brothers in 1153.

[7] Dormeier (1979), pp. 1 and 160.

[8] *Chronique de l'abbaye de Saint-Trond*, VI, 8, ed. C. de Borman (Liège 1877), I, 79. See also Guibert of Nogent's account of the decline of the old monasteries, cited pp. 26–7 above.

[9] *Cartulaire de l'abbaye de Saint-Aubin d'Angers*, ed. Bertrand de Broussillon (Documents historiques sur l'Anjou 1–3; Paris 1903), I, 39, 40–1, 47, 52, and 54–5, nos. 21, 22, 27, 30 and 31. See Dubois (1969), p. 30.

monks when Hugh became abbot in 1049 to over 300 when Peter the Venerable took over in 1122. It continued to grow during the twelfth century, in spite of its problems, and abbot Hugh V imposed a moratorium on the acceptance of new monks, except *ad succurrendum*, for three years.[10] St-Martin-des-Champs in the 1120s, when the future cardinal Matthew of Albano was prior, had, according to Peter the Venerable, 'almost 300 monks both inside and outside the monastery'.[11] The number of professions at Le Bec rose rapidly in the 1070s, levelled off until the 1120s, and then rose again to a new high in the late 1130s, after which they declined to about the level of 1080–1120 before going up again in the 1150s.[12]

The most impressive but least reliable figures come from the new orders and houses. Robert of Arbrissel is said to have had 300 in the great cloister at Fontevrault, and a total of 3,000 including *servi* and *ancillae Dei*, and in 1149 even a sober churchman like Suger of St Denis wrote to the pope that Fontevrault had 'by the will of God' grown to 4,000 or 5,000 nuns, which is hardly credible.[13] The fifteen Gilbertine houses in the late twelfth century varied between 20 and 140 nuns and 10 to 70 canons, with an average of just over 100 nuns and 39 canons each.[14] The founder of Afflighem gathered in various places more than 230 monks, nuns, and brothers, and according to Walter Daniel there were 640 monks, lay brothers, and lay men at Rievaulx under abbot Aelred, who himself put the figure at 300 in his *Mirror of love*.[15] One of the most convincing series of figures for a new house is in the *Book of the restoration of the monastery of St Martin at Tournai*, which began with 5 recruits in 1092, had 13 more a year later, 12 more in 1094, and a total of

---

[10] See Peter the Venerable, *Stat.* 55, in *CCM*, VI, 85 and the notes there, and Hugh V, *Stat.* 8, in *Statuts, chapitres généraux et visites de l'ordre de Cluny*, ed. Georges Charvin, I (Paris 1965), p. 43.

[11] Peter the Venerable, *De miraculis*, II, 8, in *CC:CM*, LXXXIII, 109. At St Remigius in Reims in the eleventh and twelfth centuries there were between 150 and 200 monks, according to Poirier-Coutansais (1974), pp. 13–14, and at least 100 inside servants: *Libelli de discordia inter monachis S. Remigii et S. Nicasii Remenses*, 36, ed. Hermann Meinert, in *Festschrift Albert Brackmann* (Weimar 1931), p. 284.

[12] Gibson (1978), p. 201.

[13] Baldric of Dol, *Vita Roberti de Arbrissello*, IV, 20 and 24, in *PL*, CLXII, 1054B and 1056B (*BHL* 7259), and Suger, *Ep.* 14, ed. A. Lecoy de La Marche (Société de l'histoire de France; Paris 1867), p. 264.

[14] Dugdale, *Monasticon*, VI.2, *lviii (between pp. 946–7). See Knowles and Hadcock (1971), p. 194.

[15] Franco of Afflighem, *De gratia Dei*, 12, in *PL*, CLXVI, 806B; Walter Daniel, *Vita Ailredi*, 30, ed. F.M. Powicke (MC; London and Edinburgh 1950), p. 38 (*BHL* 2644); and Aelred of Rievaulx, *Speculum caritatis*, II, 17, 43, in *CC:CM*, I, 87. See Aubert and de Maillé (1947), I, 10, and 226 n. 1, citing figures for Vaucelles (103 monks, 3 novices, and 130 lay brothers in 1152; 110 monks and 130 lay brothers in the early thirteenth century; 111 monks and 180 lay brothers in 1204/38; and 140 monks and 300 lay brothers in 1238/54); and Fergusson (1984), p. 33 n. 12, citing figures for Rievaulx, Waverley (70 monks and 120 lay brothers in 1189), and Louth Park (66 monks and 150 lay brothers in the second quarter of the thirteenth century), and (1986), p. 161.

70 by 1105, making an average of 5 recruits a year (or more, if some died or departed) for the first fourteen years.[16] Zwiefalten had 70 monks, 62 nuns, and 130 lay brothers in 1138, fifty years after its foundation. During this period 110 monks, 45 nuns, and 160 lay brothers died, showing that every year an average of about 3 monks, 2 nuns, and 6 lay brothers joined the abbey and 2 monks, 1 nun, and 3 lay brothers died.[17] At Clairvaux during the abbacy of Bernard it has been estimated that there was an average of 2 recruits a month, which made possible about two new foundations of 12 monks each every year.[18] Fulda, which had 600 monks in the late eighth century, also had about 24 entries a year in the mid-ninth and mid-eleventh centuries, but they remained concentrated in a single community.[19]

Many of these houses were exceptionally large and wealthy abbeys. A hundred monks constituted a very large community, and fifty was still a good size. Most houses probably had between ten and twenty-five members, not counting servants and hangers-on, whose numbers often equalled or exceeded that of the monks.[20] St Martin at Tournai started out with only five members, and Pontius of Léras with an 'inseparable community' of seven, which he regarded as the perfect number.[21] Some houses had only two or three members, but it was considered unwise to start with so few. When the founder of Pegau in 1090 proposed to the pope to establish a cell for six monks, Urban told him to add some others, if he could, 'because the tenor of regular discipline cannot in all ways be observed among so few'.[22] Bernard of Clairvaux in his letter to the abbot of Aulps expressed his disapproval of small houses, which he called 'those synagogues of Satan, the cells where three or four monks live without order or discipline'.[23] He probably had in mind dependencies that were used by larger houses for pastoral work and places of retreat and as centres of agricultural exploitation. When Berthold of Garsten said that there should be at least two brothers in each dependency 'for the sake

---

[16] There was in addition a community of sixty nuns. Herman of Tournai, *De restauratione monasterii s. Martini Tornacensis*, 37–8 and 69, in *MGH, SS*, XIV, 289–90, 307, and 313 n. 3. See Dereine (1948a), p. 147 and esp. d'Haenens (1962), p. 91.

[17] Berthold of Zwiefalten, *Chronicon Zwiveldensis*, 50, ed. Luitpold Wallach, in *Traditio* 13 (1957), p. 230, and in the series 'Schwäbische Chroniken der Stauferzeit' 2 (Stuttgart 1941, repr. 1978), pp. 276–8. These averages presume that the age distribution in the community remained constant. If the early recruits were younger, and their numbers greater, the averages would have evened out later.

[18] Dimier (1952), pp. 18–19.

[19] Schmid (1970), pp. 176 and 187. These figures are based on necrological entries and show an average of about twenty entries per year in these periods, but the later figure includes a greater number of clerics and non-monks.

[20] See Berlière (1931). The figures given in Knowles and Hadcock (1971), pp. 489–94, show an average of seventeen to eighteen members in all types of houses in England and Wales in the first half of the twelfth century.

[21] Hugh of Silvanès, *De conversione Pontii de Larazio*, 3, in Baluze, *Miscellanea*, I, 180.

[22] *Annales Pegavienses*, s.a. 1090, in *MGH, SS*, XVI, 243.

[23] Bernard, *Ep.* 254.1, ed. Leclercq, VIII, 156.

of reputation (*testimonium*) and of company',[24] he clearly did not expect them to maintain even a semblance of regular monastic life. Most of the reformers regarded twelve, plus a superior, as the ideal size, probably for symbolic as well as practical reasons, and were often fearful of growing too big. When Hugh of Lacerta was on his deathbed in 1157, at the age of eighty-six, he warned the eighteen monks gathered around him (of whom ten were priests and eight *conversi*) that his two greatest fears for the future of the community were more woods and new monks.[25] Hugh of Fouilloy in his introduction to the cartulary of St-Laurent-au-Bois, which at the time of his conversion had seven brothers (four canons and three *conversi*), said that 'The crowd of religious men grew and with the crowd confusion grew. For those who were many required many possessions. Discord concerning possessions arose not only between religious and secular men, but contention also often sprang up between religious men in the presence of wealth.'[26] Stephen of Obazine, whose followers numbered 150 nuns and 120 monks in the middle of the twelfth century, felt that discipline had been stronger at the beginning, 'when they were fewer in numbers and more perfect in life'.[27] This may simply be an expression of the sense of lost intimacy and enthusiasm felt by the members of a successful community that has grown and become more complex.

Restrictions in size were sometimes imposed for logistical and economic as well as for religious reasons, and a *numerus clausus* was not rare in religious communities of the eleventh and twelfth centuries.[28] The statutes of the regular canons of Hérival laid down that it might receive twenty lay brothers 'and as many literate [monks] as the revenues and resources permit',[29] and at the end of the twelfth century the abbot of St Laurence at Liège decreed that owing to lack of resources the number of monks should be reduced to forty and that no one over that number should be received unless he was able to feed and clothe himself, meaning that he must bring a sufficient endowment. The abbot particularly deprecated the practice of having lay and clerical *praebendarii* in the monastery and forbade any lay man *sub monachali habitu* to have a place in the choir, which should be restricted to forty literate and chanting monks.[30] Peter the Venerable was constantly worried about the growing number of monks at Cluny, which created severe problems in a period of rising costs and of transition from a domanial to a money economy, when the

[24] *Vita Bertholdi Garstensis*, 6, ed. Josef Lenzenweger (Forschungen zur Geschichte Oberösterreichs 5; Graz and Cologne 1958), p. 233 (*BHL* 1274).
[25] William Dandina of St Savin, *Vita Hugonis de Lacerta*, 51, in *Ampl. coll.*, VI, 1180D (*BHL* 4017).
[26] Simons (1980), p. 243. See Peltier (1946), p. 32.
[27] *Vita Stephani Obazinensis*, I, 16, ed. Aubrun, p. 70.
[28] On the *numerus clausus*, see the references in Constable and Somerville (1992), pp. 847–8, to which should be added the examples in Poirier-Coutansais (1974), pp. 13–14.
[29] *Vetera Hyreevallis statuta*, in C.L. Hugo, *Sacrae antiquitatis monumenta historica, dogmatica, diplomatica* (Etival 1725), I, 138. See Galli (1959), pp. 18–19.
[30] *Historia monasterii s. Laurentii Leodiensis*, in *Ampl. coll.*, IV, 1180AC.

finances of many old houses suffered. In his statutes he restricted to fifty the number of *prebenda* (allowances of food and drink) to be distributed daily to the poor in memory of dead monks and justified this restriction in his *Disposition of the familial affairs of Cluny* (where he also reduced the size of the loaves that were distributed) on the grounds that the dead monks might otherwise in time expel the living, 'since the revenue of a poor church cannot provide for at least three hundred living and perhaps at the same time a thousand dead'.[31]

The best guide to the internal structure of religious communities are necrological documents, which exist primarily for older communities and of which only a few have been fully analysed. A study of the 4,300 names in the necrological annals of Fulda, which cover the years from 779 to 1065, show that many monks entered as children and lived for between fifty and sixty years. At Reichenau in the late tenth century the community was divided about equally into three age groups of eighteen to twenty-eight, twenty-nine to thirty-nine, and forty to fifty and older, since some monks lived to a great age.[32] Comparable evidence is lacking for the eleventh and especially for the twelfth century, when the older type of memorial books disappeared, but some indications of the distribution of ordained and unordained monks can be derived from other sources.[33] The so-called foundation charter of Fruttuaria, which probably dates from 1015, lists the names of 301 monks from seven monasteries in France: seventy-eight from St Benignus at Dijon, thirty from Vergy, thirty-seven from Bèze, thirty-nine from St Evurtius at Toul, thirty-five from St Arnulf at Metz, forty-nine from Fécamp, and twenty-six from Jumièges, each with a prior. Of the total number 39 per cent were priests, 14 per cent were deacons, 18 per cent were subdeacons, and 29 per cent were *conversi* of the old type, that is, monks who had entered as adults and were not ordained.[34] The tendency for more monks to be ordained was noted in the early ninth century in Hildemar's commentary on the rule of Benedict, in whose time, it said, 'There were few priests and of better life than they are now.'[35] The number of ordained monks continued to grow in the eleventh and twelfth centuries. Farfa had 19 per cent unordained monks in 1047 and 10 per cent in 1097; Subiaco and Rieti, both in about 1075, had 28 per cent and 20 per cent respectively; and at Monte Cassino, which was a very conservative house, less than 30 per cent of the monks were not ordained in the

---

[31] Peter the Venerable, *Stat.* 32, in *CCM*, VI, 66–7, and *Chartes de Cluny*, V, 479, no. 4132. See Duby (1952) and (1956).

[32] Schmid (1970), p. 185, and Beyerle (1929).

[33] On the numbers of monks in the priesthood see Schmitz (1948–56), I, 287, and Dudley (1991).

[34] Kaminsky (1966), pp. 256–7, and Bulst (1973), pp. 223–36. These proportions differed considerably from house to house.

[35] Hildemar, *Expositio regulae*, 60, ed. R. Mittermüller (Regensburg, New York, and Cincinnati 1880), p. 555.

eleventh and twelfth centuries.[36] In strict old houses like Cluny, though no detailed study has been made, the proportion would probably have been still less, and also in the new reformed houses, which insisted on a longer novitiate and tended to use illiterate adult recruits as lay brothers. Unordained monks were still found in the twelfth century, however, in both reformed and old black houses.

Very little is known about the social or educational background of members of religious houses in the eleventh and twelfth centuries. More research of this type has been done for heresy than for monasticism, but with inconclusive results, except to show that heretics appear to have come from various backgrounds and that, contrary to what was once believed, many of them came from the countryside as well as from towns.[37] The Patarenes at Milan in the eleventh century, who were religious as well as social reformers, and occasionally crossed the borderline of heresy, have been described as 'socially eclectic' and included, as did their opponents, clerics, nobles, merchants, and artisans in addition to members of the rural classes.[38] Lambert le Bègue, whose father was a smith or carpenter, was said to have come 'from more humble people and uncultivated parents'.[39] There is still therefore no clear picture of the nature of the appeal of religious reform or of who chose to enter some form of religious life.

Anyone who was not married (or had been freed by his or her spouse) could in principle enter religious life, but an institution might refuse them on the grounds of *inutilitas*, which may be broadly translated as unsuitability.[40] In practice, depending upon the traditions and attitudes of individual communities and abbots, this was interpreted as covering a variety of impediments, including age (which was sometimes also set in the rule or customs), poverty, since recruits were expected to make a gift, and legal and social position. The Cistercians required a married man to obtain a document certifying that his wife had absolved him and vowed to live chastely.[41] Great men, both lay men and clerics, were normally welcomed, though they were sometimes discouraged from becoming monks on account of their secular responsibilities; monks from other houses were as a rule received only under special conditions; and

---

[36] See the figures given by Harmut Hoffmann in Dormeier (1979), pp. 9–11. Unordained monks who had entered as adults tended to spend less time in the monastery and are therefore over-represented in the necrologies. On Farfa and Subiaco, see also Schwarzmaier (1968). Ordericus Vitalis, *Historia ecclesiastica*, XIII, 45, ed. Chibnall, VI, 555, writing in 1141, when he had been at St Evroul for fifty-six years, said that he had been received *ad monachatum* at the age of eleven and became a subdeacon at sixteen, a deacon at eighteen, and a priest at thirty-three.

[37] Violante (1968), p. 176.

[38] Cowdrey (1968), p. 31. See also Miccoli (1966a), pp. 101–3, and Cinzio Violante, in *Laici* (1968), p. 619.

[39] Fredericq (1895), pp. 995–6 = Fredericq (1889–1906), II, 23–32.

[40] Lynch (1975), p. 429.

[41] *Consuetudines*, 102, in *Monuments*, ed. Guignard, pp. 219–20.

serfs were expected to have the permission of their lords.[42] This was sometimes given, especially when the lord was an ecclesiastical institution, and a serf of the nunnery of Ronceray who was permitted to become a monk at St Albinus in Angers apparently built up a considerable estate.[43] The canonist Huguccio argued that, since lordship was over bodies and not over souls, a serf could be a serf in body and a monk in soul and that the priesthood *ipso facto* conferred freedom from servitude, whether or not the lord had given permission.[44] A serf became free, according to Pollock and Maitland, 'by entering religion or receiving holy orders; it is unlawful to ordain a serf – this is forbidden by canon as well as by temporal law – but, when once ordained, he is free, though his serfdom revives if he resumes a secular life'.[45] Since the ordination of serfs both with and without the *manumissio ad tonsuram* was not rare,[46] it is probable that a number of recruits came to the religious life from the unfree classes.

Some idea of the composition and character of a small eremitical community is given in the history of Fontaines-les-Blanches, in Touraine, which was written by its abbot Peregrinus in about 1200. It was founded in 1127 by two hermits, both named Geoffrey, and joined the order of Savigny in 1134 and the Cistercians in 1147. The two Geoffreys were both from Montlouis and were joined, among others who were not named, by a cleric named William, a knight named Lambert the Big from Flanders, Lambert the Small, Gerald of Locumne, Harvey of Galardon, a priest named Ascelin, and a lay man named David 'who was pretty handy (*satis utile*) at agriculture'. Seven of this group lived until the middle of the twelfth century and five until 1158, thirty years after the foundation, so they were presumably young men at the time they joined. At least three of the original hermits refused to become monks when Fontaines entered the order of Savigny, and they were allowed to go where they wished and to keep for their lifetimes what they needed from the monastery's property. One of the Geoffreys went to live in the forest at Aiguevive and died at Montrichard; Ascelin and the other Geoffrey, who was called master Geoffrey the hermit, went to La Lande, which Rainald of Château-Renault gave him in 1140. This Geoffrey returned to Fontaines before his death, however, which marked, according to Peregrinus, 'the end of the hermits'. Meanwhile both William the cleric and Lambert the Big went to the Holy Land, where William was said to have become patriarch of Jerusalem and to have given Lambert some relics to take back to Fontaines.[47]

---

[42] Petot (1954) and Landau (1991b).

[43] *Cartularium monasterii beatae Mariae Caritatis Andegavensis*, ed. Paul Marchegay, in *Archives d'Anjou* (Angers 1843–54), III, 27–30, no. 34. See Boussard (1950), pp. 43–6.

[44] See Gilchrist (1977), pp. 315–16, and Landau (1991b), p. 191.

[45] Pollock and Maitland (1898), I, 429.

[46] Petot (1954), pp. 195 and 203–4.

[47] Peregrinus, *Historia*, I, 2–4, ed. Salmon, pp. 258–61. The story of William's becoming patriarch may have been invented to authenticate the relics. Peregrinus derived his information, he said (p. 259), from Robert of Fosseau, who entered the abbey as a boy under abbot Theobald (1149–

The reformers were great pilgrims and travellers. Many of them went to the Holy Land, and some, like William, stayed there. Among the hermits in the Holy Land who were mentioned by Gerard of Nazareth (who was a hermit himself before he became bishop of Laodicea) were a monk named John from Italy, a 'lay pilgrim' to Jerusalem named Ralph, Cosmas from Hungary, 'Hugh from across the Alps, who came to the Holy Land from across the sea for the sake of fighting', Haimo of Limoges, Bernard of Blois, a Burgundian knight named Valerius, and two nobles named William and Ralph from France, who was the lord of seventy knights.[48] Gerald of La Sauve-Majeure, who died in 1095 and whose *Life* was written by a monk who knew him personally, entered Corbie as an oblate and went on two pilgrimages, one to Italy, where he visited Rome, Apulia, Monte Gargano, and Monte Cassino, and the other to Jerusalem, where his abbot was reluctant to let him go, 'lest he remain somewhere on the way as a recluse or hermit'. He then became abbot of St Vincent at Laon, resigned to go to Poitiers, and finally settled down at La Sauve-Majeure, where he established a small community of *milites* who had gone to Compostela as pilgrims and who from strenuous fighters now became 'vigorous clearers of forests and woods'. They were joined, still according to Gerald's *Life*, by 'youths and virgins, old men and young ones', and he was surrounded at his death by 'a multitude of nobles, clerics, and lay men, and of peasants and women'.[49]

More is known about the social origins of the leaders of the reform movement, and the founders of new houses, whose *Lives* were written by their admirers, than about the members of most communities. Men like Amedeus of Hauterives, Godfrey of Cappenberg, Louis of Arnstein, Simon of Crépy, and Waldef of Melrose belonged to the high nobility of their regions; Adelelmus of La Chaise-Dieu, Hugh of Lacerta, and Pontius of Léras were *milites*, of whom other examples have already been cited; Stephen of Obazine's parents were said to have had 'a satisfactory sufficiency of life', being neither rich nor poor;[50] whereas the parents of Geoffrey of Chalard and Guy of Anderlac (whose *Life* was written in the early twelfth century, though he lived in the tenth) were described as poor and humble. Some, like Bernard of Tiron, were students at the time they entered religious life; some were priests or married lay men; others first appeared on the scene as monks, clerics, hermits, wandering preachers, pilgrims, or penitents. This diversity confirms Murray's

70) and had spent fifty years there in 1200, and from William the infirmarian, who had been there forty-two years in 1200 (p. 273).

[48] Gerard of Nazareth, *De conversatione virorum Dei in Terra Sancta morantium*, 9, 11, 17, 25–6, 33–4, 36–7, and 39, in Kedar (1983), pp. 72–5. See Jotischky (1995), pp. 17–46.

[49] *Vita Geraldi Silvae Maioris*, 7–27 and 36, in *PL*, CXLVII, 1028–42 and 1046 (quotations on 1034C, 1039C, and 1046A) (*BHL* 3417). See Zimmermann, II, 17–20. During the course of Bernard of Tiron's long and checkered career he was a hermit at least five times between periods in various monasteries: see Geoffrey *Grossus*, *Vita Bernardi Tironiensis*, in *PL*, CLXXII, 1367–1446 (*BHL* 1251).

[50] *Vita Stephani Obazinensis*, I, 1, ed. Aubrun, p. 42.

opinion that saints in the twelfth century were 'socially amphibious' and 'without social class',[51] and while this itself may be a hagiographical topos, like those in other periods that made all saints either nobles or of humble origins, it supports the general, if not always specific, accuracy of these accounts of diverse social backgrounds.

There are fewer indications of the social origins of the followers of these leaders, except that they frequently came from the noble and free classes.[52] The emphasis on this point in the sources may be in part owing to the snobbery of many medieval writers and to their satisfaction at the sight of nobles who humbled themselves by joining religious houses and performing menial tasks. The nobler they were, said Bernold of the lay men at St Blaise, Hirsau, and Schaffhausen, the lowlier were their tasks.[53] This again may have been a topos, but it would have lost its point had it not contained a measure of truth. Entire noble families and households, including children and servants, and groups of relations sometimes entered or founded religious houses at the same time. Both Bernard of Clairvaux and Amedeus of Hauterives were said to have brought with them bands of followers, and Louis of Arnstein started with his wife, chaplain, chamberlain, and five soldiers. At Obazine, a noble who came with his wife and children later became a priest, in spite of his age, and many of the women, who came from noble families and had lived in luxury, spent their time cooking and washing while the male members of the community did other work.[54] The accounts of new houses sometimes stressed their openness to people from various backgrounds and their egalitarian spirit. Herman, who allegedly converted from Judaism and became a regular canon at Cappenberg in 1129/30, remarked in the history of his conversion on the presence there of 'knowledgeable and unlettered, strong and weak, noble and ignoble' canons, among whom perhaps not the least remarkable was himself.[55] The young Norbert of Xanten was said to have been all things to all men, 'great among the great, and small among the little; illustrious among nobles,

---

[51] Murray (1978), p. 383.

[52] See Grundmann (1968); Ehlers (1973); and Wollasch (1980). Not all noble families had members in religious life, however, as is sometimes suggested. Of the families studied by Newman (1971), I, 10–11, only a few members were monks and none were regular canons, though they patronized monasteries and were buried there.

[53] Bernold of St Blaise, *Chronicon*, s.a. 1083, in *MGH, SS*, V, 439. In the *Vita Amedaei Altae Ripae*, 7, ed. M.-Anselme Dimier, in *Studia monastica* 5 (1963), pp. 293–4 (*BHL* 385b), Guigo of Albon found his nephew Amedeus, who came of the high nobility, greasing the monks' boots. On this topos, see Schreiner (1964), pp. 41–4, and Baldwin (1970), I, 255.

[54] *Vita Ludovici de Arnstein*, ed. S. Widmann, in *Annalen des Vereins für nassauische Altertumskunde und Geschichtsforschung* 17 (1882), pp. 254–5 (*BHL* 5033), and *Vita Stephani Obazinensis*, I, 29–30, ed. Aubrun, pp. 86–90.

[55] Herman, *De conversione sua*, 6, ed. Gerlinde Niemeyer (*MGH*, Quellen zur Geistesgeschichte des Mittelalters 4; Weimar 1963), p. 89. See p. 64 n. 82 above. There is a reference to a Jew who converted and became a monk in the *Vita et passione Willelmi Norwicensis*, II, 11, ed. Augustus Jessopp and Montague R. James (Cambridge 1896), pp. 93–4 (*BHL* 8926), on which see Langmuir (1984), pp. 835 and (on the date) 840.

and rustic among non-nobles; learned among the knowledgeable, and foolish among the illiterate; amiable to all'; and in his later life Norbert gathered 'into the same poverty a multitude from different nations and of different birth, nobles and non-nobles, rich men, poor men, of older and younger age, wise men, simple men, and illiterates'.[56] Gaucherius of Aureil and Stephen of Obazine were praised in similar terms for receiving both men and women and nobles and non-nobles, and Geoffrey *Grossus* said that Bernard of Tiron's hospitality extended to 'the rich, poor, deaf, weak, little children, weak women, lepers, whoever was ill; he excluded no sex and no age'.[57]

This was probably not always true in practice, but it reflected an ideal of the character of religious communities. True nobility depended on inner virtue, according to the *Mirror of virgins*, and noble lineage was not recognized as a claim to authority in the community.[58] When Amedeus of Hauterives and his followers sought admission to Bonnevaux, the abbot stressed that in Cistercian houses no concessions were made to nobles and that 'A free man is not preferred to a serf.'[59] The Cistercian novice in Aelred's *Mirror of love* expressed his warm approval that 'There is no favouritism of persons, no consideration of births. Only necessity creates diversity; only infirmity, lack of equality.'[60] Bernard's statement in his sermons on the Song of Songs that 'Nature creates all men equal' was echoed in a Bernardine text in Lincoln manuscript 201 that 'In nature no one is inferior, no one superior; no one before, no one after; no one noble, no one ignoble; but nature always creates us all equals.'[61] This encroaches on the subject of the next chapter, on the rhetoric of reform, but it is relevant to the character of the reformed communities, since it explains the reformers' dislike for the use of the title *dominus* by monks and the reluctance of some of them to take any position or enter a defined category. Gilbert of Sempringham was described in his *Life* as 'a secular man and of no ecclesiastical dignity', though he apparently wore a canonical habit and later became

---

[56] *Vita* [B] *Norberti*, I, 4, and XI, 62, in *PL*, CLXX, 1259A and 1299CD (*BHL* 6249).
[57] *Vita Gaufridi Castaliensis*, I, 6, ed. A. Bosvieux, in *Mémoires de la Société des sciences naturelles et archéologiques de la Creuse* 3 (1862), p. 100 (*BHL* 3283); *Vita Stephani Obazinensis*, I, 29, ed. Aubrun, p. 86; and Geoffrey Grossus, *Vita Bernardi Tironiensis*, XI, 92, in *PL*, CLXXII, 1421D–2A (*BHL* 1251); cf. VIII, 74, ibid., 1411C, where Bernard said he would exclude no one. Von Walter (1903–6), II, 15–16, attributed cap. 74 to writer A and cap. 92 to R. The early Cistercians, according to Nicholl (1964), pp. 161–2, were 'misfits' and 'not easy men to live with'.
[58] Bernards (1955), p. 147.
[59] *Vita Amedaei Altae Ripae*, 4, ed. Dimier (n. 53), p. 282.
[60] Aelred of Rievaulx, *Speculum caritatis*, II, 17, 43, in *CC:CM*, I, 87; cf. II, 26, 75, in *PL*, CXCV, 574C, and *CC:CM*, I, 102, where Aelred, following Gregory the Great, called the *libido dominandi* the worst passion: see Rouche (1979), pp. 326 and 329. In the illustration to the 'Rota verae religionis' (plate 5), the good abbot is described as 'Nolens dominatur', and according to the *Meditationes Godwini Salesberie*, in MS Oxford, Bodleian Library, Digby 96, fol. 45ᵛ, 'Tutius est subesse, quam praeesse.'
[61] Bernard, *Serm. 23 in Cant.*, III, 6, ed. Leclercq, I, 142, and Rochais and Binont (1964), p. 164, no. Lc 58; cf. p. 199, Lc 73: 'Ergo omnes homines natura aequales genuit, sed uariantur meritorum ordine.'

a priest and a canon.[62] Pontius of Léras remained a *conversus* all his life, and Louis of Arnstein, who was said to have scorned rank and wealth, was described as count, founder, and *conversus* together by his biographer, who admitted his astonishment 'that these three adjectives came together in one man'.[63] The rich and pious burgher Werimbold of La Vigne, who put his wife and children into monasteries and inspired many others to become monks and hermits, remained a lay man himself, while living like a monk, and devoted himself to good works.[64]

These examples may have been recorded precisely because they were exceptional, and the spirit of egalitarianism and humility of which they were an expression did not inspire many people or last very long. A distrust of low birth was almost as endemic in the Middle Ages as a suspicion of women, and accusations of raising men of humble rank to positions of trust and authority were brought both against the neo-Cluniac monasteries in Germany and, in the middle of the twelfth century, against Suger's successor Odo at St Denis.[65] The legal restriction of communities to members of noble families did not begin before the late twelfth or early thirteenth centuries, but poor and low-born candidates were refused by some houses, and Tenxwind of Andernach in a letter to Hildegard of Bingen objected that only *spectabiles et ingenuas* and not *modicos* or *pauperes* were accepted at Bingen.[66] Many houses were in fact populated entirely from the noble and free classes and nearly all of them treated rich and poor guests differently. According to a mildly scurrilous and possibly apocryphal story in Stephen Langton's commentary on the letter of James,

> It is said that P[eter] Abelard, wishing to see the order of the monks of Clairvaux, entered alone in cheap clothing and was very poorly received with the poor. The following day, however, having put on different clothing, he entered their chapter and at once exclaimed: 'If there shall come a man having a golden ring' [James 2.2] etc. And from then on they hated him.[67]

As the twelfth century progressed, the inclusion of men of high birth among the lay brothers became increasingly rare, and long before the Cistercian general chapter decreed in 1188 that the son of a knight could not become a lay

---

[62] *Vita Gileberti Sempinghamensis*, 6, 7, 29, and 55, ed. Foreville and Keir, pp. 24, 26, 92, and 130.

[63] Hugh of Silvanès, *De conversione Pontii de Larazio*, 24, in Baluze, *Miscellanea*, I, 184, and *Vita Ludovici de Arnstein*, ed. Widmann (n. 54), p. 263; cf. p. 258.

[64] *Gesta pontificum Cameracensium*, ed. C. de Smedt (Société de l'histoire de France; Paris 1880), pp. 122–39.

[65] Glaser (1965), pp. 287–8.

[66] Haverkamp (1984), pp. 544–5 and 547–8. See generally Despy (1956) and Parisse (1983), pp. 207–14.

[67] Cited from MS Paris, Bibl. nat., Lat. 14443, fol. 438, by Landgraf (1952–6), I, 15 n. 5. This passage was brought to my attention by Chrysogonus Waddell, who pointed out that the use of *Clarevallenses* suggests the story had an early origin.

brother, most of the lay brothers at La Ferté were of humble birth, and the monks noble.[68] The lay brothers of Sempringham, according to the *Life* of Gilbert written in the late twelfth century, included many men raised at Gilbert's expense and also poor men, beggars, and fugitives from serfdom 'whom the name of religion has freed'.[69] This shows that the institution of lay brotherhood opened the possibility of a new type of religious life to men who could not otherwise have become members of a religious house, but it also emphasizes the social distinction that existed, even in reformed houses, where the monks or canons, though not legally restricted to the nobility, were for the most part of higher social rank than the lay brothers.[70]

In houses affiliated with the new reformed orders, though less than in independent unorganized communities, the members were likewise distinguished by their age at the time of admission. Since one of the main objectives of the reformers was to raise the level of religious life and to attract recruits with a personal commitment to the religious life, they often refused to accept the *oblati* and *nutriti* who were such an important element in older monasteries and insisted that all new members should be, by contemporary standards, adults.[71] Ulrich in the introduction to his customs of Cluny, which was addressed to abbot William of Hirsau, referred to deformed or disabled children who were given to monasteries by lay men 'not for the sake of God but only in order to free themselves from raising and feeding them or to take more care of their other children'.[72] It was the custom at Hirsau in the late eleventh century not to receive a recruit from the lay world until he had enough beard to be shaved in the *ordo tonsurae*.[73] The earliest Cistercian legislation on this subject set the age of admission at sixteen, which was raised to eighteen by 1157. The Carthusians and Grandmontines both set twenty as the minimum age, as did Peter the Venerable for the Cluniacs, who later made an exception for the boys who participated in the liturgy.[74] The change in attitude is reflected in the fact that whereas Urban II held that a vow made

---

[68] *Recueil des pancartes de l'abbaye de la Ferté-sur-Grosne*, ed. Georges Duby ([Aix-en-Provence] 1953), p. 7. See generally, Wollasch (1980), pp. 5–6.

[69] *Vita Gileberti Sempinghamensis*, 11, ed. Foreville and Keir, pp. 36–8; cf. *Ep.* 12, ibid., p. 163.

[70] Schreiner (1964), pp. 50–2, said that by the thirteenth century the monks in reformed houses in the eastern Black Forest were *de facto* if not *de iure* predominantly noble.

[71] Blanc (1960), pp. 144–5, estimated that half of the monks in the monasteries in the lower Rhone Valley entered as boys under ten. On oblation see, in addition to the references in *Medieval Monasticism*, nos. 760–7, de Jong (1986), on the early Middle Ages; Boswell (1988), pp. 228–55 and 296–321, who said (p. 317) that 'Between the twelfth and thirteenth centuries . . . oblation waned markedly'; and Bull (1993), pp. 116–25, on south-western France. On the refusal of the reformers to accept children, see Pierre Riché, in *Pierre Abélard – Pierre le Vénérable* (1975), p. 693.

[72] Ulrich of Zell, *Consuetudines Cluniacenses*, *Ep. nunc.*, in *PL*, CXLIX, 635B–6A.

[73] William of Hirsau, *Consuetudines*, I, 2, in Herrgott, *Disciplina*, p. 380.

[74] See Peter the Venerable, *Stat.* 36, in *CCM*, VI, 70–1, and references there. See also Milis (1969), pp. 465–6, on the growing number of children at Arrouaise; Lynch (1973) on the problem of enforcing the Cistercian statutes; and Schreiner (1987), pp. 487–96.

by a child, even in ignorance, was valid, Alexander III decreed that the religious habit taken by a boy under fourteen years old was invalid.[75] The reformers also tested the vocations of their recruits by a longer novitiate than was customary in older houses, such as Cluny, where Peter the Venerable tried to increase the time of probation, as he called it, to at least a month.[76] In other established houses monks were often admitted immediately in order to prevent backsliding and assure their salvation, as when they were admitted *ad succurrendum.*

These differing practices reflected two different views of the nature and purpose of monasticism. In the reformed houses, which had higher age limits, the monks grew up in the secular world and were admitted to the community only after a substantial period of probation. They had been educated outside the monastery and had some experience of the world, normally including, if they were lay men, sexual experience, which was considered to start at the age of fourteen or soon after.[77] Most men married between the ages of fifteen and twenty-one, and women when they were about fifteen.[78] In the old houses, on the other hand, many of the monks had come as children and spent practically their entire lives *in clausura*, while those who entered as adults (the *conversi* of the old type) were sometimes admitted after a few hours or days. Although some of the new houses admitted children either as oblates[79] or with their parents, as members of families,[80] they were as a rule not regular members of the community and many of them probably departed when they became adults.

The recruits to both the old and new houses in the eleventh and twelfth centuries included clerics and monks from other houses. Charismatic preachers like Robert of Arbrissel and successful abbots like Hugh of Cluny and Bernard of Clairvaux, whose approach was said to have been dreaded by the parents of eligible sons, recruited actively for converts to their forms of religious life, and their words naturally appealed to monks or clerics as well as to lay men and women. The letter from Ivo of Chartres to the monks of Coulombs shows that they had been urged to leave their monastery for a stricter life. Bishops often entered monasteries, sometimes as a sort of retirement,[81] and monks who were formerly priests or clerics were occasionally

---

[75] Fuhrmann (1984), pp. 42–4 (cited p. 18 above), and *Decretales*, III, 31, 8, in *Corpus*, ed. Friedberg, II, 571.

[76] Peter the Venerable, *Stat.* 37, in *CCM*, VI, 71 and n.

[77] Brundage (1980), pp. 378–9.

[78] Foucault (1984), p. 129, and Bessmertny (1990), pp. 144–8.

[79] A four-year-old girl was received at the Gilbertine house of Watton at the request of archbishop Henry of York: Constable (1978), pp. 206–7.

[80] See *Vita Stephani Obazinensis*, I, 29, and II, 47, ed. Aubrun, pp. 88 and 170.

[81] See Oliger (1958), pp. 203–8, and for Cluny, Constable (1956) and for Cîteaux, Crozet (1975), who mentioned examples both of bishops who became Cistercians and of Cistercians who became bishops. Bishops who became monks lost the use of their episcopal powers but not their consecrated nature.

required to return to their former positions. A more serious problem was created by the transfer of monks or regular canons, or *transitus* as it was technically called, from one house to another.[82] The fact that many of the members of the new houses came from other monasteries, frequently without the permission of their abbots, created serious personal, legal, and political problems. Cîteaux itself, like Fountains and other new houses, was formed by a migration from an older house, and the account of its foundation in the earliest Cistercian documents may have been revised so as to play down the role of Robert, who left Molesme without permission and was required to return.[83] Bernard of Tiron was also an eremitically inclined reformer who had to return to the houses he left in search of another type of religious life.[84] Many monks found themselves caught between their duty of stability, which held them to the house where they had made their profession, and their obligation to themselves to leave a house where the rule was not observed or where they felt their salvation might be in danger. There was no satisfactory solution to this dilemma, which was further complicated by various papal privileges on the one hand forbidding specific types of transfers, as for regular canons to become monks, and, on the other, allowing some monasteries, such as Cluny, to receive monks or clerics coming from any house.[85] The compromise that was worked out, and was eventually embodied in canon law, allowed transfers to stricter but not to less strict houses, but since there was no recognized standard of strictness, the way was left open for bitter disputes.

The old stress on stability of place was thus increasingly replaced by a new concept of stability of profession, in which a monk's loyalty to the substance of his commitment was considered to override his loyalty to the house where it was first made.[86] The rule of Benedict established that no monk should be received 'from another known monastery (*de alio noto monasterio*) . . . without the consent of his abbot or a commendatory letter', and the old black monks, most of the canons, and all those who were considered less strict than the new orders adhered to this traditional position. Permissions to move were sometimes given, both orally and in writing, as a few surviving examples of commendatory letters show. In a model letter from St Hilary near Venice the abbot introduced to other monasteries a monk who wanted 'to choose a stricter life' and allowed him to transfer 'provided he chooses a stricter life in a place

---

[82] There is no satisfactory general account of the issue of *transitus* and stability from both a practical and a legal point of view, but see, among other works, Hofmeister (1928); Fina (1957); the unpublished dissertation of Roby (1971); Melville (1978); and Landau (1991b), pp. 88–91.

[83] See de Waha (1978), pp. 162–5, citing previous works, and Hallinger (1983).

[84] Geoffrey *Grossus, Vita Bernardi Tironiensis*, III, 25, and V, 39–42, in *PL*, CLXXII, 1383C and 1391C–3C (*BHL* 1251).

[85] On the reception privilege at Cluny and other monasteries, see Constable (1973), pp. 343–5, and on the celebrated Rottenbuch privilege of 1092, which served as the model for many houses of regular canons, see Mois (1953), pp. 76–7, and Fuhrmann (1984), pp. 6–8, esp. n. 9 with the text of this clause.

[86] The modern euphemism 'transferring stability' was unknown in the Middle Ages.

observing the rule of Benedict'.[87] The practice was frowned upon, however. Guibert of Nogent told of a monk who had moved to a stricter house with his abbot's permission and who was accused in the afterworld, after he died, of breaking his first profession and promise and who was required to return to earth and his first monastery and to confess his sin of perjury and desertion.[88]

Another escape valve provided in the rule was in the final chapter, which was entitled 'That not all observance of justice is established in this rule', which furnished only 'a beginning of *conversatio*'. 'Otherwise, for him who would hasten to the perfection of *conversatio*, there are the teachings of the holy fathers, of which the observance leads a man to the height of perfection.' This was frequently interpreted as allowing monks to move to an eremitical way of life. Peter Damiani, for instance, argued in a letter to an abbot who had protested the reception of one of his monks that life in a monastery was a preparation for the desert and that the monastery was a *transitus* and *hospitium* rather than a *mansio* or *habitatio*. 'Monks who remain unmoving in a monastery should be tolerated; but those who move to the desert with an ardent spirit should be exalted with commendations and praise . . . The former defend what they have; the latter bring back booty.'[89]

Most of the monastic reformers, while condemning and even prohibiting transfers from their own houses, asserted the right of monks to move from a less strict to a stricter house.[90] The Grandmontines, who consistently tried to avoid any cause of friction or controversy, were almost alone in refusing to accept transfers from other monasteries.[91] Bernard of Clairvaux found himself in the thick of this dispute. The first letter in his collection, which marked his entry into the religious polemics of his time, concerned the issue of his cousin Robert, who, after being promised to Cluny as a boy, entered Clairvaux, found the life there too hard, moved to Cluny, and finally returned to Clairvaux.[92] Bernard became involved in several acrimonious controversies over fugitives, one with the Premonstratensian Philip of Harvengt, the prior of Bonne-Espérance, to whom he denied any knowledge of the papal privilege prohibiting the reception of a Premonstratensian without a commendatory letter, and another with the abbot of St Germer of Flaix, a monastery that Bernard originally said was unknown to him (and therefore within the letter of the rule) and later claimed, when the abbot protested, was known to him

---

[87] Wilmart (1928b). The hand-writing of the manuscript apparently dates this letter to the twelfth century.

[88] Guibert, *De vita sua*, III, 19, ed. Bourgin, pp. 222–3.

[89] Peter Damiani, *Ep.* VI, 12, in *PL*, CXLIV, 392–6 (quote on 395CD) = no. 152, ed. Kurt Reindel, in *MGH*, *Briefe*, IV.4, 5–12 (quote on 12); see also *Opusc.* 15 *de suae congregationis institutis*, 29, in *PL*, CXLV, 362A.

[90] See, for instance, Statute 3 of the first general chapter of the Carthusians in 1141, in *Die ältesten Consuetudines der Kartäuser*, ed. James Hogg (Analecta Cartusiana 1; Berlin and Salzburg 1970), p. 120.

[91] *Regula Stephani Muretensis*, 40, in *CC:CM*, VIII, 87.

[92] Bernard, *Ep.* I, ed. Leclercq, VII, 1–11. See Dimier (1953).

only by name, drawing a distinction between the names (*vocabula*) and realities (*res ipsas*) of things.[93] These arguments sound thin today, as they did to his opponents in these disputes, and Bernard's basic position was that a fugitive who sincerely believed that his soul was in danger could not be turned away. In his treatise *On precept and dispensation* Bernard defined the three grades of obedience 'as of necessity owing to the fear of hell or owing to the holy profession', of charity 'from the love of God', and 'when an imposed task is received in the same spirit in which it is ordered'. Later in this treatise he formulated the doctrine of stability based not on place but on the promises of profession: 'For if these cannot be preserved in a particular place owing to the excessive depravity and irreligiousness of others living there, I advise without hesitation, under the guidance of the spirit of liberty, transfer to another place where a man will not be prevented from fulfilling his vows to God, which his lips expressed.' As an experienced abbot and spiritual adviser, Bernard warned against fickleness and urged a monk who was in this position to obtain, if possible, the permission of his abbot, but ultimately he must follow the dictates of his conscience.[94]

This view was accepted, with occasional misgivings, by serious churchmen and spiritual writers. In a letter allegedly from Lanfranc to abbot Ralph of St Vito at Verdun the author cited himself as a hypothetical example of a monk who had sworn never to leave his monastery but who did so when he found that 'I could not save my soul there.'[95] Ivo of Chartres advised the abbot of the Trinity at Vendôme, if necessary, to give a monk who wanted to leave 'permission . . . to save his soul in another monastery'.[96] An interesting case concerning a transfer from a secular to a regular canon arose in the early twelfth century in the cathedral chapter of Utrecht when a former canon named Ellenhard, who three years earlier had become an Augustinian canon in the diocese of Trier, claimed the right to return and to recover his benefice on the grounds that he had left without the permission of the bishop of Utrecht, though his real reason was his dislike for the poverty of the regular canons. The canons of Utrecht, knowing 'that many men in the conprovincial churches have transferred to a higher life without the permission of their bishops and were not received when they later returned', decided to consult the neighbouring chapters of Liège, Münster, and Minden. The chapter of Minden in its reply hesitantly recommended that Ellenhard be taken back but given only food and clothing, not his prebend, but the other two chapters said that he must remain in his monastery, since no one can return from a

[93] Delhaye (1953), and Bernard, *Epp.* 67–8, ed. Leclercq, VII, 164 and 166.
[94] Bernard, *De praecepto et dispensatione*, VII, 16, and XVI, 44–51, ed. Leclercq, III, 264 and 283–8 (quote on 284).
[95] Lanfranc, *Ep.* 60, in *PL*, CL, 550A. The authenticity of this letter was questioned by Helen Clover and Margaret Gibson in their edition of *The Letters of Lanfranc Archbishop of Canterbury* (OMT; Oxford 1979), pp. 184–5, but cf. Leclercq (1965a), p. 218.
[96] Ivo, *Ep.* 82, in *PL*, CLXII, 104A; cf. *Ep.* 78, ibid., 100CD.

stricter life, even if entered improperly. This was also the view of the canon (and later provost) Meingot of Utrecht and of Reimbald of Liège, who discussed the case in his *Stromata* and argued that in view of the superiority of the poverty and common life of regular canons Ellenhard might not return 'from perfection to imperfection'.[97]

The differing views expressed in this case, mostly by secular canons, show the direction in which ecclesiastical opinion was moving. Later in the century Stephen of Tournai approved of the transfer of some Grandmontines to the Cistercian abbey of Pontigny, saying that the better must always be preferred to the good and that even if the Grandmontines were regular canons (and thus prevented by papal privilege from becoming monks) he would not recall them from the stricter life or impede the spirit of liberty.[98] The Cistercians also experienced problems of this type. Among the letters in the collection of Philip of L'Aumone is one from a monk of Clairvaux to pope Alexander III seeking his protection and permission to serve God 'more freely and unrestrictedly' in solitude.[99] Monastic life thus became increasingly a matter of personal choice and freedom. A prior of Sainte-Barbe who became a Premonstratensian wrote to his former colleagues that he left 'in order that my soul may always be in my own hands, that is, that my life and mind may be before me in my sight, so that I may be mindful of God's commands, as follows "and I have not forgotten thy law" [Psalm 118.61, 109, 153]',[100] and Gervase of Louth Park said in his testament that he left St Mary at York for Fountains 'seeing that his former life did not suffice for him . . . He went to the desert in order to lead the life he had long desired, with the peace he had long wished for, among the harshness of the rocks and the hollows of the valleys.'[101] A few voices were also raised on behalf of monks who found monastic life too harsh. In the 1120s cardinal Stephen of Ostia advised the abbot of a disgruntled monk either to modify the rigour of the discipline or, if the monk's behaviour was insupportable, to allow him to live in a cell of the monastery or 'to give him permission to save his soul', presumably by going elsewhere.[102] Wibald

---

[97] *Oorkondenboek van het Sticht Utrecht tot 1301*, ed. S. Muller and A.C. Bouman, I (Utrecht 1920–5), pp. 235–50, nos. 262–8, and Reimbald of Liège, *Stromata*, in *CC:CM*, IV, esp. 86.

[98] Stephen of Tournai, *Ep.* I, ed. Desilve, pp. 3–16 (dating it 1178/80). This appears to be the same case discussed by Peter of Celle in his *Epp.* II, 175–6, in *PL*, CCII, 633A–6A.

[99] Philip of L'Aumône, *Ep.* 2 (of Clairvaux collection), in *Bibliotheca patrum Cisterciensium*, ed. Bertrand Tissier (Bonnefontaine and Paris 1660–9), III, 239. In *Ep.* 30 (of the Clairvaux collection), ibid., 249–50, Philip interceded with the abbot of St Ghislain on behalf of a monk and his nephew who wanted to return to their abbey.

[100] *Ampl. coll.*, I, 784A.

[101] Gervase of Louth Park, *Testament*, ed. Charles H. Talbot, in *Analecta sacri ordinis Cisterciensis* 7 (1951), p. 40.

[102] Henry Francigena, *Ep.* 6, ed. Botho Odebrecht, in *Archiv für Urkundenforschung* 14 (1936), pp. 244–5. See also the abbot's reply (*Ep.* 7), blaming the situation on the 'evil customs' introduced by his predecessors. The letters may not be authentic, but the collection dates from Pavia probably in the early 1120s. There are significant variants in the Oxford manuscript, including that the monk should save his soul 'with his associates'.

of Corvey gave a troublesome monk the choice of staying or leaving, and he left the monastery, Wibald said, 'joyful and laughing'.[103]

In practice it was probably not difficult to move to a less strict house or even give up religious life entirely, and many people tried their vocations in monasteries and then left, with or without the permission of their superiors. Peter of Blois wrote in alarm to a Carthusian who wanted to leave in order to celebrate mass every day, urging him to remain in the life of solitude and contemplation to which he was bound 'by the vow of religion and the bond of stability'. If he must leave, Peter wrote, he should join the order of Cîteaux, where 'there is a highly tested school of religion, the highest use of modesty, regularity of ways, feeling of fraternity, peace of soul, communication of all men, mutual complaisance, vigour of discipline, love of obedience, bond of love, subjection of the flesh, display of hospitality, liberty of lamenting, nocturnal watches, quiet of meditation, and devotion of psalmody'. In his letter concerning a woman who said she had been forced to become a nun, Peter stressed that religious life should be voluntary, comparing the lesser freedom of carnal marriage to the greater freedom of spiritual marriage.[104] While he did not go on to conclude that she should therefore be released from her nunnery, his view reflects the growing emphasis in the twelfth century on the voluntary nature of monasticism.

This freedom was a mixed blessing, since it imposed on individuals the hard decision of whether to enter or remain in religious life and of what type of life to choose. When Norbert refused the invitation of the pope to remain at the papal court, which he considered unsuited to his age and penitential status, he said that 'He would willingly and entirely obey if he ordered him to be a canon, or a monk, or a hermit, or even a travelling pilgrim', and he in fact accepted a papal commission to preach.[105] Stephen of Grandmont, on the other hand, refused to be classified at all and maintained to the end, for himself and his followers, his own way of life. Stephen of Obazine hesitated between the monks and canons and between the Carthusians and Cistercians, as did Pontius of Léras, some of whose followers wanted to establish a monastery for virgin nuns, perhaps on the model of Fontevrault. The Cistercians did not always accept communities that wanted to join their order. When Waldsassen first asked, 'St Bernard refused the request, citing the defect of the monks', by which he probably meant their small number rather than their moral failings; and Gilbert of Sempringham was said to have established his own order only after being rejected by the Cistercians, whose monastic rigour

---

[103] Wibald, *Ep.* 172, in *Monumenta Corbeiensia*, ed. Philipp Jaffé (BRG 1; Berlin 1864), p. 292; cf. *Ep.* 220, ibid., pp. 338–9.
[104] Peter of Blois, *Epp.* 54 and 86, ed. J.A. Giles (Bibliotheca patrum ecclesiae Anglicanae 5; Oxford 1847), I, 162–3 and 265–6.
[105] *Vita* [B] *Norberti*, IV, 23, in *PL*, CLXX, 1272C–3A (*BHL* 6249).

he attributed to their recent origins.[106] When the founder of Fontaines-les-Blanches was ill, the hermits considered several alternatives, including becoming regular canons or black monks affiliated with Bonneval or Marmoutier, and finally decided on Savigny, 'a famous monastery, from which have already come forth many other monasteries, of which the abbots meet in the chapter. The [monastic] order flowers again there, and their good name resounds everywhere.'[107] Some of them did not want to become monks, however, and resettled elsewhere as hermits. Fontaines-les-Blanches later, with other Savigniac houses, joined the Cistercians, who had a high reputation for good order as well as strictness. Behind this evidence lay many difficult though unrecorded individual decisions. The number of visions, miracles, and dreams offering guidance in such matters shows that the question of whether to move to another house or order or to become a hermit or go on a pilgrimage could be long and painful.

These decisions were not always between 'old' and 'new', and some of the great old houses such as Monte Cassino and Marmoutier were also held in high esteem, though they never became centres of orders. Cluny still had the highest reputation among the 'new' old houses, but monasteries like St Victor at Marseilles were also influential and prestigious. The best-known of the new (or 'new' new) orders in the mid-twelfth century were the Cistercians, Carthusians, Savigniacs (before they joined the Cistercians), Grandmontines, and (among the regular canons) Premonstratensians. But other orders and individual houses had a high reputation on a local basis and established spheres of influence, such as Fontevrault in central France, the Gilbertines in England, Camaldoli and Vallombrosa in Tuscany, and the canons of Rottenbuch and neo-Cluniac monks in Germany. Kings, great nobles, and regional prelates were in a position to steer new foundations in one direction or another. Otto of Bamberg founded nine houses of Cluniacs, two of Cistercians, and one of Premonstratensians in addition to others of which the affiliation is unknown. Otto of Freising in his own diocese established only houses of regular canons. Louis of Arnstein apparently chose the Premonstratensians because he had a cousin who had founded a Premonstratensian house.[108] These decisions may also have been influenced by policy factors, such as the willingness to perform pastoral work or to accept the control of a bishop or advocate. It was probably easier (and cheaper) to transform a parish church or a hermitage into a house

---

[106] *Fundatio monasterii Waldsassensis*, 7, in *MGH, SS*, XV.2, 1092, and *Vita Gileberti Sempinghamensis*, 13, ed. Foreville and Keir, pp. 40–2. At least some of these accounts of unsuccessful attempts to join the Cistercians may have been fabricated to satisfy the requirement that unaffiliated houses join a recognized order.

[107] Peregrinus, *Historia*, I, 6, ed. Salmon, p. 264. Cf. the description of the monks of Savigny and Clairvaux in whom the Gospel seemed to live again in Hugh of Kirkstall, *Narratio*, p. 20, cited p. 53 above.

[108] *Vita Ludovici de Arnstein*, ed. Widmann (n. 54), pp. 252–3.

of canons than of monks, and in some regions canons fitted better than monks into the emerging urban structures.[109] There were no clear dividing lines between the various forms of religious life, according to Christopher Brooke, who concluded that in the end many slight differences added up to major divisions.[110]

Personal influence and connections were often paramount. Men like Gerard of Brogne, Dunstan of Canterbury, Richard of St Vanne, and William of Dijon had established spheres of personal influence in the tenth and eleventh centuries, and the abbacies of Odilo and Hugh corresponded to the greatest period of Cluniac expansion. By the time Hugh died almost no one could remember the time when he had not been abbot of Cluny, which extended its influence both by establishing dependencies and through the customaries that were compiled in the second half of the eleventh century. Cluniac influence in Germany spread from Anchin, Siegburg, St Blaise, and particularly Hirsau, all of which followed Cluniac customs without being dependent on Cluny.[111] At the turn of the twelfth century Cluniac customs were introduced at St James in Liège and in 1107 into the old abbey of St Trond, where a copy of Bernard of Cluny's customary was made in the late 1160s, when it was no longer used at Cluny itself.[112] A modified version of Bernard's customary, made at Sahagún, was found in the twelfth century in many monasteries in Portugal, where the adoption of Cluniac customs was usually followed by an increase in the number of grants from lay benefactors.[113] The high prestige of Cluniac monasticism among the laity thus seems to have been a factor in the spread of Cluniac customs and, very likely, in the use of the term Cluniac for all old black monks.

In the early twelfth century the principal promoters of reform were wandering preachers like Robert of Arbrissel, Bernard of Tiron, Vitalis of Savigny, and Norbert of Xanten, who clearly exercised great influence not only in attracting people to the religious life but also in founding new houses. In the second quarter of the century, no one could touch the influence of Bernard of Clairvaux, who almost single-handedly assured the survival and success of the order of Cîteaux, which otherwise seems to have resembled other small regional eremitical orders. Bernard stands out as one of the few figures of his time (or, indeed, of any time) who was equally important as a writer and as

---

[109] Herbert (1985) and Postles (1993). See also Mortimer (1978) on the patronage of Augustinian and Premonstratensian houses by the family of Glanville.

[110] Brooke (1985), p. 129.

[111] In addition to Hallinger (1950–1), *passim*, see Feine (1954–5), pp. 81–2, on Cluniac influence in Germany; Semmler (1959), pp. 124–5; Massini (1946), pp. 150–2, on the diocese of Basel; and Violante (1979–81), and other essays in *Cluny in Lombardia* (1979–81), on north Italy, where most Cluniac dependencies were founded by lay lords in the last quarter of the eleventh century.

[112] See Stiennon (1951), pp. 281–6, and (1955), pp. 66–71, and Constable (1977a), pp. 216–23, with further references.

[113] Mattoso (1968), pp. 271–4 and 351.

a man of affairs. While he may have been somewhat less influential than some writers have suggested, since he by no means always got his way, it is clear that few contemporaries could resist his moral force and powers of persuasion. His conversion of Conrad III to the Second Crusade was considered the miracle of miracles by his biographer Philip of Clairvaux.[114] He seems to have almost instinctively resonated and responded to the enthusiasms and concerns of his contemporaries. At his behest founders rivalled each other in establishing and endowing Cistercian abbeys, and recruits flocked in to populate them. This success cannot be attributed entirely to Bernard's charismatic powers, since the Cistercian way of life and the constitution of the order clearly met the desires of many individuals and the needs of institutions that required, owing both to force of numbers and also sometimes to pressure from ecclesiastical authorities, a more structured type of life.[115] But Bernard knew how to make the most of this in presenting a combination of contemplation and action and of community life and solitude that corresponded to the religious sensibilities of his age.

The Cistercians were part of a broader movement, however, and must be seen in relation to other orders and individual houses that were inspired by the same ideals, and that were therefore at the same time rivals and emulators of Cîteaux. It must also be seen in relation to a long tradition of monastic development, going back through Molesme to Cluny, St Benignus of Dijon, and Marmoutier, and through them to the reforms of Benedict of Aniane and beyond, and also to Vallombrosa and the eremitical congregations of central Italy.[116] These inter-institutional currents are at the heart of medieval monastic history but have only begun to be studied because they often show themselves only as fragments in customaries and necrological documents and because many scholars have tended to concentrate on the histories of individual houses and orders rather than on inter-monastic tendencies.[117] In Germany in the twelfth century Cluniac features were found not only in known neo-Cluniac houses like Hirsau, from where they spread to other communities of monks, but also among the regular canons of Rottenbuch and Marbach and also, through Paulinzelle, in Cistercian abbeys like Georgenthal and Ichtershausen in Thuringia.[118] The earliest rules for canons, drawn up in the eighth and ninth centuries, drew on the rule of Benedict, and the regular canons of the twelfth century resembled contemporary reformed monks in many specific ways. The Premonstratensians in all probability made use of the customaries of Bernard of Cluny and of Hirsau as well as the *Summary of the charter of*

---

[114] Philip of Clairvaux, *Vita prima Bernardi*, VI (= *Miracula*), I, IV, 15, in Bernard, ed. Mabillon, II(6), 2289B (*BHL* 1225).
[115] Delaruelle (1967–8), p. 44, suggested that the Cistercians marked a transition between the traditional form of religious life and that of the itinerant hermits.
[116] See esp. Schneider (1960–1) and pp. 204–5 and 312 below.
[117] Wollasch (1973a), pp. 104–9, and Schieffer (1988).
[118] See Hofmeister (1938); Mois (1953), pp. 73–5; and Falck (1958).

love and early Cistercian legislation; the customs of Marbach, which were compiled about 1122/36, incorporated elements from Cluny, Hirsau, and St Rufus; and the constitutions of Arrouaise, of which the first redaction dates from about 1135, included Cistercian, Premonstratensian, and some Cluniac elements.[119] The rule of the little house of canons at Hérival drew on the rules of Caesarius of Arles, Benedict, and Columban as well as on the Premonstratensian and Grandmontine statutes.[120] When the first abbot of Rolduc in 1119 wanted to make the life of the canons stricter, he took various rules, according to the annals of Rolduc, 'from the customs of monks'; and when in 1141 the fourth abbot decided that the customs that 'had been brought into this place from the statutes of monks' were too severe, 'he changed some and lightened others with the consent (*asspiratione*) [which may mean 'to the relief'] of everyone'.[121]

Where exactly these cross-currents came from is unknown, but there was clearly an opportunity to pick and choose in developing a particular form of religious life. Rules and customaries doubtless circulated in manuscript form, and letters of exhortation and advice flowed between the various orders and houses, but the main channels of influence seem to have been through spiritual associations and personal contacts and visits. The congregation of Monte Cassino in a round letter written probably in the mid-1070s to several German monasteries, of which only the copy to Hersfeld survives, defended their own way of observing the rule of Benedict and criticized the Cluniacs, whose tonsure and habit they considered 'altogether against the rule'. At the end they said that it would take a month to describe their own customs and institutions and that if the house in question wanted to know more it should send a monk to Monte Cassino for at least a year.[122] This is interesting evidence of how an old monastery, which had no customary through which to spread its influence, made use of periods of residence. It is unknown why the great Cluniac customaries were compiled at the time they were, and later apparently abandoned at Cluny itself, but it was doubtless associated, if only obscurely, with its rapid expansion during the second half of the eleventh century and its rivalry at that time with other types of monasticism. Lampert of Hersfeld recorded in his *Annals* that after archbishop Anno of Cologne in 1071 replaced the canons at Saalfeld with reformed monks (who followed Cluniac customs) from Siegburg and St Pantaleon, Lampert himself spent fourteen weeks at Saalfeld and Siegburg in order to see how the customs of his own abbey could

---

[119] Lefèvre (1954); Siegwart (1965), p. 50–5; and *Constitutiones canonicorum regularium ordinis Arroasiensis*, in *CC:CM*, xx, xxx–viii and xlii–iii. On the influence of the *Carta caritatis*, see Dimier (1946), esp. 241–5.

[120] Galli (1959), pp. 18–19.

[121] *Annales Rodenses*, s.a. 1119 and 1141, ed. P.C. Boeren and G.W.A. Panhuysen (Assen 1968), fols. 8ʳ and 17ʳ–18ʳ, pp. 50 and 88–90.

[122] *Die ältere Wormser Briefsammlung*, ed. Walther Bulst, in *MGH, Briefe*, iii, 13–18, no. 1, with references to previous editions and discussions, esp. Hallinger (1950–1), pp. 450–1 and 709.

be brought into closer agreement with the rule of Benedict.[123] The way of life of the monks of Vallombrosa was greatly admired, and some scholars have attributed the resemblances between Cîteaux and Vallombrosa to Stephen Harding's visit there in the 1080s. Chézal-Benoît in the diocese of Bourges was founded by a monk of Vallombrosa, who 'taught his followers to serve God in great poverty and continence', and Urban II in a bull of 1099 established that the abbey should preserve 'the institution of the regular discipline . . . that you received according to the custom of the monks of Vallombrosa'.[124] Aybert of Crépin in about 1090 visited Vallombrosa and received from the monks there 'many documents of living rightly'.[125] The monks of Afflighem sought instruction from Anchin, 'because it was more celebrated than other monasteries both for brotherly love and for the strictness of holy religion'.[126] The founder of Holy Trinity Aldgate visited Mont-St-Eloy, Chartres, and Beauvais in order to study the life of regular canons under the Augustinian rule, which he introduced into England,[127] and Odo of Tournai went to Mont-St-Eloy and Watten 'where canons of the stricter life resided', before he restored St Martin at Tournai.[128] While some of these accounts may be apocryphal and designed to show a respectable genealogy for a particular way of life, they indicate what was probably the most important single source of the inter-institutional influences in the movement of reform.

The reformers did not all have the same objectives, but austerity of life, seclusion, regularity, silence, and manual labour clearly excited admiration and imitation. Lampert of Hersfeld's account of the enthusiasm of the lay people for the new monks at Cologne, who were regarded as angels rather than men, and of the alarm aroused by Anno's reform in the older monasteries, some of whose monks fled in fear of having to lead a stricter life, sheds some interesting light on the dynamics of the reform movement, which rarely followed a smooth course. The opponents of reform were not necessarily bad men, though Lampert admitted that they included some avaricious and simoniacal pseudo-monks, but they were set in their ways and opposed to change in principle as well as in practice. When the monks of Molesme were challenged

---

[123] Lampert of Hersfeld, *Annales*, s.a. 1071, ed. O. Holder-Egger (*MGH, SSRG*; Hanover and Leipzig 1894), pp. 132–3.

[124] *Analecta juris pontificii* 10 (1869), pp. 567–8 (JL 5789).

[125] Robert of Ostrevand, *Vita s. Ayberti*, 8, in *AASS*, 7 Apr. 1, 672 (*BHL* 180). See Duvernay (1952), pp. 461–3, and Dereine (1987), pp. 302–3.

[126] *Exordium monasterii Haffligiensis*, 5, ed. V. Coosemans and C. Coppens, in *Affligemensia* 4 (1947), p. 15.

[127] *Historia fundationis*, 6–8, ed. (with the *Historia* of William of Newburgh) Thomas Hearne (Oxford 1719), III, 694–6, and in *Cartulary of Holy Trinity Aldgate*, ed. Gerald A.J. Hodgett (London Record Society 7; London 1971), pp. 225–7, citing a letter from Anselm to the abbot of Mont-St-Eloy saying that Norman was coming to study its order and customs. At Chartres and Beauvais he wrote down the customs, including lists of the canons' clothing. See Luscombe (1962).

[128] Herman of Tournai, *De restauratione monasterii sancti Martini Tornacensis*, 4, in *MGH, SS*, XIV, 277.

by their abbot Robert to follow the rule *ex integro* and *per omnia*, in the account given by Ordericus Vitalis, they replied that conditions had changed since the days of the early monks, who (in the words of St Jerome) 'changed their necessity into their desire', and that 'the better is the enemy of the good',[129] and when prior Richard of St Mary at York spoke with his abbot 'concerning the correction of his monastery, . . . the lord abbot did not receive these words very cheerfully, since it is difficult to change established ways by the novelty of virtue'.[130] The old monks, like the cellarer whom Brillat-Savarin met in the late eighteenth century in a monastery where a strict new abbot had been appointed, were inclined at first not to worry and to say with him, 'Let him be as strict as he pleases, he will never have the heart to deprive an old man either of his corner by the fire or of the cellar keys.'[131]

When they were faced with the reality of having to change their way of life, they resisted both passively and actively. The evidence of this resistance is often distorted or omitted in the sources, most of which were written by sympathizers with the reform, but it was not underestimated or ignored by the reformers themselves. Bernard of Clairvaux is reported to have said that it is easier to inform than reform, and when Peter the Venerable was asked by Innocent II to restore the ancient abbey of Luxeuil to its 'privileged and pristine integrity', he told the pope that 'In matters of religion, new houses can be founded more easily than old ones can be repaired.'[132] Even more bluntly, Suger said concerning the reform of St Geneviève at Paris that 'Irregular [canons] will never consent to [be] regular canons except by force.'[133] Persuasion, or at least a velvet glove, was often necessary, and reforms that turned out to be too harsh and too external sometimes had to be modified in order not to turn away even those who were sympathetic and willing to lead a stricter life. The monks of Dalon, for instance, to which Obazine was subjected in 1142, were 'rough in manner and lacking in judgement'. 'They wearied the simplicity of the brothers with sudden novelties and harsh reprimands and brought their spirits to bitterness.'[134] A successful reformer had to be a spiritual leader as well as a disciplinarian, and in the overall picture of the movement it is remarkable that there was not more overt resistance and

---

[129] Ordericus Vitalis, *Historia ecclesiastica*, VIII, 26, ed. Chibnall, IV, 316–18, citing Jerome, *Vita s. Pauli primi eremitae*, 5, in *PL*, XXIII, 21A. They also stressed that they performed religious services, leaving agricultural work to the peasants, and that as clerics they were entitled to pastoral revenues. See Holdsworth (1985).

[130] Hugh of Kirkstall, *Narratio*, ed. Walbran, p. 21.

[131] Brillat-Savarin (1825), Misc. 22, p. 361.

[132] Gerald of Wales, *Speculum duorum*, 1, ed. Yves Lefèvre and R.B.C. Huygens (Board of Celtic Studies, University of Wales: History and Law Series 27; Cardiff 1974), pp. 42–4, and Peter the Venerable, *Ep.* 23, ed. Constable, I, 43.

[133] Suger, *Ep.* 7, ed. Lecoy de la Marche (n. 13), p. 255.

[134] *Vita Stephani Obazinensis*, II, 7, ed. Aubrun, p. 107. This experiment lasted only a few years, until Obazine joined the Cistercians, who proved better teachers.

that the reform influenced as many institutions as it did, both old and new, without greater opposition.

The monks in older houses sometimes saw the handwriting on the wall, as at Hersfeld, where Lampert was sent to discover how they could reform themselves. They welcomed reform out of genuine conviction and agreement with the purposes of the reformers. Ralph Waldo Emerson wrote to Carlyle at one point that 'We are all a little wild here with numberless projects of social reform',[135] and the same could be said of the early twelfth century, even without substituting 'religious' for 'social' in the sense Emerson was using it. There is a real parallel between the nineteenth-century utopian communities, which combined religious and social ends, and some of the twelfth-century religious communities, which not only attracted enthusiasts and idealists but touched the hearts of many others, including old monks and lay people who had no personal inclination to enter religious life. This change of mood can be seen at Bamberg, where, according to Lampert, bishop Herman created a scandal in about 1075 by replacing the canons in the church of St James with monks from Michaelsberg, not because the canons had done any harm but simply because he preferred monks.[136] A generation later it was the turn of the monks, according to Ebo's *Life* of bishop Otto, and they decided 'by common consent of the brothers' to abolish 'the old and defective order of Amorbach', which they had been following, and to replace it with 'the new and fully religious order of Hirsau', which was 'at that time most famous for the holy rigour of its spiritual order'.[137] The old reform movements of the tenth and early eleventh centuries were by this time the old guard. In the mid-twelfth century Otto of Freising told pope Eugene III that the monks of Tegernsee, who apparently adhered to the old reform traditions of Lorraine rather than 'the modern institutions and customs', argued that 'They could neither infringe nor change in any way the ancient statutes of that monastery without a great upheaval or indeed destruction of the place, both because the advocate would oppose it and because the men of the *familia*, who are called ministerials, said they would resist it to the death.' Otto put the case before the pope, adding that he knew no evil about the abbot or the monks.[138] A few years later, in 1160, a similar situation arose at Kremsmünster when the bishop of Passau imposed a new abbot from Admont, but whereas the monks of Tegernsee were truculent, those of Kremsmünster were pathetic, humbly requesting, as the

---

[135] Cited in Edel (1978), III, 137.
[136] Lampert of Hersfeld, *Annales*, s.a. 1075, ed. Holder-Egger (n. 123), pp. 203–4.
[137] Ebo, *Vita Ottonis*, I, 19 (20), ed. Jaffé (n. 3), pp. 608–9.
[138] Meichelbeck (1724–9), I, 331. This shows that the reformed customs would have affected the rights and powers of the abbey's advocate and ministerials. On this letter see Hallinger (1950–1), p. 630, dating it 1145/6; Bauerreiss (1949–70), III, 20–1 and 109; and Glaser (1958), p. 30 n. 28a, for further bibliography. Opposition to new customs was also expressed at Lorsch (*Chronicon Laureshamense*, 142, ed. Karl Glöckner (Darmstadt 1929, repr. 1963), I, 419–20), and at St Gall (*Casus s. Galli*, Cont. II, 7, s.a. 1086, in *MGH, SS*, II, 159).

archbishop of Salzburg said in a letter on their behalf to the abbot of Admont, that they be allowed to keep

> the way of reading and chanting that they had learned from boyhood and had made into a custom . . . They also asked that if some elements could be found among them that were useful and honest and consonant with the monastic religion, these should not be abolished together with those that needed correction, since the more they knew . . . that the sound would not be discarded together with the rotten the more willingly they would follow where the pious direction led them.[139]

A threatened reform could sometimes be averted. When the pope suggested that Norbert become abbot of St Martin at Laon in 1119, for instance, he expressed his readiness provided the canons would accept his programme 'not to seek the property of others, never to seek to recover what has been taken by secular pleas or judges or complaints, not to bind someone with the chain of anathema for any injury or damage that has occurred, but . . . by a clearer understanding to live a purely evangelical and apostolic life' as imitators of Christ, contemptors of the world, voluntary poor men 'suffering opprobria, scorn, hunger, thirst, nakedness, and the like, and obeying the decrees of the holy fathers'. The canons, according to the *Life* of Norbert, were horrified at these words and at Norbert's appearance and immediately replied that

> We do not want this man over us, since our custom and that of our predecessors has not known such a master. For our possessions will be taken and not returned; we shall plead without success; and we shall issue a sentence but it will not be feared. Let us live as we are; God wishes to castigate, not to mortify.[140]

Compromises were also possible, which protected the interests of the former members of a community while gradually introducing reforms. In the middle of the eleventh century at Aix-en-Provence, where the *episcopium* included three churches, a new chapter of regular canons was established at St Saviour alongside the old canons of St Mary, who adopted a common life and whose functions were taken over, after they died out about 1080, by the regular canons.[141] At St Quiriace in Provins, where count Theobald of Champagne introduced regular canons in about 1140, there were two parallel communities until the old secular canons agreed to keep their benefices for their lifetimes and then to be replaced by the newcomers. After Theobald died in 1152, however, the remaining old canons appealed to both the new count and pope

---

[139] Hansitz (1727–55), I, 318–20. See von Meiller (1866), pp. 89 and 466. Members of the *familia* here, unlike Tegernsee, offered fidelity and reverence, but the dispute dragged on for some time before it was finally settled. For the difficulty created at Glastonbury by the abbot's effort to introduce new chants, see Florence of Worcester, *Chronicon*, s.a. 1082, ed. Benjamin Thorpe (English Historical Society; London 1848–9), II, 16–17. See Huglo (1956).
[140] *Vita* [A] *Norberti*, 9, in *MGH, SS*, XII, 678–9 (*BHL* 6248).
[141] Laurent (1952), pp. 185 and 188–90.

Adrian IV, and the two chapters were eventually separated.[142] A similar arrangement is described in Adrian's bull of 1155/9 concerning the church of Namèche, near Huy, where Cluny and the local nobles agreed 'that when the clerics died, Cluniac monks would succeed in their place'.[143]

Reforms of existing institutions almost always involved some pain and difficulty, and the reformers occasionally met with resistance and open violence. Several efforts were made to kill Norbert, and the attempt of the monks of St Gildas in Brittany to poison Abelard was presumably the result of his efforts to reform them.[144] Some or all of the previous members of a reformed house might have to be expelled. Bishop Berengar of Vic in about 1080 expelled all the canons 'on account of their bad behaviour . . . since I could not correct their life in any other way'. He then brought together a few canons 'who wished to live canonically' with other religious men, including the abbot of St Rufus at Avignon, which was an important centre of canonical reform, and held a council with these people and 'with the *majores* of this church so that I would impose on them a form of institution adapted to their state of weakness, through which they might behave better'.[145] One of the most notorious cases in the twelfth century was in 1150 at Compiègne, where the canons (who included king Louis VII's brother Philip) resisted the combined efforts of Suger and the bishop of Noyon to introduce monks. They seized the relics, barricaded the doors, cut the bell-ropes to prevent the alarm from being sounded, and were finally subdued only by a show of force. Suger later wrote to Eugene III that this and the reform of St Geneviève were the two hardest tasks imposed upon him by the pope or king.[146]

The example of Compiègne and the reforms at Tegernsee and Namèche suggest that the resistance was likely to be stronger, and more successful, when the incumbents had the support of an important individual – the king's brother or the advocate – or of a local power, such as the nobility or ministerials, whose interests were threatened by the proposed reform. Townsmen could be fickle in their religious loyalties. Lampert of Hersfeld said that the people of Cologne, who in 1071 had welcomed the new monks at St Pantaleon, were ready to kill them during the revolt in 1074 'because when the previous monks had been expelled by the archbishop, he had established there a new and unaccustomed type of religion'.[147] Many bishops and abbots, especially of old black houses, were unfavourably inclined towards the reformers, whose

---

[142] Veissière (1961), pp. 39–46.

[143] Miraeus–Foppens, II, 1172–3 (JL 10466).

[144] *Vita* [B] *Norberti*, XVI, 96, in *PL*, CLXX, 1327BC (*BHL* 6249), and Abelard, *Historia calamitatum*, ed. J.T. Muckle, in *Mediaeval Studies* 12 (1950), p. 209. See Miethke (1972), pp. 170–9.

[145] *España sagrada*, XXVIII, 290–1. On Berengar's nineteen-point reform programme, see pp. 184–5 below.

[146] See the letter from bishop Baldwin of Noyon to pope Eugene III in Duchesne, *Scriptores*, IV, 544–5, and Constable (1986a), p. 21.

[147] Lampert of Hersfeld, *Annales*, s.a. 1074, ed. Holder-Egger (n. 123), p. 190.

popularity and independence might undermine existing economic and political interests. Great institutions normally know how to defend themselves, and monasteries in the Middle Ages tended to be less squeamish about their methods than they are today. New houses often faced the hostility of the regional ecclesiastical powers or of a local monastery that did its best either to absorb or to drive away the newcomers.[148]

Resistance to reform was not always selfish or unreasonable. The replacement of secular canons by regular canons or monks, and of canonesses by nuns, raised serious questions in the minds not only of those who were directly involved, like the canons of St James at Bamberg, who pointed out to the bishop that canons were better suited than monks to serve an urban church, but also of other observers of the broader ecclesiastical scene. Ivo of Chartres wrote to the bishop of Poitiers in 1094 that by replacing canons with monks in a particular church he had injured the order of clerics and promoted the pride of monks, who should follow a single life of humility and obedience.[149] Any involuntary reform or change of order was a blow to the self-esteem both of the members of the house involved and of other members of their order. The strong feelings aroused by cases of *transitus* and the occasional insistence that a fugitive return were primarily the result of injured dignity. The canons of Sainte-Barbe in Normandy insisted that a canon who had gone to the white monks come back 'lest the order, being recent in these parts, be brought into contempt by the pretext of being less strict'.[150] Peter the Venerable was outraged when Premonstratensian canons replaced monks of St Paul in Verdun. If the monks were bad, he wrote to Matthew of Albano, let them at least be replaced by other monks, not by clerics.[151] The blow was particularly serious because monks were commonly considered, and considered themselves, superior to canons. To become a monk from a canon was a step up – which explains why so many canons were forced to become, or were replaced by, monks[152] – whereas for a monk to become a canon was a step down. In point of fact, however, many regular canons were stricter than monks, and changes from monks to regular canons were not uncommon. At the ancient house of St Antonin in Rouergue, for instance, Gregory VII installed regular canons in place of the monks who apparently observed no regular life, and at Grimberghen in the diocese of Cambrai the Augustinian canons, who 'accomplished nothing', were replaced first by monks, who suffered from poverty and per-

---

[148] Vidier (1906), p. 81.

[149] Ivo, *Ep.* 36, ed. Jean Leclercq (CHFMA 22; Paris 1949), pp. 150–2.

[150] *Chronicon de s. Barbara in Algia*, ed. R.-Norbert Sauvage, in *Mémoires de l'Académie nationale des sciences, arts et belles-lettres de Caen: Documents*, 1906, p. 35.

[151] Peter the Venerable, *Ep.* 47, ed. Constable, I, 145; see II, 130.

[152] See the *Vita Bertholdi Garstensis*, 2, ed. Lenzenweger (n. 24), pp. 228–9, describing the foundation of Garsten by marquis Otakar II, who forced many priests to become monks in Austria, where 'the habitations of monks were very rare' in the early twelfth century.

secution, and then by Premonstratensians.[153] At Frasnes-les-Goselles monks were installed in place of the canons, who had departed one by one in the late eleventh century owing to 'the intolerable poverty of the place',[154] whereas the bishop of Csanád in the early thirteenth century established secular canons in the former abbey of Ittebö because it was too poor to support either monks or regular canons.[155]

It was in many ways easier to establish a new house than to reform an existing one. A majority of houses of new strict monks and regular canons in the twelfth century were new communities formed either by a migration from an existing house, like Cîteaux and Fountains, or by a new group gathered around a nucleus of founding members, like Fontaines-les-Blanches. New houses required material as well as spiritual foundations, and even the humblest and poorest community had to have some land, buildings, books, vestments, and other supplies. The role of the material patrons, as contrasted with the spiritual founders, was often spelled out in the foundation charter, which was a record of the rights both of the community and of the patrons and their families. The *Lives* of founders and the histories of foundations, on the other hand, tended to emphasize the initiative of the spiritual founders and often played down the role of the patrons, who might lay claim to the position of advocate or other rights over the monastery,[156] which could serve as a centre of family influence. Some patrons, like Louis of Arnstein, became members of their own houses, or joined them later. Others retained important rights, such as the appointment of the superior, collation of prebends, collection of dues and revenues, exercise of jurisdiction, and the right to military service. These differed from house to house, and the efforts of the monasteries to limit and if possible abolish these rights, while still retaining the help and protection of which they occasionally stood in need, were frequently at odds with the interests of the patrons and their families in maintaining and extending their prerogatives. Throughout the eleventh and twelfth centuries, however, the combination of social prestige and of spiritual and material benefits was sufficiently attractive to inspire the patrons without whom the monastic expansion would have been impossible.[157]

The interests of the spiritual founders and material patrons occasionally clashed at the time of foundation, since even the most generous patrons as a

---

[153] Constable and Somerville (1992), and Miraeus–Foppens, I, 96–7. At St Martin of Laon the secular canons were replaced first by regular canons and in 1124 by Premonstratensians who lived 'the eremitical life under the canonical profession': Hugo (1734–6), I.1, xliii.

[154] Miraeus–Foppens, I, 670–1.

[155] *Vetera monumenta historica Hungariam sacram illustrantia*, ed. Aug. Theiner (Rome, Paris, and Vienna 1859–60), I, 22–3, no. 37.

[156] See Despy (1957) on Villers, of which the early records omit any reference to the founders, and Despy (1968) on Orval, with a reply by Grégoire (1969).

[157] According to Bouchard (1987), p. 238, 'The attempt to discover ubiquitous political and economic motivations in sources that express nothing of the kind seems more an artifact of the modern, secular and suspicious age than an insight into the way that medieval men behaved.'

rule hoped to get away as cheaply as possible, whereas many of the monks were shrewd judges of the quality of land and of building sites and insisted, occasionally with the aid of visions and miracles, on being given a location that the donors were reluctant to part with.[158] In this respect the reformers had an important advantage over the old monks because they preferred to settle on isolated and uncultivated lands that they could work themselves, whereas the old monks and canons, who spent most of their time in church and little in manual labour, required working estates in order to fill their material needs. The reformers not only wanted to live away from other people and work with their hands but also to avoid the claims and obligations, ecclesiastical as well as secular, that almost inevitably accompanied settled lands and involved their owners in disputes and lawsuits. *Qui terram habet guerram habet* was a well-known medieval motto,[159] and when they could the reformers avoided all kinds of conditional and partial tenures and insisted on full ownership and control (often expressed as *plena libertas* or *allodium*) over their lands. Hermits likewise sought to own the lands on which they lived in order to protect themselves from expulsion and oppression and from legal entanglements. The founders of Joux, according to a charter of bishop Stephen of Autun in 1104, wanted 'to live apart (*secreti*) from men and to devote themselves to manual labour without the controversy and insolence of men', and the founders of Miseray in 1112 sought to lead 'a solitary and theoretical life . . . without tithe or tribute' and free from all other claims.[160] The Grandmontines represented the logical extreme of this position in their refusal to accept any lands 'outside the boundaries of their own places' or to go to law under any circumstances.[161]

The Cistercians, Carthusians, and some others of the new monks, when they could not get previously uncultivated lands, removed the existing settlers in order to obtain lands that they could work themselves and were free of any claims. One of the best examples of this policy in England is the foundation of Revesby, where the earl of Lincoln in 1142 offered either other lands or the freedom 'to go and live where they wanted' to the men of three villages, of whom seven took the option of land and thirty-one the option of free-

---

[158] Plandé (1932), p. 30. For examples of foreseen sites, see Geoffrey *Grossus, Vita Bernardi Tironensis,* 65, in *PL,* CLXXII, 1407A (*BHL* 1251), and *Vita Gaufridi Castaliensis,* I, 1, ed. Bosvieux (n. 57), pp. 80–1. Norbert's site was already called Prémontré when he settled there, according to the *Vita* [B] *Norberti,* 39, in *PL,* CLXX, 1284B (*BHL* 6249). On the sites of new houses in the Vendômois, see Barthélemy (1993), pp. 191–4.

[159] Coulton (1929–50), III, 507–9.

[160] *GC,* XII, *instr.,* 106, and II, *instr.,* 57–9. See also ibid., 315, on Gerald of La Sauve-Majeur, who entered solitude in 1180 in order to escape *saecularia negotia.*

[161] *Regula Stephani Muretensis,* 4 and 23, in *CC:CM,* VIII, 71–2 and 81–2. According to Peter Comestor, writing in Paris in 1159/78 and basing himself on an anonymous Laon authority, contemplatives might ask for restitution but not go to law: Smalley (1979), p. 126.

dom[162] – though what they did with their freedom is unfortunately not recorded. When count William III of Nevers gave some land to Pontigny in 1156 he said that 'Since it seemed too harsh to the monks of Pontigny to expel on their account the inhabitants of this villa from their possessions, I made acceptable compensation to these men so that they left of their own accord and released the place to the monks in peace.'[163] At Rufford, when the Cistercians bought off the claims of some peasants, they specified that 'If any of them touched by a desire to serve God or forced by infirmity wishes to come to them [the monks], they will receive them as seems to them expedient.'[164] This suggests that some of them may have become lay brothers or even monks.

A new community needed buildings as well as lands. Many reformers made use of deserted churches, which gratified their sense of rebuilding the church physically as well as spiritually and at the same time reduced the possibility of invading established ecclesiastical rights or of creating new ones.[165] When Robert of La Chaise-Dieu was looking for a deserted and dilapidated church in which to live with his followers, he specified that it should be a parish church, 'lest by establishing a new oratory on someone else's property they do injury to the old places'.[166] The number of references to the occupation of deserted churches by reformers suggests that it was a topos, but the effects of the Norse and Magyar raids were still evident in some regions where the reformers were active, especially in western and central France, and the civil disturbances of the eleventh and twelfth centuries had left many deserted churches and monasteries.[167] Ordericus Vitalis said that the buildings of St Evroul returned to forest within fifty years after they were abandoned; the monks of Durham renewed and put a new roof on the church of Tynemouth, which had been deserted for fifteen years; and Robert of Knaresborough used

---

[162] *Facsimiles of Early Charters from Northamptonshire Collections*, ed. F.M. Stenton (Northamptonshire Record Society 4; Lincoln and London 1930), pp. 1–7.

[163] *Le premier cartulaire de l'abbaye cistercienne de Pontigny (XIIᵉ–XIIIᵉ siècles)*, ed. Martine Garrigues (Collection de documents inédits sur l'histoire de France. Section de philologie et d'histoire jusqu'à 1610. Série in-8° 14; Paris 1981), p. 156, no. 85.

[164] Barley (1957), p. 80.

[165] On this theme in Franciscan ideology, see Peters (1986).

[166] Marbod of Rennes, *Vita Roberti*, II, 8, in *AASS*, 24 Apr. III, 321 (*BHL* 7261).

[167] On the sense of devastation still felt in some regions in the eleventh and twelfth centuries, see the *De commendatione Turonicae provinciae*, in *Recueil de chroniques de Touraine*, ed. André Salmon (Société archéologique de Touraine I; Tours 1854), p. 306, and the *Chronicon Mauriniacense*, ed. Léon Mirot, 2nd edn (CTSEEH 41; Paris 1912), pp. 5–6. These should be compared with the late twelfth-century account of the 'good old days' in the county of Anjou in the tenth century in *Chronica de gestis consulum Andegavorum*, ed. Louis Halphen and René Poupardin (CTSEEH 48; Paris 1913), pp. 36–7. According to Herman of Tournai, *De restauratione s. Martini Tornacensis*, 6, in *MGH, SS*, XIV, 277, the old church occupied by Odo had been destroyed by vandals. See Nazet (1983), who argued that more damage was done by secularizations and mismanagement than by the Normans or Hungarians.

as his first hermitage a church in the village destroyed by king Stephen.[168] The reformers were also sometimes given established settlements and castles, as at Arnstein, which was transformed from a soldiers' *castrum* into a *domum orationis*.[169]

The wilderness and solitude in which the new houses were often said to be located was a topos based on the description of the desert as 'a place of horror and vast wilderness' in Deuteronomy 32.10. They were usually much closer than the sources suggest to settled areas and to roads and rivers, as the contradictory topos of hospitality shows. The Carthusians were almost the only organized order that seems to have sought true isolation in high places, and they often had to acquire alternative sites at lower altitudes in order to escape the cold and to grow grapes.[170] The romantic names of many Cistercian abbeys, which have led some writers to believe that they were located in distant valleys and inaccessible mountains, were chosen to indicate their spiritual, rather than their physical, beauty and solitude.[171] Even in eastern Europe and Poland the Cistercians usually settled on or near settled lands and did not play a major role in clearing new land.[172] The paradoxical combination of being cut off in spirit while close to other people in fact is brought out in the history of the abbey of Selby, which after praising in characteristic phrases the dense forest, flowing rivers, and abundant quarries, all suggesting physical isolation, said that

> The monastery sat so beautifully and so notably in its hidden retreat that the towers of the church and other roofs of its buildings . . . were visible from every side by those coming from afar along public roads . . . Whatever was brought by boat from York from across the sea or from any part of England, or was taken from York, passed before the gates of the monastery of Selby.[173]

In spite of the care that was usually taken in the choice of sites, many of the new houses had to move, sometimes more than once. No less than twenty-nine of the Cistercian abbeys in England moved at one time or another, usually to places where there was an ample supply of water.[174] There is no evidence

[168] Ordericus Vitalis, *Historia ecclesiastica*, VI, 10, ed. Chibnall, III, 328–30; *Liber vitae ecclesiae Dunelmensis*, ed. Joseph Stevenson (Surtees Society 13; Durham 1841), pp. 66–7, cf. the facsimile, ed. A. Hamilton Thompson (Surtees Society 136; Durham 1923), fol. 46ᵛ, and intro., pp. xxiii–iv; and *Vita* [A] *Roberti Knaresburgensis*, ed. Paul Grosjean, in *Anal. boll.* 57 (1939), p. 369 (*BHL* 7270d). See *Cartulaire de Saint-Jean-d'Angély*, ed. Georges Musset (Archives historiques de la Saintonge et de l'Aunis 30 and 33; Paris and Saintes 1901–3), I, 83–5, and II, 8–9, nos. 56 (*c*. 1088) and 344 (*c*. 1098), for examples of ruined churches given to monks for restoration and renewal.
[169] *Vita Ludovici de Arnstein*, ed. Widmann (n. 54), pp. 250–1. See Ehlers (1973) on this and other examples, and esp. Lewald (1976).
[170] Dubois (1971), pp. 24–6.
[171] Dimier (1944).
[172] Swiechowski and Zachwatowicz (1958), p. 143.
[173] *Historia monasterii Selebiensis*, 11, ed. Fowler (n. 2), p. [13].
[174] Donkin (1959).

supporting the old canard that the early Cistercians purposely chose unhealthy sites for the spiritual health of the monks, and they were in fact more concerned than most orders with the problems of sanitation and water supplies.[175] A community might outgrow its original site, or need new or different types of land. The hermitage of Le Reclus moved 'from an arid and unfertile place . . . to a richer and more commodious place' when it joined the Cistercians, and Clairvaux itself moved in 1135/6 owing to its need for vineyards.[176] Some moves were motivated by the hostility of neighbours or by the excess of admiring visitors. The two houses of St Martin and St Nicholas at Tournai apparently both relocated on account of the proximity of the town, and Mortemer in Normandy moved from an exposed location to 'a more secret valley . . . far from the disturbance of secular men and removed from [their] sight'.[177] Solitary life was not without its dangers. A hermit at Vicogne was strangled and thrown into a well, and one at Windberg was murdered by a jealous companion who was 'moved by envy of the greater grace divinely granted to him, and grief that he [himself] appeared unequal'.[178] The problems were multiplied in eastern Europe, and the Cistercians from Walkenried moved to Pforte from Schmölln because it 'was unsuited to their way of life owing to the closeness of the barbarians, the persecution of wicked men, and the difficulty of the location', in addition to the fact that 'Religion would have no succession there since there were few or no recruits on account of the barbarity of the people.'[179]

Even after a satisfactory permanent site was found for a new community, there were many difficulties to be surmounted before it could be called an established house. Among these were the need to choose a recognized rule and way of life. The dislike of the ecclesiastical authorities for independent and unaffiliated houses, and their fear of the growing diversity of forms of religious life, culminated in the decree of the Fourth Lateran Council in 1215 requiring anyone who wanted to enter religious life to choose a house of an

---

[175] Gougaud (1930), pp. 1–13, and Dimier (1943–4) and (1955b).

[176] *GC*, XII, *instr.*, 264 and 270; d'Arbois de Jubainville (1858), p. 120; and Robert Fossier, in *Bernard de Clairvaux* (1953), pp. 101–3.

[177] Herman of Tournai, *De restauratione monasterii s. Martini Tornacensis*, 39, in *MGH, SS*, XIV, 291 (it was later required to return); *Fundatio monasterii s. Nicolai de Pratis Tornacensis*, 3, in *MGH, SS*, XV.2, 1114; and *Fundatio monasterii Mortuimaris*, 10, ed. J. Bouvet, in *Collectanea ordinis Cisterciensium reformatorum* 22 (1960), p. 153. The abbey of Silvanès moved 'owing to the arrogance of lay men and many other inconveniences', according to Hugh of Silvanès, *De conversione Pontii de Larazio*, 23, in Baluze, *Miscellanea*, I, 183–4. See also the old French history of the regular canons of Wigmore, who moved when their original location became 'trop estreit et hidous', in Dugdale, *Monasticon*, VI.1, 346.

[178] *Historia monasterii Viconiensis*, 6, in *MGH, SS*, XXIV, 296, and *Historiae Windbergenses*, 3, in *MGH, SS*, XVII, 562. In the late twelfth century two successive hermits were murdered at the priory of Franchard near Fontainbleau: see Stephen of Tournai, *Ep.* 188, ed. Desilve, p. 230, and Estournet (1913), pp. 296–7.

[179] See the charter of bishop Odo of Naumburg in 1140 in *Urkundenbuch des Klosters Pforte*, ed. Paul Boehme, I (Geschichtsquellen der Provinz Sachsen 33; Halle 1893), p. 4, no. 3.

approved order and any new religious house to follow the rule of an approved order.[180] Long before this, however, communities were faced with the problem of finding a rule suited to their needs and desires. Permanent buildings were needed, and the means to construct them had to be found, since few communities had the necessary resources or skills to build a church and conventual buildings entirely by themselves. The chronicler of Ebrach said that 'An outstanding monastery was built, where formerly there were dens of robbers, with such speed and zeal that the entire work was completed, with the help of God, in the seventh year.'[181] Elsewhere the work dragged on for years and was a constant drain on the energy and resources of the community. The changes in architectural styles of the buildings sometimes reflect the development of the order, as among the Cistercians, whose first buildings usually show the persistence of regional architectural features. In the second quarter of the twelfth century the dominance of Clairvaux II and Fontenay indicate the increasing centralization of the order and gave way in the later twelfth century to the influence of Gothic.[182] Changes like these had practical repercussions for individual houses, which had to import workers and designers from considerable distances.

There was in addition the constant problem of recruits, especially as the first generation of members of a new community died out and was replaced by new and different members who did not share the memories and ideals of the early years. Communities occasionally split, both old ones like Molesme and St Mary at York, and new ones like Fontaines-les-Blanches. The prestige of a new house might look more attractive to new recruits than its way of life proved in reality. Ordericus Vitalis said in his account of the early history of the Cistercians that 'Mixed with the good men were hypocrites, who clad in white and various costumes deceived men and made a great spectacle to the people. Many men wanted to resemble the true worshippers of God in form but not in virtue; and by their numbers they disgusted those who observed them and made the proven cenobites look more despicable.'[183]

The most significant and dangerous period of institutional development usually came in the second generation, after the death or departure of the founders and their immediate followers, who provided both inspiration and guidance.[184] The Grandmontines were exceptional in successfully following

---

[180] IV Lateran (1215), 13, in *Conc. oec. decreta*, p. 242 (cited p. 2 n. 8 above).

[181] *Fundatio monasterii Ebracensis*, in *MGH*, *SS*, xv.2, 1040.

[182] Beuer (1957) and Elm (1994), pp. 16–17, with further references. See p. 39 n. 172 above for references on the generational shifts in Cistercian art and architecture.

[183] Ordericus Vitalis, *Historia ecclesiastica*, VIII, 26, ed. Chibnall, IV, 326. See p. 64 above on the misfits at Petershausen, and Luchaire (1899), p. 129, on the measures taken by the bishop of Nantes against an unordained hermit who celebrated mass.

[184] Hostie (1972), pp. 314–15, proposed, largely on the basis of the histories of modern orders, a life-cycle starting with a period of gestation (10–20 years) and followed by periods of consolidation (20–40 years), spread (100 years), stabilization (100 years), and decline and extinction (50–100 years).

the life and words of their founder, without adopting another rule or customs, and even they were forced to write down his precepts as the living memory of his principles and way of life died out. Stephen of Tournai may have expressed a deeper truth than he knew when he said that they must be called *vitales* because they followed the *Vita* of their founder. This process of institutionalization was almost inevitably accompanied by a sense of loss of intimacy and dedication among the older members, who looked back on the early years as a golden age. There is a moving passage in the *Life* of Stephen of Obazine saying that Stephen's discipline was strongest at first, when his followers were 'both fewer in number and more perfect in life'. It then went on, 'And since no law of any order was held to be fixed, the institutes of the master were in place of a law, which taught only humility, obedience, poverty, and discipline and, above all, continual love . . . This law was promulgated then, and no attention was paid to pharisaical traditions.'[185]

Almost every new house that survived and flourished later went through a painful period, sometimes amounting to an institutional crisis, as it grew in wealth and numbers and had to adopt a rule and develop customs and traditions.[186] This was often also the time when an account of its foundation and early history, which was no longer enshrined in the memories of its members, was written down in the light of, and sometimes to justify, the subsequent developments. A crisis of confidence might be caused by a lack of material resources or of recruits, as seems to have taken place early in the history of Cîteaux, before the arrival of Bernard and his followers,[187] or by a migration of a group of members to another house. The difficulties in the order of Savigny, such as its quarrel with Furness, which looks on the surface like a rebellious daughter-house asserting its independence, were in part the result of deep-seated constitutional weaknesses and were not entirely solved by its entry into the order of Cîteaux.[188] The crises at Arrouaise, Rottenbuch, Springiersbach, and other houses of regular canons in the middle of the twelfth century seem to have been brought on by a lack of constitutional and economic development to match their growing size and complexity after the deaths of the founders.[189]

Some of the most serious of these problems were associated with lay brothers. The first known case, at Sempringham, began in about 1165 and was not finally settled until 1178. It involved both pope Alexander III and

---

[185] *Vita Stephani Obazinensis*, I, 16, ed. Aubrun, p. 70.
[186] D'Haenens (1962), pp. 102–3, said that outside opinion concerning St Martin at Tournai shifted from initial enthusiasm to hostility to indifference. See also Dereine (1959), p. 44.
[187] See [Ducourneau] (1932–3), (5) pp. 178–80.
[188] See the letters from Hugh of Rouen to Henry of York and from Aelred of Rievaulx to the Cistercian general chapter, ed. Léopold Delisle, in *Journal of the British Archaeological Society* 6 (1851), pp. 422–4. Cf. Dugdale, *Monasticon*, V, 247, no. 4.
[189] Milis (1969), p. 591; Mois (1953), pp. 304–5; and Pauly (1962), pp. 59–64. On Springiersbach, see also Erkens (1987), pp. 30–40.

king Henry II in addition to a number of bishops, who rallied to the support of the elderly patriarch of English holy men and who have been followed by modern scholars in their condemnation of the lay brothers.[190] The merits of the matter are still not entirely clear, but the early support given to the lay brothers by the pope and Thomas Becket suggests that there may have been some justification for their charge of scandal and harsh treatment. Burchard of Bellevaux's treatise on the beards of lay brothers, which was written in the early 1160s, shows that there were complaints about the Cistercian lay brothers.[191] The Cistercians, Premonstratensians, and Grandmontines all experienced serious problems with their lay brothers. Among the Cistercians the cause appears to have been the inferior status and menial duties of the lay brothers, whereas among the Grandmontines, who were neither clerics nor monks and who clung to their eremitical and lay status, the difficulty seems to have been in the changing character of the order, and especially the growing number of priests in relation to lay brothers during the second half of the twelfth century and the control over secular affairs exercised by lay brothers, whom the priests served almost as chaplains.[192] Whatever the precise reasons for these problems, they show that the lay brothers were not an unmixed blessing for the new houses.

The diversity of types of religious life in the twelfth century, even when it was accepted in theory, introduced tensions and rivalries that were unknown in early medieval monasticism. The perception of a hierarchy of strictness put many communities and individuals into a painful position, and the charismatic individuality of the founders heightened the competition by fostering a sense of the special character of each community. The development of orders created constitutional problems, just as the institution of lay brothers had unforeseen consequences for the internal structure of religious communities. As these and other problems were faced and overcome in separate houses and orders, there was an overall, unconscious movement towards greater uniformity and traditional solutions. In the long run this reduced the extent of difference not only among the new houses and orders but also between them and the old houses, which at the same time moved along parallel lines, pushed by the influence both of shared ideals and problems and by the spirit of competition. As the age of experiment drew to a close, and the more radical reformers moved into new and different types of activities, traditional ideals and institutional patterns reasserted themselves within the monastic order and brought the great period of change and development to an end.

[190] See *Vita Gileberti Sempinghamensis*, 25, ed. Foreville and Keir, pp. 76–84, and intro., pp. lv–lx, and references there and in Constable (1995b) and Golding (1995), pp. 40–51.

[191] Burchard of Bellevaux, *Apologia de barbis*, in *CC:CM*, LXII, 151–224, and intro., pp. 138–9, and, generally, Donnelly (1949) and McGuire (1983b), p. 56.

[192] Becquet (1960), pp. 295 and 322–3. The papacy redressed the balance in favour of the clerics and in the thirteenth century the lay brothers revolted. On transfers to the Cistercians, which were defended by Peter of Celle and Stephen of Tournai, see p. 105 and n. 98 above.

4

THE RHETORIC OF REFORM

THE original texts concerned with the reform of religious life in the eleventh and twelfth centuries are filled with references to liberty and the spirit of liberty; to solitude and poverty; to the integrity, rectitude, perfection, purity, simplicity, and strictness of the rule; to the imitation of Christ, the apostolic life, and the primitive church; and to exile and peregrination. Almost the entire spiritual message of the movement is summed up in the precepts *Scito te ipsum, Nudus nudum Christum sequi*, and *Habe caritatem et quod uis fac*,[1] and in the maxims *Diversi sed non adversi*, truth against custom, and the aging world nearing its end. A few biblical texts were cited again and again as stimuli to a life of personal reform and withdrawal from the world, above all 'If any man will come after me, let him deny himself and take up the cross and follow me' from Matthew 16.24 and 'If thou wilt be perfect, go sell what thou hast and give to the poor' from Matthew 19.21, and the corresponding passages in Mark and Luke, together with Paul's dictum that 'Where the spirit of the Lord is, there is liberty' in 2 Corinthians 3.17 and his censure in Philippians 2.21 of those who 'seek the things that are their own; not the things that are Jesus Christ's'. The parable of the sower and the episode of Christ's visit to the house of Mary and Martha were used to illustrate the rewards of those who dedicated themselves to Christ, and the description in Acts 2.44 and 4.32 of the apostles and early Christians who had 'but one heart and one soul' and 'all things in common' set the standard for Christian community life. The writers of saints' *Lives* and other works of spirituality constantly used metaphors of ascent and descent, birth, growth, aging, and death, and images drawn from the world of the senses, of flowers, plants, and trees, of seas, storms, and harbours, and of fires dying down and flaring up again, and they had a rich vocabulary of topoi going back to Antiquity to describe almost every aspect of the personal lives of the saints, such as the nobleman made

---

[1] Variations on these maxims, which will be referred to below, include *Nosce te ipsum, Pauper pauperem Christum sequi*, and *Dilige et quod vis fac*. The importance of formulaic and mythical thought and models in Antiquity and the Middle Ages has been studied by various scholars, including Hadot (1983), pp. 37–40, and Stock (1983), pp. 16, 58, and *passim*, who stressed the role of texts as organizers of thought and action in the eleventh and twelfth centuries.

humble, and the nature of their monasteries, which resembled paradise, the Garden of Eden, and the heavenly Jerusalem.[2]

Together these may be called the rhetoric of the reform, which shaped the thinking not only of people at the time but also of later scholars, who have taken them at face value without always recognizing their rhetorical character. Rhetoric, like ritual, has a bad name today. It implies form without substance and words without conviction. Political rhetoric has come to mean almost the opposite of truth – what politicians say without sincerity. Paul contrasted ten thousand words said with the tongue with the five words said with understanding (1 Corinthians 14.19), which was another popular biblical text in the twelfth century, and Robert of Arbrissel in his letter to Ermengard of Brittany warned against prayers said with the lips but not with the heart.[3] Like propaganda, which also played a part in the ecclesiastical politics of the eleventh and twelfth centuries,[4] rhetoric suggests the art of persuading for selfish and partisan ends. It often holds up a mirror to what people want, however, and shapes their actions as well as their thoughts, and it cannot be neglected by historians. Rhetorical images and devices lie on the borderline between illusion and reality. Just as the image of the pipe-smoking professor in a tweed jacket with leather elbow-patches – a topos if there ever was one – both reflected and shaped the clothing and behaviour of university teachers, so the images and language studied in this chapter shaped the realities of medieval religious life. People were well aware of this in the Middle Ages, when rhetoric was esteemed not only as an academic discipline going back to classical Antiquity but also as an essential tool for men of affairs who wanted to influence behaviour.[5] The art of writing persuasive letters and giving convincing speeches was essential to the conduct of practical affairs, and many of the reformers were masters of rhetorical techniques. Bernard of Clairvaux's unique combination of sincerity and eloquence, which drew on many of the tricks of the rhetorician's trade, swept countless men and women into the religious houses of Europe, swelled the ranks of the crusading armies, and more than once induced hard-headed rulers and prelates to act against their own best interests and judgement. The mere sound of his voice as a preacher was enough in some cases to move to tears people who could not understand his words.[6]

Rhetoricians tend to make use of time-tested formulas and techniques, such as the *captatio benivolentiae*, which is still used by speech-makers today, and

---

[2] See Thoss (1972), p. 2, and Dronke (1986b), pp. xii–xix and 11–22, who said that topoi guided argument in medieval logic and *inventio* in medieval rhetoric (p. xix).
[3] Robert of Arbrissel, *Sermo ad comitissam Britanniae*, ed. J. de Petigny, in *Bibliothèque de l'Ecole des chartes* 15 (3 S. 5) (1854), p. 232. See pp. 34–5 above and 201 below.
[4] Constable (1983) and the references in n. 23 below.
[5] On the revival of interest in and study of rhetoric in the twelfth century, see Janet Martin, in *Renaissance and Renewal* (1982), pp. 538–40, and bibliography on pp. 566–8, and more generally, Kristeller (1983).
[6] On Bernard's preaching, see Constable (1994a), pp. 145–6 and 149–50. On the epithet *doctor mellifluus* see p. 25 n. 117 above and Leclercq (1953a), pp. 184–91.

it is often hard to say, as in a sermon, what exactly is new or when it was first written. None of the precepts, maxims, or images cited at the beginning of this chapter were new in the twelfth century, and the originality lies in the way they were used and the response they evoked. Consider these three characteristic quotations. 'The man of God Benedict wrote his rule in clear language; he expressed in it no hidden teaching, nothing obscure. Therefore it needs not exposition but admonition'; the abbot 'began to observe strictly the strictness of the regular order, so that nothing whatever of those things which the rule of saint Benedict orders was omitted'; and the description of some monks as 'lovers of the new Christian poverty' and as seeking 'naked to follow Christ and poor to imitate the Poor Man'. These passages could all have been written in the twelfth century, yet the first comes from the ninth century *Life* of Eigel of Fulda, the second (which refers to abbot Maiolus of Cluny) from the eleventh-century *Life* of Burchard of Vendôme by Odo of St Maur, and the third (which refers to the followers of Richard of St Vanne) from the eleventh-century chronicle of Hugh of Flavigny.[7] Examples like these make it difficult to speak about the distinctiveness or novelty of twelfth-century spirituality. It is likewise hard to establish whether later *Lives* of early saints reflect the attitudes of the time they were written or when the protagonist lived. Reference has already been made to the view of poverty in the early thirteenth-century *Life* of Robert of Molesme and to the statement about the poverty of the parents of Guy of Anderlac, who lived in the tenth century but whose *Life* was written in the twelfth century. It says in the eleventh-century *Life* of Hugh of Anzy-le-Duc, who died in about 930, that 'Many people of both orders and sexes flocked from various places to the same place [Anzy], requesting humbly and devoutly the consoling words of the very holy man, imploring that they be made his companions by large and spiritual supplies of his prayers and other benefits.'[8] While this could be true of the early tenth century, it sounds, especially the request for consolation and prayers rather than miracles, like the description of a hermit in the second half of the eleventh century. Passages like this are a reminder that scholars must be cautious in interpreting passages that may be less original and authentic (in its medieval sense) than they appear at first sight.

Rhetoric influenced the form as well as the content of spiritual writings. It was especially suited to speeches, including sermons, and to letters. A branch of rhetoric known as the *ars dictandi* or *dictamen*, which was cultivated in both

---

[7] Candidus, *Vita Eigilis Fuldensis*, 10, in *MGH, SS*, XV.1, 228 (*BHL* 2440); Odo of St-Maur, *Vita Burcardi comitis*, 4, ed. C. Bourel de la Roncière (CTSEEH 13; Paris 1892), p. 11; and Hugh of Flavigny, *Chronicon*, II (= *Vita Richardi*), 3–4, in *PL*, CLIV, 201A and 202B (*BHL* 7219), cited in Dauphin (1946), p. 61 n. 2, with *Vita Richardi*, 4, in *AASS OSB*, VI.1, 520 (*BHL* 7220).

[8] *Vita Hugonis Enziacensis*, III, 15, in *AASS*, 20 Apr. II, 765 (*BHL* 4004). The reference to Odilo of Cluny in the past (IV, 29, ibid., 769) suggests that it was written as Cluniac propaganda under abbot Hugh. See Zimmermann, II, 78 and 80, on the date.

French and Italian monasteries in the eleventh and twelfth centuries, was devoted to the writing of letters.[9] The distinction between speeches and letters was less clear at that time than it is today, since letters were frequently read aloud to their recipients, as were charters, of which the introductory harangues, or *arengae*, as they were called, were small rhetorical compositions. Among monastic letters, special subgenres were formed by letters of vocation proposing entry to religious life, letters of recruitment praising a particular house or order (and sometimes urging a change), and letters of encouragement to monks and nuns whose resolution was weakening. The form of a letter by its nature allowed an expression of personal opinion and could be used for a book or pamphlet, which can be called an epistolary treatise. These, like other works in epistolary form, were not sent and delivered like real letters, and the inscription to a recipient was more like a dedication than an address or salutation. Many forms of minor literary production were also influenced by rhetoric, such as the moral tales or *exempla* that were used in sermons and were later extracted and gathered into collections, and the accounts of dreams, visions, and prophecies, which often have a formulaic character while at the same time serving a propagandistic purpose and giving advice to individuals in moments of personal crisis.[10] Collections of miracle stories were put together to serve institutional purposes, such as the cult of a particular saint or the popularity of a place of pilgrimage, and also to promote particular ways of life and liturgical practices. The collection of miracles by Peter the Venerable, for example, can be seen as a piece of Cluniac propaganda, but it also promoted certain spiritual attitudes and devotions, such as confession and prayers for the dead, and the distribution of its manuscripts shows that it was copied in Cistercian and Carthusian as well as in Cluniac houses.[11]

One of the most striking examples of the influence of rhetoric on the forms of religious literature in the eleventh and twelfth centuries was the popularity of debates, dialogues, and disputes, or, as they were sometimes called, the *altercatio* or *conflictus*.[12] It was usually between two individuals, to whom names might be given or who were simply called 'Master' and 'Pupil', as in

---

[9] See the references in Constable (1976a), pp. 35–6.
[10] Lanfranc, *Ep.* 17, ed. Helen Clover and Margaret Gibson (OMT; Oxford 1979), p. 94, told of a monk who apparently had a vision urging him to leave his monastery.
[11] See Giles Constable, in *Petrus Venerabilis* (1956), pp. 220–36, and the list of manuscripts in Peter the Venerable, *De miraculis*, in *CC:CM*, LXXXIII, pp. 35*–56*.
[12] More rarely they were called *certamen*, *causa*, or simply *colloquium*: see Walther (1920), p. 3, who studied the *Streitgedicht*. See among other works de Lubac (1959–64), II.2, 201; Glaser (1965), p. 292; Schmidt (1976), pp. 121–4 and 174–80, on late Antiquity; Arduini (1985), p. 89, on Honorius *Augustodunensis*; Davenport (1988) on Middle English dialogues in the twelfth to fourteenth centuries; Abulafia (1989); von Moos (1989a), who said that 'a new culture of problematizing dialogue' tended to replace the commentary in the late twelfth century (p. 199) and (1989b) on the *ars dialogica* in the twelfth century; Ronquist (1990), who stressed the equality of interlocutors and 'spirit of tolerance and open inquiry' in twelfth-century dialogues (pp. 242 and 245); and Mews (1991), pp. 77–9. Southern (1995), p. 145, said that 'Progress through contradiction was the scholastic method.'

the *Bridlington dialogue*, or between two qualities, such as reason and the soul in Adam of Dryburgh's *Soliloquy*. A few involved more than two people, like Abelard's *Dialogue between a philosopher, a Jew, and a Christian*. Some may have originated as genuine discussions or conversations about the nature of religion and the religious life, but they dealt with all sorts of subjects, including the lives of saints', like Herbord's dialogue on Otto of Bamberg, and secular topics like the dispute between 'O' and William of St Emmeram over astrology and music and the debates, of which there were several versions, between a cleric and a knight over who was the better lover.[13] Rupert of Deutz went to Laon in 1117 in order to debate with the masters there over the nature of God's will, and in 1128 he disputed with Herman the converted Jew over the honour paid to images.[14] Some of these discussions may have actually taken place, like that of Odo of Tournai with a Jew from Senlis at Poitiers in 1100. Both Ademar of Chabannes and Peter the Deacon implied that their debates respectively with the prior of La Chiusa in 1029 and with a Cistercian monk before the emperor Lothar III at Lago Pesole in 1137 were real, but they were both such consummate falsifiers that it is hard to believe anything beyond that they tried to give an impression of an actual dispute.[15] The *Dialogue between two monks* of Idungus of Regensburg is also too good to be true, especially since Idungus, who was a Cluniac before he became a Cistercian, was fully able to sustain both sides.[16] The use of the dialogue form was in most cases a literary device allowing a writer to raise and refute objections in the same work and to make his points more convincing.

Discussions of this type were not always controversies, and there are many references in the spiritual literature of the eleventh and twelfth centuries, especially in letters, to amicable private conversations about religious matters. Bruno of Cologne in a letter to his friend Ralph, the future archbishop of Reims, described a talk they had with One-eyed Fulco (probably the poet Fulco of Beauvais) in a garden at Reims in about 1080. They spoke about

---

[13] The 'O' in the dialogue with William of St Emmeram on astronomy and music may have been Otloh of St Emmeram: see Schauwecker (1964), pp. 224–32. On the debate between a cleric and a knight, see Oulmont (1911), who mentioned two Latin and four vernacular versions.
[14] Herman the Jew, *De conversione sua*, 3, ed. Gerlinde Niemeyer (*MGH*, Quellen zur Geistesgeschichte des Mittelalters 4; Weimar 1963), pp. 76–9. See p. 64 n. 82 above on this work, and, generally, Magrassi (1959), pt 3, and Silvestre (1968).
[15] Odo of Tournai, *Disputatio contra Judeum Leonem nomine de adventu Christi filii Dei*, in *PL*, CLX, 1103–12, and tr. Irven Resnick (Philadelphia 1994), pp. 29–30 and 114 n. 167, on the scholarly disagreements concerning these disputes. Abulafia (1989) denied the reality of the *Dialogus inter Christianum et Iudeum de fide catholica*, whereas Southern (1995), pp. 228–30, argued for the authenticity of the dialogue between Everard of Ypres and the Greek 'Ratius' in 1193, which Häring (1953) believed was fictitious. On a debate between a Cathar and a Waldensian in 1208, mentioned in MS Toulouse, Bibl. mun., 609, fol. 198, see John Mundy, in *Renaissance and Renewal* (1982), p. 242 n. 19.
[16] Idungus, *Dialogus duorum monachorum*, ed. Huygens, pp. 91–186. See also the 'dialogues' between the old and the new monks reported by Ordericus Vitalis, *Historia ecclesiastica* (pp. 212–13 below) and by Hugh of Kirkstall, *Narratio* (pp. 53–4 above and p. 154 below).

'the false delights and passing riches of the world and also the joys of eternal glory', and then and there they decided to leave the world and become monks.[17] A follower of Anselm named Elmer, who was a monk at Christ Church Canterbury and prior from 1128 to 1137, mentioned 'the sweet discussions (*colloquia*) about the salvation of our souls, when by our words to each other we raised ourselves to the love of the heavenly city'.[18] Bernard of Clairvaux spoke with his friend Hugh of Vitry about his becoming a monk even when he was in bed, and Peter the Venerable wrote to his secretary Peter of Poitiers that they spoke together 'more frequently and intimately than others . . . about the contempt of the world and love of heavenly things'.[19]

Dialogue and dialectic – the science of doubt, as it has been called – played a fundamental part in the thought processes of the eleventh and twelfth centuries. It underlay the discipline of disputation that developed in the schools and was applied to almost every branch of intellectual inquiry, including religious and spiritual questions, and it helps to explain the popularity of oxymora like busy leisure, concordant discord, powerless power, learned ignorance, ancient youth, and wealthy poverty.[20] It involved the division and distinction of individual issues and looking at them from different points of view. Berengar of Tours cited Augustine in support of his defence of the importance of dialectic, which he equated with reason and regarded as necessary for salvation. 'It belongs to the great heart to take refuge in dialectic in all matters, since to take refuge in it is to take refuge in reason, wherefore he who does not do so, since he is made according to reason in the image of God, loses his honour and cannot be renewed from day to day in the image of God.'[21] The method of oppositions, by which everything had a good and a bad side, was used by Otloh of St Emmeram in the eleventh century and was applied to religious history by Anselm of Havelberg, who argued that monks were either good or bad, that a change of order was either up or down, and that the term regular canon was a logical absurdity.[22] Dialectic and rhetoric

---

[17] Bruno of La Chartreuse, *Ep.* 1.13, ed. André Wilmart, in *Revue bénédictine* 51 (1939), p. 268, and ed. anon. (Maurice Laporte) (SC 88; Paris 1962), pp. 74–6. See the fuller citation of this letter p. 257 below.

[18] Elmer of Canterbury, *Ep.* 1.1, ed. Jean Leclercq, in *Anal. mon.*, II, 63. See ibid., p. 163, for a mid-twelfth-century letter from a monk of Le Bec to Clement the Englishman referring to the intimate colloquium 'quod ad inuicem de mutua dilectione habuimus'.

[19] Geoffrey of Auxerre, *De vita et miraculis Bernardi*, 11, ed. Robert Lechat, in *Anal. boll.* 50 (1932), pp. 94–5 (*BHL* 1207) (cf. William of St Thierry, *Vita prima Bernardi*, I, III, 13–14, ed. Mabillon, II(6), 2101C–2D (*BHL* 1211)), and Peter the Venerable, *Ep.* 58, ed. Constable, I, 182.

[20] On busy leisure, see Leclercq (1963a), p. 151; Constable (1980), p. 88; and p. 59 above. According to Gregory the Great, *Dialogi*, 2, *praef.*, ed. Umberto Moricca (FSI 57; Rome 1924), p. 72, Benedict 'necessit igitur scienter nescius et sapienter indoctus'.

[21] Berengar of Tours, *De sacra coena contra Lanfrancum*, 23, ed. W.H. Beekenkamp (Kerkhistorische Studien 2; The Hague 1941), p. 47. Cf. the opposing view of Peter Damiani, *De divina omnipotentia*, 7, ed. André Cantin (SC 191; Paris 1972), pp. 416–18; see intro. p. 231.

[22] Schauwecker (1964), pp. 224–32; Fina (1956–8), (4) pp. 282–5; and Schreiber (1942), p. 60.

played a role both in the Investiture Controversy and in the solution that was worked out in the early twelfth century. They may also have contributed to a spirit of tolerance. Paul's controversial statement in 1 Corinthians 11.19 that 'There must be also heresies' was interpreted in the first half of the twelfth century to mean that the orthodox must be forced by heresies to discover the truth, which thus emerges out of challenge and dispute.[23]

Many of the issues associated with the movement of religious reform were shaped by this approach and were presented in terms of rhetorical figures and contrasts rather than (as they were in reality) as matters of degree or even shades of difference within a common tradition. Much of the polemical literature was an effort at self-definition as much as an attack on a clearly formulated enemy.[24] Keen debates over the nature of the primitive church, the apostolic life, the desert fathers, and the rule of Benedict were conducted by monks who had no real knowledge of the early church and none of whom followed the rule to the letter, and they were doubtless more aware of this than some of the scholars who have taken their arguments literally. Writers in the twelfth century were rarely literal-minded. Their danger, as some of the biblical commentators knew, was to lose sight of the letter in a series of allegorical speculations linked by resemblances that seem fanciful today but were full of meaning at the time. These writers were completely sincere in their use of images, comparisons, and opposites and at the same time fully aware of other levels of interpretation that come closer to modern ideas of reality. They hurled abuse at other types of monks and canons and argued passionately over the respective superiority of different forms of religious life, of which in other contexts they were quite ready to recognize the validity and value.[25] This was not inconsistency, as it may now appear, or a failure to see the forest for the trees or to keep their heads in the heat of the battle. It was the way they thought and wrote, and it coloured how they dealt in their writings with many aspects of the reform movement.

The polemical literature must therefore be seen as presenting a genuine but partial and distorted picture of the realities as the writers saw them. Most of it was written between 1120 and 1160, and aside from brief works and miscellaneous references, of which some have come to light relatively recently and others may still exist in manuscripts,[26] it consists of some twenty works by twelve known writers. Among the black monks (most of them Cluniacs or neo-Cluniacs) were Rupert of Deutz, Peter the Venerable, Hugh of Rouen,

---

[23] Grundmann (1967), pp. 155–8. On the importance of the *ars dictandi* in the Investiture Controversy, see esp. Reinke (1937), pt IV, 30 and 89–90 and Robinson (1978), p. 67.

[24] See Bynum (1995), p. 215.

[25] Many reformers were apparently indifferent, for instance, concerning the choice of rule or order until after it was made.

[26] Such as the treatise *Adtendite a falsis prophetis*, ed. Engels (1975), who attributed it to Abelard, and the reply written in 1156/63 to the provost of St Euphemia in Piacenza by the abbot of St Marco in Piacenza, published by Motta (1985), pp. 237–40.

Matthew of Albano, and Boto of Prüfening; among the old canons, Theobald
of Etampes; among the regular canons, Gerhoh and Arno of Reichersberg,
Philip of Harvengt, and Anselm of Havelberg; and among the Cistercians,
Bernard of Clairvaux, who stands out here as elsewhere as the single most
important figure, and Idungus of Regensburg.[27] To these must be added a
number of anonymous works, such as the Cistercian document that is
embodied in Peter the Venerable's Letter 28; a monastic reply to Theobald
of Etampes; the treatise *On the truly apostolic life*, which has been variously
attributed to Rupert of Deutz, Honorius *Augustodunensis*, and an anonymous
monk of Brauweiler; the *Reprehensio* (or *Riposte*) published by Wilmart, who
attributed it to Hugh of Rouen; the *Rescriptum* (or *Nouvelle réponse*) published
by Leclercq; the dialogue *On the eating of birds*; and a few long poems like
that of Pagan Bolotinus against false hermits. Some writers of importance,
like Ivo of Chartres in his letters and Abelard in his sermon on John the
Baptist and his letter on the liturgy to Bernard of Clairvaux, discussed specific
aspects of the dispute in a way that left no doubt about their feelings; but
these works were not polemics in the sense of attacking one position while
defending another, any more than the many writers of letters, sermons, saints'
Lives, spiritual treatises, and other works that touch on the dispute from a
partisan point of view, and often show an animus against other views, but
that were not written primarily to make points or to discredit an opponent.
For this reason the list does not include most of the poems directed against
abuses in the church,[28] canonical collections designed to support one position
or another, interesting as they are, or such non-polemical works as the *Libellus*,
the treatise *On the professions of monks*, William of St Thierry's *Golden letter*
to the Carthusians of Mont-Dieu, or various Cistercian treatises and sermons
praising their own order, which are an important part of the broader literature
of the movement of reform but which attacked no one specifically.[29] The same
applies to various commentaries and customaries, and to the *Charter of love*
(and its *Summa*), the *Beginning of Cîteaux*, and other early Cistercian works,
which have been called polemical treatises against the black monks but are
primarily concerned with the origins of the Cistercian order, albeit from a
highly partisan position.[30] Mention should also be made of Peter Damiani's

---

[27] See the useful synoptic list of these works in Lunardi (1970), pp. 19–20, and Piazzoni (1988),
pp. 69–94. On disputes between monks and canons, see Dereine (1951), pp. 558–9.
[28] On the many allusions, frequently satirical, to both sides of the controversy in twelfth- and
thirteenth-century verse, see Walther (1920), pp. 163–5; Lehmann (1922), pp. 13–16; and
Szövérffy (1992–5), III, 106–73, esp. 167–70 on monks.
[29] See Honemann (1978), pp. 12–87 and 163–215, on the number and distribution of the manuscripts of the *Golden letter*, of which copies were in the libraries of almost all religious orders
and which was translated into many vernacular languages. The *Libellus* and *De professionibus
monachorum*, on the other hand, each survive in only one manuscript.
[30] De Waha (1978), p. 172, called the *Exordium parvum* an 'oeuvre de combat destinée à justifier
les Cisterciens dans leur polémique avec les Bénédictins'. On the dates of this and other early
Cistercian documents, see p. 38 n. 171 above.

Apology of the monks against the canons and the round letter from the monks of Monte Cassino to Hersfeld and other German monasteries, but these belong to an earlier period and had no immediate successors. They constitute what may be called the pre-history of the main body of polemics associated with the movement of monastic reform and were written at a time when the principal attention of the reformers was concentrated on the issues of clerical reform and the controversy between the empire and the papacy.

Four points stand out about these writings when they are looked at together: first, their relatively small number and total bulk, which would comfortably fit into a good-sized octavo volume; second, they were almost all written by men who by contemporary standards would have been considered reformers; third, many more were written by Cluniacs and regular canons than by Cistercians; and fourth, they were written within a period of between thirty and forty years, which corresponded to the fourth and final phase of the entire reform movement, when attention was concentrated on the nature of religious life.[31] These works, indeed, give this period some of its distinctive character in the broader movement of reform. These four points, and above all that the dispute was essentially among reformers and not, as is so often said, between old and new monks or canons, should be kept in mind in studying the two most significant groups among these writings.

The most celebrated and influential group consists of the works dealing with the differences between the Cluniacs and Cistercians and includes (on the Cluniac side) Peter the Venerable's two Letters 28 and 111 to Bernard of Clairvaux, written in the late 1120s and in 1144 respectively, the *Reprehensio* attributed to Hugh of Rouen, and the anonymous *Rescriptum*, and (on the Cistercian side) the Cistercian schedule of charges to which Peter the Venerable replied in Letter 28, Bernard's letter to his cousin Robert and *Apology*, which both date from the early or mid-1120s, and Idungus's *Dialogue of two monks*. To these can be added, in a broad sense, the defence of old black monasticism found in the works of Rupert of Deutz and Boto of Prüfening and the exchange between Matthew of Albano and the abbots gathered at Reims, though they were not Cistercians. There has been considerable scholarly debate over the dating of the earliest works in the dispute, primarily to establish who started it. The view adopted here (with which not everyone would agree) is that the Cistercian list of charges came first, followed by Bernard's letter to Robert, and then by Peter's Letter 28 and the *Apology* in an order that cannot be determined. These are in any case the works that have attracted the attention of scholars, owing largely to the celebrity of their

---

[31] The earliest may be Bernard's *Apologia* and *Ep.* 1, which Holdsworth (1994), pp. 45–8, dated 1121/2 and *c.* 1121 respectively. *Ep.* 1 is dated 1125 in ed. Leclercq, VII, 1. Garrigues (1973), p. 447, dated the *De vita vere apostolica* in the mid-1120s. The latest are probably Philip of Harvengt's *De institutione clericorum*, of which much (if not all) was written after he became abbot of Bonne-Espérance in 1157, or Idungus's *Dialogus*, ed. Huygens, p. 9, dating it 1153/5.

authors, and upon which a heavy, and perhaps excessive, weight of historical interpretation has come to rest.[32] Three centuries ago the English translator of Louis Dupin's *Bibliothèque des autheurs ecclésiastiques*, commenting on Peter's Letter 28, said that:

> Upon this whole Debate or Controversie between the Monks of Cisteaux and those of Cluny, we cannot forbear making this one Remark, that according to our old coarse English proverb, here has been a great Cry, but little Wool; a great noise and clamour about the Externals, but scarce one Word said, Pro, or Con, about the Internals of Religion.[33]

The two great protagonists (though not perhaps all their followers) might not have disagreed with the substance of this remark. Later writers, however, have found in these works, depending upon their personal points of view, a dichotomy of humanism and asceticism, interpretation and literalism, cenobitism and eremitism, contemplation and action, ritualism and liberty, and Benedictine and pre-Benedictine monasticism.[34] Some of the specific issues raised by these dichotomies will be discussed below, but such broad generalizations represent a prolongation rather than an analysis of the controversy.

A more interesting and important group within the polemical literature is formed by the works of both Cluniacs and Cistercians on one side and of canons, most of them regular but including one secular canon, on the other. These works concentrated on the right of monks to perform pastoral work (and to own pastoral revenues), the question of *transitus* from one religious house to another, and, more broadly, the respective superiority of the monastic and clerical ways of life. On these issues the principal works on the monastic side were by Rupert of Deutz, Bernard of Clairvaux, Honorius *Augustodunensis*, Hugh of Rouen, and Idungus of Regensburg and the treatise *On the truly apostolic life*, to which can be added two interesting letters by abbot Egbert of Huysburg, of which the first was addressed 'To all observers and defenders of the monastic order.'[35] On the canonical or clerical side were the works of Gerhoh and Arno of Reichersberg (especially Arno's *Shield of the canons*), Philip of Harvengt, Anselm of Havelberg, and the somewhat intemperate Oxford master Theobald of Etampes, who called a monastery 'a place and prison of the damned, that is, of monks, who damn themselves in order

---

[32] It has not been sufficiently emphasized, for instance, that Bernard's *Apologia* is not primarily directed against the Cluniacs, who are mentioned only twice, in III, 6, and IV, 7, ed. Leclercq, III, 87, and that it was probably a response to a criticism of the Cistercians made by one or more black Benedictines. See Rudolph (1990), esp. pp. 159–91.

[33] Dupin (1693–1715), IX, 95–7, Eng. tr. X, 82.

[34] See Constable (1974), pp. 37–8.

[35] *Die Reinhardsbrunner Briefsammlung*, 9, ed. Friedel Peeck (*MGH, Epistolae selectae* 5; Weimar 1952), pp. 8–9, and more completely, ed. Walter Zöllner, in *Forschungen und Fortschritte* 38 (1964), pp. 25–8.

to avoid perpetual damnation'.[36] To these can be added the letter by abbot Lietbert of St Rufus and one to the prior of La Charité-sur-Loire, the preface to a commentary on the Augustinian rule in MS Vienna, Nationalbibliothek, 2207, and a treatise *On the origin and creation of the regular canons* in MS Paris, Bibliothèque nationale, N.a.l. 368. There is even more rhetoric and polemic in these works than in those concerning the Cluniacs and Cistercians, and their tone was often embittered by transfers from one monastery to another and by the competition for tithes and oblations. But they raise some basic issues about the nature of religious life and prepared the way for a reassessment of the respective values of a life spent in seclusion and of one spent in the world.

Both the old and new monks defended the traditional monastic ideal of withdrawal as the highest form of Christian life on earth. They saw themselves as a distinct order of society, set off by their renunciation of secular life and its values, on the one hand from the laity and on the other from the clergy, who by their nature were ordained and involved in pastoral work in the world. In principle this applied to all those in holy orders. The earliest known use of the concept of the ivory tower in the sense of seclusion occurs in a sermon by Richard of St Victor, who said that among those who were out of harmony (*discordant*) with the new song of Psalm 97 were many in holy orders 'who ought to live in ivory houses, that is, to preserve chastity, like subdeacons, deacons, priests, bishops, archbishops, and who may be apostolics, regular canons, monks, hermits, recluses'.[37] The old monks argued that the status of a monk and of a cleric, though distinct, could be combined and that an ordained monk had the rights and privileges of a cleric, even if he did not exercise them. Abbo of Fleury said that a monk who was ordained a priest or a priest who became a monk should celebrate mass *in congregatione* rather than publicly.[38] The reformers, on the other hand, tended to stress the difference and held that an ordained monk was first a monk and only secondarily a cleric. For them the most important aspect of religious life was seclusion, which they normally described as *solitudo* or as living in a *desertum* or an *eremus* – terms that were used primarily to indicate a spiritual as much as a physical state and cannot therefore be taken literally without further evidence.[39]

---

[36] Theobald of Etampes, *Ep.*, in Holland (1890), p. 153, and ed. Raymonde Foreville and Jean Leclercq, in *Anal. mon.*, IV, 52.

[37] Richard of St Victor (attr. to Hugh of St Victor: see p. 22 n. 104 above), *Serm.* 13, in *PL*, CLXXVII, 926C. See Panofsky (1957), who traced the term to the Song of Songs and Sainte-Beuve and the 'idea of withdrawal, isolation, or seclusion' to Milton (p. 115).

[38] Abbo of Fleury, *Apologeticus*, in *PL*, CXXXIX, 465A.

[39] See the debate between von der Nahmer (1972) and Prinz (1974) and also Milis (1979), pp. 49–50.

Some of the most eloquent expressions of monastic rhetoric were lavished on the concept of solitude and the so-called myth of the desert. Deserts, mountains, and forests brought with them in the Middle Ages an ancient baggage of biblical, literary, and folkloristic associations with pre-Christian deities, wild beasts, and outlaws. They were places of physical and spiritual danger and at the same time of freedom and opportunity, where man was face to face with himself and with the forces of evil.[40] The desert in which the Lord found Jacob and the mountain and desert into which Christ withdrew to pray in solitude were cited in countless lives of saints and histories of monasteries, as were the examples of the desert fathers in Egypt who battled in lonely struggles against the demons. These accounts were part of the potent mythology of monastic reform, but they were not taken literally most of the time.[41] Physical solitude of the type practised by the hermit Schetzelo was very rare. Most hermits lived with at least a few companions, and the most striking aspect of their life was its freedom rather than its solitude. *Solitudo* meant a life separated from people in the world; *desertum* meant 'without people' rather than a desert in the modern sense; and *eremus* was used in both secular and spiritual texts to mean 'uncultivated', and therefore unpopulated. For the reformers these terms were expressions of their desire not only to live apart but also to work their own lands and to avoid worldly obligations. When Peter the Venerable went for a retreat into the woods near Cluny in about 1140, his 'co-hermit' Arnulf referred to their '*heremus* or rather *solitudo*', though other references show that they were plagued by visitors.[42] The Cistercian Isaac of L'Etoile described his abbey as located 'in this remote, arid, and parched solitude', though its lands were in fact well-cultivated.[43]

The concepts of solitude and the desert were increasingly spiritualized in monastic writings. Ralph Glaber in the early eleventh century referred to making the monastery of St Saturninus into 'a common hermitage in the church (*communis in ecclesia eremus*)', and a century later abbot Geoffrey of St Thierry equated the terms *eremus* and *claustrum*.[44] Ivo of Chartres in his letter to the monks of Coulombs said that 'The hidden places of forests and the peaks of mountains do not make a man holy unless he has with him a solitude of mind, peace of heart, tranquillity of conscience, and soarings in his heart without which *accidia* of mind, curiosity, vainglory, and dangerous assaults of

---

[40] On the 'desert myth' see Williams (1962), pp. 38–46; Ward (1976); and Brown (1988), pp. 216–17, and on the evil spirits and forces associated with trees, Crampon (1936), pp. 99–179.

[41] Ward (1976) argued that the desert myth was a topos in twelfth-century monasticism and developed among the Cistercians in the second and third generations of their history.

[42] Peter the Venerable, *Ep.* 125, ed. Constable, I, 321; cf. *Ep.* 127, ibid., p. 324.

[43] Isaac of L'Etoile, *Serm.* 14 *in dominica IV post Epiphaniam*, 2, in *PL*, CXCIV, 1737A.

[44] Ralph Glaber, *Vita Willelmi Fiscannensis*, 6, ed. Neithard Bulst (OMT; Oxford 1989), p. 266, and n. 3, equating *communis* and *eremus*, and Geoffrey of St Thierry, *Serm.* 9, in MS Reims, Bibl. mun., 581, fol. 35: 'Postea in heremo, id est in claustro, commorantes.'

temptations accompany all solitude.'[45] Solitude of mind thus became a sub-topos, as it were, within the broader topos of solitude. Bernard of Clairvaux praised 'the solitude of spirit, not of body', and Peter the Venerable told his secretary Peter of Poitiers, who wanted to become a hermit, that 'the solitary places where a true hermitage is alone found by true despisers of the world' were 'in the secret places of our hearts'.[46] 'Consider how poverty and baseness make a solitude in the middle of towns', said Guigo of La Chartreuse, 'riches fill the deserts with crowds.'[47] Solitude was equated with solitude of mind and heart, by which people were alone in a crowd and oblivious to what was going on in the world around them.[48]

Monastic life was generally seen in the twelfth century as a social ideal. Even more than some of the old monks the reformers approved of living alone in physical solitude only for exceptionally strong and well-prepared hermits who could resist the dangers of self-will. Ivo of Chartres said that the solitary life was inferior 'because it is voluntary and full of improper ideas', and Elizabeth of Schönau expressed a common sentiment when she said that 'There are some men who love solitude more for the liberty of their own wills than for the fruit of good work.'[49] Excessive freedom and lack of obedience were among the commonest charges against hermits, and the desire to become a hermit was sometimes regarded as a temptation from the devil. Most of the reformers favoured cenobitical life, preferably in a community large enough to maintain a strict regular life, and when they described their monasticism as eremitical they meant cut off from the world rather than resembling the life of the hermits. Some spiritual writers went further and said that for most monks a community was essential not only as a restraint on self-will but also as an environment in which to express a Christian love of neighbour. Seneca's view of man as a naturally social animal was widely cited in the twelfth century, among others by William of St Thierry, who regarded Seneca as a wise man seeking a rational life in contemplation and mastery of the soul over the body.[50] The natural equality of men was stressed by Bernard and other Cistercian writers.[51]

[45] Ivo of Chartres, *Ep.* 192, in *PL*, CLXII, 201D–2A; cf. *Ep.* 34, ed. Jean Leclercq (CHFMA 22; Paris 1949), pp. 138–41, and *Ep.* 256, in *PL*, CLXII, 260–2.

[46] Bernard, *Serm.* 40 *in Cant.*, III, 4, ed. Leclercq, II, 27, and Peter the Venerable, *Ep.* 58, ed. Constable, I, 188. The same words are found in Geoffrey of St Thierry, *Serm.* 28, in MS Reims, Bibl. mun., 581, fol. 118ᵛb.

[47] Guigo of La Chartreuse, *Med.* 307, ed. André Wilmart (Etudes de philosophie médiévale 22; Paris 1936), p. 121, with a trans. on p. 231, no. 320.

[48] Constable (1987b). According to a thirteenth-century rule for hermits, ed. Livarius Oliger, in *Antonianum* 3 (1928), p. 299, some people derived *heremita* from *hereo* (to remain or hold fast) rather than from *heremus*.

[49] Ivo of Chartres, *Ep.* 256, in *PL*, CLXII, 261C, and Elizabeth of Schönau, *Liber viarum Dei*, ed. Roth, p. 119.

[50] Déchanet (1940b); Nothdurft (1963), pp. 67, 139, and 146; Ryan (1974); and, generally on the influence of Seneca's letters in the twelfth century, Reynolds (1965), pp. 104–24.

[51] See p. 98 above.

Human love and friendship were distinctive ideals in twelfth-century spiritual writings, as were acts of charity and assistance to others, without which it was impossible to lead a full Christian life. Friendship was not only a source of enjoyment or pleasure but also a way of promoting religion, according to Brian McGuire, who wrote that 'Close friendships among men in the cloister were seen as necessary and positive within the monastic communal life.'[52] A classic exposition of the concept of Christian friendship is found in the works of Aelred of Rievaulx, who said in one of his sermons that a religious community is held together by the different qualities of its members, who joined in a common purpose.[53] An ideal of peace and social harmony is also found in the *Lives* of some of the reformers. Bernard of Tiron was praised for 'the unheard-of breadth of his love', which embraced all men and was compared to the saving power of the apostles and apostolic men; Stephen of Obazine showed his 'care and solicitude for peace not only at home but also of the entire province' and was mourned on his deathbed as 'the protector and provider of the whole province (*patria*)'; and Gilbert of Sempringham was admired for 'this marvellous unity both of persons and churches, this unheard-of communion of all things that makes one thing all and all things one, in a diversity of so many hearts and of such great monasteries'.[54]

The monastery was thus at the same time a place of peace, beauty, and social harmony and a place of solitude, located 'in a desert land, in a place of horror and of vast wilderness' and in 'the beautiful places of the wilderness', according to Deuteronomy and the Psalmist.[55] Bruno of Cologne in his letter to Ralph of Reims gave a glowing picture of the physical beauty of the setting of his hermitage in Calabria,[56] and William of Malmesbury described the abbey of Thorney, which was named 'on account of the density of the thorn-bushes', as 'the image of paradise, which in its pleasantness already resembles heaven itself'. He described the lushness of the fields and trees and the struggle, as he put it, between the efforts of nature and man, 'in which the latter produced

---

[52] McGuire (1983a), p. 222. On monastic friendship see Fiske (1970); Lodolo (1977), pp. 276–83; McGuire (1988); Morris (1989), pp. 369–71, who pointed out that *amicitia* is a broader term than 'friendship'; Haseldine (1993), with bibliography p. 393 n. 11; and, generally, Southern (1995), pp. 28–30. See p. 277 nn. 102–3 below for references on love, including the love of neighbour.

[53] Aelred of Rievaulx, *Serm.* 7 *de tempore*, in *PL*, CXCV, 248D–9B. On Aelred and friendship, see Fiske (1970), pt 18, and McGuire (1994), with references to other works.

[54] Geoffrey *Grossus*, *Vita Bernardi Tironiensis*, XIV, 130 and 136, in *PL*, CLXXII, 1441A and 1444A (*BHL* 1251; see von Walter (1903–6), II 15–16 and 44–6); *Vita Stephani Obazinensis*, II, 39, and III, 4, ed. Aubrun, pp. 158 and 198; and *Vita Gileberti Sempinghamensis*, 19, ed. Foreville and Keir, p. 54. Reformers often served as peace-makers between both individuals and groups.

[55] Auberger (1986), pp. 120–4.

[56] Bruno of La Chartreuse, *Ep.* 1.4, ed. Wilmart (n. 17), p. 265, and ed. anon. (n. 17), p. 68. See [Laporte] (1960–7), I, 265, and the parallel sentiments in Guigo of La Chartreuse, *Med.* 113, 260, and 273, ed. Wilmart (n. 47), pp. 23 and 37, who said that Guigo 'était sensible à la beauté de la création et des créatures en particulier'.

whatever the former forgot'.[57] William did not say where the thorn-bushes went, but his description is an example of the ancient topos of the *locus amoenus* that was used to describe the locations of new monasteries and that drew on biblical as well as classical sources, above all the description in the Song of Songs 4.12–15 of the enclosed garden where 'Thy plants are a paradise of pomegranates with the fruits of the orchard' and where there was 'a well of living waters, which ran with a strong stream from Libanus'.[58] It is impossible to say how much truth and how much fancy was involved in the use of phrases like these. Monasteries were often in genuinely beautiful places; they had enclosed cloister-gardens with fountains and running water; and monastic agriculture imposed some order on the surrounding lands, which filled the needs of the monks by way of food and timber. The monastic estates furnished the opportunity for manual labour, which was an important feature of the religious programme, and they were also a source of mental refreshment and inspiration and a prefiguration on earth of the paradisiacal beauty of the future. These aspects mingled in the minds of the beholders (as they did in biblical commentaries) and produced an impression of beauty and order that was no less real to them than those of solitude, harshness, and danger.

Nature was viewed with ambivalence, both as benevolent, as at Thorney where it struggled with man to produce what the abbey needed, and as threatening in a spiritual as well as material sense. Hugh of Fouilloy in his treatise *On the cloister of the soul* rang the changes between images and reality and after describing paradise as a celestial monastery, where the angels lived in bliss, he went on to describe a material monastery, as he called it, in similar terms. The monks, like the angels, love the order of future felicity, lack few things, and do without the few things they need. 'They conquer nature, since they lead a heavenly life on earth, are free for contemplation, and desire to see God.' Nature for Hugh represented man's physical needs, which tie him to earth, but he also praised nature as a source of beauty and goodness and compared the garden of heaven to that of a monastery, where 'The greenness of the lawn in the middle of the material cloister refreshes the eyes of the monks and makes them more eager to read.'[59] Miro of Ripoll was inspired to leave the world by hearing the songs of birds at dawn, which could only be the work of God. 'Who will give me powers to concord in imitation of these animals? What an internal harmony is formed by the points of the virtues!

[57] William of Malmesbury, *Gesta pontificum*, IV, 186, ed. N.E.S.A. Hamilton (RS 52; London 1870), p. 326. Cf. the much earlier description of Solignac in the *Vita Elegii Noviomagensis*, I, 16, in *MGH, SS rerum Merov.*, IV, 682 (*BHL* 2474).

[58] See Stock (1972), pp. 133–7, who defined the *locus amoenus* as 'the description of a pleasant place or a paradise according to rhetorical rules' (p. 133); Thoss (1972); Lodolo (1977); and Fox (1988), p. 438. The analogous *loc aizi* is frequently found in twelfth-century vernacular poems.

[59] Hugh of Fouilloy, *De claustro animae*, IV, 32 and 34, in *PL*, CLXXVI, 1169D and 1172D. On this work, see Grégoire (1962).

Where, my beloved, do you desire me to make my nest in order to say farewell to the world?'[60] The songs of the birds represent here a celestial harmony of virtues that is to be found in the monastery where Miro will nest like a bird. Abbot Gilbert of Holland contrasted the location of his abbey with those of the desert fathers:

> A secret, cultivated, well-watered, fertile place, and a wooded valley resounds in springtime with the sweet songs of birds, so that it can revive the dead spirit, remove the aversions of the fastidious soul, and soften the hardness of the undevout mind. These in brief either depict for you the signs of future happiness or reveal some remnants of the first [happiness] that the integrity of the human condition received amid the pleasures of paradise.[61]

Here the paradisiacal nature of the monastery is demonstrated in both its backwards- and its forwards-looking aspects.

The sense of harmony between the saints and nature included wild animals, which was another ancient and paradoxical topos, suggesting the pre-lapsarian peaceable kingdom and conditions after the Second Coming.[62] Like the beauty of nature, which flows from both its own spontaneous fruitfulness and man's efforts at cultivation, the animals come of their own accord to serve the holy man and have to be controlled and tamed by him. William Firmat forbade the animals to eat the vegetables in his garden, fed fish from his hands, and was guided on his first pilgrimage by a crow. 'The man Firmat was so gentle that birds that flee the sight of man would take food from his offering hand and lying hidden under his clothing would moderate the cold of winter.'[63] The harmony of man and nature was also shown by the topos of worshipping and learning in the open air. Romuald as a young man, as he himself related cheerfully (*hilariter*), according to Peter Damiani, used to recite the Gospel wandering about his hermitage, saying twenty psalms under one tree and thirty or forty under another.[64] Marbod of Rennes pictured rural life as a prelude to paradise in one of his poems,[65] and Bernard of Clairvaux was said to have learned by meditating and praying 'in the woods and in the fields' and to have had no other masters than the oak-trees and beeches.[66] He wrote in about 1125 to Henry Murdac, who later became archbishop of York, 'Believe me who knows: you will find more in the forests than in books. Woods and stones

---

[60] *Vita Mironis*, in *España sagrada*, XXVIII, 306 (*BHL* 5971).
[61] Gilbert, *Tractatus* 7, II, 4, in Bernard, ed. Mabillon, II(5), 376C. See Mikkers (1963), p. 273.
[62] Boas (1948), pp. 82–5.
[63] *Vita Guillelmi Firmati*, 1 and 3, in Pigeon (1892–8), II, 403, 405, and 413 (*BHL* 8914).
[64] Peter Damiani, *Vita Romualdi*, 4, ed. Giovanni Tabacco (FSI 94; Rome 1957), pp. 20–1 (*BHL* 7324).
[65] Marbod of Rennes, *Carm.* 28, in *PL*, CLXXI, 1665D–6A. See Boas (1948), p. 109 n. 60.
[66] William of St Thierry, *Vita prima Bernardi*, I, 4, 23, in Bernard, ed. Mabillon, II(6), 2109AB (*BHL* 1211). See Gilson (1961), pp. 36–41, and Constable (1980), p. 90 n. 169, with references on this passage, which was cited among others by Petrarch.

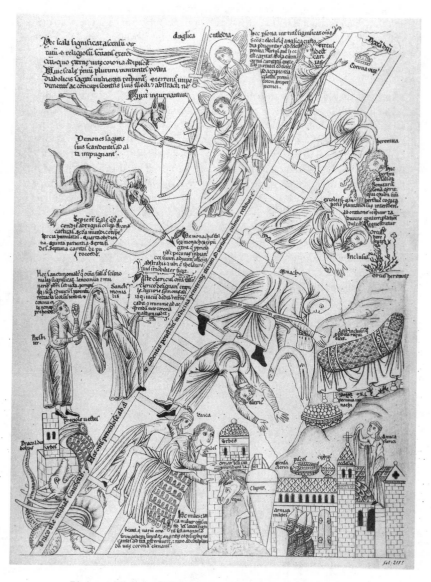

Plate 1   Herrad of Hohenbourg *Hortus deliciarum*, fol. 215^v

Plate 1   This illustration from Herrad of Hohenbourg's *Garden of delights*, which was completed in the early 1180s, depicts the ladder of virtues and religious exercises by which the crown of eternal life is attained and of which the seven steps are chastity, contempt of the world, humility, obedience, patience, faith, and love, which is described both as virtue and as containing the other virtues. The ladder is in fact concerned less with virtues than with vices, which are shown as arrows shot by demons in the service of the dragon or devil, who is in the bottom left-hand corner. Only one 'person of virtue', standing at the top of the ladder on the left, represents the saints and elect who receive the crown. The other persons are all described as 'false' or 'unfaithful' and are shown falling off the ladder: the hermit on account of his preoccupation with his garden, which distracts him from prayer and contemplation; the recluse because he sleeps and talks too much; the monk because he is diverted by possessions and money; the cleric on account of his drinking, luxury, simony, and other vices; and the lay knight and woman because they love worldly adornments and are guilty of fornication, avarice, and pride. To the right of the falling figures can be seen the hermit's garden, the recluse's bed, the monk's money, the cleric's girlfriend and table, set with food and drink, and the knight's town, horses, shield, and armed soldiers. On the left side of the ladder are a priest and a nun who has been seduced by the priest's enticements and gifts and dragged down by worldly pomp and wealth. On the ladder itself is written that 'the medicine of penance' can restore to 'the height of the virtues' those who are falling. See Coulton (1929–50), II, xx–xxi and plate 6; Katzenellenbogen (1939), pp. 22–6; Yvonne Labande-Mailfert, in *Laici* (1968), pp. 498–501; and the edition by Rosalie Green, Michael Evans, Christine Bischoff, and Michael Curschmann (Studies of the Warburg Institute 36; London and Leiden 1979), I, 201.

Plates 2-3   The Floreffe Bible is generally dated to the third quarter of the twelfth century, though some scholars believe it is earlier. Under the illustration on fol. 3^r is written 'An exemplar of good ways of life (*morum*) is given in this figure', and around it there is a metrical inscription recalling the language of the story of Mary and Martha in Luke 10.38–42 and reading 'These depictions are a sign of the two lives, of which the first is the practical and the second the theoretical (*theorica*) life. The first groans, implores, grieves, and labours by suffering. It is troubled by care while it wanders around many things. The other rejoices and takes pleasure while it contemplates. For it has discerned the one thing, for which it has already spurned many things.' The theoretical or contemplative life is shown by a series of episodes from the life of Job around a central design of two concentric circles, with love in the middle between faith and hope (surrounded by an inscription saying that 'Faith establishes, hope cools, unction cleanses hearts') and the seven virtues produced by the gifts of the Holy Spirit. The active life is represented by three scenes showing a woman feeding a hungry man, a man clothing a naked man who is sitting by a fire, and a woman caring for a prisoner in jail. Under the illustration on fol. 4^r is written 'This teaches the hidden things of the divine mysteries' and around it: 'God keeps each [life] for His servants because as a poor man He serves in order that they may learn to be assimilated to Him in such a form. He transforms Himself, and He reforms their hearts. They spurn the things that perish in order that they may see the good things that survive. Every faithful person hopes for this part (*partem*) from the heavens, if this life is redeemed by deeds of faith.' The illustration has two large scenes, one above showing the transfigured Christ holding a scroll with 'Fear not' and the other below showing the Last Supper. Together these illustrations demonstrate visually as well as verbally that the two lives are not mutually exclusive but are correlated in the process of individual salvation. See Katzenellenbogen (1939), pp. 37–8; Cahn (1982), pp. 196–7 and 265, with further bibliography; and Constable (1995a), pp. 57–8, upon which the above account is based.

Plate 2 Floreffe Bible (MS London, British Library, Add. 17738, fol. 3ᵛ)

Plate 3   Floreffe Bible (MS London, British Library, Add. 17738, fol. 4ʳ)

Plate 4   Hugh of Fouilloy, *De rota verae religionis* (MS Heiligenkreuz, Stiftsbibliothek, 226, fol. 146ʳ)

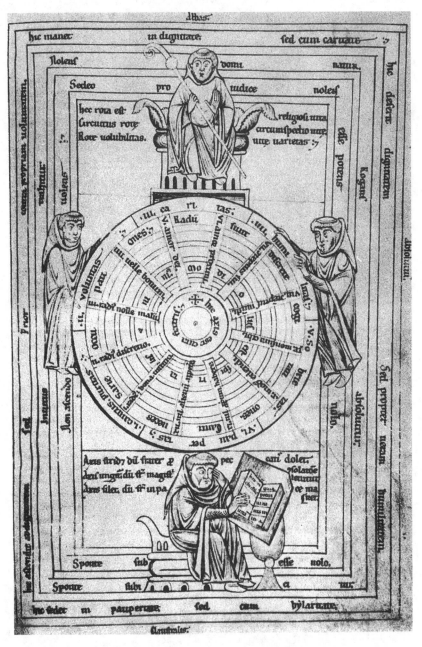

Plate 5 Hugh of Fouilloy, *De rota verae religionis* (MS Heiligenkreuz, Stiftsbibliothek, 226, fol. 149ʳ)

Plates 4-5   The text of Hugh of Fouilloy's *On the wheel of true religion* is a commentary on two diagrams or illustrations, of which those in the Heiligen-kreuz manuscript are among the earliest and best of several versions. Though commonly described as the wheels of good and bad religion, in the manuscripts they are called the wheels of the life of a religious man and of the hypocrites. The rims of each wheel are divided into six sections, each with two spokes. The rim and spokes are described respectively as discerning thoughts and necessary occupations (on the wheel of religious life) and as feelings of the spirit and worldly actions (on the wheel of hypocrites). The hub of the wheel of religious life is inscribed 'This axis is the care of the brother', and the sections of the rim and the respective spokes are labelled purity (good intention and discretion), will (avoiding evil and desiring good), love (love of God and love of neighbour), humility (contempt of self and contempt of the world), sobriety (moderation of food and manner of eating), and poverty (having nothing of one's own and seeking nothing belonging to another). The wheel of hypocrites has on the hub 'This axis is the perversity of the brother', and the sections of the rim and the respective spokes are cunning (care in acquisition and diligence in preservation), avarice (rapacity and tenacity), pride (contempt and disobedience), negligence (forgetting oneself and confusion of spirit), idleness (sloth and food belonging to another), and scarcity (casting out and casting down). See Katzenellenbogen (1939), pp. 70–2, mentioning other manuscripts (p. 72 n. 1), to which can be added Oxford, Bodleian Library, Bodley 188; de Clercq (1960) with the text of Hugh's treatise and illustrations from MS Brussels, Bibl. royale, II, 1076; and Caviness (1983), pp. 113–14, who compared the stability and instability of the two wheels.

Plate 6   This illustration from the account of early Cistercian history in the commentary on the Apocalypse by Alexander of Hales dates from the thirteenth century, but it presents the tradition of Cistercian origins as it was formulated in the documents and accounts composed in the second and third quarters of the twelfth century. Among the points to be noticed are the prominence given to manual labour, the clothing of the working monks, the presence among them of at least one untonsured novice or lay man, and the differing colours of the robes of the four abbots of Clairvaux, La Ferté, Morimond, and Pontigny on the right. On fol. 54^v of the same manuscript there is an illustration with (from left to right) three scenes from the life of Benedict in Gregory the Great's *Dialogues*, II, 1 and 8: the devil breaking the bell of the monk Romanus, who is bringing bread to Benedict; a white-robed priest bringing a refection at Easter to Benedict, who is seated amid the birds and beasts; and Benedict in his monastery instructing a crow to remove some poisoned bread.

Plate 7   The frescoes in the chapter room of the abbey of the Trinity at Vendôme were published by Hélène Toubert (1983), who considered them evidence of the influence on art of the Gregorian reform and associated them with the visit to Vendôme of pope Urban II early in 1096. The scene in the illustration is the second from the left and shows the miraculous catch of fishes in the lake of Tiberias (John 21.1–9), with ten disciples (rather than seven, as in the Gospel story) in the boat and Peter walking on the water to the right (not included in the illustration). All the apostles except Judas are thus present, and their role as fishermen in the boat of the church, of which Peter is the head, is emphasized. On the left of this scene is the supper at Emmaus and on the right, in succession, three scenes showing the investiture of Peter, the mission of the apostles (recalling the mosaic in the Lateran palace, which has the text beginning 'Euntes docete' from Matthew 28.16–20 and stands for the pope surrounded by bishops), and the ascension of Christ.

Plate 8   This painting of St Francis in the desert by Giovanni Bellini is fully discussed and placed within its medieval context by John Fleming (1982). See also p. 327 below.

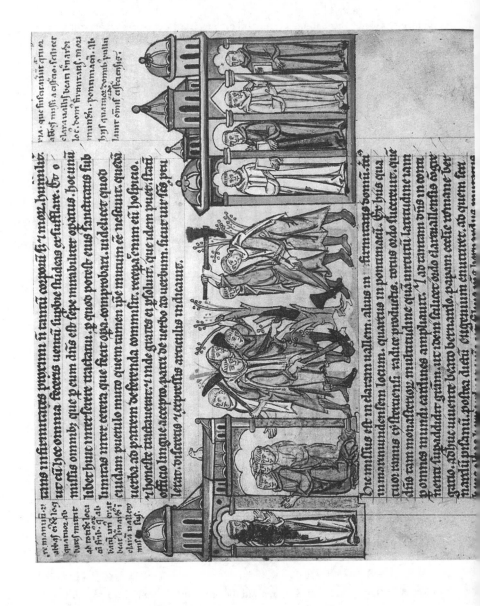

Plate 7 Vendôme, Abbey of the Trinity, Chapter Room

Plate 8 Giovanni Bellini, *St Francis in the Desert*
(New York, Frick Collection).

will teach you what you cannot hear from masters.'[67] Bernard's purpose here was anti-scholastic, if not anti-intellectual, since he contrasted the teaching of men with his own meditation and suggested that there was more to be learned alone in the country than in the towns and schools.[68] Here (though not in all his works) he adumbrated Shakespeare's 'tongues in trees, books in the running brooks, sermons in stones'.

Nature in the twelfth century was often equated with the divine order of things and was depicted as a 'very grave and active' personification in the works of writers like Bernard of Chartres and Alan of Lille.[69] As such it played a central part in the cosmic process of continuous creation and recreation and more specifically in the ideology of the movement of religious reform. William of St Thierry in his *Golden letter* cited Seneca's adage that 'Our undertaking is to live according to nature (*Propositum nostrum est secundum naturam vivere*)' in order to indicate a life in which man has rediscovered his original nature, as it was in the Garden of Eden.[70] Nature here, like *humanitas*, was the true nature or virtue of man, and it was parallel to *ratio* in the sense of divine reason and the creation of man in the image of God as a rational being.[71] Nature and reason were contrasted, however, in the late eleventh-century *Life* of St Romanus by Fulbert of Rouen, who wrote in a passage stressing the dangers of discord and the harmony of birds and animals who fly and graze together that 'By being in agreement with itself irrational nature [the birds and animals] surely show how much harm rational nature [man] does through discord, since the latter loses by the intention of reason what the former naturally preserves.'[72] Suger used the terms reason and nature in a somewhat different sense in his treatise *On the consecration of the church of St Denis*, where he praised reason for bridging the disparity between divine and human things, which seemed divided by a lowly origin and contrary nature but were

---

[67] Bernard, *Ep.* 106.2, ed. Leclercq, VII, 266–7; see also *Ep.* 523 to Aelred of Rievaulx, ed. Leclercq, VIII, 486–8.

[68] On the perceived opposition between the cloister and the school, see Delhaye (1947), p. 228, and Leclercq (1961c).

[69] Alan of Lille, *De planctu naturae*, 6, ed. Nikolaus Häring, in *Studi Medievali* 3 S. 19 (1978), p. 826. See Boas (1948), pp. 80, 88–94, and 117–18; Lewis (1967), pp. 41, 44, 46, and 71; and Stock (1972), pp. 77–87.

[70] Déchanet (1940b) pointed to similar uses by Abelard and later by Bonaventura, for whom naturalism was the same as the love of God.

[71] Aelred of Rievaulx, *Speculum caritatis*, I, 23, 65, in *CC:CM*, I, 40. On *humanitas* in the eleventh and twelfth centuries see Petré (1948), pp. 200–21; Sprandel (1962), pp. 24–8; and von Moos (1965), pp. 276–8. The term continued to have its older meaning of mercy and kindness, as in Suger, *Vita Ludovici Grossi*, 24, ed. Henri Waquet (CHFMA 11; Paris 1929), p. 174.

[72] Fulbert of Rouen, *Vita Romani*, in MS Paris, Bibl. nat., Lat. 13090, fol. 123: 'que si sollerter aspicimus nimirum sibi concordando irrationales natura indicat, quantum malum per discordiam rationalis natura committat, dum uidelicet ista rationis intentione perdit quod illa naturaliter custodit', as transcribed in Lifshitz (1988), pp. 203–4 (*BHL* 7313). Man is equated here with reason and animals with non-reason.

united into 'a pleasing accord of one superior moderated harmony'.[73] When Bruno of Querfurt described Romuald as 'the father of the rational hermits' he was using *rationabilis* to mean intentional, as contrasted with capricious, or 'reasonable' as it is often used today, as when 'Be reasonable' is used as the opposite of rash or foolish.[74] The references to 'the tested life of the holy fathers' in the papal privileges for Rottenbuch and other houses of regular canons and to 'the more tested life' of the Cluniacs in the forged charter of about 1100 for Hasungen likewise meant that the religious life was proven, approved, and in this sense reasonable.[75] Bernard of Tiron directed that everything should be done 'according to reason'; bishop Atto of Florence declared in a charter freeing a monastery from various dues that 'The order of reason demands, and the authority of the holy law approves, that what was previously done at the prompting of charity and the instinct of piety should not be turned to an evil use'; and Hugh Sotovagina of York said that the religious life at Cluny was marked 'by the design of reason'.[76] From the highest levels of philosophy to the lowest levels of material affairs, therefore, reason was equated with the life of monks, and it was no accident that in his *Soliloquy concerning the instruction of the soul* Adam of Dryburgh had Reason defend the strict monastic life against the complaints of the soul.[77]

Reason was seen as an essential part of religious life and of the reform of man. The monastic reformers of the eleventh and twelfth centuries would have agreed with the seventeenth-century divine Benjamin Whichcote that 'There is nothing so intrinsically Rational, as Religion is; nothing that can so Justify itself; nothing, that hath so pure Reason to recommend itself; as Religion hath.'[78] Reason was coupled with nature, authenticity, and truth in various texts dealing with the changes in the liturgy in the twelfth century. The abbots in their reply to Matthew of Albano in 1132 said that they had

---

[73] Suger, *De consecratione*, 1, ed. A. Lecoy de la Marche (Société de l'histoire de France; Paris 1867), p. 213, and tr. Panofsky (1946), p. 83.

[74] Bruno of Querfurt, *Vita quinque fratrum*, 2, in *MGH, SS*, XV.2, 718. See Leclercq (1962b), p. 311.

[75] See the privileges of Urban II for Rottenbuch in 1092 (JL 5459) and St Paul in Narbonne in 1093 (JL 5482) in *PL*, CLI, 338B (and better in Mois (1953), p. 76) and 360B (see n. 168), and of Siegfried of Mainz for Hasungen, allegedly in 1081, in *Mainzer Urkundenbuch*, ed. Manfred Stimming, 1 (Darmstadt 1932), p. 257, no. 358. See Hallinger (1958–60), esp. pp. 227–43.

[76] Geoffrey Grossus, *Vita Bernardi Tironiensis*, XI, 103, in *PL*, CLXXII, 1428B; cf. XI, 104, ibid., 1428CD (*BHL* 1251); Soldani (1741), p. 266; and MS London, British Library, Cotton Vitellius A. xii, fol. 135ʳa. Other poems in this collection were published by Thomas Wright, *The Anglo-Latin Satirical Poets and Epigrammists of the Twelfth Century* (RS 59; London 1872) and Boutemy (1937).

[77] Adam of Dryburgh, *De instructione animae*, in Pez, *Thesaurus*, I.2, 337–72, and in *PL*, CXCVIII, 845–72.

[78] Benjamin Whichcote, *Moral and Religious Aphorisms*, ed. Samuel Salter (London 1753), no. 457. Richard Baxter, *Saints' Everlasting Rest*, pt IV, 8, sect. VII, 5, in his *Practical Works*, ed. William Orme (London 1830), XXIII, 342, said that 'Meditation also putteth reason into his strength. Reason is the strongest, when it is most in action.' I owe these references to Geoffrey Hill.

changed some practices that were in accord with custom but not with reason; the Cistercians claimed that their liturgical revisions in the 1140s emulated nature more than usage and that 'Reason makes our [version] different from others'; and Bernard of Clairvaux said that 'not new and trivial but surely ancient and authentic things' should be heard in the liturgy.[79] Harvey of Bourg-Dieu in his treatise *On the correction of certain readings* cited the ancient adage, which went back to the church fathers, that Christ said He was the truth, not that He was custom. Harvey's purpose was to abolish customs not in accord with truth and to return to 'the pure truth as it was promulgated from the beginning by the evangelists and the prophets'.[80] Hildebert of Lavardin in a letter written about 1124 concerning hereditary canonries wrote after citing Jesus's saying 'I am the way, and the truth, and the life (John 14.6)', that 'He did not say, I am custom … We should therefore, since Christ is truth, follow truth rather than custom, since reason and truth always exclude custom.'[81] In these texts, truth, nature, reason, authenticity, and antiquity stood together as allies, and almost equivalents, in the battle of the reformers against custom, usage, novelty, and triviality.

Perhaps the most striking example of the use of the concept of reason, linked with those of nature, equilibrium, and authority, in the context of monastic reform was in a speech to the monks of Molesme that was attributed by William of Malmesbury to Stephen Harding:

> By reason the supreme Author of things has made all things; by reason He rules all things; by reason the fabric of the heavens is rotated; by reason even the stars that are called wandering [the planets] are turned; by reason the elements are moved; by reason and equilibrium our nature should subsist. But since through neglect (*desidia*) it often falls away from reason, many laws have been proposed from time to time; most recently a rule came forth by divine inspiration through the blessed Benedict that was to bring back the vagaries (*fluxum*) of nature to reason; although it includes certain things of which I am unable to penetrate the reason, I consider it necessary to acquiesce to [its] authority. For reason and the authority of the holy writers are one

[79] *Documents inédits pour servir à l'histoire ecclésiastique de la Belgique*, ed. Ursmer Berlière, I (Maredsous 1894), pp. 109–10, and ed. Stanislaus Ceglar, in *Saint-Thierry. Une abbaye du VIe au XXe siècle. Actes du colloque international d'histoire monastique. Reims-Saint-Thierry, 11 au 14 octobre 1976*, ed. Michel Bur (Saint-Thierry 1979), p. 348, and the treatise, perhaps by Guy of Charlieu, on the *Cantum quem Cisterciensis ordinis ecclesiae cantare consueverant*, ed. F.J. Guentner (Corpus scriptorum de musica 24; Rome 1974), p. 44; and Bernard, *Ep.* 398.2, ed. Leclercq, VIII, 378. Bernard again stressed authenticity in his *Ep. de revisione cantus Cisterciensis*, edited with the treatise on the *Cantum*, p. 21. See Chrysogonus Waddell, in *Renaissance and Renewal* (1982), pp. 106–7.

[80] Harvey of Bourg-Dieu, *De correctione quarundam lectionum*, ed. Germain Morin, in *Rev. bén.* 24 (1907), pp. 39 and 43. On the concept of truth and custom, which was used by Gregory VII in the Investiture Controversy, see Ladner (1959), pp. 138–9, 298, and 410–11 and (1983a), II, 675–9, with additional references 1031–2; Schreiner (1966), p. 143 n. 61, with further references; and Morrison (1969), pp. 31, 273, and 279.

[81] Hildebert of Lavardin, *Ep.* II, 29, in *PL*, CLXXI, 251B.

and the same thing, however much they may appear to differ; for since God created and recreated nothing without reason, how can it be that I should believe that the saintly fathers, that is the followers of God, declared anything against reason, as if we should put our trust in authority alone? Bring forth therefore either the reason or the authority for those things you have devised [the customs of Molesme], although not much credence should be given if some human reason is alleged that can be destroyed by arguments of equal force. Give examples, therefore, in conformity with the rule that is based on reason and authority, as it was dictated by 'the spirit of all just men'. But if you cannot do this, you claim in vain the prerogative of Him whose teaching you scorn to follow.[82]

It would require a whole chapter to comment fully on this remarkable passage, which encapsulates the twelfth-century view of the role of reason both in the macrocosm of the creation and running of the universe and in the microcosm of the nature and activities of man, who reflects the reason of the universe and subsists, like nature, by the balance or equilibrium of the elements.[83] This anthropocentrism provided the framework for William's (or Stephen Harding's) view of the rule of Benedict as designed to restore the lost equilibrium in man by bringing nature back to reason, from which it had departed. The use of *revocare* and especially *recreare* rather than the more common terms of reform, revival, and regrowth emphasized the importance of God's continuing work (which was personified in various ways and was later defined as His conserving or sustaining grace) in recreating what He had originally created. Although William admitted that he did not understand it fully, he insisted in principle on the identity of reason and authority in the works of the fathers and the rule of Benedict, which, as the embodiment of reason and authority, was the basis on which monastic customs must be judged and, if found not in conformity with the rule, abolished. The monks of Molesme seem to have found these arguments less convincing than William, for he went on to say that most of them 'refused to receive the new things because they loved the old ones'. Only eighteen, including the abbot Robert and Stephen himself, agreed 'that superfluous matters should be omitted and only the essence (*medulla*) of the rule should be observed' and decided, since they could not observe the purity (*puritas*) of the rule at Molesme, to leave and establish a new monastery at Cîteaux. Reason, like all good rhetorical devices, was impartial, however, and in the version of the speech of the monks of Molesme given by Ordericus Vitalis, in reply to Robert rather than Stephen, they cited reason in defence of custom, saying that the holy doctors who had preceded them had handed down 'reasonable causes' for the differences

---

[82] William of Malmesbury, *De gestis regum Anglorum*, IV, 334–5, ed. William Stubbs (RS 90; London 1887–9), II, 381–2. The phrase *spiritu omnium justorum* comes from Gregory the Great, *Dialogi*, II, 8, ed. Moricca (n. 20), p. 93.

[83] These remarks replicate in part those in *Renaissance and Renewal* (1982), pp. 61–2 and n. 130, and are indebted to John Callahan, who also assisted with the translation.

between the early monks and themselves and that 'reason required' them, as monks, to be devoted to liturgical rather than to agricultural or manual labour.[84]

Both medieval monks and modern scholars have discussed at length the question of the observance of the rule of Benedict, which had been the touchstone of monastic reform since at least the ninth century.[85] The modern debate has turned in particular on the meaning of the terms *ad litteram* and *litteraliter*, which convey an impression of phariseeism and rigidity. Peter the Venerable in Letter 28 mentioned the letter that killeth and the spirit that quickeneth of 2 Corinthians 3.6, and when in the *Dialogue of two monks* the Cistercian defended his way of life as coming from ancient sources, the Cluniac replied that 'Since you Cistercians judaize, following the killing letter (*occidentem litteram*) of the rule, you therefore diligently study the authorities pertaining to the pure letter (*ad puram litteram*) in order to defend your judaizing through them.'[86] It has been claimed, in order to refute this charge, that *ad litteram* was used only in later sources and by writers who were hostile to the reform and that at the beginning of the movement the most frequently used terms were *districtio* (as in the *Life* of Burchard of Vendôme), *medulla* and *puritas* (as by William of Malmesbury), *rectitudo*, *per omnia*, *ex integro*, *arctius*, *perfectius*, and *simpliciter*, most of which convey an impression of strictness and a concern for the essence rather than literalism in the modern sense.[87] *Ad litteram* was used by Bernard himself in the 1120s,[88] however, and by Ordericus Vitalis in his description of the early Cistercians written in the mid-1130s,[89] and it was probably not taken by contemporaries either in an unfavourable sense (unless combined with 'killing') or in the narrow modern sense of literally, since they all knew that no monks kept the rule of Benedict 'to the letter' and that the reformers departed from it in almost as many ways as the old monks. The differences between what people said and what they did bothered people at that time less than they do now, so long as their hearts were in the right place, which is what really concerned them in the observance of the rule. Gerald of Salles, whose *Life* was written probably at least a century after his death in 1120 but brought together various earlier themes, was

---

[84] Ordericus Vitalis, *Historia ecclesiastica*, VIII, 26, ed. Chibnall, IV, 318–20.

[85] Leclercq (1971a), pp. 129–35, spoke of the 'sort of cult of the rule' (p. 135) that developed in the tenth century.

[86] Idungus, *Dialogus*, III, 15, ed. Huygens, p. 444.

[87] See among others Salmon (1954), p. 278 and n. 4, who said that *ad litteram* appeared only in late sources; Spahr (1955); Dimier (1959), p. 404; Schneider (1960–1), p. 181; Lekai (1982); and Goodrich (1984).

[88] Bernard, *Apologia*, VII, 14, ed. Leclercq, III, 93; cf. *De praecepto et dispensatione*, XVI, 49, ed. Leclercq, III, 286. See Dimier (1959), p. 411.

[89] Ordericus Vitalis, *Historica ecclesiastica*, VI, 19, and VIII, 26, ed. Chibnall, III, 338, and IV, 322; cf. IV, 312 (*ex integro*) and 316 (*per omnia*). For later uses by Philip of Harvengt and Robert of Torigny, see Giles Constable, in *Renaissance and Renewal* (1982), p. 57 n. 111.

said to have established in his nine monasteries a 'manner of living in food
and clothing exactly (*ad unguem*) according to the rule of St Benedict; none
of the precepts less, none more, none repeated, none omitted'. Gerald
himself was described in a mixture of models and images as resembling
Hilarion, Anthony, Christ, John the Baptist, and Paul.

> All of him was on fire, and he set others on fire . . . He inflamed many; he
> summoned many into the desert; he built many places where he ordained that
> the law of St Benedict should be preserved down to the least point (*ad minimum
> iota*). What more? He loved Christ, he preached Christ, he imitated Christ, he
> ascended to Christ.[90]

The reform movement in practice was eclectic, and its leaders selected
within the monastic tradition elements that suited their vision of the nature
of religious life and justified them in the name of authenticity and morality.
They in particular stressed common life and manual labour owing to their
concern for poverty and simplicity. Monks, Hugh of Fouilloy said, were like
angels and man before the fall, because they had few material needs and no
property and denied themselves even those things required by their bodies.
They wanted to be poor and naked, following the poor and naked Christ,
where poverty and nakedness meant being stripped and exposed as well as
without money or clothes.[91] They wanted, like the apostles after the death of
Christ, to have 'one heart and one soul' and all things in common, for they
knew, as Gibbon said of the early Germans,[92] that 'Their poverty secured their
freedom' and that only people without possessions could step fully outside the
network of reciprocal obligations and secular duties that inevitably
accompanied the ownership of property, and especially of land, in the Middle
Ages. When Gerard of Brogne was offered some money, he feared to lose 'the
security of his poverty' and to become, like a rich man, anxious for his
wealth.[93] The reformers were therefore less concerned with indigency than
with expropriation, the state of neither having nor wanting any property,
which was a central feature of their programme.[94] For them, the basic contrast
was not between having or not having money but between *proprius* and *communis*, between something that was one's own and something that was shared.
According to the arenga of a charter of 1155, 'How quietly men would live,
if two words were taken from the centre, that is, "mine" and "yours" '; and
the customs of Marbach laid down that a religious should use the term *suus*

[90] *Vita Giraldi de Salis*, II, 12 and 18, in *AASS*, 23 Oct. X, 257C and 258D (*BHL* 3547).
[91] Châtillon (1974) and Constable (1979).
[92] Gibbon (1896-1902), I, 223.
[93] *Vita Gerardi Broniensis*, 20, in *MGH*, *SS*, XV.2, 670 (*BHL* 3422).
[94] Rousseau (1957), pp. 97-128, and the works cited n. 102 below. See also Adam (1927), p. 174,
on *meum et tuum* in the works of Ratherius of Verona. Turner (1972), pp. 403-5, emphasized
the importance of poverty as a social equalizer. On monastic poverty in the east, see Herman
(1941).

only for his parents or his sins.[95] Personal renunciation of property was not incompatible with institutional wealth. The two were indeed sometimes associated, as in the *Life* of abbot Theodoric of St Hubert in the Ardennes, who when he came found the abbey 'naked and desolate in exterior things' and 'the interior face foul and disordered' and discovered that external revenues and internal religion grew together.[96] Even the strictest reformers had no objection to an adequate institutional endowment, from which the monks could support themselves by their own labour, just as the clergy were supported by pastoral revenues and the laity by the various types of secular revenues.

Begging was generally regarded as unsuitable for monks, and the examples of it that can be cited were usually in extreme cases. Adelelmus of La Chaise-Dieu was called a *mendicus* when he went on a barefoot pilgrimage to Rome in the 1060s, but his poverty was so strict that he refused to accept the alms he was offered.[97] Abbot Andrew of Chezal-Benoît went on begging trips (*mendicando*) both in the vicinity and in England when his monks were in need; Vitalis of Savigny was twice called a *mendicus* in his obituary roll; and Pontius of Léras offered if necessary to make himself a beggar for beggars.[98] These should probably not be taken literally, however, since begging was opposed in principle because it brought monks into contact with the world and implied a lack of faith in God to supply their needs. Abelard strongly criticized abbots who went about begging – today it would be called fund-raising – and who took more care of bodily than of spiritual matters,[99] and the Grandmontines, consistent as always, stressed in their statutes that God never deserts His followers and always provides for the truly poor. If they were hungry, therefore, they should first approach the bishop, and if he did nothing after two days, two brothers might go out begging.[100] This stress on

---

[95] *The Cartulary and Charters of Notre-Dame of Homblières*, ed. Theodore Evergates a.o. (Medieval Academy Books 97; Cambridge, Mass., 1990), p. 145, no. 71, which went on to say that the church therefore invented charters 'for the concord of its sons' and to calm controversies by giving everyone their rights, and *Consuetudines Marbacenses*, XXXIV, 74, in Siegwart (1965), p. 141.

[96] *Vita Theoderici Andaginensis*, 17 and 20, in *MGH, SS*, XII, 46 and 48 (*BHL* 8050). See de Moreau (1946–52), II, 282.

[97] *Vita Adelelmi Casae-Dei*, 4, in *España sagrada*, XXVII, 834 (*BHL* 72). The term *mendicus* used here and in other sources may simply mean 'poor'.

[98] *Rouleaux des morts*, pp. 170 and 307–8, and *Vita Pontii de Larazio*, 17, in Baluze, *Miscellanea*, I, 183. The hermit Robert of Knaresborough used a disciple or servant, walking with bare feet and leaving blood on the ice, to collect alms for the poor: *Vita* [A and B] *Roberti Knaresburgensis*, ed. Paul Grosjean, in *Anal. boll.* 57 (1939), pp. 372 and 387–9 (*BHL* 7270d and 7270ef).

[99] Abelard, *Regula*, ed. T.P. McLaughlin, in *Mediaeval Studies* 18 (1956), pp. 282–3; cf. his shame at begging in the *Historia calamitatum*, ed. J.T. Muckle, in *Mediaeval Studies* 12 (1950), p. 201. Isaac of L'Etoile, *Serm.* 50, in *PL*, CXCIV, 1860D, attacked monks who begged or engaged in commerce rather than supporting themselves by their own work and resources.

[100] *Regula Stephani Muretensis*, 11–13, in *CC:CM*, VIII, 76–8. Anselm of Canterbury expressed his trust in God to provide for his monks, according to Eadmer, *Vita Anselmi*, 28, ed. Richard Southern (MT; London and Edinburgh 1962), pp. 47–8 (*BHL* 525).

economic precariousness as an aspect of faith in God was characteristic of the Grandmontines, whose begging was sharply criticized by Stephen of Tournai, who praised the Cistercians because they never begged even when they were in great need.[101] Medieval theologians and moralists consistently preferred Matthew's version of the beatitude 'Blessed are the poor in spirit' to Luke's 'Blessed are the poor' and insisted that fiscal poverty mattered less than the desire to be poor.[102] The chronicler of Petershausen was exceptional in putting beggars and the poor, as such, among the blessed, since it was generally held that what mattered was to be a *pauper Christi* or *Dei*, who had become voluntarily poor, rather than simply to be a beggar without resources.[103] The contrast between the voluntary and involuntary poor was a commonplace in twelfth-century spiritual writings and was reinforced by Seneca's view of poverty as the willing rejection of property, which was cited by William of Conches, Gerald of Wales, and Peter Comestor.[104] In the commentary on the Psalms attributed to Bruno of La Chartreuse, *paupertas spiritu* in the beatitude referred to humility of soul, not to economic poverty, and the poor in spirit were those 'who even though they abound in worldly possessions take no pride and put no hope in them but distribute them generously to the indigent'.[105] The idea of wealthy poverty was often cited. Hildebert of Lavardin in his letter to William of Champeaux, congratulating him on his conversion to the true Christian philosophy, cited the example of the wealthy poverty of Diogenes in his tub, and William of St Thierry in the *Golden letter* said that a monk who was well-suited to his poverty in his cell was rich.[106] The stress on the concept of voluntary or spiritual poverty by these writers does not mean that they closed their eyes to the problem of indigency or to

[101] Stephen of Tournai, *Ep.* 1 and 148, ed. Desilve, pp. 5–6 and 173. James of Vitry, *Vita Mariae Oigniacensis, prol.*, in *AASS*, 23 June v, 548c (*BHL* 5516), said that the beguines in the diocese of Liège never begged.

[102] On the distinction between voluntary and involuntary poverty, see Constable (1985b), pp. 109–11, and references there. On the term *pauper*, see the influential article of Bosl (1963), who argued that in the early Middle Ages *pauper* meant weak and unprotected rather than economically poor, and Leclercq (1967), and on monastic poverty generally, in addition to the works cited in *Medieval Monasticism*, nos. 999–1004, Mollat (1978) and Little (1978). By the twelfth century *pauper* usually meant poor in the economic sense, but Peter the Venerable, *Ep.* 173, ed. Constable, I, 410, put the *impotentes et pauperes* between agricultural labourers and widows as groups needing protection.

[103] *Casus monasterii Petrishusensis, praef.*, 23, ed. Otto Feger (Schwäbische Chroniken der Stauferzeit 3; Lindau and Constance 1956), p. 36. According to von Dmitrewski (1913), p. 56 n. 18, the term *pauperes Christi* was first used by Ambrose, *Ep.* 21.33, in *PL*, XVI, 1060B, who also insisted on using *in spiritu* in the first beatitude in his *Expositio Evangelii secundum Lucam*, V, 53, in *CC*, XIV, 153. The poverty of Christ later became a topos, and *pauperes Christi* a standard term for monks: see Bolton (1977) and Bosl (1981).

[104] Nothdurft (1963), pp. 67–71.

[105] Bruno of La Chartreuse (attr.), *Expositio* on Ps. 21, in *PL*, CLII, 727A.

[106] Hildebert of Lavardin, *Ep.* I, 1, in *PL*, CLXXI, 142A; cf. *Ep.* I, 4, ibid., 145C, and William of St Thierry, *Ep. ad fratres de Monte Dei*, 48, ed. Davy, p. 97. See von Moos (1965), pp. 106–7.

the sufferings of the involuntary poor, which all Christians were obliged to relieve.[107] Only a few of the reformers, like the Carthusians, regarded alms-giving, like begging, as an improper activity for monks, who were supposed to be cut off from the world.[108] Most of them would have agreed with the self-serving sentiment of the Archpoet that 'God himself is in the poor', and they gave in the hope of future reward, of which the miracle of St Martin's charity was a constant reminder.[109] A few went further and asserted that the poor had rights. Abelard in his sermon on alms distinguished the voluntary poor, to whom the beatitude referred, from those who were poor 'by force rather than by will, in things rather than in spirit, unwilling rather than will-ing', and who, he said, were entitled to alms. 'For when we minister some necessities to those who are in need, we return to them what is theirs, we do not distribute what is ours. We pay the debt of justice rather than fulfil the works of mercy.'[110] This view was developed in the later twelfth century into a doctrine that justified even theft by the poor, if they were in real need, on the grounds of the moral obligation to give alms (of which the act of theft was a venial anticipation) and of the community of property in times of want, which was also cited by Abelard.[111] For many of the reformers and founders of new houses in the early twelfth century charity was a personal as well as an institutional duty, as in the old monasteries. Geoffrey *Grossus* cited Bernard of Tiron's 'liberality in poverty (*largitas in paupertate*)' as one of his three forms of bloodless martyrdom and repeatedly stressed his hospitality and gen-erosity to all who were in need.[112] Hamo of Savigny was described as 'the father of the poor, the defence of the oppressed, the consoler of the grieving, the staff of the infirm, the supporter of the needy, the prompt intercessor and effective liberator of those in prison, and finally the strenuous performer of all piety and mercy'.[113] This list, like that of Hamo's negative qualities cited in the first chapter, is clearly rhetorical and may bear no relation to Hamo's actual activities, but it reflected an important ideal, and one that was often in conflict with the desire of the reformers for seclusion and withdrawal. Some of them were sufficiently roused by the sight of poverty and suffering not only to sympathize with and relieve it but also to identify with it and imitate

---

[107] Réginald Grégoire, in *Monachesimo* (1971), p. 183, showed the growing awareness of the pov-erty of others in eleventh-century saints' lives.

[108] Michel Mollat, in *Monachesimo* (1971), p. 212.

[109] Archpoet, I, st. 31, ed. Heinrich Watenphul and Heinrich Krefeld (Heidelberg 1958), p. 50, as cited by Peter Dronke, in *Renaissance and Renewal* (1982), pp. 585–6. On St Martin, see p. 40 and n. 178 above.

[110] Abelard, *Sermo* 30 *de eleemosyna*, ed. Victor Cousin (Paris 1844), pp. 550–1, and *PL*, CLXXVIII, 564A–9C. Van den Eynde (1962), p. 45, related this passage to that on the nuns' poverty in the *Historia calamitatum*, ed. Muckle (n. 99), p. 206.

[111] See Lottin (1942–60), III, 299–313, and esp. Couvreur (1961).

[112] Geoffrey *Grossus*, *Vita Bernardi Tironiensis*, XI, 92, in *PL*, CLXXII, 1422B; cf. VIII, 70, and XIV, 130, ibid., 1409BC and 1441AC, on his charity and hospitality (*BHL* 1251).

[113] *Vita Hamonis Saviniacensis*, 36, ed. E.P. Sauvage, in *Anal. boll.* 2 (1883), p. 541 (*BHL* 3752). See Zimmermann, II, 33–5.

it in their own lives.[114] Thus the concepts of spiritual and material poverty came together in a crisis of conscience created by the growth of economic poverty in the eleventh and twelfth centuries and instilled a new meaning and intensity, of which the results fully emerged only later, into the ascetic and spiritual poverty of the early reformers.

There was a similar interaction between the theory and the reality of pilgrimage and exile, or peregrination and expatriation, which also played a large role in the rhetoric of the reform. For if all Christians were travellers on the road to heaven, and the entire church was seen as peregrinating, monks and nuns, who had permanently left their homes and entered a state of spiritual and physical exile, represented even more clearly the highest form of pilgrimage.[115] In the early Middle Ages, this was often literally true, since ascetic wandering and homelessness were recognized forms of religious life, especially among the insular monks who set out from their homes in Ireland and England and spent their entire lives on the continent.[116] The stress on stability in the ninth and tenth centuries tended to keep strict monks in their monasteries, but they often felt, and sometimes succumbed to, the temptation to make a pilgrimage or join a crusade.[117] As the ideal of physical stability weakened in the eleventh and twelfth centuries and was replaced by a more personal view of stability of profession, the ideal of peregrination reemerged, and many of the hermits and reformers of that time were wanderers in body as well as in spirit, spending periods in ascetic exile away from their homes and going on pilgrimages to Rome, Compostela, and the Holy Land. Drogo of Seburg when he was still a boy set out on a 'voluntary peregrination', and the anchoress Christina made 'a peregrination across the sea' from her home among the West Saxons to Wareham in England.[118] Goscelin of St Bertin in his *Book of encouragement*, which was addressed to the English recluse Eve who went to Angers and lived with Harvey, included a section on 'The salvation of peregrinating saints', in which he cited many of the standard biblical texts on peregrination and said, addressing Eve, 'You also among all the pilgrims and poor people of the Lord have left your country not only in the spirit of poverty and renunciation of worldly pleasure but also by the distance of lands so that the more you are exiled the more closely you can commend yourself in the ear of the Lord.'[119]

---

[114] See Michel Mollat, in *Monachesimo* (1971), pp. 41–2, and Bolton (1977), pp. 100–1, who suggested on the basis of the work of Mary Douglas that those who voluntarily assumed poverty saw their bodies as surrogates for society and the church.

[115] Congar (1954), pp. 192–4.

[116] Von Campenhausen (1930) and Hughes (1960).

[117] Constable (1976b) and (1977b).

[118] *Vita Drogonis Seburgi*, I, 3, in *AASS*, 16 Apr. II, 439 (*BHL* 2337), and John of Ford, *Vita Wulfrici Haselbergiae*, 56, ed. Maurice Bell (Somerset Record Society 47; n.p. 1933), p. 82 (*BHL* 8743–4).

[119] Goscelin of St Bertin, *Liber confortatorius*, ed. Charles H. Talbot, in *Anal. mon.*, III, 37–8.

Goscelin here associated Eve's physical exile with the spiritual renunciation that was emphasized by the monastic reformers, who looked on pilgrimage in rather the same way they looked on solitude. Most of them valued the spiritual more than the physical ideal of pilgrimage. For Bernard of Clairvaux, 'The object of monks is to seek out not the earthly but the heavenly Jerusalem, and this not by proceeding with their feet but by progressing with their feelings.' And he wrote to the bishop of Lincoln about a cleric who had stayed at Clairvaux rather than continue on a pilgrimage to Jerusalem that 'Your Philip, wishing to go to Jerusalem, found a short-cut and swiftly arrived where he wished to go', that is, the heavenly Jerusalem at Clairvaux. Monastic life for Bernard was thus a *peregrinatio* in which the monk travelled with his heart while remaining stable in his body.[120] He is perfect 'to whom the whole world is an exile', said Hugh of St Victor, who stressed, like John of Salisbury, that to the wise man and the philosopher the world is a foreign land.[121] William of St Thierry also spoke of life as 'a peregrination of this generation . . . of those fighting on earth', which men should always be ready to leave 'for our homeland and city and for the home of our eternity'.[122]

Images of movement and struggle permeate the spiritual writings of the twelfth century: the soul on its way to salvation moves up and down, to and fro, in and out, there and back, always fighting against the forces of evil and secular life, climbing a mountain, finding its way like Dante through a forest, crossing dangerous terrain, sailing over stormy seas, ever hoping to find a safe haven in a monastery before reaching its final destination in heaven. Images like these are found throughout Christian history – and are still used by many preachers – but there was a marked tendency in the twelfth century to spiritualize and internalize the journey and the struggle and to generalize the motif of travel and quest, as in the search for the Holy Grail. What had previously been a war against the external forces of evil and the devil was now increasingly seen as an internal struggle against the evil proclivities of man. This was not new, but it was more marked than before, and was used for all aspects of religious life, like the images of ascent and descent that were applied to transfers from one monastery to another.[123]

A more distinctive feature of the late eleventh and twelfth centuries, and particularly, though not exclusively, of the reformers, was the concern in the *Lives* of saints with inward and humble virtues, and on work in the world, as in the *Life* of Robert of La Chaise-Dieu, and a reduced emphasis on heroic

---

[120] Bernard, *Ep.* 64.1–2, and 399, ed. Leclercq, VII, 157–8, and VIII, 379–80. See Leclercq (1964b), pp. 82–4.

[121] Hugh of St Victor, *Didascalicon*, III, 19, ed. Charles J. Buttimer (Catholic University of America Studies in Medieval and Renaissance Latin 10; Washington 1939), p. 69, and John of Salisbury, *Policraticus*, VII, 13, ed. C.C.J. Webb (Oxford 1909), II, 145. See Delhaye (1947), p. 240.

[122] William of St Thierry, *Ep. ad fratres de Monte Dei*, 65, ed. Davy, p. 114.

[123] On Anselm of Havelberg's use of *ascendere* and *descendere* in cases of *transitus*, see Fina (1956–8), (2) pp. 217–18 and (4) pp. 282–3.

asceticism and ostentatious wonder-working.[124] Such saints still existed, like the Camaldolese monk Dominic *Loricatus*, who took his name from the metal plates he hung on his body and whose practice of flagellation while reciting the psalms has been considered the origin of the penitential discipline, as it was called, though earlier examples can be found,[125] and the hermit Schetzelo, whose isolation and nakedness excited the admiration of Bernard of Clairvaux.[126] The physical mortifications of Robert of Arbrissel, Bernard of Tiron, Stephen of Grandmont, and other reformers were usually presented, however, as an expiation of personal guilt and as an identification with the sufferings of Christ rather than as a battle against external forces of evil. In winter Stephen of Obazine immersed himself in water and wore his clothes frozen owing to his 'sole desire of suffering', so that in this and other ways, his biographer said, 'The good athlete condemned himself in his body for the sake of Christ, so that his spirit might be saved on the day of the Lord'; and Pontius of Léras 'was totally converted to penance and shed rivers of tears night and day in order to wash away the stains of his crimes'.[127] Personal penitential devotions, sometimes of great physical severity, became frequent in the twelfth century and later, outside as well as inside monasteries, but they were characteristically practised in private and sometimes in secret, so that they were discovered only after death, and were regarded as expressions of personal piety and guilt rather than of a general battle against evil or the conquest of the body. Public displays of asceticism were not as a rule admired by serious churchmen. Bernard of Clairvaux gave a classic depiction in the *Steps of humility* of the monk who fasted and groaned 'with singularity but without sincerity' and who was grievously deceived, Bernard said, when the more innocent monks admired him and called him blessed; and Hugh of Marchiennes, who died in 1158, was said to have hated 'with a perfect hate those singularities and singular abstinences in food and clothing, which pertain more to vanity than to utility'.[128]

Bernard's picture of a hypocritical ascetic is so vivid that the reader can almost see him, coughing and spitting in his corner and examining his body in order to see how emaciated it was, and can easily forget that he is a type and a topos, who may have existed in reality but who also filled a social niche, like an exhausted runner today breaking the tape or crawling to the finish line

---

[124] Schmeidler (1927) and, more generally, Constable (1982a) and (1992b).

[125] Peter Damiani, *Vitae Rodulphi et Dominici Loricati*, 8, in *PL*, CXLIV, 1015A–16B (*BHL* 2239). See also Damiani's praise of self-mortification in *De perfectione monachorum*, 2, ed. (with *De divina omnipotentia*) Paolo Brezzi (Edizione nazionale dei classici del pensiero italiano 5; Florence 1943), p. 210, and of flagellation in *De laude flagellorum*, in *PL*, CXLV, 682D–3A.

[126] Herbert, *De miraculis*, II, 3–7, in Bernard, ed. Mabillon, II(6), 2383D–8D.

[127] *Vita Stephani Obazinensis*, I, 2 and 5, ed. Aubrun, pp. 44 and 52, and *Vita Pontii de Larazio*, 2, in Baluze, *Miscellanea*, I, 180. See pp. 25–6 above for other examples of suffering.

[128] Bernard, *De gradibus humilitatis et superbiae*, XIV, 42, ed. Leclercq, III, 48–9, and tr. George B. Burch (Cambridge, Mass., 1940), p. 209, and *Vita Hugonis Marchianensis*, 8, ed. Henri Platelle and Robert Godding, in *Anal. boll.* 111 (1993), p. 326 (*BHL* 4031d).

at the end of a race. Mortification of the flesh was considered admirable when it was practised out of love and sincerity, and in private, but not when it was displayed in the search of praise. Richard of St Victor in his sermon on Psalm 64 said that the new religious orders were truly 'the beautiful places of the wilderness' and every day marvellously enriched their members 'not in the flesh but in the spirit'. 'For while they lacerate the flesh, they enrich the spirit; while they weaken the flesh, they strengthen the spirit; while they take a little away from the flesh outside, they add a lot to the spirit inside.'[129] Such practices were in particular a sign of the desire to suffer with and for Christ, which was a marked feature of the spirituality of the age, together with a general devotion to the humanity of Christ and His life on earth. A desire not only to follow, as commanded in the New Testament, but also to copy and almost to replicate the life of Christ, down to the last detail, is stressed in almost all the spiritual writings of the eleventh and twelfth centuries.[130] Christ was an institutional as well as a personal model and was cited to justify many activities and changes in society. His life on earth had long been used to show that He instituted and served in all the ranks of the clerical hierarchy, and it was now used systematically, as in the *Libellus*, to justify the various orders and professions in the church.[131] The ideal of the imitation of Christ was thus a powerful solvent of the traditional view of the superiority of a life of withdrawal and an impetus towards the acceptance of social pluralism and the validity of different types of work in the world. As such it entered into the debates over the respective merits of an exclusively secluded life of contemplation and a mixed life of contemplation and action.

No conscious aspect of the reform movement was more important than the desire to imitate Christ and live the life of the Gospel. The reformers wanted 'to run after Christ in the tracks of the Fathers', according to the speech attributed by Ordericus Vitalis to Robert of Molesme; in the treatise *On the truly apostolic life* the Gospel was called the rule of rules, and the rule of Benedict its summary; and for Stephen of Grandmont the rules of Basil, Augustine, and Benedict all grew from the Gospel, 'the source and beginning of all rules' and 'the first and principal rule of the Christian religion', to which Stephen said his followers should cling 'like tendrils to the true vine of Christ'.[132] To the discontented monks of St Mary at York, in whom the Gospel seemed dead and impossible, it lived again (*revixit*) in the monks of

---

[129] Richard of St Victor (attr. to Hugh of St Victor), *Serm.* 72, in *PL*, CLXXVII, 1127C.

[130] Constable (1995a), pp. 143–248, esp. 169–93.

[131] *Libellus*, 4 and 33, ed. Constable, pp. 10–12 and 60, and intro., p. xxi. See generally Wilmart (1923) and Reynolds (1978).

[132] Ordericus Vitalis, *Historia ecclesiastica*, VIII, 26, ed. Chibnall, IV, 314; *De vita vere apostolica*, 5, in *Ampl. coll.*, IX, 1016; and *Regula Stephani Muretensis, prol.*, in *CC:CM*, VIII, 66–7. Stephen characteristically told his followers that if they were asked what rule they followed or to what order they belonged they should say that they were of the Gospel. See Leclercq (1961a), pp. 81–90, on the Gospel as the source of monastic rules.

Savigny and Clairvaux. Behind the rule of Benedict, which was the measure of their life at St Mary, stood the Gospel, which the rule tried to put into practice. 'Let us return (*recurramus*), if it is possible, O venerable father', they said to the abbot, 'to the Gospel truth, to the Gospel perfection and peace.'[133] In this passionate desire to recover a lost purity lay one of the most powerful inspirations of the movement of personal and institutional reform. It swept away all aspects of religious life that were not seen as in conformity with the Gospel message of personal perfection and reform in the image of Christ. This sense of the past, projected into an idealized future,[134] supplied the rhetoric of reform both with an inexhaustible wealth of models drawn from the bible and the history of Christianity and with a stern standard of authenticity and truth as weapons against the corrupt encrustations of subsequent generations.

The movement of return to the sources showed itself on every level, beginning with a concern for the textual accuracy of the bible, the liturgy, and other religious texts. Although to modern critics the techniques used may seem naive, they mark an important step in the history of scholarship as well as of spirituality and extended, in a tentative way, to legal and literary texts, which were revised in the twelfth century on the basis both of a comparison of manuscripts and of what would now be called hypothetical editorial conjectures, when scribes used their knowledge of Latin and sense of a text to correct it. The most impressive example of this concern for accuracy in the religious field was the great bible of Stephen Harding, in four volumes, of which the text was prepared by three or four correctors.[135] A note next to the text of Acts 10.6 reads: 'In two old and very truthful histories we do not find this verse: "He will tell thee what thou must do." '[136] A similar concern for tradition and accuracy based on the manuscripts was shown in the Cistercian revision of the liturgy, which made use of manuscripts from Metz and Milan, and in collections of *opera omnia*, which were rare in the Middle Ages and of which the manuscript of the works of Augustine from Clairvaux is an example.[137] This editorial and textual activity reflected a practical desire for authenticity and consistency in monastic life and liturgy. 'You know how greatly false songs in the church of God distress me', wrote Peter the Venerable, who changed the time of the celebration of Prime in the infirmary chapel at Cluny in order not to sing the hymn 'Iam lucis orto sidere' in the dark and thus tell a lie in the presence of God.[138] Bernard in his letter on the

---

[133] Hugh of Kirkstall, *Narratio*, ed. Walbran, I, 19–20. See pp. 53–4.

[134] On the concept of the mystic life as a return to and anticipation of paradise, see Eliade (1952), pp. 219–21.

[135] MSS Dijon, Bibl. mun., 12–15. See Oursel (1926), pp. 17–29 and 63–70, and pl. 3–21, who dated it 1098–1109 (p. 22); Lang (1939–40); de Lubac (1959–64), II.1, 268; and Cahn (1962–4).

[136] MSS Dijon, Bibl. mun., 15, fol. 73ᵛ: 'In duobus uetustissimis et multum ueracibus hystoriis non inuenimus hunc uersum, hic dicet tibi quid te oporteat facere.'

[137] De Ghellinck (1950).

[138] Peter the Venerable, *Ep.* 124, ed. Constable, I, 318, and *Stat.* 61, in *CCM*, VI, 93. See Szövérffy (1979).

liturgy to the monks of Montiéramey said that 'The undoubted meanings should be resplendent with truth, pour forth justice, urge humility, teach equanimity . . . The song . . . should make the meaning of the letter not empty but fruitful.'[139] This concept of the fruitful meaning of the letter spreading truth, justice, humility, and equanimity helps to explain the parallel concern of the reformers for the letter of the rule, which was part of a general battle for truth and authenticity against falsehood and custom.[140]

The bible, as the book of truth and salvation above all others, was the great arsenal of reform rhetoric.[141] It has been said of medieval writers that 'They thought and spoke and wrote the thoughts and words and phrases of the bible.'[142] Monks above all heard the words of the bible every day. Bertrand of Grandselve 'at the beginning of his conversion' meditated daily on the Scriptures and wept torrents of tears at the name of Jesus, and Hamo of Savigny took the bible with him for reading and meditation when he went out to tend the pigs.[143] They tried to live the bible in every aspect of their personal and institutional lives. Christ's command to deny oneself, take up the cross, and follow Him was 'the *summa* of the monastic religion', and His counsel of perfection, to sell what one had and give to the poor, expressed the perfect philosophy of Christ, which could never be countermanded.[144] Gerard of St Albinus at Angers was said to have carried His cross voluntarily (*sponte*), like Christ, outdoing Simon, who carried his as a duty, and to have 'deviated in no respect . . . from the path of the Lord, since he voluntarily abjured some things that are allowed and banished since his infancy all things that are prohibited'.[145]

The reformers inhabited the beautiful deserts and gardens of Deuteronomy, the Psalms, and the Song of Songs; they lived together in unity, as in Psalm 132, and led a common life 'with one heart and one soul' as in Acts; and they followed Paul's prescription to seek the things of Jesus Christ.[146] Freed by the Lord, like the wild ass in Job 39.5, and called unto liberty in the spirit of

[139] Bernard, *Ep.* 398.2, ed. Leclercq, VIII, 378, and other works cited in n. 79 above.
[140] See nn. 80–1.
[141] Leclercq (1966). Chrysogonus Waddell in a talk on 'The Texts of the Proper St Bernard Office' given at Kalamazoo in May 1990 stressed that the Cistercians read the glossed bible, and heard, rather than read, the bible. Cf. the published version in Waddell (1992). Southern (1995), p. 132, said that 'What the world received was not the bare text of the bible but the text as interpreted in the schools.'
[142] Maitland (1890), p. 476.
[143] *Vita Bertrandi Grandis Silvae*, 2, in *AASS*, 23 Oct. X, 245C (*BHL* 1305), and *Vita Hamonis Saviniacensis*, 19, ed. Sauvage (n. 113), pp. 522–3 (*BHL* 3752).
[144] On the use of these texts in the early Middle Ages, see Angenendt (1972), pp. 130–5, and for examples of their later use, *De professionibus monachorum*, in Martène (1736–8), II, 482; Hildebert of Lavardin, *Ep.* I, 1, in *PL*, CLXXI, 142B; and *Oorkondenboek van het Sticht Utrecht tot 1301*, ed. S. Muller and A.C. Bouman, I (Utrecht 1920–5), p. 236, no. 262.
[145] *Miracula Girardi sancti Albini Andegavensis*, in *AASS*, 4 Nov. II.1, 506D (*BHL* 3549).
[146] See the commentary on Ps. 132.1 in Hugh of Barzelle, *De cohabitatione fratrum*, ed. John Morson, in *Anal. mon.*, IV, 119–40, and, on the use of Philip. 2.21 in the Investiture Controversy, Miccoli (1958), p. 50 n. 1 = (1966a), p. 106 n. 23.

liberty by Paul, they were the other Moses, Elijah, and John the Baptist, and above all the other Christ, of Whose life every detail prefigured some aspect of theirs.[147] They had chosen the one necessary thing with Mary, who was commonly identified with contemplation, as her sister Martha was with action.[148] They knew from the parable of the sower that the reward of those who left their homes and families for Christ and took 'the more perfect treasure of voluntary poverty' would be a hundredfold, while that of the clergy would be sixtyfold and that of the laity only thirtyfold. Philip of Harvengt cited this parable in conjunction with Matthew 19.21 to drive the lesson home.[149] They looked at themselves and others with a single or simple eye, which was the opposite of double or duplicitous. Peter the Venerable especially liked the text from Matthew 6.22, 'If thy eye be single, thy whole body shall be lightsome', which he used to justify small differences in monastic observance, saying in his Letter 28 that 'If [your] intention is good, all [your] deeds will be righteous.'[150] In Letter 111 he associated it with the injunction in 1 Corinthians 16.14, 'Let all your things be done in love', and with the Augustinian maxim, 'Have love and do what you will', which was often cited to justify an inward-oriented morality.[151] In spite of Bernard's warning in *On precept and dispensation* that the single eye must see with prudence as well as good will and never call evil good or good evil,[152] the eye became identified with love in a spiritual as well as a secular sense. Adam of Dryburgh said in his sermon on St Stephen, 'It is an old proverb: Where [there is] love, there [is] the eye; and this is true, but not truer than this, which is similar to it: Where [there is] no feeling, [there is] no sight.'[153]

Precepts like this, though not found in the bible, took on a quasi-biblical authority when associated with biblical texts and in the context of a bible-based spirituality. The same is true of the models of the apostolic life and the primitive church, which were derived almost entirely from the bible and were the most powerful spurs to institutional reform after the example of Christ and the precepts of the Gospel and St Paul. The New Testament presents two pictures of the life and activity of the apostles after the death of Christ: one,

---

[147] On Job 39.5, see p. 61 n. 65, and on Gal. 5.13 and 2 Cor. 3.17, Constable (1985b), pp. 101–6.

[148] On Mary and Martha, see Constable (1995a), pp. 3–141.

[149] Philip of Harvengt, *De institutione clericorum*, 5: *De obedientia clericorum*, 30, in *PL*, CCIII, 904D. On the use of Matt. 13.8, see Miccoli (1966a), pp. 5–6, and Quacquarelli (1953), esp. ch. 6.

[150] Peter the Venerable, *Ep.* 28, ed. Constable, I, 60; cf. *Ep.* 144, ibid., I, 358. In both the Douai and King James translations of the bible, *simplex* is translated as 'single': see Lewis (1967), p. 171.

[151] Peter the Venerable, *Ep.* 111, ed. Constable, I, 281. On *Habe caritatem* (or *Dilige*) *et quod uis fac*, see James (1902), pp. 80 and 361; Gallay (1955); and John Benton, in *Renaissance and Renewal* (1982), p. 293 and n. 93.

[152] Bernard, *De praecepto et dispensatione*, XIV, 35–6, ed. Leclercq, III, 278–9; cf. XIV, 40–1, ibid., 280–2.

[153] Adam of Dryburgh, *Serm.* 3 *in die s. Stephani*, 4, in *PL*, CXCVIII, 286A. See Petit (1934), p. 99.

of which the most influential account was in Acts 2.42–7 and 4.32–7, showed a highly cohesive community living together, with shared property, common ceremonies, and a single purpose;[154] the other, of which the description is more widely scattered, presented the apostles' work of spreading the Gospel, as in Mark 16.15, where Christ told the apostles 'Go ye into the whole world and preach the gospel to every creature', and in Galatians 2.7–9, where Paul described the apostleships of the Jews and the Gentiles. Today the primary emphasis is on the second picture, but in the early Middle Ages the first picture predominated, and the community life of the apostles was universally regarded as the model for monks. Missionaries were called apostles, and the papacy was apostolic, but before the twelfth century the apostles were seen above all as the first monks and the term apostolic life almost invariably meant monastic life, with a stress on poverty, charity, and manual labour, which the first apostles were thought to have practised.[155] The decree of the council of Rome in 1059 imposing chastity and a common life on clerics, which was repeated a decade later, urged them to 'strive most greatly to arrive at the apostolic, that is the common life'.[156] There were signs of a change about the turn of the century, however, in part on account of the preaching and pastoral work of the reformers, who began to be called apostles. When Bernard of Tiron's right to preach was challenged because, as a monk, he was dead to the world, he replied that he came 'to the permission to preach . . . through the virtue of mortification', which would benefit his listeners, and later he received from the pope both the *officium* of preaching, baptizing, hearing confessions, and performing other pastoral work and permission to receive pastoral revenues, since he held the place (*vices*) of the apostolate and was vicar (*vicarius*) of the apostles,[157] which clearly referred to what would today be called apostolic work. The significance of the representation of the apostles as fishermen was presumably not lost on the monks of the Trinity of Vendôme (plate 7). Bernard of Clairvaux used the term apostle in this new sense in his *Life* of Malachy, whose wandering barefoot preaching was 'the apostolic form' and who was 'the true heir of the apostles'. Bernard meant a strict monastic

---

[154] See Martin (1972) and Bori (1974) on the history of the summary statements in Acts.

[155] Spätling (1947); Vicaire (1963); Frank (1971); Bori (1974), pp. 145–78; Grundmann (1976), pp. 58–60; and, especially on the twelfth century, McDonnell (1955) and Chenu (1954), repr. in (1957), pp. 225–51. On the terms *apostolus* and *vita apostolica*, see Dewailly (1948) and Leclercq (1961a), pp. 63–80, and (1961b), pp. 14 and 38, who said that *vita apostolica* was rarely used in patristic and early medieval sources and was applied to poverty and common life in the eighth and ninth centuries. In the east, according to Rousseau (1957), p. 53, 'apostolic' referred to the sanctity rather than the activity of the apostles.

[156] Rome (1059), 4, in Mansi, XIX, 898A, which was repeated with insignificant differences in Rome (1069), 4, ibid., 1025C.

[157] Geoffrey *Grossus, Vita Bernardi Tironiensis*, VI, 54, and VII, 59, in *PL*, CLXXII, 1399C and 1403A (*BHL* 1251). The historicity of these accounts is doubtful, but not Geoffrey's use of the terms *apostolatus* and *apostoli* in reference to preaching.

life, however, when he said that the Cistercians had professed the apostolic life and represented apostolic perfection.[158] Norbert was called 'a truly apostolic man' after he expelled a demon from a girl, and later he chose to follow the rule of Augustine rather than the eremitical, anchoretical, or Cistercian ways, 'for he already hoped to lead the apostolic life, which he had received in preaching and which he gathered had been ordered and renewed by that holy man after the apostles'.[159] While the dates of these texts are not certain, they suggest that the new use was current in the 1120s, and the word 'truly (*vere*)' may have been included in the title of the treatise *On the truly apostolic life* (which was written in the mid to late 1120s and argued that the apostles were really monks, who derive 'from the spring of the apostles') in order to refute the idea that the true apostolic life was preaching.[160] The use of the term is often ambiguous, as in the charter of archbishop Frederick of Cologne installing regular canons at Steinfeld in 1121, where he referred to the tradition of canonical life going back to the apostles and also to the pastoral care administered by the monastery but where he associated the apostolic character of the canons with their strict common life rather than with pastoral work.[161]

 The use of the terms apostle, apostolic, and apostolic life therefore overlapped in referring to monks and canons during the first half of the twelfth century. They were also used by and applied to various heterodox groups in the senses both of common life and of ascetic preaching. Guibert of Nogent, writing about 1115, mentioned some peasant heretics 'who boasting that they observe the apostolic life favour reading only their acts'. Peter the Venerable in a letter to the archbishop of Lyon in the 1130s described some false monks who claimed to live 'the apostolic, that is the common life'. And Bernard in his sermons on the Song of Songs referred several times to the apostolic life of heretics: 'They certainly boast that they are the successors of the apostles, and call themselves apostolics, but they are unable to show any sign of their apostolate.'[162] Hugh of Rouen wrote in *Against the heretics* that 'They say they lead a common life in their houses and have women with them just like the

---

[158] Bernard, *Vita Malachi*, XIX, 43–4, ed. Leclercq, III, 348–9 (*BHL* 5188), and *Serm.* 22 *de diversis*, 2, and 27.3, ed. Leclercq, VI.1, 171 and 200, and *Serm.* 3 *in labore messis*, 7, ed. Leclercq, V, 226.

[159] *Vita* [B] *Norberti*, VIII, 47, and IX, 50, in *PL*, CLXX, 1290A and 1292B (*BHL* 6249). Norbert is commonly considered to have been one of the 'new' or 'pseudo-' apostles who attacked Abelard: see p. 25 n. 114 above.

[160] *De vita vere apostolica*, 4, in *Ampl. coll.*, IX, 1012 and 1015A.

[161] *Urkundenbuch für die Geschichte des Niederrheins*, ed. T.D. Lacomblet, I (Düsseldorf 1840), p. 191, no. 292.

[162] Guibert, *De vita sua*, III, 17, ed. Bourgin, p. 213; Peter the Venerable, *Ep.* 38, ed. Constable, I, 129; and Bernard, *Serm.* 66 *in Cant.*, III, 8, ed. Leclercq, II, 183; cf. *Serm.* 65, II, 4, and 77, II, 3, ibid., pp. 174–5 and 263. Some scholars have suggested that the *apostolici* referred to by Bernard were a specific heretical sect, but the use of the term in the Steinfeld charter shows that it could mean to resemble or be the successors of the apostles, and there is no evidence that it was systematically avoided in the late twelfth century owing to its association with heresy.

apostles (*more apostolico*)', which suggests, like Guibert, a dependence on the description of the apostles' life in Acts rather than a stress on preaching.[163] While the use of these terms thus reflects the broadening variety of types of religious life in the twelfth century, no single meaning drove out the others. The monk Martinian confidently asserted that 'The order of monks took its beginning from the order of apostles',[164] and at the end of the century Stephen of Paris in his commentary on the rule of Benedict wrote that 'The apostolic life is the life of monks living communally' and that 'The monastic order is apostolic, since the monastic life originated, as the holy fathers say, from both the apostolic doctrine and the apostolic life.'[165]

The model of the primitive church was closely related to that of the apostolic life and was based to a great extent on the same sources.[166] The two were sometimes hardly distinguished, as in the charter of archbishop Siegfried of Mainz in 1074 for the regular canons of Ravengiersburg, who were to live 'according to the example of those men who, in the primitive church, as is read in the Acts of the Apostles, said nothing was theirs but all things were common to them'.[167] It often drew on Matthew 19.21 as well as Acts, however, and tended to be broader than the apostolic life, setting a standard for personal as well as institutional perfection, based on the early history of the church. In the influential privilege of pope Urban II for Rottenbuch in 1092, it was associated particularly with the regular canons, who were praised for renewing 'the tested life of the holy fathers' and for raising up 'the institutes of the apostolic discipline that emerged at the origins of the holy church but were almost obliterated as the church grew'. After distinguishing the lives of monks and canons, which he called 'two parts of almost the same intention', Urban went on to say that whereas the part of the monks had flourished in every age, the part of the canons

> has now flowed almost entirely from the waning fervour of the faithful. This part the martyr and pope Urban established; this part Augustine ordered with

---

[163] Hugh of Rouen, *Contra haereticos*, III, 4, in *PL*, CXCII, 1289D. See also Everin of Steinfeld's letter to Bernard in *PL*, CLXXXII, 677D, and Ralph Ardens, *Hom.* 19, in *PL*, CLV, 2011A, on the use of the term apostolic life by heretics and other sources cited by Ladner (1959), pp. 364 and 402 n. 64, and Grundmann (1976), p. 60.

[164] Martinian, *Exhortatio*, I, 8, ed. H. Roux, in *Mélanges bénédictins publiés à l'occasion du XIV* centenaire de la mort de saint Benoît par les moines de l'abbaye de Saint-Jérôme de Rome* (Abbaye S. Wandrille 1947), p. 339.

[165] MS Clm 3029, fols. 74ᵛa ('Vita apostolica est uita monachorum communiter uiuentium') and 146ᵛa ('Ordo monachicus est apostolicus. Vita quippe monastica ex apostolica ut dicunt sancti patres exordium sumpsit, tam doctrina quam uita'). See Leclercq (1971b) on this work, which was written about 1200 probably by a secular cleric who was at Paris as a boy and in Italy and Monte Cassino in 1159/66.

[166] See esp. Miccoli (1966b); Olsen (1969); and the unpublished dissertation of Ditsche (1958), pp. 32–46.

[167] *Urkundenbuch zur Geschichte der jetzt die preussischen Regierungsbezirke Coblenz und Trier bildenden mittelrheinischen Territorien*, ed. Heinrich Beyer, Leopold Eltester, and Adam Goerz (Coblenz 1860–74), I, 431, no. 374. See Wirges (1928), p. 117.

his rules; this part Jerome moulded in his letters; this part Gregory ordered Augustine the archbishop of the English to establish. Therefore it should not be considered of less merit to keep this primitive life of the church, with the aid and attendance of the Holy Spirit, than to observe the flourishing religion of monks by the perseverance of the same spirit.[168]

The link between the primitive church and clerical reform was underlined by Urban's own name, which recalled the third-century pope whose alleged decree on the poverty and common life of the clergy was cited in this privilege.[169] The model of the primitive church was cited so frequently in the twelfth century that it became for some writers an historical rather than a reforming concept,[170] but in the late Middle Ages it was again widely used, together with the apostolic ideal, as a standard against which to judge the contemporary church and as a source of anti-papalism.[171]

The concept of the primitive church was based not only on the sub-apostolic period but also, if not always explicitly, on the fourth and fifth centuries, when the institutional bases of the church as it was known in the Middle Ages were laid. Many of the architectural models associated with the early church dated from this period. Some of the early twelfth-century churches in Rome are almost perfect reproductions of fourth- and fifth-century basilicas and constitute in their own way as clear a statement of the desire to return to the primitive church as Urban's references to the works of Augustine, Jerome, and Gregory.[172] From this period, too, came the models of the early monks and above all the desert fathers. The *Life* of Anthony by Athanasius, together with the works of Cassian and the *Lives of the fathers*, were second only to the bible and the rule of Benedict in their influence on monasticism in the eleventh and twelfth centuries.[173] Anthony, Paul, and the other desert fathers were repeatedly cited as models of solitude, austerity, and simplicity. Peter Damiani said that he found at Cluny in the middle of the

---

[168] *PL*, CLI, 338CD and (better) Mois (1953), pp. 76–7 (JL 5459); see n. 75 above. This celebrated passage appears in somewhat differing forms in the privileges for St Paul at Narbonne (JL 5482), St Quentin at Beauvais (JL 5496; *PU in Frankreich*, N.F. VII, 248–50, no. 14), Maguelonne (JL 5550), St Pierremont (JL 5567), and St Rufus at Avignon (JL 5763), which Dereine (1951), pp. 545–6, and (1960a), p. 906, believed was the model for the Rottenbuch privilege and which was included in Ivo, *Decretum*, VI, 411, in *PL*, CLXI, 533BC, and Gratian, *Decretum*, XIX, 3, 3, in *Corpus*, ed. Friedberg, I, 840–1. Among the many works on this privilege, see Levison (1918), citing later examples, and Fuhrmann (1984), pp. 6–8, and on its sources, which are found together in Anselm of Lucca, *Collectio canonum*, VII, 2–5, ed. F. Thaner (Innsbruck 1906–15), II, 362–7, see Dereine (1948c), p. 293, and *PU in Frankreich*, N.F. VII, 247–8, no. 14.

[169] *Decretales Pseudo-Isidorianae*, ed. Paul Hinschius (Leipzig 1863), pp. 143–6, and, on Urban's name, Claxton (1967), who said (p. 495) that 'Odo consciously and purposefully assumed the name Urban because of that early pope's association with clerical reform.'

[170] Olsen (1969), pp. 70–80.

[171] See esp. Leff (1967), p. 71, and Hendrix (1976), pp. 347–8.

[172] Kitzinger (1972), p. 101, and in *Renaissance and Renewal* (1982), pp. 638–9, and Constable (1990), pp. 55–6.

[173] Penco (1963) and, on Anthony, Leclercq (1956b) and (1961b), p. 125.

eleventh century many Pauls and Anthonies 'who although they do not occupy a habitation of solitude, gain the reward of anchorites by imitating their works'.[174] William of St Thierry said that Bernard of Clairvaux followed the early Egyptian monks and dedicated 'the first-fruits of his youth to resuscitating the fervour of the ancient religion in the monastic order'.[175] 'The vast solitudes' of north-western France became 'another Egypt' owing to the number of hermits; Adam of Eynsham's description of life at La Chartreuse in his *Life* of Hugh of Lincoln resembled that of the early monks in Egypt; and in the treatise *On the eating of birds* 'the honest custom' of the ancient monks of Egypt and Palestine was compared to 'the purest spring' from which the monastic discipline flowed.[176] The works of Jerome offered the models not only of Hilarion for monks but also of Paula and Eustochium for nuns. Martin was known above all from the *Life* of Sulpicius Severus and Benedict from the *Dialogues* of Gregory the Great, which has been called the Latin *Apophthegmata*.[177] 'How could he who was "filled with the spirit of all just men" have lacked love in establishing the rule?' asked Peter the Venerable in Letter 28, citing the *Dialogues*, II, 28, in defence of the customs of Cluny. 'Do you think', he continued, citing *Dialogues*, II, 35, 'that you can see and foresee more clearly than the eye that was able in a moment to see the entire world gathered together?'[178]

No monks who lived after Benedict were prominently cited by the reformers in the eleventh and twelfth centuries, for whom the great monks of the previous 500 years – such as Columban, Benedict of Aniane, and the abbots of Cluny – were founders and legislators rather than examples, aside from some specific episodes in their *Lives*. Consciously or unconsciously, they looked back over the long space of time from their own or 'modern' times to the models of the apostolic age and the primitive church.[179] Frederick of Cologne in his charter for Steinfeld contrasted the establishment of the canonical profession in the early church and its spread in 'modern times', as did Urban II

[174] Peter Damiani, *De gallica profectione*, 12, in *PL*, CXLV, 873C. See Resnick (1988a) on Peter Damiani's attitude towards Cluny.
[175] William of St Thierry, *Vita prima Bernardi*, I, VII, 34, and VIII, 42, in Bernard, ed. Mabillon, II(6), 2118A and 2123B (*BHL* 1211).
[176] Geoffrey Grossus, *Vita Bernardi Tironiensis*, III, 20, in *PL*, CLXXII, 1380D (*BHL* 1251); Adam of Eynsham, *Magna vita Hugonis*, I, 7, ed. Decima Douie and David Farmer (OMT; Oxford 1985), I, 23 (*BHL* 4018); and *De esu volatilium*, in Pez, *Thesaurus*, II.2, 564A. On the description of the diocese of York as a Syria in the *Historia monasterii Selebiensis*, see p. 88 above.
[177] Viller and Rahner (1939), p. 267.
[178] Peter the Venerable, *Ep.* 28, ed. Constable, I, 93. On this vision, see Viller and Rahner (1939), p. 273, who said that Benedict saw God from afar, and n. 50, disagreeing with Butler's view that he saw God close by and directly, and the edition of Gregory's *Dialogi* by Adalbert de Vogüé (SC 251, 260, and 265; Paris 1978–80), II, 240–1n, who called it a vision of the smallness of the world.
[179] On the concept of modernity in the twelfth century see Freund (1957), pp. 111–13; Stock (1972), p. 228 and n. 81, and (1983), p. 456; Guenée (1976–7), who suggested (p. 30) that for twelfth-century historians modernity covered about the previous fifty years; and other references in Constable (1989), p. 164.

implicitly in the Rottenbuch privilege when he spoke of the revival of a life that had emerged in the early church but almost disappeared as it grew.[180] Suger in his *Life* of Louis VI contrasted 'the modernity of our times' with 'the antiquity of many times' in the past, and Walter Map defined 'our times' as modernity or the course of a century, beyond which memory became unclear.[181]

This sense of 'our' or modern times emerged in the second half of the eleventh century and brought with it (and may have been partly produced by) a realization of historical change and of the difference between the past and the present, which was usually seen in a less favourable light than the past. Almost everyone in the eleventh and twelfth centuries thought that the world was growing old and that things were going from bad to worse as the end approached[182] – a feeling that is not unknown today. Prophets of doom abounded, and millenarianism was in the air, though it was less widespread than it became in the thirteenth century. It can be seen in the popularity of prophetic visions and literature, including the prophetic books of the bible and the Sibylline prophecies,[183] and more literally in the depictions of the Second Coming, Last Judgement, and end of the world on the walls of countless churches. Norbert of Xanten said that he thought the Antichrist would come 'in this generation, which is now', though Bernard of Clairvaux, who recorded Norbert's views in a letter of 1124, found his reasons unconvincing.[184] It was therefore wise to prepare for the end. According to Otto of Freising, some people loved the world more than ever, presumably on the principle of eat, drink, and be merry, but others were moved to seek heaven.[185] Count Stephen of Boulogne made a grant to the abbey of Furness in 1126 'because the bounds of our age are daily breaking and falling into decay, and all the pomps of this transitory world, and the flowers, rosy crowns, and palms of flourishing kings, emperors, dukes, and all rich men wither, all built-up structures are reduced to rubble, and everything hastens with a rapid pace towards death'.[186] Otto of Bamberg founded monasteries because he wanted

---

[180] See nn. 170–1 above.

[181] Suger, *Vita Ludovici Grossi*, 28, ed. Henri Waquet (CHFMA 11; Paris 1929), p. 230, and Walter Map, *De nugis curialium*, I, 30, ed. and tr. Montague R. James, rev. C.N.L. Brooke and R.A.B. Mynors (OMT; Oxford 1983), p. 122. See Chenu (1957), p. 81.

[182] On the endemic tension in the Middle Ages between an idealized past and a degenerate present, see Boas (1948), and on the idea that the world was growing old, Grundmann (1927), pp. 76–81; Chenu (1957), pp. 76–7; and Miccoli (1966a), pp. 301–3. On twelfth-century messianism and apocalypticism, see Alphandéry (1912), who stressed the poverty and purity of apocalyptic groups, and, on its eleventh-century background, Fried (1989).

[183] Smalley (1966).

[184] Bernard, *Ep.* 56, ed. Leclercq, VII, 148. On twelfth-century views of Antichrist, see de Lubac (1959–64), II.1, 532–9.

[185] Otto of Freising, *Historia de duobus civitatibus*, VII, 9, ed. Adolf Hofmeister, 2nd edn (*MGH, SSRG;* Hanover and Leipzig 1912), p. 320.

[186] Dugdale, *Monasticon*, V, 247, no. 4.

to promote chastity and other holy works 'now . . . at the end of the world'.[187] Many sought to leave the world in order to be better prepared for its end, joining monasteries, becoming hermits, recluses, or pilgrims, or occasionally, in more radical circles, gathering in groups, often of twelve, around a leader who was assimilated to Christ. 'Almost everyone [is] now rashly running to monastic life', wrote Heloise in her letter to Abelard on the religious life. 'They are received in a disorderly way and live in a more disorderly way, and they establish as law whatever customs they wish with the same ease with which they scorn the unknown rule that they profess.' After saying that women should not have to bear a burden too heavy for men, she continued:

> We see that the world is now growing old, and that men have lost, with other things of the world, the pristine strength of nature, and in accordance with the word of Truth [Matthew 24.12] the charity not only of many but also of almost everyone has grown cold, so that now those very rules that were written for the sake of men must either be changed or tempered to fit the quality of men.[188]

Heloise thus saw the contemporary changes in religious life as part of the great sweep of history, viewing both its popularity and its decline as fulfilments of age-old prophecies and of ineluctable forces of change. Gilbert of Holland drew a similar contrast in his treatise addressed to Roger of Byland where, after contrasting the fertile location of his abbey with the arid deserts of the early monks, he went on to say that they supported themselves by handicrafts rather than by agriculture. 'They accommodated themselves to their times, and we accommodate ourselves to ours. This age of ours, which is becoming worse and worse (*in deterius vergens*), brings other customs.'[189] The situation was not hopeless, however, as Gilbert stressed in the passage cited above, where he said that the beauty of his abbey revealed not only the remnants of the primordial happiness of man in the Garden of Eden but also the signs of happiness to come. The return to the past thus presented itself as an anticipation of the future and introduced a note of optimism into an otherwise gloomy picture. For Honorius *Augustodunensis* 'the mutability of things' pointed the way towards the time when the troubles of the present would be changed 'into a better state' in the future, and even a sober lawyer like Gratian accepted that additions were made to canon law 'by the council of perfection . . . after the apostolic institutes' in such areas as the celebration of the sacraments, the celibacy of the clergy, and the marriage of members of the same family, which was 'not prohibited in the evangelical and apostolic precepts'.[190]

---

[187] Herbord, *De Ottone ep. Bambergensi*, i, 18, in *Monumenta Bambergensia*, ed. Philipp Jaffé (BRG 5; Berlin 1869), p. 717 (*BHL* 6397).

[188] Heloise, *Ep.* 5, ed. J.T. Muckle, in *Mediaeval Studies* 17 (1955), p. 246.

[189] See n. 61. On mutability, see Bruno of Segni, *Hom.* 143, in *PL*, CLXV, 860CD, and Burchard of Bellevaux, *Apologia de barbis*, II, 11, in *CC:CM*, LXII, 170, cited p. 299 below.

[190] Honorius *Augustodunensis*, *Elucidarium*, III, 78, ed. Yves Lefèvre (Bibliothèque des Ecoles françaises d'Athènes et de Rome 180; Paris 1954), pp. 462–3 (see Arduini (1985), pp. 78–9) and

The contrast between the pessimistic, backwards-looking view of history and the optimistic, forwards-looking view can be seen in the various systems of historical ages, which were dear to the hearts of twelfth-century theologians and historians, who were heirs both to the ancient traditions of successive empires, world-weeks, and ages of various metals, starting with gold and going down to iron, and also to the Christian systems based on the Old and New Testaments, the Trinity, various trilogies and quaternities of law, grace, and peace, and above all the six days of Creation, which were used by Origen and made familiar by the works of Augustine and later writers.[191] They also invented schemes of their own, making use of almost any system of twos, threes, fours, fives, sixes, or sevens that could be applied to history, especially those with prophetic significance, like the four beasts of Daniel or the four horses, seven seals, and seven trumpets of the Apocalypse.[192] Philip of Harvengt in his treatise *On the dream of Nebuchadnezzar* proposed two systems, one based on the seven parts of the statue seen by Nebuchadnezzar (head, chest, arms, stomach, thighs, shins, and feet) and the other on its five materials (gold, silver, copper, iron, and clay), both of which showed the progressive deterioration from the earliest age, of the head or gold, to the present age, of the feet or clay.[193] In his treatise *On the institution of clerics*, however, of which one section was on obedience, Philip presented a more standard system based on the days of Creation and the ages of man, where each age marked a grade of obedience, culminating in the perfect obedience of the sixth and final age, which corresponded to man's old age, when pride is conquered and sanctity, continence, and purity flourish.[194] Rupert of Deutz, and with him Hugh of St Victor, Otto of Freising, Gerhoh of Reichersberg, and Anselm of Havelberg, shared this optimistic vision of ages succeeding each other under the guidance of the Holy Spirit (which was Rupert's special contribution) and progressively promoting the spiritual and material welfare of mankind.[195]

Gratian, *Decretum*, *dictum post* XXXV, 1, in *Corpus*, ed. Friedberg, I, 1263. See Klinkenberg (1969) on the theory of the changeability of law.

[191] See Boas (1948), pp. 177–81; Luneau (1964); and Constable (1989), pp. 166–8.

[192] Towards the end of the twelfth century a few writers began to play the dangerous game of predicting when these prophesies might become true: see Geoffrey of Auxerre, *Expositio in Cantica Canticorum*, ed. Ferruccio Gastaldelli (Temi e testi 19; Rome 1974), pp. cxxiv–v, and Daniel (1986), p. 181.

[193] Philip of Harvengt, *De somno regis Nabuchodonosor*, in *PL*, CCIII, 585B–8C. See Boas (1948), pp. 181–4.

[194] Philip of Harvengt, *De institutione clericorum*, 5: *De obedientia clericorum*, 5–27, in *PL*, CCIII, 849B–98C.

[195] See generally de Lubac (1959–64), II.1, 519–55; Funkenstein (1965); and Peter Classen, in *Renaissance and Renewal* (1982), pp. 403–11; and (on Rupert) Van Engen (1983), pp. 287 and 340–1; (on Hugh) Southern (1970–3), (2), stressing his 'dynamic view of history' (p. 168) and calling him 'a prophet of a new age', who saw 'upward movement in every department of life' (p. 172); (on Otto) Peter Classen, in *Renaissance and Renewal* (1982), p. 401; (on Gerhoh) Meuthen (1959) and Classen (1960), pp. 108–14, on his equation of the seven ages of the

Anselm of Havelberg in particular, whose justification of diversity in the church has already been discussed, stressed the improvement of the successive ages.

> Thus the faith of the Holy Trinity has been measured out by degrees according to the strength of believers, and it has been distributed as it were in parts, and growing into completion it is at last perfect. In the same way no one or uniform [status] but many and multiform statuses are found [in the period] from the advent of Christ to the day of Judgement, which is called the sixth age and in which one and the same church, with the Son of God now being present, is renewed ... Therefore let no one be surprised or dispute that the unvarying God has distinguished the church of God by differing laws and observances [into periods] before the law, under the law, and under grace, so that the signs of the spiritual graces, to reveal increasingly the truth itself, would properly grow according to the progression of the times, and thus from period to period the knowledge of truth would grow with the accomplishment of salvation; and thus at first some good things were proposed, then better things, and finally the best things.[196]

This concept of progress was associated with an acceptance of change and innovation.[197] 'New' was still used in a pejorative way, and changes were condemned as novelties. There was a sense of deference towards the past, as when Wibald of Corvey wrote to Manegold of Paderborn that so much had already been written 'that it is impossible to say anything new' and that even heretics 'do not invent new things but repeat old ones'.[198] At the same time there was a realization that some innovations were desirable, even when they restored what had previously existed. William of St Thierry in his *Golden letter* to the Carthusians of Mont-Dieu condemned as impious those who objected to the very word novelty, 'being old themselves and not knowing how to think new things in an old mind'. 'This novelty', William said, referring to the Carthusian way of life, 'is not a new vanity, for it is the substance (*res*) of ancient religion, the perfection of piety based on Christ, the ancient legacy of the church of God.'[199] Robert of La Chaise-Dieu was called a 'new saint' who overturned 'the old order of sanctity'.[200] The earliest name for Cîteaux was

---

church with the seven trumpets of the Apocalypse and seven gifts of the Holy Spirit and relating Gerhoh to Rupert and Anselm of Havelberg; and (on Anselm) Schreiber (1942); Fina (1956–8), (5) pp. 33–40; and Funkenstein (1965), pp. 60–7.

[196] Anselm of Havelberg, *Dialogi*, I, 6 and 13, in *PL*, CLXXXVIII, 1148BC and 1160AB, and ed. Gaston Salet (SC 118; Paris 1966), pp. 64 and 116.

[197] See Boas (1948), pp. 175 and 201–3; Smalley (1975); Guy Beaujouan, in *Renaissance and Renewal* (1982), p. 485; and other works cited in Constable (1989), pp. 160–3.

[198] Wibald, *Ep.* 167, in *Monumenta Corbeiensia*, ed. Philipp Jaffé (BRG 1; Berlin 1864), p. 278.

[199] William of St Thierry, *Ep. ad fratres de Monte Dei*, 9, ed. Davy, p. 72. See Piazzoni (1988), p. 180.

[200] Marbod of Rennes, *Miracula Roberti Casae-Dei*, in *Nova bibl.*, II, 652 (*BHL* 7262). See p. 24 above.

the 'new monastery'; and Bernard entitled his treatise on the Templars *In praise of the new army*.[201] The Cistercians were called new men in a newness of life by Nicholas of Montiéramey, and they were thought to be 'more religious than others because they were more recent and of a stricter rule' by Gilbert of Sempringham, who sought to put them in charge of his work owing to 'the rigour of the order and the newness of their conversion'.[202] The ideal of the new man (*novus homo*) was based on the example of Christ and the precepts of St Paul and exercised a powerful influence on religious and political thought in the twelfth and thirteenth centuries.[203]

Among the most interesting advocates of change and progress was Joachim of Fiore, who worked out an elaborate pattern of interlocking and overlapping historical systems based on the two testaments, the three members of the Trinity, and the seven seals of the Apocalypse. Above all, he brought the future age into time and history, since unlike his predecessors, who saw the present as the final age, which would end in the Second Coming, Joachim saw the present as the age of the Son, which comes between the age of the Father and the approaching final age of the Holy Spirit. More than any other thinker in the twelfth century, Joachim looked forwards rather than backwards, and it was on his vision of the future that his reputation as a prophet, among both contemporaries and later Joachimites, rested.[204]

The interest of these historical speculations for the historian of religious reform lies in the role that was attributed to religious orders both in the final age and, for Joachim, especially in ushering it in. Peter of Celle in his treatise *On the discipline of the cloister* saw four overlapping, and by implication successive, disciplines, each with a different design: that of the philosophers, who wanted human fame and glory and found the secrets of nature; that of the Jews, who wanted earthly goods and found wealth; that of the Christians, who wanted the hope and forgiveness of grace and found the promise of present and future life; and finally that of the hermits and monks, who wanted the summit of grace and glory and found the fruit partly of action and partly of contemplation.[205] The Cistercians were thought to play a special part in this process of historical development. For Bernard they were the Psalmist's 'gen-

---

[201] *Chartes et documents concernant l'abbaye de Cîteaux, 1098–1182*, ed. J. Marilier (Bibliotheca Cisterciensis 1; Rome 1961), p. 36, no. 5, and following, and Bernard, *De laude novae militiae*, ed. Leclercq, III, 213–39. See Spahr (1955). Adam of Dryburgh praised the novelty of the Premonstratensians in his *De ordine, habitu, et professione canonicorum*, VI, 2, in *PL*, CXCVIII, 489D.

[202] Nicholas of Montiéramey, *Ep.* 35, in *PL*, CXCVI, 1627A, and *Vita Gileberti Sempinghamensis*, 13, ed. Foreville and Keir, p. 40.

[203] See Moltmann (1965); Le Goff (1973), pp. 98–9; and Dronke (1986a), p. 10.

[204] On Joachim, see the bibliography (since 1954) in West (1975), I, xix–xxiv; the bibliographical articles of Bloomfield (1957), repr. in West (1975), I, 29–92; Mikkers (1958); and Daniel (1986); and the works of Grundmann (1927); de Lubac (1959–64), II.1, 437–58; Reeves, esp. (1958) and (1961); and Wessley (1990).

[205] Peter of Celle, *De disciplina claustrali*, 8, in *PL*, CCII, 1113B–14B.

eration of them that seek' the Lord following the generations of those who either did not seek or were sought by the Lord,[206] and for Joachim, who was a Cistercian himself before he founded his own reformed order, they were the mediators between action (Scholastica) and contemplation (Mary) and were 'zealous above all religious men' in both preaching and silence.[207] The mixture of action and contemplation, which Peter of Celle also stressed, was a distinctive feature for Joachim of the transition from the present to the final age, when the existing religious orders would disappear and be replaced by pure contemplatives.[208] Joachim's speculations about the role of the 'spiritual men (*viri spirituales*)' who concerned themselves with preaching and contemplation during the period of transition, which for him was the present time, marked one of the high points of reform ideology in the twelfth century. Even more than Anselm of Havelberg and those who saw the new religious orders as coming at the end, and as a culmination, of the successive ages of history,[209] Joachim attributed to them a central role in the process of history itself and in the unfolding of God's plan for the emergence of a final and purely spiritual age dominated by the Holy Spirit.

[206] Bernard, *Serm. 3 in labore messis*, 2 and 9, ed. Leclercq, v, 223 and 227, citing Ps. 23.6.
[207] Joachim of Fiore, *De vita Benedicti*, 15, ed. Cipriano Baraut, in *Analecta sacra Tarraconensia* 24 (1951), p. 68. On Joachim's monastic activity as part of 'the pre-history of the future', see Grundmann (1927), p. 69, and Wessley (1990).
[208] See Reeves (1958) on the Augustinian hermits and (1961) on the Jesuits, who saw themselves as fulfilling Joachim's prophecies.
[209] Godfrey of St Victor in his sermon on Song of Songs 4.7, in Riedlinger (1958), pp. 188–93, divided the history of the church since the time of Christ into stages of innocence, justice, and glory, marked respectively by beauty without guilt, greater beauty with grace, and greatest beauty with glory.

5

THE REALITIES OF REFORM: (1) WITHIN THE COMMUNITY

THE previous chapter was concerned with the hopes and ideals of the reformers, how they saw themselves and were seen by others. This and the following chapter will study how these ideals were put into practice, first within the monasteries and other religious communities that formed the immediate framework of their daily lives and, second, in their relations with the world outside their walls and the bounds of their enclosures, especially with bishops and lay lords, and with economic conditions. The gap between the rhetoric and the reality is probably more apparent now than it was then. People today are inescapably the heirs of the Renaissance sense of the distance of the ancient world and also of nineteenth-century historicism, with its stress on the past. In the eleventh and twelfth centuries people were more conscious of continuity, though they saw history in terms of distinct periods, each with its own character, and they were deeply conscious of the difference between themselves and the form in which they were created and lived in the Garden of Eden and between the church of their own time and that of the apostolic age. The belief that they could bridge this gap, however, and recover both the paradisiacal harmony and integrity of man before the fall and the holy way of life described in the Gospels was a major source of inspiration for the movement of reform and one of the few bright signs in a world that they otherwise saw as deteriorating and hastening towards its end. It is hard today to see much resemblance between the apostles in the New Testament and the monks of Savigny and Clairvaux in whom the Gospel lived again for the unhappy members of St Mary at York;[1] but for them these monks showed that it was possible after almost exactly eleven hundred years (as they were well aware), to live a life based on that of Christ and like that of His followers in its stress on community, harmony, and humility in an atmosphere of seclusion, in and yet not of this world.

That some of these aspirations were incompatible with the traditional institutions that they tried to reform seems hardly to have occurred to people at the time, or only dimly, as in Bernard of Clairvaux's cry that he was the chimera of his age, neither one thing nor another.[2] When they could not find

[1] Hugh of Kirkstall, *Narratio*, ed. Walbran, p. 20. See pp. 53–4 and 153–4 above.
[2] Bernard, *Ep.* 250.4, ed. Leclercq, VIII, 147.

what they wanted in the older institutions, they boldly set out and established new ones, often of a similar type, and called them old. Truly new institutions are almost as rare as new religions, and it should be no surprise that for as long as they could the reformers worked within an existing institutional framework and that this framework showed a remarkable flexibility and resilience, and only later cracked as the more radical nature of some of the pressures put upon it became clear. A few recognizably new institutions, such as the military orders and the system of lay brothers, emerged within the period of the reform movement, but the larger breaks represented by the reordering of Christian values in the late twelfth and early thirteenth centuries, and by the mendicants on one hand and the organized heresies on the other, came later and were accompanied by a reassertion within the ranks of the monks, including the reformers, of many traditional characteristics. This is why, looking backwards, what was in reality a major reassessment of the nature of religious life and of the ideal of Christian perfection looks like only an episode in the history of monasticism, and is often treated as such by scholars. Some of the matters that bulked large in the eyes of contemporaries now look rather petty – 'a great Cry but little Wool', as the English translator of Dupin's *Auteurs ecclésiastiques* put it[3] – but they sprang from a confident belief that monasticism represented the highest ideal of life on earth and could, with good will, effort, and occasionally some pain, be brought back to the ideal of the Gospel as it was embodied in the rule of Benedict and the other rules of religious life.

'You know,' wrote Peter the Venerable to his monks at St Martial in Limoges probably about 1150, 'that almost every aspect of religious life that the new men of our age seem to have, takes its origin from you and receives its matter and form from you.'[4] Though this comes from a prejudiced source, it is an excellent statement of the conservative character of much of the work of the reformers, who must be seen in a tradition of monastic life going back for centuries. This has been emphasized by scholars who have studied monastic customaries, necrologies, and liturgical sources rather than the polemical and programmatic writings, which tend to stress the radical differences between the old and new monks, and especially between the Cluniacs and Cistercians. When the focus is moved to what the monks and canons, and the nuns and canonesses, were actually doing in their churches, chapter-houses, refectories, dormitories, and other conventual buildings, the differences between them are seen to be within a common tradition, with specific differences of one sort or another that were often the result of small changes over time. This type of constant change and adjustment is most apparent in the liturgy, but it affected all aspects of monastic life. From this point of view, what changed under the impact of the reform movement in the eleventh and twelfth centuries was the rate rather than the character of change, which was

[3] See p. 134 above.
[4] Peter the Venerable, *Ep.* 159, ed. Constable, I, 384.

still made up of many relatively small points.[5] Kassius Hallinger applied this view to the reforms of the post-Carolingian period in his work entitled *Gorze-Kluny*, which remains, in spite of its defects, among the most important contributions to the history of medieval monasticism to appear since the Second World War. Hallinger laid particular emphasis on the objective differences that lay behind the monastic disputes and controversies of the tenth and eleventh centuries. 'The "psychological" opposition to Cluny . . . should in the last analysis be understood as the expression of underlying *objective* tensions', he said, underlining the 'objective', and, 'Brought to a common formula, one can say that it was a matter of contrast between old and new.'[6]

The clearest examples of these types of differences are found in the customaries, of which a corpus of new editions, planned to fill about thirty volumes, is in course of publication. They also show the resemblances between the customs in various houses and throw light on the associations and affiliations between them. No less important in this respect is the evidence of necrological documents, known as obituaries, memorial books, and books of life (*Libri vitae*), which list the names of the people for whose salvation a religious community offered prayers,[7] including not only members of the community and its benefactors but also members of other communities that had entered into an association of prayer. Better than any other type of source these lists show the network of relationships between religious houses and with secular society. The surviving necrologies from eight Cluniac houses, for instance, most of which date from between the mid-eleventh and late twelfth centuries, list some 90,000 different names and not only provide a reasonably secure list of Cluniac monks, in the strict sense of monks who belonged to houses legally dependent on Cluny and who made their professions to the abbot of Cluny, but also show the range of Cluniac connections with non-Cluniac houses and individuals all over Europe.[8] Hugh of Cluny is said to have used unions and confraternities as a way of extending the influence of Cluny,[9] and Peter the Venerable continued and expanded the practice, establishing agreements for reciprocal prayers, among many others, with the Cistercians, Carthusians, and Premonstratensians. Bernard of Clairvaux wrote to Peter in 1149 that at the general

---

[5] See pp. 184–99 below.

[6] Hallinger (1950–1), pp. 419 and 422. This approach was applied to the Cistercians by Hallinger's student Bruno Schneider (1960–1). Previously, Berlière (1900–1), p. 267 n. 1, and Storm (1926), pp. 18–19, criticized the work of Giseke (1886) for overemphasizing, as they saw it, the 'material' or 'objective' differences between Cluny and Cîteaux.

[7] See the introduction to Molinier (1890) and Lemaître (1980–92), I, 17–20, on the types of entries in French necrological documents. In memorial books and *Libri vitae*, the names usually appear as they were entered, in arbitrary order or groups; in necrologies, they are listed under the day of death, on the anniversary of which special prayers were offered and liturgical obligations, including the distribution of food to the poor, were observed.

[8] See Wollasch (1967) and (1979) and the Cluniac necrologies published in Wollasch (1982), and, on the distribution of the necrologies, Müssigbrod (1988).

[9] Cowdrey (1965), p. 155.

chapter in Cîteaux 'memorial was made of you as of a special lord, both a father and a most beloved friend, and of all your [monks] both alive and dead'.[10] The association made in 1142 between Cîteaux and Prémontré included provisions not only for reciprocal liturgical commemoration but also covering *transitus*, the location of monasteries, tithes, the acquisition of property, and the settlement of disputes.[11] It was signed by four Cistercian and four Premonstratensian abbots and amounted to a treaty between the two orders. The association between Fécamp and St Benignus at Dijon, made in 1180/8, harked back to their common founder William of Dijon and stressed the unity of the two houses: 'Just as many limbs make a single body, so by the cement of love each church since its foundation constituted a single fold in Christ.'[12] The fact that a hundred and eighty monasteries in all appear on the fourteen surviving Cistercian commemoration lists shows the extent of these associations.[13]

The associations between the Cistercians and the Cluniacs and between the Cistercians and the Premonstratensians came, probably not by accident, close to the time when the controversies between these orders were at their height and when, to judge from the polemical writings alone, they hardly seem to have been on speaking terms. Both monks and canons were ready to remember in their prayers the members of houses with whom they were quarrelling in writing. These associations thus give substance to the expressions of reciprocal esteem and love and the verbal acceptance of diverse but not adverse, which might otherwise appear to be pious sentiments covering a reality of disdain and dislike. The customaries also show a willingness to borrow from communities whose behaviour was excoriated in polemical works. The reformers took freely from both the customs and the liturgy of Cluny as well as from the *Charter of love* and other early Cistercian programmatic works. Many houses were called Cluniac, and some, especially of nuns, were called Cistercian, without having any formal affiliations with these orders. In practice if not in theory all those who followed the rule of Benedict agreed on the need for some interpretation, which they covered by distinguishing what was regarded as essential – the integrity or purity of the rule – from what was changeable. According to Hildebert of Lavardin, the difference between moveable and immoveable prescriptions and prohibitions depended on whether or not they were sanctioned by eternal law, and Peter of Celle in *On the discipline*

---

[10] Peter the Venerable, *Ep.* 152, ed. Constable, I, 373; cf. *Ep.* 149, ibid., I, 366. See also the agreements between Cluny and Prémontré in *Bibliotheca Praemonstratensis ordinis*, ed. F.-J. Le Paige (Paris 1633), pp. 321–2, and between Cluny and La Chartreuse in *Recueil des plus anciens actes de la Grande-Chartreuse (1086–1196)*, ed. Bernard Bligny (Grenoble 1958), pp. 64–9, nos. 23–4.

[11] Gerits (1964) and Spahr (1966).

[12] Laporte (1963), p. 40.

[13] Wollasch (1973c), pp. 211–22. Nineteen of these, including Cluny, were on all lists, and thirty-four on ten or more. St Evroul was associated with eighty-seven monasteries in the eleventh and twelfth centuries: Laporte (1956), p. 144.

of the cloister distinguished between what he called the *substantia* and the *accidentalia* in religious life, saying that both Benedict and Augustine were holy and that the claustral discipline of monks and canons agreed on some points and differed on others.[14] Heloise wrote to Abelard in the letter cited above that with the passage of time rules had to be adapted and changed, and an eloquent statement of the need to modify in practice the application of religious rules was made by Peter the Venerable in Letter 28, where he stressed that since the rule was founded on love, it must be changed by love, of which the one and only office was 'to seek the salvation of mankind in all ways'.[15] According to the *Bridlington dialogue*, which derived from the *Questions* of Richard of St Victor, the superiors of Augustinian houses should moderate all the ecclesiastical decrees in accord with the rule of love, and even Bernard of Clairvaux and Aelred of Rievaulx agreed that man-made rules, unlike divine commandments, could be modified.[16] The same point was made in a different way in the introduction to the *Ancrene riwle*, which distinguished the inner divine from the outer man-made rules. 'The inward rule is always alike. The outward is various, because every one ought so to observe the outward rule as that the body may therewith best serve the inward.' Religion, it continued, lies 'not in the wide hood, nor in the white, nor in the black, nor in the gray cowl', but in being pure and unstained by the world.[17]

Many other examples of such sentiments could be cited. Together they constitute a collective topos of good will and tolerance, like the single eye, against which it was hard to argue, even when it was used (as it often was) in a self-serving manner to justify individual and sometimes clearly illegitimate lapses in the observance of the rule. It represented a genuine aspect of the diversification of religious life in the twelfth century, when it sometimes seemed that only a few ecclesiastical bureaucrats really cared what rule was observed, or to what order a house belonged, provided the way of life was austere and simple and threatened no existing interests. This climate of tolerance must be balanced by a recognition of the bitter quarrels and rivalry over points that even at the time were sometimes recognized as relatively unimportant, the passionate concern for a common observance within each order, and

[14] Hildebert of Lavardin, *Ep.* II, 53, in *PL*, CLXXI, 280D, and Peter of Celle, *De disciplina claustrali*, 2, in *PL*, CCII, 1103D–4B.

[15] Peter the Venerable, *Ep.* 28, ed. Constable, I, 98; cf. *Ep.* 111, ibid., I, 291, deploring that differences of food and clothing had damaged the love between monks and calling for a single eye that would not look for difficulties.

[16] Robert of Bridlington (attr.), *Bridlington Dialogue*, 3, ed. anon. (London 1960), pp. 26–7 (on this passage, and the sources of the work, see Colker (1962), pp. 186–9 and 208); Bernard, *De praecepto et dispensatione*, III, 6–8, ed. Leclercq, III, 257–9; and Aelred of Rievaulx, *Disputatio*, ed. André Wilmart, in *Revue d'ascétique et de mystique* 23 (1947), p. 273. Guibert of Nogent, *De sanctis et eorum pigneribus*, I, in *CC:CM*, CXXVII, 85, said that customs of psalmody and fasting might differ in action but not in faith.

[17] *Ancrene riwle*, intro., ed. and tr. James Morton (Camden Society 57; London 1853), pp. 5 and 11. See p. 66 n. 95 above on the date and title of this work.

the fierce attachment of individual houses to their own traditions and their readiness to criticize others for doing things differently. Anselm told a new monk at Canterbury to preserve 'the customs of our order . . . as if established by God', and the letter from the monks of Monte Cassino to Hersfeld and other German monasteries showed not only their dislike of the Cluniac habit and tonsure but also their sense of living a life that must be experienced and shared in order to be learned.[18] Implicitly they rejected the type of great written customary that was associated with Cluny in the second half of the eleventh century. The purpose of these and other customaries is still not entirely certain.[19] They may have been intended as records of how monastic life was lived in a particular house, a sort of public declaration of how it did things and a monument to collective pride. They may also have been motivated by an unspoken urge to stop further tampering and say, 'This is it.' They may have been intended to impose uniformity among the dependencies of a monastery, or have had a broader purpose of propagating a particular way of life, outside as well as inside an order, as the monks of Monte Cassino seem to have feared. The evidence of the surviving manuscripts of the Cluniac customaries shows that they were in fact often revised, both at Cluny and elsewhere, and that within the order they were replaced during the twelfth century by a more flexible system of abbatial statutes, which were normally issued with the consent of the chapter, or at least of the senior members (*seniores*), and of the decrees of the general chapters, of which the first known meeting was in 1132.[20] Many of the reformed houses of the twelfth century had no customaries and relied on the statutes and decrees of the general chapters, and increasingly on visitation, to ensure uniformity within their orders.[21]

A desire for uniformity within the monastic order dated from at least the early ninth century and reflected the concern of the rulers at that time for the high standard of the prayers offered for their own salvation and the well-being of the kingdom.[22] The ancient comparisons of monks to angels, to cherubim who unite in offering praise to the Lord, and to ants and bees who work together with a common purpose reflected the ideals of regularity and unanimity that figured so largely in the monastic reform movement. William of St Thierry in his treatise *On the nature and dignity of love*, after citing the usual biblical texts in favour of common life (and a few less common ones, like Luke 12.32) said that monks should have no house of their own but only

---

[18] Anselm, *Ep.* 335, ed. Schmitt, V, 272, and, for the letter from the monks of Monte Cassino, p. 110 and n. 122 above.

[19] Tönnies (1909) distinguished three meanings in the term 'custom': what is actually done, rules of conduct, and a will. See also Hallinger in the intro. to *CCM*, I, and (1980), where he traced *consuetudo* as an enlargement and modification of the rule.

[20] Iogna-Prat (1992). On Cluniac general chapters, see the intro. to *CCM*, VI, pp. 22–3, and on abbatial statutes, Constable (1976c).

[21] Schreiner (1992), esp. pp. 321–5 on visitation.

[22] See the Carolingian customaries in *CCM*, I, 333 (*Capitula in Auuam directa*), 341 (*Capitula notitiarum*), and 425 (*Legislatio Aquisgranensis*).

the house of the Lord, no property, no bodies, no will of their own: 'They sleep together, rise together, pray together, recite psalms together, and read together.'[23] The Cistercians were required to have the same liturgical books in all their houses, and successive general chapters emphasized the importance of uniformity throughout the order.[24] It has been said that a Cistercian monk could not only have joined in the liturgy of any Cistercian house but also have found his way in the dark from the dormitory to the church for the night offices.

This stress on uniformity was the single most important element in the making of an order, which is otherwise hard to define with any precision in the twelfth century.[25] In the eyes of the papal curia, the criterion for belonging to a monastic order was adherence to a recognized rule, and this was made the law of the church at the Fourth Lateran Council in 1215.[26] But in the twelfth century there were no recognized orders based on rules. The only two indisputable examples, upon which both contemporaries and later scholars agree, were the Cluniacs and the Cistercians, and even their character is less clear than might be wished. The order of Cluny evolved gradually out of a personal union of independent houses under a single abbot into a legal union consisting of a mother-abbey with dependent priories, each of which (even if they were nominally abbeys) was part of a single monastery and of which all the monks were professed to the abbot of Cluny. It thus combined the two ancient principles of a personal union, which became indissoluble, and of dependencies founded from a mother-house, which now included previously independent houses, but just how and when this took place is unclear.[27] In the first half of the eleventh century the houses were still linked primarily by a personal subjection to Odilo, who in all but one of the documents concerned with Peterlingen, for instance, was called not the abbot of Cluny but the abbot of Peterlingen.[28] Other aspects of the Cluniac order grew out of its special relation with the papacy. The Cluniac Urban II in 1096 referred to Beaulieu and St-Martin-des-Champs as limbs (*membra*) of the monastery of Cluny, and

---

[23] William of St Thierry, *De natura et dignitate amoris*, IX, 24, in *PL*, CLXXXIV, 395CD.

[24] *Carta caritatis prior*, 3, and *Capitula Cisterciensis ordinis*, 10, in *Textes de Cîteaux*, pp. 92 and 122, and statutes 2 and 3 attributed to the general chapter in 1134, in Canivez, *Statuta*, p. 13. See p. 38 n. 171 above.

[25] Dubois (1968b) and (1985), p. 64.

[26] Hourlier (1974), p. 53, said there was no clear distinction between members of an order and priories: 'Seul l'usage détermine les cas où l'on est en présence d'un ordre.'

[27] Schreiber (1910), I, 76 and 177–8; Hourlier (1950), (1964), pp. 174–5, and (1979), p. 440; Lemarignier (1950), pp. 322–3 and (1953), p. 172, who dated the idea of a Cluniac 'order' from 1024/7; Violante (1960), pp. 192–4; Wollasch (1973a), pp. 155–6, (1973c), pp. 227–9, and (1985), pp. 330–1; Mehne (1977), p. 287 n. 346; and Dubois (1985), p. 41, who dated the *ordo cluniacensis* from 1100.

[28] Cousin (1950) and Endemann (1967), p. 15. It is uncertain what the monks of Hasungen had in mind when they chose the 'order' of Cluny in the late eleventh century, but it probably meant a monastic or liturgical way of life rather than a constitutional body: see Hallinger (1958–60), p. 227.

the earliest examples of a papal *privilegium commune* applying to an abbey and all its dependencies were granted to Cluny in the early twelfth century and may have fostered as well as recognized its development into a single entity.[29] Peter the Venerable in his letters referred to Cluny and its dependencies several times as an *ordo*, *congregatio*, and *res publica* and, in the mid-1140s, once as an *universitas* and once as a *corpus*, a term he also used in a charter for the priory of Longpont about 1140.[30]

Both Camaldoli and Vallombrosa in the course of the eleventh century developed from personal into juridical unions, and Paschal II used the term *corpus* for Camaldoli and its dependencies in 1113, calling it a *corpus unum sub uno capite*.[31] The Cistercians, on the other hand, were never an order in this sense, since each abbey was an autonomous unit, subject to visitation by the house from which it was founded and obliged to attend the annual general chapters at Cîteaux. Peter the Venerable referred to the Cistercians three times as an *ordo* and once as a *universitas*, though in some ways the term *multitudo*, which Bernard used for the Cluniacs, applied better to his own order, which never constituted a legal unity.[32] In practice the contrast between the organization of the two orders was probably less than it looks in theory, for while the abbot of Cluny tried in vain to hold together a conglomeration of houses each of which in fact had considerable independence, the abbot of Cîteaux exercised considerably more control over Cistercian abbeys than their technical autonomy might suggest. Ordericus Vitalis in his history of the Cistercians down to 1135 said that sixty-five abbeys arose 'which are all with their abbots subject to the archimandrite of Cîteaux',[33] and in the *Dialogue of two monks* the Cistercian more or less reversed the usual view of the two orders when he said that 'All our monasteries are as if a single *corpus*', using the very term that Peter the Venerable used for Cluny, 'because they are ruled by one head with a counsel received every year in our chapter, which makes the religion of our order durable', whereas the Cluniac order, he said, was without a head

[29] *Bullarium sacri ordinis Cluniacensis*, ed. Pierre Symon (Lyon 1680), pp. 24 and 29, and *PL*, CLII, 468D and 470B (JL 5648 and 5652). See Schreiber (1910), I, 76, and Hourlier (1979), p. 440.

[30] Peter the Venerable, *Ep.* 134, ed. Constable, I, 339 (and other examples cited in the index, ibid., II, 400, s.v. Cluny) and *Le cartulaire du prieuré de Notre-Dame de Longpont* (Lyon 1879), pp. 69–70, no. 8. See also the intro. to Peter the Venerable, *Statuta*, in *CCM*, VI, 23. Peter used the term *ordo* for an individual monastery and for all black monks in *Ep.* 159, ed. Constable, I, 384–5. Cantarella (1979–81) studied Peter's use of the terms *congregatio* and *societas* and suggested (pp. 393–4 and 420–1) that the exclusion of the Italian Cluniac houses from the *corpus cluniacense* showed that it was not a comprehensive term and that the 'ideological' and 'institutional' structures did not necessarily match.

[31] *PL*, CLI, 323A (Urban II for Vallombrosa) and *PL*, CLXIII, 331C (Paschal II for Camaldoli) (JL 5433 and 6357). See (on Vallombrosa) Miccoli (1960), pp. 133–8, and (1966a), pp. 47–8 and 67–73; and (on Camaldoli) Wilhelm Kurze, in *Monachesimo* (1971), pp. 409–12.

[32] Peter the Venerable, *Epp.* 150 and 181, ed. Constable, I, 370, 371, and 424, and Bernard, *Ep.* 387, ed. Leclercq, VIII, 356 (= Peter the Venerable, *Ep.* 148, ed. Constable, I, 363). See Mahn (1945), esp. p. 68, and Wollasch (1973a), pp. 158 and 179.

[33] Ordericus Vitalis, *Historia ecclesiastica*, VIII, 26, ed. Chibnall, IV, 324.

and disorganized, with each house doing what it wanted.[34] In practice, therefore, the two systems were parallel, and in the area of monastic government, it has been said, 'Cîteaux only brought to full development the germ already implanted in the system of Cluny.'[35]

The policy of requiring houses to adopt a recognized rule, and later to join an order, was an expression of the desire for uniformity, but it was never very effective in preventing the proliferation of many forms of religious life, aside from the pressure it put on new houses to adopt some sort of rule, nor did it seriously hinder the recognition and acceptance of diversity by most churchmen. It represented an important tendency in official ecclesiastical circles, however, to try to impose some degree of institutional order on the movement of reform and to bring together the bewildering variety of reform into a few relatively clear categories. More than this, it reflected a serious concern, which was expressed in the decree of 1215, over the introduction of confusion into the church. The apparent ambiguity between an acceptance of diversity and a desire for uniformity should not trouble historians who live in an age when there is likewise much talk, not necessarily insincere, about unity and common ends but when the realities of life seem to be controlled by competition and hostility. The divisiveness within the medieval church was strengthened by the ancient tradition of the independence of religious houses, which since the early days of monasticism recognized only the vague supervision of the diocesan bishop, from which many were freed by the papacy in the early Middle Ages, and which tended to regard any interference in their affairs as an improper threat to the regularity and purity of monastic life. Apart from a tendency on the part of the reformers to assert their respect for the authority of the bishop and to see the exemption of older monasteries as a source of pride and secular involvement, the old and new houses stood together in opposing any external control and in asserting their right to run their own affairs. Even within orders the general chapters and visitors, as the records of both the Cluniac and the Cistercian orders show, had great difficulty in imposing their regulations on all the houses.

The strongest sources of institutional individuality and local independence were the control of the community over the choice of a superior and the restrictions imposed on his or her freedom of action, both of which grew in the course of the twelfth century.[36] The abbot of Gembloux wrote an interesting letter in 1182 to the archbishop of Cologne concerning the procedure for electing the abbot of Marmoutier. After gathering the priors of all cells located within a distance of one month's journey, the community alone, after fasting,

---

[34] Idungus, *Dialogus*, III, 31, ed. Huygens, pp. 451–2.
[35] See the intro. to de Montalembert (1896), I, xxxv. This introduction to the English translation was attributed to Francis Gasquet but was really written by Edmund Bishop and Elphege Cody: see Knowles (1934), p. 309 n. 1, and (1956), p. 252.
[36] On the material in this paragraph, see Constable (1982b).

giving alms, and visiting the body of St Martin, chose twenty or thirty monks 'of saner counsel (*sanioris consilii*)'. These electors chose the new abbot while the other monks waited in the chapter-house, reciting the litany and praying 'until the agreement of the electors is established on a suitable person', who swore, before he was installed, to observe the entire custom of the abbey 'up to a dotted i and a single detail'.[37] This report is of interest for several reasons in addition to the fact that the abbot of Gembloux and archbishop of Cologne were interested in the procedure for electing the abbot of a distant monastery like Marmoutier. A month's travel represented some 600 miles, estimating about twenty miles a day, and the report shows both the wide range of the cells of Marmoutier and the serious effort made to gather all the monks, who alone participated in the election. The procedure shows in its liturgical aspects a search for guidance both from God and St Martin and in its constitutional aspects an application of the provision in the rule of Benedict for the election of the abbot by part of the community choosing 'with saner counsel', who here became the representatives of the whole group. The oath to uphold the customs of Marmoutier, finally, imposed a restraint upon the authority of the abbot that was at variance both with the spirit of the rule and with the practice in the early Middle Ages, when abbots completely controlled their monasteries and expected total obedience from the monks.

In this respect Marmoutier represented a tendency that was going on in religious houses all over Europe, though it is rare to know as much about the electoral procedure as this letter reveals. There was a steady, though not always successful, effort, based on the rule and supported by canon law, to exclude outsiders from abbatial elections and consecrations and to avoid even a semblance of control by any lay or ecclesiastical authority, especially in the ceremony of investiture with the pastoral staff. At Cluny in the first half of the eleventh century, under Odilo, the abbot was elected in the presence of the bishop, who presented the staff, but by the end of the century the bishop was invited the day after the election to bless the new abbot, who received his staff from the prior.[38] Similarly at Hirsau, in the course of the eleventh century, the prior apparently replaced the bishop in presenting the staff to

---

[37] Guibert of Gembloux, *Ep. ad Philippum archiepiscopum Coloniensem*, in *Thes. nov.*, I, 609AC. There is an interesting description of a controversy over the consecration of an abbot of Marmoutier in the late eleventh or early twelfth centuries in the unpublished treatise *De professionibus abbatum*, in MS Paris, Bibl. nat., Lat. 2342, fol. 161^{r-v}. See also the account given by William of St Denis in his *Dialogus apologeticus*, 16, ed. André Wilmart, in *Revue Mabillon* 32 (1942), p. 109, of the election of Suger's successor at St Denis, where the monks gathered on the day Suger died, when the king and six bishops were still apparently there, and chose the twelve *seniores* who elected Odo. See Glaser (1965), pp. 306–8.

[38] *Liber tramitis*, II, 19, 144, in *CCM*, X, 208–10, and Bernard, *Ordo Cluniacensis*, I, 1, in Herrgott, *Disciplina*, pp. 135–6. See Hallinger (1950–1), pp. 568–72, and (1958–60), pp. 244–67; Iogna-Prat (1992), pp. 39–43; and Kohnle (1993), p. 28, who stressed the continued importance of designation by the predecessor.

the abbot-elect.[39] At Fleury in the thirteenth century the abbot-elect himself took the staff from the altar.[40] The procedure established in the rule of Benedict for the choice of the superior either by the whole community acting together or by part of it acting with saner counsel was also increasingly used in non-monastic elections, including houses of regular canons,[41] and was made general (substituting *praepositus* for *abbas*) in the *Decretum* of Gratian and the decrees of the Fourth Lateran Council, which equated saniority with majority in the formula *maior vel sanior pars*, thus recognizing the principle of majority rule, although it still accepted the validity of elections by scrutiny, compromise, and inspiration.[42]

In orders like that of Cluny, where every house (even those with the nominal rank of abbey) was in theory a branch of the mother-abbey, the superiors were all appointed by the abbot. In the Cistercian order, where every house was in principle a self-governing abbey, the *Charter of love* entrusted the election to the monks of each community, acting with the abbots of daughter-houses (which had a recognized interest in the superior of their mother-house) and with the advice and assent of the abbot of their mother-house.[43] In practice the abbot of Cîteaux both appointed and dismissed the superiors of Cistercian houses. Peter the Venerable wrote to abbot Rainald of Cîteaux on behalf of a group of monks whose abbot he had deposed and who were on their way to Cîteaux to ask him to restore their previous abbot or appoint a new one.[44] The most serious exceptions to the rule of election by the community was when the superior was appointed or nominated by his predecessor, especially in new houses of which he was also the founder. This had been common practice in the early Middle Ages, and persisted especially in new and reformed houses owing both to the need to avoid controversy in a young community and to the prestige and influence of the founder. The authority of the superior was in fact probably greater in some of the new houses than in older monasteries, where there was an established tradition of procedures

---

[39] William of Hirsau, *Constitutiones Hirsaugienses*, II, 1, in Herrgott, *Disciplina*, pp. 475–6, and Henry IV, no. 280 (1075), in *MGH, Dipl.*, VI, 360, who established that the dean or prior would take the *virga regiminis* from the altar and give it 'without any contradiction' into the hand of he 'whom the entire congregation of monks chose for themselves'. Cf. Hallinger (1950–1), p. 572, and Reimann (1991), pp. 105–6.

[40] *Consuetudines Floriacenses*, 25, in *CCM*, IX, 315.

[41] See, for instance, the provisions for free election and self-investiture in the charter of Godfrey of Brabant for Parc abbey in 1129 in Miraeus–Foppens, I, 91. The independence of such procedures was sometimes undercut by the requirement of 'consent' of outside authorities, as at Siegburg, where the archbishop really controlled the election: see Semmler (1959), p. 295.

[42] Gratian, *Decretum*, Dist. 61, 14, in *Corpus*, ed. Friedberg, I, 232, and IV Lateran (1215), 24, in *Conc. oec. decreta*, pp. 246–7. The *maior et melior pars* were equated in Lanfranc, *Decreta*, 82, in *CCM*, III, 61. On these developments, in addition to the references in *Medieval Monasticism*, nos. 598–606, see Maleczek (1990), pp. 119–24.

[43] See the *Carta caritatis posterior*, 21, in Canivez, *Statuta*, p. xxix; cf. *Carta caritatis prior*, 11, in *Textes de Cîteaux*, p. 101.

[44] Peter the Venerable, *Ep.* 120, ed. Constable, I, 313–14; see the notes in II, 180–1. Peter did not suggest that there was anything unusual or improper in this.

and restrictions. Berno, the first abbot of Cluny, designated 'with the consent of the monks' his kinsman Guy and his disciple Odo to succeed him in the several monasteries of which he was abbot, and in many twelfth-century houses a new superior was designated or even took over the administration of a house while his predecessor was still alive.[45] There was sometimes at least a show of reluctance. When Robert of Newburg was asked by the senior monks (*seniores*) on his deathbed in 1153 to designate a successor, he replied that they would follow not his but their own opinion and that they would choose Walter, and when Geoffrey of Chalard was asked ' "Why, lord, do you not indicate to us the name of him who may be held worthy to succeed you in the pastoral office after your death? Do you wish that there should be a controversy among the brothers?" he replied, "I am unwilling. Be quiet and expect the Lord, for He will take mercy on His poor." '[46]

The members of religious communities were also able to control their superiors by exercising the right to be consulted in important matters, which was embodied in the rule but had been generally disregarded by early medieval abbots, who tended to behave in an autocratic manner. It was increasingly enforced in the eleventh and twelfth centuries, however, and developed from a right of the monks to be consulted into a right to give their consent to all decisions of common concern, especially those relating to property and membership in the community.[47] All the known statutes of the abbots of Cluny in the eleventh and early twelfth centuries were issued with the consent, and sometimes at the request, of the monks, and in 1154 the pope required Peter the Venerable to recover some priories and revenues that he had alienated 'without the counsel and consent' of his monks.[48] Alexander III even recognized the right of an individual monk to sue his abbot and to have the costs of the suit paid by the monastery.[49] The use, especially in some regions, of the title *prior* or *prepositus* in place of *abbas* may reflect a shift in the position

---

[45] See the so-called 'testament' of Berno in 926 in *Bibl. Clun.*, col. 9, and *PL*, CXXXIII, 854C; cf. *Chartes de Cluny*, I, 273, no. 277. For later examples of the designation of an abbot during his predecessor's lifetime, see the *Historia fundationis* of Aldgate, 13–14, ed. Thomas Hearne (with the *Historia* of William of Newburgh) (Oxford 1719), III, 704–5, and in *Cartulary of Holy Trinity Aldgate*, ed. Gerald A.J. Hodgett (London Record Society 7; London 1971), pp. 231–2, and the *Chronicon de s. Barbara in Algia*, ed. R.-Norbert Sauvage, in *Mémoires de l'Académie nationale des sciences, arts et belles-lettres de Caen: Documents*, 1906, p. 49. According to the *Vita* [B] *Norberti*, 16, in *PL*, CLXX, 1329AB (*BHL* 6249), Norbert after his departure from Prémontré sent the *eligendi facultas* and *de electione sua uoluntas*, but this may have indicated his wish that they elect a successor rather than a designation.
[46] *Vita Roberti Novi Monasterii*, 9, ed. Paul Grosjean, in *Anal. boll.* 56 (1938), p. 354 (*BHL* 7268), and *Vita Gaufridi Castaliensis*, II, 10, ed. A. Bosvieux, in *Mémoires de la Société des sciences naturelles et archéologiques de la Creuse* 3 (1862), p. 110 (*BHL* 3283).
[47] In addition to the references in Constable (1982b), pp. 198–202, see Gransden (1975); Dubois (1982); and Felten (1988), p. 271.
[48] *PL*, CLXXXVIII, 1070C (JL 9888). Cf. the bull of Alexander III in 1174, in *PL*, CC, 967BC (JL 12334). See also the intro. to Peter the Venerable, *Statuta*, in *CCM*, VI, 22, and Constable (1976c), pp. 157–8.
[49] Gregory IX, *Decretales*, V, I, 11, in *Corpus*, ed. Friedberg, II, 735.

of the superior from a ruler to a first among equals, who governed with the cooperation of the community, though custom and tradition were also involved.[50] Rupert of Deutz in his commentary on the rule of Benedict cited a letter from the archbishop of Cologne to the bishop of Laon objecting to the use of *abbas* by Augustinian canons and saying that 'by right and by custom' abbot referred to the superiors of monks, but the author of the customs of Springiersbach and Rolduc defended the use of the *abbas* for the superiors of houses of canons.[51] Aelred of Rievaulx especially warned against the *libitudo dominandi*, and Stephen of Obazine was said never to have acted without consultation, if only with a member of the community or a servant. His biographer contrasted this behaviour with that of superiors 'who fear not to undertake great and arduous affairs without counsel and who therefore fail rather than succeed, and who scorn to follow the good advice of someone else, if presented in advance, because it might seem not to have been initiated by themselves'.[52]

The normal means of consultation was with the entire community gathered in the chapter or, on minor affairs, with the monastic officials. Many monasteries appear to have had a group known as *seniores* or *maiores*, though very little is known about their character. They may have been simply, as the name implies, the senior monks, but they seem sometimes to have been sort of a standing committee, as at Newburg, or an *ad hoc* committee, like those chosen at Marmoutier to elect the abbot.[53] The abbot at Cluny and, later at Fleury, was elected by the *spiritales fratres* and at Hirsau by a counsel of *seniores*.[54] They were clearly a group that could and did represent the interests of the community and were an important development in the constitutional controls over superiors. Yet more important, in the long run, was the institution of general chapters, which included the superiors of all the houses belonging to an order. The history of such meetings is obscure, and they were not entirely new in the twelfth century.[55] Abbots were accustomed to meeting together on a provincial basis at diocesan synods, which they were required to attend unless their houses were specifically exempted by the papacy. At Limoges in the first half of the eleventh century, during diocesan synods, 'The bishop orders the abbot of St Martial to sit next to him in the other seat. All the

[50] See Arnaldi (1959) and Bautier (1987) on the terms *prior* and *prepositus*. Mattoso (1968), p. 204, remarked on the use of *prior* rather than *abbas* in twelfth-century monasteries in Portugal.

[51] Rupert of Deutz, *In regulam sancti Benedicti*, IV, 2, in *PL*, CLXX, 526C–7C, and *Consuetudines canonicorum regularium Springiersbacenses-Rodenses*, XLV, 298, in *CC:CM*, XLVIII, 156. See Pauly (1958), p. 107, and Van Engen (1983), p. 325.

[52] *Vita Stephani Obazinensis*, II, 17, ed. Aubrun, p. 126.

[53] See Hilpisch (1956), pp. 223–8; Dubois (1982), pp. 22–5; Felten (1988), p. 271; and Constable (1992a). In the *Libelli de discordia inter monachos s. Remigii et s. Nicasii Remenses*, I, 20, ed. Hermann Meinert, in *Festschrift Albert Brackmann* (Weimar 1931), p. 285, which date from 1111, the abbot chose twelve wiser monks and twelve senior lay men and promised to do what they advised.

[54] See nn. 38–9 above.

[55] See in general, in spite of their age, Schreiber (1910), II, 325–31, and Hourlier (1936).

abbots standing by hold their pastoral staffs in their hands.'[56] It is probable that on such occasions they discussed matters of common concern. The abbots of the congregations of Camaldoli and Vallombrosa apparently met together at times in the eleventh century, but these meetings were never very large, and their character is uncertain.[57] Special meetings of abbots, often on a regional basis, were more frequent in the twelfth century. The abbots of the province of Reims, meeting at Reims in 1131 and at Soissons in 1132, decided on some important measures of reform, including the abbreviations in the liturgy to which Matthew of Albano objected; the meetings of abbots from Saxony in 1149 and at Saalfeld in 1148/50 were also concerned with improving monastic discipline.[58] General chapters of the heads of Cluniac houses met in 1132, 1140, 1144, and 1150.[59] Neither the institution of general chapters nor the system of sending visitors, as they were called, to inspect individual houses originated with the reformers or were restricted to the new orders. Gerald of Wales in the *Mirror of the church* praised both the Cistercian and the Cluniac systems of visitation.[60] But they reached their highest development in the reformed orders of the twelfth century, and especially in the order of Cîteaux, of which the annual general chapters were the model from which the institution passed into the general structure of the church in the thirteenth century.[61] The Fourth Lateran Council specifically required the abbots and priors of every kingdom and province to meet every three years in order to discuss 'the reformation of the order and the regular observance' and to appoint visitors who were empowered to correct abuses and, if necessary, to recommend the removal of superiors.[62]

In spite of these restrictions on their independence and power, many abbots still behaved inside their abbeys like arbitrary rulers and outside like great lords. At the turn of the eleventh century Theodore of Amorbach criticized the harshness and cruelty of some superiors, who ruled by force.[63] Their rule

[56] *Ordo Lemovicensium de diligentia corporis Domini sive de sinodo bis in anno ab episcopo celebrando*, ed. Léopold Delisle, in *Notices et extraits des manuscrits de la Bibliothèque nationale et autres bibliothèques* 35.1 (1898), p. 270. On diocesan synods and the obligation of abbots to attend, see Schreiber (1910), I, 215–24.

[57] Hourlier (1936), pp. 78–82, and Duvernay (1952), pp. 435–8. There were between nine and ten houses affiliated with Vallombrosa in 1073: Quilici (1941–2), (3) p. 97; and there were seventeen Camaldolese houses by 1105: Wilhelm Kurze, in *Monachesimo* (1971), p. 413.

[58] The acts of the councils of 1131–2 are edited by Ursmer Berlière in *Documents inédits pour servir à l'histoire ecclésiastique de la Belgique*, I (Maredsous 1894), pp. 91–110, and by Stanislaus Ceglar, in *Saint-Thierry. Une abbaye du VIᵉ au XXᵉ siècle. Actes du colloque internationale d'histoire monastique. Reims-Saint-Thierry, 11 au 14 octobre 1976*, ed. Michel Bur (Saint-Thierry 1979), pp. 312–50. On the meetings of abbots from Saxony, see Meyer (1956).

[59] See the intro. to Peter the Venerable, *Statuta*, in *CCM*, VI, pp. 22–3.

[60] Gerald of Wales, *Speculum ecclesiae*, II, 29, ed. John S. Brewer a.o. (RS 21; London 1861–91), IV, 93.

[61] Mahn (1945), pp. 197–216.

[62] IV Lateran (1215), 12, in *Conc. oec. decreta*, p. 241. On the visitation-system, see Coulton (1929–50), II, 197.

[63] Dümmler (1894), p. 14 n.3.

was often referred to as *imperium*.[64] Adalbero of Laon said that Cluniac monks were soldiers serving their lord king Odilo of Cluny, and in the chronicle of St Hubert an abbot in the mid-eleventh century was said to have 'ruled like the ruler of a military undertaking over all those who were fighting for God under the regular discipline'.[65] The customs of Fruttuaria, which were related to those of Cluny and were compiled in the late eleventh century, show the abbot exercising arbitrary powers of punishment and showing favour to individual monks by promoting them in the chapter, refectory, and church and by handing out tidbits in the refectory.[66] The growing institutionalization of monasticism at this time, which can also be seen in the development of profession and benediction, likewise took the form of vows, which were inevitably compared to oaths of loyalty to a superior in secular society. In addition to the customs of Springiersbach and Rolduc, which were compiled in 1123, the canons swore to be 'faithful and obedient to my lord and prelate like a vassal and a subordinate (*feudalis et subditus*)', and when the Cistercian Philip of L'Aumône resigned as abbot in 1170/1 he freed the monks 'from the bond of your profession'.[67] Julian of Vézelay referred in his sermon on the Last Judgement to 'the chains of profession' and to the charters 'which the abbot placed on the altar when he made us monks, to be kept as evidence either of our salvation or our damnation'.[68] Many abbots received from the papacy the right to wear one or more of the distinctive signs of episcopal authority, such as the dalmatic and sandals, to which the mitre and gloves were added in the second half of the eleventh century, and the ring, tunic, and cross in the twelfth.[69]

These outer appearances of power and independence were to some extent at odds with the internal restrictions on abbatial authority and with the less authoritarian view of the position of abbot that was favoured especially among the reformers, who also objected to the exemption of monasteries from episcopal supervision. Abbots in the early Middle Ages expected to be feared and obeyed rather than loved and followed, but there were signs of change already in the first known commentary on the rule of Benedict, written in the early ninth century by Smaragdus, who said that the abbot should combine the

---

[64] Felten (1988), pp. 181–92.

[65] Adalbero of Laon, *Carmen ad Rotbertum regem*, lines 114–15, ed. Claude Carozzi (CHFMA 32; Paris 1979), p. 8, and *Cantatorium sive Chronicon s. Huberti*, 10, ed. Karl Hanquet (Commission royale d'histoire. Recueil de textes pour servir à l'étude de l'histoire de Belgique; Brussels 1906), p. 28.

[66] *Consuetudines Fructuarienses-Sanblasianae*, IIIa, 11, 438, in *CCM*, XII.2, 44.

[67] *Consuetudines canonicorum regularium Springiersbacenses-Rodenses*, XLII, 271, in *CC:CM*, XLVIII, 146n, and Philip of L'Aumône, *Ep.* 11 (of Clairvaux collection), in *Bibliotheca patrum Cisterciensium*, ed. Bertrand Tissier (Bonnefontaine and Paris 1660–9), III, 244. On oaths of fidelity and subordination between ecclesiastics, see Thomassin (1864–7), IV, 440–7.

[68] Julian of Vézelay, *Serm.* 21, ed. Damien Vorreux (SC 192–3; Paris 1972), II, 474 and 480.

[69] Salmon (1955), pp. 49–55, who listed (p. 51 n. 54) over a hundred grants from the tenth to the twelfth centuries.

severity of a father with the solicitude of a mother, and maternal imagery was applied to abbots in various black monastic sources in the eleventh and twelfth centuries.[70] This more solicitous and less authoritarian view of the abbot is found especially in the works of Bernard of Clairvaux and other Cistercian writers, who called the abbot a brother and sister as well as father and mother, and is related to the new devotion to the human Christ, who was seen as the model for religious superiors.[71] Philip of Harvengt in *On the institution of clerics* stressed that a superior can be imitated only if 'he strives most greatly to be loved and shows himself to his brothers as amiable and pleasing'.[72] Obedience was still important in the twelfth century, but in a spirit less of subservience and abnegation of personal will than of humility and voluntary subjection. This can be seen in the doctrine of *transitus*, which imposed on the individual monk the responsibility for carrying out his religious obligations, and it appears again in the inwardness of monastic spirituality. Francis specifically forbade his followers to obey an order contrary to their way of life or to the salvation of their souls.[73]

In a matter like this, and in other aspects of what may be called the internal constitution of religious houses, there was no strict division between the old and new houses or between monks and canons. In a general way it can be said that old black houses were more likely to have abbots who were exempt from episcopal control and who felt responsible only to God and themselves in ruling over monks who owed them complete obedience and that houses of reformed monks and regular canons more often had a superior who was called a prior, provost, or prelate rather than an abbot, who recognized the authority both of the diocesan bishop and of a mother-house and a general chapter, and who felt obliged to consult with other members of the community in making important decisions. There were so many exceptions to this generalization, however, as to make it almost meaningless. Some of the most aggressive assertions of the rights of election and consultation, and the sharpest restrictions on abbatial power, were found in the old black houses, which often (and perhaps partly for this reason) elected elderly abbots who felt one at heart with the monks who had chosen them. Many of the new houses, on the other hand, and especially the independent communities that characterized the reform movement in its beginnings, were governed by highly authoritarian superiors, whose moral authority gave them almost arbitrary powers over their followers and who appointed their successors in a manner that would have

---

[70] Smaragdus, *Expositio in regulam s. Benedicti*, II, 30, in *CCM*, VIII, 74. See also p. 67 above.
[71] Cf. Gammersbach (1956), who tended to exaggerate the contrast between the 'monarchical' view of the abbot at Cluny, which he traced to Germanic influence, and the 'paternal' view at Cîteaux, which he attributed to canon law and the Gregorian reform.
[72] Philip of Harvengt, *De institutione clericorum*, 5: *De obedientia clericorum*, 41, in *PL*, CCIII, 933D.
[73] Francis of Assisi, *Regula prima*, 5, in *Analekten zur Geschichte des Franciscus von Assisi*, ed. Heinrich Boehmer (Sammlung ausgewählter kirchen- und dogmengeschichtlicher Quellenschriften N.F. 4; Tübingen 1930), p. 4; cf. *Regula bullata*, 10, ibid., p. 23.

been intolerable in an older establishment. The reformers' sense of superiority and conviction of righteousness, indeed, inspired many of the attacks on the old monks and embittered the tone of the polemics, which tended to concentrate on small but conspicuous, and for this reason deeply felt, differences in religious life and organization.[74]

The nature of these differences, which affected canons as well as monks and made up the substance of the reform movement for many contemporaries, as well as for later scholars, is best seen in some specific programmes. Bishop Berengar of Vic, for instance, laid down nineteen points in his charter of 1080 requiring the canons of his cathedral to (1) celebrate the sacraments and holy offices 'according to the custom of religious men', (2) wear religious habits, (3) be silent in the church, refectory, and dormitory 'unless there is an urgent need' to speak, (4) wear surplices in these places and in the cloister, (5) eat without complaint the food served in the refectory, (6) give the leftovers to the poor, (7) correct in chapter any improprieties at table or elsewhere, (8) leave the choir in an orderly fashion, (9) have no concubines and preserve their chastity 'as much as they could', (10) not hawk, dice, sling, or hunt, (11) attend the liturgical hours, (12) hasten to church when the signal was given, (13) avoid bad language or gestures, (14) give tithes from all their communal property to the hospice for the poor, (15) take the ecclesiastical grades for which they qualified, (16) sleep in the dormitory, and (17) remain in the cloister until after the chapter unless they were specifically excused by the prior. Two final points were concerned with the judgement of transgressors by the bishop, prior, and *maiores* and the expulsion from the chapter of simoniacs and excommunicates by the bishop, who agreed to admit no one to a canonry 'without the common counsel of the canons'.[75] This final concession is the only point in the programme showing, what the remainder of the charter confirms, that it arose out of discussions and may have been more of a compromise than its form suggests. The extent of the changes was so great, however, that the canons had to be expelled by the bishop before the reform could be carried through.

Like most reforming programmes, this one tells us more about the canons before they were reformed than afterwards. In many respects they behaved like lay men: wearing no distinctive clothing, sleeping in separate houses and rooms (sometimes with their mistresses), engaging in secular occupations and amusements, complaining about the food, and using vulgar words and gestures. They performed some religious duties, both in the church and in the chapter, but negligently, and they were reluctant to enter ecclesiastical grades that would presumably have imposed further obligations and restrictions.

[74] See Dimier (1955a); Zimmermann (1973); and Leclercq (1986), who examined the principal substantive issues between the old and new monks.

[75] *España sagrada*, XXVIII, pp. 290–1. See p. 115 above.

Bishop Berengar, like other eleventh-century bishops,[76] wanted to make them more like monks and to set them off from the rest of society in their dress, behaviour, and way of life and by making them fulfil their ecclesiastical obligations like religious men, which involved imposing common life, chastity, and silence and may have included, as the use of the term 'custom' suggests, changing the liturgy. Urban II in the 1090s forbade the canons of Marbach, St Saturninus at Toulouse, and Rodez to have any private property or to leave their enclosure without the permission of the provost or of the entire community.[77]

The most significant programme of monastic reform was that of the Cistercians, which can be studied not only in their own early documents but also in the list of criticisms embodied in Letter 28 of Peter the Venerable, who called it an 'invective' and suggested that it had been drawn up by some monks at Clairvaux, though not necessarily by Bernard, to whom his letter was addressed.[78] It covered twenty points, which Peter listed, as he said 'in the order in which they have been placed by you': (1) the reception of novices, (2) the use of furs, (3) the wearing of trousers when travelling, (4) the type of bed-coverings, (5) the number and types of meals, (6) the readmission of runaway monks, (7) fasting, (8) manual labour, (9) the reception of guests, (10) the property-list kept by the abbot, (11) liturgical genuflections or *metanea*, (12) the meals of guests, (13) the blessing given by senior to junior monks, (14) the doorkeeper, (15) the doorkeeper's greeting to visitors, (16) the repetition of vows, (17) the reception of monks from other houses, (18) exemption from episcopal jurisdiction, (19) the possession of tithes and first-fruits, and (20) the possession of castles, villas, serfs, tolls, and the like.[79] The first point to strike the reader of this list, to which the remainder of Peter's letter is a detailed reply, and also of the Vic list, is its apparently random order, for which there is no ready explanation. The second is the mixture of significant issues, such as the novitiate, *transitus*, and exemption, with matters so trivial that they are found nowhere else in the polemical literature of the period. It is hard to believe that even the most literal-minded observer of the rule of Benedict really bothered over who kept the list of the abbey's possessions or over the age of the doorkeeper or the precise terms with which he greeted visitors. The inclusion of points like these helps to explain the bitter and exasperated tone of some of Peter's reply, which began: 'O the new

[76] See, for instance, Soldani (1741), pp. 254–5, where bishop Atto of Florence in 1036 tried to impose on his chapter a programme of obedience and common life and property, and Magnou (1958), App. 1, *pièce justif.* 2, for the charter of bishop Isarnus of Toulouse in 1073 requiring the canons of his cathedral to lead a common life, to have no private property, to eat and dress according 'to the form of the apostolic institution', and to go out only with the prior's permission.

[77] *PL*, CLI, 455AB, 479CD, and 546D (JL 5629, 5660, and 5805).

[78] On the character of this 'invective', see the notes to Peter the Venerable, *Ep.* 28, ed. Constable, II, 170–1.

[79] Peter the Venerable, *Ep.* 28, ed. Constable, I, 53–6.

breed of pharisees that has come again to the world, who separate themselves from others, prefer themselves to others, and say that the prophet predicted that they would be called "Do not touch me" (John 20.17) because I am clean (Job 33.9).'[80] A third point is that the list makes no reference to common life, chastity, silence, the liturgy (except genuflections), and other standard issues of monastic reform, presumably because the Cluniacs were known to be above reproach in these matters. In attacking Cluny, therefore, the reformers took on an opponent quite unlike the canons of Vic, and they concentrated on points of detail precisely because there was no serious disagreement on many of the substantial issues. This list gives in many ways a better picture of the programme of monastic reform in the first generation than some of the later Cistercian documents, of which the dates and nature are uncertain. Both the *Charter of love* and the *Little beginning* (or *Beginning of the monastery of Cîteaux*) probably date in their present forms from the middle of the twelfth century. The former is concerned primarily with the organization of the order. The latter deals with its early history and includes a chapter on 'The institutes of the Cistercian monks coming from Molesme', referring to the purity and rectitude of the rule and the monks' desire to own lands only 'for their own use'.[81] The collection of three documents known individually as the *Beginning of Cîteaux* (or the *Summary of the beginning*), the *Summary of the charter of love*, and the *Chapters* (*Capitula*), which were long believed to be later abbreviations of the *Charter of love* and the *Little beginning*, may go back to the 1130s.[82] After two historical and four organizational sections, there are twenty paragraphs, numbered from seven to twenty-six, dealing with: (7) lay brothers, (8) fugitives, (9) the foundation of new houses, (10) liturgical books, (11) clothing, (12–15) food and its provision 'from the labour of the hands, the cultivation of lands, and the nourishing of herds', (16) the enclosure of monks, (17–18) exclusion of women from monasteries and granges, (19) avoidance of secular society, (20–2) lay brothers, and (23–6) various prohibitions of types of revenues, pastoral work, precious metals, gems and silk, and sculpture and painting except on wooden crucifixes.[83] This list corresponds at some points with that in Peter the Venerable's letter, and also with Ordericus Vitalis's accounts of the speech made by abbot Robert to the monks of Molesme and the history of the Cistercians down to 1135, but the differences between them show that they do not derive from a common source. Ordericus, in addition to stressing the observance of the rule *ex integro, per omnia*, and *ad litteram* and many of the usual points concerning food, clothing, silence, and manual labour, also

---

[80] Ibid., I, 57.

[81] *Textes de Cîteaux*, pp. 77–8. See p. 38 n. 171 above on the dates of these and other early Cistercian documents.

[82] See p. 38 and n. 171 above.

[83] *Textes de Cîteaux*, pp. 121–5.

mentioned the Cistercian rejection of dyed cloth and trousers, their privacy and refusal to admit even other monks to their services, and their selection 'with ingenious foresight' of names for their abbeys 'which by the sweetness of the name alone invite the hearers to experience quickly the great blessedness that is indicated in that place by so special a name'.[84]

Matters of food figured largely in most reform programmes, and in the polemical literature, but they need not be studied in detail here.[85] The principal points at issue were the number and types of meals (especially the additional snacks known as *pittantia*), the dishes served, how they were (or were not) cooked, and above all the eating of meat, animal fat, and birds. Stephen of Obazine forbade even sick monks to eat meat and on one occasion enraged some lay workers on the church by throwing out their meat.[86] On the whole there was little disagreement on these points. Although the example of Christ was cited in the *Reprehensio* to justify the eating of meat by the pastoral clergy,[87] no one defended meat-eating by monks. Even the flesh of birds, though not specifically forbidden in the rule, was to be avoided, according to the treatise *On the eating of birds*, which was written from the point of view of the old black monks.[88]

The issue of bed-covers likewise does not require a lengthy study, except insofar as it raises the broader question of sleeping arrangements, and the requirements of a common life, which included both a common refectory and a common dormitory. The almost universal preference for dormitories over individual sleeping cells is probably explained by the high value placed on common life and uniform behaviour, including participation in the night offices, as well as by the general fear of sexual misbehaviour. Individual sleeping cells had been the rule for monks in the early church, however, as the reformers certainly knew from the *Lives* of the early monks, and lasted in most parts of the Christian world until the sixth, and in Spain and Ireland until the seventh, century.[89] After that they were found among solitary hermits and recluses and in exceptional cases, like that of William of Gellone, who had a private cell for his genuflections and flagellations, which would have disturbed the sleepers in a dormitory and offended the sense of privacy that was supposed to surround such devotions.[90] There were private places at Cluny in the eleventh and twelfth centuries for monks who wanted to engage

[84] Ordericus Vitalis, *Historia ecclesiastica*, VIII, 26, ed. Chibnall, IV, 324–6.
[85] In addition to the references in *Medieval Monasticism*, nos. 818–21, see Dimier (1955a), pp. 168–73; Zimmermann (1973), pp. 58–62; and, more generally, on the diet in eastern and western monasteries, Dembiska (1985).
[86] *Vita Stephani Obazinensis*, II, 14, ed. Aubrun, p. 116.
[87] *Reprehensio*, 22, ed. Wilmart, p. 331. See Charles H. Talbot, in *Petrus Venerabilis* (1956), pp. 72–80, defending Wilmart's attribution to Hugh of Rouen.
[88] *Dialogus de esu volatilium*, in Pez, *Thesaurus*, II.2, 545–66, esp. 557AB.
[89] De Vogüé (1965) and Zimmermann (1973), p. 145.
[90] *Vita Willelmi Gellonensis*, III, 30, in *AASS*, 28 May VI, 809A (*BHL* 8916).

in private prayer and mortifications,[91] and even such a pillar of the conventional church as Suger had built for himself at St Denis a little cell, about ten by fifteen feet in size, where 'He was free for reading and tears and contemplation in the hours allowed to him.'[92] These were not sleeping cells, however, and, in spite of the importance attached by the reformers to private prayer and devotions, only the Carthusians made individual cells part of their regular way of life.[93]

Clothing, on the other hand, was a bitter source of controversy, above all the type of cloth and its colour, or, more correctly, lack of colour, since most of the reformers wore woollen robes made of undyed cloth that was variously described in the sources as white or grey depending, presumably, on the colour of the sheep and the cleanliness of the garments.[94] Undyed cloth had in fact long been used by hermits in both the east and the west, such as the monks of Camaldoli, Vallombrosa, and Fonte Avellana and by St Neophytus in Cyprus, whose typikon said that the monks should wear 'poor downtrodden grey' rather than black.[95] The illustrations of early Cistercian monks in the manuscripts from Cîteaux show them both in grey and in brown habits,[96] and even a century later in the illustration of early Cistercian abbots in Alexander of Hales's *On the Apocalypse* they are wearing robes of different colours (plate 6). Rupert of Deutz in his commentary on the rule of Benedict referred to the clothes worn by the new monks as 'off-white and of doubtful and uncertain colour' and remarked that 'Perhaps if we had used white clothes they would now use black',[97] suggesting that it was adopted simply out of a desire to be different. Peter the Venerable wrote sarcastically in Letter 28:

---

[91] *Vita s. Anastasii*, 4, in *PL*, CXLIX, 428D–9A (*BHL* 405) and Peter the Venerable, *De miraculis*, I, 20, in *CC:CM*, LXXXIII, 60–1. See Constable (1975a), pp. 131–3.

[92] William of St Denis, *Vita Sugerii*, 2, ed. A. Lecoy de la Marche (Société de l'histoire de France; Paris 1867), p. 393.

[93] See esp. Hocquard (1948), pp. 8–11, and (1951).

[94] See the *Reprehensio*, 30, ed. Wilmart, p. 340, and, among secondary works, Oppenheim (1932); Dimier (1955a), pp. 178–82; Zimmermann (1973), pp. 103–4 and 115–16; and Constable (1987a), pp. 816–31.

[95] Hallinger (1950–1), p. 700. For Neophytus, see the forthcoming collection of *Byzantine Monastica Typika*, ed. John Thomas, no. 45, C15.

[96] MSS Dijon, Bibl. mun., 170, fols. 20ʳ, 59ʳ, and 75ʳ, and 173, fols. 41ʳ and 167ʳ. Some of these may have been overpainted later. See Duvernay (1952), p. 405, and Schneider (1965), pp. 271–8, dating the change of colour in 1103. The clothing of the Cistercians was referred to as grey in Reginald of Durham, *Vita Godrici*, LXXVI, 164, and LXXXIV, 177, ed. Stevenson, pp. 174 and 185; *Vita Gaufridi Saviniacensis*, 10, ed. E.-P. Sauvage, in *Anal. boll.* 1 (1882), p. 367 (*BHL* 3285); William of Ebbelholt, *Ep.* II, 46 and 48, in *Scriptores rerum Danicorum medii aevi*, ed. J. Langebek (Copenhagen 1772–1878), VI, 60–1; *Annales Rodenses*, s.a. 1144, ed. P.C. Boeren and G.W.A. Panhuysen (Assen 1968), fol. 18ᵛ, p. 92; and Idungus, *Dialogus*, III, 38, ed. Huygens, p. 460, where the Cistercian habit was said to be neither black nor white but grey. See plate 6.

[97] Rupert of Deutz, *In regulam s. Benedicti*, III, 13, in *PL*, CLXX, 521CD. See Van Engen (1983), p. 317, who dated this work about 1125 and called this passage 'perhaps the earliest extant record of the white Cistercian habit'.

You saints, you singular men, you only true monks in the whole world, since all others are false and corrupt, you set yourselves alone among all according to the interpretation of the name, whence you also arrogate a habit of unaccustomed colour, and in distinction from all the monks of almost the entire world, you present yourselves in white among those who are in black.[98]

Some of the reformers tried to defuse the issue. Otto of Freising said that some monks wore black 'in order to express contempt for the world . . . but others who want no disputes over the colour or thickness are accustomed to wear white or grey or other [colours], but lowly and rough',[99] and Norbert stressed that the rule of Augustine covered all that was necessary for salvation.

> Because if there is a controversy among some spiritual men concerning the colour or the thickness or the softness of clothes, let those who take the opportunity of disparaging on this account indicate from this rule, let them indicate, I say, from the institution of the Gospel and the apostles, where the whiteness, blackness, softness, or thickness is described in giving a precept, and then they should be believed.

Norbert could not resist adding, however, that the canons wore white like the angels and wool like penitents and linen in the sanctuary, though he stressed that their doing so was not in order to derogate others.[100] The use of expensive white clothing was condemned in the *Mirror for virgins*,[101] and Tenxwind of Andernach, which was a daughter-house of Springiersbach, objected to the long white veils worn on feast-days by the nuns of Bingen, who also wore gold crowns with crosses and looked like brides. Hildegard in her reply said that virgins wore white to signify their marriage to Christ.[102] According to the abbess of the Camaldolese house of Pratavecchio the nuns of Rosano, near Florence, were allowed to wear black habits because 'they hated to be under the order of Camaldoli so greatly that she could not induce them to this [to wear white] without a great scandal'.[103] Peter the Venerable said in Letter 111, written in 1144, that:

> I have seen I know not how many black monks laughing at a white monk whom they meet as if he were a monster and showing by their voices and gestures that they are amazed as if a chimera or centaur or some travelling marvel came before their eyes. I have on the other hand seen white monks who were pre-

---

[98] Peter the Venerable, *Ep.* 28, ed. Constable, I, 57.

[99] Otto of Freising, *Historia de duobus civitatibus*, VII, 35, ed. Adolf Hofmeister, 2nd edn (*MGH SSRG*; Hanover and Leipzig 1912), p. 372.

[100] *Vita* [B] *Norberti*, 9, in *PL*, CLXX, 1293A (*BHL* 6249). See Petit (1939), p. 20. Cf. Arno of Reichersberg, *Scutum canonicorum*, in *PL*, CXCIV, 1505B, on which see Capitani (1962). According to the *Ancrene riwle*, intro., ed. Morton (n. 17), p. 11, the apostle James spoke in his order neither of white nor of black.

[101] Bernards (1955), pp. 161–3. See also Guibert, *De vita sua*, I, 14, ed. Bourgin, p. 50.

[102] Haverkamp (1984), pp. 543–4 and 547.

[103] Passerini (1876–7), p. 212; cf. p. 216, where a witness said that he knew two nuns whom he saw at Rosano came from Pratavecchio because they wore white.

viously talking and constantly telling each other what was going on suddenly become quiet when a black monk comes by and take the precaution of silence for themselves as if from enemies who are searching for the secrets of enemies.[104]

The strength of feeling roused by this issue would be hard to understand were it not for two special factors. The first was the importance traditionally attached to the monastic habit, which was considered almost equivalent to monastic life itself, as the deathbed ceremony of becoming a monk *ad succurrendum* shows. The monastic costume was compared to that of Christ and the apostles. Every aspect had a symbolic significance, often in comparison with the cross and the appearance of the angels and cherubim.[105] Any variation was therefore a serious matter. In the treatise *On preserving the unity of the church*, which was written in the early 1090s, perhaps at Hersfeld, the monks of Monte Cassino raised objections to the Cluniac habit, which was particularly criticized in the form it was worn by the monks of Hirsau.

> There has been a long struggle and discord among monks concerning the monastic costume, and among those who seem to be more religious in their display, among those, I say, the name that is the double costume is so solemn and celebrated, and so holy and venerable, that other monks living in monasteries are thought to be of no merit or moment by these men, unless they wear this double robe of confusion.

Fifty years later these words might have been written by a Cluniac criticizing the innovations and claims to special sanctity of the Cistercians. The writer then defended the traditional monastic habit, comparing it to the cross of Christ in Luke 14.27, which referred to the cross both of His passion and of His entire life, to which He was fixed 'by the virtues of all the disciplines. In the sign of the cross, therefore, is described not only the whole life and institution of the monk but every Christian action.' He compared the monastic habit to the mysteries of the cross: its breadth to love, its length to perseverance, and its height to contemplation. 'For just as the name monk is a certain term of mystery, so is the cowl a certain strength of sacrament.'[106]

The second factor that exacerbated the dispute over clothing was the ancient symbolism of black and white – a symbolism that can still be seen in Hudson's chapter on 'Snow and the Quality of Whiteness' and in Melville on 'The Whiteness of the Whale'.[107] Christ appeared in a white garment at the transfiguration, and white was worn by the angels, and by Christ, the elders, and

---

[104] Peter the Venerable, *Ep.* 111, ed. Constable, I, 285–6.
[105] See pp. 191–2 below and the *De vita vere apostolica*, 4, in *Ampl. coll.*, IX, 1025–6.
[106] *De unitate ecclesiae conservanda*, II, 42, in *MGH, Libelli*, II, 276–8. The author went on to say that the short monastic tunic, with bare arms, had become rare because so few monks worked with their hands. On this work see Zafarana (1966) and Robinson (1978), pp. 94–5.
[107] W.H. Hudson, *Idle Days in Patagonia*, ch. 8, and Herman Melville, *Moby Dick*, ch. 42: 'Symbolize whatever grand or gracious thing he will by whiteness, no man can deny that in its profoundest idealized significance it calls up a peculiar apparition to the soul.'

those who win the victory in the Apocalypse. White was associated with glory, resurrection, victory, and exaltation, and also with purity, innocence, chastity, and love, and with joy, success, happiness, and goodness.[108] Adam of Dryburgh said that the regular canons wore white robes 'in the brightness of future remuneration' and in witness of the promise that they would pass 'from whiteness to whiteness ... from the merit to the reward, so that if in the present we wear the albs of justice we can confidently hope to wear in the future the albs of glory'.[109] Black, on the other hand, was associated with abjection, contempt of the world, penance, self-abasement, humility, failure, servitude, and sadness.[110] For Matthew of Rievaulx, white was gold and black was silver; for Abelard, white was favourable and black, adverse: 'The blackness, that is of bodily tribulations, easily turns the minds of the faithful from the love of worldly things, raising them to the desires of eternal life, and often draws them from the tumultuous life of the world towards the secret of contemplation.'[111] Philip of Harvengt praised black clothing as a sign of inner life, though he also said that white clothing (which, as a Premonstratensian, he wore himself) showed 'the grace of remission that has been received' and 'the hoped-for glory of celestial joy'.[112] Not all regular canons in the twelfth century wore white, however. At Rolduc they wore black, and pope Adrian IV in 1155 confirmed the decision of Eugene III, when a Premonstratensian was installed as abbot of St Pierremont in Lorraine, that he should not impose the white habit and that the canons should continue to wear black.[113] The reason for this may been respect for tradition or a desire to spare the canons the humiliation of being forced to change their habit, but it shows that even a Cistercian pope did not insist upon changing the colour of their robes.

Some other aspects of clothing and appearance, while less important than that of colour, should also be mentioned.[114] The triple habit of the Cistercians was praised in the *Dialogue of two monks* because it was in the form of a cross

---

[108] Ott (1899), pp. 1–18; Oppenheim (1932), pp. 33–43 and 100; Dronke (1984), pp. 64–5; and the sources cited in Constable (1987a), p. 829, to which can be added Nicholas of Montiéramey, *Ep.* I, 50, to Peter of Celle, in *PL*, CCII, 474D; *Reprehensio*, 30, ed. Wilmart, p. 340; and *Vita Hamonis Saviniacensis*, 55, ed. E.P. Sauvage, *Anal. boll.* 2 (1883), p. 557 (*BHL* 3752).

[109] Adam of Dryburgh, *De ordine*, III, 10, and IV, 2, in *PL*, CXCVIII, 468AC and 470D.

[110] Ott (1899), pp. 19–33; Oppenheim (1932), pp. 29–32 and 100; and the sources cited in Constable (1987a), p. 829 n. 192.

[111] Matthew of Rievaulx, *De albo ordine et nigro*, ed. André Wilmart, in *Rev. bén.* 52 (1940), pp. 63–4, and Abelard, *Ep.* 4, to Heloise, ed. J.T. Muckle, in *Mediaeval Studies* 15 (1953), p. 85; cf. his *Regula* for religious women, ed. T.P. McLaughlin, in *Mediaeval Studies* 18 (1956), p. 281, where he recommended a sad woollen habit 'of black penitence'.

[112] Philip of Harvengt, *De institutione clericorum*, 4: *De continentia clericorum*, 100 and 127, in *PL*, CCIII, 803BC and 838D.

[113] *Annales Rodenses*, ed. Boeren and Panhuysen (n. 96), fol. 2ʳ, p. 26, and *PL*, CLXXXVIII, 1373A (JL 9969). See Parisse (1968), p. 362.

[114] On monastic clothing in the eleventh and twelfth centuries, see Hallinger (1950–1), pp. 661–734.

and had six wings, which resembled the cherubim and contrasted with the four wings of the Cluniac habit.[115] It was compared to an onion in the *Metamorphosis of Golias*.[116] Ailbert, the founder of Rolduc, was said to have worn 'a moderate habit, neither very cheap nor handsome, but tighter and shorter than is the modern use, hardly touching the top of his feet, such as the clergy used when religion was flourishing in ancient times'. Under his tunic he wore a hair shirt, and he never wore shoes except to celebrate mass.[117] This description identified Ailbert with the older and, as he believed, apostolic custom and set him off, on the one hand, from the contemporary clergy and monks who wore long and flowing robes and, on the other hand, from the ostentatious poverty and ragged clothing of some reformers, like Robert of Arbrissel, who according to Marbod of Rennes entirely rejected the regular habit and dressed in skins and a cloak, with half-covered legs, bare feet, a long beard, and his hair cut across his forehead, 'so that they say you are missing only the staff of the attire of a lunatic'.[118] This may have been the usual costume of hermits and of pilgrims, penitents, and beggars, but not of monks, who were supposed to be distinguished from the rest of society by the modesty as well as the simplicity of their dress. Robert of Knaresborough had no shoes and wore an old white cowl over ragged clothes and ate only greens and a special bread made of four parts of barley-meal and one part ashes. When he joined the monastery of Headley the monks said that 'This singular man is hard for us to see, since he is contrary to our works and entirely different in habit and in food.'[119]

Among other disputed points of clothing were the use of linen, which was considered luxurious except for priests at the altar, and the wearing of shirts, shoes, and above all trousers or underpants, which figure prominently both in the polemical literature and in anti-monastic satires.[120] According to the rule of Benedict, trousers were to be issued to monks when they travelled, but, implicitly, not at other times. They were increasingly common, however,

---

[115] Idungus, *Dialogus*, III, 46, ed. Huygens, p. 465. See also the explanation of the symbolism of the Cistercian habit in Otto of Freising, *Historia*, VII, 35, ed. Hofmeister (n. 99), p. 372, and, generally, Gobert of Laon, *De tonsura et vestimentis et vita clericorum*, ed. M. Hélin, in *Le musée belge. Revue de philologie classique* 34 (1930), p. 153.

[116] Huygens (1962), p. 771.

[117] *Annales Rodenses*, ed. Boeren and Panhuysen (n. 96), fol. 3ʳ, p. 30.

[118] Marbod of Rennes, *Ep.* 6, in *PL*, CLXXI, 1483CD. See von Walter (1903–6), I, 186. Many of the monks illustrated in the manuscripts from Cîteaux cited n. 96 above are wearing ragged clothes, as they are in plate 6.

[119] *Vita* [A] *Roberti Knaresburgensis*, 5, ed. Paul Grosjean, in *Anal. boll.* 57 (1939), p. 371–2 (*BHL* 7270d).

[120] See Van Haeften (1644), pp. 495–7 (V, 4, 5–6); Gougaud (1930), pp. 24–36; Lecoy (1942–3), pp. 10–14; and Zimmermann (1973), pp. 93–4 and 356–9. Curtius (1963), p. 124, said that 'In the squabbles of the twelfth century, breeches play a painful part.' See p. 310 n. 59 below for a 'joke' involving the lack of trousers. In the New Revised Standard version of the bible, according to Metzger (1991), p. 374, the 'breeches' in Ex. 28.42 are translated by 'the somewhat cumbersome "undergarments" '.

and came to be considered an essential attribute of modesty, and their use was sanctioned by custom and by miracles and *exempla*.[121] The saintly abbot Constable of La Cava gave his trousers to a poor man and received another pair from the Lord, and a monk who was waylaid by robbers was allowed by his abbot to give up all except his trousers.[122] The use of trousers appeared among the Cistercian charges against Cluny and was defended by Peter the Venerable on the grounds of necessity, cleanliness, and modesty.[123] The refusal of the Cistercians to wear trousers, even when travelling, gave rise to some unpleasant jokes concerning their presumed immodesty and desire for women.[124] The issue was certainly overblown and perhaps manufactured, like the question of what Scotsmen wear under their kilts, since the monks working out of doors in the illustrations in the manuscripts from Cîteaux are depicted wearing trousers.

Peter the Venerable's reference to cleanliness (*munditia*) raises another point that may be mentioned with regard to both the old and the new monks, who are sometimes said to have encouraged personal filth as a form of asceticism. While it is true that they saw virtue in a verminous hair shirt and luxury in a warm bath, there is no evidence that they esteemed dirtiness for its own sake, any more than that the Cistercians purposely chose unhealthy locations for their abbeys. Some of the reformers, on the contrary, encouraged cleanliness. Geoffrey of Chalard, who all his life wore a hair shirt, chains, and an iron belt, wore clean clothes and washed himself. According to his biographer, 'He wanted all his clothes . . . to be clean, and he frequently cleaned himself, and he considered that to have something dirty was the vice of negligence, not an indication of goodness.'[125] A certain concern for health in matters of food, clothing, and sleep accompanied the reaction against mortification for its own sake and was part of what has been seen as a humanizing trend in the religious life of the twelfth century. Peter the Venerable, like Heloise, regarded the monks of his own time as more fragile than the early monks,

---

[121] Hildegard of Bingen remarked on the growing use of trousers in her *Explanatio regulae s. Benedicti*, in *PL*, CXCVII, 1062C. See also Philip of Harvengt, *De institutione clericorum*, 4: *De continentia clericorum*, 55, in *PL*, CCIII, 734D and 736B.

[122] *Vita Constabilis Cavensis*, in *Rerum italicarum scriptores*, ed. L.A. Muratori (Milan 1723–51), VI, 232C (*BHL* 1926), and *Chronicon Novaliciense*, II, 11, ed. G.H. Pertz (*MGH, SSRG;* Hanover 1846), p. 28. See Lecoy (1942–3), pp. 10–12. In the *Miracula s. Benedicti*, I, 26, ed. Eugène de Certain (Société de l'histoire de France; Paris 1858), p. 59, a guardian accused Benedict of being lazy when some bracelets were stolen and said, 'It is of no concern to me if they steal your breeches if you do not defend the bracelets.'

[123] Peter the Venerable, *Ep.* 28, ed. Constable, I, 64–5; see the note in II, 117.

[124] Ordericus Vitalis, *Historia ecclesiastica*, VIII, 26, ed. Chibnall, IV, 314, 318, and 324; Walter Map, *De nugis curialium*, I, 25, ed. and tr. Montague R. James, rev. C.N.L. Brooke and R.A.B. Mynors (OMT; Oxford 1983), pp. 100–2; and *De grisis monachis*, lines 49–50, in *The Latin Poems Commonly Attributed to Walter Mapes*, ed. Thomas Wright (Camden Society 16; London 1841), p. 56; see also pp. 17 and 158. The rejection of *femoralia* except when travelling was described among the *aspera* of Cistercian usages by William of Malmesbury, *De gestis regum Anglorum*, IV, 336, ed. William Stubbs (RS 90; London 1887–9), II, 382.

[125] *Vita Gaufridi Castaliensis*, I, 9, ed. Bosvieux (n. 46), p. 107.

whose abstinence was heroic, and argued in favour of making some allowances for this fragility, and even in the strict new orders there was a recognition of the damage done to health by excessive asceticism and of the need for food, sleep, sanitation, and hygiene.[126] The Cistercian Galland of Rigny, writing in the second quarter of the twelfth century, said that a monk who was unable to work in the fields owing to the heat should choose some work to do in the shade or in the monastery and, if he could not celebrate all the liturgical feasts, should observe at least All Saints. 'Just as all other feasts are included in the feast of All Saints', Galland wrote, 'all the other [virtues] are contained in the virtue of charity.'[127]

The treatment of the hair and beard was also a matter of significance, in view of their ancient religious and folkloristic associations. Since clerics did not as a rule wear a distinctive dress except when celebrating the sacraments, their tonsure and shaving were often the only signs of their clerical status. Monks were supposed to wear both a distinctive costume and to have a broader tonsure or crown than clerics, and to shave if they were ordained, but there were so many exceptions to these rules, and such great negligence in their observance, that it was often difficult (as it is once again today) to tell a cleric or a monk from a lay man. Almost all the reformers of the eleventh and twelfth centuries, and many churchmen who were not reformers, wanted to reassert the distinctive character of monks, of which tonsure was a sign, and therefore insisted on the broad tonsure. The chronicler of Lorsch, who was writing in the late eleventh century on the basis of earlier material, clearly considered the broad tonsure of the monks of Hirsau, like their large cowls, a sign of ostentatious piety, much as the white clothing of the reformers was regarded in the following century.[128] Richard (or Hugh) of St Victor criticized monks who went around with small tonsures, long hair, and clothing with sleeves coming down to the ground; the author of *On the truly apostolic life* compared the broad tonsure of monks to the crown of thorns; and Arno of Reichersberg in his *Shield of the canons* (which is also attributed to Anselm of Havelberg) advocated a large tonsure rather than a little circle on the top of the head 'as was at one time the custom of heretics', and was still in use.[129] It is hard to know to what extent this campaign was successful, but it was undercut by the ordination of most monks and the tendency to identify the monastic and

---

[126] Peter the Venerable, *Stat.* 11, in *CCM*, VI, 51, and, generally, Zimmermann (1973), pp. 147–9, 234–5, and 459.

[127] Galland of Rigny, *Liber proverbiorum*, 13, ed. Jean Châtillon, in *Revue du moyen âge latin* 9 (1953), p. 47; cf. 105.

[128] *Chronicon Laureshamense*, 142, in *Codex Laureshamensis*, ed. Karl Glöckner (Darmstadt 1929, repr. 1963), I, 420. There is a reference to the difference in tonsure and dress in the alleged debate between the Cistercian monk and Peter the Deacon before the emperor Lother in 1137: Peter the Deacon, *Altercatio pro cenobio Casinensis*, in Caspar (1909), p. 270.

[129] Hugh of St Victor (attr.), *Serm.* 49, in *PL*, CLXXVII, 1038CD; *De vita vere apostolica*, 5, in *Ampl. coll.*, IX, 1025; and Arno of Reichersberg, *Scutum canonicorum*, in *PL*, CXCIV, 1503CD (see n. 100 above).

clerical tonsures. Idungus of Regensburg in the *Dialogue of two monks* identified the two tonsures in order to assert the right of monks to the clerical
office. 'The life of the monks is apostolic', he said, 'their habit is angelic, and
the crown they have is both the mark of perfection and the clerical sign.'[130]

The significance of beards was less obvious, but they entered the religious
disputes in two different contexts. The full or long beard (*barba prolixa*) was
worn by Robert of Arbrissel, Bernard of Tiron, and other reformers probably
in imitation of penitents and of early hermits and holy men and perhaps also,
as Marbod suggested, as a consciously a- or anti-social gesture.[131] But it was
also worn by worldly prelates like Henry of Winchester (who was a Cluniac
monk as well as a bishop) and by the dandified monks who were criticized in
an anonymous Cistercian text.[132] The other context in which beards appeared
in a reforming context was on lay brothers, who were often called *barbati*
owing to the beards they wore in order to distinguish them from the ordained
members of their communities. In the Cistercian order, to generalize from the
beards of the lay brothers of Rosières to whom Burchard of Bellevaux
addressed his *Apology on beards*, they were between one and a half and two
inches long, which at times approximated the beards of the monks, who
according to early Cistercian statutes shaved only seven times a year.[133] Some
lay brothers had much longer beards, however, like that in which a secret
letter to the empress Mathilda was concealed.[134] The beards of the lay brothers
were considered a mark of their low status and menial occupations, and, in
spite of Burchard's efforts to find every good point he could say about them,
he frankly admitted at one point that the beardless clerics were suited to
the holy offices while 'you who have beards are deputed for ploughs and
mattocks'.[135]

The presence of bearded lay brothers was a characteristic mark of a
reformed community in the early twelfth century, though in the new orders
the date of their introduction may have been later than was once believed.[136]
Some houses probably admitted them only when the founding members died
or departed and the community became more clericalized and unable to do

---

[130] Idungus, *Dialogus*, III, 37, ed. Huygens, p. 460.
[131] See the references in the intro. to Burchard of Bellevaux, *Apologia de barbis*, in *CC:CM*, LXII,
121–3. One of the holy men described by Gerard of Nazareth, *De conversatione virorum Dei
in Terra Sancta morantium*, 11, in Kedar (1983), p. 72, 'shaved his head with an uneven tonsure
and his beard in such a way that he appeared to be a moron'.
[132] John of Salisbury, *Historia pontificalis*, 40, ed. and tr. Marjorie Chibnall (MT; London and
Edinburgh 1956), p. 79, and the Cistercian text published in Rochais and Binont (1964),
p. 143, no. Lc 32, criticizing monks who wore tunics with long sleeves and had flowing hair,
a small tonsure, and a full beard.
[133] Burchard of Bellevaux, *Apologia de barbis*, II, 1, in *CC:CM*, LXII, 162; cf. intro., pp. 126–7.
[134] *Chronicon de s. Barbara in Algia*, ed. Sauvage (n. 45), p. 51.
[135] Burchard of Bellevaux, *Apologia de barbis*, II, 6, in *CC:CM*, LXII, 167.
[136] There is a large secondary literature on lay brothers: see *Medieval Monasticism*, nos. 768–75,
and especially Leclercq (1965b) and Dubois (1968c). On problems with lay brothers, see pp.
123–4 above.

all its own work. Lay brothers also appeared in older monasteries, where they took over duties previously performed by lay *famuli* or servants, but it is not certain that they ever became a closed and segregated caste, as is found in the highly organized new orders like the Cistercians and Carthusians. The lay brothers sometimes held responsible positions, performed administrative functions, and appeared as witnesses on charters, but they were always a group apart from and in principle inferior to the clerical monks. They did not join the monks in church, though they had a religious life of their own based on an ideal of poverty, patience, and obedience.[137] At Fountains in the late twelfth century there was 'a certain lay brother of singular grace and piety named Sunnulphus, a simple and illiterate man, but the Lord instructed him. He had his conscience in place of a book, the Holy Spirit for an instructor, and reading in the book of experience, he grew daily in knowledge of holy matters, having also the spirit of revelations.'[138] This is a good example of the type of simple and unpretentious piety, marked by a tendency towards mystical experiences, that characterized the Cistercian saints of the thirteenth century.[139]

The old black monasteries normally had both *famuli* and *servientes*, who were basically hired servants, and also a host of lay familiars, friends, converts, devotees, co-brothers and co-sisters, corrodians, *prebendarii*, and the like who had entered into an association with the community entitling them to burial and prayers, to food, clothing and sometimes also lodging, and to participate in or at least attend the services. Occasionally they were also entitled to become members of the community when they wished.[140] The new houses refused all such hangers-on, whom they regarded, often with justice, as a source of contacts with lay society and of distraction, if not corruption, from the proper concerns of monks. Few of them were able to break entirely with such a firmly established pattern, especially of having lay servants and workers. Cîteaux seems to have had servants almost from its origins, and the general chapters at an early date recognized their presence in other houses, not without regret.[141] Lay men worked on the church at Obazine, and one of the miracles at the tomb of Geoffrey of Chalard concerned a member of the *familia* who served the canons as a baker.[142] Recluses required servants unless all their

---

[137] On the activities of lay brothers, see Dubois (1982), pp. 31–2, and Platt (1969), pp. 76–7, who argued that in England the lay brothers served as supervisors rather than as labourers, and on their religious life, Mikkers (1962) and Leclercq (1965b), pp. 248–58.

[138] Hugh of Kirkstall, *Narratio*, ed. Walbran, pp. 118–25. Sunnulphus was friendly with abbot Ralph, to whom he gave advice and whose death he predicted.

[139] See esp. Roisin (1947) and p. 24 n. 110 above.

[140] See pp. 85–6 above.

[141] Statutes published under the year 1157, 42, in Canivez, *Statuta*, p. 65. See Dubois (1968c), pp. 217–21. The untonsured workers in plate 6 may be either novices or lay men. The fact they have no beards shows that they were not lay brothers.

[142] *Vita Stephani Obazinensis*, II, 14, ed. Aubrun, p. 116, and *Vita Gaufridi Castaliensis*, III, 16, ed. Bosvieux (n. 46), p. 119.

needs were met by members of a community on which they depended, and most hermits had at least one servant. A much-respected hermit like Robert of Knaresborough had four *famuli* or *servi*, of whom two dealt with agriculture, one with this house, and one with collecting alms for the poor.[143] There were doubtless a few very poor houses with no lay servants or dependants, but the rule of Benedict was usually interpreted as requiring not their abolition but their separation from the monks, as Peter the Venerable attempted to do in his Statute 24.[144]

The same was true of children, who formed an important element in many old black houses but were excluded from most of the reformed houses, which accepted as recruits only adults at least sixteen, or sometimes twenty, years old.[145] Some of the strict old houses tried to do the same, as at Cluny, but the boys there had an established place in both the liturgy and the community and were not entirely abolished.[146] It was a common practice, furthermore, and presumably a source of revenue, for religious houses to educate boys who had no intention of remaining in the community. The Cluniac priory of Sauxillanges, where Peter the Venerable was an oblate, accepted a boy to be raised in the monastery until he was between seven and ten years old, and the *Regula clericorum* of Peter *de Honestis* shows that even relatively strict canons were prepared to raise and educate boys.[147] Some reformed houses accepted children either as oblates or as members of families. The Gilbertine nunnery of Watton accepted a four-year-old girl at the request of the Cistercian archbishop Henry of York, and lived to regret it; and at Obazine the boys were required at the age of five to move from the women's monastery to the *statio puerorum*. According to Stephen's biographer, they 'approached both divine knowledge and angelic purity the more purely because they had nothing of the impure heat of the world'.[148] This practice presumably ceased when Obazine joined the Cistercians, who permitted only monks and novices to be educated within their abbeys.[149] The rules drawn up by the abbot Fulgentius of Afflighem for the nuns of Forest-les-Bruxelles in about 1110 forbade them to attract 'a multitude of infants or little girls' whose 'girlish levity', he said, might destroy the holiness of the nuns.[150]

[143] *Vita* [A] *Roberti Knaresburgensis*, 6, ed. Grosjean (n. 119), pp. 372.
[144] Peter the Venerable, *Stat.* 24, in *CCM*, VI, 61. See Constable (1973).
[145] See Pierre Riché, in *Pierre Abélard – Pierre le Vénérable* (1975), pp. 689–701, and pp. 100–1 above.
[146] Peter the Venerable, *Stat.* 56 and 66, in *CCM*, VI, 85–6 and 97. See Constable (1992a).
[147] *Cartulaire de Sauxillanges*, ed. Henry Doniol, in *Mémoires de l'Académie des sciences, belles-lettres et arts de Clermont-Ferrand* 34 (N.S. 3; 1861), p. 1068, no. 895, and Peter *de Honestis*, *Regula clericorum*, II, 26, in *PL*, CLXIII, 729B, on which see Dickinson (1950), pp. 44 and 165, and Charles Dereine, in *DHGE*, XII, 387.
[148] *Vita Stephani Obazinensis*, II, 49, ed. Aubrun, pp. 170–2.
[149] Statutes published under the year 1134, 78, in Canivez, *Statuta*, p. 31.
[150] Miraeus–Foppens, I, 78.

This exclusion of children was motivated not only by a concern for the maturity of the monks or nuns and to protect them from sexual temptation but also by a desire for peace and quiet in the cloister. Silence is mentioned frequently in the rule of Benedict and figured prominently in programmes of monastic reform.[151] The first known description of a system of sign-language or finger-speech is found in the section on 'the manner of silence' at Baume in the *Life* of abbot Odo of Cluny by John of Salerno, and at Cluny great emphasis was put on silence, which was the subject of four of the reforming statutes of Peter the Venerable.[152] The abbots from the province of Reims in 1131 and 1132 insisted on silence both at table and in the cloister,[153] and the hermit Godric of Finchale 'invented for the use of silence . . . various types of signs, of which he taught the meanings to his servants, so that he learned to express and say whatever he wished by signs and nods'.[154] In order to avoid any unnecessary speech, the Cistercians developed an elaborate sign-language, which is still used in their monasteries.[155] Some contemporaries, indeed, were aware that fingers could be as garrulous and lewd as tongues, and the Carthusians avoided signs when possible and preferred to speak in words when something had to be said.[156]

Relatively few of the differences between the old and new monasteries arose out of the observance of the rule of Benedict, which clearly expected monks to accept oblates and have lay dependants and made no reference to lay brothers. These were matters not, as they are pictured in the polemical literature, of regularity in the strict sense of the term, but of differing views of the nature and purpose of religious life. Although the Cistercian in the *Dialogue of two monks* attacked the Cluniac abbots who did not eat with the guests and pilgrims, as the rule required, he must have known that this was rarely done, and for obvious reasons, even in houses that claimed to follow the rule in every respect.[157] Abelard specifically approved of this change, and Hildegard of Bingen, referring to the requirement that the abbot receive all the guests and wash their hands and feet, sensibly remarked that 'At that time the monks

---

[151] See Gougaud (1930), pp. 14–23; Salmon (1947); and Dimier (1955a), pp. 166–8.
[152] John of Salerno, *Vita Odonis Cluniacensis*, I, 32, in *Bibl. Clun.*, col. 27BC, and (another version) *PL*, CXXXIII, 57AB, and Peter the Venerable, *Stat.* 19–22, in *CCM*, VI, 57–60, and (on silence in small monasteries) *Stat.* 42, ibid., p. 72. See Jarecki (1981) and, on sign-language generally, Van Haeften (1644), pp. 605–8 (VI, 3, 11); Martène (1736–8), IV, 826–37 (V, 18); Gougaud (1930), pp. 14–23; Van Rijnberk (1953); and Davril (1982).
[153] See the editions of Berlière (n. 58), pp. 93 and 107, and Ceglar (n. 58), pp. 315–16 and 342.
[154] Reginald of Durham, *Vita Godrici*, LVIII, 127, ed. Stevenson, pp. 136–7; cf. LIX, 128; LXXXVI, 182; CXI, 217; and CXVIII, 227–8, ibid., pp. 137–8, 190, 230, and 241.
[155] Barakat (1975) and Jarecki (1988).
[156] Abelard, *Regula*, ed. McLaughlin (n. 111), p. 246, and Philip of Harvengt, *De institutione clericorum*, 6: *De silentio clericorum*, 23, in *PL*, CCIII, 982A–3B. See Gougaud (1930), pp. 18 and 23, and Van Rijnberk (1953), pp. 10–11.
[157] Idungus, *Dialogus*, II, 20–2, ed. Huygens, pp. 414–17.

had not yet felt the tumult of visiting outsiders.'[158] In matters like this the reforming passion for the integrity of the rule and the triumph of truth over custom silently gave way to the interests of practicality and tradition, which played a much larger role in the realities of reform than the rhetoric alone suggests.

This can clearly be seen in some of the changes in the liturgy, or work of God, as it was called in the rule of Benedict, which was the principal occupation of religious men and women throughout the Middle Ages.[159] 'Nothing should be put before the work of God', said the rule. To an outsider, and especially to an outsider not raised in a liturgically oriented tradition, the liturgy appears to be almost unchanging, and the changes that were made from time to time look comparatively unimportant. Though conservative scholars have sometimes encouraged this view, nothing could be further from the truth except in the personal sense that people became attached to their own liturgical traditions and were often reluctant to change. In fact, there were constant changes in the liturgy, both great and small, throughout the Middle Ages, and one reason that so little is known about early medieval worship is that outdated liturgical books were discarded or revised without consideration for later historians. The earliest surviving breviary of Cluny, of which there must have been at one time hundreds if not thousands of copies, dates from the late eleventh century.[160] Every aspect of the liturgy was subject to constant revision, as Guéranger knew when he referred to 'the incorrigible mania of the French for ceaselessly retouching the liturgy'.[161] Modern liturgists, as at the Second Vatican Council, have distinguished between the unchangeable substance of the liturgy, which must be preserved, and its changeable accidents, which can be simplified or abolished; and various 'laws of liturgical evolution' have been worked out, positing that the liturgy develops on the one hand from simplicity and multiplicity to unity and uniformity and on the other hand from simplicity and sobriety to richness and prolixity.[162] Many changes may indeed have resulted from a systematic development brought about by countless anonymous emendations and additions, together with some major changes; others were associated with institutional developments, such as the desire for liturgical uniformity within an order or a change

[158] Abelard, *Regula*, ed. McLaughlin (n. 111), p. 257, and Hildegard, *Explanatio regulae s. Benedicti*, in *PL*, CXCVII, 1061D. On the mandatum at Cluny, see Peter the Venerable, *Ep.* 28, ed. Constable, I, 71–2, and notes in II, 118.

[159] See Hausherr (1947) on the term *opus Dei*, which in early spiritual literature applied to monastic life generally and was later used, as in the rule of Benedict, for the liturgy and prayer.

[160] It was taken in the mid-twelfth century to the new monastery of St Taurin at l'Echelle-Saint-Aurin, and later to other monasteries, showing the Cluniac expansion into the region between the Somme and Oise: see Hourlier (1959).

[161] Guéranger (1878–85), I, 246.

[162] Baumstark (n.d.), pp. 17–25. A third 'law' posits the growing use of the bible, of which earlier texts show less influence than later ones (pp. 64–5).

or reform within a particular house; yet others, including some of the most interesting, were the consequence of deliberate efforts to fit the liturgy to the varying religious desires of people living at different times.[163] This is true of many liturgical changes today, and of those in the twelfth century, when a serious effort was made both to reduce the length of the liturgy and to make it more meaningful to the participants.

Over the five centuries following the compilation of the rule of Benedict, the monastic liturgy had tended to expand partly, perhaps, owing to an organic process but primarily because the members of religious communities tended to devote more time to worship as they became free from the necessity of supporting themselves. In some houses, which did not last very long in the west, prayers were offered continuously by rotating shifts of monks. Scholars are not in agreement over whether Benedict of Aniane and the monastic reformers of the early ninth century expanded, as was long believed, or reduced the amount of time spent in worship, but there is no question that they set the standard for strict regular houses, such as Cluny, during the following two centuries, when the liturgy continued to grow for two specific reasons, which have already been mentioned in other contexts. One was the growing number of ordained monks who celebrated mass every day, which at Cluny in the twelfth century reached the point where private masses interfered with the attendance at the conventional mass.[164] The other was the practice of liturgical commemoration for the dead, and often also the living, which included the recitation of prayers and psalms and charitable distributions to the poor, for the spiritual benefit not only of members of the house but also of benefactors, familiars, and the members of other communities associated with it.[165] These developments affected almost every aspect of life in religious houses. In architecture, provision had to be made for more altars;[166] in the economy, the wherewithal for charitable distributions had to be found; above all, in the liturgy, the offices were greatly prolonged. On some days at Cluny in the late eleventh century almost five times the number of psalms prescribed in the rule were recited. Of these four were recited at each office except compline 'for the familiars (*pro familiaribus*)' and were therefore known as the familiar psalms.[167]

---

[163] Fassler (1993), p. 82.

[164] See, on Cluny, Peter the Venerable, *Stat.* 6 and 72, in *CCM*, VI, 46 and 102, and generally, in addition to other works in *Medieval Monasticism*, nos. 853–60, Nussbaum (1961), pp. 126–7; Grégoire (1967–8), with a bibliography on the history of private masses (p. 548 n. 115); Häussling (1973); and Angenendt (1983) and (1984), esp. pp. 180–1. According to Simonin (1961), pp. 8–9, the growth of private at the expense of conventual masses at Cluny reflected the concern for individual and affective piety.

[165] In addition to the old but still useful book of de Berlendis (1743), p. 389, see Angenendt (1984), pp. 196–8, and Cowdrey (1984).

[166] There were twenty-one altars at St Gall in the early ninth century: see Horn and Born (1979), I, 127, 131–5, 190–2, 204, and 208–12. The number of chapels at Clairvaux grew from thirteen in the second church (1135/6) to seventeen in the third (rebuilt in the 1170s).

[167] Peter the Venerable, *Stat.* 31, in *CCM*, VI, 66, and the relevant notes.

The tendency to enlarge the liturgy was characteristic of strict houses in the tenth and eleventh centuries and was almost universally admired. While Cluny had its critics at that time, as has already been seen, its long liturgy was widely praised and imitated. Damiani and Anselm stressed the severity of its order, of which the liturgy was the most important part. Damiani compared it to the primitive church, calling the Cluniac monks so many Pauls and Anthonies, and said that the Holy Spirit rather than human intervention must have formed 'so strict and so frequent' an order, of which the length, he continued, scarcely left the monks more than half an hour daily to talk in the cloister.[168] Since chatting in the cloister was generally condemned at that time, Damiani doubtless intended this as a compliment, but it underlined the fact that the monks at Cluny, and in other houses with long liturgies, had very little time for other occupations. Matthew of Albano in his reply to the abbots at Reims in 1131, who proposed some abbreviations, praised the rigour of the morning offices in winter as a form of asceticism, and the length of the liturgy was cited in the *Reprehensio* as a reason for allowing additional food and sleep to the monks, who might otherwise have suffered physical collapse.[169] It is noteworthy that neither Damiani nor Anselm, in spite of their undoubted admiration for Cluny, decided to become monks there, perhaps in part because they wanted a less exclusively liturgical life, and a few years later the first signs appeared of an open reaction, which later became a central feature of the reformers' programme.

In this as in other respects, Robert of Arbrissel was a bell-wether when he wrote to countess Ermengard of Brittany that prayer should be brief and from the heart and that many hypocritical monks and clerics simulated long prayers in order to please men.[170] The abbots at Reims defended their proposals to reduce the number of psalms and ceremonies in similar terms, citing 1 Corinthians 14.19 that five words spoken with understanding were better than ten thousand words without understanding.[171] The future monks of Fountains contrasted reciting the Gospel with living it; Miro of Ripoll stressed the spiritual danger of monks who spent their entire lives in the choir praising God with their lips; and as the century advanced other voices joined in.[172] There was even a reaction against the daily celebration of mass. Herbert of Bosham in his *Life* of Thomas Becket, who out of reverence did not celebrate every day, wrote that 'Some [priests] consecrate every day but others on certain

---

[168] Peter Damiani, *Ep.* VI, 5, in *PL*, CXLIV, 380AB, and *De gallica profectione*, 12, in *PL*, CXLV, 873C. See Resnick (1988a).

[169] See the editions of Berlière (n. 58), pp. 101–2, and Ceglar (n. 58), p. 331, and *Reprehensio*, 25, ed. Wilmart, pp. 334–5.

[170] Robert of Arbrissel, *Sermo ad comitissam Britanniae*, ed. J. de Petigny, in *Bibliothèque de l'Ecole des chartes* 15 (3 S. 5) (1854), pp. 232–3.

[171] See the editions of Berlière (n. 58), p. 109, and Ceglar (n. 58), p. 346.

[172] Hugh of Kirkstall, *Narratio*, ed. Walbran, p. 20, and *Vita Mironis*, in *España sagrada*, XXVIII, 309 (*BHL* 5971). See also *Exordium magnum Cisterciense*, I, 20, ed. Bruno Griesser (Series scriptorum s. ordinis Cisterciensis 2; Rome 1961), p. 75 = Turk (1948), p. 91.

days' and distinguished between legal priests, who like the *pontifex* (Christ) in Hebrews 7.27 'needeth not daily (as the other priests) to offer sacrifices', and evangelical priests who offered daily for the sins of themselves and others.[173] When Master Alexander wanted to leave the Carthusians because they did not celebrate mass every day, Peter of Blois pointed out that neither did the early hermits or Benedict, who was not even a priest and who went without mass for long periods. Each Carthusian had his own cell 'in order more freely to have time for contemplation and prayer', Peter wrote. He also praised 'the freedom of groaning, nocturnal watches, quiet of meditation, and devotion of psalmody' of the Cistercians, whom he said Alexander should join rather than a monastery of black monks.

> What sweetness or devotion would you find among those in whom the muttered and confused repetition and stuffing of psalms has turned into vomiting. Paul said, Let us recite the psalms in our spirit; let us also recite the psalms in our mind. If there is no devotion in those reciting the psalms, even though they may repeat the same psalm a thousand times, it is not a joyful and decorous praise.[174]

The attention to devotion can also be seen in an emphasis on simplicity in the architecture and decoration of monastic buildings, which is exemplified in the *Apology* of Bernard, and the desire for less sumptuous and, as they saw it, more fitting ecclesiastical furnishings. The so-called *Chapters of the Cistercian order* permitted 'no sculptures and only paintings on the crosses, which should only be of wood', and the *Institutes of the general chapter* forbade sculptures and paintings in Cistercian churches and monastic offices, 'because when the utility of good meditation is concentrated on these the discipline of religious seriousness is often neglected', and also established that 'We have painted crosses which are of wood.'[175] Robert of Arbrissel asked on his death-bed for the wood of the holy cross,[176] and Peter the Venerable decreed that the cross presented to sick monks should be made of wood rather than of gold and silver because it was 'more rational and devout' for such crosses to be made of the material on which Christ was crucified, and it would avoid any falseness when 'Behold the wood of the cross' was said. He did not condemn crosses of gold and silver, he said, 'but the preciousness of metal, which

---

[173] Herbert of Bosham, *Vita s. Thomae*, III, 13, ed. James C. Robertson (RS 67; London 1875–85), III, 208–9 (*BHL* 8190). See Angenendt (1983), pp. 215–16, who called this criticism astonishing 'weil sie die Praxis des frühen Mittelalters schlichtweg abtut und zielsicher zum Wesen des neutestamentlichen Opfers zurückkehrt'.

[174] Peter of Blois, *Ep.* 86, ed. J.A. Giles (Bibliotheca patrum ecclesiae Anglicanae 5; Oxford 1847), I, 265–6.

[175] *Capitula Cisterciensis ordinis*, 26, in *Textes de Cîteaux*, p. 125, and *Instituta generalis capituli apud Cistercium*, ed. J.-A. Lefèvre, in *Collectanea ordinis Cisterciensium reformatorum* 16 (1954), p. 260.

[176] Andrew of Fontevrault, *Vita altera Roberti de Arbrissello*, VII, 38, in *PL*, CLXII, 1076B (*BHL* 7260).

raises the minds of the simple to greater veneration of the holy cross, is different from the worthlessness of wood, which moves the souls of the spiritual to more fervent devotion towards the cross and the crucifix'.[177] Within less than a century a movement that started as an almost personal hesitation grew into a chorus of criticism from all sides of the monastic world. Not only were the defenders of the traditional liturgy, like Matthew of Albano, put on the defensive, but many of them sympathized with the criticisms. When Peter the Venerable reduced the number of familiar psalms, he gave as the reason 'the wearisome and for many even hateful multiplicity of familiar psalms that has gradually grown for many reasons',[178] and towards the end of the century abbot Warinus of St Albans, another great old abbey, carried out what the chronicler described as 'a cutting off of the superfluity in the divine service'.[179] The long liturgy did not disappear, but it became more of a personal devotion than an institutional commitment. Aybert of Crépin celebrated two masses and recited nine lessons and 150 psalms every day, in addition to performing 100 genuflexions and fifty prostrations; the Cistercian Robert of Newburg recited 150 psalms a day and was known 'for the prolixity of his meditations and prayers'; and for Hugh of Lincoln private devotions were in many ways more vivid than corporate worship.[180] In Adam of Dryburgh's *Soliloquy on the instruction of the soul*, Reason defended psalmody when the soul complained at its length.[181] But these were not obligations, and Aybert's biographer archdeacon Robert of Ostrevand admitted that Aybert's devotions 'would be onerous and burdensome for someone who did not do [them] from the spirit (*ex spiritu*)'. Among the first elements to be cut were the familiar and other psalms, prayers for the dead, anniversary masses, and various ceremonies that were regarded as superfluous, though subsequently some were reintroduced into the liturgies from which they had been banished.[182] Abelard objected to the abolition of the suffrages seeking the support of the saints, and the Cluniac in the *Dialogue of two monks* said that the entire Cistercian service, aside from the mass and vespers, was shorter than the Cluniac prime

---

[177] Peter the Venerable, *Stat.* 62, in *CCM*, VI, 94. Luke of Cosenza in his *Life* of Joachim of Fiore, in Grundmann (1977), p. 357, referred to the *candelabra lignea* at Corazzo.

[178] Peter the Venerable, *Stat.* 31, in *CCM*, VI, 66; cf. *Stat.* 67, ibid., p. 98. In his *Ep.* 124., ed. Constable, I, 318, Peter wrote that his new hymn for St Benedict was shorter than the previous one 'owing to the boredom of the singers'.

[179] Thomas of Walsingham, *Gesta abbatum monasterii s. Albani*, ed. Henry T. Riley (RS 28d; London 1867–9), I, 212–13; cf. II, 101 and 420, for similar efforts by later abbots. I owe this reference to C.R. Cheney.

[180] Robert of Ostrevand, *Vita Ayberti*, II, 14, in *AASS*, 7 Apr. I, 674D (*BHL* 180); *Vita Roberti Novi Monasterii*, 4, ed. Grosjean (n. 46), p. 347; and (on Hugh of Lincoln) Pfaff (1989), p. 26.

[181] Adam of Dryburgh, *De instructione animae*, I, 7, in Pez, *Thesaurus*, I.2, 352, and *PL*, CXCVIII, 855BC.

[182] As of prayers and masses for the dead into the Cistercian liturgy, on which see Kovács (1951); Laurent (1954); and Waddell (1971), p. 87, who said that the daily office for the dead was introduced between 1127/8 and 1134.

with the litany and additions.[183] A few communities did without the liturgy altogether, like the canons of Hérival, of whom the founder, a priest named Engibaldus, 'judged that he was unworthy of the sacraments of the church and was determined, against the custom of the church, not to build a church in his place, not to celebrate mass, never to communicate, and not to sing the psalmody according to the rite of the church'.[184]

This was extreme, and some of the reformers hesitated before making any cuts in the liturgy. When Bernard of Tiron's followers complained that 'the multifold prolixity of the familiar psalms' kept them from the task of producing food, he consented to omit them only after God had sent a sign, in the form of a particularly long sleep after eight days of prayer, that He 'preferred them to acquire food for themselves by working than to devote themselves to such multifold psalms'.[185] This hesitation, and the need for divine approval, showed Bernard's doubts, which were shared by many monks in the first half of the twelfth century. The author of the *Reprehensio*, after defending the Cluniac practice of going back to bed after matins so that the monks would not be sleepy all day, said that the Cistercians slept the night through because they had shortened the liturgy. 'The familiar psalms, the vigil for the dead, the glorious songs which the church received are hardly sung, but you spend the whole night in sleep after the pure and few psalms have been run through.'[186] These words reflected the attachment most monks felt for their traditional liturgies, and their sadness at changing them. Some of the strongest resistance to reform was generated by a desire to retain a traditional liturgy, as when the monks of Kremsmünster asked to be allowed to keep their way of reading and chanting when an abbot from Admont was imposed on them.[187] Earlier, at Glastonbury, a riot almost broke out when abbot Thurstan tried to introduce a new liturgy.[188]

The reformers wanted not only to reduce the length of the liturgy, in order to make it less tedious and to allow more time for private prayers and devotions, but also to make it more meaningful by changing its content and manner of chanting. The Cistercians carried out their revision of the liturgy in two stages, of which the first, in the early twelfth century, concentrated on the authenticity of the texts and the second, in the 1130s and 1140s, dealt

---

[183] Abelard, *Ep.* 10, in *PL*, CLXXVIII, 339C, and ed. Edmé Smits (Groningen 1983), p. 245, on which see Waddell (1983–5), I, 371, and Idungus, *Dialogus*, II, 3–4, ed. Huygens, p. 406; cf. II, 8, ibid., p. 408, on the prostration.

[184] *Vetera Hyreevallis statuta, prol.*, in *Sacrae antiquitatis monumenta historica, dogmatica, diplomatica*, ed. C.L. Hugo (Etival and Nancy 1725), I, 135. See Choux (1952), pp. 152–6, and Galli (1959), p. 8.

[185] Geoffrey *Grossus, Vita Bernardi Tironiensis*, VII, 61–2, in *PL*, CLXXII, 1404AC (*BHL* 1251). See Martène (1736–8), IV, 51DE (I, 4, 19), and Van Dijk (1949), p. 177.

[186] *Reprehensio*, 25, ed. Wilmart, p. 335.

[187] Eberhard of Salzburg, *Ep.* to Godfrey of Admont, in Hansitz (1727–55), I, 318–20. See pp. 113–14 above.

[188] See p. 114 n. 139 above.

with their sense and meaning, judged by the standards of nature and reason.[189] The earliest Cistercian liturgical books probably came, through Molesme, from Marmoutier, where they drew on the Cluniac observance established there by Maiolus in the tenth century. It has been argued that the Cluniac *ordo missae* was adopted at Cîteaux and La Chartreuse precisely on account of its sobriety and simplicity, but the accompanying ceremonies were progressively pruned.[190] The first revision started soon after they reached Cîteaux and is associated particularly with the name of Stephen Harding, who was abbot from 1109 to 1134. It consisted, first, in removing all elements not mentioned in the rule of Benedict, and, second, in reforming the chant on the basis of a gradual and antiphonary from Metz and of an Ambrosian hymnal. These changes met with the approval of some contemporaries, such as William of Malmesbury, who praised the Cistercians for making no additions to the canonical hours except the vigil for the dead (which had been abolished at first but was reintroduced about 1130) and for using the Ambrosian hymns 'as much as they can ascertain from Milan'.[191] Abelard, on the other hand, was outraged and attacked the new hymnal in a letter addressed to Bernard of Clairvaux probably soon after 1132: 'You who have newly emerged and rejoice greatly in novelty have established by various new decrees that the holy office should be performed among yourselves differently from the entire custom of both clerics and monks.' He went on to criticize their 'novelty and singularity' and in particular their omission of many familiar hymns and the introduction of new ones.[192] Enough Cistercians apparently shared this view that a second revision was commissioned, probably after the death of Stephen Harding, and was completed under the aegis of Bernard by 1147, when the letter already cited, attributing the changes to nature and reason, was written.[193] By this they meant that many of the texts were revised to eliminate inconsistencies and falsehoods, as Bernard advocated in his letter to the monks of Montiéramey and Peter the Venerable accomplished by his changes to the liturgy in the infirmary chapel at Cluny and his new hymns for St Benedict.[194] At the same time many old texts, of which the loss was deplored by Abelard and in the *Reprehensio*, were restored, and the final

---

[189] See Marosszéki (1952) and above all the various works of Waddell, to which all students of twelfth-century liturgy are indebted. See also Dubois (1992), reviewing Choisselet and Vernet (1989).

[190] Tirot (1981), pp. 115–16.

[191] William of Malmesbury, *De gestis regum Anglorum*, IV, 336, ed. Stubbs (n. 124), II, 383.

[192] Abelard, *Ep.* 10, in *PL*, CLXXVIII, 339AB, and ed. Smits (n. 183), pp. 244–5. See Waddell (1984), I, 64–90.

[193] See Bernard, *Ep. de revisione cantus Cisterciensis*, ed. F.J. Guentner (Corpus scriptorum de musica 24; Rome 1974), pp. 21–41, and p. 143 above.

[194] Waddell (1984), I, 68, and Szövérffy (1979), p. 190, who said that the purpose was to make the liturgy 'more "effective", reasonable, and "fitting"'.

result resembled the traditional hymnal more closely than the first revision.[195]

Some important changes were made at the same time in the manner of chanting, to which one of the earliest references was in the treatise *On the institutes of his own congregation* by Peter Damiani, who warned against reciting the psalter 'rapidly (*velociter*)', as was done in many monasteries.[196] He may have had in mind the tendency to reduce the length of the very long pauses – some of them long enough to recite the Lord's prayer two or three times – that characterized the traditional chanting of the psalms and generally to speed up the liturgy, which was mentioned in the twelfth century by Peter the Venerable and Bernard and especially in the so-called *Institutes of the fathers* from St Gall, which dates from about 1200 but was based on a Bernardine text: 'We do not extend the psalmody excessively, but we chant roundly and in a lively manner (*rotunde et viva voce*). We sound the meter and the end of the verse together, and we close together. No one holds [i.e. prolongs] the last note, but closes quickly. After the meter we make a good pause.'[197] Just what these prescriptions meant in practice is not known, nor how long 'a good pause' was, except that it was shorter than the earlier pauses.

Some idea of the effect of the new manner of chanting, as it filtered down in the course of the century, is given by abbot Peregrinus in his history of Fontaines-les-Blanches, where he said that under his predecessor Robert, who was a specialist in the liturgy, 'We were accustomed to sing all the psalms, hymns, and songs more loftily, more protractedly, and, as I should put it, more solemnly than, to tell the truth, we can ever persuade the monks of our time [to do].'[198] It is again uncertain what Peregrinus meant by the terms *altius*, *productius*, and *solemnius*, except that he felt that the chanting in his youth was slower, with longer pauses, and thus more dignified. There is a hint of wistfulness in the passage, and of an old man's irritation at the impatience of the young. When Peter the Venerable imposed a moderate pause (which, though shorter than some of the previous very long pauses, prolonged rather than shortened the liturgy), he gave as his reasons, first, to eliminate the confusion of the chanters who started and ended at different times; second, to alleviate the work of the singers; and, third, to allow 'that the understanding itself (*intellectus ipse*) should be reformed by pausing together as in a certain common silence'.[199] Such changes were therefore designed not only to save

---

[195] See p. 285 below on the textual revisions of some hymns.
[196] Peter Damiani, *Op.* 15 *de sue congregationis institutis*, 30, in *PL*, CXLV, 362D.
[197] Van Dijk (1950), p. 105, with discussion on pp. 106–8, saying (p. 107) that 'The positive side of those rules is difficult to describe but they seem to contain exactly what Peter the Venerable wanted to change in the customary psalm singing of the Cluniac monasteries.' The *bona pausa* may have been equivalent to the *mediocris repausatio* in Peter the Venerable, *Stat.* 1, in *CCM*, VI, 40–1.
[198] Peregrinus, *Historia*, I, 12, ed. Salmon, p. 272.
[199] Peter the Venerable, *Stat.* 1, in *CCM*, VI, 42.

time and make the liturgy less onerous but also to allow the chanters to understand what they were saying. A reflection of this concern may be found in the change in the wording of Benedict's rule that in psalmody 'our mind should harmonize with our voice' to the formulation of Adam of Dryburgh and Francis of Assisi that 'the voice should harmonize with the mind'. The change may have been unintentional, or even unconscious, but it reflects the view that the text should express, rather than shape, the inner attitude of the monks, whose prayers should come from their hearts rather than their lips.[200] Peter the Chanter in his *Abbreviated word* wrote

> Let there be no order to multiply matins, psalms, or prayers, unless there be devotion. Likewise, the traditions concerning various ways of chanting, reciting the psalms, and reading that are handed down in different monasteries and churches of clerics constitute a sort of schism and division of unity, since in all matters we should as much as possible preserve unity, which is the bond of ecclesiastical peace.[201]

This text forms a fitting conclusion for this chapter, since Peter presented here in the context of the liturgy a paradigm of the problem of the reformers, who wanted to promote both unity and devotion and were faced with the countless differences between individual monasteries and churches. They knew, as Peter the Venerable told the monks of St Martial in the text cited at the beginning, that almost all their matter and form came from the past, into which they dipped even more deeply in the hope of finding models to use in reshaping the present and the future. They were caught in practice, however, as the customaries, necrologies, and liturgical books show, in an ongoing tradition that could be changed in only relatively minor ways and that bound them, whether they liked it or not, to other religious men and women whose way of life they criticized and condemned and yet who resembled them, and whom they resembled, in many ways. They all shared a respect for the traditional monastic ideals while feeling a need to play a greater part in achieving their salvation, a desire for a more personal religious experience, and an obligation to promote the salvation of others as well as themselves. The members of the older communities were tied both by their own traditions and by their spiritual and material associations with society outside their enclosures, which brought many thousands of people in touch with a side of religious life that would otherwise have been closed to them. Yet the abandonment of the old necrologies and memorial books shows the decline of this aspect of religious life, even among those for whom it was part

---

[200] Adam of Dryburgh (also attributed to Guigo II of La Chartreuse), *De quadripartito exercitio cellae*, 35, in *PL*, CLIII, 878C, and de Boer (1957–8). See Constable (1986b), pp. 19–20, with further references. Odo of Cluny, speaking of the liturgy in *Vita Geraldi Auriliacensis*, II, 9, in *PL*, CXXXIII, 676BC, wrote 'Et cum debeat voci mentis intelligentia conuenire, nos facimus currere uocem post leuitatem.mentis' (*BHL* 3411).

[201] Peter the Chanter, *Verbum abbreviatum*, 79, in *PL*, CCV, 236CD.

of their *raison d'être*, and the growth, in lay as well as in monastic society, of more personal types of religion. The reformers saw the dangers of such ties and tried to cut themselves off, in their way of life and in their liturgy, from the world which they both loved and feared and with which they had to come to terms before coming to terms with themselves. For them and for the members of the old communities the problem of their own salvation, embodied in a specific form of religious life and relation to the rest of society, were inextricably mixed with the problem of the salvation of others. A parallel problem lies before educators in the modern world in considering how far they can and should extend their activities outside their institutions without imperilling the values for which they stand and their proper function in society, which often asks more of institutions than they can legitimately perform. These are questions to which there are no absolute answers and to which each generation, in the twelfth century as today, must find its own solutions.

6

THE REALITIES OF REFORM:
(2) MONASTIC ACTIVITIES AND RELATIONS
WITH SECULAR SOCIETY

SOME of the most interesting differences between the old and new houses in the twelfth century, and between the various types of new houses, were in their relations with the outside world. For while they all shared an ideal of withdrawal and seclusion, it was carried out in different ways. The reformers in particular tried to assert the distinctive character of their way of life and to cut themselves off as fully as possible from contacts with people living in the world. Although they could not be entirely self-sufficient economically and occasionally needed both the sacramental services of a bishop and the secular assistance of lay lords, they tried as much as possible to run their own affairs and to assume no responsibilities, like pastoral work or even charitable occupations, outside their walls. The older types of monks and hermits were also cut off in principle, and some of them, as in strict houses like Cluny, might go for years without setting foot outside their monastic enclosures, but their extensive liturgical commitments bound them closely to the outside world both spiritually, through intercessory prayer, and materially, since they did not produce their own food. In the early days of monasticism, furthermore, when relatively few monks were ordained, most houses were dependent on the clergy for the celebration of the sacraments, as communities of women still are today. This changed as more monks were ordained, and the construction and acquisition of churches by monasteries involved them in pastoral work, which might be performed by monks. The growth of their estates in the early Middle Ages also imposed secular responsibilities, which in the post-Carolingian period were often carried out by lay officials known as advocates, who developed in the course of the tenth and eleventh centuries from comparatively humble monastic functionaries into hereditary office-holders exercising a significant influence over the internal as well as the external affairs of monasteries.

Land remained the basic source of support for both secular lords and ecclesiastical institutions throughout the eleventh and twelfth centuries. The arenga of a charter for the Cluniac house of Sauxillanges reads 'Men may come and men may go but land goes on forever.'[1] The nature of landed estates, however, and how they were worked, varied from period to period all over Europe. All medieval religious communities occupied some land, but they differed in how it was organized and worked and what revenues were collected. The new houses sought to cultivate their lands by the labour of their own members and lay brothers, whereas the older monasteries mostly had servile dependants and divided their lands into those worked directly for their own support, and occasionally by the monks themselves, and those held by share-cropping or for rents.[2] The question of the status of the workers on monastic estates is uncertain. A Cluniac charter of 1103/4 referred to peasants 'who, freed from the yoke of servitude, have been emancipated by the service of St Peter',[3] and Peter the Venerable in his Letter 28 to St Bernard maintained that monks treated their dependants better than lay lords and demanded only what was due. 'They hold male and female serfs not as serfs but as brothers and sisters, receiving defined obligations from them according to their capacity and allowing them to suffer no hardships.'[4] According to the *Libellus*,

> The monks who live in towns and villages are often seen to deal with secular matters, make decisions in public lawsuits, have male and female serfs who owe a head tax, judge, rule, protect, raise the sons of their serfs as future serfs, have lands held by tenants, rent out lands, hope for and exact revenues therefrom, judge the cases of individuals like secular judges, impose laws on their lands and men, all of which seems to be secular and hardly religious. But of such men I shall say what I think. I do not believe all this was made up by them for cupidity but for the utility of the serfs and tenants. For we see many men fleeing cruel masters and taking refuge under the lordship of churches, and there is no cupidity but very great mercy in protecting and defending them.[5]

The reformers wanted to sweep away these involvements with the outside world and to restore a type of simple and unworldly life that they associated with the early days of the church. By stressing manual labour and poverty, which for them was a practical as well as spiritual ideal and one of the greatest safeguards of their independence and way of life, they sought to avoid the obligations and controversies that accompanied the ownership of secular prop-

---

[1] This is a loose translation (with apologies to Tennyson's *The Brook*) of 'Generatio uadit et generatio uenit, terra autem in aeternum stat', in *Cartulaire de Sauxillanges*, ed. Henry Doniol, in *Mémoires de l'Académie des sciences, belles-lettres et arts de Clermont-Ferrand* N.S. 3 (1861), p. 883, no. 567.

[2] Genicot (1943–95), I, 106, said of reserve land in the period before 1200 that 'L'organisation domaniale a subi sur ce point des modifications quantitatives mais non structurelles'; Hägermann (1981) showed the continuity of monastic economy at Prüm from the late ninth to the thirteenth centuries; and Lohrmann (1983a), p. 198, contrasted the economic organization of the old and new monks. See also Fichtenau (1991), p. 348.

[3] *Chartes de Cluny*, V, 179, no. 3822; cf. IV, 819, no. 3649.

[4] Peter the Venerable, *Ep.* 28, ed. Constable, I, 86. See Flach (1886–1917), I, 466–7.

[5] *Libellus*, 2, ed. Constable, p. 41.

erty. Abelard said that monks who lived from the labour of others (*de alieno labore*) rather than of themselves (*de proprio labore*) lost their God-given liberty,[6] and the distinction between the work of others and of oneself ran through the entire economic programme of the reformers. For the hermit Godric of Finchale it was not enough to lead a poor life supported by someone else's resources (*de stipite aliena*), and he was determined 'to acquire for himself the necessities of sustenance by his own labour'.[7] The *Little beginning* of Cîteaux, after citing the early practice concerning the distribution of tithes, said that 'Since in this arrangement they [the Cistercians] found no reference to the monk, who owns his lands from which he lives by the labour of himself and his animals, they therefore refused to usurp unjustly for themselves those things that belonged to others.'[8] The Cistercians and other early reformers for the most part rejected not only churches and their revenues, such as tithes, first-fruits, oblations, and burial dues, but also secular possessions like manors, serfs, rents, tolls, the revenues from mills and ovens, and other types of property that they regarded as not 'in accord with monastic purity'.[9] The Grandmontines owned only the land on which their buildings stood and from which they supported themselves and held no property outside the boundaries of their own houses. They were forbidden to build on land belonging to monks, for instance, 'for some of them love you greatly and show you many kindnesses, but the heads of monasteries often change, and some may later by frequent claims wish to recover what others have given away.'[10] Not all the reformers were so strict, and both Obazine and the Savigniacs owned various types of property that were prohibited by strict reformers and that created problems when they joined the Cistercian order.[11] In the long run, however, very few were able to live entirely by the labour of their own hands without any outside help or sources of revenue.

The early monks had supported themselves not only by agriculture but also by manufacture such as basket-making, and manual labour formed a basic part of monastic life according to the rule of Benedict, which established that 'Idleness is the enemy of the spirit, and the monks should therefore be occupied at certain times working with their hands and again at certain times reading

---

[6] Abelard, *Serm.* 33 *de s. Joanne baptista*, in *PL*, CLXXVIII, 587C. On the distinction between *proprius* and *communis* and between *meum* and *tuum*, see pp. 146–7 above.

[7] Reginald of Durham, *Vita Godrici*, XXVI, 62, ed. Stevenson, p. 74. Gerard of Nazareth, *De conversatione virorum Dei in Terra Sancta morantium*, 17, in Kedar (1983), pp. 72–3, referred to hermits in the east who refused to accept *alienas diuitias*.

[8] *Exordium parvum*, 15, in *Textes de Cîteaux*, p. 77. See Schreiber (1948b), p. 356, on the Cistercian refusal to own parish churches and Constable (1964), pp. 138–40, for other examples.

[9] *Exordium Cistercii*, 23, in *Textes de Cîteaux*, p. 124. The date of this document is disputed, and it may have been written in the early 1150s. See p. 38 n. 171 above.

[10] Stephen of Muret, *Regula*, 33, in *CC:CM*, VIII, 84.

[11] *Vita Stephani Obazinensis*, II, 12, ed. Aubrun, pp. 112–14, and Buhot (1936), pp. 113–17 and 121.

holy works.'[12] Manual labour was less important than the work of God, however, and monks who had other means of support tended to spend more time
in the liturgy.[13] The *Notitia Arnonis* of 790 referred to a cell 'in which the
monks live by the labour of their hands',[14] but this was probably owing to
poverty or asceticism, and in many strict houses of the ninth and tenth centuries manual labour took on a formal character, and the monks were primarily
supported by estates worked by lay dependants. According to the treatise *On
preserving the unity of the church*, the short working habit of monks disappeared
in the eleventh century

> because few or no monks of this time are diligent in labour or the exercise of
> work in the manner of the fathers, although among the ancient fathers it was
> customary to receive no one into their company unless he proved himself worthy
> by the exercise of work, which the efforts of prayers and readings made
> especially strong against the attacks of sin.[15]

In traditional monastic spirituality work was seen less as a good in itself
than as an antidote to idleness and pride and as a reparation for sin. Peter
the Deacon in his commentary on the rule, written in 1137, said that 'Bodily
labour is the guide (*dux*) of humility',[16] and Geoffrey of St Thierry described
work and grief as the two legacies of Adam, saying (perhaps in reaction to
the reformers' stress on manual labour) that the devil sent the urge to work
too much as a temptation in order to lure monks away from their liturgical
obligations.[17] The author of the *Rescriptum* contrasted the view of the new
monks – 'those men', as he called them – who dug the ground with ploughs
and hoes, ground the food that perishes, interrupted contemplation, and whose
institute was called vanity and the evil of the day, with that of the old monks –
'these men' – who cultivated the mind with psalms and prayers, produced
the food that lasts, continued contemplation, and whose institute was called
piety and the vision of peace. 'We think that man is justified through faith
without the works of the law', he wrote, citing Romans 3.28. 'The highest
virtue is therefore contemplation, the highest profession of contemplatives,
into the first step of which we ascend when we have been separated from all
the activity and vanity of worldly affairs.'[18] According to Ordericus Vitalis,
writing after 1135, the monks of Molesme replied in similar terms when their

---

[12] *Reg. Ben.*, 48. Jones (1964), pp. 931–2, described the insistence on work in the rule of Benedict
as a reform. On monastic work, see Martène (1736–8), IV, 65–73 (I, 6); Dimier (1955a),
pp. 173–8; Prinz (1965), pp. 532–7; and Dubois (1990).

[13] Delaruelle (1948).

[14] *Salzburger Urkundenbuch*, I: *Traditionscodices*, ed. Willibald Hauthaler (Salzburg 1910), p. 8.
See Prinz (1965), p. 405.

[15] *De unitate ecclesiae conservanda*, II, 42, in *MGH, Libelli*, II, 279. On this work see p. 190 above.

[16] Peter the Deacon, *In explanatione regule sanctissimi patris nostri Benedicti*, in *Bibliotheca Casinensis* 5 (1894), p. 124.

[17] Geoffrey of St Thierry, *Serm.* 23 and 30, in MS Reims, Bibl. mun., 581, fols. 87ʳa and 125ᵛa.
See n. 56 below and p. 271 n. 63 below on the temptations, respectively, to avoid and to
perform manual labour.

[18] *Rescriptum*, ed. Leclercq, pp. 85–7.

abbot Robert reproached them for not working with their hands: 'It is established in France by the decrees of rulers and by ancient custom that peasants do rural work, as is suitable, and serfs perform servile tasks; monks, however . . . who fight for the king of kings . . . devote themselves daily to pure and suitable activities, as reason demands, in accordance with the precepts of the elders.'[19]

The *opera servilia* were generally regarded as suitable only for the unfree classes of society, and not for monks, whose work consisted of intellectual and charitable activities.[20] Peter the Venerable said that manual labour was inferior to the spiritual exercises and holy studies that in his day served to ward off idleness in monks, especially those who lived not in woods and deserted places, like the Cistercians, but in towns and other places where they could not go out without meeting lay people of both sexes. His statute 'partially' restoring manual labour for the Cluniacs restricted it to the cloister or to places 'where it can be done honestly, far from the sight of lay men'.[21] Peter gave a clear exposition of the place in monastic life of intellectual and evangelical work in his letter to the hermit Gilbert of Senlis, to whom he wrote, after praising meditation, prayer, and holy readings,

> You should know, however, dearly beloved, that these are hard, and that it is not easy for anyone to pass his life entirely in these efforts. Therefore manual labour should follow these three, in order that when the mind has come down, exhausted with spiritual things and drawn down from the top to the bottom by the weight of the flesh, it should turn not to the idle talk of men but to the blessed exertion of the body. Since your perpetual reclusion prohibits the planting of trees, watering of seeds, and performance of rural work, the hand can be turned, what is more useful, from the plough to the pen; pages can be ploughed with holy letters in place of ploughing fields; the seedbed of God, sown on the sheet of the word, can fill the hungry readers with the ripe crops of perfect books and multiplied fruits; and the celestial bread can thus drive out the deadly hunger of the soul. So, clearly so, you can become a silent preacher of the holy word, and with a silent tongue your hand will resound with shouting voices in the ears of many people . . . Profession [makes] you a hermit; devotion makes you an evangelist, so that you may win by your labours what you cannot [win] in person.[22]

The ideal of religious life here resembles that in the letter cited above from the Carthusian Bernard of Portes and shows that the work even of a hermit could extend to the world outside his hermitage through his writings, without

---

[19] Ordericus Vitalis, *Historia ecclesiastica*, VIII, 26, ed. Chibnall, IV, 320.

[20] Chenu (1940).

[21] Peter the Venerable, *Epp.* 28 and 111, ed. Constable, I, 70–1, 97, and 283, and *Stat.* 39, in *CCM*, VI, 73–4. On work in the Cluniac customaries, see Redonet (1919), pp. 107–10, and David Knowles, in *Petrus Venerabilis* (1956), pp. 12–13.

[22] Peter the Venerable, *Ep.* 20, ed. Constable, I, 38–9. The content of this passage may be a topos, but the formulation is by Peter, who in *Ep.* 54, ibid., I, 174, put *aeuangelizare* for *annuntiare et praedicare* in a citation from Is. 52.7, showing that he equated the two activities.

speaking or leaving his cell. The strictest reformer would have had no quarrel with this, aside perhaps from the substitution of intellectual for agricultural labour as the necessary balance in the life of an enclosed religious.[23] The popular topos of the noble labourer reflected the traditional view of work as an inheritance from Adam and a source of humility.[24] The noble hermit Theobald was said in his *Life* by abbot Peter of Vangadizza to have come down with his companions (*devoluti sunt*) 'to the most vile and laborious work of peasants, such as carrying stones, cutting wheat in the field, cleaning stables, and especially making charcoal for the work of blacksmiths'.[25] A more positive attitude towards physical labour can be found, however, in some tenth-century *Lives* of saints, where the wealth and productivity of their monasteries were praised, and also in the works of Ratherius of Verona, for whom work was a religious, moral, and social duty for everybody, including monks.[26] For Marbod of Rennes part of Robert of La Chaise-Dieu's new order of sanctity was that he came down from a purely contemplative life 'to active and human affairs and finally to the work of a stone-mason'.[27] Bernard of Clairvaux regarded work as a duty towards God, a source of spiritual refreshment, and an antidote for idleness. By the labour of their hands monks fed Christ in the form of the poor, according to Bernard, for whom work, together with retreat and voluntary poverty, was one of the three distinguishing marks of a monk.[28] Most of the new orders required their members to work in one way or another. 'Nothing is more laborious than not to labour', according to Guigo of La Chartreuse,[29] who attributed this saying to Augustine. Its source is unknown, but it showed the attitude towards manual labour that was later embodied in the Benedictine motto *Ora et labora*.[30]

The emphasis on manual labour was sometimes accompanied by a prejudice against other types of work, especially intellectual work outside the monastery. A distrust of secular schools and their methods of teaching was widespread in monastic circles in the twelfth century. Rupert of Deutz wanted to go in person to Laon in order to refute the teaching of the masters there; Peter the Venerable contrasted the type of wisdom 'that disputes inquisitively about

---

[23] On the concept of the learned hermit, see Bickel (1916) and Kantorowicz (1965). For Bernard of Portes, see p. 59 above.

[24] See the criticism of monastic commerce and begging in Isaac of L'Etoile, *Serm.* 50, in *PL*, CXCIV, 1860CD, and, on the topos of the noble worker, p. 97 above.

[25] Peter of Vangadizza, *Vita Theobaldi eremitae*, 4, in *AASS OSB*, VI.2, 160–1 (*BHL* 8031). See pp. 41 and 61 above on charcoal-burning.

[26] Prinz (1965), pp. 532–40, and Adam (1927), esp. pp. 76–104, on Ratherius of Verona.

[27] Marbod of Rennes, *Miracula Roberti Casae-Dei*, in *Nova bibl.*, II, 652 (*BHL* 7262). See pp. 24–5 above.

[28] Bernard, *Serm.* 3 *in psalmum 'Qui habitat'*, 4, and *Ep.* 42 (*De officio episcoporum*), IX, 37, ed. Leclercq, IV, 396, and VII, 130. On Bernard's view of work and poverty, see Vignes (1928) and Holdsworth (1973), who stressed the new Cistercian ethic of work.

[29] *Consuetudines Cartusiae*, XIV, 5, in [Laporte] (1960–7), IV, 102; see the notes in V, 240–4, citing the parallel sentiment expressed by Peter the Venerable, *Ep.* 20, ed. Constable, I, 34.

[30] Leclercq (1961b), pp. 140–4.

created things in the philosophical manner' with the type 'that devoutly and earnestly seeks knowledge of the Creator'; and Bernard of Clairvaux in *On consideration* said that it is easier to find God in prayer than in disputation.[31] Norbert of Xanten 'cried out in his words and his deeds that he knew nothing "but Jesus Christ, and Him crucified" (1 Corinthians 2.2)'.[32] These men were all highly educated, and their words cannot be taken at face value, but they express a deeply felt attitude about the nature of intellectual inquiry and the proper activities of monks. When Robert of Bethune was a young man, he 'turned his spirit to hagiography' away from studying the poets and philosophers,[33] and in a sermon to the scholars at Toulouse in the late twelfth century the Cistercian Helinand of Froidmont cited both the dictum of Jerome that 'It is better not to know than to learn with danger' and the example of Benedict, who withdrew from the world 'not knowing and wisely untaught'. Real knowledge, Helinand said, is not found by studying the liberal arts at Paris, the classical writers at Orléans, the legal codices at Bologna, the medicine chests at Salerno, or the spirits of astrology at Toledo but only in the book of life, 'which is also the book of knowledge'. He then said that when the future bishop William of Montpellier was a monk at Grandselve (and was apparently tempted by secular studies) he had a vision in which Bernard of Clairvaux appeared and led him to a high mountain next to Jerusalem and told him to climb it in order to learn – which he was about to do when his vision was ended by the ringing of the bell for vigils.[34] This attitude was embodied in official policies such as the general prohibition in the 1130s for monks or secular canons to teach Roman law or medicine and the Cistercian statute forbidding any member of the order to write a book without the permission of the general chapter.[35] It is also reflected in a certain anti-intellectualism, of which a good example is found in the *Dialogue* of Everard of Ypres, who became a Cistercian, probably in the 1180s, after having studied with Gilbert of La Porrée and taught at Paris. One of the disputants, a visiting Greek scholar named Ratius, remarked on the dislike of monks for any discussion of subtle or intellectual matters (*intellecta*). Everard himself felt like a fish out of water in the monastery on account of his studies and teaching. 'It is almost the profession of monks neither to teach nor to learn', he said. 'His [Everard's] difference of studies created a discord of spirits. For they

[31] Peter the Venerable, *Ep.* 94, ed. Constable, I, 250; Bernard, *De consideratione*, V, 14, 32, ed. Leclercq, III, 493. Everard of Ypres in his dialogue with Ratius said of Bernard, citing this passage, 'De quo uere praedicatur quod plura didicerit orando quam disputando et plura sub fago quam in disputationis areopago', in Häring (1953), p. 275. See pp. 140–1 above.

[32] *Vita* [B] *Norberti*, IX, 54, in *PL*, CLXX, 1295A (*BHL* 6249).

[33] William of Wyecombe, *Vita Roberti Betun*, I, 3, in *Anglia sacra*, ed. Henry Wharton (London 1691), II, 300.

[34] Helinand of Froidmont, *Serm.* 15, in *PL*, CCXII, 603B–D. On anti-intellectual dreams and visions, see Kottje (1969), p. 161.

[35] Somerville (1976), pp. 105–6, and the Cistercian statute published under the year 1134, 58, in Canivez, *Statuta*, p. 26.

would have preferred him to cut wood or to gather and harvest crops than to unravel the knotty problems or dubious points of theology.[36] The preference of monks in the twelfth century for a traditional type of bible-based theology and their dislike for the rationalistic tendencies of scholastic disputation, however much they used the same techniques in their own polemical works, were studied by Jean Leclercq, who showed that it would be a mistake to see this as a generally hostile attitude to intellectual activity or originality. Rupert of Deutz was an immensely prolific and consciously innovative commentator on Scripture, and Bernard of Clairvaux was a skilled writer and rhetorician in spite of his ignorance of the type of speculative theology taught by Gilbert of La Porrée.[37] Many of the reformers promoted reading and wrote books, treatises, and letters – and not always, as was required among the Cistercians, with the permission of the general chapter. Isaac of L'Etoile repeatedly deplored the lack of books 'and most greatly of commentaries' in the library of his abbey, and Richalm of Schönthal regarded books as the great enemies of vain thoughts and evil spirits, who tried to keep monks from reading by making them sleepy, sending a flea, or finding other things for them to do. 'The best thing to do is to read', said Richalm, 'and you too should therefore read, read, read.'[38] And read they did, to judge from contemporary manuscripts and library catalogues from both old and new houses. Since the acquisition of books was costly, and their manufacture slow, the presence of a book in a library, while no proof that it was read, is an indication of an interest in its contents.[39] A study of the writings of the reformers shows their interest in the Greek fathers, including Origen, and also in Abelard and Gilbert of La Porrée, who in spite of their condemnations were both read and cited, though not always openly.[40] Gratian was probably a monk, though not perhaps a Camaldolese, as has been said, and his works were widely read and cited by monks.[41] The Cistercians studied not only the bible and texts of the liturgy but also, and more surprisingly, arithmetic, on which the works of Odo of Morimond, William of Auberive, and Geoffrey of Auxerre are still partly unpublished and which may have been inspired by a concern for the music of the liturgy. In the second half of the twelfth century

---

[36] Everard of Ypres, in Häring (1953), pp. 247 and 287.

[37] Cf. John of Salisbury, *Historia pontificalis*, 8, ed. Marjorie Chibnall (MT; London and Edinburgh 1956), p. 15, who called Bernard *eloquentissimus*, and Everard of Ypres, in Häring (1955), p. 148.

[38] Isaac of L'Etoile, *Serm.* 18 and 22, in *PL*, CXCIV, 1749D and 1761B, and Richalm of Schönthal, *Liber revelationum*, I, 112, in Pez, *Thesaurus*, I.2, 458; cf. I, 6, 11, 80, and 109, ibid., 391–2, 395, 443, and 456.

[39] See Kottje (1969) on the importance of regional traditions rather than innate tendencies in monastic movements.

[40] For references on the interest in Origen in the twelfth century, see Constable (1995a), p. 170 n. 157, and p. 308 below.

[41] Gouron (1985), pp. 228–9; Kuttner (1988), p. 6; and Southern (1995), pp. 281–318, esp. 286–8 on the man and his work.

Cistercians also wrote several treatises on *dictamen* or the art of letter-writing, which was of growing importance in the conduct of public affairs.[42] By this time the members of the new orders, in spite of their continued resistance to certain types of theology, had moved into the mainstream of intellectual history and, like other monks, increasingly looked outside their monasteries for their academic training and interests, leaving manual labour and agriculture to the lay brothers and secular dependants.[43]

The economic success of the reform programme in its early years, when the monks worked their own lands by themselves or with the help of lay brothers, probably surprised no one more than the reformers themselves. It illustrates Marc Bloch's point that the economic results of religious developments are usually more interesting than their alleged motives, precisely because they are unexpected and unsought-for. Writing about the Cistercians, Bloch said that

> No order at its origins was more completely disengaged from preoccupations of secular activity or more firmly enclosed in a quasi-eremitical asceticism. But precisely because this asceticism had its original aspects, the material activity of the white monks was engaged in new ways; the very intransigence of their rule made their houses into agents of economic transformation of unparalleled importance.[44]

Later scholars have tended to put less emphasis on the originality of Cistercian economic activity or on their importance in opening new lands on the internal or external frontiers of Europe. It has already been seen that when they could the members of the new orders occupied cleared lands. Already in the first half of the twelfth century the Cistercians and Premonstratensians in some regions accepted cultivated estates, and they often settled closer to established communities than the topoi used in the sources imply.[45] The Cistercians in the west supported themselves by animal husbandry, which did not require clearing new lands, and by the sale of wool and other produce. A statute in 1157 forbade them to charge more when they sold on credit.[46] At a time, however, when the older houses in settled areas were being given fewer entire domains and more scattered grants of revenues and partial rights over lands,[47] many new houses acquired large consolidated tracts of waste or unused land (the *desertum* or *eremus*), as in the north of England, and managed them by direct exploitation, which yielded handsome returns, since old houses were

[42] Guy Beaujouan, in *Renaissance and Renewal* (1982), p. 483, and Constable (1976a), p. 35, citing the works of C.V. Langlois and S.J. Heathcote.

[43] See on the Cistercians d'Arbois de Jubainville (1858), pp. 109–10.

[44] Marc Bloch, reviewing J.W. Thompson, *An Economic and Social History of the Middle Ages*, in *Annales* 1 (1929), p. 258.

[45] See Wiswe (1953), pp. 40–6, and Despy (1974–5), pp. 61–4.

[46] Waddell (1993), p. 398. See generally Martin (1893–4), pp. 91–103; Duby (1953), p. 71; Grandmottet (1958), p. 13; and the bibliographies in Elm (1994), pp. 12–13.

[47] Lot (1913), p. cxi, and Genicot (1936), pp. 139–42.

increasingly caught in an economic squeeze between rising prices and fixed revenues and services from dependent labourers.[48]

Artificial wastes and deserts were created by expelling the inhabitants, and also by warfare. An estate belonging to the monastery of Moirax in the diocese of Agen was for three years reduced *in heremum* by viscount Peter of Gabarret, 'adding new evils to his old ones'.[49] The charters concerning the expulsion of the inhabitants to make way for the monks of Revesby, Rufford, and Pontigny throw some light on the obscure world of the relation of religious houses to the rural population.[50] Caesarius of Heisterbach said in a story mentioned above that 'A certain powerful and noble man wished to build a house of our order on his land and, when he found a place suited to religious life he ejected its inhabitants partly by payment and partly by threats.' The new abbot, 'fearing that it might not please God that poor men were deprived of their possessions in such a way', prayed for guidance and was reassured by hearing a voice reciting 'Thou hast given an inheritance to them that fear thy name' (Psalm 60.6). He thus realized that it was God's will 'that undevout men should be expelled from these possessions and that fearful and God-praising men should be located there'.[51] The Cistercians were not alone in following this unpopular practice. There is a reference in the *Life* of Hugh of Lincoln to offering either new lands or their freedom to the inhabitants of lands close to a Carthusian house, and a charter of 1133 from the diocese of Bourges referred to a church and houses built by a hermit 'in the cottages where the peasants had lived'.[52] The practice may have attracted attention owing to the resistance it encountered, and it was not followed by all new houses. When a new building was needed at Obazine in the mid-twelfth century, for instance, Stephen (who was noted for his skill in such matters) rejected a location where there were many peasants, 'who would have created a great danger of souls if they had been left, but no less great a sin if they had been removed'.[53]

Direct exploitation was the secret of the economic success of many of the new communities, but the precise arrangements varied from house to house and changed with time. At first the members frequently produced their own food, as at Tiron, where they had to ask Bernard to reduce the amount of

---

[48] Donkin (1964), pp. 105–7; Waites (1967), who showed that many of the lands granted to the Cistercians in north-east Yorkshire were listed as waste in Domesday Book; and Lohrmann (1983a), pp. 198 and 231–6. On the problems of Cluny in the first half of the twelfth century, see Duby (1952).
[49] *Chartes de Cluny*, V, 265, no. 3915.
[50] See pp. 33–4 and 118–9 above and Colvin (1951–3); Waites (1961), pp. 652–3; Despy (1974–5), p. 65; and Morris (1989), p. 256.
[51] Caesarius, *Dialogus*, IV, 53, ed. Strange, I, 232.
[52] Adam of Eynsham, *Magna vita Hugonis*, II, 5, ed. Decima Douie and Hugh Farmer (OMT; Oxford 1985), I, 61–2 (*BHL* 4018), and *GC*, II, *instr.*, 60, where the pluperfect may mean the cottages were already deserted.
[53] *Vita Stephani Obazinensis*, II, 17, ed. Aubrun, p. 126; see II, 53, p. 178, on Stephen's skill as a manager in rural and domestic affairs.

psalmody in order to allow time for work.[54] The illustrations in the early manuscripts from Cîteaux also leave no doubt that the monks themselves worked in the forests and fields, as does the illustration to the account of early Cistercian history in Alexander of Hales's *On the Apocalypse* (plate 6), which also includes some untonsured novices or lay workers. Bernard of Clairvaux is said by William of St Thierry to have performed manual labour, and his brother Guy, though married, planned to give up his property and work with his hands, like a peasant, in order to support his family.[55] Isaac of L'Etoile delivered a sermon to his monks while they were resting in the shade of an ilex during a break from their work, and abbot Richalm of Schönthal, who died in 1217, worked with the monks, ploughing and reaping and building the monastery.[56] The canons of Arnstein, according to the *Life* of the founder count Louis, worked together 'in social and blessed communion and in manual labour'.[57] There was also a renewed stress on work in some of the old houses, as at Cluny, but rarely to the same extent as among the reformers, and also on work by female religious. Paulina, the founder of Paulinzelle, who died in 1107, lived in a chapel in the woods and worked with her hands all the time, even when she was praying; and the nuns of Lippoldsberg, who in 1095/1102 swore to follow the rule of the monks of Hirsau, said that 'Since we women who are incarcerated for the sake of our sins cannot perform the manual labour which saint Benedict required of men in his rule, we promise to fulfil with a ready spirit insofar as we can St Jerome's instructions for nuns concerning manual labour.'[58]

It was not easy to avoid contacts with lay society and to maintain a high level of community religious life while performing agricultural labour and other necessary economic activities. The Cistercian in the *Dialogue of two monks* attributed the number of guests in Cistercian houses, which was criticized by the Cluniac, in part to the organization of the order, with its annual general chapters and system of visitation, and in part to economic need: 'Since we have neither peasants nor the revenues of money called *census*, we have ourselves to sell what must be sold and to buy what must be bought. We go to the nearer markets to buy cheaper things, you [go] to more distant [markets] in order to buy more precious things.'[59] There were several ways out of this

---

[54] See p. 204 above.

[55] William of St Thierry, *Vita prima Bernardi*, III, 11, and IV, 23, in Bernard, ed. Mabillon, II(6), 2099CD and 2109AB (*BHL* 1211).

[56] Isaac of L'Etoile, *Serm.* 24, in *PL*, CXCIV, 1768D–9B, and Richalm of Schönthal, *Liber revelationum*, I, 21 and 106, in Pez, *Thesaurus*, I.2, 408 and 458, who said that the demons tried to make him feel ill in order to avoid work. Cf. n. 17 above for the temptation to do manual labour.

[57] *Vita Ludovici de Arnstein*, ed. S. Widmann, in *Annalen des Vereins für nassauische Altertumskunde und Geschichtsforschung* 17 (1882), p. 260 (*BHL* 5033).

[58] Sigeboto, *Vita Paulinae*, 21, in *MGH, SS*, XXX.2, 919 (*BHL* 6551), and *Mainzer Urkundenbuch*, ed. Manfred Stimmung, I (Darmstadt 1932), p. 310, no. 405.

[59] Idungus, *Dialogus*, III, 52, ed. Huygens, p. 467.

dilemma, all of which were followed in differing degrees by individual houses and orders. The first, and most striking, was the use of lay brothers, or *conversi* of the new type, who have already been discussed and who constituted a distinct category of men concerned with agricultural and other outside activities, leaving the monks free for worship and prayer.[60]

Closely associated with the institution of lay brothers was that of granges or *curtes*. They were in principle isolated estates worked by lay brothers, as are found among the Cistercians and Premonstratensians, but in practice they were often like the cells, deaneries, and priories of older houses, where a few religious, or even only one, administered an estate of which the main purpose was to produce food for the mother-house.[61] The new houses normally established granges when they acquired lands that owing to their size or distance from the community could not be worked by the resident members. It is uncertain when exactly granges were first set up. The Premonstratensians seem to have had them before the Cistercians, perhaps because, as regular canons and clerics, they were less determined than the reformed monks to support themselves.[62] The earliest reference to a Cistercian grange in England is in 1145/6, but of the 120 Cistercian granges that were eventually established in Yorkshire alone, three-quarters date from before 1200.[63] The middle and second half of the twelfth century was likewise the principal period for establishing granges on the continent. The abbey of Chaalis on the plain of France set up its first grange, at Vaulerent, in 1145/50, on nearby lands it had acquired in 1136 and 1138, and during the next fifty years it organized a total of some fifteen granges within a radius of 100 kilometres from the mother-house.[64] This evidence suggests that the system of granges, like lay brothers, was not an essential feature of the reform movement but a development that

---

[60] On *conversi* and lay brothers, see pp. 77–81 above.

[61] The character and nomenclature of granges varied according to the region, period, and type of religious house to which they belonged: Martin (1893–4), pp. 58 and 67–9; Fossier (1955), pp. 264–5; Waites (1961), p. 630; and Golding (1995), pp. 394–419. In England, and especially in Yorkshire, it was 'a large and . . . predominantly arable farm', according to Bishop (1936), p. 193; 'a small farm centred about the necessary buildings for residence and storage and the barns and shelters for horses, cattle, sheep, and fowl', according to Donnelly (1954), p. 405; and 'a directly cultivated and relatively consolidated land-holding with its own nucleus of farm buildings', according to Donkin (1963), p. 186, and (1964), p. 95, who went on to say (pp. 110–11) that 'Tenants, from whom labour services could, if necessary, be claimed, were never entirely absent.' See also Platt (1969), p. 93, who said that 'The grange, perhaps even from its very beginnings, was a mixed community in which lay brothers, supervisors, servants, and tied peasantry equally played their parts.' See the bibliography in *Medieval Monasticism*, nos. 677–84, and Elm (1994), p. 15 n. 34.

[62] Lohrmann (1983b), p. 213, said that Prémontré had twenty-six *curtes* in 1138, twenty-nine in 1147, and thirty in 1188.

[63] Donkin (1960), p. 149, and (1964), p. 102.

[64] Higounet (1965), pp. 17–19. According to Lohrmann (1980), p. 119, fifteen Cistercian granges were created north of the Beauvaisis between 1140 and 1150, and according to Martin (1893–4), pp. 56 and 67, five Cistercian abbeys in the Haute-Marche established about forty granges in the second half of the twelfth century.

occurred during the second generation as a way of reconciling the need for economic support with the desire for a secluded life of prayer. While it solved some problems, it created others. Some granges consisted of scattered holdings and were worked from their origins by lay dependants and were only administered by lay brothers, or even by a monk. They were subject to internal disputes and often quarrelled with the mother-house. Granges that had chapels or acted as hospices resembled in many respects the small dependencies that the reformers sought to avoid.[65]

An interesting example of a grange that developed out of a hermitage was at La Lande, where Geoffrey and Ascelin, two of the founders of Fontaines-les-Blanches, settled after Fontaines joined the order of Savigny in 1134, and where they lived as hermits for the rest of their lives. Rainald of Château-Renault, at the request of his lord Theobald IV of Champagne and Blois, gave La Lande to Geoffrey the hermit in 1140, 'after he separated himself from the society of the monks of Fontaines', together with 'whatever I hold there, that is jurisdiction over thieves (*latronum*) and capital offences (*forisfactum sanguinis*)' – he did not say how Geoffrey was expected to exercise these rights –, pannage in the forest of Blimars, and wood for heating and building. After Geoffrey's death, the property apparently passed to the bishop of Chartres, who in about 1150, at the request of Bernard of Clairvaux 'and other religious men', gave it to Fontaines, which in 1147 had joined the order of Cîteaux, for use as a grange (*ad opus grangiae*). Subsequently it received some alms from Peter of Candes, to whom John of Salisbury, when he was bishop of Chartres from 1176 to 1180, wrote that 'You should not by your alms of La Lande (*eleemosyna tua de Lauda*) compel the monks of Fontaines to celebrate against the form of the order of Cîteaux, but the holy office which the monks agreed to celebrate for the salvation of yourself and your ancestors should be sufficient for your devotion.'[66] This account, which is pieced together from the history and charters of Fontaines, leaves many unanswered questions, but it illustrates the origins of the grange, the interest taken in it by some of the greatest men in France, and the problems created by its acceptance of support from a lay noble.

The food and buildings needed by growing communities created pressures to seek additional revenues and to use outside labour. A small community, which in its early years made use of an existing church or chapel and wooden

---

[65] On the use of hired lay workers and serfs see Martin (1893–4), pp. 61, 67–9, and 77; Wiswe (1953), pp. 98–103; Graves (1957), pp. 6–7; Higounet (1965), p. 41, who said that Vaulerent was worked by lay brothers until 1248; Platt (1969), pp. 76–94; and Lohrmann (1983b), p. 219, who said that the Premonstratensians had serfs before 1150. On the existence of chapels in granges, see Chalvet de Rochemonteix (1888), pp. 36 and 43, who said that in the second half of the twelfth century many granges became little monasteries and described them (p. 36) as 'de sortes d'abbayes au petit pied'; Martin (1893–4), p. 58; and Fossier (1955), p. 262.

[66] Peregrinus, *Historia*, I, 6, and II, 2, 3, 7, and 9–10, ed. Salmon, pp. 265, 284, and 286–8 (reading *Lauda* for *Landa*).

structures,[67] could probably get by without using lay builders, but as the number of members grew, even if they continued to do some cutting and carting of wood and stone, they had to make use of outside designers and workmen. The surviving examples of early reformed monasteries show that the first buildings as a rule adhered to regional architectural traditions, which suggests that they were made, as at Obazine, by local workers, whose meat Stephen indignantly threw out. After a generation, however, the houses belonging to orders like the Cistercians, Premonstratensians, and Grandmontines show, in spite of regional variations, sufficient uniformity of ground-plan and design to indicate, if not any strict central direction, a desire to conform to an established pattern or ideal and to follow a single manner of construction. Although it is rarely possible to tell from the architecture alone to which order a religious house belonged, it expressed a spiritual as well as an architectural ideal, and the reconstruction or remodelling of a church or conventual buildings was sometimes the most conspicuous sign of the reform of an existing house and reflected the intention of the reformers to impose a new way of life.[68] The size and elegance of many of these buildings, in spite of their simplicity, could hardly have been achieved without using designers and workers from outside the community, or without the expenditure of substantial funds, which had to be raised by the sale of surplus produce unless they were given by a benefactor.

Even the smallest and poorest communities needed, in addition to buildings, at least a few books, which had to be acquired by gift or purchase if they could not be produced at home. Books (like boots and belts) required the skins of animals, of which the reformers refused to eat the flesh. They either had to sell or give away the meat, therefore, or acquire the skins by purchase or barter, both of which involved contacts with the outside world. The production of manuscripts required prototypes as well as time and skill, and there was an active exchange of manuscripts among religious houses in the twelfth century. Peter the Venerable wrote to the Carthusians in 1136/7 asking for a volume of the letters of St Augustine 'because by accident a bear ate a large part of ours in one of our dependencies'.[69] The size and splendour of the early Cistercian manuscripts pose a problem for scholars because they are at vari-

---

[67] The canons of Beckford used a church outside their enclosure until they built one of their own: see the *Chronicon de s. Barbara in Algia*, ed. R.-Norbert Sauvage, in *Mémoires de l'Académie nationale des sciences, arts et belles-lettres de Caen: Documents*, 1906, p. 33.

[68] Kunze (1925), pp. 405–35, stressed the influence of Hirsau and said that the architecture of monasteries in the middle Elbe region reflected the expansion of neo-Cluniac monasticism. Hahn (1957), pp. 81–2, and Stiegman (1988), p. 28, emphasized the unity of the Cistercian style and plan, but other scholars, such as Bilson (1909), pp. 187–8, argued that this might better be called a manner of building than a style, since it incorporated elements found in previous buildings. According to Horn and Born (1979), II, 333–47, on the other hand, the basic continuity in the monastic plans of St Gall, Cluny, and Cîteaux corresponded to the continuity of monastic customs.

[69] Peter the Venerable, *Ep.* 25, ed. Constable, I, 47; see the notes in II, 112.

ance with the alleged poverty of Cîteaux in its early years, when, according to some accounts, it was on the verge of extinction, before the arrival of Bernard and his followers. A poor community could not have afforded to produce such magnificent manuscripts, nor to hire professional scribes, as has been suggested, to work in the scriptorium. It is possible that the stress on poverty and artistic puritanism was to some extent a characteristic of the second generation of the Cistercian order and was directed against its own origins as well as against other monasteries and orders.[70]

When other sources of support failed, or were insufficient, a reformed house might resort to the expedient of accepting either prohibited types of revenues or distant lands that it could not work itself and therefore rented or had cultivated by hired or dependent labourers. During the first generation of the reform movement there were signs of a serious effort to observe the economic regulations, as in the episodes of the gems bought by Suger from some Cistercians who were forbidden to keep them and the refusal of the Carthusians to accept a gift of silver from count William II of Nevers.[71] In 1133 the Cistercians of Ourscamp received a field in exchange for some tithes given them by Louis VI 'because the institution of the Cistercian order altogether refused to hold this revenue'.[72] Archbishop Wichmann of Magdeburg cited the fact that the Premonstratensian abbey of St Mary at Magdeburg 'was not accustomed to have infeudated men' as evidence against a knight who claimed to hold one of its estates as a fief.[73] Already in the 1130s, however, the Cistercians and other reformed houses began to accept both ecclesiastical and secular revenues and other types of property that they had originally refused.[74] An interesting example of this is found in the *relatio* sent by bishop Ulger of Angers to pope Innocent II on behalf of the canons of La Roë and their abbot John – 'the poor man John and his very poor place' – against the monks of the Trinity at Vendôme, who claimed a chapel that the canons had been given and had held without opposition for over thirty years. The case was complicated, and its merits questionable, but it ended in 1136 when the pope confirmed La Roë's possession of the chapel, which was endowed, according to Ulger, with

---

[70] See Stratford (1981), who suggested that the decoration of the Stephen Harding Bible and Gregory's *Moralia* was the work of a professional lay artist, and Rudolph (1990), pp. 157 and 187. See p. 39 n. 172 above for references on the second generation in Cistercian art history.

[71] Suger, *De administratione*, 32, ed. A. Lecoy de La Marche (Société de l'histoire de France; Paris 1867), p. 195, and Guibert, *De vita sua*, I, 11, ed. Bourgin, pp. 33–4.

[72] *Cartulaire de l'abbaye de Notre-Dame d'Ourscamp*, ed. H. Peigné-Delacourt (Mémoires de la Société des antiquaires de Picardie. Documents inédits concernant la province 6; Amiens 1865), pp. 75 and 283–4, nos. 111 and 462. See Luchaire (1890), pp. 238–9, no. 521. When Mortemer joined the Cistercian order in 1137 it gave Beaumont to Longueville because, having been blessed by the pope, it could not become a grange: *Relatio quomodo domus Mortuimaris sit fundata*, 20, ed. J. Bouvet, in *Collectanea ordinis Cisterciensium reformatorum* 22 (1960), p. 155.

[73] J.G. Leuckfeld, *Antiquitates Praemonstratenses* (Magdeburg and Leipzig 1721), p. 99, no. 29. See Uhlhorn (1894), p. 367, on the refusal to accept infeudated land.

[74] For tithes, see Constable (1964), pp. 191–2, and Despy (1974–5), pp.76–8. On corrodies and burials, mostly in the thirteenth century, see Williams (1991), pp. 104–7.

various revenues, including rents, ovens, mills, and market dues 'which were taken from the demesne and from the portion (*mensa*) of the same lord [the founder], which he could freely have given to one of his knights or to a client, had he wished, or to a mime or an actor, had he wished to act lightly'. The secular character of the chapel's revenues is underlined by the fact that the pope forbade the canons to live there 'because it is known to be unsuitable for the use of religious men'. The real basis for giving the chapel to John was his poverty. As Ulger put it: 'He is alone, powerless, and poor: alone, he is assailed by many; powerless, he is surrounded by powerful men; and poor, by rich men.'[75] This chapel represented a type of property that the reformers wanted to avoid, but it was apparently the principal source of support for a small ascetic community; and many other new houses seem to have been in the same position.

This case also illustrates the sort of legal dispute in which new houses, in spite of efforts to avoid litigation, almost inevitably became involved through their ownership of property to which there were conflicting claims. The very process of cultivation and land-clearing often created claims, as at the former villa of Maisons-en-Beauce, which a monk of Morigny named Baldwin acquired in 1102, when it was deserted, and settled with almost eighty *hospites oblatiarii*. As soon as it became productive, claims were made for various dues and payments, which Baldwin resisted as best he could both by pleading and by paying. He travelled all over the Beauce by foot or horse, or in a cart when his legs hurt, seeking grain to buy off the claims and to free the lands from these burdensome customs. 'May God reward him who acted well, honestly, and faithfully', wrote the chronicler of Morigny.[76] Though Morigny was a house of black monks, Baldwin's problems resembled those of any community that was trying to establish a grange. Hermits ran into similar difficulties. William of Stuteville, the constable of the castle of Knaresborough, disliked having a hermitage on his hunting grounds and expelled the hermit Robert from his cell, calling him a hypocrite (*simulator*).[77] In this case William changed his mind, and the story may have been invented to illustrate his conversion, but there were many examples of the harassment of hermits and houses of reformed monks and canons, who were forced to move, to make a settlement, or to go to the law to protect themselves from the claims of former owners and present neighbours.[78] The monks of Pontigny in 1140 gave up some prop-

[75] On La Roë, which was founded by Robert of Arbrissel, see Ulger of Angers, *Relatio pro monasterio Rotensi adversus monachos Vindocinenses*, in Baluze, *Miscellanea* (1st edn), II, 200–9 (quotes on 200 and 201–2) and (for the bull of Innocent II) 209–12 = *PL*, CLXXIX, 265B–6D (JL 7755).

[76] *Chronicon Mauriniacense*, I, 2, ed. Léon Mirot, 2nd edn (CTSEEH 41; Paris 1912), pp. 5–6.

[77] *Vita* [A] *Roberti Knaresburgensis*, ed. Paul Grosjean, in *Anal. boll.* 57 (1939), p. 373 (*BHL* 7270d).

[78] See the accounts of the legal battles of Chaumouzey (against the founder's brother) in Seher of Chaumouzey, *Primordia Calmosiacensia*, 2, in *Documents rares ou inédits de l'histoire des Vosges*,

erty in and around the castle of Ligny-le-Châtel 'in order to avoid the disturbance of secular men', according to a charter of count William II of Nevers,
who declared in the arenga that 'He who does not by the law of equity seek
and preserve temporal peace between himself and his neighbour cannot reach
the highest peace that is Christ.'[79]

In order to avoid disputes and litigation, the Grandmontines were forbidden
to make charters recording gifts 'for the sake of pleading at law (*placitandi*)'
or to bring legal suits. They were allowed to receive annual gifts for only as
long as the donors wished and to remind them once if they failed to pay.
After that they were to keep quiet and be grateful for what they had received.[80]
Later in the twelfth century Peter Comestor said that 'It is not permitted nor
is it suitable for perfect speculatives [that is, contemplative monks] who have
put all things aside and "naked follow the naked Christ" to seek what is theirs
by any legal proceeding. But they may request by themselves or by friends.'[81]

Some of the most bitter controversies arose over the payment of tithes.
Although tithes were in principle a universal obligation, and owed to God
rather than to man, they were in practice considered a pastoral revenue and
were divided between the parish priest and the bishop, and over the centuries
many tithes had come into the possession of monasteries and lay lords. They
were regarded as the sustenance of the poor, and Ivo of Chartres in his letter
to the monks of Coulombs argued that they could legitimately be owned by
those who had made themselves poor for the sake of Christ.[82] Reformed houses
in the first half of the twelfth century, including some entire orders like the
Cistercians and Premonstratensians, received privileges either giving them
their own tithes or freeing them from the obligation to pay tithes from goods
produced by themselves or for their own use, especially from lands that were
newly cultivated and from which no tithes had previously been paid. As the
new houses prospered, however, and acquired lands from which tithes had
customarily been paid, and which they did not always work themselves, the
refusal to pay led to some serious conflicts, of which that between the Cluniac
monks of Gigny and the Cistercians of Le Miroir was one of the longest and
most violent.[83] This dispute ended, as did others, in a compromise by which

ed. L. Duhamel (Paris 1868–82), II, 15–16; of Fontdouce (against La Chaise-Dieu, Fontevrault,
and others) in *De origine monasterii Fontis Dulcis*, in *RHGF*, XIV, 525; and of La Couronne
(against Fontevrault) in a charter of bishop John of Séez in 1129, ed. Paul de Fleury, in *Archives
historiques de la Saintonge et de l'Aunis* 7 (1880), pp. 32–4, no. 4.

[79] *Le premier cartulaire de l'abbaye cistercienne de Pontigny (XIIe–XIIIe siècles)*, ed. Martine Garrigues (Collection de documents inédits sur l'histoire de France. Section de philologie et d'histoire jusqu'à 1610. Série in-8° 14; Paris 1981), p. 158, no. 86.

[80] Stephen of Grandmont, *Regula*, 23–4, in *CC:CM*, VIII, 81–2.

[81] Smalley (1979), pp. 126–7.

[82] Ivo of Chartres, *Ep*. 192, in *PL*, CLXII, 199D–200B. On this and other material in this paragraph,
see Constable (1964).

[83] This controversy, which began in 1135/7 and was not settled until 1155, involved at least
three popes and many lesser authorities: see Constable (1960).

the Cistercians agreed to pay an annual rent in place of the tithes formerly paid to Gigny. At about the same time, pope Adrian IV introduced the policy, which was later generalized, of restricting the freedom to noval tithes, which had not previously been paid, and thus requiring new houses either to pay or to reach a specific settlement concerning existing tithes.

The spread of the reform movement, and its economic success, thus brought with it not necessarily a decline, as it was seen at the time and by later scholars, but unforeseen difficulties and changes. The two central decades of the twelfth century saw a shift in the economic history of most of the new houses and orders, after which they began, on the one hand, to rely increasingly for economic support on lay brothers and the system of granges and, on the other, to accept various types of properties and revenues that they had originally refused and to conform more closely than they had at their beginnings to the traditional model of monastic economic organization. During these years many of the new houses became richer than the old ones, which were going through a difficult financial period, and the Cistercians in particular were widely accused, even by the pope, of deserting their early economic principles and of becoming rich at the expense of others.[84] The Grandmontines paradoxically, as they were aware, compiled their first customary, which embodied the principles of strict poverty and economic precariousness advocated by their founder Stephen, at the very time when they were receiving numerous gifts and charters and when the difficulties with their lay brothers, which erupted in the crisis of 1185–8, were beginning to develop.[85] Gerald of Wales, who admired the Grandmontines more than most of the new orders, gave an interesting account of this process in his *Mirror of the church*:

> With the passage of time the dispensing advice of older and more mature men tempered the statutes that had been made at the beginning without discretion or consultation and with excessive harshness. So that at present they are allowed to possess, like the Cistercians, as many ploughs and tools, cattle and sheep, broad lands and pastures as they need. They also accept with gratitude the ecclesiastical benefices given them by the faithful with charitable generosity, but not the cure of souls, which they renounce and refuse on account of the accompanying dangers. In this they resemble both the Cluniacs and the Carthusians, just as they differ greatly from the Cistercians in the said excessive quantity both of moveable and of immoveable property. And they are neither ashamed nor afraid to possess churches, which they had previously refused and feared with greater devotion and religious perfection, just as in recent times the order of Cîteaux, desiring at last to return to its vomit, not without grave scandal, resembles both the Cluniacs and the Grandmontines in this matter.[86]

---

[84] Hoffmann (1910), p. 700, divided Cistercian economic history into three periods, of which the second began about 1150. On these developments, see pp. 217–20 above.

[85] See esp. Becquet (1956), dating the first customary prior to the crisis of 1185–8, and (1960) on the crisis.

[86] Gerald of Wales, *Speculum ecclesiae*, III, 21, ed. John S. Brewer a.o. (RS 21; London 1861–91), IV, 256.

Among the interesting points in this passage are the parallels between the economic organization of the black monks (whom Gerald called Cluniacs) and the new orders of Cîteaux, Grandmont, and La Chartreuse, the condemnation of the wealth of the Cistercians, especially their possession of churches, and the approval Gerald expressed for the Grandmontines' departure from their early statutes in extending their possessions and for their refusal to exercise the cure of souls, which he considered dangerous.

Some of the reformers, at least during the early years of the movement, hoped to restore the diocesan bishop's rights of visitation and control as they had existed during the early days of monasticism and been established by the council of Chalcedon in 451. One of the harshest criticisms of Cluny in the Cistercian 'invective' to which Peter the Venerable replied in his Letter 28 was that it had its own bishop, meaning that it was exempt from the authority of the diocesan bishop and could ask any bishop to perform the necessary sacramental functions. The restoration of episcopal control over monasteries, however, involved the risk of the type of external interference in monastic affairs that the old privileges of exemption had sought to prevent, and that the reformers themselves sought to avoid; and exemption in fact, if not in name, crept into the reform programme by the back door. The possession of parochial churches and revenues was also high on the list of Cistercian charges against Cluny, and more generally the exercise of pastoral work by monks, which the reformers considered to be the special responsibility of secular clerics, who were therefore alone entitled to receive pastoral revenues. Not all the reformers, however, especially among the regular canons, refused to perform pastoral work, and many had pastoral and caritative inclinations that involved them in preaching and good works and brought them into contact with the world outside their communities.

The performance of pastoral work by monks and their possession of spiritual revenues (*spiritualia*) such as tithes, first-fruits, and oblations were controversial owing not only to their economic consequences but also to their bearing on the question of the status of monks and their relation to the clergy.[87] The situation was further complicated because many monasteries possessed prebends in cathedrals and collegiate churches. They were thus members of the chapter and expected to receive the revenues of the prebend, though to what extent they performed the associated duties is uncertain.[88] The lines of division on this controversy cut across the usual distinctions of old and new monks and of conservatives and reformers. The old black monks, including reformed orders like the Cluniacs, tended to assert in principle the right of ordained monks to perform pastoral work and to receive pastoral revenues, though in practice they might decide not to do so or not be authorized by the bishop,

---

[87] See Constable (1964), pp. 145–85, and pp. 132–5 above for some of the writers on either side of this issue.

[88] Imbart de la Tour (1891), p. 527, and, on the Cluniac prebends at Abbeville, Peter the Venerable, *Ep.* 102, ed. Constable, I, 264, and notes in II, 289–90.

who had charge of all pastoral work in the diocese. Canons and the clergy generally, on the other hand, tended to deny the right even of ordained monks to preach and perform the cure of souls, which was the prerogative of clerics. The reformers were divided and sometimes ambiguous. The regular canons, as clerics, asserted their right to perform pastoral work and, on this basis, claimed a higher rank of perfection than monks, but those whose rules imposed a degree of seclusion as great or greater than that of monks sought to avoid contacts with secular society and often refused to perform pastoral work or receive pastoral revenues. The earliest Premonstratensian statutes, which were compiled about 1131/4 and may have been influenced by the Cistercians, forbade the possession of 'altars to which the cure of souls belongs unless they can be [made into] abbeys'.[89] It is hard to draw a clear line in practice between the old and new monks, or between the conservatives and reformers, with respect to the performance of pastoral work. Some of the strongest critics of the monastic performance of pastoral work came from the ranks of the regular canons. The reformed monks were also divided. For the most part they wanted to reassert the distinctive character of the monastic order and agreed with the clergy that pastoral work was not the proper concern of monks, who were supposed to be withdrawn from the world and devoted to prayer. They were reluctant, however, to regard this as evidence of a lower spiritual standing than clerics. Many reformers, furthermore, had strong evangelical instincts and engaged, both with and sometimes without proper authorization, in preaching and pastoral counselling, such as hearing confession and administering penance, and also in the public celebration of the sacraments.

Ordination was generally regarded as a *sine qua non* for the exercise of any cure of souls, including preaching, which further required (unless it had been granted with the ordination, as to parish priests) the special permission of the bishop or the pope. For an unordained monk or lay man to preach or celebrate the sacraments was a sign of grave error, if not of heresy, and even for a cleric to preach without proper authorization might lead to problems, as Bernard of Tiron and Norbert of Xanten discovered, though bishops seem to have been relatively tolerant in this respect. Hermits like Robert of Arbrissel, Vitalis of Savigny, and Bernard of Tiron were well-known preachers, and many obscure hermits were more interested in the right to preach than to celebrate the sacraments.[90] Bernard of Clairvaux was careful to insist that his preaching outside his monastery was properly authorized, and the Cistercian commitment to preaching and pastoral work in the late twelfth century prepared the way for the role of the mendicants in the thirteenth century, when preaching

---

[89] *Les premiers statuts de l'ordre de Prémontré. Le Clm. 17.174 (XIIᵉ siècle)*, ed. Raphaël Van Wae-felghem (offprint from *Analectes de l'ordre de Prémontré* 9; Louvain 1913), p. 45. See Colvin (1951), p. 252 n. 3 (and pp. 13–14 on the date), and Constable (1964), pp. 155–6.

[90] Etienne Delaruelle, in *Eremitismo* (1965), pp. 215–19, and Van Moolenbroek (1990), pp. 170–2 and 218–35.

took on 'something of a sacramental nature'.[91] The proportion of ordained monks increased steadily through the early Middle Ages, and by the thirteenth century it was common to equate the monastic and clerical tonsures and to regard all monks as automatically clerics.[92] It was never a requirement for monks to be ordained, however, except as a matter of policy in individual houses or orders, and there is evidence in vernacular literature of a continued awareness among the laity that monks were not necessarily priests and that they were distinct from clerics.[93] Not even all abbots were ordained. In the ninth century abbots were apparently expected to be priests, in part for the convenience of their communities, and the council of Poitiers in 1078 required 'That deacon abbots who are not priests should be made priests or lose their positions,' but as late as the thirteenth century Bernard of Monte Cassino considered it a 'new law' to require abbots to be priests.[94]

While the general trend towards ordination is clear, it is hard to establish precise figures except in houses for which there are necrologies or obituary lists distinguishing between ordained and unordained monks. The surviving figures for the twelfth century suggest that in independent old black monasteries as many as a quarter or a third of the monks were still not ordained, whereas in houses of reformed orders like the Cluniacs the proportion was probably lower and perhaps, by the end of the century, not more than 5 or 10 per cent.[95] The proportion of ordained members in new communities depended on the nature of the house and the origins of the recruits. Canons were in the nature of things ordained, and the Carthusians seem to have had a higher percentage of priests than the Cistercians, although they celebrated mass more rarely. The number of priests in Cistercian abbeys may have grown during the twelfth century owing in part to the division between the monks and the unordained lay brothers.[96] Houses that originated in migrations from liturgically oriented monasteries, like Cîteaux and Fountains, presumably had more priests than communities that were at first primarily or even exclusively lay. Of the nine named original members of Fontaines-les-Blanches, two were hermits, two were lay men (one a knight), and two were clerics (one a priest), and the first obituary of the order of Grandmont, which covers the years from 1120 to 1160, lists 23 priests and 130 brothers.[97] These differing proportions of ordained and unordained members are a useful reminder of the variety within the

[91] Rouse and Rouse (1979), pp. 52–61 (quote on p. 61).
[92] Bock (1952), esp. pp. 389–91, and Leclercq (1963b), pp. 19–20.
[93] Merk (1914), p. 210.
[94] See Rome (826), 27, and Poitiers (1078), 7, in Mansi, XIV, 1007, and XX, 498, and, on Bernard of Monte Cassino, Nussbaum (1961), p. 91.
[95] See pp. 93–4 and 200 above on the percentages of ordained monks in religious communities in the eleventh and twelfth centuries.
[96] Lucet (1954), pp. 274–7, and Leclercq (1963b), pp. 16–19.
[97] Peregrinus, *Historia*, I, 2, ed. Salmon, p. 259, and Dereine (1960b), p. 330.

reform movement and of the danger of classifying the new monks and canons together in contrast to the members of older houses.

Even in houses where there was a high proportion of priests and deacons, the position and office of a monk remained distinct from the ordained ranks of the ecclesiastical hierarchy. In some necrologies and witness-lists the names are accompanied by the indications *monachus et presbyter*, *monachus et diaconus*, or simply *monachus* or *conversus*. A monk who became a bishop remained a monk and was expected to live like a monk in all but specific matters such as obedience, clothing, and property, to which exceptions were defined by canon lawyers in the tenth and eleventh centuries.[98] The position of monk-priests was less clear. They were considered to be ordained to the church of the monastery of which they were members, and they were entitled to celebrate mass there and to minister to other members of the community and also, presumably, to pilgrims and lay people who came to the church, provided that it did not infringe on the sacramental rights of parochial or baptismal, as they were called in some areas, churches.[99] Their right to celebrate in private chapels and oratories not belonging to the monastery and above all to serve as parish priests, unless specifically authorized to do so by the bishop, was much less clear and was not officially approved by the papacy until the end of the twelfth century.[100] It was accepted in practice, however, and recognized in canon law, partly on the basis of texts that were forged, probably in the mid-eleventh century, specifically in order to justify the exercise of the *cura animarum* by monks. Some of these were cited a century later in the *Decretum* of Gratian, who accepted a limited right of monks to perform pastoral work and receive spiritual revenues, subject to the control of bishops, and who was followed by later canonists.[101] In spite of regional variations, there were few parts of Europe in the twelfth century where monks did not serve in parish churches.[102]

Almost three-quarters of the private churches referred to in French royal charters between 840 and 987 belonged to monasteries,[103] and the number

---

[98] Oliger (1958), esp. pp. 48–60, 69, and 82–91.

[99] See among other works the old but still useful Thomassin (1864–7), III, 316–17.

[100] Henry (1957), pp. 165–6; Fransen (1957), pp. 265–70; Oliger (1958), pp. 78–80; Constable (1964), pp. 146–7, citing Berlière (1927b), p. 351, and Hofmeister (1953–4), pp. 255 and 272; and Devailly (1975). The work of de Marca (1708), pp. 960–4, is still of use, though written from an episcopal and Gallican point of view.

[101] Gratian, *Decretum*, XVI, 7, *dictum post* 38, in *Corpus*, ed. Friedberg, I, 811. See Dereine (1954) and Constable (1965).

[102] Berlière (1927b); Schmitz (1948–56), I, 342–6 (with bibliography on 342 n. 22); Choux (1952), pp. 75 and 129 (on the diocese of Toul); Chibnall (1967) (on England and Normandy); Toubert (1973), pp. 900–11 (on central Italy, where most parishes were served by secular priests), and (1977), p. 428 (on monastic churches in Italy that were served by monks); Devailly (1975), pp. 265–8; and Avril (1976–80), pp. 256–89. On the empire, see the opposing views of Semmler (1959), pp. 267–81, who maintained that monastic *cura* was relatively widespread, and Oediger (1960), who said it was unusual (at least in the diocese of Cologne) before 1200.

[103] This conclusion is based on the charts distributed at the Spoleto conference in 1980 and published in Lemarignier (1982), pp. 770–5.

grew rapidly in the eleventh century, particularly during the reform movement, when many lay proprietors gave their churches not to the bishop, to whom they properly belonged, but to monks whose ownership of churches, though technically no less improper than that of lay men, was acceptable to all except the strictest reformers.[104] Churches belonging to monasteries were more easily and cheaply served by ordained monks than by clerics, though the question of the performance of pastoral work by monks was in principle distinct from that of their possession of parochial churches, since the former was a matter of the status of monks and the latter of proprietary rights. The Cistercians in the list of charges reproduced in Peter the Venerable's Letter 28 addressed themselves to the question of possession, since they doubtless knew that the monks of Cluny did not serve in churches:

> Why do you own parish churches, first-fruits, and tithes, which according to canon law all belong not to monks but to clerics? They have been given to those whose office it is to baptize, preach, and administer other [sacraments] pertaining to the salvation of souls, so that they need not engage in worldly affairs but that, since they work in the church, they may live off the church, since the Lord says that 'The labourer is worthy of his hire.' But why do you usurp this, when you do none of these things which we have mentioned? And since you do not perform the labour, why do you receive the labourer's hire?[105]

This implies that if the Cluniacs had served in the churches from which they drew revenues, the situation would have been less serious, though by doing so they would have laid themselves open to criticism of another sort. The secular cleric or canon Theobald of Etampes argued in a letter to archbishop Thurstan of York that since monks were inferior to priests, they might not rule churches or administer the sacraments any more than a servant might rule a mistress. If they did so, it was on account of the scarcity of priests, not of any general rule of the church. 'No churches or tithes properly belong to them . . . but like the early monks they should live from the labour of their hands and from the common lot that is God.'[106] Theobald was no friend of monks or of monastic reform, but on this point he was not only historically correct but also in agreement with many of the reformers. The regular canons Anselm of Havelberg, Philip of Harvengt, and Gerhoh of Reichersberg all asserted the distinction between monks and clerics and the superiority of clerics and argued that monks were excluded from clerical functions, though Philip and Gerhoh seem to have recognized that monks who in fact performed the cure of souls might receive spiritual revenues.[107] In this case, it seems, two wrongs made a right, or at least a lesser wrong.

---

[104] Devailly (1975), pp. 263–4, stressed the regional and chronological differences in the number of parish churches given to monasteries, and Aubrun (1986), pp. 81–5.

[105] Peter the Venerable, *Ep.* 28, ed. Constable, I, 56. The biblical citation is from Luc. 10.7 and 1 Tim. 5.18.

[106] Theobald of Etampes, *Improperium cuiusdam in monachos*, ed. Raymonde Foreville and Jean Leclercq, in *Anal. mon.*, IV, pp. 52–3.

[107] Constable (1964), pp. 158–65.

The defenders of monastic possession of churches and performance of pastoral work showed the relative weakness of their case by relying on the de facto situation and on forgeries. Several small canonical collections were compiled in the eleventh and twelfth centuries specifically to justify the performance of pastoral work and possession of parochial revenues by monks.[108] Peter the Venerable in Letter 28 based his defence of Cluniac possession of tithes, first on papal privileges and confirmations, second on the liturgical services performed by monks, who like the Levites had no worldly inheritance, and third on the right of a bishop to turn a church into a monastery and to endow it with the episcopal share of pastoral revenues. On this basis he concluded that 'We possess freely, justly, and canonically the churches and all their goods that bishops have given us without sale.'[109] The case was easier to make when the monks performed the cure of souls. Rupert of Deutz, writing in the early 1120s, went further and argued that monks who were also clerics were entitled to preach, baptize, absolve sins, and celebrate mass.[110] The author of the *Libellus* said that monks and canons who lived near men were entitled to the revenues given them by lay men who received the sacraments and pastoral instruction in their churches.[111] Honorius *Augusto-dunensis* reached a similar conclusion, more cautiously, by distinguishing between the clerical and lay offices and between the monastic and regular (canonical) professions, which he considered 'titles of merit, not of office, since they signify contemptors of the world'. A monk or canon who was a cleric might therefore preach 'not from his rule but from his office'.[112] Idungus in his *Argument about four questions*, written in 1144/5, also distinguished the *monachatus* from the *clericatus*, saying that a monk might also be a cleric and, as such, if duly authorized, might preach and live off tithes and oblations.[113] Writing at about the same time, the canonist Roland Bandinelli, the future pope Alexander III, said that a monk who had both the sacerdotal *ordo* and the episcopal *licentia* might perform pastoral work; and in the *Summa Parisiensis*, which dates from about 1160, this argument was presented as one of three different justifications for allowing monks to exercise clerical offices.[114] This was a face-saving compromise, since it

---

[108] See Constable (1965); Paxton (1985); and Picasso (1993), with references to other such collections. On the forgeries attributed to popes Gregory and Boniface, see also Dereine (1954), pp. 308–9, and Kuttner (1968), p. 504.

[109] Peter the Venerable, *Ep.* 28, ed. Constable, I, 81–2.

[110] Rupert of Deutz, *Altercatio monachi et clerici quod liceat monacho praedicare*, in *PL*, CLXX, 537C–42C. See Endres (1906), p. 146, and Constable (1964), pp. 173–5. This work is dated 1119/22 by Van Engen (1983), pp. xix and 312.

[111] *Libellus*, II, 14, ed. Constable, p. 26; see VI, 47, p. 82.

[112] *Quaestio utrum monachis liceat praedicare*, in Endres (1906), pp. 147–50. See Constable (1964), pp. 175–6, and Van Engen (1983), p. 312 n. 46.

[113] Idungus, *Argumentum*, 1 and 9, ed. Huygens, pp. 345 and 366–8.

[114] *Die Summa magistri Rolandi*, ed. Friedrich Thaner (Innsbruck 1874), pp. 36–45, and *The Summa Parisiensis on the Decretum Gratiani*, ed. Terence McLaughlin (Toronto 1952), p. 177,

agreed with the strict reformers and conservative clerics that monks as such might not administer the sacraments but recognized with the old monks and moderate reformers that ordained monks who were properly authorized had all the rights of clerics.

This solution left the regular canons in an anomalous position, since as clerics they were undoubtedly entitled to perform sacramental functions but as cloistered religious living under a rule, and as reformers seeking to avoid contacts with lay society, they often refused to perform pastoral work and were sometimes prohibited from doing so by bishops.[115] When the provost of Lesterps in the late eleventh century complained to Ivo of Chartres that the bishop of Limoges had forbidden regular canons 'both the rule of parishes and the confession of penitents', Ivo replied that, while he personally thought that all clerics should lead a regular life, the bishop was responsible for the cure of souls in his diocese and should be asked to entrust it to the older and more experienced members of the community, since not all regular canons were suited for pastoral work.[116] The fact that four houses of regular canons, including Lesterps, acquired about a hundred parish churches in the diocese of Limoges between 1070 and 1140 may explain the attitude of the bishop, who doubtless felt that his control over the pastoral care of his diocese was threatened.[117] The episcopal charters for houses of regular canons in the diocese of Liège between 1091 and 1151 show that the right to exercise the cure of souls was granted primarily to houses in remote areas, where pastoral work was needed, and not to others.[118] The Augustinian canons of St Botulph at Colchester were authorized by pope Paschal II in 1116 to preach and administer baptism and penance and to own tithes, and according to the *Libellus* the moderate regular canons of St Quentin at Beauvais and St Victor at Paris, like the moderate monks 'who live next to men', went out 'to teach and govern the people' and lived off revenues and tithes from the faithful.[119]

The attitude towards pastoral work of strict regular canons, like the Premonstratensians, varied regionally. In France and England they seem for the most part to have resembled the reformed monks and to have refused both the possession of churches and the cure of souls.[120] In the empire, on the other hand, and especially in Bavaria and the diocese of Salzburg, they nor-

which presented arguments based on the growing number of ordained monks, the combination of the offices of cleric and monk, and specific grants to some abbots. On Alexander III, see Fransen (1957), p. 266.

[115] Avril (1976–80), pp. 489–501.
[116] Ivo of Chartres, *Ep.* 69, ed. Jean Leclercq (CHFMA 22; Paris 1949), pp. 304–8.
[117] Becquet (1972), pp. 113–14.
[118] Dereine (1952), pp. 70–1 and 92.
[119] Dugdale, *Monasticon*, VI.1, 106–7 (JL 6529) and *Libellus*, VI, 47, ed. Constable, p. 82. See Constable (1964), p. 154, citing Dickinson (1950), p. 101 n. 2, on the authenticity of this bull.
[120] Lemarignier (1949), reviewing the work of Dereine; Dickinson (1950), pp. 232–41; and François Petit, in *Vita comune* (1962), p. 469.

mally engaged in pastoral work and were expected and even required to do
so by the bishops.[121] It may be no accident that some of the strongest critics
of the cure of souls by monks and supporters of the prerogatives of canons
were regular canons from the east, like Anselm of Havelberg, who was himself
active in pastoral work.[122] Archbishop Frederick of Cologne in the charter
installing Augustinian canons at Steinfeld in 1121 specifically transferred 'the
parochial care of which the dispensation belongs to this monastery to the
chapel at the entrance to the same house', where the laity could come for the
sacraments,[123] and Calixtus II in 1123 authorized the canons of Springiersbach,
who had established themselves in 'a solitary spot' in 1107, to preach, administer the sacraments and penance, and visit the sick.[124] The conclusion that the
regular canons were more open to pastoral work in the empire than in other
parts of Europe is confirmed by the papal and episcopal charters in Hugo's
Sacri et canonici Praemonstratensis annales. The rights to celebrate the sacraments, preach, baptize, and bury were granted in varying forms to Dünnwald
by the archbishop of Cologne in 1117, Ilbenstadt by the archbishop of Mainz
in 1123 (confirmed by Innocent II in 1139), Varlar by the bishop of Münster
in 1129 (confirmed for the burial rights only by Innocent II in 1142), Ursberg
by the bishop of Augsburg in 1130, Knecksteden by the archbishop of Cologne
in 1134, and Wadgassen by the archbishop of Trier in 1135 (confirmed by
Eugene III in 1152).[125] In 1140, Otto of Freising gave Schäftlarn four churches
'with the cure of souls',[126] and Innocent II gave Etival 'the rule over the souls
of both clerics and lay parishioners of the churches with all their possessions
. . . and the cures of those receiving churches from your hands'. This was
confirmed in 1147 by Eugene III, who went on to specify that they might
institute either canons or secular priests in these churches, without consulting
the bishop, archdeacon, or dean. 'They thus receive from you both the cure
of souls and the prebend and are responsible for their actions neither to the
bishop nor to the archdeacon nor to the dean.'[127] This was in all respects an

---

[121] Schmale (1959), pp. 47–9; Dereine (1960a), pp. 911–14; Semmler (1959–61), p. 169, who said
that the canons of the *ordo novus* were more open to the *cura animarum* than those of the *ordo
antiquus* and cited the canons of Hördt, who at first refused and later undertook pastoral work;
Siegwart (1965), pp. 289–316; and Bosl (1979), on which see Weinfurter (1980–1), p. 384,
who attributed the *cura animarum* of canons to a new perception of priests and the church.

[122] Berges (1956), p. 39.

[123] *Urkundenbuch für die Geschichte des Niederrheins,* 1 (Düsseldorf 1840), p. 192, no. 292.

[124] *Urkundenbuch zur Geschichte der jetzt die preussischen Regierungsbezirke Coblenz und Trier
bildenden mittelrheinischen Territorien,* ed. Heinrich Beyer, Leopold Eltester, and Adam Goerz
(Coblenz 1860–74), 1, 510, no. 451, and *Bullaire du pape Calixte II,* ed. Ulysse Robert (Paris
1891), 11, 219–20, no. 414 (JL 7079). Differing views on the extent to which the canons exercised this privilege were expressed by Dereine (1948b), pp. 424 and 429; Pauly (1962),
pp. 30–7; and Semmler (1956), pp. 107–8.

[125] C.-L. Hugo, *Sacri et canonici ordinis Praemonstratensis annales* (Nancy 1734–6), 1.1, ccccxxxix
(Dünnwald); dclxi–ii (Ilbenstadt; JL 8060); 1.2, dcli–ii (Varlar; JL 8241); dccvii (Ursberg);
ii (Knecksteden); dcxix–xxii (Wadgassen; JL 9585).

[126] Ibid., 1.2, cccclxxxii.

[127] Ibid., 1.2, dxlii–iv (JL 8109 and 9128).

exceptional privilege and in effect granted the abbot of Etival episcopal powers over the churches belonging to his abbey. No comparable privileges, aside from a few grants of burial rights, were made to Premonstratensian houses elsewhere.

The varying attitudes of monks and regular canons towards pastoral work is also reflected in the design of their churches and conventual buildings. The absence of large western portals, of internal divisions and decoration, and of bell-towers (which were prohibited by the Cistercians) showed the desire of many communities to be cut off from lay society and pastoral work, while the growing number of altars was a response to the need of ordained monks to celebrate mass within the community.[128] A lack of transepts, on the other hand, which in monastic churches served to link the church with the cloister, and the presence of a great west door and galilee, extensive decoration, and internal divisions such as a choir-screen, which separated the clergy from the laity, all indicated the openness of a church to the laity, both pilgrims and parishioners, and tended to characterize the churches of old black monks and of secular canons more than those of reformed monks and regular canons. The screen dividing the choir from the nave in the church of the Cistercian abbey at Maulbronn has been considered evidence of the increasing receptivity of the Cistercians to the laity, though it may have served to separate the monks from the lay brothers.[129]

Every part of a monastery – the size and design of the chapter-house, refectory, and dormitory, and the presence or absence of a separate residence for the abbot – tells something about the way of life in the community. The reference in the chronicle of Zwiefalten to building 'a refectory of the bearded brothers with a dormitory' shows that they were lay brothers of the new kind, who were segregated from the monks, and the situation of the residence for women in some of the new houses reflected the changing attitudes towards the female element in the community.[130] The type of portal and porch was an indication of the participation of a church in the religious, legal, and social functions that took place in or before the doors of the church. Recent research has confirmed the view that the colourless, decorated glass in the windows of Cistercian churches had symbolic meaning and was not the result simply of economy or artistic puritanism.[131] The size and location of the guest-house and hospital indicated the role played by the caritative works in the life of a

---

[128] Hubert (1966) associated galilees with the role of the laity; see also his article in *Laici* (1968), pp. 470–87. Crozet (1944), pp. 233–4, remarked on the absence of west portals on Grandmontine churches.

[129] Some scholars consider this screen an addition to the original structure, but it is apparently original. Jean Hubert, in *Vita comune* (1962), I, 108, assumed it served to separate the laity from the monks. See generally Zarnecki (1954), pp. 111–13

[130] Berthold of Zwiefalten, *Chronicon*, 10, ed. Luitpold Wallach, in *Traditio* 13 (1957), p. 200, and in the series 'Schwäbische Chroniken der Stauferzeit' 2 (Stuttgart 1941, repr. 1978), p. 174. See above pp. 69–70 and 73 on buildings for women.

[131] Lillich (1993).

community. When Miro of Ripoll came to the house of regular canons where he decided to live he was favourably impressed by the well-built *domus infirmorum* and 'praised the charity of the religious men'. His own love grew greater every day, according to his *Life*, and 'produced the feelings not only of love for his neighbour but also of alms for the poor. When he violently chastised his own body and performed the greatest penance and admirable virtues, he implanted the germs of piety not only in the hearts of the canons but also in the inhabitants of the neighbouring villas.'[132] This passage shows that the house was less isolated than other passages in Miro's *Life* suggest and that his association of self-mortification with brotherly love and alms-giving served as an example to the laity and as a type of silent preaching by example that was in its own way no less eloquent than the writings of the hermit Gilbert of Senlis.

The concern of the reformers for charity and good works was often in conflict with their desire for seclusion, and a few, like the Carthusians, refused to distribute alms at their houses or to have an almoner.[133] Hermits occasion-ally turned away guests, and according to an unpublished Mary-legend of uncertain date, a Cistercian monk who sinned by leaving his monastery in order to help relieve the injustice and hunger in the world was saved only by the intervention of the Virgin.[134] Even if the purpose of this story was to reinforce the monastic commitment, it shows that at least some monks thought that they should do more to assist other people.[135] These charitable inclinations were for the most part fulfilled within the traditional framework of care for travellers and pilgrims and the poor and sick, with occasional special distri-butions in times of need. Many of the new houses were located not far from roads and settlements,[136] and their histories and the *Lives* of their founders and early members are filled with references to charitable activities. Stephen of Obazine was said to have contracted debts of over 3,000 solidi (most of which were later forgiven) in order to feed over 3,000 poor men daily between Easter and harvest time during a severe famine.[137] When Waldef, the future abbot of Melrose, was a canon at Nostell and later prior of Kirkham, 'Religion flourished internally in the regular discipline, the distribution of alms, the reception of guests, and great diligence in the display of much humanity', and after he became a Cistercian at Melrose he continued to show charity to the

---

[132] *Vita Mironis*, in *España sagrada*, xxviii, 308 and 312 (*BHL* 5971).
[133] *Consuetudines Cartusiae*, xx, 1 and 6, in [Laporte] (1960–7), iv, 112 and 117; cf. the notes in vi, 349. On Guigo's opposition to works of charity and hospitality, see the anon. article (probably by Maurice Laporte) in *Théologie* (1961), p. 487.
[134] MS London, British Library, Harley 2851, fols. 85ʳ–6ʳ. See Ward and Herbert (1883–1910), ii, 401, 670–1, 748, and iii, 503.
[135] See pp. 148–50 above on the doctrine of charity.
[136] See pp. 120–2 above on the locations of new houses.
[137] *Vita Stephani Obazinensis*, ii, 26, ed. Aubrun, p. 142.

poor and was responsible for a miraculous increase of food during a famine.[138] Pontius of Léras likewise cared for the poor during a famine, and at other times, since 'It was an established custom of that house and those brothers, and held almost as a law, to receive everyone in the hospice, to nourish the needy, to restore the poor, to clothe the naked, to bury the dead, and to carry out other works of mercy and piety.'[139] While passages like this are found in the *Lives* of monastic saints at all times, they are especially prominent in the *Lives* of some of the twelfth-century reformers.

Two points that may be mentioned in particular are the sense of personal obligation attached to charitable activities, which differed from the primarily liturgical character of traditional monastic charity, and the personal identification of the reformers with the sufferings of the poor. The Patarene leader Arialdus of Milan wanted 'to fulfil in action whatever he read in the holy books' and, after washing and drying the feet of a poor man, lay on the ground and put his head under the man's feet, 'and in this way he made the beggar and poor man tread under foot himself [who was] modestly rich'.[140] Stephen of Obazine gave one of his two habits to the children of a poor man in whose house he spent the night; Adelelmus of La Chaise-Dieu devoted himself to the care of the pilgrims, the sick, and the naked while he was still a soldier, before he entered religious life; and Pontius of Léras, regretting his evil actions while he was a knight, gave up his property and appeared on Palm Sunday at Lodève, 'naked and unshod', with a wooden lock around his neck, like a thief, beaten by the man who led him, and confessed his sins publicly to the bishop and people.[141] Here, as in Miro of Ripoll, can be seen the association of self-imposed suffering with concern for the sufferings of others.

These charitable activities inevitably entailed contacts with lay people and work outside the monastic enclosure. The greater freedom of hermits to preach and work in the world was one reason so many reformers chose their type of life. Vitalis of Savigny during his seventeen years as a hermit devoted himself to making peace, providing food and clothing to the poor, giving hospitality, finding husbands for prostitutes, and caring for lepers.[142] This problem was especially acute for religious women, who were considered at the same time to need stricter enclosure than men and to be particularly called to acts of mercy. The widow Paulina 'was so intent on the six works of mercy, such as

---

[138] Jordan (Joscelin) of Furness, *Vita Waldevi Furnesiensis*, II, 21, and IV, 51–9, in *AASS*, 3 Aug. I, 255F and 262D–3F (*BHL* 8783). See Zimmermann, II, 533–5 and 536–7, who called the author Joscelin. The monks of Fountains fed 'great crowds of poor people' during a famine: Hugh of Kirkstall, *Narratio*, ed. Walbran, I, 48.

[139] Hugh of Silvanès, *De conversione Pontii de Larazio*, 16, in Baluze, *Miscellanea*, I, 182.

[140] Andrew of Strumi, *Vita Arialdi*, 15 and 17, in *MGH*, *SS*, XXX.2, 1060 (*BHL* 673).

[141] *Vita Stephani Obazinensis*, II, 39, ed. Aubrun, p. 162; *Vita Adelelmi Casae Dei*, in *España sagrada*, XXVII, 833 (*BHL* 72); and Hugh of Silvanès, *De conversione Pontii de Larazio*, 5, in Baluze, *Miscellanea*, I, 181.

[142] *Rouleaux des morts*, pp. 283–4.

caring for the sick, visiting those in prison, and giving hospitality and other exercises of the active life that in these not many of the conjugal order were superior, even if a few were equal'.[143] Two out of the three acts of charity depicted in the Floreffe Bible are performed by women (plate 2), as are half of those shown around the St Gall door of the cathedral at Basel.[144] The spread of alms-houses, leprosaries, and hospitals, of which many were founded and supported by the laity and run by canons and canonesses, has been called one of the great innovations of the twelfth century.[145] Already before the turn of the century they attracted benefactions that earlier would probably have been given to monasteries, which also had hospices. Ralph of Déols in about 1072 gave the canons of St Silvanus at Levroux (*de Leproso*)

> the men and women belonging to my lordship who are afflicted with the fire of St Silvanus and, hoping to recover their health, seek the protection of the blessed confessors Silvanus and Silvester and of the other saints who rest in that church, and who will lie in the loggia (*porticus*) of that church with others who are ill in the same way.

He also gave their children and the taxes, payments, and customs they owed to him 'in life and in death'.[146] When a division was made at Flône in 1118 between the revenues 'for the hospital of the poor' and for the monks, the charter specified,

> Let no one say that by this division we wished to make parts of one body or two heads, [since] we are striving rather to be together one body and limbs, and since there can and should be no hospice without a church and no church without a hospice, we shall administer the whole more suitably, each carrying the burdens of the other, when the parts of each [house] have been properly distributed.[147]

Though this was specifically called a hospital for the poor and was probably what would today be called an alms-house, various references to hospitals in northern France and the Low Countries show that care was taken of the sick as well as the indigent.[148] The earliest statutes for hospitals and leprosaries

---

[143] Sigeboto, *Vita Paulinae*, 7, in *MGH, SS*, XXX.2, 914 (*BHL* 6551).

[144] See p. 40 n. 178 above.

[145] Fonseca (1962) and Bienvenu (1966–7), (3) p. 202.

[146] *Recueil général des chartes intéressant le département de l'Indre*, ed. E. Hubert (offprint from *Revue archéologique de Berry*; Châteauroux and Paris 1899), p. 191, no. 38. A woman *cruribus contracta et brachiis* lay for many days in the *porticus* of this church, according to the *Miracula s. Silvani*, 5, in *Catalogus codicum hagiographicorum latinorum . . . qui asservantur in Bibliotheca nationali Parisiensi* (Brussels and Paris 1889–93), II, 131. On St Silvanus, see *Vie des saints*, IX, 445–6. The fire of St Silvanus was probably erysipelas, according to Neithard Bulst, but St Silvanus was also appealed to in cases of epilepsy and leprosy.

[147] 'Documents relatifs à l'abbaye de Flône', ed. M. Evrard, in *Analectes pour servir à l'histoire ecclésiastique de la Belgique* 23 (1892), p. 290, no. 5.

[148] See the charters in Miraeus–Foppens, I, 177–8 (1138); II, 963–4 (1124); III, 688–9 (1148); and IV, 514–15 (1140).

date from the second half of the twelfth century and stress the care and consideration to be shown to inmates.[149] The predominance of cures among the miracles of twelfth-century saints, many of whom were religious reformers, also reflects the growing attention given to the sick.

The new monks and canons sometimes performed public works and acted generally for the public benefit. Marbod of Rennes did not say what Robert of La Chaise-Dieu did as a stone-mason, which may have been simply an act of humility, but Guibert of Nogent described a former knight who became a monk at Flaix and asked permission, when he was sent to a cell in the Vexin, 'to restore the road of public travel, which had broken down'.[150] The pious lay man Werimbold repaired and maintained bridges and abolished tolls in addition to rebuilding and endowing the hospital for the poor at Cambrai, and Raymond of Toulouse built a hospice and two bridges at Toulouse.[151] Wulfstan of Worcester by his preaching promoted peace and the abolition of the slave trade between Bristol and Ireland, and Norbert as a young man combined preaching with reconciling enemies and 'bringing established dislikes and wars to peace'.[152] Hamo of Savigny, who died in 1179, persuaded kings, princes, and nobles to build churches, chapels, and bridges, to help the poor, and to perform 'other works of mercy'. In 1167 he intervened to make peace between Henry II and Louis VII, and later he imposed on Henry a penance that included clothing 300 poor men.[153] This type of involvement in public affairs can be seen on a large scale in Bernard of Clairvaux and on a small scale in the hermit Wulfric of Hazelbury, who worked as a local ombudsman.[154]

Activities of this kind were nothing new for medieval saints and holy men, whose role as mediators was well established in medieval society and still persists in some parts of the Mediterranean world.[155] Abbots were more and more involved in public affairs since the time of the Carolingians,[156] and in the twelfth century Suger of St Denis and Wibald of Corvey were among the

---

[149] See the statutes for the hospital at Aubrac (1162), 1–2, and the Hôtel-Dieu at Angers (*c.* 1200), 8, in *Statuts d'Hôtels-Dieu et de léproseries*, ed. Léon le Grand (CTSEEH 32; Paris 1901), pp. 16–17 and 24.

[150] Guibert, *De vita sua*, I, 21, ed. Bourgin, p. 81.

[151] *Gesta pontificum Cameracensium*, ed. C. de Smedt (Société de l'histoire de France; Paris 1880), pp. 130–7 (see p. 99 above), and *Vita Raimundi Tolosani*, ed. C. Douais, in *Bulletin de la Société archéologique du Midi de la France* 13–14 (1894), pp. 160–1. Raymond, who was active from about 1080 to 1118, was a cantor at St Saturninus but married 'lest he break out in worse things' and later became a canon of St Saturninus. For references to bridge-building in the *Moniage Guillaume*, see Schenck (1984), pp. 170 and 175.

[152] William of Malmesbury, *Vita Wulfstani*, II, 15, 16, and 20, ed. R.R. Darlington (Camden Society 3 S. 40; London 1928), pp. 38, 40, and 43–4, and *Vita [B] Norberti*, V, 27, and VI, 31–6, in *PL*, CLXX, 1276A and 1278B–82A.

[153] *Vita Hamonis Saviniacensis*, 20, 27, and 33, ed. E.P. Sauvage, in *Anal. boll.* 2 (1883), pp. 523–4, 532, and 536 (*BHL* 3752).

[154] Mayr-Harting (1975).

[155] Brown (1979) and Black-Michaud (1975), pp. 94–5.

[156] Felten (1980), p. 80; cf. pp. 140–1 and 174.

most influential statesmen of their day. The responsibilities of these men were to some extent the result of their positions as heads of great monasteries, whereas many of the reformers, who avoided obligations of this type and sought to leave the world, were at the same time driven by a seemingly irresistible inner urge to improve it by preaching, advising, and working actively to promote the salvation and ameliorate the conditions of those still living in the world. The new orders, as Joachim of Fiore saw it, thus mediated in God's work of ushering in a new and better age, both actively through their work among lay men and passively through their contemplation. The most impressive examples of the formal combination of worldly activity and a religious vocation were the military orders and the lay brothers and sisters, who were occupied, within the scope of a consecrated life, with activities that would previously have been regarded as suitable only for the laity. There is a logical connection between Bernard's descriptions of himself as a chimera, who was neither a cleric nor a lay man and who had given up the monastic way of life but not the habit, and of the Templars as both monks and soldiers, since each expressed his sense of the novelty and incongruity, in traditional terms, of what amounted to new forms of religious life.[157] Regular canons combined the qualities of monks and clerics, and lay brothers were at the same time monks and peasants, since for them agricultural activity, like fighting in the military orders, took the place of worship and prayer in the life of monks.[158]

The new houses were therefore involved with the outside world owing both to the desires of some of their members and to the requirements of material existence. In particular they could not escape connections with their benefactors, whose gifts entitled them, at least in their own eyes, to special consideration, and with bishops, whose authority over the religious houses in their dioceses was generally recognized by the reformers. During the early Middle Ages, and especially in the tenth and eleventh centuries, many monasteries had been granted privileges guaranteeing the right to control their property and internal affairs, especially the selection of a superior. This was often combined with the delegation to the officials known as advocates of immediate control over external affairs, including the exercise of jurisdiction and performance of military service and other public responsibilities. These grants were regarded as measures of reform designed to protect monasteries from undue interference in their affairs by local magnates, secular or ecclesiastical, since bishops tended to abuse their powers over monasteries. The privileges concerned with secular powers are commonly called immunities and those concerned with episcopal powers, exemptions, but the distinction, though useful, is not rigid. Grants of this type were made by popes, emperors, and kings and also by bishops and lay lords, such as William of Aquitaine, who

---

[157] Bernard, *Ep.* 250.4, ed. Leclercq, VIII, 147, and *De laude novae militiae*, ed. Leclercq, III, 213–39.
[158] See pp. 74–5 and 77–80 above on the military orders and lay brothers.

in his foundation charter for Cluny established an influential model for monastic reform in the west by freeing the monks from the worldly power of himself and his family and of all secular and ecclesiastical authorities and putting it under the immediate protection of the apostles Peter and Paul and the papacy.[159] A monastery with a privilege of this type was called free. The earliest references to the *libertas monasticae religionis* are found in the privileges granted by Louis the Pious to monasteries in the first half of the ninth century.[160] From about the middle of the ninth century monasteries began to be granted to the Roman church and put under papal protection, which was variously called *tuitio*, *protectio*, and *defensio*.[161] Over the years various types of liberties developed that were identified with the authority that granted or guaranteed them, or the region or monastery with which they were associated. Thus there were Roman (or papal), imperial, and royal liberties; regional liberties granted by archbishops and bishops, especially in the empire, and by a few secular princes.[162] There were also what may be called congregational liberties, like those of Cluny and, in spite of the hostility of the reformers to special monastic privileges, of Cîteaux and Prémontré.

The monastic sources of the eleventh and twelfth centuries are filled with references to liberty in the sense of the privileges of a particular religious house or group of houses. References to general liberties such as the *libertas Romana*, *libertas Cluniacensis*, or *libertas Moguntinensis* are also found, though less frequently, and as constitutional concepts they have been largely constructed by later scholars on the basis of individual privileges. Besides the question of who granted them, the three key questions about them – to which there are still no clear answers – are what they contained, to whom they applied, and by whom they were guaranteed. To these is connected the more general question of whose interests they served, since it is not always certain who took the initiative in issuing a privilege, how it was drawn up, or even, when it was given to a monastery with dependencies, exactly to whom it applied.[163] It may seem obvious now that the monasteries themselves sought such privileges – and it is clear that in many cases they did, even to the point of drawing up a text for approval – but they also served the interests of the

---

[159] *Chartes de Cluny*, I, 126–7, no. 112. Boshof (1976), p. 99, considered this charter to be in the tradition of grants to monasteries in the west Frankish kingdom in the second half of the ninth century.

[160] Büttner (1957), pp. 20–2.

[161] Boshof (1976), pp. 20, 76, etc. On royal monasteries in Germany in the tenth and eleventh centuries, see Bernhardt (1993), esp. pp. 70–5.

[162] Such as the so-called liberties of Cologne, Mainz, Speyer, and Worms in the Rhineland and of Passau, Bamberg, and Salzburg in the east. See Dereine (1965) on Cambrai; Erkens (1987), pp. 38–40, on Trier; and Jordan (1941–2) on the monastic policy of Henry the Lion, which was one of the best examples of a regional liberty guaranteed by a secular prince.

[163] These questions were raised in a comprehensive manner by Schreiber (1910) and were also studied by Stengel (1910) and Brackmann (1912), esp. in his review of Schreiber in the *Göttingische gelehrte Anzeigen* 175 (1913), pp. 275–90.

grantors and guarantors. The patrons and benefactors of a new house, for instance, often sought to have their rights over it embodied in a privilege issued by a lofty authority. From this point of view, the rule observed by the house, or the order to which it belonged, was less important than its local position and immediate needs in determining the nature of a privilege,[164] which was designed for the particular house to which it was granted even when it followed a common pattern and used common formulas. Among these the most frequent were the right to own and control its property and to select, sometimes subject to the approval of the grantor, its abbot, monastic officials, and advocate. Some privileges seem to have been directed primarily against lay proprietary rights and the institution of advocacy, whereas others, especially those granted by the papacy, were concerned more with the powers of the diocesan bishop and guaranteed the control of the monks over their internal affairs.[165] The privileges often overlapped and occasionally conflicted; some were forged; and many are lost. Liberty for these houses was a practical as well as a theoretical matter, as abbot Peregrinus of Fontaines-les-Blanches recognized when he said that his house had a triple liberty, of which one part came from the Holy Spirit and was embodied in the Gospels, the second part was contained in the papal privileges both for Fontaines and for Cîteaux and Savigny, and the third part consisted of the grants of nobles, bishops, and other 'worldly powers', as he called them.[166] Without a complete series of these privileges it is often impossible to establish the position of a monastery in its regional setting and its relation not only to local lords and the diocesan bishop but also to the pope and king and to a monastic order and other houses.

One way to protect a religious house was to establish a *salvatio* or safe area around it. In 1080 cardinal-bishop Peter of Albano, acting on behalf of Gregory VII, established an area around Cluny within which no act of violence could be committed. He forbade anyone to attack or disturb Cluny, its inhabitants, or 'those fleeing within the established boundaries'; he abolished all bad customs and warned 'the soldiers (*milites*) living in the villa of Cluny' to make no trouble, especially 'because the closer they live the more they should avoid injuring the servants of God'.[167] 'The boundaries of the sacred ban' and 'certain limits of immunity and security' were redefined by Urban II in 1095 and confirmed and extended by Lucius II in 1144.[168] A more modest *salvatio* was established around the church of Meunet, which had suffered 'many bad

---

[164] Mois (1953), pp. 2–3, 51–6, and 149, studied the case of the Rottenbuch, which, though a house of canons, had privileges like those of Hirsau and resembled in its constitutional position one of the papal proprietary monasteries in Swabia.

[165] Cf. Anton (1975), esp. pp. 89–92.

[166] Peregrinus, *Historia*, II, *praef.*, ed. Salmon, pp. 273–4.

[167] *Bibl. Clun.*, col. 512BD; *Chartes de Cluny*, IV, 677, no. 3549. See Constable (1992c), p. 156.

[168] *Bibl. Clun.*, coll. 518–20 and 1383B–4A; *Chartes de Cluny*, V, 41 and 439, nos. 3689 and 4085 (JL, I, 681 and 8621).

things' from the brothers Tedbad and Odo of Issoudun, with whom the abbot of St Sulpicius at Bourges agreed that an archer acting for the monastery should shoot an arrow in all directions from the choir of the church and that a cross should be placed where the arrows landed 'as a sign of the *salvatio* of that church'. No one living within the area owed any service or obligation to the brothers, who kept their rights, however, over any of their dependants (*consuetudinarii*) who moved into the area. They gave up all other rights within the area and agreed to use no force there so that 'Everything may remain safe and peaceful.'[169] Both sides gained in this agreement. The monastery got a promise of security and peace for its church; the lay lords got, in addition to fifty shillings, a recognition of their rights over their men who lived outside the *salvatio* and who moved into it.

Every freedom and protection in the Middle Ages involved a corresponding dependency, and through the concessions and privileges granted to monasteries the patrons and donors acquired rights as well as obligations.[170] In Lorraine, for instance, the royal *libertas* given to monasteries in the tenth and eleventh centuries involved a strict dependence on the king, and a noble who made a grant of a regular abbacy did not necessarily give up all of his powers over a monastery.[171] In central Italy in the eleventh century even explicit guarantees of freedom in foundation charters did not exclude implicit control by the founders and their descendents.[172] The key questions in the dispute over the patronage of the nunnery of Rosano near Florence, in which evidence covering the entire twelfth century was given, were who founded and endowed the house and had the church consecrated, who defended it, who controlled or consented to the appointment and removal of the superior, who had rights to hospitality, who received and made grants from the nuns' property, to whom oaths and fealty were made, and for whom prayers were offered.[173] The patronage of churches was thus an economic and political as well as religious matter.[174]

This is not to say that all grants of property and privileges to monasteries were motivated by worldly considerations. The explicit purpose was almost always to promote the spiritual welfare of the donors and their families by means of prayers, liturgical commemoration, burial, admission, or some other sort of association with the community, though these motives also had their

---

[169] *Essai de reconstitution du cartulaire A de Saint-Sulpice de Bourges*, ed. Louis de Kersers (Mémoires de la Société des antiquaires du Centre 35; Bourges 1913), p. 201, no. 108.

[170] Howe (1988), pp. 334–6 ('Piety and profit were not necessarily seen as incompatible'), and Holdsworth (1991), p. 5.

[171] Margue (1988), p. 56, and Parisse (1989), pp. 189–90. See generally Boshof (1976), p. 5.

[172] Howe (1992), pp. 20 ('Guarantees of monastic independence . . . may not always be what they appear') and 30–3.

[173] Passerini (1876–7), pp. 209–10, 215–16, 342, 391, 398, etc.

[174] See, on England, Chibnall (1988) and Holdsworth (1991), pp. 8–9.

self-serving side and imposed obligations on the members of the house.[175] For this reason many lay men took a serious interest in the standard of life in the monasteries with which they were associated. It is a mistake to see the clergy as supporters and the laity as opponents of religious reform in the eleventh and twelfth centuries. The contrary was probably closer to the truth, and some of the most ardent supporters of the reform movement were found among lay men who believed that their spiritual welfare depended upon their support for monasteries. They were naturally encouraged in this belief by the clergy. In about 1145 Roger of Valognes confirmed a grant of a third of a knight's fief made to the priory of Binham by his father Peter and his kinsman Walter 'before he was made a monk'. Roger made the grant for the souls of his father, mother, himself, and his wife and children and 'for the common salvation of all our men both living and dead' and also on the advice of many wise men, including archbishop Theobald of Canterbury,

> who showed me by reasonable and very true arguments that it was very just for a noble and generous man who has a fief of six knights to grant to God and the holy church for the salvation of himself and his men the land not only of a third part of a knight but also of an entire knight and more, and who added that if his heir tries to take away the gift that acts almost like a bridge, by which his father may cross, between the father and paradise and if the heir as much as he can disinherits his father from the celestial kingdom, then he who has shown himself not to be a son, because he killed his father, will not justly obtain the rest of the inheritance.[176]

This charter shows the difficulty of guaranteeing the permanence of grants to monasteries, which needed constant support and protection to defend their possessions and privileges. Great and distant protectors like popes and kings were not always very effective on a local level, and were not perhaps intended to be at the time a privilege was granted, when the monks were probably more concerned with the freedoms granted by a privilege than with their defence. The early grants of Roman liberty, like that of Cluny, stressed the protection of the apostles as much as that of the pope, and communities regularly looked to their patron saints for protection. During the eleventh and twelfth centuries, the influence on the local level of both the papacy and the monarchies expanded, partly through the monasteries that sought their support and protection and, in the case of the papacy, paid a small annual rent as a sign of dependency and the privileges it guaranteed.[177] Some of the regional diocesan liberties in the empire gave back to the bishops, through their right to approve the choice of abbots and advocates, powers that they had lost, or had been

---

[175] 'The acquisition of spiritual capital rivalled in importance the acquisition of material capital', according to White (1988), p. 152. See also Bouchard (1987), pp. 229–44; Howe (1988), pp. 332–3; Holdsworth (1991); and, on the empire, Arnold (1991), pp. 62 and 145.
[176] Stenton (1961), pp. 260–1, with a translation and discussion on pp. 38–40.
[177] See Lemarignier (1950) and (1957).

severely curtailed, by papal privileges of exemption.[178] Above all, through the institution of advocacy, lay men who had started as officials concerned with carrying out the secular responsibilities of religious communities became in the course of time protectors who exercised a wide variety of jurisdictional and quasi-governmental powers technically in the name of the institution but increasingly in their own name as hereditary holders of the position.

The very privileges of immunity and exemption that were designed to protect monasteries from interference in their affairs were thus often a source of further problems, and they roused the hostility of reformers in the early years of the reform movement.[179] Bernard of Clairvaux sharply criticized exemption in his treatise *On consideration*, which was addressed to pope Eugene III, and in other works.[180] And the Cistercian authors of the 'invective' against Cluny asserted that its freedom from the diocesan bishop was absurd, unjust, and opposed to both the law of the church and 'the custom of the whole world': 'For where do you get chrism? Holy orders? The consecration of churches and the blessing of cemeteries? Or lastly all those things that cannot be performed canonically without a bishop or the order of a bishop? Certainly in these things you exceed the rule not only of monks but also of all Christians.' These questions were largely rhetorical, since the Cistercians were certainly aware of exemption, even if they disapproved of it, but they reflected a widespread feeling that it was a source of pride and irregularity among monks, who in accordance with the decree of the council of Chalcedon should be subject to the diocesan bishop. Peter the Venerable in his reply argued that Cluny had always been subject only to the pope and authorized to receive 'chrism, oil, holy orders, the consecrations of churches and cemeteries, and other similar things from any catholic bishop' and also that the apostolic see had granted similar rights to many monasteries before and after Cluny. He cited in particular two letters of Gregory the Great showing that the purpose of the privilege was to protect monks from the oppression of bishops.[181]

Both positions were historically correct, but they referred to different periods of history: the reformers looked back to the early church, when monasteries were brought under the control of bishops, and the black monks to the period from the sixth to the eleventh century, when bishops frequently abused their powers over monks. By the early twelfth century, largely as a consequence of the reform movement of the previous century, the situation had again changed, and a new generation of bishops, who took their pastoral powers and responsibilities more seriously than their predecessors, raised their

---

[178] See Semmler (1959), pp. 198–212, on the *libertas Coloniensis*.
[179] On episcopal opposition to exemption, see the material gathered (from a Gallican point of view) by de Marca (1708), pp. 311–12.
[180] Bernard, *De consideratione*, IV, 14, and *Ep.* 42 (*De officio episcoporum*), IX, 33–7, ed. Leclercq, III, 442, and VII, 127–31. See Jacqueline (1953) and Bligny (1960), pp. 364–5, who suggested that Bernard's opposition to exemption was a personal policy.
[181] Peter the Venerable, *Ep.* 28, ed. Constable, I, 56 and 79–81.

voices against the independence of monasteries. And they now met with a more sympathetic response from the papacy, which had previously tended to support the monks against the bishops and to treat any episcopal efforts to infringe the rights of an exempt house as an affront to its own authority. Cluny's problems under abbot Pontius in the early twelfth century, and his eventual deposition, may be in part attributable to this change and particularly to the fact that Calixtus II, who had been archbishop of Vienne, may have shared the bishops' feelings about the extent of Cluny's privileges, in spite of his close connections with Cluny and with Pontius personally.[182] The reformed monks were not therefore alone in their opposition to monastic exemption. Gilbert of La Porrée was cited in the *Abbreviated word* of Peter the Chanter as having said that exempt abbots were schismatics,[183] and Peter of Blois, writing to pope Alexander III in the name of archbishop Richard of Canterbury in about 1180, bitterly attacked monastic exemptions and abbots who refused to obey their archbishops and bishops:

> We know that many Roman pontiffs granted these exemptions on account of the quiet of monasteries and the tyranny of bishops, but matters have now been reversed. For monasteries that have obtained the benefit of this most damnable liberty, either by apostolic authority or, which is more frequent, by adulterated bulls, incur greater unquiet, disobedience, and need; and therefore many houses that are most outstanding in holiness and religion either wish never to have these immunities or immediately reject those that they have.[184]

The control by monasteries over parish churches was a particular thorn in the side of the bishops, who felt, not without justice, that it interfered with their responsibility for the cure of souls. The reform movement thus had the double and in some respects paradoxical effect, as Schreiber pointed out, of increasing both the number of parish churches held by monks and the pressure from bishops to renew the old rulings concerning their control over the cure of souls.[185] The bishops on the whole objected less to the possession of churches in itself than to the appointment and control of parish priests, who were thus removed from the normal framework of diocesan authority. Though this was not normally part of exemption, it was protected by the freedom from episcopal control of exempt houses and added fuel to the bishops' dislike

---

[182] On Pontius, the episcopate, and Calixtus II, see White (1958); Tellenbach (1963), esp. pp. 31–6; Fresco (1973), pp. 138–40; and for a different view, the reprinted articles of Bredero (1985), esp. pp. 27–113 and 277–326, who dated the opposition to Cluniac privileges from the time of Hugh and saw Pontius as a reformer whose policies fostered opposition at Cluny and in the Roman curia.

[183] Peter the Chanter, *Verbum abbreviatum*, 44, in *PL*, CCV, 139D.

[184] Peter of Blois, *Ep.* 68, ed. J.A. Giles (Bibliotheca patrum ecclesiae Anglicanae 5; Oxford 1847), I, 204–5. Earlier in the letter he complained (in Richard's name) that whereas Rome owned many monasteries, Canterbury had only St Augustine's, which the pope had now usurped. Gerald of Wales also criticized exemption, mentioning Bernard's opposition, in the *Speculum ecclesiae*, II, 16–17, ed. Brewer (n. 86), IV, 60–3.

[185] Schreiber (1910), II, 17.

for the high-handed ways of monks. The compromises that were made in the eleventh and early twelfth centuries paralleled in many respects the great compromise which was worked out at the same time between the church and the empire concerning investitures and were based on a distinction between the spiritual and temporal aspects of the priestly position.[186] This was spelled out in a bull of Calixtus II for the church of Modena in 1121, which confirmed the decision of Urban II

> concerning the priests who are appointed to the churches in the parishes belonging to monasteries ... that the abbots should not install priests in the parish churches that they hold without the advice of the bishops, but the bishops should commit the cure of the parish to the priest with the consent of the abbots in such a way that the priests may be accountable to the bishop for the cure of the parish and may be subject to the abbot for the temporal possessions belonging to the monastery, and thus the rights of each will be preserved.[187]

A similar arrangement was worked out a few years later when the parish church of Bertrée in the diocese of Liège was given as a priory to Cluny. The prior owned the prebend of the parish priest and after consultation presented it to a suitable priest, who was responsible to the archdeacon, as the representative of the bishop, 'for the investiture of the altar, the cure of souls, and his own sins'.[188] The rights of the monastery, like those of a lay proprietor, were thus restricted to patronage or presentation, which concerned the secular property rather than the spiritual office of the priest and which was more acceptable to bishops and reformers than the powers previously exercised by monasteries.[189] By the middle of the twelfth century, as the passage cited above from Gerald of Wales's *Mirror of the church* shows, most of the reformed orders had abandoned their early opposition to the possession of churches.

When the reformers were faced with the realities of episcopal visitation and control, they also revised their views on exemption. Bernard of Clairvaux's opposition to the Cluniac candidate for the bishopric of Langres in 1138 may have been motivated in part by his sense of the need for a sympathetic bishop in the diocese in which Clairvaux was situated,[190] and in his treatise *On precept and dispensation* Bernard defined with care the legitimate sphere of ecclesiastical authority over monasteries. The privileges for individual Cistercian houses therefore embodied specific rights based both on the needs of each house and

---

[186] See Constable (1977a), p. 214 and references there, and Avril (1976–80), p. 461, who discussed the distinction between *temporalia* and *spiritualia* in eleventh-century charters applying to parishes.

[187] *PL*, CLXIII, 1201A, and Robert, *Bullaire* (n. 124), I, 321, no. 219 (JL 6894). See JL 5751 for the sentence of Urban II.

[188] *Chartes de Cluny*, V, 336, no. 3976. See Constable (1977a) and Dereine (1983b) on grants of monasteries to Cluny in the Hesbaye and Hainault.

[189] The standard work on patronage and presentation is Thomas (1906). See also Kurze (1966), esp. pp. 474–90 on England, France, and Spain, and Hyams (1987) on England.

[190] Constable (1957).

on the principles set forth in the founding documents of the order (which were themselves revised to reflect its needs) and in the statutes of the general chapters.[191] In effect they restricted without abolishing the ordinary rights of bishops in matters like the election and consecration of abbots, visitation, and diocesan synods.[192] The 'exemption' of the Cistercians was thus based on a series of individual privileges. Cistercian abbeys remained technically subject to the bishops and swore obedience to them, but they enjoyed a degree of practical independence that was hardly less than that of exempt houses.[193]

The regular canons were likewise never given a formal grant of exemption, but they received privileges that varied from region to region and in effect guaranteed their freedom from diocesan bishops. In the first of his two privileges of 1090 and 1092 for the canons of Rottenbuch Urban II said that they should receive ordinations, consecrations, and chrism from the bishop of Freising, their diocesan, provided he was in communication with the see of Rome, and, if he was not, from any bishop. Since the bishop of Freising was excommunicated at that time, and throughout the Investiture Controversy, Rottenbuch had effectively the same freedom in these matters as the Cluniacs.[194] A similar privilege subjecting the canons to the diocesan bishop only if he was in communion with Rome was granted by Honorius II in 1128 to Floreffe (and expanded by Innocent II in 1138 to permit it otherwise to go to any bishop) and by Innocent II in 1134 to Frankenthal, which was the earliest house of strict regular canons in the middle Rhine area.[195] The provost of Steinfeld was authorized by the archbishop of Cologne to hold synods and exercise power in its parish 'unless something happens requiring the presence of the bishop', and its parish and two others were freed 'from all census and episcopal service or synod'. Gottesgnaden was freed by the archbishop of Magdeburg from all obligations except attending the episcopal council.[196] Innocent II confirmed these privileges respectively in 1136 and 1138, when he also gave Prémontré the right to celebrate mass during a diocesan interdict 'with excommunicates excluded and the doors closed'.[197] These grants of mis-

---

[191] Brackmann (1912), p. 78: 'Selbst der Inhalt der Privilegien für die Cisterzienserklöster ist in dieser Zeit recht verschieden gestaltet . . . Was das Formular bestimmt, ist durchaus die besondere Rechtslage des einzelnen Stiftes, nicht das *privilegium commune* des Ordens.' Pfurtscheller (1972), on the other hand, concluded (pp. 147–8) that the *privilegium commune* applied to all Cistercian houses from the beginning.

[192] Mahn (1945), pp. 89–101, and Pfurtscheller (1972), pp. 37–66 and 89–128.

[193] Mahn (1945), pp. 81–4 and 119–52, and Schreiber (1948b).

[194] Mois (1953), pp. 55–66. On the reception of gifts from excommunicates, see Mordek (1983), p. 200.

[195] Hugo, *Annales* (n. 125), I.1, lii–iii (JL 7323 and 7924), and Semmler (1956), pp. 109–10.

[196] These are known from papal confirmations issued in 1136 and 1138 respectively: Hugo, *Annales* (n. 125), I.1, dxxii (JL 7801) and dxcvi (JL 7921). In 1138 and 1139 Innocent II freed Vicogne and Averbode from all obligations except the episcopal synod: ibid., I.2, dclxxxiii (JL 7925), and I.1, cxvi (JL 8000).

[197] Ibid., I.1, xiii (JL 7926). Weinfurter (1977), pp. 89–96, called this the *libertas Praemonstratensis*, on which the later *libertas Magdeburgensis* was based.

cellaneous privileges culminated in 1148 in the great charter of Eugene III for Etival, which was completely removed from the authority of the bishop and given quasi-episcopal powers.[198] Together these privileges, granted by both bishops and popes, established a practical exemption that safeguarded the right of the canons to live in accordance with their customs. Most of these charters came from the empire, where their development matched the broader pattern of papal grants to monasteries. Of the total of ninety grants of papal protection to monasteries in Bavaria, three date from the eleventh century, fifteen from the first quarter of the twelfth century, forty-four from the second quarter, and twenty-eight from the second half.[199] Such grants were less common in France and rare in England, where relatively few houses of regular canons were exempt.[200]

Lay advocates presented an even greater threat than bishops to the independence of religious houses, even when they were technically appointed by and subject to the control of the community.[201] The terminology of advocacy, protection, custody, defence, jurisdiction, and guard (*tuito*, and later *ditio* and *guarda*), and of the various people who exercised these powers, and their deputies, is immensely complicated and is only beginning to be clarified by computer-based studies of their use in particular regions. An analysis for the area of modern Belgium has shown that up to the year 1000 *advocatio* was still basically a monastic office, while *protectio* and *tuitio* were associated with immunity as aspects of public authority, but that after 1000, and especially in the twelfth century, their use and meaning began to overlap.[202] The term advocate also continued to be used in the non-technical sense of assistant and supporter, as in a charter for Nostell in 1121/7 from Henry I, who wished 'always to have the poor of Christ as advocates in the heavenly court'.[203] The question is further complicated by the use of modern terms like *Reichsvogtei*, *Herrenvogtei*, *Kastvogtei*, *Schirmvogtei*, and *Schutzvogtei* for particular types of advocacy, such as noble or seigniorial advocacy (when a house had more than one advocate), protective advocacy without jurisdiction, and general protection by a ruler or king.[204] It is clear in a general way, however, that most monasteries, and particularly those in the empire, including those that wanted to be free from lay contacts and controls, occasionally required assistance in administering their estates and protecting them from enemies and were therefore willing to have a protector upon whom they could when necessary call

[198] Hugo, *Annales* (n. 125), I.2, dxlv–vi (JL 9128), cited pp. 234–5 and n. 127 above.
[199] Bauerreiss (1949–70), III, 103.
[200] Dickinson (1950), p. 162.
[201] In addition to the works cited below, see the regional studies cited in *Medieval Monasticism*, nos. 639–51, esp. the work of Senn (1903) on France.
[202] Genicot (1984b).
[203] *Early Yorkshire Charters*, ed. William Farrer, continued by Charles T. Clay (Yorkshire Archaeological Society. Record Series. Extra Series 1–10; [Wakefield] 1936–65), III, 130, no. 1428.
[204] On some of these terms, see Tellenbach (1928), pp. 143–7, and Mayer (1950), p. 213.

for help. On this basis many lay lords were able to establish a measure of control over monasteries, even though its exact form varied from region to region and time to time.

The attitude of the reformers towards advocacy varied between England, France, and the empire. As an institution advocacy was unknown in England and Normandy, owing both to the power of the dukes, who kept high justice in their own hands, and to the action of the Gregorian reformers.[205] Some of the rights over monasteries asserted by nobles during the reign of Stephen, however, resembled those of advocates on the continent, and they may have represented a parallel effort to establish regional principalities.[206] But the term advocacy and its English derivative advowson referred primarily to the right of patronage and presentation, not to the types of powers exercised by advocates elsewhere. Also in France, advocacy as such did not present a major problem for monasteries in the twelfth century, though from time to time vague claims to protection and guard were put forward by powerful lords. Some lay lords had given up voluntarily, or under pressure from the reformers, the powers that they had previously exercised.[207] In the Narbonnais, the advocates remained monastic functionaries who were responsible for representing their institutions before public tribunals and never developed into hereditary noble protectors, and in Burgundy, where advocates acted mainly as ad hoc protectors, both the institution and term *advocatus* disappeared in the twelfth century.[208] Many monasteries, like Cluny, never had an advocate. Its appeal for help to Louis VII in the 1160s was based on his responsibilities as king rather than as the special protector of Cluny.

The situation was entirely different in the empire, where rulers and lords in the eleventh and twelfth centuries used the institution of advocacy to extend their jurisdiction and powers over lands belonging to monasteries, which were centres of family influence as well as of intercessory prayer and burial.[209] Such monasteries are referred to by German historians as *Adelskloster*, *Dynastenkloster*, *Familienkloster*, *Hauskloster*, *Stammkloster*, and *Sippekloster* in order to emphasize their close connection with noble families and clans, and also as *Pfalzstifte* when they were actually founded in the chapel of a familial castle

---

[205] Yver (1963–4) and Hyams (1987), pp. 451–2.
[206] King (1984), p. 137. It may be significant that the prelates who opposed these developments came from the circle of the Cluniac bishop Henry of Winchester.
[207] See Magnou (1964), pp. 126–9, on Moissac, where the old lay rights of *dominium* were replaced by patronage in the eleventh and twelfth centuries, and Guillot (1972), pp. 128–61, on the relations of the count of Anjou with the abbey of St Albinus at Angers.
[208] Magnou-Nortier (1974), pp. 623–7, and Richard (1954), pp. 68–71.
[209] Advocacy in Germany was two centuries behind that in Lorraine, northern France, and Flanders, according to Mayer (1950), pp. 185–214, and spread in the Low Countries from the eleventh to the thirteenth centuries, according to de Moreau (1946–52), II, 222–3. See Wollasch (1987) on the concept of the *Hauskloster* and the close relations between noble, episcopal, and reformed monastic circles in south Germany in the eleventh century; Leyser (1988), p. 160; Arnold (1991), pp. 84, 145, 164, and 196; and Reynolds (1994), pp. 445–6, on the tendency in the empire for advocacies to become benefices.

or *castrum*, which then had the combined character of a centre of religious as well as political power.[210] The position of advocate in these houses was as a rule hereditary within the family of the founder, which was able in return for continued protection and support to exercise jurisdiction over the monastery's lands, to pocket some of its revenues, and frequently to influence or control the choice of the superior and other monastic officials. Through the institution of advocacy many families were able to salvage some of the powers and revenues that they had lost during the Investiture Controversy as a result of the attack on lay rights over churches.[211]

The struggle of monasteries in the empire to limit and control the hydra-headed monster of lay influence ran parallel in its nature and course to the Investiture Controversy. While ideally the monasteries might have liked to abolish lay rights altogether, they had to balance their desire for independence against their need for protection, and their efforts were directed towards limiting the power of advocates and establishing control over their appointment. They forged documents when they had to; they revised charters and histories to play down the role of a founder whose heirs might claim rights; and they turned elsewhere for help when they could. When on one occasion in the late eleventh century the canons of St Servatius at Maastricht were unable by their own efforts to recover an estate which the count of Louvain had given to one of his knights, 'It at last pleased the blessed Servatius to act as an advocate for himself.' He therefore appeared in a vision to a hermit who so frightened the knight by predicting his uncle's death that he not only restored the estate but gave his other property to the canons and went on a pilgrimage to Compostela.[212] Monasteries tried in particular to restrict the power of advocates to the jurisdiction that monks were unable to exercise themselves and to limit their emoluments to the profits from this justice, often defined as the third penny. In order to prevent the division of advocacy and the appointment of sub-advocates, the monks also asserted their right to appoint as advocate preferably whomever they wished but at least a single member of the founder's family. Some monasteries tried to transfer the responsibilities of the advocate to their own ministerials or officials drawn from the monastic *familia* of unfree lay dependants, thus in effect restoring the situation that had existed in the ninth and tenth centuries, when advocates had been monastic officials without any independent powers. The ministerials were no less likely to abuse their powers than the advocates, however, and the monks sometimes found that

---

[210] Genicot (1965), pp. 98–9 and 122: 'Les abbayes n'ont pas été pour les dynastes que des mausolées, quand ils les dotaient, ou des foyers d'intercession, quand ils les enrichissaient. Elles ont été aussi des points d'appui, des centres d'influence; elles ont fourni aux territoires une de leurs pierres angulaires.' Störmer (1973), pp. 357–74, discussed the *Sippenklöster* as the *Herrschaftsobjekt* of the founding family.

[211] See in particular Hirsch (1967).

[212] *Gesta s. Servatii*, 58, ed. Friedrich Wilhelm (Munich 1910), p. 136 (*BHL* 7637).

they had jumped from the frying pan into the fire.[213] Another risky step was to seek an over-advocate who was sufficiently powerful and prestigious to frighten potential oppressors but too far away, or too busy, to oppress the monks himself. Some territorial rulers, including ecclesiastics, used this sort of general or 'umbrella' advocacy (known as *Schutz-* or *Schirmvogtei*) to promote their own interest. During the first half of the twelfth century the monastic liberty of Mainz in effect replaced the power of lay advocates by combining the ecclesiastical and secular authority of the archbishop, who exercised a general advocacy over all the monasteries in his diocese.[214]

The standard-bearers in the struggle to bring advocacy under control in Germany in the second half of the eleventh century were the Cluniac and neo-Cluniac houses that directly or indirectly drew on the Cluniac tradition of having no advocate but sought to restrict rather than abolish the institution.[215] The contrast can be seen between the two Cluniac houses of Romainmôtier and Peterlingen, which were located not far from each other respectively in the modern Franche-Comté and in Switzerland. Romainmôtier had no advocate after it was granted to Cluny, while Peterlingen had an advocate chosen by the monastery and installed by the abbot of Cluny.[216] In the diocese of Mainz the main effort was to abolish lay control and to guarantee free choice of the abbot and advocate.[217] Even the alleged charter of archbishop Siegfried for Hasungen in 1082, in which the canons 'by divine inspiration chose the order of the most holy religion of Cluny', and which, as a forgery made about 1100, might have omitted any reference to an advocate, provided for the choice of the advocate and limited his powers to justice and judgement.[218] A few years later the advocacy of the new Cluniac priory of Bertrée was held, through the prior, from the church of Cluny by the founder's brother and his heirs. They were obliged to uphold the provisions of the foundation charter, to protect the liberty of the allod, and to defend it from evil men. They were forbidden to appoint any other advocate or sub-advocate and had no authority over the church's men and no jurisdiction unless specifically summoned by the monks. In return the advocate received half of the

---

[213] See p. 113 on the ministerials who threatened to resist to the death the reform of Tegernsee.
[214] Mayer (1950), p. 207, and Falck (1956), pp. 27 and 58, who said (p. 39) that after 1133 the term *libertas* disappeared and was replaced by *protectio*.
[215] Hallinger (1950–1), pp. 258–9, and 573–97, and Bulst (1973), pp. 198–201.
[216] Chapuis (1940), pp. 191–209, esp. 191–201 on Romainmôtier; Mayer (1963), esp. pp. 84–5 and 114 on the advocacy of Peterlingen; Büttner (1964), p. 284 (Peterlingen); Endemann (1967), pp. 7–29 (Romainmôtier) and 33–6 (Peterlingen); Heinemann (1983), pp. 129–31, who said that Romainmôtier had a *defensio* rather than *advocatia*.
[217] Büttner (1949), esp. p. 50.
[218] *Mainzer Urkundenbuch*, ed. Stimmung (n. 58), pp. 257–8, no. 358. On this charter, which was forged probably *c.* 1100 and was influenced directly from Cluny, see Büttner (1949), p. 47, and Hallinger (1958–60).

two revenues known as the *districtio* and *restauratio* and the third penny from any pleas with which he assisted.[219]

A number of Cluniac and neo-Cluniac houses were founded in southern Germany and northern Italy in the second half of the eleventh century by nobles who kept the hereditary right of advocacy, to which there were no objections provided the monks could control the advocate and he did not abuse his powers or claim the right of investiture.[220] This alliance between the local aristocracy and the reformed papacy was encouraged by pope Leo IX, who came from a noble family in the diocese of Toul, and developed during the Investiture Controversy into a religious, political, and social symbiosis of monks and nobles, linking monastic reform, subjection to Rome, and noble advocacy.[221] The famous privilege for Hirsau in 1075 marked the high point of a delicate balance between the freedom of the monks to control their property and advocate and to choose their abbot (who was given his staff by the prior), the hereditary right of advocacy within the family of the founder, the over-advocacy of the king, and the Roman liberty guaranteed by the pope.[222] It might appear, as some scholars have suggested, that the nobles got the lion's share in this arrangement, but the strength of the monks' position is shown by the example of Zwiefalten, which was founded from Hirsau in 1089 and held successive privileges from popes Urban II, Paschal II, and Calixtus II confirming the right of the monks to choose the advocate, like the abbot, by common consent or saner counsel and to replace him 'if he is found useless to the monastery'.[223] They did just this in 1130, when they removed duke Henry the Proud as advocate because he was too occupied with other business and chose in his place his brother Welf, who swore to respect the monastery's privileges and to resign if asked to do so. The chronicler later remarked that no advocate helped the abbey except for his own profit. 'Money was always our principle advocate', he said; 'it was our king and lord.'[224]

In spite of this progress in limiting the powers of advocates and establishing control over their appointment, monasteries continued to have difficulties with their advocates, as the number of twelfth-century German forgeries dealing

---

[219] Constable (1977a), pp. 203 and 204–6, generally on advocacy.

[220] According to Bauerreiss (1949–70), II, 94–5, the principal difference between the Trier/ Regensburg and Cluny/Hirsau reform circles lay in the attitude towards lay investiture. See also Violante (1979–81), pp. 621 and 657 on Italy.

[221] Wollasch (1961), pp. 422–3, and Jakobs (1968), pp. 239–41 and 278; cf. pp. 75 and 233.

[222] Henry IV, no. 280, in *MGH, Dipl.*, VI, 360. See Mayer (1950), pp. 50–62; Hallinger (1950– 1), pp. 564–5 and 840–3; Jakobs (1961), pp. 154–67; and Cowdrey (1970), pp. 198–9, with references to previous works.

[223] *Germania Pontificia*, ed. Albert Brackmann, II: *Provincia Moguntinensis*, I (Berlin 1923), pp. 220–1, and *Bullaire*, ed. Robert (n. 124), II, 18, no. 286 (JL 6958).

[224] Berthold of Zwiefalten, *Chronicon*, 34–7 and 44, ed. Wallach (n. 130), pp. 217–18 and 225 (see notes on 243–4), and (Stuttgart 1941, repr. 1978), pp. 232–8 (capp. 29–32) and 260 (cap. 38).

with advocacy show.[225] The new houses therefore fell heir, in spite of their strong opposition to lay control over their affairs, to a situation that often forced them to make compromises limiting the powers of advocates. Complete freedom from advocacy was rarely specified even in Cistercian charters and is found nowhere in the statutes of the Cistercian general chapters.[226] There was no specific reference to advocacy in the foundation charter of Camp, the first Cistercian abbey in the diocese of Cologne, established in 1122, and it was freed from the worldly authority of the archbishop, but it remained under his protection, like other monasteries in the diocese.[227] The term advocacy was also avoided when Orval was founded in 1131, but the count of Chiny was called *conservator et defensor iuris* in charters of 1153 and 1173.[228] Although there is no reference to the founder in the early records of Villers, perhaps in order to avoid a claim to advocacy, the duke of Brabant appeared as *protector* in the mid-twelfth century.[229] In what ways the positions of conservator, defender, and protector differed from that of advocate is unknown, and in the twelfth century the use of these terms began to overlap in the Low Countries.[230] They seem to have acted in a reserve capacity, as the names imply, and were called upon when needed, and without remuneration, and they were probably less involved than the old type of advocates in the normal administration of justice and control over monastic property. Some Cistercians in Germany themselves exercised high justice and comital powers in order to prevent an advocate from doing so,[231] but they recreated in this way the problem of worldly involvement that the institution of advocacy was designed to avoid. They still needed protection, and in the second half of the twelfth century Frederick Barbarossa assumed a general advocacy of all Cistercian houses in the empire, which had been adumbrated but never formalized in the charters of Conrad III. It was ineffective outside the areas of direct Hohenstaufen authority and never entirely superseded the general defence exercised by various territorial lords over the monasteries in their principalities or excluded the continuing claims of lesser lords, but it gave a distinctive character to the constitution of the Cistercian order in the empire.[232]

The relationships between regular canons and lay lords in the empire were marked by an even greater degree of variety, ranging from the complete absence of an advocate through a series of compromises designed, as in houses of monks, to control his appointment and limit his powers. A characteristic

[225] Hirsch (1967), p. 102, and Mayer (1950), pp. 22–4.
[226] Pflüger (1958) stressed the rarity of references to freedom from advocacy in twelfth-century Cistercian sources.
[227] Semmler (1959), pp. 197–8.
[228] Despy (1968); cf. Grégoire (1969), esp. pp. 776–90, and Genicot (1984b), pp. 9–10.
[229] Despy (1957), p. 13.
[230] See p. 249 above.
[231] Hirsch (1967), pp. 123–4.
[232] Ibid., pp. 99–151; Engelmann (1933), p. 68; Chapuis (1940), pp. 89–109; Mayer (1950), pp. 213–14; and Schlesinger (1962), II, 563–9.

arrangement was established at Rolduc, where the superior had 'the power of pleading and judging' and the founder and his son agreed 'that they and their successors should protect and defend the church, its property, and the *familia* only for the salvation of their souls', that is, without remuneration. They were to hold no pleas 'as from their own power' but were entitled to the third penny if their help was requested. This *institutio libertatis*, as it was called, was confirmed by the bishop of Liège and revised in 1145 to specify that if the founder's descendents lost their liberty and were therefore unable to hold the advocacy, the canons might choose their own advocate.[233] Differing arrangements might apply to a mother-house and its dependencies. Innocent II gave the canons of Arnstein the right to choose their own advocate; but in one of their dependencies, where the archdeacon resigned his rights and the advocacy was given by the count of Katzenellenbogen 'in perpetual liberty' to the canons and the founder, the archbishop of Trier took it 'under the protection (*tuitio*) of himself and his successors' in return for an annual census.[234] Here again there is no indication of the real difference between the advocacy given up by the count and the protection exercised by the archbishop. Rottenbuch, like the reformed monasteries in Swabia, depended on the papacy, but most of the houses of regular canons founded or reformed by archbishop Conrad of Salzburg depended on the bishop and chapter.[235] The papal privileges for Premonstratensian houses published by Hugo show that Arnstein and Varlar chose their own advocates; that the local bishop was advocate for Averbode, Bellelay, and Wadgassen, and the local duke for Tongerloo; and that at Osterhofen the advocate was to demand no unjust exactions. Only after 1152 did two bulls respectively free Roth from the power of an advocate or any lay man and declare that Steingaden 'should have no advocate'.[236] In three successive privileges granted by three different popes to Ilbenstadt in 1139, 1144, and 1147, the first established that there should be no advocate 'against the will of the canons (*invitis fratribus*)', the second that no one should usurp the advocacy and that the house 'should remain free as before and quiet from any advocacy'; and the third 'that no advocate should be established for you in the future without your common assent and that

---

[233] *Annales Rodenses*, s.a. 1144, ed. P.C. Boeren and G.W.A. Panhuysen (Assen 1968), fol. 4ʳ, p. 36, and *Beredeneerde inventaris der oorkonden en bescheiden van de abdij Kloosterrade*, ed. G.D. Franquinet (Maastricht 1869), p. 9, no. 7.

[234] Hugo, *Annales* (n. 125), I.1, cxx (JL 8239), and *Vita Ludovici de Arnstein*, ed. Widmann (n. 57), p. 262 (*BHL* 5033). The archbishop received a gold penny and twelve silver pennies of Coblenz annually to confirm this protection, which was described as 'beschirmet' in the old German translation of this life.

[235] Mois (1953), p. 150.

[236] Hugo, *Annales* (n. 125), I.1, cxvi (Averbode, 1139; JL 8000); ccxvi (Bellelay, 1142; JL 8211); I.2, cclxxxiii (Osterhofen, 1146; JL 8970); ccccxlviii (suspect for Roth, 1152; JL †9618); dxxxviii (Steingaden, 1156; JL 10180); dxciv (Tongerloo, 1146; JL 8885); dclii (Varlar, 1142; JL 8241); and dcxxxi (Wadgassen, 1152; JL 9585). Many charters, like those for Lac-de-Joux studied by Endemann (1967), pp. 37–8, contained no reference to advocacy.

your church should always remain, as it was in the past, free and quiet without the disturbance of any advocate'.[237] Clearly the canons, like others, wanted to have their cake and eat it too, that is, to have no advocate unless one was needed.

The variety of these arrangements, and the complexity of the relationships, show more clearly than any programmatic documents how the reform movement worked in practice and how the reformers had to compromise with the realities of medieval life. A complete picture of the movement must take into account these endless regional variations and the individual arrangements in economic organization and relations with the local community. This chapter has concentrated on the second and third parts of the liberty as defined in the history of Fontaines-les-Blanches, that is, the rights and possessions granted by the papacy and by secular powers, which constituted the foundation on which the way of life and worldly position of a community was based. The next chapter will study the first part, the liberty of the Holy Spirit, which formed the spiritual basis of the reform movement.

---

[237] Hugo, *Annales* (n. 125), I.1, dclxiii–v (JL 8060, 8669, and 9113).

7

THE SPIRITUALITY OF REFORM

I N the closing years of the eleventh century, shortly before his death in
1101, Bruno of Cologne, who had been *scholasticus* and chancellor of the
cathedral chapter at Reims, wrote a letter from his hermitage in Calabria to his
friend and former colleague at Reims, Ralph *Viridis*, urging him to remember

> how one day, when you and I and one-eyed Fulco were together in the orchard
> next to Adam's house, where I was then living, we talked for some time, as I
> remember, about the false delights and passing riches of the world and also
> about the joys of eternal glory. Whence, inflamed by holy love, we promised,
> swore, and decided to leave the fleeting things of the world on the next day and
> to seek eternal things and to receive the monastic habit. And this would have
> been done soon if Fulco had not departed for Rome, and on his return we put
> off many things that should have been done. What with the delay and other
> things that came up, the holy fire slackened, the spirit grew cold, the fervour
> vanished.

Although the description of this episode, which took place probably in the
1070s, was influenced by literary models, it gives a vivid picture of the infec-
tious sense of enthusiasm and urgency that inspired religious reformers in the
late eleventh century. One can almost see the three men discussing together
and then eagerly taking an oath, before the pressure of worldly commitments
reasserted itself. Ralph went on to become archbishop of Reims. Fulco was
an archdeacon or subdeacon, perhaps at Beauvais, and a prolific writer of prose
and verse. Bruno, on the other hand, left Reims soon after 1080, when he
was about fifty years old, and went first to Molesme and then to La Chartreuse, where he founded one of the strictest and most famous of the new
monastic orders. A few years later he was summoned by his former pupil,
pope Urban II, to Italy, where he became a hermit, and wrote this letter to
Ralph, in which he went on to describe the beauty and fertility of his hermitage and the joys of living there. 'The solitude and silence of the hermit confer
on those who love them a benefit and holy joy that only those who have
experienced them know ... Flee, therefore, my brother, all those concerns
and miseries and transport yourself from the tempest of this world to the
safety and peace of a port.' If he did not give up the world for the love of

257

God and hope of future rewards, Bruno wrote, let him do so out of necessity and fear of future punishment.[1]

A few years later, in 1115, Norbert of Xanten, when he was about thirty-five years old and had, like Bruno, some twenty years to live, was converted during a thunderstorm from his worldly life as a secular canon of St Victor at Xanten. According to his *Life*, which was written probably in the 1150s, 'He did not suddenly change his habit, or immediately leave the world', but he began to wear a hair shirt under his robe. 'Then, however, gradually and slowly, the interior sword of the word of God, penetrating the depths, burning the senses (*urens renes*), and examining the hearts, began from the inside to reform from one thing to another what had been falsely deformed.'[2] Norbert was then ordained a deacon and a priest and embarked on his career first as a wandering preacher, reformer, and founder of the Premonstratensian canons and subsequently as archbishop of Magdeburg.

Later in the twelfth century a prior of Sainte-Barbe, a house of regular canons in Normandy, resigned in order to become a Premonstratensian and wrote a letter to his former colleagues comparing his previous and present lives and explaining his reasons for leaving Sainte-Barbe, where he had lived (he thought) for over sixty years and which he still loved and did not want to harm or criticize. He admitted that the life in his new house was less peaceful than he might have wished owing to the proximity of a fortress and a royal road and the consequent number of visitors, but he praised 'the harmonious and unanimous tranquillity' of the canons and the harshness and poverty of their way of life in contrast to the soft and luxurious life of the world, to avoid which, and to repair and recover the grace of his first way of life, 'I came to this place of miserable poverty, this monastery of copious indigence, in which almost everything except the ways of the inhabitants seem uncultivated and impolite.' He came 'so that my soul may always be in my hands, that is, that my life and mind may be in my sight before me, so that I may be mindful of the commands of God'. He was eager to improve his life, he said, but could not find 'the form of improvement that would lead more securely to this life'. It therefore pleased him to adopt a way of life in which, since his colleagues were his superiors, he was raised to the height of their virtues rather than lowered into vice.[3]

---

[1] Bruno of La Chartreuse, *Ep.* 1, ed. André Wilmart, in *Rev. bén.* 51 (1939), pp. 265–8, and ed. anon. (Maurice Laporte) (SC 88; Paris 1962), pp. 70–6 (quotes on pp. 70 and 74–6). On Fulco of Beauvais, see the intro. to his *De nuptiis Christi et ecclesiae*, ed. Mary I.J. Rousseau (Catholic University of America: Studies in Medieval and Renaissance Latin Language and Literature 22; Washington 1960), pp. 1–2, 6, and 14.

[2] *Vita* [B] *Norberti*, I, 7, in *PL*, CLXX, 1260D–1A (*BHL* 6248). See Lefèvre (1961), who compared the accounts of Norbert's conversion in *Vitae* A and B. It would be interesting to study the relation of storms to decisions to enter religious life: see Somerville (1981–2) on the thunderstorm that 'propelled Martin Luther into a monastery'.

[3] *Ampl. coll.*, I, 782–4. See Dereine (1947), p. 371, on the poverty of the early Premonstratensians, and *Chronicon de s. Barbara in Algia*, ed. R.-Norbert Sauvage, in *Mémoires de l'Académie nationale des sciences, arts et belles-lettres de Caen: Documents*, 1906, on Sainte-Barbe.

The themes found in these three accounts of individual conversions range from a traditional emphasis on love of God, fear of hell, and contempt for the world to a highly inward experience, self-examination, and voluntaristic drive towards a new form of religious life.[4] They are found in many sources of the late eleventh and twelfth centuries and give an idea of the continuities and changes in the spirituality of the age. Contemporaries as well as later scholars were puzzled by the question of why so many people at this time turned away from a life in the world or in another religious house, sometimes (as with these three) at a relatively advanced age. A monk named Onulf, who taught at Speyer in the eleventh century, addressed this question in a rhetorical *ratiocinatio* based on the proposition, of which he analysed the various parts, that many men gave up their secular occupations for the stricter life of the monks. They did so, he said, 'because they prefer to lead a quiet life with the monks, having previously been bound in the world by many necessities'. Among these he listed oppression, poverty, debts, enemies, and illness, which they avoided by becoming monks, 'because everything needed for both food and clothing is equitably distributed for all those who profess the common life in a cloister'. Some monks returned to the world because their minds were evil or their former ways too strong; some, who had been monks since youth, left on account of inexperience; but those who persisted, Onulf said, 'taste and feel in the present how sweet is the Lord'.[5] A monk who entered Lérins in the eleventh century said that he wanted to emulate those 'whom he saw to be, though placed in the world, in a way outside the world' and who lived far from both the pleasures and the possibility of sin, 'as secluded, quiet, and silent foreigners from the tumult of the human republic'. He could escape the eternal fires that his growing sins had prepared for him only by renouncing his secular burdens and escaping like someone saved from a shipwreck 'into the quiet bosom of a monastery'.[6]

The importance of monasteries as places of penance for the laity is illustrated by a vision related to pope Leo IX by a citizen of Narni, who saw a long procession of people dressed in white, with white hair and faces, and was told by one of them that they were sinful souls who were not yet worthy of celestial joys and were on their way from Marmoutier to Farfa and other

---

[4] William James, in a letter written in 1902 to C.W. Eliot concerning *The Varieties of Religious Experience*, accepted that no narrative of conversion was literally true: 'Everyone aims at reproducing an ideal type which he thinks most significant and edifying. But in a general account of religious experience I think these inaccuracies of detail of no great moment; for ideals are *pointed to* by experience (*and reached* in some cases)': Perry (1935), II, 337–8. Morrison (1992a) is concerned more with 'how people made sense of conversion' than with conversion experiences (pp. xi–xii).
[5] The relevant sections of Onulf's *Colores rhetorici* are edited by Wattenbach (1894), pp. 371–2.
[6] *Cartulaire de l'abbaye de Lérins*, ed. Henri Moris and Edmond Blanc (Paris 1883), pp. 16–17, no. 18. There are some interesting examples of the preoccupation with sin, death, hell, and judgement in eleventh-century charters from Portugal in Mattoso (1968), pp. 281–3.

holy places as a penance.[7] The twelfth-century preacher Peter of Poitiers told a story in one of his sermons about a father who was enraged that his son had entered a Cistercian abbey and threatened to destroy it. When his son offered to return if his father abolished from his lands 'the custom that a son might not die before his father', however, the older man saw the point and became a monk himself.[8] Sources like these – a rhetorical treatise, the arenga to a charter, a vision, and a preacher's *exemplum* – are natural repositories for conventional wisdom and commonplaces. They are cited here rather than in the chapter on rhetoric because they express the mixture of religious and secular motives, and of hope and fear, that was also found in letters, biographies, histories, and spiritual writings.

Guibert of Nogent in the history of his own life gave an account of the conversions of the viscount of Chartres, Everard of Breteuil, who became a monk at Marmoutier, of count Simon of Crépy, who entered the monastery of St Claude and died at Rome, and of Bruno of Cologne, the beginning of whose conversion, as he called it, he attributed to the worldliness of archbishop Manasses of Reims.

> These people laid the foundations of the conversions of that time. Crowds of men and women continually joined them; every order immediately came together. What shall I say of their ages, when ten- and eleven-year-old children meditate the thoughts of age and bear greater chastisements than a youthful age should suffer? In these conversions took place what used to occur in the ancient martyrs, that a greater liveliness of faith is found in weak and tender bodies than in those in whom the authority of age and learning flourishes.[9]

In this passage can be seen what Stock called 'the sense of cultural discontinuity' between a corrupt present and a pure past and also between the innocence of youth and the worldliness of age.[10] Very little is known about what fostered this sense and promoted conversions, but the role of charismatic preachers like Bernard of Clairvaux, whose approach was feared by the parents of susceptible sons, was certainly of great significance.[11] The word was also spread by private conversations like that described by Bruno and by letters of monastic vocation, of which a few have survived.[12] Both men and women were inspired by an awareness of their own sinfulness and unworthiness,

---

[7] Wibert, *Vita Leonis IX*, II, 8, in *Pontificum romanorum . . . vitae*, ed. J.M. Watterich (Leipzig 1862), I, 161 (*BHL* 4818).
[8] MS Paris, Bibl. nat., Lat. 14593, fol. 45ʳ. On this manuscript see Bourgain (1879), pp. 329–30, and Hauréau (1890–3), III, 68, who referred to another copy of this sermon in MS Lat. 14470, fol. 284ʳ.
[9] Guibert, *De vita sua*, I, 9–11, ed. Bourgin, pp. 24–36 (quote on p. 35). On Simon of Crépy, see Cowdrey (1994), comparing Guibert's account with that in the *Vita Simonis*, which depicted a less rapid conversion.
[10] Stock (1983), p. 504.
[11] On Bernard as a popular preacher, see Constable (1994a), pp. 145–6.
[12] Leclercq (1955).

which drove them to punish themselves with self-inflicted sufferings and to put the world and its temptations behind them, and also by an optimistic faith in the possibility of repairing the damage by bridging the gap – the *regio dissimilitudinis* or region of difference, as it was called[13] – between their present degenerate condition and the perfect form in which they had been created and of preparing themselves for salvation, of which some of the joys could be experienced in the peace and quiet of religious life.

These differences of individual backgrounds and aspirations fostered the variety of minds that Peter the Venerable deplored in his Letter 111 to Bernard of Clairvaux:

> I see that some of both our sheep [the Cluniacs] and your sheep [the Cistercians] have taken up sworn battles against each other and that those who ought to live with one spirit in the house of the Lord have withdrawn from mutual love. I see that they are of the *familia* of the same lord, from the army of the same king, and are called Christians and monks by the same name. I see them, bound not only by the link of a common faith but also by the yoke of the same monastic rule, cultivating the field of the Lord with many and different toils. And although they are joined by the Christian name, as I said, and united by the monastic profession, only some concealed and execrable variety of minds divides them and separates them from that sincere unity of hearts in which they appear to be joined.[14]

This was written from the point of view of a strict black monk who accepted a diversity of customs but still believed in the basic unity of the monastic order and way of life. Not until half a century later did the implications of the new spirituality begin to become clear, both for the institutional structure of monasticism and for the emergence of new forms of religious life.

The most important elements in the formation of this ideal from the point of view of its influence on religious life were spiritual liberty, inwardness or interiority, and the search for a life modelled on the Gospels and specifically on the human life of Christ, and it is with these that this chapter is primarily concerned. A sense of the contrast between internal and external ran through the religious life and institutions of the eleventh and twelfth centuries and inspired a new awareness of the possibility of inner freedom and knowledge.[15] The ideal of institutional freedom from external control and influence, which

---

[13] On the *regio dissimilitudinis*, see Gervais Dumeige, in *Dictionnaire de spiritualité*, III (Paris 1954–7), coll. 1330–46; Courcelle (1963), pp. 278–9 and 623–40; Javelet (1967), I, 15, 266–85, and 456–7; and Diers (1991), pp. 92–8.

[14] Peter the Venerable, *Ep.* 111, ed. Constable, I, 277.

[15] Fulbert of Chartres, *Ep.* 126, ed. Frederick Behrends (OMT; Oxford 1976), p. 226, wrote in 1027 to archbishop Robert of Rouen, who had been attacked by duke Robert I of Normandy, that 'si abstulet exteriora, interiora non potuit', and Ordericus Vitalis, *Historia ecclesiastica*, III, ed. Chibnall, II, 74, said that in 1059 'exterior power' was granted by the duke to the new abbot of St Evroul and 'interior cure of souls' was commended by the bishop of Evreux; see ibid., II, 144–6, and IV, 254. I owe these examples to Olivier Guillot.

was the watchword of ecclesiastical reform in the eleventh century, has already been studied. It was paralleled by the ideal of internal and spiritual freedom, which opened the way for a basic reshaping of the church in the twelfth century. The first part of the triple liberty of the hermits at Fontaines-les-Blanches was that which was held through the Holy Spirit and was guaranteed, according to abbot Peregrinus, by the Gospels and the Acts of the Apostles.[16] The most important reference to freedom in the New Testament, however, was in 2 Corinthians 3.17, where Paul said that 'The Lord is a spirit. And where the spirit of the Lord is, there is liberty.' Encapsulated in the phrases 'spirit of liberty' and 'liberty of spirit', which were used interchangeably, this text was cited in countless monastic and spiritual writings to show that man, who was created in the image of God, was spiritually free and to contrast the true freedom of those who served God with the false freedom in the world, where men served men.

The classic statement of inner freedom and of the superiority of private to public law was the canon *Duae sunt leges*, which first appeared about 1110 and was included in the *Decretum* of Gratian under the name of pope Urban II but of which the origins and authenticity are debated by scholars, who date it somewhere in the late eleventh or early twelfth century but who agree in stressing its striking originality and interest.[17]

> There are two laws, he said: one public, the other private. Public law is that which is confirmed in the writings of the holy fathers, like the law of the canons, which is handed down on account of transgressions . . . Private law is that which is written in the heart at the inspiration of the Holy Spirit, as the Apostle said of those 'Who show the work of the law written in their hearts' [Romans 2.15] and 'For when the Gentiles who have not the law, do by nature those things that are of the law; these, having not the law, are a law to themselves' [Romans 2.14].

A secular canon may therefore become a monk or regular canon, because, the text continued,

> No reason requires him to be constrained by public law since he is led by private law. For private law is more worthy (*dignior*) than public law. The spirit of God is indeed the law, and those who act in accordance with the spirit of God are led by the law of God, and who can properly resist the Holy Spirit? . . . 'Where the spirit of God is there is liberty' [2 Corinthians 3.17], and if you are led by the spirit of God, you are not under the law.[18]

---

[16] Peregrinus, *Historia*, II, *praef.*, ed. Salmon, p. 273 (see p. 242 above).

[17] See Eschmann (1944), pp. 100–1, who dated *Duae sunt leges* before Urban II; Dereine (1951), pp. 548–9, who suggested that it was a canon of the council of Clermont; Kuttner (1968), p. 504; Chenu (1969), pp. 60–1; Landau (1991a), pp. 52–96, who described it as 'ein erstaunlicher Text' (p. 60) and said that it first appeared about 1110 but may go back to an oral pronouncement, possibly a sermon, of Urban (p. 69); and Tellenbach (1993), p. 317.

[18] Gratian, *Decretum*, XIX, 2, 2, in *Corpus*, ed. Friedberg, I, 839–40. On the distinction between *privatus* and *publicus*, which emerged about 1000, see Genicot (1984a), pp. 162–3.

It would be hard to exaggerate the importance of this canon, which as an official statement of the doctrine of Christian freedom influenced not only lawyers like Alexander III, Huguccio, and Johannes Teutonicus but also theologians like Thomas Aquinas.[19]

The sense of a direct relationship with God in the decision to enter religious life was of central importance in early monasticism and in the lives of many individual saints, but it tended to be less prominent in the early Middle Ages, when many monks and nuns were given to monasteries as children by their parents and when the emphasis in worship was on collective prayer and liturgical ceremonies. The essence of religious life for early medieval monks was the elaborate celebration of the liturgy and the steady recitation of the psalms, which were later cut back gradually, and occasionally painfully, since they still suited the spiritual needs of many people. In the early Middle Ages, greater attention was paid in the *Lives* of hermits, whose way of life tended to be more voluntary and spontaneous than that of monks and nuns, to their visible sufferings and austerities than to their inner state of heart or private devotions, but in the eleventh and twelfth centuries there were signs of a growing desire for a personal relationship to God, Who was more interested in people's thoughts and motives than in their actions, which were of concern primarily to man. The preference of many reformers for the eremitical life was owing to its freedom, which permitted a more personal type of religious life than was possible in most monasteries, rather than its isolation and unworldliness, which were in fact often less than in religious communities. When Gerard of St Albinus was sent by his abbot 'outside the monastery to the cells of the abbey', according to his *Life*, 'He engaged in spiritual exercises as much more freely as more privately.'[20] In the early eleventh century, a hermit and ascetic like Romuald broke with the pattern of liturgical celebration by a community. He himself sometimes recited the psalter wandering in the woods. He urged his followers to read with concentrated attention and for as long as they could, saying that the reader should feel before God as he would before the emperor.[21] The view of God as a mighty king who wanted strict obedience and conformity from His subjects was deeply rooted in Christianity, and has not entirely disappeared today. In about 1084 Anselm of Canterbury wrote to the abbess and nuns of Wilton that they should keep a watch on their innermost thoughts as well as their exterior actions and 'should not think that an improper thought is less displeasing to God than a reprehensible action is to man'.[22] God looked into people's hearts and intentions and took a personal interest in them. He was seen as a father and mother and, in the person of

---

[19] See Eschmann (1944), p. 120, and Landau (1991a), pp. 84–8.
[20] *Vita Girardi s. Albini Andegavensis*, in *Chroniques des églises d'Anjou*, ed. Paul Marchegay and Emile Mabille (Société de l'histoire de France; Paris 1869), p. 99 (*BHL* 3548).
[21] Bruno of Querfort, *Vita quinque patrum*, in *MGH, SS*, xv.2, 738.
[22] Anselm, *Ep.* 185, ed. Schmitt, IV, 70.

Christ, as a friend and model. Robert of Arbrissel in his letter to countess Ermengard of Brittany in 1109 said that good works, prayers, and fasting were useless if they were performed for the sake of praise of men rather than of God, Who 'pays attention not to the words but to the heart of the person who prays'.[23]

These themes recurred frequently in the sermons of abbot Geoffrey of St Thierry, among whose listeners may have been the future Cistercian William of St Thierry and perhaps also some lay people.[24] Speaking of God as He was described in 2 Chronicles 20.17, where the prophet wrote, 'O Juda and Jerusalem, fear you not nor be you dismayed', Geoffrey said that 'A pious and sweet father seeks to be loved, not to be feared. Those who fear are serfs. Those who desire are mercenaries. Those who love are sons. He Who is a father and has the affection of a father knows no serfs, hates mercenaries, and receives sons into their inheritance.' Elsewhere Geoffrey said that 'The memory and recollection of divine goodness should break into and penetrate to the interior senses of the spirit where man lives, where reason knows, and where it ought to be rooted, and when rooted, to be enlarged.' Of the crucifixion, he said, 'There is in the act or in that account, if you love, nothing that does not move, that does not penetrate and enter the spirit.' When Elijah went into the desert in 3 Kings 19.4 he 'left exterior things and progressed to interior things', and of the saints 'that are converted to the heart' in Psalm 84.9 Geoffrey said that men hear what God says to them by interior hearing and that 'conversion to the heart' meant 'to the doctrine given from heaven that they receive not out of the mouth of someone else but, with the Holy Spirit guiding them, from the fount of their own heart'. 'Confession that simply tells a story with the mouth is useless and fruitless unless confession of the heart is added. This is the anxiety and inward bitterness in which we alone confess to God.' Christ acted first and instructed afterwards, showing what is owed to truth and suited to integrity. 'Examples are more powerful than words, and in practice it is more to teach by deed than to speak by voice.'[25]

Sentiments of this kind are often found in sermons and have echoed from pulpits for centuries, and it is not certain that the passages cited here were original to Geoffrey. Their interest is because they represent a type of spirituality that was still relatively new in the early twelfth century, when God was more commonly presented in terms of power and fear than of love and compassion and when there was less stress than later on the direct relation between

[23] Robert of Arbrissel, *Sermo ad comitissam Britanniae*, ed. J. de Petigny, in *Bibliothèque de l'Ecole des chartes* 15 (3 S. 5) (1854), p. 232.
[24] Geoffrey of St Thierry was abbot of St Thierry at Reims from 1112 to 1120 and of St Nicasius from 1120–31, when he became bishop of Châlons-sur-Marne. Most of his sermons (see Abbreviations) were addressed to monks, but a few, like Sermon 30, in MS Reims, Bibl. mun., 581, fol. 125'b, seem to have been delivered to a secular congregation.
[25] These passages are from Sermons 11, 12, 15, 22, 23, 29, and 31, in MS Reims, Bibl. mun., 581, fols. 44'a, 45'a, 58'b, 78'a, 80'a, 120'a, and 135'a.

God and man and on man's personal responsibility to Him. This responsibility was sometimes mediated through others, whose words and example in this life and whose intercessory prayers in the next were greatly valued, and through the saints, who assisted with visions and miracles, and above all through Christ and the Virgin Mary, both of whom intervened directly to help individuals at critical moments in their lives. It was still a basically personal responsibility, however, of which the consequences were born in eternity by the individual. The prior of Sainte-Barbe left his former monastery in order that his soul might always be in his own hands. When Robert of Bethune was called to the bishopric of Hereford from the priory of Llanthony in 1131, the 'spiritual man', as his biographer called him, felt like Adam driven out of paradise. 'How is it that while I am free and my own I enter into servitude and torments as though I had my eyes open and my own free will?' he asked. 'If obedience is less than will, how do we try to choose what is better? Behold a smooth way from the left-hand side leads to flight and a wood on the right [leads] to a hiding-place.' In this way Robert expressed his anguish at being caught between his desire to stay at Llanthony and his duty to become bishop. *Nolo episcopari* was not a topos for him but a serious expression of his desire to remain withdrawn from the world, and it was only after a severe conflict within himself (unassisted, in this case, by any supernatural visions or voices) that he finally accepted.[26] By the end of the century this type of inner reliance and self-examination was well established in monastic spirituality. Francis of Assisi wrote that 'After God gave me some brothers, no one showed me what I ought to do, but the Almighty Himself revealed to me how I ought to live according to the form of the holy Gospel.'[27]

The rule of Benedict required a monk to reveal any evil thoughts or deeds to his abbot 'by humble confession'.[28] The importance of confession in the late eleventh century is shown by the story of one of Lanfranc's miracles by Osbern of Canterbury, who recounted it at length, he said, 'so that the great-ness of the miracle might be recognized in proportion to the greatness of the sin and the love of confession might become sweeter in the hearts of listeners the more effective the height of its power appears'. The story concerns a young monk of Christ Church who committed many sins while possessed by an evil spirit and was cured by confessing to Lanfranc, who at one point was so pleased at the confession that he covered the monk's hands with kisses and gave alms to 300 poor men for his salvation. Recognizing the power of con-fession, Lanfranc said to the evil spirit that 'Although you are a liar and a father of lies, you nevertheless bear witness willy nilly to this truth and attest

---

[26] William of Wyecombe, *Vita Roberti Betun*, I, 12, in *Anglia sacra*, ed. Henry Wharton (London 1691), II, 305–6.
[27] Francis of Assisi, *Testamentum*, 14, in *Opuscula*, ed. Cajetan Esser (Bibliotheca franciscana ascetica medii aevi 12; Grottaferrata 1978), p. 310.
[28] *Reg. Ben.*, 7.

that this young man is not what he was because whatever he failed to do through the negligence of his frailty or did by diabolical attack is absolved through confession.'[29] In the eleventh and twelfth centuries the practice of confession was rarer among lay people than in monasteries, but lay confession was promoted by the masters of the school of Laon, and especially by William of Corbeil, and was well established by the middle of the twelfth century.[30] In the section on 'How the conscience should be examined' in the *Penitential book* of Alan of Lille, he compared the priest to a doctor and the sinner to a sick man who 'before he goes to his doctor, that is his own priest, should look into the corners of his conscience to see what sins are there'.[31] The concern for self-examination culminated in the canon *Omnis utriusque sexus* of the Fourth Lateran Council, which required all faithful Christians to confess their sins to their own priest at least once a year.[32]

There was a tendency in the twelfth century to interiorize and spiritualize all aspects of monastic life and morality. This may have been a reaction against the rigidity and exteriority of the early medieval penitential codes, which took deeds at face value with no account of intention, and perhaps also against the literalism of some of the reformers and heretics, whose stress on the letter rather than the spirit of the law was considered pharisaical by many of the older monks. A religious rich man was considered poorer than an avaricious beggar because religious poverty in the twelfth century was poverty in spirit, a lack of desire for property, rather than an absolute lack of material possessions. Like inner solitude, it brought people together rather than separating them. This view was marked by rhetorical and literary features that make it hard to distinguish reality from the ideal. The topos of interior solitude was an expression of the suspicion of physical solitude felt by many reformers, who shared the opinion of Bernard of Clairvaux that true solitude was 'in the mind, not in the body; in intention, devotion, and spirit', and it was also equivalent to a type of quasi-mystical spiritual withdrawal found in many saints and holy men who could turn their gaze inwards and remain oblivious to their surroundings and external events.[33] Bernard's failure to notice the rich trappings when he travelled from Clairvaux to La Chartreuse or to see the lake of Geneva while riding beside it for a day was the result not, as has been said, of his insensitivity to natural beauty or lack of observation, let alone his

---

[29] Osbern, *Miracula s. Dunstani*, 19. ed. William Stubbs, in *Memorials of St Dunstan, Archbishop of Canterbury* (RS 63; London 1874), pp. 144–50 (quotes on pp. 148 and 151) (*BHL* 2345). There are briefer accounts of this miracle in Eadmer, *Miracula s. Dunstani*, 16, ibid., pp. 234–8 (*BHL* 2347) and in Milo Crispin, *Vita Lanfranci*, XIV, 35, in *PL*, CL, 54B–5A (*BHL* 4719). See MacDonald (1926), pp. 171–4.

[30] See Murray (1993), pp. 78–9.

[31] Alan of Lille, *Liber poenitentialis*, in *PL*, CCX, 299C.

[32] IV Lateran (1215), 21, in *Conc. oec. decreta*, p. 245.

[33] Bernard, *Serm.* 40 *super Cantica*, 4, ed. Leclercq, II, 27. Aelred of Rievaulx, *Speculum caritatis*, II, 24, 70–3, in *CC:CM*, I, 99–101, distinguished the inner curiosity of monks from their outer curiosity, which observed the splendour of buildings and decorations.

deep cowl or physical suffering, but of his intense inner concentration, as his biographer made clear. 'The prior [of La Chartreuse] most greatly admired in him that the abbot, that servant of God, so circumscribed his eyes externally and occupied his spirit internally that he did not observe for the space of such a journey what he himself [the prior] had seen at the first glance.'[34] The topos of interior pilgrimage was of practical application as well as spiritual significance. Bernard used it to discourage monks from going on pilgrimages or the crusades. 'For the object of monks', he wrote to the abbot of St Michael in Thiérache, 'is to seek out not the earthly but the heavenly Jerusalem, and this not by proceeding with the feet but by progressing with the feelings.'[35] Guigo of La Chartreuse urged, 'Let others go to Jerusalem, and you to humility and patience. For you thus go outside the world; he goes within it.'[36] The image of man as an inner traveller or pilgrim, embarked on a journey of desire and search, as in the legends of the Holy Grail, pervaded the popular mentality of the late Middle Ages and early modern period, down to and beyond the *Pilgrim's progress*.[37]

Many obstacles had to be overcome in the course of this journey, especially by monks, who were more exposed than others to both inner and outer enemies. Whoever wished to ascend the mountain must follow Christ and the truth, wrote Richard of St Victor in the *Lesser Benjamin*, referring to the mountain of the Lord in Psalm 23.3: 'The way that leads to the summits of this mountain is hard, hidden, and unknown to many.' But the labour of the journey and the difficulty of the ascent should not discourage the climber, since Jesus is transfigured on top.[38] The monk was presented as engaged in a battle between the forces of good and evil, or as a lonely fighter in the struggle against the enemy inside and outside himself.[39] Goscelin of St Bertin in his *Book of encouragement* cited Paul's statement in 2 Timothy 3.12 that

---

[34] Alan of Auxerre, *Vita secunda Bernardi*, XVI, 45, in Bernard, ed. Mabillon, II(6), 2438BD (*BHL* 1232). The *stramentum animalis* was described as *minus praeferens paupertatem* ('not displaying poverty'). Parallels to the account in William of St Thierry, *Vita prima Bernardi*, I, IV, 20, ibid., col. 2106CD, where after a year in the novices' cell Bernard was unaware of the roof, are found in the *Verba seniorum*, IV, 16, and VII, 19, in *PL*, LXXIII, 866C and 896D–7A. Among many secondary references to these episodes, especially the lake of Geneva, see Symonds (1875), p. 14; Duby (1979), p. 88; John Benton, in *Renaissance and Renewal* (1982), pp. 268–9; Gurevich (1985), pp. 61–2; Dalarun (1985), p. 237; Christopher Brooke, in Norton and Park (1985), p. 19; Constable (1987b), pp. 30–1; and Rudolph (1990), p. 112, who called them 'hagiographical devices'.

[35] Bernard, *Ep.* 399, ed. Leclercq, VIII, 379–80.

[36] Guigo of La Chartreuse, *Meditatio* 262, ed. André Wilmart (Etudes de philosophie médiévale 22; Paris 1936), pp. 111 and 232, and ed. anon. (Maurice Laporte) (SC 308; Paris 1983), p. 184.

[37] See Ladner (1967), p. 245, on 'a shift from the stationary to the wayfaring and missionary *habitus*' among monks between the eleventh and twelfth centuries; Gardiner (1971) on the theme of inner pilgrimage 'human and destinal' (p. 1); and Stock (1983), p. 478.

[38] Richard of St Victor, *Beniamin minor*, 77–8, in *PL*, CXCVI, 55C–6A (quote on 55CD).

[39] See Boas (1948), pp. 41–4, on these themes and on the distinction between prelapsarian 'innocence' and virtue and goodness.

'All that will live godly in Jesus Christ shall suffer persecution' and commented that 'If they are not bodily struggles, they are spiritual. The former are external, the latter are internal . . . The enemy attacks more powerfully when he conceals his attack than when he comes out with an open front.'[40] It was therefore essential to face the enemy and fight openly and not to retreat or pretend that no battle was necessary. Abbot John's statement in the *Lives of the fathers* that 'He who does not fight will neither fall nor overcome' was cited by Fulbert of Chartres.[41] Changes were rung by many writers on Paul's words in 2 Timothy 2.5 that 'He also that striveth for mastery is not crowned except that he strive lawfully' and Gregory the Great's statement in the *Dialogues* that 'There is no palm of victory without the labour of struggle.'[42] An entry in the mortuary roll of Bruno of Cologne called him 'O knight of Christ, who departed the victor of the battle; how well you strove, since you overcame by striving';[43] and Peter the Venerable in 1134 wrote to his secretary Peter of Poitiers, who wanted to live in a solitary retreat: 'The laurels of victory are given not to him who flees but to him who stands, not to him who yields but to him who resists; not to him who succumbs, but to him who conquers.'[44]

It was a small step from this recognition of the inevitability of struggle in the spiritual life to the view found in several twelfth-century writers that 'Where the grief is graver the crown is greater' or that 'Where the labour is greater the glory should be greater.'[45] Gerald of Wales went further, attributing to Gregory the Great a statement that 'The labour of battle is therefore protracted, so that the crown of victory will in this way become greater.'[46] Onulf of Speyer in the eleventh century cited as a commonplace that 'It may be great to be a good man among good men; it is far greater to preserve innocence among evil men',[47] and according to Rainald the hermit the critics of solitary life said that 'He who has not been good among bad men is not perfect.'[48] Bernard of Clairvaux praised Hugh of Rouen for leading a good life among evil men, saying that 'He who is good among good men has sal-

---

[40] Goscelin of St Bertin, *Liber confortatorius*, 2, ed. Charles H. Talbot, in *Anal. mon.*, III, 51.

[41] Fulbert of Chartres, *Rithmus de abbate Iohanne*, ed. Frederick Behrends (OMT; Oxford 1976), p. 269, no. 153, citing the *Vitae patrum*, V, 10, 27.

[42] Gregory the Great, *Dialogi*, III, 19, ed. Umberto Moricca (FSI 57; Rome 1924), p. 187. See Herbert of Losinga, *Ep.* 13, ed. R. Anstruther (Caxton Society; Brussels and London 1846), p. 24; Abelard, *Ep.* 4, ed. J.T. Muckle, in *Mediaeval Studies* 15 (1953), p. 84; Geoffrey *Grossus*, *Vita Bernardi Tironiensis*, XIV, 138, in *PL*, CLXXII, 1444D (*BHL* 1251); and Hugh of Silvanès, *De conversione Pontii de Larazio*, 17, in Baluze, *Miscellanea*, I, 182.

[43] Obituary roll for Bruno of La Chartreuse, 24 (St Peter at Chartres), in *PL*, CLII, 562C; cf. *Rouleaux des morts*, p. 157.

[44] Peter the Venerable, *Ep.* 58, ed. Constable, I, 187.

[45] Fulco of Beauvais, *Vita Blandini*, ed. A. Poncelet, in *Anal. boll.* 7 (1888), p. 155 (*BHL* 1369), and Bernards (1955), p. 94.

[46] Gerald of Wales, *Speculum duorum*, ed. Yves Lefèvre and R.B.C. Huygens (Board of Celtic Studies, University of Wales: History and Law Series 27; Cardiff 1974), p. 180, with notes on the quote, which the editor could not find in the works of Gregory the Great.

[47] Onulf of Speyer, *Colores rhetorici*, in Wattenbach (1894), p. 378.

[48] Morin (1928), p. 109.

vation; [he who is good] among bad men also [has] praise. The former is of as great facility as it is of security; the latter is of as great virtue as it is of difficulty.'[49] In the polemics of the twelfth century this served as an argument for the superiority of clerics, who fought in the world, over monks, who fought in the cloister. Philip of Harvengt said that 'To flee from the middle of Baby-lon and be saved is as much safer as it is easier; but to be crowned victor in the middle of Babylon is as much grander as it is harder; so that monastic perfection, although commendable for merit, is considered as much lower as it is easier than clerical [perfection].'[50]

Behind this polemical use of what had become almost a rhetorical topos lay a significant change in the concept of virtue and the respective values of life in the world and in the monastery. Philip no less than Bernard, however, knew that the real fight was against the innate vices. These were often presented as external enemies or spirits, as in the *Book of revelations* of abbot Richalm of Schönthal, who would have sympathized with Luther's view that the devil was close when Christ was present and that 'When the devil harasses us then we know ourselves to be in good shape.'[51] According to Richalm, 'Whatever good we say or do is from good spirits; and whatever bad, from bad [spirits], so that I hardly know what I am saying for myself.' Bad spirits attacked evil men less than virtuous men and tried to distract them from interior to exterior concerns. When a good man was reading, they sent fleas and sleepiness; sick-ness when he was working; yawns, sleepiness, and all manner of distractions to divert him from what he should be doing. These were all externalizations of internal weaknesses, however, and Richalm was fully aware of the constant struggle against the natural tendency to depravity, helplessness, and ignorance, against which the best defence was holy reading, the sign of the cross, and the remembrance of the love and beauty of Christ, which warded off even the spirit of fornication. 'I think that I myself am already a wanderer and fugitive on earth', Richalm wrote, 'blown by every wind, so that no part of me would stay together, if the cross alone did not hold me together.'[52]

This concentration on the inner life of monks paralleled the tendency in moral theology to emphasize the importance of intention in the doctrine of sin and of repentance in the doctrine of confession and penance. Christians, and especially monks, had long known that virtue lay in the will and vice in the assent to evil. Athanasius in his *Life* of Anthony, which was as familiar to monks as the *Lives* of Martin and Benedict, said that the strength of the soul lay in its power of understanding and its fault in departing from the form

---

[49] Bernard, *Ep.* 25.1, ed. Leclercq, VII, 78.
[50] Philip of Harvengt, *De institutione clericorum*, 4: *De continentia clericorum*, 99, in *PL*, CCIII, 802AB, and see below p. 290.
[51] Oberman (1989), p. 106, citing *Tischreden* 5, no. 5284.
[52] Richalm of Schönthal, *Liber revelationum*, 1, 3 and 5, in Pez, *Thesaurus*, I.2, 387 and 391. On the magical power of the cross, see Flint (1991), pp. 174–5.

in which it was created.[53] Virtue thus depended on the will, and divinity lay within the self. Cassian applied this to chastity in his *Institutions*, where he wrote, citing Basil, that 'In this he understood that incorruption of the body lies not so much in the abstinence from women as in the integrity of heart, which by fear of God or by love of chastity preserves in perpetuity the truly incorrupt holiness of the body.'[54] Abelard and other theologians in the early twelfth century tended to interiorize and subjectivize all morality and gave a new meaning to the concepts of consent, intention, and good faith.[55] Guilt was a matter of the will's consent to evil, not of evil deeds in themselves, and was expiated by remorse rather than by public shame and punishment. John of Salisbury said in the *Policraticus* that hunting, of which he generally disapproved, could be useful and honest depending on the place, time, manner, person, and cause, under which he mentioned need, utility, and honesty. The substance of an act is coloured by the attitude of mind (*affectus mentis*), John said, citing Ambrose's *On offices*: 'For your attitude, as a wise man said, "gives a name to the deed", which is made a crime "not of itself but from its cause".'[56]

Some twelfth-century moralists stressed contrition in their teachings concerning the forgiveness of sins and reserved to God both the remission of the guilt and the divine punishment for sin, thus reducing the role of priests to declaring the divine pardon, granted at the moment of inner repentance, and to imposing the ecclesiastical punishments of penance and excommunication.[57] True confession for Geoffrey of St Thierry was not with the mouth but with the heart and consisted of inner anxiety and bitterness rather than the outer story told to the priest. Hugh of St Victor and other theologians still asserted that Christ's grant to Peter of the power of the keys conferred on all priests the power not only to declare the pardon granted by God but also, through confession and absolution, to remit the divine punishment. According to Hugh, 'The sin itself, that is the debt of damnation, is absolved in confession.'[58] Bernard of Clairvaux likewise recognized that the grant of the keys gave the clergy the power to bind and loose in heaven as well as on earth, but in his teaching on penance he resembled Abelard and other contemporaries in stressing the importance of inner repentance and contrition of heart.[59]

[53] Athanasius, *Vita Antonii*, 20, in *PG*, xxvi, 874AB. See Viller and Rahner (1939), p. 88, and MacDermot (1971), pp. 49, 63, 79, and 203.

[54] Cassian, *Institutiones*, vi, 19, ed. Jean-Claude Guy (SC 109; Paris 1965), p. 284.

[55] See in particular Lottin (1942–60), i, 421–65, and iv, 309–486; Blomme (1958), esp. pp. 163 and 338; Javelet (1967), i, 459–61; and Chenu (1969), pp. 17–32 and 59.

[56] John of Salisbury, *Policraticus*, i, 4, ed. C.C.J. Webb (Oxford 1909), i, 31–3.

[57] Anciaux (1949), pp. 275–95. The inscription on the ladder of virtues in Herrad of Hohenbourg's *Hortus deliciarum* stressed the power of 'the medicine of penitence' (plate 1).

[58] Hugh of St Victor, *De sacramentis*, ii, 14, 8, in *PL*, clxxvi, 568A. See Anciaux (1949), pp. 295–302.

[59] Anciaux (1949), pp. 248–53 and 291.

There was at this time a remarkable development, as C.S. Lewis called it, in the concept of conscience, which 'passed from the witness-box to the bench' and became 'the inner law-giver', without entirely losing its earlier meaning of knowledge and awareness, which survives in the term consciousness.[60] Paul said in 2 Corinthians 1.12 that 'the testimony of our conscience' was the glory of those who lived 'in simplicity of heart and sincerity of God, and not in carnal wisdom but in the grace of God'. This passage was often cited in the spiritual writings of the first half of the twelfth century, where the distinction between *conscientia* as inner awareness and as moral arbiter is not always clear. For Bernard of Clairvaux in his first sermon on the annunciation, 'the testimony of our conscience' was 'when the [Holy] Spirit itself attributes testimony to our spirit', above all the three beliefs that God alone pardons sins, permits the performance of good works, and grants eternal life.[61] And the anonymous author of a Cistercian treatise *On conscience*, arguing that the human will was the cause of salvation and damnation, called attention to 'how the man full of God said that his conscience was his glory, as if he understood it fully and himself in it (*tanquam eam plene intelligens, et se in ea*).'[62] On the level of daily life, however, Bernard knew that conscience was not infallible, as when he asked in the fiftieth sermon on the Song of Songs, speaking of the temporal cares that interfere with spiritual concerns, 'How often is a book put aside with a good conscience [that is, believing it the right thing to do] in order to sweat at manual labour?'[63] *Conscientia* meant knowledge or awareness in a letter written to the pope in 1119 by archbishop Ralph of Canterbury, who denied various accusations, saying that 'God knows and my soul knows that my entire conscience is free from this spot of transgression',[64] and also in the sermons of Geoffrey of St Thierry, who called conscience a good field to till, praised the secure life 'where there is a pure conscience', warned against the danger of a solitary life without 'repose of heart, tranquillity of conscience, and soarings of the heart', and urged his listeners to preserve an immaculate conscience for God. Christ, Geoffrey said, 'had the form but not the conscience of a serf because although He had the form of a man He did not have a conscience of sin', where *conscientia* must mean awareness.[65] Alan of Lille's injunction that

---

[60] Lewis (1967), pp. 191–4. See Chenu (1969); Potts (1980); and Murray (1991).

[61] Bernard, *Serm.* 1 *in annunciatione*, 1, ed. Leclercq, v, 13.

[62] *De conscientia*, 1, 2, in *PL*, CLXXXIV, 554B. See Delhaye (1954) on this (pp. 92–6) and two other treatises on conscience.

[63] Bernard, *Serm.* 50 *super Cantica*, II, 5, ed. Leclercq, II, 81. The hermit on the ladder of virtues in Herrard of Hohenbourg's *Hortus deliciarum* is distracted from prayer and contemplation by his garden (plate 1).

[64] Hugh (the Chanter) of York, *Historia archiepiscoporum Eboracensium*, ed. Charles Johnson, rev. M. Brett, C.N.L. Brooke, and M. Winterbottom (OMT; Oxford 1990), p. 104.

[65] Geoffrey of St Thierry, *Serm.* 8, in MS Paris, Bibl. nat., Lat. 13586, p. 19, and *Serm.* 27, 30, and 36, in MS Reims, Bibl. mun., 581, fols. 108ᵛb, 124ʳb, and 158ʳb. See also *Serm.* 9, 10, and 12, in MS Paris, Bibl. nat., Lat. 13586, pp. 22, 28, and 29, and *Serm.* 15 and 21, in MS Reims, Bibl. mun., 581, fols. 56ᵛa and 77ʳb. Note the similarity with Ivo's warning against solitude cited pp. 63 and 136 above.

the sinner should search the corners of his conscience before confession likewise refers to knowledge. These threads came together in the teaching of
Thomas Aquinas, who defined conscience in his *Summa* as 'the act by which
we apply our knowledge to the things that we do'.[66] Thomas said in his questions *On truth* that

> A righteous conscience binds simply and perfectly against the order of a prelate,
> 'simply' because its obligation cannot be removed, since such a conscience
> cannot be put aside without sin, and 'perfectly' because a righteous conscience
> binds in such a way not only that he who does not follow it incurs a sin but
> also that he who follows it is immune from sin, however much the order of a
> prelate may be opposed.[67]

Conscience here was both the witness and the judge.

For many of the new monks prayer and spiritual devotions were a matter
of direct communication of the inner self with God rather than of participation
in community worship and psalmody, which for them came from the lips
rather than the heart. There was a widespread desire to spend less time in
church, not only for practical reasons, as among the followers of Bernard of
Tiron, who had to raise their own food, but also for spiritual reasons, to allow
more time for private prayer and devotions. Adam of Perseigne, in his treatise
On mutual love, which was written towards the end of the twelfth century for
a community of nuns, probably at Fontevrault, described the labour of those
who obtained purity in meditation and sweetness in prayer, by which they
speak 'as a friend to a friend'.[68] The attraction of solitude, and also its dangers,
lay in the freedom of hermits to devote themselves to private religious exercises, which often included violent displays of emotion inspired by feelings of
guilt and weakness and also, more rarely, of joy and exaltation. The passionate
self-mortifications of Dominic *Loricatus* and the desire to suffer of his biographer Peter Damiani, who led the way in this as in other respects, were inspired
by a sense of sin and personal inadequacy as well as by a need to battle against
the external forces of evil. Both Dominic and, to a lesser degree, Damiani
practised self-flagellation, which became a custom in many monasteries, where
it was known as the discipline, and also among later associations of lay flagel-
lants. It was not a punishment in a specific sense but rather a way to show
grief and to expiate the sins of oneself and others.[69] 'The holy mind should

---

[66] Thomas Aquinas, *Summa theologica*, I, 79, 13 *conclusio*, in *Opera omnia*, V (Rome 1889), p. 281.
See Lewis (1967), p. 194.
[67] Thomas Aquinas, *Quaestiones disputatae de veritate*, 17, 5 *responsio*, in *Opera omnia*, XXII.2 (Rome
1972), p. 527. See Potts (1980), pp. 33–5, and Murray (1991), p. 37.
[68] Adam of Perseigne, *De mutuo amore*, XXIII, 74, ed. Gaetano Raciti, in *Cîteaux* 31 (1980),
p. 337.
[69] Martène (1736–8) IV, 229–33 (II, 11); Leclercq (1962c); and, on the thirteenth century, Meersseman (1962).

not fear to share the cross of Christ in blows', wrote Damiani, 'nor be ashamed of His contumely in nakedness of body.'[70]

Tears were among the most admired qualities of spiritual men and women, who were described as weeping copiously and frequently at the memory of their own sins.[71] 'Who would not weep there where each person, reminded of his own weakness within his conscience, can hardly speak for tears?', asked Arnold of Regensburg in his treatise *On the miracles of St Emmeram*, which dates from 1035/7.[72] Peter Damiani especially praised Romuald's gift of tears, which he compared to contemplation.[73] John of Lodi was said to have been given two sources of tears, one upper, which overflowed out of desire for heaven, and the other lower, by which his soul showed its fear of eternal punishment. 'First he wept so that he might not be led to punishment; afterwards he began to weep most bitterly because he was far from the kingdom.'[74] Ulrich of Zell wept for his own sins and the labours of his exile, and also because 'We who are called monks are many in number but few in merit.'[75] Peter of Avranches urged all monks to weep 'because prayer softens God but tears compel Him', and for Peter Comestor 'An abundance of tears was the sign of conversion from a perverse heart.'[76] Adam of Perseigne in *On mutual love* compared tears to a second baptism and praised the 'virtue of tears', of which he classified five types.[77] Some monks could probably turn their tears on and off at will, and Aelred of Rievaulx in his *Mirror of love* praised tears as 'a most pleasing and most acceptable sacrifice to God' but also warned that they were no substitute for obedience to His commands.[78]

The contemplation of death was a constant reminder of human mortality and of the need for repentance. When Harold's daughter Gunnilda returned to secular life after being a nun, Anselm wrote her that her parents were dead, and also her lover count Alan the Red.

---

[70] Peter Damiani, *Opusc.* 43 *de laude flagellorum*, 6, in *PL*, CXLV, 685B.
[71] Berlière (1927a), pp. 210–13, and Steidle (1938).
[72] Arnold of Regensburg, *De miraculis s. Emmerammi*, *praef.*, in *PL*, CXLI, 991D, and *MGH, SS*, IV, 546 (*BHL* 2541). See Zimmermann, III, 90, on the date.
[73] Peter Damiani, *Opusc.* 13 *de perfectione monachorum*, 12, and *Opusc.* 15 *de suae congregationis institutis*, 26, in *PL*, CXLV, 307–9 and 358–9. See Tabacco (1954), pp. 332–3 and 335, with further references.
[74] *Vita Joannis Laudensi*, III, 15, in *AASS*, 7 Sept. III, 165E; see also IV, 23, ibid., 168A (*BHL* 4409). Bernard of Tiron had an exceptional gift of tears, according to Geoffrey *Grossus*, *Vita Bernardi Tironiensis*, XI, 101–2, in *PL*, CLXXII, 1427C–8A (*BHL* 1251); and even a traditional black monk like Suger was said to have wept in his cell: William of St Denis, *Vita Sugerii*, 2, ed. A. Lecoy de La Marche (Société de l'histoire de France; Paris 1867), p. 393.
[75] *Vita Udalrici*, 68, in *AASS*, 10 July III, 158B (*BHL* 8370).
[76] *Vita Petri Abrincensis*, 14, ed. E.P. Sauvage, in *Anal. boll.* 2 (1883), p. 497 (*BHL* 6689), and Peter Comestor, *Serm.* 69 *in festo s. Magdalenae*, published among the works of Hildebert of Lavardin, in *PL*, CLXXI, 675C.
[77] Adam of Perseigne, *De mutuo amore*, VI, 15 and 18, ed. Raciti (n. 68), pp. 311 and 315.
[78] Aelred of Rievaulx, *Speculum caritatis*, II, 20, 63, in *CC:CM*, I, 95.

Go now sister; put yourself with him in the bed where he now lies; collect his worms in your bosom; embrace his corpse; kiss closely his naked teeth, for his lips are already consumed with putrefaction. He certainly does not now care for your love, in which he delighted while he was living; and you shudder at his putrid flesh that you wanted to use.[79]

A scholar unfamiliar with this passage might well date it long after the late eleventh century, owing to its almost brutal concentration on the sensual aspects of death, which was characteristic of late medieval spirituality, but it was also popular in the twelfth century. Arnulf of Boheries in about 1200, while stressing that a monk must attend to 'the prayers that are commanded' before his private prayers and devotions, urged him to meditate on his own death and burial and on how his body would turn to dust and be eaten by worms. 'The highest philosophy is the continual meditation of death.'[80]

As the prayers of monks became more passionate and introspective, and moved outside the framework of the established liturgy, they tended to become more personal and systematic. The early twelfth-century collections of Anselm's prayers, which were accompanied by a prologue and letters explaining their use, have been called revolutionary because they were written by a single writer who served as 'an active spiritual guide, one who composes prayers to meet specific devotional requirements'.[81] The hermit Godric of Finchale, 'since he was greatly burdened by the accustomed multitude of prayers, had reckoning stones, with which he calculated their numbers, in order that owing to ignorance he might not omit any'.[82] Others arranged their prayers around the hours of the day, and the episodes in the life of Christ, anticipating the books of hours that appeared in the thirteenth century and played an important role in the late Middle Ages.[83] Goscelin of St Bertin urged the recluse Eve in the late eleventh century to 'consecrate all hours to the passion of Christ. In the middle of the night adore [Him] captured and imprisoned; in the morning, scourged; at the third hour, crucified', and so on throughout the day and the passion of Christ.[84] The meditations of a twelfth-century monk, probably a Cistercian, took him through seven days, each devoted to some aspect of the life of Jesus, and Adam of Dryburgh associated each canonical hour with an episode in Jesus's life.[85] At the same time the concept of spiritual exercises, which had long been used for physical asceti-

---

[79] Anselm, *Ep.* 169, ed. Schmitt, IV, 47–8. See Wilmart (1928a).
[80] Arnulf of Boheries, *Speculum monachorum*, 2, in *PL*, CLXXXIV, 1178A.
[81] Bestul (1984), p. 360.
[82] Reginald of Durham, *Vita Godrici*, CVIII, 213, ed. Stevenson, pp. 225–6.
[83] See Aston (1984) on 'devotional literacy' in the late Middle Ages. According to Nobels (1911), pp. 455 and 457, the association of the liturgical hours and parts of the mass with stages in Christ's passion was known in Christian Antiquity and was revised and elaborated in the twelfth century.
[84] Goscelin of St Bertin, *Liber confortatorius*, ed. Talbot (n. 40), p. 83.
[85] Leclercq (1944–5), pp. 2–3 and 11–19, and Adam of Dryburgh, *De ordine*, IX, 8, in *PL*, CXCVIII, 526B–7A.

cism, began also to be applied to prayer. Guigo of La Chartreuse referred in his customs to prayer, reading, meditation, and contemplation as *exercitia spiritualia*,[86] and William of St Thierry used the term five times in his *Golden letter*, where he also used *vitam ordinare*. 'Learn . . . to be master of yourself according to the laws of the common institute', William wrote, addressing the Carthusians of Mont-Dieu, 'to order your life, to compose your habits, to judge yourself, to accuse yourself to yourself, and often to condemn and to punish yourself.'[87] Arnulf of Boheries in his *Mirror of monks* said that someone who was moved by a desire for a better life should examine his own thoughts, speech, and actions 'as though he were looking at his face in the mirror of the interior man'. He should carefully consider the offices, psalmody, prayer, readings, mass, and labour in order to determine 'not what he is doing but for what reason he came'. He should go over every day what he had done wrong, both privately and publicly, in thought, speech, and action, since to be perfect a life must be voluntary, naked, and clean. 'Voluntary, that is, of his own will and decision. Naked, so that he may confess his sin nakedly, as he performed [it]. Clean, that he should not publish his sin like Sodom; but he should accuse himself of many things and with a single intent.'[88]

The most famous expression of this requirement for self-examination was the Socratic motto 'Know yourself', which was cited in the twelfth century as *Nosce te ipsum* or *Scito te ipsum*.[89] It was the subtitle of Abelard's *Ethics*, and it was placed on the abbey of Corvey when it was rebuilt by Wibald.[90] For Bernard of Clairvaux, *Nosce te ipsum* was a *sententia* from heaven, and self-knowledge was the beginning of the process of personal salvation, to which the two main routes – 'the ways of life' shown to man by God in Psalm 15.11 – were confession, in which all things were cleansed, and obedience, in which the virtues were consolidated. 'The first path and the first step on this way [of confession] is knowledge of oneself', which requires a man to know what he has done, what he deserves, and what he has let go. 'What is more vile, O noble creature, the image of God, the likeness of the Creator, than to befoul your flesh with carnal enticements and to lose a flood of pleasure for the sake of fleeting pleasure?'[91] Self-knowledge was thus at the root of conscience or consciousness in its basic meaning of inner knowledge or awareness of oneself. For Richard of St Victor the ascent of the mountain of the Lord –

---

[86] Guigo of La Chartreuse, *Consuetudines*, XXIX, 3, in [Laporte] (1960–7), IV, 136; see II, 525–7, and VI, 541–3, saying that real methodical prayer came at the end of the twelfth century.

[87] William of St Thierry, *Ep. ad fratres de Monte Dei*, 52, ed. Davy, p. 101; see 10, 33, 42, 57, and 76, ibid., pp. 73, 88–9, 94, 106, and 123. See Pinard de la Boullaye (1950).

[88] Arnulf of Boheries, *Speculum monachorum*, in *PL*, CLXXXIV, 1175A–6B.

[89] See Boas (1948), pp. 123–7; Bertola (1959); Javelet (1959), p. 25, and (1967), I, 368–71; Courcelle (1963), pp. 281–2, and (1974), pp. 237–91; Chenu (1969), pp. 41–6; Morris (1972), pp. 64–95; and Bennett (1979).

[90] Wibald, *Ep.* 167, in *Monumenta Corbeiensia*, ed. Philipp Jaffé (BRG I; Berlin 1864), p. 287. See Heckscher (1937), p. 220, and Courcelle (1974), p. 290 n. 271.

[91] Bernard, *Serm.* 40 *de diversis*, 3, ed. Leclercq, VI.1, 236.

the journey of life – was one of self-knowledge. 'Climb this mountain, learn to know yourself,' he wrote in the *Lesser Benjamin*.[92] Hugh of St Victor said in *On the pledge of the soul* that 'Your eye sees nothing well if it does not see itself. For when it is highly perceptive in contemplating itself, no outwardly strange likeness or false fancy of truth can deceive it.'[93] Self-knowledge was the starting point of the general principle of progression from material to immaterial knowledge, as Hugh explained in his commentary *On the celestial hierarchy of Denis the Areopagite*, where he said that the human body uses corporeal signs 'in order to be guided from visible things to the imitation and contemplation of invisible things. To imitation, by the exercise of virtue; to contemplation, by the knowledge of the truth.'[94] William of St Thierry also stressed the need for self-knowledge in order to penetrate the truth of one's own conscience. Commenting on the passage in the Song of Songs 1.7 that 'If thou know not thyself, O fairest among women, go forth, and follow after the steps of the flocks', William wrote: 'Blessed conscience, which always says Lord Jesus in the same spirit, whatever it encounters, whatever it attacks.' 'Know yourself because you are My image, and so you can know Me, whose image you are, and you will find Me within yourself. If you will be with Me in your mind, then I shall recline with you, and from there I shall pasture you.' If someone does not know himself, in Solomon's words, he must go forth and follow, 'As if He said: go forth from Me and My similitude into the place of dissimilitude, or from yourself into the lonely places of concupiscence or curiosity.' 'But let this not be so, O bride of Christ, let you rather recognize yourself; let you be ready to discern yourself.'[95] In this passage William linked together, and almost identified, three basic features of the twelfth-century spirituality: self-knowledge, conscience, and the creation of man in the image of God.

For Bernard there were two books written in man: one of recollection written in the conscience, where the soul read its history, and one of faith written in the heart, where the soul found certainty, through the Holy Spirit, in the proofs of God's goodness.[96] To these was added the book of experience, which represented the sphere of action besides those of recollection and faith. Already in the eleventh century Otloh of St Emmeram took up Cassian's concept of *experimentum* and stressed the importance within an individual

---

[92] Richard of St Victor, *Beniamin minor*, 78, in *PL*, CXCVI, 56A.

[93] Hugh of St Victor, *De arrha animae*, in *PL*, CLXXVI, 954C. See Javelet (1959), p. 227.

[94] Hugh of St Victor, *In hierarchiam coelestem s. Dionysii Areopagiticae*, 2, in *PL*, CLXXV, 948A. See Javelet (1959), pp. 148–50. In the *Didascalicon*, VI, 5, ed. Charles H. Buttimer (Catholic University of America: Studies in Medieval and Renaissance Latin 10; Washington 1939), p. 123, Hugh said that 'By contemplating what God has done, we recognize what we ought to do.'

[95] William of St Thierry, *Super Cantica*, in *PL*, CLXXX, 493C–4B. In his *In epistolam ad Romanos*, III, 12, ibid., 595B, William again linked self-knowledge with the creation of man in the image of God. See Javelet (1959), p. 25, and Courcelle (1974), pp. 253–7.

[96] Leclercq (1964a).

monk of the personal experience of divine power, grace, and love.[97] Guigo of La Chartreuse said that a visit from Christ was understood only when it was read in the book of experience, which in the works of some Cistercian writers took on a quasi-technical meaning of a personal and almost physical awareness of the presence of God in the soul, like Onulf of Speyer's description of monks who tasted and felt the sweetness of the Lord.[98] Experience in this sense was almost equivalent to mystic union with God. But it was also used in a simpler sense, closer to the modern use of experience, to refer to the link between moral theory and practice, which was not abstract or absolute but was based on activity in the world.[99] Experience was thus at the same time the application of moral precepts in action and the basis on which the precepts were founded. This was what the monks at St Mary of York meant when they said that the rule of Benedict set forth the Gospel 'not as an allegorical exposition but in simple experience and the visible exhibition of work'.[100] The lay brother Sunnulphus, who had his conscience for a book and the Holy Spirit for a teacher, 'grew daily in his knowledge of the saints, reading in the book of experience', presumably by observing the holy men around him.[101] A simpler type of experience was involved in the desire of the faithful to see the eucharist, which led to the practice of elevating the host, and to have relics in transparent crystal containers.

Love of God, love of man, and love of self were indissolubly linked in the monastic spirituality of the twelfth century, and human friendship led to and reflected friendship with God.[102] Bernard of Clairvaux in his treatise *On loving God* traced the four steps by which love progressed from man's love of himself for his own sake, to love of God for man's sake, to love of self for God's sake, and finally to love of God for God's sake.[103] For Richard of St Victor, the love of God was reflected in the love of man, whose love was the image of

[97] Schauwecker (1964), p. 102.
[98] Hallier (1969), pp. 120–34.
[99] Stock (1975), citing Bernard, *Serm.* 5 *super Cantica*, 8, and *Serm.* 36 *super Cantica*, 6, ed. Leclercq, I, 24, and II, 8, and other Bernardine texts on experience. See de Lubac (1959–64), I, 585–6, on Bernard's effort to apply rather than explain the Scriptures, and Borst (1992), pp. 80–1, on *experientia* and *experimentum*, which he defined as 'a method of realizing mental principles through action, of proving conviction through deeds'.
[100] Hugh of Kirkstall, *Narratio*, ed. Walbran, p. 15.
[101] Ibid., p. 118. See p. 196 above.
[102] According to the inscription on the ladder of virtues in Herrad of Hohenbourg's *Hortus deliciarum*, 'Only the virtue of love, which contains the other virtues, leads to receiving the crown of the celestial prize' (plate 1). See Rousselot (1908), esp. pp. 3–4 on twelfth century, 43–9 on Hugh of St Victor, and 49–55 and 76–7 on Bernard; Lewis (1936), esp. pp. 87–111 on the twelfth century; Chenu (1969), pp. 33–9; Leclercq (1979), pp. 27–85; and Morris (1989), pp. 368–9. On friendship, see the works cited p. 138 n. 52 above, esp. Fiske (1970) and McGuire (1988).
[103] Bernard, *De diligendo Deo*, VIII–X, 23–9, ed. Leclercq, III, 138–44. On the linked loves of God and neighbour, see Hugh of Fouilloy, *De rota verae religionis*, II, 10, in de Clercq (1959–60), p. 19, and plate 5, where *amor Dei* and *amor proximi* are the two spokes in the section of the rim of the wheel of true religion labelled *caritas*.

the Holy Spirit, not *in* or *ad* but *secundum imaginem*.[104] Among the favourite precepts of spiritual writers at that time was *Dilige et quod vis fac* or *Habe caritatem et fac quicquid vis*, which derived ultimately from St Augustine and expressed the belief that people who loved properly, that is, loved God first and other people, including themselves, in relation to God, could behave as they wished without fear of doing evil, because their actions would be informed by love.[105] Its implications in practice were much like those of the Golden Rule. The motto on the seal of the Norman priory of Sainte-Barbe (the letter of whose former prior was cited above) – *Si recte vivis fac mihi quod tibi vis* – seems to mean 'Do unto me what you wish for yourself provided you live rightly', which is probably the same as loving rightly.[106] Love, liberty, and life went together, and proper love was the essential concomitant of the freedom to live as one wanted. 'Love and do what you will' was therefore a multi-purpose slogan in the monastic polemics of the twelfth century and was used by innovators who wanted to break out into new forms of religious life and by conservatives who tried to defend the established ways. Peter the Venerable associated it with the single eye of the Gospel, with Paul's injunction to do all things in charity, and the dispensing power of the abbot to adjust the observance of the rule of Benedict.[107] The canon Hugh Farsit of Soissons argued in a letter criticizing the innovations of the Premonstratensians that the holier and better observances established by men lead the soul to the love of God and must be preserved because the law exists for the feeble, not for the just.[108] This suggests that the concept was being used to justify innovations, but its more radical implications for stepping outside the framework of normal behaviour did not emerge until later.[109] Caesarius of Heisterbach hinted at this danger when he remarked in his *Dialogue of miracles*, before giving an account of an act of theft by a saintly provost of Cologne, that 'Many things are allowed to saints that are prohibited to people who are not saints. Where the spirit of the Lord is, there is liberty. Whence the authority: Have love and do what you will.'[110]

The monk's greatest inspiration to love, model for reform, and ally in the struggle against internal and external enemies was Christ, Whose humanity took on a new importance in the eleventh and twelfth centuries both as an

---

[104] Richard of St Victor, *Beniamin maior*, V, 11, in *PL*, CXCVI, 180B, cited by Javelet (1967), I, 423–5.

[105] Gallay (1955); Chenu (1969), pp. 28–9; and John Benton, in *Renaissance and Renewal* (1982), p. 243 n. 93.

[106] *Chronicon de s. Barbara in Algia*, ed. Sauvage (n. 3), pp. 23–4.

[107] Peter the Venerable, *Ep.* 111, ed. Constable, I, 281.

[108] Constable (1994b), pp. 261–2.

[109] James (1902), p. 80: 'Saint Augustine's maxim, *Dilige et quod uis fac* – if you but love [God], you may do as you incline – is morally one of the profoundest of observations, yet it is pregnant . . . with passports beyond the bounds of conventional morality'; cf. p. 361.

[110] Caesarius, *Dialogus*, VI, 5, ed. Strange, I, 352.

object of devotion and as an example for imitation.[111] The emphasis in early medieval spirituality, and for most early monks, was on Christ's divinity, which made possible the divinization of man, and on His royalty, which overcame the forces of evil, though there were always individuals, especially in the regional spiritual traditions in Syria and Ireland, who emphasized the tender aspects of His humanity and suffering service. A more exclusive concentration on the human life of Christ and a passionate devotion to His humanity became general in the eleventh century and were exemplified in men like Romuald and Damiani, for whom Christ was the object not only of reverence and worship but also of love and inspiration. 'Whoever embraces Christ with a constant love in the recess of his heart', wrote Damiani in his *Monastic institution*, 'whoever meditates continually on the mystery of His passion for the sake of imitation, for this person Christ will surely become "a bundle of myrrh . . . and will abide within his breast" [Song of Songs 1.12].'[112] Passages like this can be found in the writings especially of the reformers, including Bernard and his followers, whose devotion to the human Jesus has been studied by many scholars. But it also appears in the works of black monks and must be considered, in varying degrees, a general characteristic of monastic spirituality at that time. According to a monk named Martinian, who may have lived at Rebais or Marmoutier in the late eleventh or early twelfth centuries, the true monk should always have Christ before his eyes like the mirror used by a woman to see if she is properly dressed. 'For Christ is not only the mirror but also the fount of all the good which the monk acquires from his contempt of this vanity.'[113] The biographer of Gerald of Salles, writing long after his death, said that he 'loved Christ, preached Christ, imitated Christ, and rose to Christ'.[114] This devotion concentrated especially on the childhood and death of Christ – His most human periods – and on His poverty and sufferings, although the other aspects of His life on earth were frequently cited. Some of the tenderest expressions in art as well as in literature were reserved for the baby and the child Jesus and for His mother Mary. Several treatises and letters were devoted exclusively to His infancy and boyhood, of which the best known is that by Aelred of Rievaulx *On the boy Jesus when he was twelve years old*. The most passionate displays were reserved, however, for His crucifixion, which drew on the well-springs of love and pity and also on the desire of His followers to show their devotion by relieving His sufferings and, insofar as they could, by participating in them. 'If you love', Geoffrey of St Thierry said of the crucifixion in one of his sermons, 'there is nothing

[111] See Constable (1995a), pp. 169–217, and esp. 179–93, on the material in this paragraph.
[112] Peter Damiani, *Institutio monialis*, 3, in *PL*, CXLV, 735CD.
[113] Martinian, *Exhortatio*, II, 14–15, ed. H. Roux, in *Mélanges bénédictins publiés à l'occasion du XIVe centenaire de la mort de saint Benoît par les moines de l'abbaye de Saint-Jérôme de Rome* (Abbaye S. Wandrille 1947), pp. 342–3.
[114] *Vita Giraldi de Salis*, II, 18, in *AASS*, 23 Oct. X, 258D (*BHL* 3547). See *Rouleaux des morts*, pp. 279–81, on this *Life*, which, though late, incorporated contemporary sources.

in the act or in the account that does not move, does not penetrate and enter the spirit'.[115] Bernard of Clairvaux wrote in 1138 to the future abbot Hugh of Bonneval, who was still a novice and fearful of the harshness of Cistercian life, that he should consider the sufferings of Christ on the cross and

> suck not the wounds but the breasts of the Crucified One. He will be as a mother to you, and you as a son to Him, and the nails that will pass through His hands and feet to yours will to some extent be unable to harm the Crucified One to the same degree (*nec pariter Crucifixum laedere aliquatenus poterunt*).[116]

The poor of Christ were not only those who had given up their property for His sake but those who 'Naked followed the naked Christ', shared His sufferings, carried His cross, whipped themselves as He was whipped, and in a few exceptional cases bore the marks or stigmata of the wounds of His passion.[117]

This devotion to the humanity of Christ penetrated every aspect of the life of the church at that time. It can be seen in the liturgy, in the cult of the eucharist and the elevation of the host, in the new hymns to the Sacred Heart, of which the earliest is attributed to a Premonstratensian canon of Steinfeld, and in the Palm Sunday processions carrying the sacrament, which began in the eleventh century and later developed into the official celebration of Corpus Christi Day.[118] It can be seen in the devotion to the cross, the holy lance, and the five wounds of Christ,[119] and, most clearly, in iconography. The figure of Christ on the cross changed from a crowned, erect, alive, and victorious Saviour in the early Middle Ages to a slumped and wounded dead man, Who began to appear both in painting and sculpture on the walls of many parish churches,[120] and in the little bronze and wooden crucifixes that played an increasing role in monastic and later lay spirituality. Peter the Venerable in his letter concerning the death of his mother Raingard, who was a nun at Marcigny, gave an account of how on her deathbed she asked to have 'a cross with an image of the Lord brought to her' and how 'she brought the effigy of the Lord to her mouth, and licking His feet with her tongue, pressed it with the whole strength of her body on her face', adoring His passion, death,

---

[115] Geoffrey of St Thierry, *Serm.* 23, in MS Reims, Bibl. mun., 581, fol. 80[r]a.

[116] Bernard, *Ep.* 322, ed. Leclercq, VIII, 257. See Constable (1995a), p. 204 (misnumbered Ep. 332). Chrysogonus Waddell pointed out that the second *crucifixus* may refer to Hugh (i.e. the nails will harm him less if they come through the hands and feet of Christ), but the previous *crucifixus* can only be Christ, and both words are capitalized in Leclercq's edition. See also n. 125 below.

[117] See Constable (1995a), pp. 199–217.

[118] See Lanfranc, *Decreta*, 25, in *CCM*, III, 22–5, and notes there on the Palm Sunday procession; Wilmart (1932a), esp. p. 371 on the elevation of the host; and Schreiber (1940) and (1941) on the Sacred Heart.

[119] See Wilmart (1932a), pp. 138–46, and Constable (1995a), pp. 209 (on the wounds) and 210–16 (on the cross).

[120] According to Delaruelle (1971), pp. 149–50, parish churches began to have crucifixes in the twelfth century: 'L'intimité du fidèle avec son Seigneur en croix n'a donc commencé qu'à une époque relativement tardive.'

and wounds and holding it until she died. 'Believing that she saw not the image but [Christ] Himself on that cross, it could not be taken from her embrace.'[121] Raingard seems innocently to have fallen into the error of which the Premonstratensian Herman, who was a convert from Judaism, accused the Christians in the alleged debate in 1128 with Rupert of Deutz, who replied that

> We do not cherish the image of the crucifix or of anything as the deity, but by the form of the cross we represent to ourselves by pious devotion . . . the passion of Christ that should be adored, so that while we picture His death externally through the likeness of the cross, we are also incited internally to love of that Man, and remember constantly that He Who was entirely without sin suffered such an ignominious death for our sake, we ponder constantly by pious consideration how many things we who are involved in many and mighty sins ought to suffer for love of Him.[122]

Aelred of Rievaulx likewise stressed the importance of representations of the crucifix in his treatise on the life of recluses. 'An image of the Saviour hanging on the cross should be enough for you on your altar. It represents to you His passion which you imitate; it invites [you] by its spread arms to His embraces, in which you delight; and it pours out to you from its naked breasts the milk of sweetness in which you find consolation.'[123]

There is in this and other accounts of personal devotion to Jesus an emotional and sensual quality that may offend modern religious sensibilities and is often passed over, if not entirely suppressed, in scholarly accounts and translations, though it was an essential and inescapable aspect of medieval and early modern piety.[124] It appears in Onulf's reference to the monk's tasting and feeling the sweetness of the Lord, in Ivo's description of thirsting after the fountain of life with the mouth of the heart, and in Bernard's advice to suck the breasts of Christ.[125] To contemporaries the taste, touch, sight, smell, and sounds associated with the spiritual life were certainly more real than they

---

[121] Peter the Venerable, *Ep.* 53, ed. Constable, I, 169.

[122] Herman, *De conversione sua*, 3, ed. Gerlinde Niemeyer (*MGH*, Quellen zur Geistesgeschichte des Mittelalters 4; Weimar 1963), p. 80. Herman went on to say that for ignorant people images supplied the place of books. See p. 64 n. 82 above on this work. Theophilus, *De diversis artibus*, 3, ed. C.R. Dodwell (MT; Edinburgh and London 1961), pp. 63–4, which is dated by Van Engen (1980), p. 162, in the mid-to-late 1120s, said that representations of the passion should inspire sympathy and pity in the beholder. See the description by Elizabeth of Schönau, *Liber visionum*, I, 48, ed. Roth, p. 24, of her vision of the dying Christ on the cross, which inspired pity, sadness, and tears.

[123] Aelred of Rievaulx, *De institutione inclusarum*, 26, ed. Charles Dumont (SC 76; Paris 1961), p. 104; see 11, pp. 72–4, on the special devotion to Christ during Lent. See also the *Ancrene riwle*, ed. and tr. James Morton (Camden Society 57; London 1853), p. 137, on contemplating and kissing the crucifix. See p. 66 n. 95 above on this work.

[124] Grundmann (1961), pp. 412–14.

[125] In *The Letters of Saint Bernard of Clairvaux*, tr. Bruno Scott James (Chicago 1953), p. 449, Bernard's *suge non tam uulnera quam ubera Crucifixi* is translated 'draw life from the wounds of Christ'.

are for modern people, who have inherited from the eighteenth century (rather
than from the Puritans, as is sometimes thought) a tendency to separate
religion and piety from sensuality and sexuality.[126] For a monk or nun in the
Middle Ages who tasted the milk from the breasts of the Virgin or of Christ,
felt the warmth of His embrace, saw His beauty and that of His saints, smelled
the odour of sanctity, or heard the angelic choirs the sensation was even more
intense than purely physical sensations are today.

This reality can be seen particularly in the accounts of mystic visions and
ecstatic meditations, which were so vivid that they had the force of actual
experiences, like the figure of Christ on the cross for Raingard. Rupert of
Deutz as a young man, when he was still a monk at the abbey of St Laurence
at Liège in the late eleventh century, had several such experiences, of which
the most striking was when he embraced a wooden image of Christ on the
cross above an altar in the church and while kissing Him felt His mouth open
'in order that I might kiss Him more deeply'.[127] According to an anonymous
monk, Jesus should be fed by Mary, who gives milk and food, and by the
monk, who 'ministers to Him what is needed as much as he can' and who
'receives the Boy in his hands and embraces Him, mingling sweet kisses'; and
the Carthusian Hugh of Lincoln expressed his passionate desire to have held
and kissed the feet of Jesus on the cross and 'to have held close to my heart
anything which His hands or any part of His body has touched'. In particular
he wanted to gather and taste the sweat that flowed from Christ's human body
'as something sweeter than honey'. 'How greatly are they to be pitied who
esteem anything else sweet, or desire anything except to cleave lovingly to
such a lover, and lovingly to obey Him. To my mind nothing can seem hard
to a man who has through meditation experienced His sweetness, and sweetly
digested it in the depths of his heart.'[128] There is no evidence that the appeal
of this sensual imagery was restricted to the celibate members of society or
was the result, as has been suggested, of the enforced chastity of monks and
nuns, which was no greater in the eleventh and twelfth centuries than it had
been in the early Middle Ages, when such sentiments were unknown. It was
rather the sign and expression of their sense of the reality of the humanity of
Jesus and of their desire to identify with Him in all possible ways. Mystical
experiences of this type have been described as part of the love-affair of the
soul with God, bringing the individual into direct contact with the absolute.
They were of central importance in bridging the gap between God and man
and in moving man away from the love of his own body towards the love of
Christ. Again and again in his sermons on the Song of Songs Bernard of

---

[126] Davie (1976), esp. pp. 1491–2.
[127] Rupert of Deutz, *Super Mattheum*, 12, in *CC:CM*, XXIX, 382–3. See Haacke (1980) and Van
Engen (1983), pp. 51 and 350–1.
[128] Leclercq (1944–5), pp. 11 and 13, and Adam of Eynsham, *Magna vita Hugonis*, IV, 3, ed.
Decima Douie and David Hugh Farmer (OMT; Oxford 1985), II, 14–15 (*BHL* 4018).

Clairvaux stressed the need for this type of fleshly love – *amor iste carnalis* – for the human Christ, by which 'the fleshly life [of the body] is shut out and spurned and the world is conquered'.[129] It was the precious gift of Christ to man and an essential part of the continuity between the material and spiritual worlds that alone led to salvation.

The importance of the humanity of Christ, as distinct from His divinity, is illustrated by the final *Meditation* of Guigo of La Chartreuse, who said that

> Man ought to follow only God, but he is able [to follow] only man. Man was therefore assumed so that in following what he can he also follows what he should. Likewise, it is of profit to conform only to God, in Whose image he was made, but he is able [to conform] only to man. God was therefore made so that when he conforms to man, to whom he can, he also conforms to God, from Whom he profits.[130]

A similar view is found in an early twelfth-century sermon attributed to Godfrey of Bath, who said that Christians must follow the way of love shown them by Christ. 'The Apostle did not order us to imitate God in divinity, since in truth we cannot by our nature, but in participation.'[131] Bernard said in his second sermon for Lent that 'The Lord is indeed sublime, but He is not presented to you, thus: His greatness is praiseworthy but not imitable', and in his first sermon for the birth of St Victor that 'We more safely emulate the more solid than the more sublime and things that are redolent more of virtue and less of glory.' And speaking of the incarnation in his first sermon for Christmas Bernard said that 'Power requires subjection, and majesty [requires] admiration, [but] neither of them imitation. Let, O Lord, the goodness, to which man who was created in Your image can be conformed, appear, since we neither can imitate nor is it suitable to emulate the majesty, the power, the wisdom.'[132] The ideal of the imitation of Christ was here applied specifically to the humanity rather than the divinity of Christ, but it embraced all aspects of His life on earth.

One of Bernard's most important disagreements with Abelard was over the precise effect of the incarnation on man and its role in salvation history. Abelard stressed the instructional role of the incarnate Wisdom of God in his *Christian theology*, composed in 1121/6, where he interpreted John 1.14 to mean that 'This Wisdom became incarnate in order that the knowledge of Wisdom might truly live in us through illumination. In this flesh that He assumed He perfectly instructed and showed us both, as I have said, by the

---

[129] Bernard, *Serm.* 21 *super Cantica*, V, 9, ed. Leclercq, I, 120.

[130] Guigo of La Chartreuse, *Meditatio* 476, ed. Wilmart (n. 36), p. 172, and ed. anon. (n. 36), p. 306. On *conformari/reformari*, see Stock (1983), p. 435.

[131] Published in *Sancti Aurelii Augustini . . . sermones inediti*, ed. D.A.B. Caillau (Paris 1836–42), II, 85–6. See *PL*, *Suppl.*, II, 876. On the attribution to Godfrey of Bath, see Morin (1893); Bonnes (1945–6), p. 174; and Bethell (1969a), p. 684.

[132] Bernard, *Serm.* 2 *in quadragesima*, 1; *Serm.* 1 *in natali s. Victoris*, 2; and *Serm.* 1 *in nativitate Domini*, 2, ed. Leclercq, IV, 245–6 and 360, and VI.I, 31.

way of His life and also by the passion of His death and likewise by the glory of His resurrection and ascension.'[133] He returned to this subject in his commentary on Romans, written in 1133/7, where he said that

> It seems to me that we are justified in the blood of Christ and reconciled to God in this, that, through this singular grace that has been shown us, His son received our nature and persisted up until death in teaching us by both word and example [and] He bound us to Himself more closely by love, so that aroused by so great a benefit of divine grace, true charity will not fear to bear anything.[134]

The view that the effect of the life of Christ lay in the hearts and minds of men, to whom He brought love and knowledge, was inadequate for Bernard, who stressed in his treatise *On the errors of Abelard* that the real work of Christ was that of liberation and regeneration. He not only taught and showed righteousness and love but bestowed and infused them. 'Neither the examples of humility nor the signs of love are anything without the sacrament of redemption.'[135] Yet Bernard expressed views very close to those of Abelard in some of his writings, as in the twenty-ninth sermon *On various matters*, where he said that 'Consideration of the incarnation of Christ and His entire existence in the flesh and most greatly of the passion most powerfully promotes this affective love of the heart';[136] and in his sermon on Holy Wednesday he said that the imitation of Christ by those who voluntarily gave up their property and followed Him was 'the strongest evidence that both the passion of the Saviour and the similitude of humanity are of use to me'. 'Here is the savour, here is the fruit both of labour and of grief.'[137] Alan of Auxerre described Bernard himself as 'an eager imitator of the goodness of the Lord',[138] and he referred to Christ as an example not only of suffering, poverty, and prayer but also of patience, obedience, humility, love, goodness, temperance, resistance to temptation, fasting, and other Christian virtues.[139] Bernard did not therefore deny the role of Christ in imparting knowledge and arousing love, but he never lost sight of His prime role as a redeemer. The two roles went together, as Guerric of Igny stressed in his second sermon on the annunciation, saying that God's love for man, which He showed by becoming a man for the sake of man, aroused the love of man for God and that 'the likeness

---

[133] Abelard, *Theologia christiana*, 4, 63, in *CC:CM*, XII, 292. See Mews (1985), p. 131, on the date. Murray (1967), p. 126, said that for Abelard the atonement involved not only the death of Christ but 'His whole life culminating in His death'.

[134] Abelard, *In epistolam Pauli ad Romanos*, II, in *CC:CM*, XI, 117. See Southern (1963), p. 96, with a somewhat different translation, and Mews (1985), p. 132, on the date.

[135] Bernard, *Ep.* 190 (*Tractatus de erroribus Abaelardi*), IX, 23–5, ed. Leclercq, VIII, 36–8 (quote on 38).

[136] Bernard, *Serm.* 29 *de diversis*, 2, ed. Leclercq, VI.1, 211.

[137] Bernard, *Serm. in feria IV hebdomadae sanctae*, 12, ed. Leclercq, V, 65.

[138] Alan of Auxerre, *Vita secunda Bernardi*, XXIV, 65, in Bernard, ed. Mabillon, II(6), 2456D (*BHL* 1232).

[139] Bernard, *Serm.* 3 *in laudibus Virginis*, 14; *Serm.* 4 *in adventu*, IV, 7; and *Serm.* 2 *in die pentecostes*, 5, ed. Leclercq, IV, 45 and 187, and V, 168.

and nature of a neighbour in the humanity of God' nourished man's love for his neighbour. 'The conception of the Virgin was not only mystical but also moral', he continued, 'because the sacrament is for the redemption and the example is for imitation, so that you plainly cancel the grace of the sacrament in yourself if you do not imitate the virtue of the example.'[140]

An echo of this dispute is found in the changes made in the traditional text, which went back to at least the ninth century, of the hymn *Conditor alme siderum* when it was introduced into the second Cistercian hymnal, compiled between 1134 and 1147.[141] The second stanza, which read 'You, grieving that the present time (*saeculum*) would perish by the destruction of death, saved the feeble world [by] giving a remedy to the guilty', was changed in the Cistercian version to, 'Grieving for men who are subject to the laws of death, You were made a man and restore life in Your blood.' The three points to be noticed here are the substitution of 'men' for 'the present time', the specific reference to the incarnation (*factus homo*), and the change from God's giving a remedy to His restoring life in His blood, which emphasized both His humanity and the sacramental character of the gift. The changes in the fourth stanza, which was based on Philippians 2.10, restored Paul's reference to the infernal as well as the celestial and terrestrial knees that bow at the name of Jesus. And in the fifth stanza the Cistercian version put 'Preserve us in time in which we are for a long time strangers' in place of the traditional 'Preserve us in time from the weapon of the treacherous enemy.' While each of these changes was small, they reflected distinctive (though not necessarily new) aspects of twelfth-century spirituality and brought out respectively the sacramental significance of the incarnation, the universal mastery of Christ, and the view of man as a wanderer. Changes like these help to relate the developments in theology and spirituality to the movement of religious reform and to show how the new monks saw the life they led.[142]

The new mood can be seen most clearly in the revived stress in the twelfth century on the description in Genesis of the creation of man in the image and likeness of God and on the associated doctrine of the natural dignity of man.[143] The salvation of man no longer depended entirely upon the power and mercy of God, whose favour had to be won, like that of a great king, by

---

[140] Guerric of Igny, *Serm.* 2 *de annuntiatione dominica*, 4, in *PL*, CLXXXV, 122C–3A. He went on to stress that God is both a father and a mother.

[141] For the material in this paragraph, see Waddell (1984), I, 57–60, and II, 65.

[142] See also the changing relation of voice and mind in the liturgy cited p. 207 above.

[143] On the medieval concept of the dignity of man and his creation in the image of God, see Garin (1938); Otto (1963) on the *imago*-concept; Javelet (1967), I, 247–9; Trinkaus (1970), I, 179–89; Kristeller (1972), p. 5, distinguishing the medieval and Renaissance concepts; Stock (1983), p. 323; and Morris (1989), pp. 317 and 367, citing Ivo of Chartres. On Grosseteste, who 'found in the personal union of the divine and human natures in God the Word the explanation for the personal union of the spiritual and material in man', see Dales (1977), pp. 569–72 (quote on 569), and Southern (1986), p. 189, who said that he had a special symbol to mark passages in his reading on the dignity of man.

constant worship and prayer, since the imitation of Christ's humanity held out hope that with God's help man might recover the perfection in which he was created and abolish the difference between his original and his present condition. This was the region of dissimilitude, which was described sometimes in biblical terms as a captivity and more commonly in geographical terms as a foreign or strange land that had to be crossed in the journey – the process of renewal and reformation – of the soul from unlikeness to likeness.[144] Whatever it was called, the difference was essentially personal and of man's own creation, as William of St Thierry made clear when he spoke of man's going forth from God's likeness into the place of unlikeness and from himself into the lonely places of concupiscence and curiosity.[145] It was the result of the freedom given by God to man, who can choose either the way leading to reformation and salvation or that leading to deformation and damnation. 'The true nobility of man is to submit himself voluntarily (*sponte*) to the allegiance of the Creator', according to a charter of about 1070; the author of the Cistercian treatise *On conscience* said that the human will was the cause of salvation and damnation; and for some writers this power of choice constituted the main feature of the dignity of man and his difference from animals.[146] The themes of human exaltation and depression were therefore complementary, and it is no accident that Innocent III planned to write as a pendant to *On the misery of the human condition* a treatise on man's dignity, which would have given a more confident and optimistic impression of the possibility of salvation.[147]

For centuries monks had heard the call of Leo the Great in the first sermon for Christmas: 'Recognize, O Christian, your dignity', and his admonition, based on 1 Corinthians 6.15, to 'Remember of Whose head and of Whose body you are a member.'[148] These words took on a new reality in the works of writers like Hugh of St Victor, who said in the *Didascalicon* that the contemplation of truth and the practice of virtue were the two things that could restore the divine likeness in man. Man like God, Hugh continued, is wise and just, though (unlike God) not unchangeably so, and he performs a divine action in striving to restore his nature and a human action in following the needs of his humanity.[149] Richard of St Victor made the same point in his *Greater Benjamin*, where after stressing the need to examine oneself and others, he said that

[144] On the *regio dissimilitudinis*, see pp. 261 and 276 above.
[145] William of St Thierry, *Super Cantica*, in *PL*, CLXXX, 493C–4A, cited p. 276 above.
[146] *Cartulaire de l'abbaye cardinale de la Trinité de Vendôme*, ed. Charles Métais (Paris 1893–1905), I, 336, no. 202. See Bloch (1963), p. 329 n.2, on this charter, and generally Lottin (1942–60), I, 222.
[147] At least four humanist works on the dignity of man were planned as pendants to Innocent's treatise: Garin (1938), p. 123, and Trinkaus (1970), I, 174.
[148] Leo the Great, *Tractatus* 21, 3, in *CC*, CXXXVIII, 88. See Chrysogonus Waddell, in *Renaissance and Renewal* (1982), p. 91.
[149] Hugh of St Victor, *Didascalicon*, ed. Buttimer (n. 94), p. 15.

Anyone can easily learn from their own experience, I think, how greatly this examination of souls is able either to raise [a barrier] against vice or to arouse to good. Know, O man, I ask, your dignity; think about that excellent nature of your soul, how God made it in His image and similitude, how He raised it above every fleshly creature.[150]

Bernard of Clairvaux in his second sermon on the nativity of Christ likewise called on man to recognize his dignity and described the condition of man as above that of all other creatures.[151] William of St Thierry continued his praise of self-knowledge in his commentary on the Song of Songs 1.7, which was cited above, by saying that man will find the kingdom of God within himself if he purifies and exerts himself: 'O image of God, recognize your dignity; let the effigy of the Author shine forth in you. You are vile to yourself, but you are a precious object.' Though he has departed from his true image and is covered with false ones, he can caste them off and recover the image in which he was created by knowing his real nature. 'Stand fast in your position, lest you succumb, lest you fall. The strength of your station is the knowledge of grace ... Blessed person and joyful man, who has in the house of his heart and in the treasury of his conscience this glory and the riches of this grace.'[152]

In order to make the process of reformation more comprehensible and accessible than it was in the abstract language of soteriological theology, it was often described in simple and homely images derived from everyday life and observation. Anselm said that 'The image is so worn and blotted out by faults, so darkened by the smoke of sin, that it cannot do what it was made for unless you renew and refashion it.'[153] He thus suggested that like a dark picture or old medallion the soul would benefit from a thorough cleaning. Aelred of Rievaulx in the *Mirror of love* said that 'The reformation of the image [of God in man] will be perfect if no forgetfulness corrupts memory, if no error casts a shadow over knowledge, and if no cupidity obstructs love.'[154] For him, therefore, a good memory, accurate knowledge, and proper love made the reformation of man possible. Other writers used the images of putting on new clothes and of pressing softened wax into the matrix of a seal to describe how the image could be restored and the individual Christian reformed, and also how the faithful could be formed.[155] Basil of Caesarea in his so-called *Long Rules* said that 'While the mind is still easy to mould and

---

[150] Richard of St Victor, *Beniamin maior*, III, 13, in *PL*, CXCVI, 123A.

[151] Bernard, *Serm. 2 in nativitate Domini*, 1, ed. Leclercq, IV, 252.

[152] William of St Thierry, *Super Cantica*, in *PL*, CLXXX, 494C–5B. See Javelet (1959), p. 25, and Dales (1977), p. 569.

[153] Anselm, *Proslogion*, 1, ed. Schmitt, I, 100, and tr. Benedicta Ward (Harmondsworth 1973), p. 244.

[154] Aelred of Rievaulx, *Speculum caritatis*, I, 5, 14, in *CC:CM*, I, 18.

[155] See Javelet (1967), I, 83 and 366–7; Bynum (1979), pp. 82–3; and Giles Constable, in *Renaissance and Renewal* (1982), p. 46. Dante used the image of wax and seal in the *Paradiso*, II, 132, VIII, 127–8, and XIII, 67–9.

pliable as wax, taking the form that is impressed upon it, it should be exercised from the very beginning in every good discipline.'[156] And Eadmer wrote that Anselm 'compared the time of youth to wax that has been properly tempered for impressing a seal'. A boy is too soft to take an impression, and an old man is too hardened, but 'Between them is the youth and the young man, aptly tempered between softness and hardness. If you instruct him, you will be able to mould him to what you want.'[157] This shows the importance of the example and instruction of a teacher, who stood in the place of Christ for a student and set him on the right path. According to Philip of Harvengt, 'The cleric cannot conform more expressly to Christ [and] the disciple to the master unless he strives not only to follow in his footsteps but also to imitate his way of life, so that the Gospel text may be said of him that "If any man minister unto me, let him follow me" [John 12.26].'[158]

For people in the twelfth century the greatest hope of salvation lay in this reform and renewal of the soul according to the image of God in which it was created and on which the contemporary view of the dignity of man was primarily based. In intellectual circles, however, and especially among some of the teachers at Chartres, there was also discussion of the doctrines of hierarchy, deification, and microcosm, all of which placed man in a larger setting and held out the hope of human perfectibility.[159] These were rarely used in a developed form in monastic spirituality, which was based more on the bible than on works of ancient philosophy, and when found in works addressed to monks they usually derived from the writings of philosophically minded fathers like Gregory of Nyssa. The popularity and influence of some of the works of the Greek fathers in the twelfth century was in great part because they presented doctrines concerning the nature of man that were congenial to, if not identical with, the views of Latin writers in the west. Guerric of Igny's reference in one of his sermons to the birth of the man Christ 'in the outer world of our body, which is also customarily called the minor world (*minor mundus*)',[160] reflected the view of man as a microcosm enclosing within his person the elements of the macrocosm of the world. It has already been seen that a similar view inspired the speech attributed to Stephen Harding by William of Malmesbury, where the reason of the universe was equated with that of the rule of Benedict.

---

[156] Basil, *Long Rules*, R. 15, in *Ascetical Works*, tr. M. Monica Wagner (The Fathers of the Church 9; Washington 1950), p. 267.

[157] Eadmer, *Vita Anselmi*, I, 11, ed. R.W. Southern (MT; Edinburgh and London 1962), pp. 20–1 (*BHL* 526).

[158] Philip of Harvengt, *De institutione clericorum*, 4: *De continentia clericorum*, 63, in *PL*, CCIII, 749D.

[159] Garin (1938), p. 139, and Dales (1977), p. 558, who saw the concept of man's unity and excellence as 'a variation on the theme of man the microcosm'.

[160] Guerric of Igny, *Serm. 2 de annuntiatione dominica*, 5, in *PL*, CLXXXV, 123D.

For average Christians the greatest influence of these views was probably in the realm of art, where they could see, in addition to the standard representations of God in human form, which were constant reminders that man was created in His image (since it never occurred to them that their image of God might have derived from the image of man!), occasional representations of man in a circle or a diagram that stressed his ideal form and relation to the proportions of the universe.[161] Some scholars have suggested that the *homo quadratus* of this type, and its philosophical background in the doctrine of the macrocosm and the microcosm, were related to the design of buildings, and especially the new churches that were built up *ad quadratum* out of squares, triangles, and circles and may have been seen as miniature embodiments of the perfection of divine proportions. It may have also been related to the appearance in art at that time of a greater naturalism in the representations of man, and especially the singling out of various parts of the body according to their functions, which paralleled the organological view of society as a body composed of interdependent social and functional categories.[162] While a casual viewer would not have been likely to draw any profound conclusion from such representations, they confirmed a sense of the place of man in the broad structure of the universe and the relation of the human body, as well as the soul, to the divine standard of perfection.

These views on the relation of God and man were an important element in what has been called the optimism of the twelfth century.[163] The growing confidence in the possibility of salvation can be seen not only in religious writings but also in secular works, including charters, where there was greater emphasis than previously on optimistic themes like the goodness of God, the value of good works and intercession, and the church as the image of the heavenly Jerusalem and the instrument of salvation.[164] Above all, the full imitation of Christ's humanity opened a number of ways in which spiritual reformation and renewal could be achieved. Individual aspects of Jesus's life on earth had long been cited to justify particular activities and functions, but now for the first time His entire earthly life presented a challenge to the ideal of withdrawal that had long been considered the standard of Christian perfection. The life of Christ on earth was seen as presenting the perfect example of a life that combined contemplation with action in the world. Anselm of Havelberg wrote in his *Apologetic letter* that Christ 'presented in His own single person the example of both lives in the form of the highest contemplation and in the form of perfect action, and offered Himself as the

[161] Caviness (1983).
[162] Davy (1964), pp. 189–90, and Ladner (1965), pp. 41–5.
[163] Javelet (1967), I, 296–7 and 451–4, and Southern (1970a), p. 58, who contrasted the mood of the early fourteenth century with 'the optimism which had buoyed up the efforts of the previous two centuries'. See also Southern (1995), p. 56.
[164] Mattoso (1968), pp. 283–7.

norm of living rightly in deeds and in words to all Christians and especially to His apostles'. He went on to give a sarcastic description of simple monks

who think the contemplative life is to sit idly in cloisters with joined hands and folded sleeves, to have idle nourishment, to receive idle clothing, to walk as they wish from corner to corner with a light step, to explore with cunning inquiry the going and coming of the abbot and the absence and presence of the prior, to investigate with a wandering curiosity from passers-by what is going on out-side, to confuse everything by an intricate multiplicity of signs, with the tongue quiet and the restless hand usurping its place, and, to conclude briefly, to abound idly in everything beyond necessity and to live idly by abounding.[165]

Just as the apostle Paul was 'more sublime and worthy' than the hermit Paul of Thebes, Anselm continued, so 'a cleric who lives well and regularly is without doubt always to be put ahead of even the best monk'. That clerics who committed crimes were sent to monasteries also showed the superiority of clerics to monks, he argued earlier, as did the fact that clerics who sought to become monks, 'fleeing the narrow path which leads to the homeland', had to be returned.[166] For Philip of Harvengt it was 'much easier to achieve mon-astic than clerical perfection, and much more precious, and therefore rarer, to find a good cleric than a good monk',[167] and Gerald of Wales said in the *Mirror of the church* that, although the contemplative life was more secure, the active life when holy and honest was more useful and glorious.[168] Although these opinions came from sources that were unfavourable to monks and were clearly prejudiced, it is interesting that they were expressed at all.

Similar views, without necessarily the same conclusions, are found in works written by monks, above all in the *Golden letter* of William of St Thierry, who praised the virtue and glory of 'the most powerful ambidextrous men', as he called them, who were both free for contemplation and prepared for outside work 'for the truth of carrying out love'. For him this combination of love and faith was 'the one necessary thing' that Jesus praised in Mary of Bethany, 'to whom much was forgiven because she loved much', and was therefore still in a monastic context, but the concept of the ambidextrous prelate who was both contemplative and active had an influence on later medieval thought and prepared the way, like the *vita biformis* praised by Hildebert of Lavardin, for the emergence in the thirteenth century of the ideal of a mixed life of action and contemplation.[169] For some authors the active and contemplative lives alternated in the same person, and for others action was itself a way to sal-

---

[165] Anselm of Havelberg, *Epistola apologetica*, in *PL*, CLXXXVIII, 1133B and 1135BC.

[166] Ibid., coll. 1125C–6A, 1136C, and 1137B.

[167] Philip of Harvengt, *De institutione clericorum*, 4: *De continentia clericorum*, 122, in *PL*, CCIII, 832B; see 86, col. 780B, on the claims of monks to greater dignity and merit, and p. 269 above.

[168] Gerald of Wales, *Speculum ecclesiae*, I, 4, ed. John S. Brewer a.o. (RS 21; London 1861–91), IV, 18.

[169] William of St Thierry, *Ep. ad fratres de Monte Dei*, 12 and 71, ed. Davy, pp. 74–5 and 119–20. See von Moos (1965), p. 133, and Constable (1995a), pp. 67 and 91, with further references.

vation and an essential preparation for contemplation. The author of a homily attributed to Theodulf of Orléans but probably written in the eleventh or twelfth century described the works of the active life as 'one mansion and one part of Syon, that is of the holy church' and said that 'By these examples, brothers, you can have confidence and certain hope of the promised judgement of God in the future.' The contemplative life, on the other hand, was

> of a few men, that is of monks, hermits, recluses, and some clerics and lay men whose mind is so fixed on God that it wants nothing else in the world . . . We cannot come to this life unless we have first fully and perfectly performed the works of the active life, since the one precedes the other, which is reached through the merits and works of the [active] one, just as the love of God is reached through the love of neighbour.[170]

The clearest expressions of the increasingly positive view of the active life in the eleventh and twelfth centuries concerned bishops who became monks, and vice versa. In 1072, when archbishop Siegfried of Mainz entered a monastery, the clergy and people of Mainz sent a letter imploring him to return. To leave the world and follow Christ is praiseworthy, they said, for those 'who live only for themselves, who have accepted no care for cultivating the vineyard of the Lord Sabaoth, and for whom it is enough to save only themselves, since they have to render an account of no one except themselves'. Siegfried, however, occupied an office like that of the apostles, who did not desert the cure of souls because they bore the cross of Christ. 'Every order, every dignity, every profession is below the apostolic dignity. There is nothing in the world more eminent or closer to God than the episcopal life, to which every monk and recluse, every cenobite and hermit gives way as being less.'[171] Arguments of this sort probably weighed with Robert of Bethune in the internal struggle between his desire to remain a regular canon and his duty to become a bishop, and also with Otto of Bamberg when he wanted to become a monk at Michaelsberg, of which the abbot said it would be useless for 'such a man, so necessary to the church and to the poor of Christ, to enter the silence of a monastery'. 'What monk is of such perfection that we can compare his merits and poverty to your wealth?'[172]

There were also signs of reassessing the value of a lay life of activity in the world. Already in the tenth century Odo of Cluny praised the life of Gerald

---

[170] 'Il Codice Casanatense 1338. Sette homelie inedite di Teodulfo d'Orléans', ed. Umberto Moricca, in *Bilychnis. Rivista di studi religiosi* 32 (1928), p. 255. It is interesting that the author recognized that clerics and lay men could lead a contemplative life. In the thirteenth century Thomas of Eccleston, *De adventu fratrum minorum in Angliam*, 11, ed. A.G. Little (Collection d'études et de documents 7; Paris 1909), p. 65, referred to a brother Giles who was *laicus sed contemplativus*.

[171] *Udalrici Babenbergensis codex*, Ep. 39, in *Monumenta Bambergensia*, ed. Philipp Jaffé (BRG 5; Berlin 1869), pp. 82–3.

[172] Herbord, *De Ottone episcopo Bambergensi*, I, 30, ibid., pp. 726–7.

of Aurillac, saying that a good lay man was better than a bad monk,[173] and Ratherius of Verona warned a would-be monk that it was better to be a lay man in dress and a monk at heart than, as was often the case, a monk in dress and a lay man at heart.[174] Gregory VII likewise recognized the need for active lay princes in his letter to Hugh of Cluny deploring the entry to monastic life of Hugh of Burgundy. 'You have taken and received the duke into the peace of Cluny, and you have deprived a hundred thousand of a protector . . . God-fearing monks, priests, soldiers, and not a few poor men are, by the mercy of God, found in various places, but princes who love and fear God are found hardly anywhere else in the west.'[175]

These arguments were mostly *ad hominem* and *ad occasionem*, but they show the direction in which the winds of opinion were blowing. The concern of Miro of Ripoll to find a monastery that avoided the dangers of a life spent exclusively in the choir and offered some opportunity for Christian action was shared by Bernard of Clairvaux in his treatises *On consideration* and *On the steps of humility*, and the example of Bernard's own life combined a central focus on faith and love of God with activities both inside and outside his monastery. In his first sermon on the feast of Saints Peter and Paul, Bernard said that the apostles had taught him not how to fish or make tents, nor to read Plato or Aristotle, but to live, and above all to suffer evil, do good, and persevere unto death.[176] His biographers referred to his desire to harvest souls and convert sinners and described how 'his greatest concern for the salvation of the many' conflicted in his heart with his humility.[177] Joachim of Fiore probably had Bernard in mind when he described the Cistercian order as a mediator, like Scholastica and the Virgin, between action and preaching, on one hand, and quest and silence, on the other.[178] Bernard was the most eloquent spokesman and influential practitioner of a view that combined faith with action, but always with a primacy of faith, and that was at the time widely shared, even by those who opposed him in the monastic polemics of the day. The author of the *Rescriptum* refuting the Cistercian criticisms of the old monasticism wrote, quoting Romans 3.28, that 'We account a man to be justified by faith, without the works of the law', and when the Cluniac in the

---

[173] Odo of Cluny, *Vita Geraldi Auriliacensis*, II, 8, in *PL*, CXXXIII, 675B; cf. I, 8, where Odo said that a lay man could carry a sword in order to defend others, and II, 2, where bishop Gauzbert advised Gerald to remain in lay life, ibid., 647C and 670C (*BHL* 3411).

[174] Ratherius of Verona, *Exemplar ad Petrum Veneticum*, in *Miscellanea Cassinense* 1 (1897), II.3: *Monastica*, p. 17.

[175] Gregory VII, *Reg.*, VI, 17, ed. Erich Caspar (*MGH, Epistolae selectae* 2; Berlin 1920–3), p. 423–4. See Cowdrey (1970), pp. 144–7.

[176] Bernard, *Serm.* 1 *in sollemnitate apostolorum Petri et Pauli*, 3, ed. Leclercq, V, 188–90.

[177] William of St Thierry, *Vita prima Bernardi*, I, V, 26, in Bernard, ed. Mabillon, II(6), 2110D–11A (*BHL* 1211), and Geoffrey of Clairvaux, *Vita prima Bernardi*, III, VII, 28, ibid., col. 2210C (*BHL* 1214).

[178] Joachim of Fiore, *Vita s. Benedicti*, 15, ed. Cipriano Baraut, in *Analecta sacra Tarraconensia* 24 (1951), p. 68.

Dialogue between two monks asked what made men good and holy, the Cistercian replied, 'Nothing except faith, that which works through love in accordance with knowledge.'[179]

The combination of spiritual inwardness, with its stress on faith, love, liberty, and knowledge, and the imitation of Christ, with its ideal of a mixed life of action and contemplation on earth, ushered in a new era in the history of Christian spirituality and opened new paths of Christian perfection. As an ideal of lay sanctity emerged, a few voices were heard saying that monks were no better than lay men and even that all men were monks. If the virtues of monks were indeed inner virtues, it was possible for a pious lay man no less than a monk to be poor in spirit, solitary in mind, and a seeker for salvation. According to the *Book of teaching* of Stephen of Grandmont,

> All Christians who live in unity can be called monks, especially those who according to the Apostle are more removed from secular affairs and think only about God [cf. 2 Timothy 2.4] ... Whoever holds to the rule of God can be saved, with or without a wife, which cannot be done under the rule of Benedict; for it is of great perfection, but the rule of St Basil is of greater perfection. It is all taken from the common rule, however, that is, of the Gospel.[180]

Whether or not these are Stephen's own words, which may be doubted, they express a point of view that reached its full development in the early thirteenth century in the works of James of Vitry, who said that 'We do not consider religious only those who renounce the world and go over to a religious life, but we can also call regulars all the faithful of Christ who serve the Lord under the evangelical rule and who live in an orderly way under the one highest and supreme Abbot.' For James the entire body of the faithful was like a gigantic religious community under God the abbot. Unlike Stephen of Grandmont, who still accorded a certain primacy to those who renounced the world and thought only about God, James regarded no order or profession as more pleasing to God than the order of priests, who ministered to the spiritual needs of the faithful.[181]

In the interiorization of virtue, in the stress on inner responsibility and a direct relation to God, and in the consecration of the way of life of every faithful Christian lay the essence of what has been called the individualism of the twelfth century, which may be better described as personalism, since it involved a sense of the importance of the inner *persona* rather than a view of society, in modern terms, made up of distinct units marked by a self-awareness of their differences from other people.[182] A few signs of a sense of artistic and

---

[179] *Rescriptum*, ed. Leclercq, p. 87, and Idungus, *Dialogus*, II, 59, ed. Huygens, p. 436.

[180] Stephen of Grandmont, *De doctrina*, in *CC:CM*, VIII, 5–6.

[181] James of Vitry, *Historia occidentalis*, 34, ed. John F. Hinnebusch (Spicilegium Friburgense 17; Fribourg 1972), pp. 165–6. See p. 7 above.

[182] Javelet (1967), I, 454–7. On individualism in the twelfth century, see Morris (1972) and (1980); Bynum (1982b); and Olsen (1987), who stressed (p. 137) 'a sense of personal responsibility

intellectual individuality showed themselves in the emerging pride of author-ship and the signing of works of art by their makers, and in the concept of the distinctive gifts and talents – the *genius* – given by God to different people.[183] Life-like portraiture, which was virtually unknown in the early Middle Ages, also reappeared at about this time.[184] These had little impact, however, on the traditional pattern of anonymity that shrouded most artistic activity. Theophilus in the preface to the first book of his treatise *On the various arts* said that the artist's gift came from God: 'Let no one glorify himself, as if it were received of himself and not Another.'[185] In relation to other men and women, people in the twelfth century were still primarily mem-bers of groups,[186] but in relation to God and themselves they were seen more and more as free and independent beings who were responsible for their own spiritual welfare and had to make their own religious decisions. They were on their own before God and, oppressed by a sense of their own guilt and unworthiness, they felt a waning confidence in the power of others to assist them. There is something paradoxical in the fact that the doctrine and practice of indulgences, which in principle served to fill this gap by allowing the accumulation of merits for the future, emerged at the same time that their deeper spiritual justification was being questioned. When Stephen of Obazine built a new church in 1156 he refused to allow the bishop to give the usual indulgences to those who assisted, since they offered what God alone could give. 'Our own sins still oppress us,' he said, 'and we cannot relieve those of others.'[187] This sense of personal responsibility, and the waning belief in the value of intercessory prayers, may have contributed to the emergence in the second half of the twelfth century of the concept of purgatory as a place where the process of penance and salvation could continue between death and the Last Judgement and where, in effect, the Christian was given a last chance.[188] It promoted the appeal of many Christians to the saints and the Virgin to help overcome their own incapacity and do for them what they felt unable to

---

for one's own spiritual progress'. Strathern (1988), p. 57, defined the western concept of the individual (as contrasted with eastern concepts) as a single entity 'bounded and integrated and set contrastively against other such wholes'. Macfarlane (1979), as his subtitle suggests, was less concerned with religious than with social, economic, and legal history; cf. the critique by White and Vann (1983).

[183] See Otto Pächt, in Pächt, Dodwell, and Wormald (1960), p. 172, who considered the traditional view of the anonymity of medieval art a dangerous half-truth; Klotz (1976); and Schapiro (1977), p. 22.

[184] Morris (1972), pp. 87–90.

[185] Theophilus, *De diversis artibus*, I, *praef.*, ed. Dodwell (n. 122), p. 2.

[186] Brian Tierney reviewing Morris (1972), in *Journal of Ecclesiastical History* 24 (1973), p. 296, said that 'The period treated ... could just as well be called an age of corporatism as an age of individualism. The two things are not necessarily contradictory. Medieval men came to an enhanced awareness of their individual selves precisely through interaction with their fellow-men in tightly-knit communal groups.' See also Bynum (1982b), pp. 90–5.

[187] *Vita Stephani Obazinensis*, II, 18, ed. Aubrun, p. 130.

[188] Le Goff (1981), p. 386.

do for themselves, and it may also have contributed, more obscurely, to the darker sides of heresy and witchcraft, which were seen as forms of inner perversion.[189] This feeling of loneliness lent an urgency to the spirituality of the age. 'Brief are the days of man, until he is roused by the prick of conscience from penance and conversion either internally by the spirit or externally by man', said Bernard of Clairvaux, according to his disciple Geoffrey. 'Nothing is more precious than time, but, alas, nothing is held more cheaply today.'[190] The author of the *Life* of Louis of Arnstein also said that 'Nothing is more precious than time, which once it has elapsed by whatever cause or order, cannot be had again for the price of gold or silver nor by any effort.'[191] Ben Franklin would have agreed, though for him the results of the loss were temporal rather than eternal.

Urged by this sense of passing time, hurrying towards both their own deaths and the end of the world, and prodded by their consciousness of sin, countless men and women in the twelfth century were nonetheless encouraged to believe that through the grace of God and the example of Christ they could cross the bridge between this life and paradise, as Theobald of Canterbury put it, and abolish the region of dissimilitude by reforming themselves into the perfect image of God in which they had been created. An unbroken thread, connected by the example of Christ, led from the physical life on earth to the ethereal life in heaven, and the life of the senses flowed imperceptibly into the life of the soul. Knowledge of self, shaped by experience and the example of others, formed the inner consciousness that rose to the knowledge of God, in the same way that love of self rose through love of neighbour, expressed in service, friendship, and hospitality, to love of God, making a seamless whole involving the entire human being. It was at this point that rhetoric and reality met. The spirit of liberty and the imitation of Christ, together with *Scito te ipsum*, *Nudus nudum Christum sequi*, and *Dilige et quod vis fac*, became a way of life that expressed the cooperation of body and soul, knowledge and love, intellect and will, and contemplation and action in the inner journey of each human being on the way to salvation.

---

[189] See K. Erikson (1966), p. 136, who drew (p. 50) some parallels between the Puritans and medieval people.

[190] Geoffrey of Igny, *Declamationes ex s. Bernardi sermonibus*, XLIV, 53 and 54, in Bernard, ed. Mabillon, II(5), 633D and 634A.

[191] *Vita Ludovici de Arnstein*, ed. S. Widmann, in *Annalen des Vereins für nassauische Altertumskunde und Geschichtsforschung* 17 (1882), p. 245 (*BHL* 5033).

8

THE BROADER SETTING

THE purpose of this final chapter is to relate the movement of religious reform to other aspects of the history of the eleventh and twelfth centuries, not to explain its causes, which were buried too deeply in the hearts of contemporaries for even themselves, let alone later scholars, to understand.[1] In 1928 Freud wrote to Lytton Strachey that

> It is impossible to understand the past with certainty because we cannot discover men, their motives, and the nature of their souls, and therefore cannot interpret their actions. Our psychological analysis is insufficient even for those who are close to us in space and time, unless we can make them the subject of searching studies for many years, and even then it breaks down on the incompleteness of our knowledge and the clumsiness of our synthesis. So that with respect to peoples of past times we stand as to dreams for which we are given no associations, and only lay men [by which Freud meant those without professional training] could ask us to interpret such dreams as these.[2]

Since these words were written some progress has been made in understanding the motives and mentalities of people in the past, but least of all in the areas of change, where, as Freud put it, the associations or points of reference are either missing or deceptive. C.S. Lewis wrote about the ideal of love in the twelfth century that

> What is new usually wins its way by disguising itself as the old. The new thing itself, I do not pretend to explain. Real changes in human sentiments are very rare – there are perhaps three or four on record – but I believe that they occur, and that this is one of them. I am not sure that they have 'causes', if by a cause we mean something which would wholly account for the new state of affairs, and so explain away what seemed its novelty.[3]

Changes in the field of religious life or sentiments are among the most difficult of all aspects of human experience to understand. 'The history of religion is a history of feeling, rather than of reason,' said Arthur Darby Nock,

---

[1] References in this chapter to previously cited sources can be located in the index.
[2] Sigmund Freud, *Briefe 1873–1939*, 2nd edn, ed. Ernst and Lucie Freud (Frankfurt 1968), p. 399. See Holroyd (1968), II, 615–16.
[3] Lewis (1936), p. 11.

who added (perhaps not without a touch of malice), 'So it is that people are but little troubled by inconsistencies between their beliefs and their instincts.'[4] The distinctions between feeling and reason and between belief and instinct hardly apply to the twelfth century, when the idea that religion could be studied apart from human nature as a whole would have been incomprehensible and when the recognition of transcendence was part of being human. It is distinctly modern and western to think of human beings as having a basically secular nature, to which a body of thoughts or attitudes called religion may or may not be added. The ideas that God 'exists' or that religious people 'believe in' Him were called 'somewhat blasphemous' and 'a modern aberration' by Wilfred Smith, who stressed that for most Christians in the past faith was a total commitment, 'a saying "Yes" ' to the fact that through Christ they could become what they were intended to be.[5] To have truly said 'No' to Christ in the Middle Ages would have been a sign not of heresy but of madness. No one at that time questioned that man was a spiritual being and naturally religious, in the modern sense, as Leclercq put it, 'that God exists and that man can enter into relation with Him'.[6] The term *religio* meant not a body of personal beliefs but a way of life through which people expressed their commitment to God. The focus here, therefore, is not on faith itself, or the lack of it, but on the changes in the ways and forms in which faith was expressed.

In studying the relationship between individuals and institutions in a period of change, it is helpful to bear in mind the concept of *seelische Weite* that was developed by the nineteenth-century social historian Karl Lamprecht and used by his student the art historian Aby Warburg, for whom the Warburg Institute is named. It may be translated as psychic range or breadth – the capacity for expansion of the soul or spirit – which tended to widen in periods of change and transition when, as Warburg's biographer Ernst Gombrich put it, 'new stimuli which can no longer be absorbed by the old and customary groups of associated ideas' rush in and produce 'a "dissociation", the breaking-up of mental balance and a feeling of crisis till a new idea can serve as a "dominant" point of crystallization'.[7] The twentieth century may some day be considered such a period, as was the fifteenth century in Italy, which Warburg saw not in traditional terms as a clash between old and new but as a time when 'Tendencies which appear to be irreconcilable to the modern observer could exist quite peacefully side by side not only in the same milieu but even in the same person.' He cited the examples of 'the predilection of Florentine merchants for the devotional art of the north' and the concern of worldly-wise Renaissance

[4] Nock (1972), p. 963.
[5] Smith (1979), pp. 38, 138, and 168, and (1983), p. 11.
[6] Leclercq (1979), p. 2.
[7] Gombrich (1970), p. 34.

businessmen for their eternal welfare.[8] Henry Adams in *Mont St Michel and Chartres* referred to this quality in the twelfth and thirteenth centuries as an elasticity that embraced, he said, a far wider range of radical contradictions than were found at the time he himself was writing in the late nineteenth century.[9] The rate of change and innovation in such periods imposed great strains on institutions, which were under pressure to function in ways for which they were not intended or designed. Two modern examples that come to mind are the university and the jury, both of which developed in the twelfth century in order to serve the needs of society but which are less suited, in spite of their adaptation over time, to meet all the demands that are put upon them by the different circumstances of the present. In the twelfth century, this was the situation of religious institutions, which had evolved in the early Middle Ages to meet the religious needs of people at that time and were then, within a comparatively short period, faced with the different demands and requirements of people who were themselves caught between the traditions that had shaped their ways of life and thought and their own deepest feelings about themselves and their obligations to God and their neighbours.

The idea of rapid change is not in favour among historians today, and especially medievalists, who tend to look for continuity and 'long duration', as it is called in France. The interest in slow change and deep structures is in part a reaction against earlier scholars who tended to emphasize the impact on history of events and individuals and in part, and more profoundly, the result of the pervasive influence on historical thinking of science, and especially of biology, which regards change as slow and perceptible only over long periods of time. Not all scientists accept this view, however. 'Gradualism is a culturally conditioned prejudice, not a fact of nature', according to the biologist Stephen Gould, who suggested that species developed not only by the slow accumulation of tiny differences but also by punctuational changes caused by catastrophes of which the nature is still largely unexplained. 'Species are stable entities with very brief periods of fuzziness at their origin.'[10] It is possible that in history, in spite of periods of long continuity, there were also times of rapid change, when more stimuli, to use Gombrich's phrase, came in and were absorbed with greater difficulty.

Change was seen as part of the nature of the world in the eleventh and twelfth centuries, which were ushered in around the year 1000 by 'an age of forgetting', when the perception of discontinuity created an image of the tenth century as a period of confusion and destruction.[11] The growing acceptance of historical change and development by theologians and historians, which was

[8] Ibid., pp. 134, 168, and 171.
[9] Adams (1936), p. 356.
[10] Gould (1980), pp. 195 and 213; cf. 243, where he said that 'Orthodoxy can be as stubborn in science as in religion' – or, it may be added, in history.
[11] Geary (1994), p. 29.

discussed above, was related to a broader sense of the mutability of man and the world. Bruno of Segni in his homily on Luke 19.1, where Jesus 'walked through Jericho', said that Jericho stood for the moon, 'of which the mutability is so great that it never stays in the same state' and which in turn signifies the world 'of which the mutability is constant . . . For to say nothing of heaven, and time, and the days and months and years that always revolve and repeat themselves, neither the air, nor the land, nor the sea, nor men themselves perpetually preserve their form (*figura*).' Jesus Himself, Bruno concluded, received this mutability when He took on humanity.[12] The illustrations in the Heiligenkreuz manuscript of Hugh of Fouilloy's *On the wheel of true religion* suggest the mutability of fortune, especially the two monks climbing and falling on the wheel of false religion (plate 4). The change was not always random or cyclical. Burchard of Bellevaux said that 'changes of times require changes of customs'; Gilbert of Holland emphasized the accommodation of monks to differing conditions; and for Honorius *Augustodunensis* 'the mutability of things' pointed the way to improvements in the future.[13]

The concept of generational change enjoyed a certain currency in the Middle Ages. The Arab proverb that 'Men resemble their times rather than their fathers' was of Greek origin, and the saying 'Do not force your children to follow your ways, because they have been created for an age different from yours', was attributed to Socrates or Plato.[14] The idea is still popular today. F. Scott Fitzgerald wrote that 'Some generations are close to those that succeed them; between others the gap is infinite and unbridgeable.'[15] Recently it has been studied by sociologists and historians, who have remarked, like Fitzgerald, that it seems to be more marked in some periods than in others. Citing Karl Mannheim on 'The Problem of Generations', David Riesman wrote that 'It is only in certain countries and in certain epochs that historical events, as unconsciously transmitted through parents to their children, lead to a generational gap rather than a smooth and silent succession – a gap across which the young cannot easily talk to the old who grew up in a different world.'[16] It is unknown what forms these age-linked interests, but in times of change and stress, like a war or a plague, the common experiences of people of a

[12] Bruno of Segni, *Hom.* 143 *in dedicatione ecclesiae*, in *PL*, CLXV, 860CD. See Neale (1856), p. 109.
[13] Burchard of Bellevaux, *Apologia de barbis*, II, 11, in *CC:CM*, LXII, 170, and, for Gilbert and Honorius, pp. 140 and 163 above.
[14] This saying apppears twice, attributed once to Socrates and once to Plato, in Gutas (1975), pp. 115 and 137. I am indebted for this reference to John Callahan, who pointed out the parallel in the so-called *Sayings* of Menander, no. 452. The proverb 'Men resemble their times more than their fathers' (see Michael Prestwich in the *English Historical Review* 81 (1966), p. 110) is of Greek (probably Platonic) origin, according to Franz Rosenthal, and is the title of a book in medieval Arabic.
[15] F. Scott Fitzgerald, 'The Scandal Detectives', in his *Stories*, ed. Malcolm Cowley (New York 1951), p. 309.
[16] Riesman (1964), p. 309.

particular age seem to create similar reactions, making what may be called a cultural generation.[17] Such a pattern of generational change fits the chronology of the movement of religious reform between about 1040 and 1160, when, as seen above, four overlapping but distinguishable areas of reform activity and concern marked the successive periods from 1040 to 1070, 1070 to 1100, 1100 to 1130, and 1130 to 1160. These naturally did not involve the entire population at any one period, any more than generational changes in later ages, when mass education and communication made possible a broader diffusion of common ideas, but they involved a sufficient proportion of the articulate and religiously active population to deserve historical recognition and to be seen in relation to other changes at that time and in the preceding and following periods, when the focus of spiritual interest and activity moved to other fields and objectives.

The eleventh and twelfth centuries were by common consent a period of relatively rapid and significant change in many aspects of human affairs, including areas that seem to be relatively impervious to change and characterized by continuity. 'If the European mind and character be considered in itself and in its achievements', wrote David Knowles, 'a greater gulf, in the sphere alike of speculation and practical achievement, separates the thirteenth from the ninth than separates the sixteenth from the thirteenth centuries'; and Arno Borst called the eleventh century 'the grand turning-point of the Middle Ages, the beginning of differentiation and stabilization in all regions of living'.[18] Studies of volcanic activity have shown that the climate at that time was relatively warm in comparison with the preceding and the following periods, especially the so-called 'Little Ice Age' from about 1350 to 1700.[19] The warmth had profound effects for agriculture, industry, commerce, and the associated activities on both land and sea. Combined with some of the technological innovations of the preceding period, it made possible what has been called an agricultural revolution, especially in the eleventh century, which Lynn White described as 'a moment of primary mutation in the forms of human life . . . No more fundamental modification in a man's relation to his environment can be imagined: he ceased to be nature's child and became her exploiter.'[20] 'Dominion over his environment', as Sybille Bedford put it, 'became the hallmark of man.'[21] Countless changes took place at this time in the fields of politics, economy, thought, and law, and above all in society. As

---

[17] See generally Spitzer (1973) and esp., on the Middle Ages, Herlihy (1974).

[18] Knowles (1936), p. 310, and Borst (1992), p. 130. Morris (1989), p. 3, called the period after 1050 'the Europe of tradition, "the world we have lost"', whereas to go back before 1050 is to enter a region which is by comparison alien to our own'.

[19] Hammer, Claussen, and Dansgaard (1980). Cf. *Proceedings* (1963), pp. 85–6, where the 'Little Climatic Optimum' was dated 1000–1300 and the 'Little Ice Age', 1550–1850, and pp. 50–68 for a general bibliography on historical climates.

[20] White (1967), p. 98.

[21] Sybille Bedford, *A Visit to Don Otavio* (London 1982), p. 22.

the last vestiges of tribal structures, based on a sense of community that bound its members together, disappeared in the post-Carolingian period, a more mobile and competitive society, fostered by the increase of population and development of trade and towns, began to emerge, and much of the variety of the personalized and oral society of the early Middle Ages was replaced by the rule of law, public authority, and written texts.[22] 'Of all the centuries', said Maitland, 'the twelfth is the most legal.'[23] Among the results of these developments were, on the one hand, the appearance after about the year 1000 of new social groupings, including urban guilds and a consolidated family structure, and, on the other hand, the emergence of the anonymous poor and the urban crowd, with the accompanying sense of alienation and *anomie* and the polarization of society and threats of disorder.[24] The growing exclusiveness of the nobility was paralleled by that of the guilds and other groups that sought to protect the status and interests of their members.

It is hard to say precisely how these developments affected the organization of religious life, or the attitudes of people towards themselves and others, but they suggest that the changes studied in this book were not isolated from other developments in society. The movement of religious reform may indeed have been the most conspicuous part of a mighty iceberg of change, largely unseen though widely sensed, that came close to wrecking the ship of the medieval church. This metaphor begs many questions, but it expresses in brief compass the idea that much of what was happening lay below the level of conscious change and controversy and that the traditional church was near to a danger that it neither fully saw nor understood but that created an ever-widening gap between its institutions and many faithful Christians. The reformers realized at least some aspects of the danger and tried to avert it by bringing the institutional forms of religious life back into contact with the needs and values of people who might otherwise have been permanently alienated.

The difficulty of their task was increased, especially in the early years of the reform movement, by the failure to understand its real nature and cause, which was commonly considered to be the decline of religious institutions from their original perfection and the moral defects of their members. There had always been critics of monks, but now for the first time the values of monastic life and the status of monks in society were seriously called into question, in part because their intercessory role was less highly valued than previously and perhaps also because they were thought to have failed in their mission. There was a rising tide of criticism among serious churchmen and

---

[22] On the implications of some of these developments, see Genicot (1967); Clanchy (1979); Stock (1983), esp. p. 87; and Reynolds (1994), pp. 478–9.

[23] Pollock and Maitland (1898), I, 111. Cf. Haskins (1927), p. 218.

[24] On family structure in the eleventh and twelfth centuries, see Bullough (1969); Herlihy (1970); Wheaton (1975); Moore (1980); and White (1988), pp. 201–4.

writers, not only satirists, who accused monks and nuns of hypocrisy, idleness, selfishness, avarice, lust, and worldly ambition. 'Many crimes are committed under the guise of religious life', wrote Boncompagno in the first half of the thirteenth century, 'since feigned religious life is an incentive to sin and a cover of every iniquity'.[25] This view has been shared by scholars who are either so sympathetic to monasticism (or to one of its branches) that they see any defect as a decline or so hostile that they are always ready to believe the worst of its adherents. These two approaches share a common moral ground and pessimistic view of human nature. Dean Inge regarded 'the mysticism of the cloister' as 'the least satisfying to the energetic and independent spirit of our countrymen' and was the first to express 'the melancholy reflection', as he put it, that 'in religion nothing fails like success', which was echoed by scholars as different in their approaches as Haskins and Knowles, who said that 'The Cistercians were, as others before them had been, ruined by their own success.'[26] Moralists in the twelfth century were less inclined to blame success in itself, at least during the first half of the century, but were acutely aware of the dangers presented by wealth and were quick to criticize not only its misuse in the form of luxury and soft living but also the desire for wealth, from which no religious house or order was immune. Avarice figured among the principal charges against the Cistercians from the middle of the twelfth century on.[27] The tendency of the reformers to internalize virtue attached an even greater stigma to property-mindedness than to property, and the humble rich man who was poor in spirit was more admired than the avaricious beggar who constantly sought money. They were therefore ready to see the major fault of contemporary religious institutions, including those of which the individual members were poor, in the constant concern for material resources.

The tension between the requirements of material support and the desire for withdrawal from the world and dedication to God was at the heart of medieval monastic history, and most of the reformers tried to cut the ties that linked religious houses to the world outside their enclosures. They looked back to the age of the primitive church and of the early monks, before the alliance between monasticism and secular society that emerged in the seventh century and before the Carolingian kings made abbots into great lords and government officials. By the ninth century monasticism was firmly linked to the world, as monasteries fell under the control of lay nobles, who saw them as centres of power as well as of intercessory prayer for themselves and their families, and as monks became involved in pastoral work and in prayers for outsiders. The great 'Books of life' or memorial books, some of which contain about 40,000 names, show the extraordinary network of prayer that connected

[25] Boncompagno, *Rhetorica novissima*, VII, 2, in *Bibliotheca iuridica medii aevi*, ed. Augusto Gaudenzi (Bologna 1891–1913), II, 275. I owe this reference to Robert Benson.
[26] Inge (1899), p. 197, and (1925), p. 190; Haskins (1927), p. 36; and Knowles (1969), p. 89.
[27] See pp. 33–4 above.

religious communities with families and individuals all over Europe. Monasteries also performed an essential social role as hospices for travellers and the sick, centres of charitable distributions to the poor and needy, schools and repositories of learning, and even as institutions of credit. These activities were not necessarily the result of secularization and decline, any more than the involvement of modern academic institutions in non-academic affairs is intrinsically corrupt, but they reflected a distinctive view of the nature of society and of the role within it of religious institutions. It resembled in some respects the system of charistikia in Byzantium, where monasteries were entrusted to lay men who were in principle responsible for the secular affairs of the community, permitting the monks to live a monastic life, but who often used the monasteries for their own purposes.[28]

The fact that many of the strictest and most admired monasteries in Europe became involved in these activities shows that the system was accepted in theory, even if it was liable to abuse in practice. Bishop Adalbero of Laon's charge that Odilo of Cluny was the prince of a new army of the warlike order of Cluniac monks reflected the involvement of reformed monasteries in the eleventh century with promoting the peace and truce of God and freeing churches from lay proprietors.[29] The frescoes in the chapter-house of the abbey of the Trinity at Vendôme, which probably date from the visit of pope Urban II in 1096, showed the investiture of St Peter and the mission of the apostles, themes that were close to the hearts of reformers like abbot Geoffrey, and reflected the involvement of monks in the ecclesiastical politics of the day (plate 7).[30] Almost a century later Walter Map in his *Courtiers' trifles* told stories of nobles who became monks at Cluny but who returned to secular life in order to defend their family lands.[31] He may have had in mind someone like Humbert *miles atque Cluniensis monachus* who made a grant to Cluny in 1066 or William II of Clérieu, abbot of St Felix at Valence, who after his brother's death left his monastery and married and made a grant to Cluny in 1191.[32] Map's stories may be untrue, but they show the kind of obligations still felt by black monks, even in a strict monastery, and of the responsibilities that tied them to secular society. The associations between monasteries and the laity known as *societas* and *familiaritas* involved a wide range of reciprocal obligations. The most important of these was intercessory prayer, which was a basic feature of early medieval society and was the principal reason monasteries continued to be founded and supported by both lay men and clerics, who believed that the eternal welfare of themselves and their families depended

---

[28] See Lemerle (1967) and Ahrweiler (1967). The practice, like advocacy, was open to abuse and was modified and largely abolished in the twelfth century.

[29] Hoffmann (1964), pp. 45–7 and 85, and Reynolds (1984).

[30] Toubert (1983), esp. pp. 316–17.

[31] Walter Map, *De nugis curialium*, I, 13–14, and IV, 7, ed. and tr. Montague R. James, rev. C.N.L. Brooke and R.A.B. Mynors (OMT; Oxford 1983), pp. 36–41 and 340–5.

[32] *Chartes de Cluny*, IV, 514, and V, 713–14, nos. 3408 and 4351.

on the prayers of monks and on the charitable distributions made on their behalf. Burial in a monastery, and especially as a member of the community, in a monastic habit, was among the most sought-after privileges a monastery could grant.

The reformers wanted to sever all these ties and go back to a time in history when religious houses were entirely cut off from the world. One of the most perceptive insights in the *Libellus* was that the differences between the types of monks and canons who lived far from, close to, and among other men were no less important than those between the formal types of religious life. Even though living in the desert was a topos, and many of the new communities were in fact located close to roads and settlements and attracted all kinds of visitors as well as recruits, they prized the ideal of solitude and unworldiness; and the strict new houses in principle excluded all the servants, children, hangers-on, and affiliated members, as they may be called, who were found in older monasteries. They attempted to abolish, or at least to reduce, the spiritual and material obligations to benefactors, to reject the traditional services and hospitality to kings and bishops, and to restrict the role of advocates to remote and unremunerated protection. Some houses were so anxious to avoid contacts with lay society that they reduced the general obligations of charity and hospitality and located their alms-houses and hospices at a distance from the community. Ordericus Vitalis in his brief account of the history of the Cistercians down to 1135 said that 'They firmly bar their entrances and fully protect their privacy. They admit no monk of another church into their interiors, and do not allow them to enter with them into the church for mass or other services.'[33] They refused to receive for confession, communion, or burial anyone except a guest or one of their own hired servants (*mercenarii nostri*) who was dying in the monastery.[34] It was presumably a refusal of hospitality that brought down upon them the wrath of Brunellus the Ass in the *Mirror of fools*.

Even ties that were not incompatible with strict seclusion were reduced, especially those created by intercessory prayer and spiritual associations, though they reappeared at an early date. The reformers cut down the number of familiar psalms said on behalf of benefactors, the liturgical celebration of anniversaries, and other practices that were considered incompatible with monastic seclusion. John of Salisbury when he was bishop of Chartres forbade a benefactor of Fontaines-les-Blanches to require a mass 'against the form of the Cistercian order'.[35] They did this not only on account of the contacts with outsiders, and the financial temptations that accompanied such associations, but also, and more importantly, because of the changes in spirituality, which put a greater emphasis than previously on interior attitudes and on an immedi-

---

[33] Ordericus Vitalis, *Historia ecclesiastica*, VIII, 26, ed. Chibnall, IV, 326.
[34] *Capitula Cisterciensis ordinis*, 24, in *Textes de Cîteaux*, p. 124.
[35] Peregrinus, *Historia*, II, 9, ed. Salmon, p. 287.

ate relation between God and each believer. Confidence in the value of inter-cessory prayer did not disappear, and monks continued to offer prayers on behalf of deceased sinners, as they still do today, but the balance of spiritual responsibility in society, as it were, shifted from the community to the individ-ual, so that the process of salvation, even in purgatory, was seen as a lonely affair, in which the sinner could look for only limited help from other people. At the same time as various activities that had previously been personal and private, such as education and the care of the sick and the poor, were becoming public and organized, one of the few activities that in the early Middle Ages had been institutionalized, prayer and worship, was de-institutionalized and became more personal. Thus on the one hand the social role of monasteries was reduced by eliminating many of their traditional connections with the outside world, while on the other hand the ground was cut from beneath their broad spiritual function by the emphasis on interiority and personal religious responsibility.

It is uncertain whether the reformers were aware of the consequences of their programme and policies or to what extent they were consciously inspired by new spiritual needs rather than by their view of the decline of existing religious institutions and the moral weaknesses of their members. The concern of the reformers was with personal reform and salvation rather than with the future of the church. For them, a strict and secluded life was the shortest and safest way to heaven, and they did not fully see that it was narrower than the earlier and broader way. There was an element of moral earnestness and self-righteousness in the reformers, as in many revolutionaries, that did not endear them to everyone and made it difficult, in spite of their openness and desire to bring salvation to all, to come up to their standards. They were accused of hypocrisy, and were themselves often unable (and sometimes unwilling) to avoid the type of pastoral, caritative, and educational activities that they condemned in other monks. When these activities broke out of the framework of traditional religious life and became embodied in independent institutions, such as hospitals and schools, the implications of the reform movement for the welfare of others became clearer, but in the eleventh and twelfth centuries it tended to assert the exclusive character of monasticism while at the same time enlarging the range of other types of religious life, especially the eremitical communities, the military orders, and the new insti-tution of lay brothers and sisters, which made possible a form of religious life for men and women who were not monks or nuns. From their origins, how-ever, these were regarded as less praiseworthy than those who were insti-tutionally and spiritually committed to a life that was in principle fully with-drawn from the world and devoted to God.

Had the reformers been questioned about their motives and desires, most of them would have said that they wanted to follow the Gospel, and above all the example of Christ, and to observe the rule of Benedict, which for them embodied the Gospel. They would have pointed to the apostles and the early monks to show the possibility of this ideal, and to contemporaries who seemed to them to lead lives that conformed to these ideals. They might also have mentioned some models outside the tradition of western Latin monasticism, and especially the Greek and Armenian monks from the east, the monks and hermits of southern Italy, and the remaining representatives of Celtic religious life who persisted in Ireland and in parts of England and northern France. It is possible to see the movement of reform at least in part as the result of the introduction, or reintroduction, into Latin monasticism of non-Latin traditions and even of non-Christian influences from Islam and Judaism, where parallel tendencies can be found in the twelfth century. Jewish thought and biblical studies were taken seriously by Christian intellectuals during the first half of the twelfth century,[36] but there is no evidence of Jewish influences on religious life, in spite of some conversions both to and from Judaism, like that of Herman of Cologne, whether or not the account of his conversion is strictly historical. The tendency towards mysticism and internalization of piety in twelfth-century Judaism suggests that there were parallels rather than influences between the development of the two religions at this time,[37] since on the whole the twelfth century was a period of growing hostility to Jews and Muslims and of a developing consciousness of Christian identity.

Of the possible non-Latin influences on the movement of reform the most interesting and important came from the east, since there is extensive evidence of the admiration for the eastern monks who travelled and settled in the west or whom the reformers visited, especially in Italy.[38] Bruno of Cologne's glowing account of hermit life in southern Italy has already been cited; William of St Thierry referred to 'the light from the east (*orientale lumen*)' in the introduction to the *Golden letter*; Otto of Freising compared the transfer of religion, in the sense of religious life, from east to west to the transfers of power and wisdom, and cited as proof that there were in his own time more holy men in France and Germany than formerly in Egypt; and Joachim of Fiore described the movement of monasticism from east to west and its return with the Cistercians to the Greeks in southern Italy.[39] Many eastern monks

---

[36] See Smalley (1952), esp. pp. 145–56; Grabois (1975); Jean Leclercq, Nikolaus Häring, and Marie-Thérèse d'Alverny, in *Renaissance and Renewal* (1982), pp. 76, 194, and 428, with further references; and Abulafia (1989).

[37] John Benton, in *Renaissance and Renewal* (1982), p. 292, with references to the works (in Hebrew) of Seligmann Baer and Haim Hillel Ben-Sasson.

[38] See Piolin (1879–80), p. 533, on recluses from the east; Huyghebaert (1951); Schreiber (1954–5), pp. 107–12; McNulty and Hamilton (1963); Demus (1970), pp. 19–44; and Sansterre (1983) on Greek and eastern monks at Rome from the sixth to the ninth century.

[39] William of St Thierry, *Ep. ad fratres de Monte Dei*, 7, ed. Davy, p. 70; Otto of Freising, *Historia de duobus civitatibus*, VII, 35, ed. Adolf Hofmeister, 2nd edn (*MGH, SSRG*; Hanover and Leipzig 1912), p. 372; and Joachim of Fiore, *Vita s. Benedicti*, 9, ed. Cipriano Baraut, in *Analecta sacra Tarraconensia* 24 (1951), pp. 55–6, with further references to Joachim's works in p. 56 n. 16.

came to the west in the tenth and eleventh centuries, including at least three named Simeon, of whom one, who was born in Armenia, visited Pisa, Lucca, Piacenza, Pavia, Vercelli, Turin, and Novalese and then went to Aquitaine, Gascony, Spain, Galicia, Compostela, Brittany, and Tours before he returned to Mantua and Polirone, where he settled and died in 1016.[40] The interest and admiration were apparently reciprocal, since several monks from southern Italy and the east were attracted 'to the doctrine . . . of father William' of St Benignus at Dijon, including a bishop named Barnabas who 'lived for many years under his teaching in this monastery'.[41] The recluse Olardis of St Amand received the veil from patriarch Sophronius II of Jerusalem when he was in the west, perhaps in 1059.[42] These visitors sometimes took advantage of their hosts and were not always welcome, as at the hospice of the oratory of St Bartholomew at Hildesheim, which was founded in 1024 by bishop Godehard, who according to his biographer Wolfher had no use for travellers

> who wander about the kingdoms and regions either in the monastic or canonical or even in the Greek habit, whom he smilingly called Peripatetics in the manner of Plato . . . to whom, however, for the name of Christ which they professed, he gave what was necessary for two or at the most three days and whom, when shoes and clothes had been given, he asked to leave so that they should not forget the customary course of their ways.[43]

Eastern monasticism had a lasting influence in the west. Monks from Calabria settled at Cologne and founded Bertscheid near Aachen, the first abbey of Orval, and the cell of St James in the diocese of Toul. The second founder of Windberg learned 'the discipline of the eremitical life under the instruction of St Gregory, who was said once to have been archbishop of the Armenians but then followed voluntary poverty and peregrination around Passau in the hope of a richer heavenly reward'.[44] In 1067 Hugh of Cluny invited the hermit Anastasius, who came from Venice and knew both Greek and Latin, to come to Cluny, where he was 'an exemplar of a good way of life' by his prayers, fasts, and annual solitary retreats, during which 'he macerated himself beyond measure with prayers, fasts, vigils, and genuflections', before he moved on after some years.[45] The rule of Basil was known and admired in the west, and reformers like Romuald, Gerald of La Sauve-Majeure, Bruno of Cologne,

---

[40] *Vita Simeonis*, v, 46, in *AASS*, 26 July VI, 332B (*BHL* 7952). See *Vita Gregorii ep. Nicopolitani*, in *AASS*, 16 March II, 457C–8D (*BHL* 3669), and Wolff (1978), pp. 181–7, on other monks who travelled between east and west.

[41] *Chronicon s. Benigni Divionensis*, ed. E. Bourgaud and J. Garnier (Analecta Divionensis 9; Dijon 1875), p. 152. Cf. McNulty and Hamilton (1963), p. 199.

[42] Serbat (1912), pp. 205–6 (211 on the date), and Détrez (1951), p. 22.

[43] *Vita posterior Godehardi*, 20, in *MGH*, *SS*, XI, 207 (*BHL* 3582).

[44] *Historiae et annales Windbergenses*, 3, in *MGH*, *SS*, XVII, 561. See Huyghebaert (1951), pp. 100–2, and *GC*, XIII, *instr.*, 477–9, for a charter of 1097 concerning the *pauper* and *exul* Ursus of Benevento, on whom see Choux (1952), p. 151.

[45] Walter, *Vita Anastasii*, in *PL*, CXLIX, 428C–9A (*BHL* 405). See Pigeon (1892–8), II, 339–44.

Stephen of Grandmont, and Bertrand of Grandselve were familiar with Basilian monasticism in southern Italy, which had close ties with northern France especially after the establishment of Norman rule.[46] A few western monks may also have visited monasteries in the east, including Sinai, where they found some of the tendencies that they admired at home. There were some interesting parallels, on which the forthcoming corpus of Byzantine monastic typika will throw more light, between eastern and western monasticism at this time, though so far as is known none of the major reformers had any direct experience of Byzantine monasticism at its centres in Mt Athos or Constantinople.

The evidence of intellectual, cultural, and commercial contacts shows that there were also opportunities for indirect influences.[47] 'The channels of communication between east and west . . . often ran beneath the surface', wrote Haskins, 'and many of the contacts were occasional or accidental, so that the process of transmission often eludes us.'[48] The writings of some of the Greek fathers had survived in the west both through earlier Latin writers like Hilary of Poitiers and through translations, and were known at Cluny, for instance, in the tenth and eleventh centuries.[49] In the twelfth century there was a significant rise of interest and influence, and the works of Gregory of Nyssa, Epiphanius, Nemesius, Chrysostom, Maximus Confessor, John of Damascus, and the Pseudo-Denis, to mention only the most important, were read and cited by western spiritual writers like William of St Thierry, Bernard of Clairvaux, Hugh and Richard of St Victor, Gerhoh and Arno of Reichersberg, Isaac of L'Etoile, and Peter Lombard.[50] The reformers found in these works a congenial emphasis on the primacy of the invisible, on exemplarism and resemblance as the basis of hierarchical degrees, and on the rise of the soul to God by the use of sensible symbols.[51] Bernard was particularly influenced by Origen, whose imagery and psychological approach to the bible resembled his own.[52] The fact that some of Origen's teachings had been condemned, like those of Abelard, did not seem to disturb his readers. Elizabeth of Schönau in one of her visions consulted the Virgin about 'that great doctor' Origen and was told that, because his errors arose not from malice but from excessive zeal, his punishment was not severe.[53]

[46] Ordericus Vitalis, *Historia ecclesiastica*, III, ed. Chibnall, II, 94, 100–2, and 126–8; *GC*, III, *instr.*, 184–5, for a reference to the rule of St Basil in a charter of 1130. See Hamilton (1975), pp. 184–5, on Romuald and Byzantine monasticism.
[47] See Schreiber (1954–5) on pilgrims, relics, the liturgy, and other indirect contacts between east and west, and Southern (1970a), p. 80, on the *Philosophia mundi* by William of Conches, which was read at Constantinople in 1165.
[48] Haskins (1929), p. 160, and ch. 8 generally on 'Contacts with Byzantium'.
[49] Dutton (1980), pp. 450–1.
[50] See the chapter on 'Orientale lumen' in Déchanet (1940a), and the review by von Ivánka (1940); and Jean Leclercq and Marie-Thérèse d'Alverny, in *Renaissance and Renewal* (1982), pp. 80 and 430–3.
[51] Javelet (1967), I, 28–51 (on Richard of St Victor) and 148–9 (on Hugh of St Victor).
[52] See Bardy (1945); Leclercq (1949) and (1951a); de Lubac (1959–64), I, ch. 4; and Deroy (1963).
[53] Elizabeth of Schönau, *Visiones*, III, 5, ed. Roth, pp. 62–3. See p. 216 above.

The routes of transmission and translation of these works are still obscure and may have varied according to the content of the works. Some were brought to the west by Greek monks. A few translations were made in the east; other texts came through Sicily and Spain; and yet others, including some important spiritual writings, through Hungary. A translation of the *On the orthodox faith* by John of Damascus, which was attributed to Basil, was made by Cerbanus in Hungary and reached Clairvaux in the twelfth century, probably carried by monks of Admont or Rein, by way either of Rome or of Reichersberg, Reims, and Paris, or possibly through Peter of Vienna.[54] A similar obscurity surrounds the sources of Byzantine influence on western religious art, for which the evidence is almost entirely stylistic. In the early twelfth century western art was apparently hit by what has been called a wave of Byzantine stylistic influence, which was followed by lesser waves marked by a growing admixture of classical elements and of artistic independence.[55] Almost nothing is known about how it got there.[56] It is uncertain, for instance, whether the frescoes at Berzé-la-Ville near Cluny and the manuscript of Ildefonsus now at Parma, both of which show strong resemblances to Byzantine painting, were made by eastern artists working at Cluny or by western artists who learned the style and technique of Byzantine art either in the east or in Italy.[57] The existence of these works of art in a Byzantine style, however, like the hermit Anastasius and the manuscripts of works of the Greek fathers, shows that there was a sympathy and demand for Greek culture at Cluny in the eleventh and twelfth centuries.

It is harder to make a case for Celtic influence in view of the comparatively low esteem in which Irish monks were held by most of the reformers. Bernard of Clairvaux had nothing good to say of native Irish monasticism in his *Life* of Malachy, whom he praised precisely for reforming it according to continental norms, and Peter the Venerable in his letter to Innocent II about the reform of Luxeuil gave a sorry account of the decay of monasticism in one of the great old Irish foundations on the continent.[58] The tradition of Irish asceticism and peregrination had not died out, however, and seems to have revived in the tenth and eleventh centuries, when a number of Irishmen came to the

---

[54] Häring (1950), and Buytaert (1951), pp. 20–9, and (1965), p. 309, with references to his previous works on the translations of John of Damascus.

[55] According to Kitzinger (1966), p. 37, Wilhelm Koehler introduced the concept of 'a great wave of Byzantine stylistic influence which powerfully affected the pictorial arts of Western Europe in the first half of the twelfth century'. Demus (1970), pp. 108–18 and 163, also remarked on the 'tidal wave' of Byzantine influence carrying the 'two revolutionary ideas' of the articulated body and animated figure. Grabar (1968), II, 377–85, studied various eastern motifs found in western works of art in the eleventh century.

[56] See Schapiro (1964), p. 43; Kitzinger (1966), p. 38, on the contacts between east and west in the second half of the eleventh century; and Demus (1970), pp. 19–44, on various types of transmission.

[57] Schapiro (1964), pp. 41–53, and Demus (1970), pp. 112–15.

[58] Peter the Venerable, *Ep.* 23, ed. Constable, I, 43–4.

continent and were greeted, like the Greeks, with admiration tempered by some reservations.[59] They were in touch especially with the monastic reformers in Lorraine in the tenth century and gathered in communities at Metz, Verdun, and Cologne, as did monks from the east. Some of them established monasteries, like Waulsort; others lived as hermits and recluses, like the abbot Columban, who was a recluse at Ghent in 957, Paternus, who spent many years as a recluse at Paderborn and died in 1058, and Marianus Scotus, who left Ireland in 1067 and went to Bamberg and Regensburg.[60] 'A certain religious priest, by nation an Irishman (*Scottus*), by profession a monk, and by name John' was installed by bishop Altmann of Passau as a recluse in a church that he reformed at Altmann's command (which came to him in a vision) by expelling the clerics and introducing monks.[61] The ascetic practices of the reformers resembled those of the Celts in several respects, including the chaste concubinage of Harvey and Eve and of Robert of Arbrissel and his followers and the ascetic immersions of Godric of Finchale and Aelred of Rievaulx, who may have had direct contact with Irish monks.[62] Dominic *Loricatus* resembled the early Irish monks in praying with his arms extended, in the form of the cross,[63] and while this was probably a parallel rather than an imitation it suggests that there were similarities in the area of spirituality, and some of the Irish monks of the ninth and tenth centuries showed a notable love of nature, devotion to God, and tenderness towards Jesus, whom St Ide wanted to nurse as a baby in her cell.[64] Other characteristic themes are found in a letter written in 1117 by Reimbald of Liège for a pilgrim named Dermot, who was on his way from Ireland to Jerusalem and who wanted to urge others to go likewise from Babylon to Jerusalem: 'You see that I have made myself an exile for God; you see that this cross is not only the one on my garment but that I bear the cross of Christ. You see that I take flight to God not only in Jerusalem but everywhere, because He is everywhere.'[65] This short passage presents a striking mixture of old and new themes, including some that are characteristic of traditional Irish spirituality, but its significance is uncertain without knowing how much of it was written by Dermot and how much by

---

[59] Among the references in *Medieval Monasticism*, nos. 393–406, most of which are concerned with the early Middle Ages, see esp. Gwynn (1940) and Bethell (1969b), pp. 113–14. Bauerreiss (1949–70), II, 168–71, referred to a second wave of Irish monks who came to the continent at this time. On the adventures of the lay poet Moriuht, who set up as a grammarian in Rouen and was mocked by the satirist Garnerius for (among other things) wearing kilts which *genitalia cuncta patebant*, see Omont (1894) and Musset (1954), pp. 250–4.

[60] *De Columbano abbate*, in *AASS*, 15 Feb. II, 847–8, and *De Paterno recluso*, in *AASS*, 10 Apr. I, 886–7. See *Vies des saints*, II, 217–18 and 340, and IV, 222.

[61] *Vita Altmanni Pataviensis*, 38, in *MGH, SS*, XII, 240–1 (*BHL* 313).

[62] See on syneisactism p. 68 above; on ascetic immersions, Reginald of Durham, *Vita Godrici*, XXXIII, 74, ed. Stevenson, pp. 85–6; Reynolds (1968), pp. 561–2; and Smith (1969).

[63] Peter Damiani, *Opusc.* 15 *de sua congregatione*, 18, in *PL*, CXLV, 351A. See Rordorf (1995), pp. 95–8, on positions of prayer in the early church.

[64] Jackson (1951), p. 306.

[65] Reimbald of Liège, *Itineraria*, 5–7, in *CC:CM*, IV, 3–5 (quote on 4).

Reimbald, who was in close touch with the religious movements of his time. It is hard to know what to make of this material, since any evidence of influence is ambiguous, leaving a series of similarities that suggest shared interests and sympathies rather than causal connections. In two complementary articles on cross-cultural influences in the Middle Ages the Islamists Hamilton Gibb and Gustave von Grunebaum suggested that one culture takes from another only those elements that are congenial to its needs and values and for which there is prior preparation and receptivity. It is therefore wiser to think in terms of convergences and parallels than of influences or borrowings.[66] In the area of thought, where Christians and Muslims drew on a common classical heritage and differed primarily in their principles of selection, western thinkers in the eleventh and twelfth centuries tended to take from Islamic culture elements that were related to their own thought, some of which originally came from the west. A similar experience can be seen in the nineteenth and early twentieth centuries, when the style of many artists showed an affinity with primitive art, often without conscious influence,[67] and when people turned to Zen and Hindu mysticism because Christianity had to a great extent lost touch with its own mystical tradition. In each case there was a conditioning and anticipation that prepared the way for the reception of elements from another culture. For the historian the question of the nature of the predisposition and preparation is more important than that of the specific elements taken. In the field of religion in the eleventh and twelfth centuries, von Grunebaum wrote that 'The focusing of piety on Mohammed is paralleled by the focusing of piety on Jesus and the dominance gained in Islam by hope and love over fear in man's relation to God recurs in Latin Christendom as does the channelling of the religious life into lay orders of various kinds.'[68] There were also signs in twelfth-century Byzantium of tendencies parallel to those in western spirituality and of interest in western philosophical writers, which suggest that there was a broader religious and intellectual meeting ground than is sometimes thought.[69] Eustathius of Thessalonica wrote in his *Life* of Philotheus of Opsicium, which dates from the twelfth century, that it was harder and more worthy to achieve salvation in the world than in solitude – a view that was shared by several writers in the west.[70] The idea that there were parallel trends at the same time in eastern and western Christianity, in Islam, and to some extent in Judaism raises interesting ques-

---

[66] Gibb (1964) and von Grunebaum (1964).
[67] This point was made by the exhibition on ' "Primitivism" in 20th Century Art' held at New York, Detroit, and Dallas in 1984–5. According to Berenson (1960), p. 178, Matisse denied the influence on his work of the Cambodian art with which he was surrounded in his studio.
[68] Von Grunebaum (1964), p. 104.
[69] Eustathios of Thessalonica, *Opuscula*, ed. G.L.F. Tafel (Frankfort 1832), p. 148. See Kazhdan and Franklin (1984), pp. 151–2.
[70] This point was made with reference to the tenth and eleventh centuries by Hallinger (1950–1), who concentrated on the specific differences between monasteries and groups of monasteries.

tions for students of comparative religion and puts into doubt whether any one of them were the result of influences from one on another. It shows, on the contrary, that the movement of reform in the west must be seen in a setting of far-reaching changes, still not fully studied or understood, that disposed the reformers to be sympathetic to similar aspects in other monastic or religious traditions.

The similarities among the reformed orders and communities, and between many of the old and new houses, should probably also be seen as parallels rather than as influences, even when there is evidence of borrowing. The old view that monastic reform originated and spread from a single centre of influence, such as Cluny in the tenth century, Vallombrosa and Camaldoli in the eleventh, or Cîteaux in the twelfth, is thus replaced by a view of these monasteries as the most prominent examples of tendencies that appeared in many houses, which differed (like modern universities and colleges) in specific ways but shared the same basic concerns. The changes in old black houses in the twelfth century, like those in older universities today, are easier to understand as responses to a broad pattern of development than as the result of influences or attacks. Throughout the history of Christian monasticism certain activities and patterns of behaviour were embodied in various rules, customaries, and lives of saints, and in the traditional way of life in particular communities, and they were admired and imitated as expressions of the highest ideals of life on earth. The real extent of inter- and cross-monastic borrowings in the eleventh and twelfth centuries will become clearer when the editions of monastic customaries and necrologies are complete, but enough is already known to show that no house can be studied in isolation. The monks of Cîteaux in the twelfth century, like those of Cluny in the tenth, did not stand at the beginning or the end of the line of monastic development, but in the middle, surrounded by other monks who shared their feelings, even when they did not express them in exactly the same way or with the same vehemence.

There was at all times within the monastic world a higher degree of continuity and similarity than of change and difference. The customs, organization, and liturgy of Cîteaux show how much it took over from earlier monasticism and that it was part of a broad movement.[71] Cîteaux in its turn was freely pillaged by other monks, who took from it what they wanted and sometimes even called themselves Cistercians without being members of the order, and also by regular canons, who gathered elements from various sources.[72] Occasionally such borrowing may have been unconscious, but for the most part it was deliberate and purposeful, as when Norbert said that the annual

---

[71] See pp. 109 and 204–5 above and esp. Duvernay (1952) and Schneider (1960–1) and, on the liturgy, Waddell (1971) and other works. Van Damme (1962), p. 111, said that both in their common and in their distinctive features the Cistercians came at the end of the monastic movement started by Benedict of Aniane.

[72] See pp. 109–10 above.

general chapter at Prémontré was held 'at the similitude and example of the Cistercians', although this may be a later justification, built into his *Life*, of a practice that had independent origins.[73] It is uncertain to what extent even such an explicit borrowing should be described as influence, however, because the concept of general chapters was in the air at that time. Just as cooks collect and revise recipes, and put them into cookbooks that they call their own, so the reformers in the twelfth century put together from various sources a way of life that reflected shared values and tastes and yet can legitimately be considered their own.

The eclectic character of the reform movement is illustrated in the *Life* of Aybert of Crépin, which was written shortly after his death in 1141 by archdeacon Robert of Ostrevand, perhaps with an eye on his canonization.[74] Aybert's father was a *miles*, and his parents were 'both of free condition and honest persons'. He 'changed his life and left the world' when he was a young man, in about 1080, and following the example of a hermit named Theobald went to live in a deserted place with a priest of the abbey of Crépin named John. Early in the pontificate of Urban II he went to Italy with John and the abbot of Crépin 'for the sake of confirming the liberty of his monastery'. They went barefoot and used their mule for pilgrims rather than themselves. In Italy they visited Vallombrosa, 'where they found monks of marvellous continence and excellent life ... who strove to keep them with themselves for ever', observed the rule of Benedict 'firmly and perfectly', lived by the labour of their hands, and afflicted their bodies 'in the hope of heavenly life'. They were fervid, charitable, pious, and holier than any monks the travellers had seen before, and from them, according to Robert, 'They received, as they themselves bore witness, many documents for living rightly (*documenta recte vivendi*).' After his return Aybert had a dream directing him to become a monk at Crépin, where he spent twenty-five years, first as provost and then as cellarer, before he retired to a cell 'in order to have time more freely for divine praises and prayers and to subdue his body more harshly'. When visitors were attracted by his reputation for holiness, he became a priest 'in order better to advise the people who came to him'. Later he was specifically authorized by Pascal II and Innocent II to hear confessions and impose penances. Each day he celebrated two masses, made 100 genuflections and 50 prostrations, and recited 150 psalms interspersed with nine readings, 'which would be burdensome and heavy for anyone not doing it from his spirit', said Robert, who called him a martyr for carrying the cross of Christ in will and deed and a confessor for praising God with his heart, mouth, and good works. He refused to receive or touch any money. So many people of all ranks and walks

---

[73] *Vita* [B] *Norberti*, XVI, 101, in *PL*, CLXX, 1330C (*BHL* 6249).

[74] Robert of Ostrevand, *Vita Ayberti*, in *AASS*, 7 Apr. I, 671–7 (*BHL* 180). The quotations in the following paragraph are from I, 3, 5, and 7, and II, 11, 14, and 16, pp. 671–4 and 676. See Trelcat (1924), pp. 63–9, and Lamma (1961), p. 75.

including bishops, monks, and hermits, came to him that his hermitage resembled a besieged castle or town, and people who could not confess to him in private did so in public with everyone listening. They snatched relics from his clothes and received spiritual bread from him when he had no food to give. His entire life, according to Robert, was 'martyrdom, miracle, consolation of the suffering, relief of sinners, labour and penance, and love and fear of Him Who terrifyingly said in the Gospel, "He who wishes to follow Me" [cf. Matthew 16.24]'.

Aybert's *Life* illustrates almost every aspect of the reform movement seen from a personal rather than an institutional point of view. If its authenticity were not well established, its veracity might be questioned, like that of the *Life* of the twelfth-century Venetian saint Peter Acotantus, which is said to have been written by a nineteenth-century Viennese scholar in order to show off his knowledge of hagiographical topoi.[75] In the course of his long life, which covered over two generations of the reform movement, Aybert embraced at least four of the most characteristic aspects of the reform: from about 1080 to 1090, he was an independent hermit, unordained but apparently literate; from about 1090 to 1115, he was a monk, still unordained but serving the needs of his monastery; and finally, from about 1115 to 1141, he was both an ordained hermit 'living under the rule of the lord abbot of Crépin' and a charismatic preacher and holy man. There is no indication of why he originally left secular life or whether he was influenced by any known reformer, though he came to the attention of two and perhaps three popes. At the beginning of his career, he was associated with two hermits, one independent and the other a monk and priest. His biographer stressed above all the influence upon him of the monks of Vallombrosa. The 'many documents' that he received from them may have included customaries, liturgical books, and spiritual writings, or perhaps consisted simply of the example of their way of life, which doubtless influenced his own decision to become a monk but hardly explains his involvement in monastic administration. From this he went on to his third and most remarkable career as a hermit priest and holy man. It was the freedom rather than the solitude of eremitical life that seems to have appealed to him, and neither he nor his biographer suggested that his pastoral activities or the enthusiastic crowds interfered with his liturgical obligations and private devotions. On the contrary, he was regarded as a follower of Christ precisely for combining privation and suffering for himself with service and pastoral work to others. The martyrdom, labour, and penance to which he was impelled by his mingled fear and love of God were miraculously transformed into a consolation and comfort for others.

A *Life* like this, whether or not it corresponded exactly to reality, brought together in a single person the spiritual themes and ways of life that have

---

[75] *Vita Petri Acotanti*, ed. Georg Zappert (Vienna 1839). See Fichtenau (1975), pp. 283–6. Even if this work is a forgery, it is made up of authentic fragments to which Zappert gives references.

been analysed separately in this book and shows how the psychic range of the reformers combined seemingly inconsistent attitudes and actions in the same person and milieu. While Aybert was in many ways an improbable figure, he was admired by his contemporaries and seems never to have encountered any serious criticism. His *Life* helps to explain why the old and new monks often quarrelled more bitterly over small points than over major issues, on which there was a large measure of agreement. The fact that they all drew on a common monastic tradition and that even individual aspects of the reform programme can be traced to earlier reforms gave a high degree of prominence to small differences. Relatively few of the criticisms levelled at the old monks touched on what were regarded as the fundamentals of religious life, and those that did concerned issues either on which there was no serious disagreement, such as the quality of recruits to monastic life and the amount of time spent in private prayer and devotions, or on which the reformers themselves later compromised, such as the sources of economic support and relations with the diocesan bishop. Although the reform programme as a whole can be seen as the visible peak of an iceberg of even broader contemporary change, the issues that figured prominently in the polemical writings were not symptomatic of greater issues below the surface. They were more (to use another metaphor) like pieces of floating wood, which look larger and more dangerous than they are. It is striking in this connection that the two real innovations in monastic organization, the lay brothers and general chapters, apparently roused almost no opposition and were accepted by both old and new houses. Even the controversy over black and white clothing flared up largely owing to its symbolic importance. The heat generated in the polemical literature must therefore be understood in relation to the more irenic and generous spirit shown in other contexts by people like the Cistercian Amedeus of Hauterives, who praised Cluny even when leaving it for Bonnevaux, the prior of La Chartreuse who advised Stephen of Obazine to join the Cistercians rather than the Carthusians, the prior of Sainte-Barbe who became a Premonstratensian, the Cluniacs who supported and helped the Cistercians and Carthusians, and the regular canon who tried in the *Libellus* to see the best in all the contemporary orders and professions and related each to an episode in the Old Testament and in the life of Christ.[76]

When attention is concentrated on the general features of the reform movement and on the similarities rather than the differences of its parts, it takes on a different character than when it is broken down into various factions, each critical of the other, as if it were a family quarrel within the monastic order. When, furthermore, the similarities with other branches of Christianity and with non-Christian religions are seen not as influences or borrowings but

[76] *Vita Amedaei Altae Ripae*, 5, ed. M.-Anselme Dimier, in *Studia monastica* 5 (1963), p. 288 (*BHL* 385d); *Ampl. coll.*, I, 787BC; *Vita Stephani Obazinensis*, I, 27, ed. Aubrun, p. 82; Constable (1975b); and *Libellus*, ed. Constable, p. xxiv.

as affinities and parallels, it no longer looks exclusively Latin and western or even, perhaps, exclusively Christian. Some scholars have proposed that the movement was part of the progressive Christianization of Europe and the assertion, after centuries of contamination with pagan elements, of the essentially individualistic message of Christian perfection embodied in the Gospels, which was thus somehow discovered in the eleventh and twelfth centuries after centuries of being hidden and veiled.[77] This view would have appealed to the twelfth century. Though put forward in another form, it corresponds to the historical theology of writers like Rupert of Deutz, Anselm of Havelberg, and especially Joachim of Fiore, who saw a progressive unfolding of the divine plan for salvation culminating in the appearance of new religious orders inspired by the teaching of the Gospel. The comparative study of mass conversions from one religion to another suggests that the final wave of converts adheres to 'an alternative orthodoxy' consisting of 'populism and vernacular language development, mysticism with its antinomian and anticlerical implications, and communal and fraternal organizations'.[78] This fits various aspects of the religious development of the twelfth century, including the emergence of heretical groups, but the formal process of conversion to Christianity in western Europe, except on its edges, had been completed so long before the twelfth century, and the informal conversion was still so incomplete, that it is difficult to attribute the movement of reform either to the internal conversion of people who had previously been Christians only in name or to a sudden influx of recent converts, even if this contributed in part to its character.

If the reform is seen as an adjustment or accommodation to the religious needs of those who formerly had no place in the official organization and views of Christianity, these people were less likely to be recent converts than men and especially women who, while faithful Christians, had been excluded from positions of influence in the early medieval church and who were able through the reform movement to create a larger place for themselves by changing its structure and values. The many signs of malaise in twelfth-century society, including the isolation and persecution of Jews, heretics, and lepers, may be associated with various forms of dislocation and deprivation.[79] It has been said that 'a situation of felt deprivation' is a necessary pre-condition of all organized social movements, both secular and religious, and that the less clearly the nature of the deprivation is perceived – when it is a vague unhappiness rather than a specific lack or complaint – the more the movement will

---

[77] See for instance Chenu (1957), pp. 245, 251–2, and 273, and Le Goff (1986), p. 70. Cf. Morris (1989), p. 580, who said that between 1050 and 1250 Christianity immensely increased 'in its impact upon hearts and minds', and Milis (1992), pp. 80–1, who suggested stages or steps from external/formal to internal/individual conversion.

[78] These words are taken from a paper on 'The Conversion Factor and the Spirit of Islam and the Rise of the Protestant Ethic' by Richard Bulliet of Columbia University.

[79] See Moore (1987), who studied the attitudes towards heretics, Jews, and lepers, and Douglas (1991), citing the work of Mark Pegg.

be religious and compensatory rather than a solution to the problem.[80] The form of deprivation can vary. Marxists have looked at economic deprivation and emphasized the importance of poverty in the movement of reform.[81] Other scholars have stressed political and social deprivation, such as the distinction in the early Middle Ages between *potentes* and *pauperes*, who were without power rather than without money.[82]

The rise of affective mysticism and devotion to the human Christ in the twelfth century was attributed to sexual deprivation by Herbert Moller, who suggested that the lack of men, especially in northern France, north-west Germany, and the Low Countries, created 'an unbalanced sex composition of the remaining population of young and middle-aged adults', who married late or never married, and thus fostered 'a regression to the state of a love-craving child and blissful feelings of union with God'. Quite apart from its pejorative view of women and of mysticism, and the fact that the devotion to the humanity of Christ was at this period equally marked among men as among women, this argument is based upon too many a priori arguments to be accepted without further evidence, even if Moller is correct that a development of this type must be seen not 'as a summation of individual psychological phenomena' but 'as a process of conceptual and symbolic communication and interaction'.[83] Among other types of deprivation was the desire of many people to exercise the religious prerogatives previously reserved for monks and nuns and for the clergy.[84] Chenu argued in the conclusion to his book on the awakening of the conscience in the twelfth century that the assertion of spiritual liberty and personalization was an evangelical reaction against the feudal oath that for centuries had been the 'real sacrament of collective life'.[85] For Janet Nelson there was a double reaction: one of ecclesiastical reform, which stressed organization and conformity in belief and practice against the mobility and uncertainty of the eleventh and twelfth centuries, and the other of the heretics who were squeezed out by the pressures to conform. 'Twelfth-century heresy was in an important sense anti-structural', she wrote, 'this was why the issue of obedience was crucial, and why doctrine was not necessarily involved.'[86]

Interesting and stimulating as these views are, they suffer from two weaknesses, both of which have been touched on before. The first is the difficulty of seeing the reform primarily as a reaction against the values and structures of early medieval society, which was different but not more hierarchical or exclusive than the society that emerged during the eleventh and twelfth cen-

---

[80] Glock (1964).
[81] Such as Werner (1953) and (1956).
[82] See Bosl (1963) and pp. 146–50 above.
[83] Moller (1971), pp. 312, 331, and 332–3.
[84] Van Engen (1986a), p. 537.
[85] Chenu (1969), p. 79; see also (1957), pp. 44 and 255. Cf. Reynolds (1994), who argued against the prevalence of feudalism (and especially fiefs and vassals) in early medieval society.
[86] Nelson (1972), p. 74.

turies. It is therefore impossible to distinguish the reformers from the heretics (at least before the second half of the twelfth century, when many heretics were excluded from the church) on the basis of their attitudes towards structure and obedience without first answering the questions of what structures and obedience to whom. The emphasis of the Gregorian reformers on institutional unity and clerical conformity reinforced some structures at the expense of others, and in many respects the monastic reformers were as anti-structural, and as contemptuous of existing institutions and hierarchies of power, as the early heretics. A second and more serious weakness is the lack of evidence concerning the social origins of the reformers and their followers, who cannot be shown to have come primarily from the economically or politically deprived classes of society, nor from the areas, occupations, or environments, such as towns, where the effects of the economic and social changes of the eleventh century were most strongly felt. So far as is known they came from all walks of life and included haves as well as have-nots. Their stress on poverty, humility, and unworldiness was less a compensation or exaltation of their own condition than a spiritualization of virtues that they felt they lacked themselves.

For many people in the tenth and eleventh centuries security was even more important than freedom, as the number who gave themselves as *censuales* to churches and monasteries shows;[87] and they adjusted only slowly to the opportunities and risks presented by economic growth and social mobility. The modern definition of poverty emerged in the twelfth century, when *paupertas* came to mean a lack of material resources rather than of power or social position, and when moral and legal thinkers began to address themselves to the social problem of indigency.[88] The initial attitude of the reformers was to ignore the broader issue by stressing the spiritual nature of poverty and their own character not as *pauperes mundi* but as *pauperes Christi*, who for the sake of Christ had given up their desire for property as well as their possessions. By voluntarily identifying with involuntary poverty and powerlessness the reformers dissociated themselves not from the structure of early medieval society but from the consequences of its breakdown, which left people exposed in ways from which they had previously been to some extent sheltered, in spite of the hardship of their lives. In the course of the century, there was a growing emphasis on economic poverty and on the dangers of wealth and avarice. The corrupting power of money in the affairs of the church, and especially in the purchase of ecclesiastical office, was a key concern of reformers in the eleventh century, and there was a general feeling that the less monks had to do with money the better. The passionate concern with economic precariousness of Stephen of Grandmont and the refusal to handle

---

[87] See Constable (1972), p. 273, and (1977a), pp. 201–2, and more generally, on the security for new settlers, Bartlett (1993), p. 132.

[88] See Couvreur (1961) and pp. 146–50 above on poverty.

money of Aybert of Crépin and Berthold of Garsten may have been motivated by these traditional concerns and not by an objection to money as such, but they showed the way in which opinion was moving.[89]

The visible gap between wealth and poverty in twelfth-century society was not lost on the reformers, many of whom were socially concerned because they saw the suffering in the world around them. Although their first response was to imitate, and even exceed, the suffering and poverty rather than to attempt to eliminate it or cure its causes, which lay in areas where they had no knowledge or concern, they took action because they identified with those who suffered. The ragged clothing of Robert of Arbrissel and other wandering preachers was a mark not only of personal poverty and holiness but also of their desire to be at one with the people to whom much of their message was addressed and also, perhaps, to distinguish themselves from the normal type of parish preacher. By their conspicuous poverty they bore witness to their rejection of the world and devotion to God, like the apostles in Acts 4.32–3. Francis of Assisi showed his desire to break with his former life by publicly taking off the clothing that marked him as the son of a prosperous merchant. The precepts *nudus Nudum* and *pauper Pauperem* were taken literally, as when the abbot of Crépin went barefoot to Rome with the hermits John and Aybert and Pontius of Léras came to Lodève 'naked and unshod'. The topos of nobles performing menial tasks was a symbol of their repudiation of power and wealth as well as of their desire for humility and austerity. The stress on manual labour and a mixed life of work and prayer, in addition to the need of new communities to clothe and feed their members, created a type of life that in its early years, though cut off from the secular world, had more in common with the life of peasants and artisans than with that in many old monasteries. It not only satisfied to some degree the spiritual and material needs of the reformers but also made their way of life accessible to people who might have hesitated to approach an old black house. Some of the new communities seem genuinely to have welcomed all comers, and the military orders and lay brothers attracted recruits who could not have entered a regular monastery. People who change their way of life, however, do not necessarily choose one that resembles the life they seek to leave, and too little is known about the types of recruits who entered the new and old houses to draw any conclusions concerning their respective appeal to different social classes.

If the reform is seen in relation less to the structure of early medieval society than to the social, political, and economic changes of the eleventh century, several approaches are suggested by the works of psychologists, sociologists, and anthropologists. According to Erik Erikson, whose words refer to the modern world but apply equally well to the Middle Ages, 'the decrease of

---

[89] Robert of Ostrevand, *Vita Ayberti*, 15, in *AASS*, 7 Apr. I, p. 674E (*BHL* 180), and *Vita Bertholdi Garstensis*, 5, ed. Josef Lenzenweger (Forschungen zur Geschichte Oberösterreichs 5; Graz and Cologne 1958), pp. 232–3 (*BHL* 1274–82).

ritual reassurance from the ceremonial resources of a passing age and the increase of self-conscious awareness of the role of the individual' tend to produce in individuals 'an oppressive sense of responsibility in isolation'.[90] The sociologist Louis Wirth in an article on 'Urbanism as a Way of Life' emphasized 'the coincidence of close physical contact and distant social relations'.[91] People living together in towns tend to be isolated as individuals. To achieve anything they have to join with others in organized groups, through which they develop their personalities and acquire social status.[92] The medieval town thus promoted, as Le Goff put it, 'the destruction of the large family community' and created 'a ground favourable for individualism'.[93] The economic life of towns also fostered mental habits of competition and self-interest that were transferred to other areas of thought and action.[94] 'It seems a plausible proposition that people assimilate in the market-place an integrated, coherent set of values about social behavior and personal independence and that these values quickly inform the non-economic realms of individual mentalities.'[95] The development of a money economy and the growth of literacy likewise contributed to changes in moral and religious attitudes.[96] Marvin Becker based his book on eleventh- and twelfth-century Italy on 'the hypothesis ... that religion followed the exchange system in many of its particulars'. The partnership between God and man paralleled the commercial partnerships between men, and the replacement of the gifts and literal exchanges of the early Middle Ages by a system of credit marked 'a renewal of confidence' in abstract relationships that resembled the concern of the religious reformers for interiority and subjective relations with God.[97]

It is not necessary to agree with these ideas in order to consider their implications for the history of the reform movement. For while there is no evidence specifically connecting the religious reform to urbanism or economic mentalities, there is no doubt about the general increase of population and growth of towns in the eleventh century, and there may be some relation between these developments and the changes in religious life and thought. Among

---

[90] E. Erikson (1966), pp. 347–8.

[91] Wirth (1938), p. 1.

[92] Turner (1972), pp. 407–8, argued that rituals stressing community often developed when community values were breaking down. On the effects on religion of modernization, and especially bureaucracy, see Douglas (1982). Ruthven (1988), p. 120, said that in both Islamic and Christian society 'the recently urbanized ... tend to become the most aggressive and articulate defenders of religious beliefs'.

[93] Le Goff (1972), p. 96. See also Anderson (1971), p. 49, citing Lewis Mumford on the effect of urbanization.

[94] Le Goff (1986). For the urban and mercantile sense of time, see the references in Constable (1989), pp. 146–7.

[95] Shorter (1973), p. 622.

[96] Little (1978) and, on the influence of literacy in the thirteenth and fourteenth centuries, Aston (1984). According to Montagu (1957), p. 193, literacy tends to detach people from the world of everyday affairs.

[97] Becker (1981), pp. 6, 19, and 21.

political developments, the declining role of monks in public life and govern-
mental business, as secular and ecclesiastical courts were increasingly staffed
by secular clerics, probably contributed to their concentration on monastic
affairs. The apparent imbalance in the sex ratio and numerical preponderance
of women in the twelfth and thirteenth centuries has been attributed to various
factors, including the longevity of women, the higher death rate of men,
especially in battle, the migration of men to the frontiers and on the crusades,
and the number of men who entered the church and religious life. This is
speculative, but unmarried women may have created a pressure for new forms
of female religious life.[98] The fact that women increasingly lost their central
position in the kinship structure of the early Middle Ages but gained new
opportunities for social and economic independence also helps to explain the
prominence in the reform movement of women, whose social role in history
seems to vary in reverse proportion to the degree of centralization and organization in society.[99] In particular, the division of society into clergy and laity
and the clericalization of monasticism marginalized the role of women in the
church and inspired the growth of distinctively female types of religious life.

Society in the eleventh and twelfth centuries came to be seen as made up
not, as earlier, of three orders of monks, clerics, and lay people but of two
orders of the laity and the clergy, which had two branches, one secular, the
clerics who worked in the world, and one regular, those who lived under a
rule.[100] The role of the regular clergy tended to be forgotten in the emphasis
on the two orders. A celebrated and influential canon in the *Decretum* of Gratian declared that 'There are two types of Christians.' The first consisted of
'clerics and those devoted to God, that is converts', who were free for the
holy office, dedicated to prayer and contemplation, and avoided all temporal
concerns. Their tonsure was a crown representing their rule over themselves
and others and a sign of their lack of possessions, since they had no private
property and had everything in common. The second type of Christians consisted of lay men who owned property, married, tilled the soil, engaged in
legal and other business, and paid oblations and tithes, 'and in this way they
can be saved if they avoid vices by acting well'.[101] Gratian attributed this canon
to Jerome, but it almost certainly dates from the eleventh century, when the
reformers sought to separate the clergy from the laity and to impose a monastic
way of life, including celibacy and common property, on clerics, who thus
became more like monks.[102] Hugh of St Victor was probably familiar with this
canon, and in his book *On the sacraments* he distinguished between the two
orders of the clergy and the laity, which were respectively concerned with

---

[98] Southern (1970b), pp. 311–18; Moller (1971), cited n. 83 above; and Bolton (1973).
[99] Shorter (1973), pp. 621–2. Some of these points were made in a talk by Claudia Koonz at
the New England Historical Association in May 1974.
[100] Constable (1995a), esp. pp. 289–323.
[101] Gratian, *Decretum*, XII, 1, 7, in *Corpus*, ed. Friedberg, I, 678. See Constable (1995a), pp. 294–5.
[102] Cox (1959), pp. 20–6; Couvreur (1961), p. 196 n. 167; and Prosdocimi (1965a).

spiritual and temporal things. These two orders corresponded to two lives, Hugh said, one earthly and physical and the other heavenly and spiritual, and 'according to the two lives', there are 'two peoples and in the two peoples two powers and in each [power] different grades and orders of dignities, and one inferior, the other superior'.[103] Stephen of Tournai in the introduction to his *Summa* on the *Decretum* also said that

> There are two people in the same city under the same king, and according to the two people, two lives, and according to the two lives, two sovereignties, and according to the two sovereignties, a double order of jurisdiction. The city is the church; the king of the city is Christ; the two people are the two orders in the church of lay men and clerics; the two lives, spiritual and physical; the two sovereignties, the priesthood and the kingship; the double jurisdiction, divine and human law.[104]

Some further lines of inquiry are suggested by the work of the anthropologist Mary Douglas, who correlated the extent of personal relationships in society, ranging from shared to private and called grid, with the extent of individualism, ranging from controlling others to being controlled and called group. A combination of strong grid and strong group, meaning a highly organized society with a low degree of individualism, as in a monastery, 'will tend to a routinized piety towards authority and its symbols; beliefs in a punishing, moral universe; and a category of rejects'. Weak group and weak grid, on the other hand, involves the withdrawal of public classification and pressures, leaves the individual free to develop a private and unritualistic cosmology, and leads to a slackening of bodily controls. 'The weaker the social constraints, the more bodily dissociation is approved and treated as a central ritual adjunct for channelling benign powers to the community. The stronger the social pressures, the more magicality in ritual and in the definition of sin.' Likewise in attitudes to wrong-doing, weak social pressures lead to a stress on wishes, intent, and state of mind, whereas strong social pressures involve a concern with the intrinsic evil and danger of wrong-doing.[105] Much of the evidence for these views is derived from tribal societies, but it offers some comparisons with medieval religious development. Peter Munz has suggested that the appearance of gnosticism may be associated with the close personal relationships and loose social structure (strong grid and weak group) in late Antiquity, when people tended to experience their bodies as being 'something very individual whose success depends upon enterprise and calculation' and

---

[103] Hugh of St Victor, *De sacramentis*, II, 2, 3–4, in *PL*, CLXXVI, 417B–18D (quote on 417D), and tr. Roy J. Deferrari (Mediaeval Academy of America, Publ. 58; Cambridge, Mass., 1951), pp. 255–6. See Prosdocimi (1965b), esp. pp. 677–8, where he raised a question about the authenticity of this passage.

[104] Stephen of Tournai, *Summa*, intro., ed. J.F. von Schulte (Giessen 1891), pp. 1–2. See Carlyle and Carlyle (1950), II, 198–9 and 225, and Prosdocimi (1965b).

[105] Douglas (1973), *passim* (quotes on pp. 87 and 130).

to see the principles governing the universe 'as multipliers of human success or failure'.[106] The strong grid and strong group of early medieval tribal society promoted monasticism, worship, and an objective view of sins and retributions, while the weakening of social structures, both grid and group, in the eleventh and twelfth centuries, correlated with the individualism and variety of forms of religious life and with a stress on interiority, private devotions, and intention. The personalism of religion contributed to the decline of mediation, intercessory prayer, and the saints and ceremonies – 'the magic of the medieval church', as Keith Thomas called it – which had long kept the forces of evil at bay.[107] The waning confidence in the efficacy of this orthodox counter-magic left the way open for the growth of witchcraft and sorcery. Some cases can be cited from the eleventh and twelfth centuries, as with heresy, but it did not become a serious matter until the late Middle Ages, when the resort to witchcraft by people who felt that they had nowhere else to turn for help was a sign of the despair and anxiety of the age.[108]

In the personalized social world of the early Middle Ages, where everyone had their place, the role of mediation and intercession between man and God was entrusted to professional religious men and women. The prayers and mortifications of monks, nuns, hermits, and holy men inclined God to look with favour both on individuals and on humankind generally, now and in the future. At the same time they mitigated the hardships of earthly life by intervening in secular affairs. The role of monks on earth was thus parallel with that of the saints and angels in heaven, with whom they were often compared and who, being close to God, like the courtiers of a great king, could intercede directly with Him on behalf of their clients. They also played a role through their tombs and relics, and by their miracles. No reader of early medieval saints *Lives* or charters, or of the liturgy, can miss the sense of immediacy and personality surrounding the saints, who often behaved as if they were alive and present. The power of saints in heaven and of monks and holy men on earth rivalled and overshadowed the pastoral work of the clergy, who were responsible for the formal framework of instruction and the sacraments that guided people in what to believe and how to behave and ushered them through both the great occasions of life and the conduct of their daily and seasonal affairs, which were attended by countless blessings and charms designed to ensure their successful outcome. For really important

---

[106] Munz (1972), p. 49.

[107] Thomas (1971), esp. pp. 25–77 and 253–79. See also the unpublished paper (dated June 1988) by Mary Douglas on 'The Problem of Evil among the Lele: Sorcery, Witch-Hunt and Christian Teaching in Africa', stressing the parallels between non-Christian and Christian magic, and Flint (1991), who argued that magic in the Middle Ages constituted 'a whole alternative world of intercession' (p. 69) and 'a Christian substitute' (p. 203) that developed both as the heir and in competition with non-Christian magic.

[108] Thomas (1971), p. 522, and Douglas (1973), p. 70. K. Erikson (1966), pp. 22 and 125, argued that in the sixteenth and seventeenth centuries deviant behaviour (such as witchcraft and crime) was related to the fear and definition of deviance.

undertakings, however, and many less important ones, and above all for the most important enterprise of all, the winning of salvation, early medieval people turned to monks and holy men, whose visible unworldliness, manifested by their seclusion, asceticism, and prayer, showed their closeness to God and almost obliged Him to accede to their requests.

The question of whether this was a proper role for monks or whether it conformed to the ideals of the Gospel or the desert fathers or to the rules of Basil or Benedict is not the concern of historians, who can only observe that it represented, with infinite variety in practice, the accepted ideal of how monks should live and what they should do for at least five centuries, down, that is, until the eleventh century, when it was seriously challenged for the first time by general changes in society and the accompanying emergence of new spiritual attitudes and forms of religious life. The old institutions were so well established, and the confidence in their ideals and traditions so strong, that for a long time the real nature of the challenge was not recognized, and its effect was to attract into religious houses all over Europe thousands of recruits seeking to remake monasticism according to the model of life they found in the early church and the rule of Benedict. The incompatibility of their aspirations with a life of withdrawal and prayer became clear only gradually, as the reformers branched out into new activities and ways of life that could not be accommodated within the existing institutions. In the second half of the twelfth century the currents of reform swept into other fields, leaving a rich and varied legacy of new orders and houses that as time went on reverted to the established patterns and way of life but were largely shorn of their role as spiritual intercessors for society and of other social functions, which were taken over by new and independent institutions.

Monks were not in principle excluded from the bipartite division of society. Indeed, it could be argued, as did some contemporaries, that by imposing a monastic way of life on all clerics the monastic order had prevailed and the clergy had been monasticized. Monks and nuns no longer constituted a distinct order of society, however, made up of men and women with superior claims to holiness. They were still admired in the later Middle Ages and played an important role in the church and Christian society, but they never recovered the central position they held before the twelfth century. Many men and women with sincere religious ideals continued to be attracted to monasticism, and they contributed to the intellectual as well as the spiritual life of the church, but the quality as well as the quantity of recruits declined, and with them the sources of material support without which religious institutions cannot survive.[109] There were signs already in the twelfth century of financial difficulties, which were the result of reduced support as well as rising costs,

---

[109] See Morris (1989), pp. 541–5, on the continued strength of monasticism in the thirteenth century, and Kristeller (1966), pp. 37–8, and (1970), on the contribution of monks to intellectual life in the fourteenth and fifteenth centuries.

and also of the attraction of donors to other types of institutions and the tendency to keep their wealth within their own families. To some extent this was a topos. Patrons are never as generous as they used to be. Monks were not alone, however, in sensing that the well-springs of generosity were drying up. Almost all the vernacular poets who praised generosity were born in the generation between 1120 and 1150 – the very time when the movement of monastic reform was at its height – and by the time they were writing, in the second half of the century, their praise was mixed with complaints at the decline of generosity.[110] In this case the topos appears to have had some truth, at least insofar as the church was concerned. Theobald of Canterbury in the first half of the twelfth century was concerned to prevent the cancellation by an heir of an ancestor's grant to a monastery, and a document of 1254 from Richmondshire harked back to the age before Innocent III, who had settled a dispute concerning legacies to the church, and recorded sadly that

> In the old days (*antiquitus*) there were men who were very devoted to God and munificent, generous, and liberal in giving tithes, produce, and oblations and in paying other dues to the holy church of God, and assiduous and benevolent towards the buildings and venerations of churches, and in all other and individual things that could more greatly please God and benefit their souls.

But now, the document continued, the executors of wills keep the property of dead men and do little or nothing for the salvation of their souls.[111] While complaints of this sort should not be taken too literally, and large benefactions continued to be made to the church, these documents seem to reflect a change of attitude towards the advantages to be gained by gifts for the benefit of a donor's soul.

The reformation of the twelfth century was a watershed in the history of the church and of Christian society as well as of monasticism and religious life. It involved a passionate reexamination of what it meant to be a Christian in a world where the traditional links between people and between the individual and God were loosened and where the boundaries between the sacred and the profane, as Peter Brown called them, were redefined within the course of less than a long lifetime.[112] The fact that monastic institutions survived the challenge, absorbing some of the changes and rejecting others, shows their strength and the need they still met in the hearts of those Christians for whom a life of withdrawal and prayer embodied the message of the Gospel and represented the way to salvation. The fact that there were also sincere Christians who no longer shared this conviction, however, and sought other ways to heaven, which seemed to them more pleasing to God than that of monks, is the measure of the religious transformation from the early to the central

---

[110] Whitney (1923), esp. pp. 202–3 and 209.
[111] *Registrum honoris de Richmond*, [ed. Roger Gale] (London 1722), pp. 101–6 (quote on p. 101).
[112] Brown (1975), p. 134.

Middle Ages. As the broad developments in society swept away the older patterns of life, leaving people exposed to the dangers as well as the opportunities of isolation and the need to form new bonds, so the changes in spirituality swept away the established bridges between God and man, who built new and inner bridges based upon a direct dependence on God, a devotion to the human Christ, and a lively sense of the degradation of the human condition and of the possibilities of redemption through reform and progressive conformity to the image in which mankind was created. The monastic life was one way to achieve this, but no longer the only or necessarily the best way. The efforts of the reformers to monasticize the world and interiorize monastic virtues ended by consecrating everyone and all human activities. When everyone who observed the rule of the Gospel and lived under the supreme abbot God was considered a regular, monks and nuns took a place beside rather than above other people. The claim that priests were superior to monks reflected a deep shift in values, and as time went on more people turned away from a life of withdrawal and asceticism towards an ideal that combined personal prayer and devotion with activity in the world and was an expression of inner faith.

These remained the hallmarks of later Christian spirituality, down until modern times, and have not entirely disappeared today under the waves of science and secularism. Bernard of Clairvaux was the great master of late medieval and early modern piety.[113] 'There was a greater gulf between Montesqieu and Bossuet than between Bossuet and Bernard of Clairvaux.'[114] Luther venerated Bernard 'above all other monks' and praised his sincerity, preaching, stress on experience, and above all his faith. 'You see that these are the words of a most Christian breast', Luther said, citing two passages from Bernard's *Life* and his treatise *On consideration*, 'that placed entire trust in Christ, utterly despairing of its [own] works.'[115] Some scholars have argued that Luther misinterpreted Bernard, but the fact remains that he and many of his contemporaries, both Protestants and Catholics, found in Bernard's works and example a spirituality that suited their own religious attitudes.[116] In his own time Bernard was not alone in his stress on faith. Such different writers as the anonymous author of the reply to the Cistercian charges against the old monks and the Cistercian in the *Dialogue* by Idungus of Regensburg held with St Paul that 'A man is justified by faith without the works of the

---

[113] Renaudet (1916), pp. 70–1, and Bremond (1915–32), III, 26.
[114] Strachey (1980), p. 48.
[115] Luther, *Tischreden* no. 4772 and *De votis monasticis*, 2, in *Werke*, IV (Weimar 1916), p. 480, and VIII (Weimar 1889), p. 601; cf. pp. 617 and 641. See *Werke*, LVIII (Weimar 1948), pp. 178–80, for other references to Bernard in Luther's works and, among secondary works, Benz (1953); Mousnier (1953); Stange (1954), pp. 5–9; and Constable (1971), pp. 38–9, with further references.
[116] Constable (1971), *passim*.

law' and is sanctified by 'nothing except faith'.[117] The spiritual teaching of
the *Imitation of Christ* and of the *Devotio moderna* derived from the twelfth
century. The debt of Ignatius Loyola to twelfth-century spirituality can be
recognized on almost every page of the *Spiritual exercises*, of which the very
title echoes the words of Bernard, Guigo of La Chartreuse, and the Victorines.[118] Bellini's painting of *St Francis in the desert* (plate 8), which has been
seen as a monument to Renaissance naturalism, is a visual parallel to the
Imitation of Christ, and belongs in the tradition of medieval teaching concerning the religious life. There is a mountain, a cave, and water, with a castellated
town in the distance and a shepherd and his flock in between. There is a wild
ass, the symbol of the holy man set free by the Lord, and a lectern for reading
and meditation with a skull on it as a reminder of human mortality. And there
is Francis himself, barefoot and in a simple habit, alone before his Maker,
standing in an attitude of prayer. Almost nothing in the religious (as distinct
from the aesthetic and artistic) content of this painting dates from after the
twelfth century. Even its naturalism, which so clearly separates it from any
painting of the twelfth century, shows the appreciation of natural beauty that
was associated with the spirituality of that time.[119] Petrarch's treatise *On the
solitary life* was inspired by traditional monastic ideals and reveals the time it
was written mainly by its references to classical writers and to non-Christian
religions,[120] and the remarkable list of 'Instructions for a devout and literate
lay man' published by Pantin from an early fifteenth-century English manuscript goes back in all its essentials to the teachings of the twelfth century,
including the devotion to 'the most sweet Jesus', Mary, and the Mary Magdalene, the references to Anselm and Godric of Finchale, the private devotional
practices, and above all the emphasis on self-abasement, fear of sin, self-
examination, and dependence on God. It lacks much of the optimism, confidence, and joyful love of twelfth-century spirituality, leaving what Pantin
called 'a rather grim and rigorist air', which resembles the piety of both the
Recusants and Puritans of the seventeenth century.[121] It thus forms a link
between medieval and modern spirituality. Edmund Gosse wrote in *Father
and Son* that his father Henry, who was a Plymouth Brother as well as an
eminent scientist, 'believed that if my brain could be kept unaffected by any
of the tempting errors of the age, and my heart centred in the adoring love
of God, all would be well with me in perpetuity';[122] and Claudel wrote to
Gide in 1912 that the two subjects for meditation were to examine one's own
life and conscience and 'to lift up, or rather to bow down, your heart towards
Christ, to read, for instance, the Seven Penitential Psalms, the resurrection

[117] *Rescriptum*, ed. Leclercq, p. 87, and Idungus, *Dialogus*, II, 59, ed. Huygens, p. 436.
[118] Brou (1949), pp. 5–6, and other works cited in the notes to Constable (1971), pp. 47–9.
[119] Fleming (1982). See p. 61 n. 65 above on the freedom of the wild ass (Job 39.5).
[120] Constable (1980).
[121] Pantin (1976).
[122] Edmund Gosse, *Father and Son: A Study of Two Temperaments* (New York 1907), p. 335.

of Lazarus, the four narratives of the Passion; to shut yourself up in your room, to take a crucifix and to kiss its feet'.[123]

These passages were written without any conscious reference to the twelfth century, but they depend heavily on its spiritual teaching. They appear at the close of this book because they are characteristic examples of the piety of the times when they were written and also illustrations of the way in which spirituality was reshaped in the twelfth century to meet the needs of men at that time and in the future. They offer no explanation for what happened, but they help scholars to understand what it meant to people both then and later. The broader context also offers no reasons or causes in Lewis's sense of some thing or things that would account for a new state of affairs and explain away what seems to be its novelty. As a part of human nature, and perhaps its deepest part, religion is not simply a variable reaction to other aspects of human experience; but the forms it took in the twelfth century relate the reform to a broad pattern of change. To people at that time the rhetoric of the recovery of a lost perfection, the ideal of personal reformation, and the details of monastic life were the essence of what religion meant as a way of life expressing a commitment to God and Jesus, and a sense, which was at first only dimly if at all perceived, of standing alone before Them. It was these feelings, and the tensions between them, that made the twelfth century into an age of experiment and transformation in religious life and sentiment and that laid the basis for the future development of Christian values and ideals.

[123] *The Correspondence between Paul Claudel and André Gide*, ed. Robert Mallet, tr. John Russell (Boston 1964), p. 182.

BIBLIOGRAPHY OF SECONDARY WORKS

Works cited without dates are listed under Abbreviations.

Books are cited in the editions used here, owing either to availability or to the inclusion of material omitted in other editions. Names including 'de' and 'von' are normally listed under the last name; names beginning with 'Van' under Van. Depending on regional and individual usage, there are some inconsistencies in capitalization and the use of a colon or full stop between the sections of a title. As a rule a colon is used between the title and subtitle of works in English and a full stop in titles in foreign languages. To avoid confusion, Latin words and phrases are put in quotation marks rather than italics.

Abulafia, Anna Sapir (1989), 'Jewish-Christian Disputations and the Twelfth Century Renaissance', *Journal of Medieval History* 15: 105–25

Adam, Alfred (1953–4), 'Grundbegriffe des Mönchtums in sprachlicher Sicht', *Zeitschrift für Kirchengeschichte* 65: 209–39

Adam, August (1927), *Arbeit und Besitz nach Ratherius von Verona* (Freiburger theologische Studien 31), Freiburg

Adams, Henry (1936), *Mont-Saint-Michel and Chartres*, Boston and New York

Ahrweiler, Hélène (1967), 'Charisticariat et autres formes d'attribution de fondations pieuses aux Xe–XIe siècles', *Recueil des travaux de l'Institut d'études byzantines* 10: 1–27

Alphandéry, Paul (1912), *Notes sur le messianisme médiéval latin (XIe–XIIe siècle)...* *avec un rapport sommaire sur les conférences de l'exercise 1911–1912 et le programme des conférences pour l'exercise 1912–1913* (Ecole pratique des hautes études: Section des sciences religieuses), Paris

Anciaux, Paul (1949), *La théologie du sacrement de pénitence au XIIe siècle* (Universitas Catholica Lovaniensis. Dissertationes ad gradum magistri in Facultate theologica vel in Facultate iuris canonici consequendum conscriptae II, 41), Louvain and Gembloux

Anderson, Robert T. (1971), *Traditional Europe*, Belmont

Angenendt, Arnold (1972), *Monachi peregrini. Studien zu Pirmin und den monastischen Vorstellungen des frühen Mittelalters* (Münstersche Mittelalter-Schriften 6), Munich

    (1983), 'Missa specialis. Zugleich ein Beitrag zur Entstehung der Privatmessen', *Frühmittelalterliche Studien* 17: 153–221

(1984), 'Theologie und Liturgie der mittelalterlichen Toten-Memoria', in *Memoria. Der geschichtliche Zeugniswert des liturgischen Gedenkens im Mittelalter*, ed. Karl Schmid and Joachim Wollasch (Münstersche Mittelalter-Schriften 48), Munich, pp. 79–199

(1994), *Heilige und Reliquien. Die Geschichte ihres Kultes vom frühen Christentum bis zur Gegenwart*, Munich

Angiolillo, Maria d'Elia (1959), 'L'epistolario femminile di S. Bernardo', *Analecta sacri ordinis Cisterciensis* 15: 23–55

Anson, John (1974), 'The Female Transvestite in Early Monasticism: The Origin and Development of a Motif', *Viator* 5: 1–32

Antin, Paul (1964), 'Une question de vocabulaire: monachisme, "monachologie" ', *Revue d'histoire ecclésiastique* 59: 89–90

Anton, Hans Hubert (1975), *Studien zu den Klosterprivilegien der Päpste im frühen Mittelalter, unter besonderer Berücksichtigung der Privilegierung von St. Maurice d'Agaune* (Beiträge zur Geschichte und Quellenkunde des Mittelalters 4), Berlin and New York

Arbois de Jubainville, Henri d' (1858), *Etudes sur l'état intérieur des abbayes cisterciennes, et principalement de Clairvaux, au XIIe et au XIIIe siècle*, Paris

Arduini, Maria Lodovica (1985), ' "Rerum mutabilitas". Welt, Zeit, Menschenbild und "Corpus Ecclesiae-Christianitatis" bei Honorius von Regensburg (Augustodunensis). Zum Verständnis eines politischen Rationalismus im 12. Jahrhundert', *Recherches de théologie ancienne et médiévale* 52: 78–108

Arnaldi, Girolamo (1959), ' "Prior" e "praepositus" nella "Vita Odonis" di Giovanni Romano', *Archivum latinitatis medii aevi* 29: 167–71

Arnold, Benjamin (1991), *Princes and Territories in Medieval Germany*, Cambridge

Aston, Margaret (1984), 'Devotional Literacy', in her *Lollards and Reformers: Images and Literacy in Late Medieval Religion* (History Series 22), London, pp. 101–33

Aston, Stanley C. (1970), 'The Saint in Medieval Literature', *Modern Language Review* 65: xxv–xlii

Auberger, Jean-Baptiste (1986), *L'unanimité cistercienne primitive. Mythe ou réalité?* (Cîteaux. Studia et documenta 3) Achel

Aubert, Marcel, and Maillé, Geneviève Aliette [de Rohan-Chabot, marquise] de (1947), *L'architecture cistercienne en France*, 2nd edn, Paris

Aubrun, Michel (1986), *La paroisse en France des origines au XVe siècle*, Paris

Avril, Joseph (1976–80), 'Recherches sur la politique paroissiale des établissements monastiques et canoniaux (XIe–XIIIe s.)', *Revue Mabillon* 264–82: 453–518

Baker, L.G. Derek (1969a), 'The Genesis of English Cistercian Chronicles: The Foundation History of Fountains Abbey, I', *Analecta cisterciensia* 25: 14–41

(1969b), 'The Foundations of Fountains Abbey', *Northern History* 4: 29–43

(1978), 'Popular Piety in the Lodèvois in the Early Twelfth Century: The Case of Pons of Léras', in *Religious Motivation: Biographical and Sociological Problems for the Church Historian*, ed. Derek Baker (Studies in Church History 15), Oxford, pp. 39–47

Baldwin, John W. (1970), *Masters, Princes, and Merchants: The Social Views of Peter the Chanter and his Circle*, Princeton

Barakat, Robert (1975), *The Cistercian Sign Language* (Cistercian Studies Series 11), Kalamazoo

Barbier, Victor (1892), *Histoire de l'abbaye de Floreffe*, Namur

Bardy, Gustave (1945), 'Saint Bernard et Origène?', *Revue du moyen âge latin*, 1: 420–1

Barley, Maurice W. (1957), 'Cistercian Land Clearances in Nottinghamshire: Three Deserted Villages and their Moated Successor', *Nottingham Mediaeval Studies* 1: 75–89

Barrière, Bernadette (1977), *L'abbaye cistercienne d'Obazine en Bas-Limousin*, Tulle

Barthélemy, Dominique (1993), *La société dans le comté de Vendôme de l'an mil au XIVe siècle*, Paris

Bartlett, Robert (1993), *The Making of Europe: Conquest, Colonization, and Cultural Change, 950–1350*, Princeton

Batany, Jean (1969), 'Les convers chez quelques moralistes des XIIe et XIIIe siècles', *Cîteaux* 20: 241–59

Bauerreiss, Romuald (1949–70), *Kirchengeschichte Bayerns*, St Ottilien

Baumstark, Anton (n.d.), *Liturgie comparée*, 2nd edn, Chevetogne

Bautier, Anne-Marie (1987), 'De "Prepositus" à "Prior", de "Cella" à "prioratus". Evolution linguistique et genèse d'une institution (jusqu'à 1200)', in *Prieurs et prieurés dans l'occident médiéval. Actes du colloque organisé à Paris le 12 novembre 1984* , ed. Jean-Loup Lemaître (Ecole pratique des hautes études, IVe section 5: Hautes études médiévales et modernes 60), Geneva and Paris, pp. 1–21

Becker, Marvin (1981), *Medieval Italy: Constraints and Creativity*, Bloomington

Becquet, Jean (1956), 'L'"Institution": premier coutumier de l'Ordre de Grandmont', *Revue Mabillon* 46: 15–32

(1957), 'Saint Etienne de Muret et l'archevêque de Bénévent Milon', *Bulletin de la Société archéologique et historique du Limousin* 86: 403–9

(1958), 'La règle de Grandmont', *Bulletin de la Société archéologique et historique du Limousin* 87: 9–36

(1960), 'La première crise de l'ordre de Grandmont', *Bulletin de la Société archéologique et historique du Limousin* 87: 283–324

(1972), 'Les chanoines réguliers de Lesterps, Bénévent et Aureil en Limousin aux XIe et XIIe siècles', *Bulletin de la Société archéologique et historique du Limousin* 99: 80–135

Bennett, John A.W. (1979), ' "Nosce te ipsum": Some Medieval Interpretations', in *J.R.R. Tolkien, Scholar and Storyteller. Essays in Memoriam*, ed. M. Salu and R.T. Farell, Ithaca, pp. 138–58

Benz, Ernst (1953), 'Luther und Bernhard von Clairvaux', *Eckhart* 23: 60–4

Berenson, Bernard (1960), *The Passionate Sightseer: From the Diaries, 1947 to 1956*, New York

Berges, Wilhelm (1956), 'Anselm von Havelberg in der Geistesgeschichte des 12. Jahrhunderts', *Jahrbuch für die Geschichte Mittel- und Ostdeutschlands* 5: 39–57

Berlendis, Franciscus de (1743), *De oblationibus ad altare communibus et peculiaribus*, 3rd edn, Venice

Berlière, Ursmer (1900–1), 'Les origines de Cîteaux et l'ordre bénédictine au XIIe siècle', *Revue d'histoire ecclésiastique* 1: 448–71 and 2: 253–90

(1927a), *L'ascèse bénédictine des origines à la fin du XIIe siècle* (Collection pax in-8° 1), Paris and Maredsous

(1927b), 'L'exercice du ministère paroissial par les moines dans le haut moyen-âge', *Revue bénédictine* 39: 227–50, and 'L'exercice du ministère paroissial par les moines du XIIe au XVIIIe siècle', ibid. 340–64

(1929–30), 'Le nombre des moines dans les anciens monastères', *Revue bénédictine* 41: 231–61 and 42: 19–42

(1931), *La familia dans les monastères bénédictins du moyen âge* (Académie royale de Belgique: Classe des lettres et des sciences morales et politiques, Mémoires in-8° 2 S. 29.2), Brussels

Bernard de Clairvaux (1953) = *Bernard de Clairvaux* (Commission d'histoire de l'ordre de Cîteaux 3), Paris

Bernards, Matthäus (1955), *Speculum virginum. Geistigkeit und Seelenleben der Frau im Hochmittelalter* (Forschungen zur Volkskunde 36–8), Cologne and Graz

(1960), 'Die Welt der Laien in der kölnischen Theologie des 12. Jahrhunderts. Beobachtungen zur Ekklesiologie Ruperts von Deutz', in *Die Kirche und ihre Ämter und Stände. Festgabe für Joseph Kardinal Frings*, Cologne, pp. 391–416

(1971), 'Die Frau in der Welt und die Kirche während des 11. Jahrhunderts', *Sacris erudiri* 20: 39–100

Bernhardt, John W. (1993), *Itinerant Kingship and Royal Monasteries in Early Medieval Germany, c. 936–1075* (Cambridge Studies in Medieval Life and Thought 4 S. 21), Cambridge

Bertola, Ermenegildo (1959), 'Il socratismo cristiano nel XII secolo', *Rivista di filosofia neo-scolastica* 51: 252–64

Bessmertny, Yuri (1990), 'Contribution à l'étude du comportement matrimonial en France aux XIIe–XIIIe siècles', in *L'homme et l'histoire* (Histoire universelle. Recherches en URSS 6), Moscow, pp. 134–56

Bestul, Thomas H. (1984), 'The Collection of Private Prayers in the "Portiforium" of Wulfstan of Worcester and the "Orationes sive Meditationes" of Anselm of Canterbury', in *Les mutations socio-culturelles au tournant des XIe–XIIe siècles. Etudes anselmiennes (IVe section)* (Colloques internationaux du Centre de la recherche scientifique), Paris, pp. 355–64

Bethell, Denis L.T. (1966), 'The Foundation of Fountains Abbey and the State of St. Mary's York in 1132', *Journal of Ecclesiastical History* 17: 11–27

(1969a), 'English Black Monks and Episcopal Elections in the 1120s', *English Historical Review* 84: 673–98

(1969b), 'English Monks and Irish Reform in the Eleventh and Twelfth Centuries', *Historical Studies* 8: 111–35

Beuer, H.V. (1957), 'Evolution du plan des églises cisterciennes en France, dans les pays germaniques et en Grande-Bretagne', *Cîteaux in de Nederlanden* 8: 269–89

Beyerle, Franz (1929), 'Eine Reichenauer Konventsliste aus der Zeit Abt Ruodmans (972–985)', *Zeitschrift für die Geschichte des Oberrheins* 81 (N.F. 42): 382–99

Bickel, Ernst (1916), 'Das asketische Ideal bei Ambrosius, Hieronymus und Augustin. Eine kulturgeschichtliche Studie', *Neue Jahrbücher für das klassische Altertum, Geschichte und deutsche Literatur und für Pädagogik* 37: 437–74

Bieler, Peter (1985), 'Words and the Medieval Notion of "Religion" ', *Journal of Ecclesiastical History* 36: 351–69

Bienvenu, Jean Marc (1966–7), 'Pauvreté, misère et charité en Anjou aux XIe et XIIe siècles', *Le Moyen Age* (1) 72 (4 S. 21): 389–424, and (2–3) 73 (4 S. 22): 5–34 and 189–216

Bilson, John (1909), 'The Architecture of the Cistercians, with Special Reference to Some of their Earlier Churches in England', *Archaeological Journal* 66: 185–280

Bishop, Terence A.M. (1936), 'Monastic Granges in Yorkshire', *English Historical Review* 51: 193–214

Black-Michaud, Jacob (1975), *Ordered Force*, Oxford

Blanc, Colette (1960), 'Les pratiques de piété des laïcs dans les pays du Bas-Rhône aux XIᵉ et XIIᵉ siècles', *Annales du Midi* 72: 137–47

Blazovich, Augustin (1954), *Soziologie des Mönchtums und der Benediktinerregel*, Vienna

Bligny, Bernard (1960), *L'église et les ordres religieux dans le royaume de Bourgogne aux XIᵉ et XIIᵉ siècles* (Collection des cahiers d'histoire publiée par les universités de Clermont, Lyon, Grenoble 4), Paris

Bloch, Marc (1963), 'Liberté et servitude personnelles au moyen âge, particulièrement en France' (1933), repr. in his *Mélanges historiques* (Bibliothèque générale de l'Ecole pratique des hautes études, VIᵉ section), Paris, I, 286–355

Blomme, Robert (1958), *La doctrine du péché dans les écoles théologiques de la première moitié du XIIᵉ siècle* (Universitas catholica Lovaniensis. Dissertationes ad gradum magistri in Facultate theologica vel in Facultate iuris canonici consequendum conscriptae III, 6), Louvain and Gembloux

Bloomfield, Morton W. (1957), 'Joachim of Flora: A Critical Survey of his Canon, Teachings, Sources, Biography and Influence', *Traditio* 13: 249–311

Blume, Karl (1914), *Abbatia. Ein Beitrag zur Geschichte der kirchlichen Rechtssprache* (Kirchenrechtliche Abhandlungen 83), Stuttgart

Boas, George (1948), *Essays on Primitivism and Related Ideas in the Middle Ages*, Baltimore

Bock, Colomban (1952), 'Tonsure monastique et tonsure cléricale', *Revue de droit canonique* 2: 373–406

Boer, Bertilo de (1957–8), 'La soi-disant opposition de saint François d'Assise à saint Bernard', *Etudes franciscaines* N.S. 8: 181–94 and 9: 57–65

Bogdanos, Theodore (1977), ' "The Shepherd of Hermas" and the Development of Medieval Visionary Allegory', *Viator* 8: 33–46

Bolton, Brenda M. (1973), 'Mulieres sanctae', in *Sanctity and Secularity: The Church and the World*, ed. Derek Baker (Studies in Church History 10), Oxford, pp. 77–95

(1977), ' "Paupertas Christi": Old Wealth and New Poverty in the Twelfth Century', in *Renaissance and Renewal in Christian History*, ed. Derek Baker (Studies in Church History 14), Oxford, pp. 95–103

Bonnes, Jean-Paul (1945–6), 'Un des plus grands prédicateurs du XIIᵉ siècle: Geoffroy du Loroux dit Geoffroy Babion', *Revue bénédictine* 56: 174–215

Bori, Pier Cesare (1974), *Chiesa primitiva. L'immagine della comunità delle origini – Atti 2, 42–47; 4, 32–37 – nella storia della chiesa antica* (Testi e ricerche di scienze religiose 10), Brescia

Borst, Arno (1992), *Medieval Worlds: Barbarians, Heretics, and Artists*, tr. Eric Hansen, Chicago

Boshof, Egon (1976), ' "Traditio romana" und Papstschutz im 9. Jahrhundert. Untersuchungen zu vorcluniazensischen "Libertas" ', in *Rechtsgeschichtlich-diplomatische Studien zu frühmittelalterlichen Papsturkunden*, ed. Egon Boshof and Heinz Wolter (Studien und Vorarbeiten zur Germania pontificia 6), Cologne and Vienna, pp. 1–100

Bosl, Karl (1963), ' "Potens" et "pauper". Begriffsgeschichtliche Studien zur gesellschaftlichen Differenzierung im frühen Mittelalter und zum "Pauperismus" des Hochmittelalters', in *Alteuropa und die moderne Gesellschaft. Festschrift für Otto Brunner*, Göttingen, pp. 60–87

(1979), *Regularkanoniker (Augustinerchorherren) und Seelsorge in Kirche und Gesellschaft des europäischen 12. Jahrhunderts* (Bayerische Akademie der Wissenschaften, phil.-hist. Kl.: Abhandlungen N.F. 86), Munich

(1981), *Armut Christi. Ideal der Mönche und Ketzer. Ideologie der aufsteigenden Gesellschaftsschichten vom 11. bis 13. Jahrhundert* (Bayerische Akademie der Wissenschaften, phil.-hist. Kl.: Sitzungsberichte 1981.1), Munich

Boswell, John E. (1988), *The Kindness of Strangers: The Abandonment of Children in Western Europe from Late Antiquity to the Renaissance*, New York

Bouchard, Constance B. (1987), *Sword, Miter, and Cloister: Nobility and the Church in Burgundy, 980–1198*, Ithaca and New York

Bourgain, Louis (1879), *La chaire française au XIIᵉ siècle d'après les manuscrits*, Paris and Brussels

Boussard, Jacques (1950), 'La vie en Anjou aux XIᵉ et XIIᵉ siècles', *Le Moyen Age* 56 (4 S. 5): 29–68

Boutemy, André (1937), 'Notice sur le recueil poétique du manuscrit Cotton Vitellius A xii, du British Museum', *Latomus* 1: 278–313

Brackmann, Albert (1912), *Die Kurie und die Salzburger Kirchenprovinz* (Studien und Vorarbeiten zur Germania pontificia 1), Berlin

Bredero, Adriaan H. (1966), *Bernhard von Clairvaux im Widerstreit der Historie* (Institut für europäische Geschichte Mainz, Vorträge 44), Wiesbaden

(1980), 'The Conflicting Interpretations of the Relevance of Bernard of Clairvaux to the History of his Own Time', *Cîteaux* 31 (Studia cisterciensia Edmundo Mikkers oblata 1): 53–81

(1985), *Cluny et Cîteaux au douzième siècle*, Amsterdam and Maarssen

(1993), *Bernardus van Clairvaux (1091–1153). Tussen cultus en historie*, Kampen

Bremond, Henri (1915–32), *Histoire littéraire du sentiment religieux en France*, Paris

Brillat-Savarin, Jean-Anthelme (1825), *La physiologie du goût*, tr. Anne Drayton (Harmondsworth 1970)

Brooke, Christopher N.L. (1964), 'Gregorian Reform in Action: Clerical Marriage in England, 1050–1200' (1956), repr. in *Change in Medieval Society: Europe North of the Alps 1050–1500*, ed. Sylvia Thrupp, New York, pp. 49–71

(1968), 'Heresy and Religious Sentiment: 1000–1250', *Bulletin of the Institute of Historical Research* 41: 115–31

(1985), 'Monk and Canon: Some Patterns in the Religious Life of the Twelfth Century', in *Monks, Hermits and the Ascetic Tradition*, ed. W.J. Sheils (Studies in Church History 22), Oxford, pp. 109–29

Brou, Alexandre (1949), *Ignatian Methods of Prayer*, tr. William J. Young, Milwaukee

Brown, Peter R.L. (1975), 'Society and the Supernatural: A Medieval Change', *Daedalus* 104.2: 133–51

(1979), 'The Rise and Function of the Holy Man in Late Antiquity' (1971), repr. in his *Society and the Holy in Late Antiquity*, Berkeley and Los Angeles, pp. 103–52

(1988), *The Body and Society: Men, Women and Sexual Renunciation in Early Christianity* (Lectures on the History of Religion N.S. 13), New York

Bruhat, L. (1907), *Le monachisme en Saintonge et en Aunis (XIᵉ et XIIᵉ siècles)*. *Etude administrative et économique*, La Rochelle

Brundage, James (1980), 'Carnal Delight: Canonistic Theories of Sexuality', in *Proceedings of the Fifth International Congress of Medieval Canon Law, Salamanca, 21–25 September 1976*, Vatican City, pp. 361–85

Buczek, Daniel S. (1971), ' "Pro Defendendis Ordinis": The French Cistercians and the New Enemies', in *Studies in Medieval Cistercian History Presented to Jeremiah F. O'Sullivan* (Cistercian Studies Series 13), Spencer, pp. 88–109

Bugge, John (1975), *Virginitas: An Essay in the History of a Medieval Ideal* (Archives internationales d'histoire des idées. Series minor 17), The Hague

Buhot, Jacqueline [Rambaud-] (1936), 'L'abbaye normande de Savigny, chef d'ordre et fille de Cîteaux', *Le Moyen Age* 46 (3 S. 7): 1–19, 104–21, 178–90, and 249–72

Bull, Marcus (1993), *Knightly Piety and the Lay Response to the First Crusade: The Limousin and Gascony c. 970–c. 1130*, Oxford

Bullough, Donald (1969), 'Early Medieval Social Groupings: The Terminology of Kinship', *Past and Present* 45: 3–18

Bulst, Neithard (1973), *Untersuchungen zu den Klosterreformen Wilhelms von Dijon (962–1031)* (Pariser historische Studien 11), Bonn

Busley, Hermann-Joseph (1958), 'Zur Frühgeschichte des von Bischof Otto I. gegründeten Prämonstratenserklosters Neustift bei Freising', in *Otto von Freising. Gedenkgabe zu seinem 800. Todesjahr*, ed. Joseph Fischer, Freising, pp. 49–64

Büttner, Heinrich (1949), 'Das Erzstift Mainz und die Klosterreform im 11. Jahrhundert', *Archiv für mittelrheinische Kirchengeschichte* 1: 30–64

(1957), 'Verfassungsgeschichte und lothringische Klosterreform', in *Aus Mittelalter und Neuzeit* (Festschrift Gerhard Kallen), Bonn, pp. 17–27

(1964), 'Studien zur Geschichte von Peterlingen', *Zeitschrift für schweizerische Kirchengeschichte* 58: 265–92

Buytaert, Eligius M. (1951), 'The "Apologeticus" of Arno of Reichersberg', *Franciscan Studies* 11.3–4: 1–47

(1965), 'Another Copy of Cerbanus' Version of John Damascene', *Antonianum* 40: 303–10

Bynum, Caroline Walker (1979), *Docere verbo et exemplo: An Aspect of Twelfth Century Spirituality* (Harvard Theological Studies 31), Missoula

(1982a), *Jesus as Mother: Studies in the Spirituality of the High Middle Ages* (Publications of the Center for Medieval and Renaissance Studies, UCLA 16), Berkeley, Los Angeles, and London

(1982b), 'Did the Twelfth Century Discover the Individual?' (1980), expanded repr. in Bynum (1982a), pp. 82–109

(1984), 'Women's Studies, Women's Symbols: A Critique of Victor Turner's Theory of Liminality', in *Anthropology and the Study of Religion*, ed. Frank Reynolds and Robert Moore (Studies in Religion and Society), Chicago, pp. 105–25

(1987), *Holy Feast and Holy Fast: The Religious Significance of Food to Medieval Women*, Berkeley, Los Angeles, and London

(1995), *The Resurrection of the Body in Western Christianity, 200–1336*, New York

Cabassut, André (1949), 'Une dévotion médiévale peu connue. La dévotion à "Jésus notre mère" ', *Mélanges Marcel Viller* (Revue d'ascétique et de mystique 25), Toulouse, pp. 234–45

Cahn, Walter (1962–4), 'A Defense of the Trinity in the Cîteaux Bible', _Marsyas_ 11: 58–62

(1982), _Romanesque Bible Illumination_, Ithaca

Campenhausen, Hans von (1930), _Die asketische Heimatslosigkeit im altkirchlichen und frühmittelalterlichen Mönchtum_ (Sammlung gemeinverständlicher Vorträge und Schriften aus dem Gebiet der Theologie und Religionsgeschichte 149), Tübingen

Cantarella, Glauco Maria (1979–81), 'Pietro il Venerabile, Cluny, i monasteri cluniacensi dell'Italia settentrionale. Un altro aspetto della crisi del monachesimo nel XII secolo?', in _Cluny in Lombardia_ (1979–81), I, 383–427

(1993), _I monachi di Cluny_, Turin

Cantor, Norman F. (1960–1), 'The Crisis of Western Monasticism, 1050–1130', _American Historical Review_ 66: 47–67

Capelle, Catherine (1959), _Le vœu d'obéissance des origines au XIIe siècle. Etude juridique_ (Bibliothèque d'histoire du droit et droit romain 2), Paris

Capitani, Ovidio (1962), 'Nota per il testo dello "Scutum canonicorum"', in _Vita comune_ (1962), II, 40–7

Carlyle, Robert W., and Carlyle, Alexander J. (1950), _A History of Mediaeval Political Theory in the West_, Edinburgh and London

Caspar, Erich (1909), _Petrus Damianus und die Monte Cassineser Fälschungen_, Berlin

Caviness, Madeline (1983), 'Images of Divine Order and the Third Mode of Seeing', _Gesta_ 22: 99–120

Chalvet de Rochemonteix, Adolphe (1888), _La maison de Graule. Etude sur la vie et les œuvres des convers de Cîteaux en Auvergne au Moyen-Age_, Paris, Clermont-Ferrand, and Aurillac

Chamard, François (1863), _Les vies des saints personnages de l'Anjou_, Paris and Angers

Chapuis, Marc (1940), _Recherches sur les institutions politiques du pays de Vaud du XIe au XIIIe siècle, 1032–1218_ (Bibliothèque historique vaudoise 2), Lausanne

Châtillon, Jean (1948), 'Le contenu, l'authenticité et la date du "Liber exceptionum" et des "Sermones centum" de Richard de Saint-Victor', _Revue du moyen âge latin_ 4: 23–51 and 343–66

(1974), 'Nudum Christum nudus sequere. Note sur les origines et la signification du thème de la nudité spirituelle dans les écrits de saint Bonaventure', in _S. Bonaventura, 1274–1974_, IV. _Theologica_, Grottaferrata, pp. 719–72

(1977), 'La crise de l'Eglise aux XIe et XIIe siècles et les origines des grandes fédérations canoniales', _Revue d'histoire de la spiritualité_ 53: 3–46

[Chautard, Jean-Baptiste] (1948), _The Spirit of Simplicity_, tr. anon., Trappist

Chédeville, André (1973), _Chartres et ses campagnes (XIe–XIIIe s.)_ (Publications de l'Université de Haute-Bretagne 1), Paris

Cheney, Mary (1980), _Roger, Bishop of Worcester 1164–1179_, Oxford

Chenu, Marie-Dominique (1940), 'Arts "mécaniques" et œuvres serviles', _Revue des sciences philosophiques et théologiques_ 29: 313–15

(1954), 'Moines, clercs, laïcs au carrefour de la vie évangélique', _Revue d'histoire ecclésiastique_ 69: 59–89

(1957), _La théologie au douzième siècle_ (Etudes de philosophie médiévale 45), Paris

(1969), _L'éveil de la conscience dans la civilisation médiévale_ (Conférence Albert-le-Grand 1968) (Publications de l'Institut des études médiévales), Montreal and Paris

(1973), ' "Fraternitas". Evangile et condition socio-culturelle', *Revue d'histoire de la spiritualité* 49: 385–400

Chibnall, Marjorie (1967), 'Monks and Pastoral Work: A Problem in Anglo-Norman History', *Journal of Ecclesiastical History* 18: 165–72

(1988), 'The Empress Matilda and Church Reform', *Transactions of the Royal Historical Society* 5 S. 38: 107–30

Choisselet, Danièle, and Vernet, Placide (1989), *Les "Ecclesiastica officia" cisterciens du XIIᵉ siècle. Texte latin selon les manuscrits édités de Trente 1711, Lubljana 31 et Dijon 114* (Documentation cistercienne 22), Reiningue

Choux, Jacques (1952), *Recherches sur le diocèse de Toul au temps de la réforme grégorienne. L'épiscopat de Pibon (1069–1107)*, Nancy

Cipolla, Carlo M. (1976), *Before the Industrial Revolution: European Society and Economy, 1000–1700*, New York

Clanchy, Michael T. (1979), *From Memory to Written Record: England, 1066–1307*, Cambridge, Mass.

Clark, Cecily (1992), 'Onomastics', in *The Cambridge History of the English Language*, II: *1066–1476*, ed. Norman Blake, Cambridge, pp. 542–606

Classen, Peter (1960), *Gerhoch von Reichersberg. Eine Biographie, mit einem Anhang über die Quellen, ihre handschriftliche Überlieferung und ihre Chronologie*, Wiesbaden

Claxton, James H. (1967), 'On the Name of Urban II', *Traditio* 23: 489–95

Clercq, Charles (Carlo) de (1959–60), 'Le "Liber de rota verae religionis" d'Hugues de Fouilloi', *Archivum latinitatis medii aevi* 29: 219–28 and 30: 15–37

Cluny in Lombardia (1979–81) = *Cluny in Lombardia. Atti del Convegno di Pontida. 22–25 aprile 1977* (Italia benedettina 1), Cesena

Colker, Marvin L. (1962), 'Richard of Saint Victor and the Anonymous of Bridlington', *Traditio* 18: 181–227

Colvin, Howard M. (1951), *The White Canons in England*, Oxford

(1951–3), 'Deserted Villages and the Archaeologist', *Archaeological Newsletter* 4: 129–31

Conant, Kenneth John (1968), *Cluny. Les églises et la maison du chef de l'ordre* (Mediaeval Academy of America, Publication 77), Cambridge, Mass., and Mâcon

Congar, Yves-Marie-Joseph (1954), 'Eglise et cité de Dieu chez quelques auteurs cisterciens à l'époque des croisades, en particulier dans le "De perigrinante civitate Dei" de Henri d'Albano', in *Mélanges offerts à Etienne Gilson* (Etudes de philosophie médiévale N.S.), Toronto and Paris, pp. 173–202

Constable, Giles (1956), 'The Letter from Peter of St John to Hato of Troyes', in *Petrus Venerabilis* (1956), pp. 38–52

(1957), 'The Disputed Election at Langres in 1138', *Traditio* 13: 119–52

(1960), 'Cluniac Tithes and the Controversy between Gigny and Le Miroir', *Revue bénédictine* 70: 591–624

(1964), *Monastic Tithes from their Origins to the Twelfth Century* (Cambridge Studies in Medieval Life and Thought N.S. 10), Cambridge

(1965), 'The Treatise "Hortatur nos" and Accompanying Canonical Texts on the Performance of Pastoral Work by Monks', in *Speculum historiale. Geschichte im Spiegel von Geschichtsschreibung und Geschichtsdeutung* (Festschrift Johannes Spörl), ed. Clemens Bauer, Laetitia Boehm, and Max Müller, Freiburg and Munich, pp. 567–77

(1971), 'Twelfth-Century Spirituality and the Late Middle Ages', *Medieval and Renaissance Studies* 5, ed. O. B. Hardison, Jr (Proceedings of the Southeastern Institute of Medieval and Renaissance Studies, Summer 1969), Chapel Hill, pp. 27–60

(1972), 'The "Liber Memorialis" of Remiremont', *Speculum* 47: 261–77

(1973), ' "Famuli" and "Conversi" at Cluny: A Note on Statute 24 of Peter the Venerable', *Revue bénédictine* 83: 326–50

(1974), 'The Study of Monastic History Today', in *Essays on the Reconstruction of Medieval History*, ed. Vaclav Mudroch and G. S. Couse, Montreal and London, pp. 21–51

(1975a), 'The Monastic Policy of Peter the Venerable', in *Pierre Abélard–Pierre le Vénérable. Les courants philosophiques, littéraires et artistiques en Occident au milieu du XIIᵉ siècle. Abbaye de Cluny, 2–9 juillet 1972* (Colloques internationaux du Centre national de la recherche scientifique 546), Paris, pp. 119–38

(1975b), 'Cluny–Cîteaux–La Chartreuse. San Bernardo e la diversità delle forme di vita religiosa nel XII secolo', in *Studi su S. Bernardo di Chiaravalle nell'ottavo centenario della canonizzazione. Convegno internazionale, Certosa di Firenze, 6–9 novembre 1974* (Bibliotheca Cisterciensis 6), Rome, pp. 93–114

(1976a), *Letters and Letter-Collections* (Typologie des sources du moyen âge occidental 17), Turnhout

(1976b), 'Opposition to Pilgrimage in the Middle Ages', *Studia Gratiana* 19 (Mélanges G. Fransen 1), Rome, pp. 123–46

(1976c), 'Monastic Legislation at Cluny in the Eleventh and Twelfth Centuries', in *Proceedings of the Fourth International Congress of Medieval Canon Law, Toronto, 21–25 August 1972*, ed. Stephan Kuttner (Monumenta Iuris Canonici, Series C: Subsidia 5), Vatican City, pp. 151–61

(1977a), 'Monasticism, Lordship, and Society in the Twelfth-Century Hesbaye: Five Documents on the Foundation of the Cluniac Priory of Bertrée', *Traditio* 33: 159–224

(1977b), 'Monachisme et pèlerinage au moyen âge', *Revue historique* 258: 3–27

(1978), 'Aelred of Rievaulx and the Nun of Watton: An Episode in the Early History of the Gilbertine Order', in *Medieval Women* (1978), pp. 205–26

(1979), ' "Nudus nudum Christum sequi" and Parallel Formulas in the Twelfth Century: A Supplementary Dossier', in *Continuity and Discontinuity in Church History: Essays Presented to George Huntston Williams on the Occasion of his 65th Birthday*, ed. F. Forrester Church and Timothy George (Studies in the History of Christian Thought 19), Leiden, pp. 83–91

(1980), 'Petrarch and Monasticism', in *Francesco Petrarca: Citizen of the World. Proceedings of the World Petrarch Congress, Washington, D.C., April 6–13 1974*, ed. Aldo S. Bernardo (Ente nazionale Francesco Petrarca. Studi sul Petrarca 8), Padua and Albany, pp. 53–99

(1982a), *Attitudes toward Self-Inflicted Suffering in the Middle Ages*, Brookline

(1982b), 'The Authority of Superiors in Religious Communities', in *La notion d'autorité au moyen âge: Islam, Byzance, Occident*, ed. George Makdisi, Dominique Sourdel, and Janine Sourdel-Thomine (Colloques internationaux de la Napoule, 23–6 octobre 1978), Paris, pp. 189–210

(1983), 'Papal, Imperial and Monastic Propaganda in the Eleventh and Twelfth Centuries', in *Prédication et propagande au moyen âge: Islam, Byzance, Occident*, ed. George Makdisi, Dominique Sourdel, and Janine Sourdel-Thomine (Penn–Paris–Dumbarton Oaks Colloquia 3, 20–2 octobre 1980), Paris, pp. 179–99

(1984), 'The Abbots and Anti-Abbot of Cluny during the Papal Schism of 1159', *Revue bénédictine* 94: 370–400

(1985a), 'The Diversity of Religious Life and Acceptance of Social Pluralism in the Twelfth Century', in *History, Society and the Churches: Essays in Honour of Owen Chadwick*, ed. Derek Beales and Geoffrey Best, Cambridge, pp. 29–47

(1985b), 'Liberty and Free Choice in Monastic Thought and Life, especially in the Eleventh and Twelfth Centuries', in *La notion de liberté au moyen âge: Islam, Byzance, Occident*, ed. George Makdisi, Dominique Sourdel, and Janine Sourdel-Thomine (Penn–Paris–Dumbarton Oaks Colloquia 4, 12–15 octobre 1982), Paris, pp. 99–118

(1986a), 'Suger's Monastic Administration', in *Abbot Suger and Saint-Denis: A Symposium*, ed. Paula Lieber Gerson, New York, pp. 17–32

(1986b), 'The Concern for Sincerity and Understanding in Liturgical Prayer, especially in the Twelfth Century, in *Classica et Mediaevalia: Studies in Honor of Joseph Szövérffy*, ed. Irene Vaslef and Helmut Buschhausen (Medieval Classics: Texts and Studies 20), Washington and Leiden, pp. 17–30

(1987a), 'The Ceremonies and Symbolism of Entering Religious Life and Taking the Monastic Habit, from the Fourth to the Twelfth Century', in *Segni e riti nella chiesa altomedievale occidentale* (Settimane di studio del Centro italiano di studi sull'alto medioevo 33), Spoleto, pp. 771–834

(1987b), 'The Ideal of Inner Solitude in the Twelfth Century', in *Horizons marins-Itinéraires spirituels (V^e–XVIIIe siècles)* (Mélanges Michel Mollat), I. *Mentalités et sociétés*, ed. Henri Dubois, Jean-Claude Hocquet, and André Vauchez, Paris, pp. 27–34

(1988), 'The Metrical Epitaph of Rusticus, Priest of Pescia (d. 1132/3)', in *Scire litteras. Forschungen zum mittelalterlichen Geistesleben* (Festschrift Bernhard Bischoff), ed. Sigrid Krämer and Michael Bernhard (Bayerische Akademie der Wissenschaften, phil.-hist. Kl.: Abhandlungen N.F. 99), Munich, pp. 103–10

(1989), 'Past and Present in the Eleventh and Twelfth Centuries: Perceptions of Time and Change', in *L'Europa dei secoli XI e XII fra novità e tradizione. Sviluppi di una cultura. Atti della decima Settimana internazionale di studio, Mendola, 25–29 agosto 1986* (Pubblicazioni dell'Università cattolica del Sacro Cuore: Miscellanea del Centro di studi medioevali 12), Milan, pp. 135–70

(1990), 'A Living Past: The Historical Environment of the Middle Ages', *Harvard Library Bulletin* N.S. 1.3: 49–70

(1992a), ' "Seniores" et "pueri" à Cluny aux Xe, XIe siècles', in *Histoire et société. Mélanges offerts à Georges Duby*, Aix-en-Provence, III, 17–24

(1992b), 'Moderation and Restraint in Ascetic Practices in the Middle Ages', in *From Athens to Chartres: Neoplatonism and Medieval Thought. Studies in Honour of Edouard Jeauneau*, ed. Haijo Jan Westra, Leiden, New York, and Cologne, pp. 315–27

(1992c), 'The Abbot and Townsmen of Cluny in the Twelfth Century', in *Church and City, 1000–1500: Essays in Honour of Christopher Brooke*, ed. David Abulafia, Michael Franklin, and Miri Rubin, Cambridge, pp. 151–71

(1994a), 'The Language of Preaching in the Twelfth Century', *Viator* 25: 131–52

(1994b), 'The Letter of Hugh of Soissons to the Premonstratensian Abbots', in *Cristianità ed Europa. Miscellanea di studi in onore di Luigi Prosdocimi*, ed. Cesare Alzati, Rome, Freiburg, and Vienna, I.1, 249–63

(1995a), *Three Studies in Medieval Religious and Social Thought*, Cambridge

(1995b), 'The Lay Brothers and Lay Sisters of the Order of Sempringham', in *Medieval Studies in Honour of Avrom Saltman* (Bar-Ilan Studies in History 4), Ramat-Gan, pp. 83–96

Constable, Giles, and Somerville, Robert (1992), 'The Papal Bulls for the Chapter of St Antonin in Rouergue in the Eleventh and Twelfth Centuries', *Speculum* 67: 828–64

Coulton, George Gordon (1929–50), *Five Centuries of Religion* (Cambridge Studies in Medieval Life and Thought), Cambridge: I. (2nd edn) *St Bernard, his Predecessors and Successors, 1000–1200 AD*; II. *The Friars and the Dead Weight of Tradition, 1200–1400 AD*; III. *Getting and Spending*; IV. *The Last Days of Medieval Monachism*

Courcelle, Pierre (1963), *Les Confessions de saint Augustin dans la tradition littéraire*, Paris

(1974), *Connais-toi toi-même de Socrate à saint Bernard*, Paris

Cousin, Patrice (1950), 'L'expansion clunisienne sous l'abbatiat de saint Odilon', in *A Cluny. Congrès scientifique. Fêtes et cérémonies liturgiques en l'honneur des saints abbés Odon et Odilon 9–11 juillet 1949*, Dijon, pp. 186–91

Couvreur, Gilles (1961), *Les pauvres ont-ils des droits? Recherches sur le vol en cas d'extrême nécessité, depuis la Concordia de Gratien (1140) jusqu'à Guillaume d'Auxerre († 1231)* (Analecta Gregoriana 111), Rome and Paris

Cowdrey, Herbert E.J. (1965), 'Unions and Confraternity with Cluny', *Journal of Ecclesiastical History* 16: 152–62

(1968), 'The Papacy, the Patarenes, and the Church of Milan', *Transactions of the Royal Historical Society* 5 S. 18: 25–48

(1970), *The Cluniacs and the Gregorian Reform*, Oxford

(1984), 'Legal Problems Raised by Agreements of Confraternity', in *Memoria. Der geschichtliche Zeugniswert des liturgischen Gedenkens im Mittelalter*, ed. Karl Schmid and Joachim Wollasch (Münstersche Mittelalter-Schriften 48), Munich, pp. 233–54

(1994), 'Count Simon of Crépy's Monastic Conversion', in *Papauté, monachisme et théories politiques. Mélanges Marcel Pacaut* (Collection d'histoire et d'archéologie médiévales 1), Lyon, pp. 253–66

Cox, Ronald J. (1959), *A Study of the Juridic Status of Laymen in the Writing of the Medieval Canonists* (The Catholic University of America: Canon Law Studies 395), Washington

Crampon, Maurice (1936), *La culte de l'arbre et de la forêt en Picardie. Essai sur le folklore picard* (Mémoires de la Société des antiquaires de Picardie 46), Amiens and Paris

Crozet, René (1944), 'L'architecture de l'ordre de Grandmont en Poitou, Saintonge et Angoumois', *Bulletins et mémoires de la Société archéologique et historique de la Charente* 2: 221–41

(1975), 'L'épiscopat de France et l'ordre de Cîteaux au XIIᵉ siècle', *Cahiers de civilisation médiévale* 18: 263–8

Curtius, Ernst Robert (1963), *European Literature and the Latin Middle Ages*, tr. Willard R. Trask, New York

Dalarun, Jacques (1985), *L'impossible sainteté. La vie retrouvée de Robert d'Arbrissel (v. 1045–1116), fondateur de Fontevraud*, Paris

Dales, Richard C. (1977), 'A Medieval View of Human Dignity', *Journal of the History of Ideas* 38: 557–72

Daniel, E. Randolph (1986), 'Joachim of Fiore and Medieval Apocalypticism: Some Current Research', *Medievalia et Humanistica* N.S. 14: 173–88

Dauphin, Hubert (1946), *Le bienheureux Richard, abbé de Saint-Vanne de Verdun, † 1046* (Bibliothèque de la Revue d'histoire ecclésiastique 24), Louvain and Paris

Davenport, W.A. (1988), 'Patterns in Middle English Dialogues', in *Medieval English Studies Presented to George Kane*, ed. Edward Kennedy, Ronald Waldron, and Joseph Wittig, Wolfeboro and Woodbridge, pp. 127–45

Davie, Donald (1976), 'The Literature of Dissent, 1700–1930' (Clark Lectures 1976), *Times Literary Supplement* 1976: 1459–60, 1491–2, and 1519–20

Davis, Ralph H.C. (1969), *King Stephen 1135–1154*, London

Davril, Anselme (1982), 'Le langage par signes chez les moines. Un catalogue de signes de l'abbaye de Fleury', in *Sous la règle de saint Benoît. Structures monastiques et sociétés en France du Moyen Age à l'époque moderne. Abbaye bénédictine Sainte-Marie de Paris 23–25 octobre 1980* (Ecole pratique des haute études, IVᵉ section 5: Hautes études médiévales et modernes 47), Geneva and Paris, pp. 51–75

Davy, Marie-Madeleine (1964), *Initiation à la symbolique romane: XIIᵉ siècle* (Homo Sapiens) Paris

Déchanet, Jean-Marie (1940a), *Aux sources de la spiritualité de Guillaume de Saint-Thierry*, Bruges

(1940b), 'Le "Naturam sequi" chez Guillaume de Saint-Thierry', *Collectanea ordinis Cisterciensium reformatorum* 7: 141–8

Delaruelle, Etienne (1948), 'Le travail dans les règles monastiques occidentales du quatrième au neuvième siècle', *Journal de psychologie normale et pathologique* 41: 51–62

(1962), 'La vie commune des clercs et la spiritualité populaire au XIᵉ siècle', in *Vita comune* (1962), I, 142–85

(1966), 'L'autel roman de Saint-Sernin (1096). Confrères, pèlerins et pénitents', in *Mélanges offerts à René Crozet*, ed. Pierre Gallais and Yves-Jean Riou, Poitiers, I, 383–9

(1967–8), 'Erémitisme et pauvreté dans la région de Toulouse au XIIᵉ siècle', in *Recherches sur les pauvres et la pauvreté au moyen-âge*, ed. Michel Mollat, Paris, VI, 40–4

(1971), 'Saint François d'Assise et la piété populaire', in *San Francesco nella ricerca storica degli ultimi ottanta anni, 13–16 ottobre 1968* (Convegni del Centro di studi sulla spiritualità medioevale 7), Todi, pp. 127–55

Delhaye, Philippe (1947), 'L'organisation scolaire au XIIᵉ siècle', *Traditio* 5: 211–68

(1953), 'Saint Bernard de Clairvaux et Philippe de Harveng', *Bulletin de la Société historique et archéologique de Langres* 12 (156): 129–38

(1954), 'Dans le sillage de saint Bernard. Trois petits traités "De conscientia"', *Cîteaux in de Nederlanden* 5: 92–103

Delmaire, Bernard (1994), *Le diocèse d'Arras de 1093 au milieu du XIVᵉ siècle*, Arras

Delooz, Pierre (1969), *Sociologie et canonisations* (Collection scientifique de la Faculté de droit de l'Université de Liège 30), Liège and The Hague

Demaret, H. (1886), 'Guda, veuve de Thiebauld comte de Fouron, recluse à Saint-Jacques au commencement du XIIe siècle', *Bulletin de la Société d'art et d'histoire du diocèse de Liège* 4: 36–50

Dembińska, Maria (1985), 'Diet: A Comparison of Food Consumption between Some Eastern and Western Monasteries in the 4th–12th Centuries', *Byzantion* 55: 431–62

Demus, Otto (1970), *Byzantine Art and the West* (Wrightsmann Lectures 3), London and New York

Depoin, Joseph (1914), *Recherches sur l'état civil, les conditions du baptême, et le mode de dénomination des enfants du IXe au XIe siècle* (offprint from *Bulletin des sciences économiques et sociales du Comité des travaux historiques et scientifiques* 1911), Paris

Dereine, Charles (1947), 'Les origines de Prémontré', *Revue d'histoire ecclésiastique* 42: 352–78

(1948a), 'Odon de Tournai et la crise du cénobitisme au XIe siècle', *Revue du moyen âge latin* 4: 137–54

(1948b), 'Les coutumiers de Saint-Quentin de Beauvais et de Springiersbach', *Revue d'histoire ecclésiastique* 43: 411–42

(1948c), 'Le problème de la vie commune chez les canonistes d'Anselme de Lucques à Gratien', *Studi gregoriani* 3: 287–98

(1951), 'L'élaboration du statut canonique des chanoines réguliers, spécialement sous Urbain II', *Revue d'histoire ecclésiastique* 46: 534–65

(1951 and 1959), 'Coutumiers et ordinaires de chanoines réguliers', *Scriptorium* 5: 107–13 and 13: 244–6

(1952), *Les chanoines réguliers au diocèse de Liège avant Saint Norbert* (Académie royale de Belgique: Classe des lettres et des sciences morales et politiques, Mémoires in-8°, 2 S. 47.1), Brussels

(1953), 'Pierre l'Ermite, le saint fondateur du Neufmoustier à Huy', *La nouvelle Clio* 5: 427–46

(1954), 'Le problème de la "cura animarum" chez Gratien', *Studia Gratiana* 2: 305–18

(1959), 'La spiritualité "apostolique" des premiers fondateurs d'Affligem (1083–1100)', *Revue d'histoire ecclésiastique* 54: 41–65

(1960a), 'Les chanoines réguliers dans l'ancienne province ecclésiastique de Salzbourg d'après les travaux récents', *Revue d'histoire ecclésiastique* 55: 902–16

(1960b), 'L'obituaire primitif de l'ordre de Grandmont', *Bulletin de la Société archéologique et historique du Limousin* 87: 325–31

(1965), 'La "libertas" des nouveaux monastères au diocèse de Cambrai sous Gérard II (1074–1094)', *Revue du Nord* 47: 118–20

(1983a), 'Les prédicateurs "apostoliques" dans les diocèses de Thérouanne, Tournai, et Cambrai-Arras durant les années 1075-1125', *Analecta praemonstratensia* 59: 171–89

(1983b), 'La donation par Baudouin III, comte de Hainaut, de Saint-Saulve près Valenciennes à Cluny (1103)', *Sacris erudiri* 20: 119–53

(1987), 'Ermites, reclus et recluses dans l'ancien diocèse de Cambrai entre Scarpe et Haine (1075–1125)', *Revue bénédictine* 97: 289–313

Deroy, Jean P.T. (1963), 'Bernardus en Origenes. Enkele opmerkingen over de invloed van Origenes op sint Bernardus' "Super Cantica Canticorum" ' (Diss. Nijmegen), Haarlem

Despy, Georges (1956), 'Les chapitres de chanoinesses nobles en Belgique au moyen âge', in *XXXVIe Congrès de la Fédération archéologique et historique de Belgique. Annales 2: Communications*, Ghent, pp. 169–79

(1957), 'La fondation de l'abbaye de Villers (1146)', *Archives, bibliothèques et musées de Belgique* 38: 3–17

(1968), 'Cîteaux et l'avouerie. La dotation primitive de l'abbaye d'Orval', *Revue du Nord* 50: 113–14

(1974–5), 'Les richesses de la terre. Cîteaux et Prémontré devant l'économie de profit aux XIIe et XIIIe siècles', *Problèmes d'histoire du Christianisme* 5: 58–80

(1983), 'Les Bénédictins en Brabant au XIIe siècle: la "Chronique de l'abbaye d'Afflighem" ', *Problèmes d'histoire du Christianisme* 12: 51–116

Détrez, Lucien (1951), 'L'érémitisme septentrional', *Bulletin du Comité flamand de France* 14: 19–41

Deug-Su, I (1992), 'I nuovi movimenti religiosi nel "De nugis curialium" di Walter Map', *Studi medievali* 3 S. 33: 537–70

Devailly, Guy (1975), 'Le clergé régulier et le ministère paroissial', *Cahiers d'histoire* 20.2 = *Aspects de la vie conventuelle aux XIe et XIIe siècles. Actes du 5e Congrès de la Société des historiens médiévistes de l'enseignement supérieur public (Saint-Etienne, 7–8 juin 1974)*, pp. 259–72

Dewailly, L.-M. (1948), 'Notes sur l'histoire de l'adjectif apostolique', *Mélanges de science religieuse* 5: 141–52

Dickinson, John C. (1950), *The Origins of the Austin Canons and their Introduction into England*, London

Diers, Michaela (1991), *Bernhard von Clairvaux. Elitäre Frömmigkeit und begnadetes Wirken* (Beiträge zur Geschichte der Philosophie und Theologie des Mittelalters N.S. 34), Münster i. W.

Dimier, Marie-Anselme (1943–4), 'Les emplacements des monastères cisterciens', *Bulletin de la Société nationale des antiquaires de France*, 1943–4: 231–8

(1944), *Clarté, paix et joie. Les beaux noms des monastères de Cîteaux en France* (La Clarté-Dieu 15), Lyon

(1946), 'A propos de la Charte de Charité. Cîteaux et Chalais', *Collectanea ordinis Cisterciensium reformatorum* 8: 241–56

(1952), 'Saint Bernard et le recrutement de Clairvaux', *Revue Mabillon* 42: 17–30, 50–68, and 69–78

(1953), 'Saint Bernard et le droit en matière de "transitus" ', *Revue Mabillon* 43: 48–82

(1955a), 'Observances monastiques', *Analecta cisterciensia* 11: 149–98

(1955b), 'Cîteaux et les emplacements malsains', *Cîteaux* 6: 89–97

(1955c), 'Mourir à Clairvaux', *Collectanea ordinis Cisterciensium reformatorum* 17: 272–85

(1959), 'Les concepts de moine et de la vie monastique chez les premiers Cisterciens', *Studia monastica* 1: 399–418

Dinzelbacher, Peter (1981), *Vision und Visionsliteratur im Mittelalter* (Monographien zur Geschichte des Mittelalters 23), Stuttgart

Ditsche, Magnus (1958), 'Die "Ecclesia primitiva" im Kirchenbild des hohen und späten Mittelalters' (Diss. Bonn)

Dmitrewski, Michael von (1913), *Die christliche freiwillige Armut vom Ursprung der Kirche bis zum 12. Jahrhundert*, Berlin and Leipzig

Dobson, Eric John (1976), *The Origins of 'Ancrene Wisse'*, Oxford

Donkin, Robert A. (1959), 'The Site Changes of Medieval Cistercian Monasteries', *Geography* 44: 251–8

(1960), 'Settlement and Depopulation on Cistercian Estates during the Twelfth and Thirteenth Centuries, especially in Yorkshire', *Bulletin of the Institute of Historical Research* 33: 141–65

(1963), 'The Cistercian Order in Medieval England: Some Conclusions', *Institute of British Geographers: Transactions and Papers* 33: 181–98

(1964), 'The Cistercian Grange in England in the 12th and 13th Centuries, with Special Reference to Yorkshire', *Studia monastica* 6: 95–144

Donnelly, James S. (1949), *The Decline of the Medieval Cistercian Laybrotherhood* (Fordham University Studies, History Series 3), New York

(1954), 'Changes in Grange Economy of English and Welsh Cistercian Abbeys, 1300–1540', *Traditio* 10: 399–458

Dormeier, Heinrich (1979), *Montecassino und die Laien im 11. und 12. Jahrhundert* (Schriften der Monumenta Germaniae historica 27), Stuttgart

Douglas, Mary (1973), *Natural Symbols: Explorations in Cosmology*, 2nd edn, London

(1982), 'The Effects of Modernization on Religious Change', *Daedalus* 111: 1–19

(1991), 'Witchcraft and Leprosy: Two Strategies of Exclusion', *Man* 26: 723–36

Dronke, Peter (1984), 'Tradition and Innovation in Medieval Western Colour-Imagery' (1972), repr. in his *The Medieval Poet and his World* (Storia e letteratura 164), Rome, pp. 55–103

(1986a), *Dante and Medieval Latin Traditions*, Cambridge

(1986b), *Poetic Individuality in the Middle Ages: New Departures in Poetry, 1000–1150*, 2nd edn (Westfield Publications in Medieval Studies 1), London

Dubled, Henri (1952), 'Bénédictins et Augustins. Note sur les chanoines réguliers de Saint-Augustin de Goldbach en Haute-Alsace', *Revue du moyen âge latin* 8: 305–22

Dubois, Jacques (1967), 'Les dépendances de l'abbaye du Mont Saint-Michel et la vie monastique dans les prieurés', in *Millénaire du Mont Saint-Michel, I. Histoire et vie monastique*, ed. Jean Laporte, Paris, pp. 619–76

(1968a), 'Quelques problèmes de l'histoire de l'ordre des chartreux à propos de livres récents', *Revue d'histoire ecclésiastique* 63: 27–54

(1968b), 'Les ordres religieux au XIIe siècle selon la curie romaine', *Revue bénédictine* 78: 283–309

(1968c), 'L'institution des convers au XIIe siècle, forme de vie monastique propre aux laïcs', in *Laici* (1968), pp. 183–261

(1969), 'Du nombre des moines dans les monastères', *Lettre de Ligugé* 1969.2 (no. 134): 24–36

(1971), 'L'implantation monastique dans le Bugey au moyen âge', *Journal des savants* 1971: 15–31

(1981), 'Une œuvre littéraire à Saint-Aubin d'Angers au XIIe siècle: "La vie de saint Girard" ', in *La littérature angevine médiévale. Actes du colloque du samedi 22 mars 1980*, Angers, pp. 51–62

(1982), 'Le rôle du chapitre dans le gouvernement du monastère', in *Sous la règle de saint Benoît. Structures monastiques et sociétés en France du Moyen Age à l'époque moderne. Abbaye bénédictine Sainte-Marie de Paris 23–25 octobre 1980* (Ecole pratique des haute études, IVe section 5: Hautes études médiévales et modernes 47), Geneva and Paris, pp. 21–37

(1985), *Les ordres monastiques* (Que sais-je? 2241), Paris

(1990), 'Le travail des moines au moyen âge', in *Le travail au moyen âge. Une approche interdisciplinaire. Actes du colloque internationale de Louvain-la-Nueve, 21–23 mai 1987*, Louvain, pp. 61–100

Dubois, Marie-Gérard (1992), 'Twelfth-Century Cistercian Usages', *Liturgy OCSO* 26.2: 79–87

Duby, Georges (1952), 'Economie domaniale et économie monétaire. Le budget de l'abbaye de Cluny entre 1080 et 1155', *Annales* 7: 155–71

(1953), 'Dangers d'une réussite', *Témoignages. Cahiers de La Pierre-Qui-Vire* 38–9: 67–75

(1956), 'Un inventaire des profits de la seigneurie clunisienne à la mort de Pierre le Vénérable', in *Petrus Venerabilis* (1956), pp. 128–40

(1979), *Saint Bernard. L'art cistercien*, Paris

[Ducourneau], J. Othon (1932–3), 'Les origines cisterciennes', *Revue Mabillon* 22: (1) 133–64, (2) 233–52; 23: (3) 1–32, (4) 81–111, and (5) 153–89

Dudley, Martin (1991), 'The Monastic Priest', in *Monastic Studies II*, ed. Judith Loades, Bangor, pp. 183–92

Dümmler, Ernst (1894), 'Über Leben und Schriften des Mönches Theoderich (von Armorbach)', *Philosophische und historische Abhandlungen des königlichen Akademie der Wissenschaften zu Berlin 1894*: 3–38

Dupin, Louis (1693–1715), *Bibliothèque des auteurs ecclésiastiques*, 2nd edn, Paris, Eng. tr., London 1692–9

Durtelle de Saint-Sauveur, Edmond (1910), *Recherches sur l'histoire de la théorie de la mort civile des religieux des origines au seizième siècle*, Rennes

Dutton, Paul Edward (1980), 'Raoul Glaber's "De divina quaternitate": An Unnoticed Reading of Eriugena's Translation of the "Ambigua" of Maximus the Confessor', *Mediaeval Studies* 42: 431–53

Duvernay, Roger (1952), 'Cîteaux, Vallombreuse et Etienne Harding', *Analecta cisterciensia* 8: 379–495

Edel, Leon (1978), *Henry James*, New York

Edwards, Kathleen (1967), *The English Secular Cathedrals in the Middle Ages: A Constitutional Study with Special Reference to the 14th Century*, 2nd edn, Manchester and New York

Ehlers, Joachim (1973), 'Adlige Stiftung und persönliche Konversion zur Sozialgeschichte früher Prämonstratenserkonvente', in *Geschichte und Verfassungsgeschichte. Frankfurter Festgabe für Walter Schlesinger* (Frankfurter historische Abhandlungen 5), Wiesbaden, pp. 32–55

Eliade, Mircea (1952), *Images et symboles. Essais sur le symbolisme magico-religieux*, Paris

Elkins, Sharon K. (1988), *Holy Women of Twelfth-Century England*, Chapel Hill and London

Elm, Kaspar (1962), *Beiträge zur Geschichte des Wilhelmiterordens* (Münstersche Forschungen 14), Cologne and Graz

(1984), ed., *Norbert von Xanten*, Cologne

(1994), 'Questioni e risultati della recente ricerca sui Cisterciensi', in *I Cisterciensi nel mezzogiorno medioevale. Atti del Convegno internazionale di studio in occasione del IX centenario della nascità di Bernardo di Clairvaux (Martano–Latiano–Lecce, 25–27 febbraio 1991)*, ed. Hubert Houben and Benedetto Vetere, Galatina, pp. 7–31

Elm, Kaspar, and Parisse, Michel (1992), ed., *Doppelklöster und andere Formen der Symbiose männlicher und weiblicher Religiösen im Mittelalter* (Berliner historische Studien 18: Ordensstudien 8), Berlin

Endemann, Traute (1967), *Vogtei und Herrschaft im alemannisch-burgundischen Grenzraum*, Konstanz and Stuttgart

Endres, Joseph Anton (1906), *Honorius Augustodunensis. Beitrag zur Geschichte des geistigen Lebens im 12. Jahrhundert*, Kempten and Munich

Engelmann, Johannes (1933), *Untersuchungen zur klösterlichen Verfassungsgeschichte in den Diözesen Magdeburg, Meissen, Merseburg und Zeitz-Wannburg (etwa 950 bis etwa 1350)* (Beiträge zur mittelalterlichen und neueren Geschichte 4), Jena

Engels, Lodewijk Joseph (1975), ' "Adtendite a falsis prophetis" (MS Colmar 128, fols. 152v/3v). Un texte de Pierre Abélard contre les Cisterciens retrouvé?', in *Corona gratiarum* (Festschrift Eligius Dekkers), Bruges and The Hague, II, 195–228

Epperlein, Siegfried (1967), 'Gründungsmythos deutscher Zisterzienserklöster westlich und östlich der Elbe im hohen Mittelalter und der Bericht des leubuser Mönches im 14. Jahrhundert', *Jahrbuch für Wirtschaftsgeschichte* 1967.3: 303–35

Erdmann, Carl (1935), *Die Entstehung des Kreuzzugsgedankens* (Forschungen zur Kirchen- und Geistesgeschichte 6), Stuttgart

Eremitismo (1965) = *L'eremitismo in Occidente nei secoli XI e XII. Atti della seconda Settimana internazionale di studio, Mendola, 30 agosto – 6 settembre 1962* (Pubblicazioni dell'Università cattolica del Sacro Cuore, Contributi 3 S.: Varia 4. Miscellanea del Centro di studi medioevali 4), Milan

Erikson, Erik H. (1966), 'Ontogeny of Ritualization in Man', in *A Discussion on Ritualization of Behaviour in Animals and Man*, ed. Julian Huxley (Philosophical Transactions of the Royal Society of London 3.251), London, pp. 337–49

Erikson, Kai T. (1966), *Wayward Puritans: A Study in the Sociology of Deviance*, New York

Erkens, Franz-Reiner (1987), 'Die Kanonikerreform in Oberlothringen', *Historisches Jahrbuch* 107: 1–43

Eschmann, Ignatius T. (1944), 'Bonum commune melius est quam bonum unius. Eine Studie über den Wertvorrang des Personalen bei Thomas von Aquin', *Mediaeval Studies* 6: 62–120

Estournet, G. (1913), 'Les chartes de Franchard, prieuré de l'ordre de Saint-Augustin près Fontainebleau', *Annales de la Société historique et archéologique du Gâtinais* 31: 275–369

Evans, Gillian R. (1978), 'A Change of Mind in Some Scholars of the Eleventh and Early Twelfth Centuries', in *Religious Motivation: Biographical and Sociological Problems for the Church Historian*, ed. Derek Baker (Studies in Church History 15), Oxford, pp. 27–38

Falck, Ludwig (1956), 'Klosterfreiheit und Klosterschutz. Die Klosterpolitik der Mainzer Erzbischöfe von Adalbert I. bis Heinrich I. (1100–1153)', *Archiv für mittelrheinische Kirchengeschichte* 8: 21–75

(1958), 'Hirsauische Einflüsse in thüringischen Zisterzienserurkunden Erzbischof Heinrichs I. von Mainz', *Archiv für Diplomatik* 4: 216–25

Falkenstein, Ludwig (1993), 'Alexandre III et Henri de France. Conformités et conflits', in *L'église de France et la papauté (X^e–XIIIe siècle)* ... *Actes du XXVIe colloque historique franco-allemand* ... *(Paris, 17–19 Octobre 1990)* (Etudes et documents pour servir à une Gallia Pontificia 1), Paris, pp. 103–76

Faral, Edmond (1924), *Les arts poétiques du XIIe et du XIIIe siècle* (Bibliothèque de l'Ecole des hautes études 233), Paris

Fassler, Margot (1993), *Gothic Song: Victorine Sequences and Augustinian Reform in Twelfth-Century Paris*, Cambridge

Faust, Ulrich (1964), 'Gottfried von Admont. Ein monastischer Autor des 12. Jahrhunderts', *Studien und Mitteilungen zur Geschichte des Benediktiner-Ordens und seiner Zweige* 75: 271–359

Febvre, Lucien (1957), 'Une question mal posée. Les origines de la réforme française et le problème des causes de la réforme' (1929), repr. in his *Au coeur religieux du XVIe siècle* (Bibliothèque générale de l'Ecole des hautes études VIe section), Paris, pp. 3–70

Feine, Hans Erich (1954–5), 'Klosterreform im 10. und 11. Jahrhundert und ihr Einfluss auf die Reichenau und St. Gallen', in *Aus Verfassungs- und Landesgeschichte. Festschrift ... Theodor Mayer*, Konstanz, II, 77–91

Felten, Franz J. (1980), *Äbte und Laienäbte im Frankenreich. Studie zum Verhältnis von Staat und Kirche im früheren Mittelalter* (Monographien zur Geschichte des Mittelalters 20), Stuttgart

(1988), 'Herrschaft des Abtes', in *Herrschaft und Kirche. Beiträge zur Entstehung und Wirkungsweise episkopaler und monastischer Organisationsformen*, ed. Friedrich Prinz (Monographien zur Geschichte des Mittelalters 33), Stuttgart, pp. 147–296

Ferguson, Wallace K. (1948), *The Renaissance in Historical Thought: Five Centuries of Interpretation*, Boston

Fergusson, Peter (1983), 'The First Architecture of the Cistercians in England and the Work of Abbot Adam of Meaux', *Journal of the British Archaeological Association* 136: 74–86

(1984), *Architecture of Solitude: Cistercian Abbeys in Twelfth-Century England*, Princeton

(1986), 'The Twelfth-Century Refectories at Rievaulx and Byland Abbeys', in Norton and Park (1986), pp. 160–80

Fichtenau, Heinrich (1975), 'Die Fälschungen Georg Zapperts' (1970), repr. in his *Beiträge zur Mediävistik*, Stuttgart, pp. 270–95

(1991), *Living in the Tenth Century: Mentalities and Social Orders*, tr. Patrick Geary, Chicago and London

Figueras, Cesáreo M. (1958), 'Acerca del rito de la profesión monástica medieval "ad succurrendum"', *Liturgica* 2: 359–400

Fina, Kurt (1956–8), 'Anselm von Havelberg. Untersuchungen zur Kirchen- und Geistesgeschichte des 12. Jahrhunderts', *Analecta praemonstratensia* 32: (1) 69–101 and (2) 193–227; 33: (3) 5–39 and (4) 268–301; and 34: (5) 13–41

348   Bibliography of secondary works

(1957), ' "Ovem suam requirere". Eine Studie zur Geschichte des Ordenwechsels im 12. Jahrhundert', *Augustiniana* 7: 33–56

Fine, Agnès (1987), 'L'héritage du nom de baptême', *Annales* 42: 853–77

Fiske, Adele (1970), *Friends and Friendship in the Monastic Tradition* (Centro intercultural de documentación: Cuaderno 51), Cuernavaca

Flach, Jacques (1886–1917), *Les origines de l'ancienne France. X^e et XIe siècles*, Paris

Fleming, John (1982), *From Bonaventure to Bellini: An Essay in Franciscan Exegesis*, Princeton

Flint, Valerie I.J. (1991), *The Rise of Magic in Early Medieval Europe*, Princeton

Fonseca, Cosimo Damiano (1962), 'Canoniche e ospedali', in *Atti del primo congresso europeo di storia ospitaliera, 6–12 giugno 1960*, Reggio Emilia, pp. 482–98

(1970), *Medioevo canonicale* (Pubblicazioni dell'Università cattolica del Sacro Cuore, 3 S.: Scienze storiche 12), Milan

(1973), 'Hugues de Fouilloy entre l' "Ordo antiquus" et l' "Ordo novus" ', *Cahiers de civilisation médiévale* 16: 303–12

Fontette, Micheline de (1967), *Les religieuses à l'âge classique du droit canon. Recherches sur les structures juridiques des branches féminines des ordres* (Bibliothèque de la Société d'histoire ecclésiastique de la France), Paris

Fornasari, Giuseppe (1981), 'Pier Damiani e Gregorio VII: dall'ecclesiologia "monastica" all'ecclesiologia "politica"?', in *Fonte Avellana nel suo millenario, I. Le origini* (Atti del V Convegno del Centro di studi avellaniti, Fonte Avellana 26–8 agosto 1981), pp. 151–244

(1986), 'Coscienza ecclesiale e storia della spiritualità. Per una ridefinizione della riforma di Gregorio VII', *Benedictina* 33: 25–50

Fossier, Robert (1955), 'Les granges de Clairvaux et la règle cistercienne', *Cîteaux in de Nederlanden* 6: 259–66

Foucault, Michel (1984), *The Care of the Self*, tr. Robert Hurley, New York

Fox, Robin Lane (1988), *Pagans and Christians*, San Francisco

Frank, Karl Suso (1971), 'Vita apostolica. Ansätze zur apostolischen Lebensform in der alten Kirche', *Zeitschrift für Kirchengeschichte* 82: 145–66

Fransen, Gérard (1957), 'La tradition des canonistes du moyen âge', in *Etudes sur le sacrement de l'ordre* (Lex orandi 22), Paris, pp. 257–75

Fredericq, Paul (1895), 'Note complémentaire sur les documents de Glascow concernant Lambert le Bègue', *Bulletins de l'Académie royale des sciences, lettres et des beaux-arts de la Belgique* 3 S. 29: 990–1006

(1889–1906), ed., *Corpus documentorum inquisitionis haereticae pravitatis Neerlandicae*, Ghent and The Hague

Fresco, Nadine (1973), 'L' "affaire" Pons de Melgueil, 1122–1126. De l'ordre à l'inquiétude dans le monachisme clunisien' (Thèse de 3e cycle, Paris I)

Freund, Walter (1957), *Modernus und andere Zeitbegriffe des Mittelalters* (Neue Münstersche Beiträge zur Geschichtsforschung 4), Cologne and Graz

Fried, Johannes (1989), 'Endzeiterwartung um die Jahrtausendwende', *Deutsches Archiv* 45: 381–473

Fuhrmann, Horst (1984), *Papst Urban II und der Stand der Regularkanoniker* (Bayerische Akademie des Wissenschaften, phil.-hist. Kl.: Sitzungsberichte 1984.2), Munich

(1988), 'Neues zur Biographie des Ulrichs von Zell († 1093)', in *Person und Gemeinschaft im Mittelalter. Karl Schmid zum fünfundsechzigsten Geburtstag*, ed. Gerd Althoff, Dieter Geuenich, Otto Oexle, and Joachim Wollasch, Sigmaringen, pp. 369–78

Funkenstein, Amos (1965), *Heilsplan und natürliche Entwicklung. Formen der Gegenwartsbestimmung im Geschichtsdenken des hohen Mittelalters* (Sammlung Dialog 5), Munich

Galbraith, Vivian H. (1934), 'Monastic Foundation Charters of the Eleventh and Twelfth Centuries', *Cambridge Historical Journal* 4: 205–22 and 296–8

Gallay, Jacques (1955), ' "Dilige et quod uis fac". Notes d'exégèse augustinienne', *Recherches de science religieuse* 43: 545–55

Galli, André (1959), 'Les origines du prieuré de Notre-Dame de Hérival', *Revue Mabillon* 49: 1–34

Gammersbach, Suitbert (1956), 'Das Abtsbild in Cluny und bei Bernhard von Clairvaux', *Cîteaux in de Nederlanden* 7: 85–101

Ganck, Roger de (1984), 'The Integration of Nuns in the Cistercian Order, particularly in Belgium', *Cîteaux* 35: 235–47

Garand, Monique-Cécile (1988), 'Les plus anciens témoins conservés des "Consuetudines Cluniacenses" d'Ulrich de Ratisbonne', in *Scire litteras. Forschungen zum mittelalterlichen Geistesleben* (Festschrift Bernhard Bischoff), ed. Sigrid Krämer and Michael Bernhard (Bayerische Akademie des Wissenschaften, phil.-hist. Kl.: Abhandlungen N.F. 99), Munich, pp. 171–82

Gardiner, Frank C. (1971), *The Pilgrimage of Desire: A Study of Theme and Genre in Medieval Literature*, Leiden

Garin, Eugenio (1938), 'La "dignitas homini" e la letteratura. Patristica', *Rinascità* 1.4: 102–46

Garrigues, Marie Odile (1973), 'A qui faut-il attribuer le "De vita vere apostolica?" ', *Le Moyen Age* 79 (4 S. 28): 421–47

Gaudemet, Jean (1982), 'Le célibat ecclésiastique. Le droit et la pratique du XIᵉ au XIIIᵉ s.', *Zeitschrift der Savigny-Stiftung für Rechtsgeschichte* 99: *Kanonistische Abteilung* 68: 1–31

Geary, Patrick J. (1994), *Phantoms of Remembrance: Memory and Oblivion at the End of the First Millennium*, Princeton

Genicot, Léopold (1936), 'L'évolution des dons aux abbayes dans le comté de Namur du Xᵉ au XIVᵉ siècle', in *XXXᵉ Congrès de la Fédération archéologique et historique de Belgique. Annales*, Brussels, pp. 133–48

(1943–95), *L'économie rurale Namuroise au bas moyen âge (1199–1429)* (Université de Louvain: Recueil de travaux d'histoire et de philologie 3 S. 17, 4 S. 20, 6 S. 25 and 49), Louvain and Brussels

(1965), 'Empire et principautés en Lotharingie du Xᵉ au XIIIᵉ siècle', *Annali della Fondazione italiana per la storia amministrativa* 2: 95–172

(1967), 'Valeur de la personne ou sens du concret. A la base de la société du haut moyen âge', in *Miscellanea mediaevalia in memoriam Jan Frederik Niermeyer*, Groningen, pp. 1–8

(1983), *Les lignes de faite du moyen âge*, 9th edn, Louvain-la-Neuve

(1984a), 'Sur la survivance de la notion d'Etat dans l'Europe du Nord au haut moyen âge. L'emploi de "publicus" dans les sources belges antérieures à l'an mil', in

Institutionen, Kultur und Gesellschaft im Mittelalter. Festschrift für Josef Fleckenstein zu seinem 65. Geburtstag, ed. Lutz Fenske, Werner Rösener, and Thomas Zotz, Sigmaringen, pp. 147–64

(1984b), 'Sur le vocabulaire et les modalités de l'avouerie avant l'an mil dans la Belgique actuelle', *Publications de la Section historique de l'Institut Gr.-D. de Luxembourg* 98: 9–32

(1984c), *Le XIIIᵉ siècle européen*, 2nd edn (Nouvelle Clio 18), Paris

Gerits, Trudo J. (1964), 'Les actes de confraternité de 1142 et de 1153 entre Cîteaux et Prémontré', *Analecta praemonstratensia* 40: 192–205

Gervers, Michael (1967), 'The Cave Church at Gurat (Charente): Preliminary Report', *Gesta* 6: 10–20

Ghellinck, Joseph de (1950), 'Une édition ou collection médiévale des Opera omnia de Saint Augustin', in *Liber Floridus. Mittellateinische Studien* (Festschrift Paul Lehmann), St Ottilien, pp. 63–82

Gibb, Hamilton A.R. (1964), 'The Influence of Islamic Culture on Medieval Europe' (1955), repr. in *Change in Medieval Society*, ed. Sylvia Thrupp, New York, pp. 155–67

Gibbon, Edward (1896–1902), *The History of the Decline and Fall of the Roman Empire*, ed. J.B. Bury, London

Gibson, Margaret (1978), *Lanfranc of Bec*, Oxford

Gieysztor, Alexander (1967–8), 'Pauper sum et peregrinus. La légende de saint Alexis en occident. Un idéal de la pauvreté', *Recherches sur les pauvres et la pauvreté au moyen âge*, ed. Michel Mollat, Paris, VI, 27–30

Gilchrist, John (1977), 'St Raymond of Peñafort and the Decretalist Doctrines on Serfdom', *Ecritos del Valdat* 7: 299–328

Gilson, Etienne (1961), 'Sur deux textes de Pétrarche', *Studi petrarcheschi* 7 (= Atti del III Congresso dell'Associazione internazionale per gli studi di lingua e letteratura italiana), pp. 35–50

Giseke, Paul (1886), 'Über den Gegensatz der Cluniazenser und Cisterzienser', *Jahrbuch des Pädagogiums zum Kloster Unser Lieben Frau in Magdeburg*, Magdeburg

Glaser, Hubert (1958), 'Versuch über die Lebensgeschichte', in *Otto von Freising: Gedenkgabe zu seinem 800. Todesjahr*, ed. Joseph Fischer, Freising, pp. 14–38

(1965), 'Wilhelm von Saint-Denis. Ein Humanist aus der Umgebung des Abtes Suger und die Krise seiner Abtei von 1151 bis 1153', *Historisches Jahrbuch* 85: 257–322

Glock, Charles Y. (1964), 'The Role of Deprivation in the Origin and Evolution of Religious Groups', in *Religion and Social Conflict*, ed. Robert Lee and Martin Marty, New York, pp. 24–36

Gnädinger, Louise (1972), *Eremitica. Studien zur altfranzösischen Heiligenvita des 12. und 13. Jahrhunderts* (Zeitschrift für romanische Philologie, Fasc. Suppl. 130), Tübingen

Golding, Brian (1995), *Gilbert of Sempringham and the Gilbertine Order, c. 1130 – c. 1300*, Oxford.

Gombrich, Ernst H. (1970), *Aby Warburg: An Intellectual Biography*, London

Goodrich, W.E. (1984), 'The Cistercian Founders and the Rule: Some Reconsiderations', *Journal of Ecclesiastical History* 35: 358–75

Goossens, Jean (1983), 'La bible et la critique du clergé liégeois du XIIe siècle dans l'"Antigraphum Petri" ', in *Pascua Mediaevalia. Studies voor Prof. Dr. J.M. De Smet*, ed. Robrecht Lievens, Erik van Mingroot, and Werner Verbeke (Mediaevalia Lovanensia I 10), Leuven, pp. 93–107

Gougaud, Louis (1921), 'Mulierum consortia. Etude sur la syneisaktisme chez les ascètes celtiques', *Eriu* 9: 147–56

(1922), 'Anciennes tradition ascétiques, 1. L'usage de voyager à pied', *Revue d'ascétique et de mystique* 3: 56–9

(1923), 'Anciennes traditions ascétiques, 2. La gymnopédie', *Revue d'ascétique et de mystique* 4: 140–56

(1928), *Ermites et reclus. Etudes sur d'anciennes formes de vie religieuse* (Moines et monastères 5), Ligugé

(1930), *Anciennes coutumes claustrales* (Moines et monastères 8), Ligugé

Goulburn, Edward M., and Symonds, Henry (1878), *The Life, Letters, and Sermons of Bishop Herbert de Losinga*, Oxford and London

Gould, Stephen Jay (1980), *The Panda's Thumb*, New York and London

Gouron, André (1985), 'Une école ou des écoles? Sur les canonistes français (vers 1150 – vers 1210)', in *Proceedings of the Sixth International Congress of Medieval Canon Law, Berkeley, California, 28 July – 2 August 1980*, ed. Stephan Kuttner and Kenneth Pennington (Monumenta iuris canonici, Series C: Subsidia 7), Vatican City, pp. 223–40

Grabar, André (1968), *L'art de la fin de l'antiquité et du moyen âge*, Paris

Graboïs, Aryeh (1975), 'The "Hebraica Veritas" and Jewish–Christian Intellectual Relations in the Twelfth Century', *Speculum* 50: 613–34

Grandmottet, Odile (1958), 'Aspects du temporel de l'abbaye d'Auberive des origines à la fin du XIIIe siècle', *Cahiers Haut-Marnais* 52: 1–13

Gransden, Antonia (1975), 'A Democratic Movement in the Abbey of Bury St. Edmunds in the Late Twelfth and Early Thirteenth Centuries', *Journal of Ecclesiastical History* 26: 25–39

Graves, Coburn V. (1957), 'The Economic Activities of the Cistercians in Medieval England (1128–1307)', *Analecta cisterciensia* 13: 3–60

Grégoire, Christian (1969), 'Les origines de l'abbaye d'Orval', *Revue d'histoire ecclésiastique* 64: 756–807

Grégoire, Réginald (1962), 'Le "De claustro animae", est-il d'un clunisien?', *Studia monastica* 4: 193–5

(1967–8), 'La communion des moines-prêtres à la messe d'après les coutumiers monastiques médiévaux', *Sacris erudiri* 18: 524–49

(1970), ' "Religiosus". Etude sur le vocabulaire de la vie religieuse', in *A Giuseppe Ermini*, Spoleto, II, 415–30

Greven, Joseph (1912), *Die Anfänge der Beginen. Ein Beitrag zur Geschichte der Volksfrömmigkeit und des Ordenswesens im Hochmittelalter* (Vorreformationsgeschichtliche Forschungen 8), Münster i. W.

Griesser, Bruno (1924), 'Walter Map und die Cistercienser', *Cistercienser-Chronik* 36: 137–41 and 164–7

Grundmann, Herbert (1927), *Studien über Joachim von Floris* (Beiträge zur Kulturgeschichte des Mittelalters und der Renaissance 32), Leipzig and Berlin

(1961), *Religiöse Bewegungen im Mittelalter. Untersuchungen über die geschichtlichen Zusammenhänge zwischen der Ketzerei, den Bettelorden und der religiösen Frauenbewegung im 12. und 13. Jahrhundert und über die geschichtlichen Grundlagen der deutschen Mystik* (Historische Studien 267) (1935), repr. with 'Neue Beiträge zur Geschichte der religiösen Bewegungen im Mittelalter' (1955), Berlin

(1962), 'Zur Vita s. Gerlaci eremitae', *Deutsches Archiv* 18: 539–54

(1963), 'Deutsche Eremiten, Einsiedler und Klausner im Hochmittelalter (10.–12. Jahrhundert)', *Archiv für Kulturgeschichte* 45: 60–90

(1967), 'Oportet et haereses esse', *Archiv für Kulturgeschichte* 49: 129–64

(1968), 'Adelsbekehrungen im Hochmittelalter. "Conversi" und "nutriti" im Kloster', in *Adel und Kirche. Gerd Tellenbach zum 65. Geburtstag dargebracht von Freunden und Schülern*, ed. Josef Fleckenstein and Karl Schmid, Freiburg, Basel, and Vienna, pp. 325–45

(1976), 'Neue Beiträge zur Geschichte der religiösen Bewegungen im Mittelalter' (1955), repr. in his *Ausgewählte Aufsätze*, I. *Religiöse Bewegungen* (Schriften der Monumenta Germaniae historica 25.1), Stuttgart, pp. 38–92

(1977), 'Zur Biographie Joachims von Fiore und Rainers von Ponza' (1960), repr. in his *Ausgewählte Aufsätze*, II. *Joachim von Fiore* (Schriften der Monumenta Germaniae historica 25.2), Stuttgart, pp. 255–360

Grunebaum, Gustav E. von (1964), 'Parallelism, Convergence, and Influence in the Relations of Arab and Byzantine Philosophy, Literature, and Piety', *Dumbarton Oaks Papers* 18: 89–111

Gryson, R. (1980), 'Dix ans de recherche sur les origines du célibat ecclésiastique', *Revue théologique de Louvain* 11: 156–85

Guenée, Bernard (1976–7), 'Temps de l'histoire et temps de la mémoire au moyen âge', *Bulletin de la Société de l'histoire de France* 487: 25–35

Guéranger, Prosper (1878–85), *Institutions liturgiques*, 2nd edn, Paris and Brussels

Guillemain, Bernard (1953), 'Chiffres et statistiques pour l'histoire ecclésiastique du moyen âge', *Le Moyen Age* 59 (4 S. 8): 341–65

Guillot, Olivier (1972), *Le comte d'Anjou et son entourage au XIe siècle*, Paris

Günter, Heinrich (1954), *Psychologie de la légende. Introduction à une hagiographie scientifique*, tr. J.F. Goffinet, Paris

Gurevich, Aaron J. (1985), *Categories of Medieval Culture*, tr. G.L. Campbell, London

Gutas, Dimitri (1975), *Greek Wisdom Literature in Arabic Translation* (American Oriental Series 60), New Haven

Guth, Klaus (1970), *Guibert von Nogent und die hochmittelalterliche Kritik an der Reliquienverehrung* (Studien und Mitteilungen zur Geschichte des Benediktiner-Ordens und seiner Zweige, Fasc. Suppl. 21), Augsburg

Gwynn, Aubrey (1940), 'Irish Monks and the Cluniac Reform', *Studies* 29: 409–30

Haacke, Rhabanus (1980), 'Die mystischen Visionen Ruperts von Deutz', in *Sapientiae Doctrina. Mélanges de théologie et de littérature médiévales offerts à Dom Hildebrand Bascour O.S.B.*, Louvain, pp. 68–90

Hadot, Pierre (1983), *Leçon inaugurale faite le vendredi 18 février 1983* (Collège de France: Chaire d'histoire de la pensée hellénistique et romaine), Paris

Haenens, Albert d' (1962), 'Moines et clercs à Tournai au début du XIIe siècle', in *Vita comune* (1962), II, 90–103

Hägermann, Dieter (1981), 'Eine Grundherrschaft des 13. Jahrhunderts im Spiegel des Frühmittelalters. Caesarius von Prüm und seine kommentierte Abschrift des Urbars von 893', *Rheinische Vierteljahrschrift* 45: 1–34

Hahn, Hanno (1957), *Die frühe Kirchenbaukunst der Zisterzienser. Untersuchungen zur Baugeschichte von Kloster Eberbach im Rheingau und ihren europäischen Analogien im 12. Jahrhundert* (Frankfurter Forschungen zur Architekturgeschichte 1), Berlin

Hallier, Amédée (1969), *The Monastic Theology of Aelred of Rievaulx: An Experiential Theology*, tr. Columban Heaney (Cistercian Studies Series 2), Spencer

Hallinger, Kassius (1950–1), *Gorze-Kluny. Studien zu den monastischen Lebensformen und Gegensätzen im Hochmittelalter* (Studia Anselmiana 22–5), Rome

(1958–60), 'Cluniacensis ss. religionis ordinem elegimus. Zur Rechtslage der Anfänge des Klosters Hasungen', *Jahrbuch für das Bistum Mainz* 8: 224–72

(1959), 'Ausdrucksformen des Umkehr-Gedankens. Zu den geistigen Grundlagen und den Entwicklungsphasen der "Instituta Conversorum" ', *Studien und Mitteilungen zur Geschichte des Benediktiner-Ordens und seiner Zweige* 70: 169–81

(1980), 'Consuetudo, Begriff, Formen, Forschungsgeschichte, Inhalt', in *Untersuchungen zu Kloster und Stift* (Veröffentlichungen des Max-Planck-Instituts für Geschichte 68: Studien zur Germania Sacra 14), Göttingen, pp. 140–66

(1983), 'Die Anfänge von Cîteaux', in *Aus Kirche und Reich. Festschrift für Friedrich Kempf*, ed. Hubert Mordek, Sigmaringen, pp. 225–35

Hamilton, Bernard (1975), 'S. Pierre Damien et les mouvements monastiques de son temps', *Studi gregoriani* 10: 175–202

Hammer, C.V., Claussen, H.B., and Dansgaard, W. (1980), 'Greenland Ice Sheet Evidence of Post-glacial Volcanism and its Climatic Impact', *Nature* 288: 230–5

Hampe, Karl (1898), 'Reise nach Frankreich und Belgien im Frühjahr 1897, III. Abt Thomas von Morigny als Verfasser des zweiten Buches des Chronicon Mauriniacense', *Neues Archiv* 23: 389–98

Hansitz, Marcus (1727–55), *Germania sacra*, Augsburg and Vienna

Häring (also Haring), Nikolaus M. (1950), 'The First Traces of the So-Called Cerbanus Translation of St. John Damascene, "De fide orthodoxa", III, 1–8', *Mediaeval Studies* 12: 214–16

(1953), 'A Latin Dialogue on the Doctrine of Gilbert of Poitiers', *Mediaeval Studies* 15: 243–89

(1955), 'The Cistercian Everard of Ypres and his Appraisal of the Conflict between St Bernard and Gilbert of Poitiers', *Mediaeval Studies* 17: 143–72

(1973), 'Hilary of Orléans and his Letter Collection', *Studi medievali* 3 S. 14: 1069–122

Haseldine, Julian P. (1993), 'Friendship and Rivalry: The Role of "Amicitia" in Twelfth-Century Monastic Relations', *Journal of Ecclesiastical History* 44: 390–414

Haskins, Charles Homer (1927), *The Renaissance of the Twelfth Century*, Cambridge, Mass.

(1929), *Studies in Medieval Culture*, Oxford

Hauréau, Barthélemy (1890–3), *Notices et extraits de quelques manuscrits latins de la Bibliothèque nationale*, Paris

Hausherr, Irénée (1947), 'Opus Dei', in *Miscellanea Guillaume de Jerphanion* (Orientalia christiana periodica 13), Rome, I, 195–218

Häussling, Angelus (1973), *Mönchskonvent und Eucharistiefeier. Eine Studie über die Messe in der abendländischen Klosterliturgie des frühen Mittelalters und zur Geschichte der Messhäufigkeit* (Liturgiewissenschaftliche Quellen und Forschungen 58), Münster i. W.

Haverkamp, Alfred (1984), 'Tenxwind von Andernach and Hildegard von Bingen. Zwei "Weltanschauungen" in der Mitte des 12. Jahrhunderts', in *Institutionen, Kultur und Gesellschaft im Mittelalter. Festschrift für Josef Fleckenstein zu seinem 65. Geburtstag*, ed. Lutz Fenske, Werner Rösener, and Thomas Zotz, Sigmaringen, pp. 515–48

Heckscher, William S. (1937), 'Relics of Pagan Antiquity in Mediaeval Settings', *Journal of the Warburg Institute* 1: 204–20

Heinemann, Hartmut (1983), 'Untersuchungen zur Geschichte der Zähringer in Burgund', *Archiv für Diplomatik* 29: 42–192

Hendrix, Scott H. (1976), 'In Quest of the "Vera Ecclesia": The Crises of Late Medieval Ecclesiology', *Viator* 7: 347–78

Henry, Charles W. (1957), *Canonical Relations between the Bishops and Abbots at the Beginning of the Tenth Century* (Catholic University of America: Canon Law Studies 382), Washington

Herbert, Jane (1985), 'The Transformation of Hermitages into Augustinian Priories in 12th Century England', in *Monks, Hermits and the Ascetic Tradition*, ed. W.J. Sheils (Studies in Church History 22), Oxford, pp. 131–45

Herlihy, David (1970), 'Family Solidarity in Medieval Italian History', in *Economy, Society, and Government in Medieval Italy: Essays in Memory of Robert L. Reynolds*, Kent, pp. 173–84

(1974), 'The Generation in Medieval History', *Viator* 5: 347–64

(1985), *Medieval Households*, Cambridge, Mass., and London

Herman, Emil (1941), 'Die Regelung der Armut in den byzantinischen Klöstern', *Orientalia christiana periodica* 7: 406–60

Hertling, Ludwig (1933), 'Der mittelalterliche Heiligentypus nach den Tugendkatalogen', *Zeitschrift für Aszese und Mystik* 8: 260–9

Hiestand, Rudolf (1988), 'Kardinalbischof Matthäus von Albano, das Konzil von Troyes, und die Entstehung des Templerordens', *Zeitschrift für Kirchengeschichte* 99: 295–325

Higounet, Charles (1965), *La grange de Vaulerent. Structure et exploitation d'un terroir cistercien de la plaine de France XII⁰–XV⁰ siècle* (Ecole pratique des hautes études, VI⁰ section: Centre de recherches historiques. Les hommes et la terre 10), Paris

Hill, Michael (1971), 'Typologie sociologique de l'ordre religieux', *Social Compass* 18: 45–64

Hilpisch, Stephanus (1928), *Die Doppelklöster. Entstehung und Organisation* (Beiträge zur Geschichte des alten Mönchtums und des Benediktinerordens 15), Münster i. W.

(1956), 'Der Rat der Brüder in den Benediktinerklöstern des Mittelalters', *Studien und Mitteilungen zur Geschichte des Benediktiner-Ordens und seiner Zweige* 67: 221–36

Hirsch, Hans (1967), *Die Klosterimmunität seit dem Investiturstreit* (Untersuchungen zur Verfassungsgeschichte des deutschen Reiches und der deutschen Kirche) (1913), repr. with *Nachwort* by Heinrich Büttner, Darmstadt

Hocquard, Gaston (1948), 'La solitude cartusienne d'après ses plus anciens témoins', *Bulletin des facultés catholiques de Lyon* 70 (N.S. 5): 5–19

(1951), 'Solitudo cellae', in *Mélanges d'histoire du moyen âge dédiés à la mémoire de Louis Halphen*, Paris, pp. 323–31

Hoffmann, Eberhard (1910), 'Die Entwicklung der Wirtschaftsprinzipien im Cisterzienserorden während des 12. und 13. Jahrhunderts', *Historisches Jahrbuch* 31: 699–727

Hoffmann, Hartmut (1964), *Gottesfriede und Treuga Dei* (Schriften der Monumenta Germaniae historica 20), Stuttgart

Hofmeister, Philipp (1928), 'Der Übertritt in eine andere religiöse Gemeinschaft', *Zeitschrift für katholisches Kirchenrecht* 108: 419–81

(1938), 'Benediktinische Quellen zu den Konstitutionen des Augustinerchorherrenstiftes Marbach', *Neues Archiv für elsässische Kirchengeschichte* 13: 59–70

(1953–4), 'Mönchtum und Seelsorge bis zum 13. Jahrhundert', *Studien und Mitteilungen zur Geschichte des Benediktiner-Ordens und seiner Zweige* 65: 209–73

(1961a), 'Die Klaustral-Oblaten', *Studien und Mitteilungen zur Geschichte des Benediktiner-Ordens und seiner Zweige* 72: 5–45

(1961b), 'Kardinäle aus dem Ordensstande', *Studien und Mitteilungen zur Geschichte des Benediktiner-Ordens und seiner Zweige* 72: 153–70

Holdsworth, Christopher J. (1973), 'The Blessings of Work: The Cistercian View', in *Sanctity and Secularity: The Church and the World*, ed. Derek Baker (Studies in Church History 10), Oxford, pp. 59–76

(1985), 'Orderic, Traditional Monk and the New Monasticism', in *Tradition and Change: Essays in Honour of Marjorie Chibnall*, ed. Diana Greenway, Christopher Holdsworth, and Jane Sayers, Cambridge, pp. 21–34

(1991), *The Piper and the Tune: Medieval Patrons and Monks* (Stenton Lecture 1990), Reading

(1994), 'The Early Works of Bernard of Clairvaux', *Cîteaux* 45: 21–61

Holland, Thomas E. (1890), 'The University of Oxford in the Twelfth Century', in *Oxford Historical Society: Collectanea*, II, 137–92

Holroyd, Michael (1968), *Lytton Strachey*, New York and Chicago

Homburger, Otto (1939), 'Untersuchungen zum Stil des Baseler Galluspforte', in *Medieval Studies in Memory of A. Kingsley Porter*, ed. Wilhelm R.W. Koehler, Cambridge, Mass., II, 537–57

Honemann, Volker (1978), *Die 'Epistola ad fratres de Monte Dei' des Wilhelm von Saint-Thierry. Lateinische Überlieferung und mittelalterliche Übersetzungen* (Münchener Texte und Untersuchungen zur deutschen Literatur des Mittelalters 61), Zürich and Munich

Hoppenbrouwers, Henricus A.M. (1964), 'Conversatio. Une étude sémasiologique', in *Graecitas et latinitas christianorum primaeva: Supplementa* 1, Nijmegen, pp. 45–95

Horn, Walter, and Born, Ernest (1979), *The Plan of St Gall*, Berkeley, Los Angeles, and London

Hostie, Raymond (1972), *Vie et mort des ordres religieux. Approches psychosociologiques* (Bibliothèque d'études psycho-religieuses), Paris

Hourlier, Jacques (1936), *Le chapitre général jusqu'au moment du Grand Schisme. Origines – développement – étude juridique*, Paris

(1950), 'Cluny et la notion d'ordre religieux', in *A Cluny. Congrès scientifique. Fêtes et cérémonies liturgiques en l'honneur des saints abbés Odon et Odilon 9–11 juillet 1949*, Dijon, pp. 219–26

(1959), 'Le bréviaire de Saint-Taurin. Un livre liturgique clunisien à l'usage de l'Echelle-Saint-Taurin (Paris BN lat. 12601)', *Etudes grégoriennnes* 3: 163–73

(1964), *Saint Odilon, abbé de Cluny* (Bibliothèque de la Revue d'histoire ecclésiastique 40), Louvain

(1974), *L'âge classique (1140–1378). Les religieux* (Histoire du droit et des institutions de l'église en Occident 10), Paris

(1979), 'L'origine du prieuré clunisien', in *Mélanges offerts à Jean Dauvillier*, Toulouse, pp. 435–41

Howe, John (1988), 'The Nobility's Reform of the Medieval Church', *American Historical Review* 93: 317–39

(1992), ' "Monasteria semper libera": Cluniac-type Monastic Liberties in Some Eleventh-Century Italian Monasteries', *Catholic Historical Review* 78: 19–34

Hubert, Jean (1966), 'Les galilées des églises monastiques de Déols et de Vouillon', in *Mélanges offerts à René Crozet*, ed. Pierre Gallais and Yves-Jean Riou, Poitiers, II, 843–9

Hughes, Kathleen (1960), 'The Changing Theory and Practice of Irish Pilgrimage', *Journal of Ecclesiastical History* 11: 143–51

Huglo, Michel (1956), 'Le tonaire de Saint-Bénigne de Dijon (Montpellier H. 159)', *Annales musicologiques* 4: 7–18

Hugo, Charles L. (1734–6), *Sacri et canonici ordinis Praemonstratensis annales*, Nancy

Huygens, Robert B.C. (1962), 'Mitteilungen aus Handschriften', *Studi medievali* 3 S. 3: 747–72

Huyghebaert, Nicolas (1951), 'Moines et clercs italiens en Lotharingie (VIIIᵉ–XIIᵉ siècle)', in *Miscellanea Tornacensia* (XXXIIIᵉ Congrès de la Fédération archéologique et historique de Belgique), Brussels, I, 95–111

Hyams, Paul R. (1987), 'Warranty and Good Lordship in Twelfth Century England', *Law and History Review* 5: 440–503

Imbart de la Tour, Pierre (1891), *Les élections épiscopales dans l'église de France du IXᵉ au XIIᵉ siècle*, Paris

Inge, William Ralph (1899), *Christian Mysticism* (Bampton Lectures 1899), London

(1925), 'Religion of the Future', *Atlantic Monthly* 135: 190–200

Iogna-Prat, Dominique (1977), 'La femme dans la perspective pénitentielle des ermites du Bas-Maine (fin XIᵉᵐᵉ début XIIᵉᵐᵉ siècle)', *Revue d'histoire de la spiritualité* 53: 47–64

(1992), 'Coutumes et statuts clunisiens comme sources historiques (ca. 990 – ca. 1200)', *Revue Mabillon* N.S. 3: 23–48

Istituzioni (1980) = *Istituzioni monastiche e istituzioni canonicali in Occidente (1123–1215). Atti della settima Settimana internazionale di studio, Mendola, 28 agosto – 3 settembre 1977* (Pubblicazioni dell'Università cattolica del Sacro Cuore: Miscellanea del Centro di studi medioevali 9), Milan

Ivánka, Endre von (1940), 'Griechische Einflüsse im westlichen Geistesleben des XII. Jahrhunderts', *Egyetemes Philologiai Közlöny* 64: 211–17

Jackson, Kenneth Hurlstone (1951), *A Celtic Miscellany*, Cambridge, Mass.

Jacobsson, Harry (1955), *Etudes d'anthroponymie lorraine. Les bans de Tréfonds de Metz (1267–1298)*, Göteborg

Jacqueline, Bernard (1953), 'A propos de l'exemption monastique', in *Bernard de Clairvaux* (Commission d'histoire de l'ordre de Cîteaux 3), Paris, pp. 339–43

Jaeger, C. Stephen (1993), 'Humanism and Ethics at the School of St Victor in the Early Twelfth Century', *Mediaeval Studies* 55: 51–79

(1994), *The Envy of Angels: Cathedral Schools and Social Ideals in Medieval Europe, 950–1200*, Philadelphia

Jakobs, Hermann (1961), *Die Hirsauer. Ihre Ausbreitung und Rechtsstellung im Zeitalter des Investiturstreites* (Kölner historische Abhandlungen 4), Cologne and Graz

(1968), *Der Adel in des Klosterreform von St. Blasien* (Kölner historische Abhandlungen 16), Cologne and Graz

James, William (1902), *The Varieties of Religious Experience*, New York and London

Jarecki, Walter (1981), *Signa loquendi. Die cluniacensischen Signa-Listen eingeleitet und herausgegeben* (Saecula Spiritualia 4), Baden-Baden

(1988), 'Die "Ars Signorum Cisterciensium" im Rahmen der metrischen Signa-Listen', *Revue bénédictine* 98: 329–99

Jäschke, Kurt-Ulrich (1970), 'Zur Eigenständigkeit einer Junggorzer Reformbewegung', *Zeitschrift für Kirchengeschichte* 81: 17–43

Javelet, Robert (1959), 'Psychologie des auteurs spirituels du XIIᵉ siècle', *Revue des sciences religieuses* 33: 18–64, 97–164, and 209–68

(1967), *Image et ressemblance au douzième siècle de saint Anselme à Alain de Lille*, Paris

Johnson, Penelope (1991), *Equal in Monastic Profession: Religious Women in Medieval France*, Chicago and London

Jones, Arnold H.M. (1964), *The Later Roman Empire, 284–602*, Norman

Jones, Charles W. (1978), *Saint Nicholas of Myra, Bari, and Manhattan*, Chicago and London

Jong, Mayke de (1986), *Kind en klooster in de vroege middeleeuwen* (Amsterdamse historische reeks 8), Amsterdam

Jordan, Karl (1941–2), 'Studien zur Klosterpolitik Heinrichs des Löwen', *Archiv für Urkundenforschung* 17: 1–31

Jotischky, Andrew (1995), *The Perfection of Solitude: Hermits and Monks in the Crusader States*, University Park

Judge, E.A. (1977), 'The Earliest Use of Monachos for "Monk" (P. Coll. Youtie 77) and the Origins of Monasticism', *Jahrbuch für Antike und Christentum* 20: 72–89

Kaminsky, Hans Heinrich (1966), 'Zur Gründung von Fruttuaria durch den Abt Wilhelm von Dijon', *Zeitschrift für Kirchengeschichte* 77 (4 S. 15): 238–67

Kantorowicz, Ernst H. (1965), 'Die Wiederkehr gelehrter Anachorese im Mittelalter' (1937), repr. in his *Selected Studies*, Locust Valley, pp. 339–51

Kastner, Jörg (1974), *Historiae fundationum monasteriorum. Frühformen monastischer Institutionsgeschichtsschreibung im Mittelalter* (Münchener Beiträge zur Mediävistik und Renaissance-Forschung 18), Munich

Katzenellenbogen, Adolf (1939), *Allegories of the Virtues and Vices in Mediaeval Art from the Early Christian Times to the Thirteenth Century* (Studies of the Warburg Institute 10), London

Kazhdan, Alexander, and Franklin, Simon (1984), *Studies on Byzantine Literature of the Eleventh and Twelfth Centuries* (Past and Present Publications), Cambridge and Paris

Kedar, Benjamin Z. (1983), 'Gerard of Nazareth: A Neglected Twelfth-Century Writer in the Latin East', *Dumbarton Oaks Papers* 37: 55–77

Kiem, Martin (1883), *Das Kloster Muri in Kanton Argau* (Quellen zur schweizer Geschichte III.3), Basel

King, Edmund (1973), *Peterborough Abbey, 1086–1310* (Cambridge Studies in Economic History), Cambridge

(1984), 'The Anarchy of Stephen's Reign', *Transactions of the Royal Historical Society* 5 S. 34: 133–53

Kitzinger, Ernst (1966), 'The Byzantine Contribution to Western Art of the Twelfth and Thirteenth Centuries', *Dumbarton Oaks Papers* 20: 25–47

(1972), 'The Gregorian Reform and the Visual Arts: A Problem of Method', *Transactions of the Royal Historical Society* 5 S. 22: 87–102

Klibansky, Raymond (1946), 'L'épître de Bérenger de Poitiers contre les Chartreux', *Revue du moyen âge latin* 2: 314–16

Klinkenberg, Hans Martin (1969), 'Die Theorie der Veränderbarkeit des Rechtes im frühen und hohen Mittelalter', in *Lex et sacramentum im Mittelalter*, ed. Paul Wilpert and Rudolf Hoffmann (Miscellanea Mediaevalia 6), Berlin, pp. 157–88

Klotz, Heinrich (1976), 'Formen des Anonymität und des Individualismus in der Kunst des Mittelalters und der Renaissance', *Gesta* 15: 303–12

Knowles, David (1934), 'Edward Cuthbert Butler (1858–1934)' (1934), repr. in Knowles (1963a), pp. 264–362

(1935), 'The Revolt of the Lay Brothers of Sempringham', *English Historical Review* 50: 465–86

(1936), 'Rashdall's Mediaeval Universities', *Dublin Review* 199: 300–14

(1956), 'Cardinal Gasquet as an Historian', repr. in Knowles (1963a), pp. 240–63

(1963a), *The Historian and Character and Other Essays*, Cambridge

(1963b), *The Monastic Order in England: A History of its Development from the Times of Dunstan to the Fourth Lateran Council, 940–1216*, 2nd edn, Cambridge

(1969), *Christian Monasticism*, London

Knowles, David, and Hadcock, Richard Neville (1971), *Medieval Religious Houses: England and Wales*, 2nd edn, London

Koch, Gottfried (1962), *Frauenfrage und Ketzertum im Mittelalter. Die Frauenbewegung im Rahmen des Katharismus und des Waldensertums und ihre sozialen Wurzeln (12.– 14. Jahrhundert)* (Forschungen zur mittelalterlichen Geschichte 9), Berlin

Kohnle, Armin (1993), *Abt Hugo von Cluny (1049–1109)* (Beihefte der *Francia* 32), Sigmaringen

Kottje, Raymund (1969), 'Klosterbibliotheken und monastische Kultur in der Zweiten Hälfte des 11. Jahrhunderts', *Zeitschrift für Kirchengeschichte* 80: 145–62

Kovács, François (1951), 'Relation entre l'"Officium defunctorum feriale" et la liturgie cistercienne primitive', *Analecta sacri ordinis Cisterciensis* 7: 78–84

Krausen, Edgar (1958), 'Bischof Otto I. von Freising, der Zisterzienser auf dem Stuhl des hl. Korbinian', in *Otto von Freising. Gedenkgabe zu seinem 800. Todesjahr*, ed. Joseph Fischer, Freising, pp. 39–48

Krenig, Ernst (1954), 'Mittelalterliche Frauenklöster nach den Konstitutionen von Cîteaux', *Analecta sacri ordinis Cisterciensis* 10: 1–105

Kristeller, Paul Oskar (1966), *Renaissance Philosophy and the Mediaeval Tradition* (Wimmer Lecture 15), Latrobe

(1970), 'The Contribution of Religious Orders to Renaissance Thought and Learning', *American Benedictine Review* 21: 1–55

(1972), *Renaissance Concepts of Man and Other Essays*, New York

(1983), 'Rhetoric in Medieval and Renaissance Culture', in his *Renaissance Eloquence: Studies in the Theory and Practice of Renaissance Rhetoric*, ed. James J. Murphy, Berkeley, Los Angeles, and London, pp. 1–19

(1993), *Greek Philosophers of the Hellenistic Age*, tr. Gregory Woods, New York

Kubie, Lawrence S. (1974), 'The Drive to Become Both Sexes', *The Psychoanalytic Quarterly* 43: 349–426

Kunze, Hans (1925), 'Die kirchliche Reformbewegung des zwölften Jahrhunderts im Gebiet der mittleren Elbe und ihr Einfluss auf die Baukunst', *Sachsen und Anhalt* 1: 388–476

Kurze, Dietrich (1966), *Pfarrerwahlen im Mittelalter. Ein Beitrag zur Geschichte der Gemeinde und des Niederkirchenwesens* (Forschungen zur kirchlichen Rechtsgeschichte und zum Kirchenrecht 6), Cologne and Graz

Kuttner, Stephan (1968), 'Brief Notes', *Traditio* 24: 504–7

(1988), 'Research on Gratian: Acta and Agenda', in *Proceedings of the Seventh International Congress of Medieval Canon Law. Cambridge, 23–27 July 1984*, ed. Peter Linehan (Monumenta iuris canonici, Series C: Subsidia 8), Vatican City, pp. 3–26

Ladner, Gerhart B. (1959), *The Idea of Reform: Its Impact on Christian Thought and Action in the Age of the Fathers*, Cambridge, Mass.

(1965), *Ad imaginem Dei: The Image of Man in Mediaeval Art* (Wimmer Lecture 16), Latrobe

(1967), ' "Homo Viator": Medieval Ideas of Alienation and Order', *Speculum* 42: 233–59

(1983a), *Images and Ideas in the Middle Ages: Selected Studies in History and Art* (Storia e letteratura. Raccolta di Studi e testi 155–6), Rome

(1983b), 'Two Gregorian Letters on the Sources and Nature of Gregory VII's Reform Ideology' (1956), repr. in Ladner (1983a), II, 665–86

(1983c), 'Vegetative Symbolism and the Concept of Renaissance' (1961), repr. in Ladner (1983a), II, 727–63

Laici (1968) = *I laici nella 'Societas Christiana' dei secoli XI e XII. Atti della terza Settimana internazionale di studio, Mendola, 21–27 agosto 1965* (Pubblicazioni dell'Università cattolica del Sacro Cuore, Contributi 3 S.: Varia 5. Miscellanea del Centro di studi medioevali 5), Milan

Lambert, Malcolm D. (1978), 'The Motives of the Cathars: Some Reflections', in *Religious Motivation: Biographical and Sociological Problems for the Church Historian*, ed. Derek Baker (Studies in Church History 15), Oxford, pp. 49–59

(1992), *Medieval Heresy: Popular Movements from the Gregorian Reform to the Reformation*, 2nd edn, Oxford and Cambridge, Mass.

Lamma, Paolo (1961), *Momenti di storiografia cluniacense* (Istituto storico italiano per il medio evo: Studi storici 42–4), Rome

Landau, Peter (1991a), *'Officium' und 'Libertas christiana'* (Bayerische Akademie der Wissenschaften, phil.-hist. Kl.: Sitzungsberichte 1991.3), Munich

(1991b), 'Frei und unfrei in der Kanonistik des 12. und 13. Jahrhunderts am Beispiel der Ordination der Unfreien', in *Die abendländische Freiheit vom 10. zum 14.*

Jahrhundert, ed. Johannes Fried (Vorträge und Forschungen 39), Sigmaringen, pp. 177–90

Landgraf, Artur Michael (1952–6), *Dogmengeschichte der Frühscholastik*, Regensburg

Lang, Augustin (1939–40), 'Die Bibel Stephan Hardings', *Cistercienser-Chronik* 51: 247–56, 275–81, 294–8, 307–13, and 52: 6–13, 17–23, 33–7

Langmuir, Gavin I. (1984), 'Thomas of Monmouth: Detector of Ritual Murder', *Speculum* 59: 820–46

Laporte, Jean (1956), 'Tableau des services obituaires assurés par les abbayes de Saint-Evroul et de Jumièges, XIIe et XIVe siècles', *Revue Mabillon* 46: 141–55 and 169–88

(1963), 'Les associations spirituelles entre monastères. L'exemple de trois abbayes bénédictines normandes', *Cahiers Léopold Delisle* 12.3: 29–45

[Laporte, Maurice] (1960–7), *Aux sources de la vie cartusienne*, La Grande Chartreuse

Laudage, Johannes (1984), *Priesterbild und Reformpapsttum im 11. Jahrhundert* (Beihefte zum Archiv für Kulturgeschichte 22), Cologne and Vienna

Laurent, Jacques (1954), 'La prière pour les défunts et les obituaires dans l'ordre de Cîteaux', in *Mélanges saint Bernard* (XXIVe Congrès de l'Association bourguignonne des sociétés savantes), Dijon, pp. 383–96

Laurent, Marie-Hyacinthe (1952), 'Chanoines et réforme à Aix-en-Provence au XIe siècle', *Studi gregoriani* 4: 171–90

Lauwers, Michel (1989), 'Expérience béguinale et récit hagiographique. A propos de la "Vita Mariae Oigniacensis" de Jacques de Vitry (vers 1215)', *Journal des Savants* 1989: 61–103

Lawrence, Clifford H. (1984), *Medieval Monasticism: Forms of Religious Life in Western Europe in the Middle Ages*, London and New York

Leclercq, Jean (1944–5), 'Les méditations d'un moine au XIIe siècle', *Revue Mabillon* 34–5: 1–19

(1949), 'Saint Bernard et Origène d'après un manuscrit de Madrid', *Revue bénédictine* 59: 183–95

(1951a), 'Lettres du temps de saint Bernard', *Studien und Mitteilungen zur Geschichte des Benediktiner-Ordens und seiner Zweige* 63: 1–7

(1951b), 'Origène au XIIe siècle', *Irénikon* 24: 425–39

(1952), 'Passage supprimé dans une épître d'Alexandre III', *Revue bénédictine* 62: 149–51

(1953a), *Études sur saint Bernard et le texte de ses écrits* (Analecta sacri ordinis Cisterciensis 9.1–2), Rome

(1953b), 'La lettre de Gilbert Crispin sur la vie monastique', in *Analecta monastica*, II (Studia Anselmiana 31), Rome, pp. 118–23

(1954), 'Epîtres d'Alexandre III sur les Cisterciens', *Revue bénédictine* 64: 68–82

(1955), 'Lettres de vocation à la vie monastique', in *Analecta monastica*, III (Studia Anselmiana 37), Rome, pp. 169–97

(1956a), 'Pierre le Vénérable et l'érémitisme clunisien', in *Petrus Venerabilis* (1956), pp. 99–120

(1956b), 'Saint Antoine dans la tradition monastique médiévale', in *Antonius magnus eremita, 356–1956*, ed. Basilius Steidle (Studia Anselmiana 38), Rome, pp. 229–247

(1958a), 'La crise du monachisme aux XIe et XIIe siècles', *Bullettino dell'Istituto storico italiano per il medio evo* 70: 19–41

(1958b), 'Le poème du Payen Bolotin contre les faux ermites', *Revue bénédictine* 68: 52–86

(1961a), *The Life of Perfection*, tr. Leonard J. Doyle, Collegeville

(1961b), *Etudes sur le vocabulaire monastique du moyen âge* (Studia Anselmiana 48), Rome

(1961c), *L'amour des lettres et le désir de Dieu. Initiation aux auteurs monastiques du moyen âge* (Paris 1957); tr. Catharine Misrahi, *The Love of Learning and the Desire for God*, New York

(1962a), 'Spiritualitas', *Studi medievali* 3 S. 3: 279–96

(1962b), 'Saint Romuald et le monachisme missionnaire', *Revue bénédictine* 72: 307–23

(1962c), 'La flagellazione voluntaria nella tradizione spirituale dell'Occidente', in *Il movimento dei disciplinati nel settimo centenario dal suo inizio* (Deputazione di storia patria per l'Umbria: Appendice al *Bollettino* 9), Perugia, pp. 73–83

(1963a), *Otia monastica. Etudes sur le vocabulaire de la contemplation au moyen âge* (Studia Anselmiana 51), Rome

(1963b), 'Le sacerdoce des moines', *Irénikon* 36: 5–40

(1964a), 'Aspects spirituels de la symbolique du livre au XIIe siècle', in *L'homme devant Dieu. Mélanges H. de Lubac*, Paris, pp. 63–72

(1964b), *Aux sources de la spiritualité occidentale* (Tradition et spiritualité 4), Paris

(1965a), *Témoins de la spiritualité occidentale* (Tradition et spiritualité 5), Paris

(1965b), 'Comment vivaient les frères convers', *Analecta cisterciensia* 21: 239–58 (also in *Laici* (1968), pp. 152–82)

(1965c), 'La vie monastique est-elle une vie contemplative?', *Collectanea cisterciensia* 27: 108–20

(1966), 'The Bible and the Gregorian Reform', *Concilium* 7: 34–41

(1967), 'Pour l'histoire du vocabulaire latin de la pauvreté', *Melto* 3 (Mélanges Mgr. Pierre Dib): 293–308

(1971a), 'Profession according to the Rule of St Benedict', in *Rule and Life: An Interdisciplinary Symposium*, ed. M. Basil Pennington, Spencer, pp. 117–49

(1971b), 'Le commentaire d'Etienne de Paris sur la Règle de S. Benoît', *Revue d'ascétique et de mystique* 47: 129–44

(1979), *Monks and Love in Twelfth Century France*, Oxford

(1983), *La femme et les femmes dans l'œuvre de saint Bernard*, Paris

(1986), 'Diversification et identité dans le monachisme au XIIe siècle', *Studia monastica* 28: 51–74

Leclercq, Jean, Vandenbroucke, François, and Bouyer, Louis (1961), *La spiritualité du moyen âge*, Paris

Lecoy, Félix (1942–3), 'Le "Chronicon Novaliciense" et les légendes épiques', *Romania* 67: 1–52

Ledru, Ambroise (1899), 'La recluse Ermecin et les recluses du Mans au XIIe siècle', *La province du Maine* 7: 337–42

Lefèvre, Jean-A. (1954), 'A propos des sources de la législation primitive de Prémontré', *Analecta praemonstratensia* 30: 12–19

(1956), 'S. Robert de Molesme dans l'opinion monastique du XIIe et du XIIIe siècle', *Analecta bollandiana* 74: 50–83

Lefèvre, Placide F. (1932), 'Les cérémonies de la vêture et de la profession dans l'ordre de Prémontré', *Analecta praemonstratensia* 8: 289–307

(1957), 'A propos du cérémonial de la vêture dans l'ordre de Prémontré', *Analecta praemonstratensia* 33: 147–56

(1961), 'L'épisode de la conversion de S. Norbert et la tradition hagiographique du "Vita Norberti" ', *Revue d'histoire ecclésiastique* 56: 813–26

Leff, Gordon (1967), 'The Apostolic Ideal in Later Medieval Ecclesiology', *Journal of Theological Studies* N.S. 18: 58–82

Le Goff, Jacques (1972), 'The Town as an Agent of Civilization, c. 1210 – c. 1500', in *The Fontana Economic History of Europe. The Middle Ages*, ed. Carlo M. Cipolla, London, pp. 71–106

(1973), 'Le vocabulaire des catégories sociales chez saint François d'Assise et ses biographes du XIIIe siècle', in *Ordres et classes. Colloque d'histoire sociale, Saint-Cloud 24-25 mai 1967*, ed. Daniel Roche and Camille E. Labrousse (Congrès et colloques 12), Paris and The Hague, pp. 93–123

(1981), *La naissance du Purgatoire*, Paris

(1986), *La bourse et la vie. Economie et religion au moyen âge*, Paris

Lehmann, Paul (1922), *Mittellateinische Verse in 'Distinctiones monasticae et morales' vom Anfang des 13. Jahrhunderts* (Bayerischen Akademie der Wissenschaften, phil.-hist. Kl.: Sitzungsberichte 1922.2), Munich

Lekai, Louis (1982), 'The Early Cistercians and the Rule of Benedict', *Mittellateinisches Jahrbuch* 17: 96–107

Lemaître, Jean-Loup (1980–92), *Répertoire des documents nécrologiques français* (Recueil des historiens de la France. Obituaires 7), Paris

(1984), *Les documents nécrologiques de l'abbaye Saint-Pierre de Solignac* (Recueil des historiens de la France. Obituaires in-8° 1), Paris

Lemarignier, Jean-François (1949), 'Spiritualité grégorienne et chanoines réguliers', *Revue de l'histoire de l'église de France* 35: 36–8

(1950), 'L'exemption monastique et les origines de la réforme grégorienne', in *A Cluny. Congrès scientifique. Fêtes et cérémonies liturgiques en l'honneur des saints abbés Odon et Odilon 9-11 juillet 1949*, Dijon, pp. 288–340

(1953), 'Hiérarchie monastique et hiérarchie féodale', *Revue historique de droit français et étranger* 4 S. 31: 171–4

(1957), 'Structures monastiques et structures politiques dans la France de la fin du Xe et des débuts du XIe siècle', in *Il monachesimo nell'alto medioevo e la formazione della civiltà occidentale* (Settimane di studio del Centro italiano di studi sull'alto medioevo 4), Spoleto, pp. 357–400

(1982), 'Encadrement religieux des campagnes et conjoncture politique dans les régions du royaume de France situées au Nord de la Loire, de Charles le Chauve aux derniers Carolingiens (840–987)', in *Christianizzazione ed organizzazione ecclesiastica delle campagne nell'alto medioevo. Espansione e resistenze* (Settimane di studio del Centro italiano di studi sull'alto medioevo 28), Spoleto, II, 765–800

Lemerle, Paul (1967), 'Un aspect du rôle des monastères à Byzance. Les monastères données à des laïcs, les Charisticaires', *Académie des inscriptions et belles-lettres. Comptes rendus 1967*: 9–28

Lenssen, Séraphin (1936–7), 'Saint Robert fondateur de Cîteaux', *Collectanea ordinis Cisterciensium reformatorum* 4: 2–16, 81–96, 161–77, and 241–53

Le Pesant, Michel (1950), 'Notes d'anthroponymie normande. Les noms de personne à Evreux du XIIᵉ au XIVᵉ siècles', *Annales de Normandie* 6: 47–74

Lesne, Emile (1910–43), *Histoire de la propriété ecclésiastique en France* (Mémoires et travaux publiés par des professeurs des facultés catholiques de Lille 6, 19, 30, 34, 44, 46, 50, 53), Lille

(1927), 'Une source de la fortune monastique. Les donations à charge de pension alimentaire du VIIIᵉ au Xᵉ siècle', in *Mélanges de philosophie et d'histoire publiés à l'occasion du cinquantenaire de la faculté des lettres de l'Université catholique de Lille* (Mémoires et travaux publiés par des professeurs des facultés catholiques de Lille 32), Lille, pp. 33–47

Levison, Wilhelm (1918), 'Eine angebliche Urkunde Papst Gelasius II. für die Regular-kanoniker', *Zeitschrift der Savigny-Stiftung für Rechtsgeschichte* 39: *Kanonistische Abteilung* 8: 27–43

Lewald, Ursula (1976), 'Burg, Kloster, Stift', in *Die Burgen im deutschen Sprachraum*, ed. Hans Patze (Vorträge und Forschungen 19), Sigmaringen, I, 155–80

Lewis, Clive S. (1936), *The Allegory of Love*, Oxford

(1967), *Studies in Words*, 2nd edn, Cambridge

Leyser, Henrietta (1984), *Hermits and the New Monasticism: A Study of Religious Communities in Western Europe, 1000–1150*, London

Leyser, Karl J. (1987), 'The Angevin Kings and the Holy Man', in *St Hugh of Lincoln*, ed. Henry Mayr-Harting, Oxford, pp. 49–73

(1988), 'Frederick Barbarossa and the Hohenstaufen Polity', *Viator* 19: 153–76

Lifshitz, Felice (1988), 'The Dossier of Romanus of Rouen: The Political Uses of Hagiographical Texts' (Diss. Columbia)

Lillich, Meredith Parson (1993), 'Recent Scholarship concerning Cistercian Windows', in *Studiosorum speculum: Studies in Honor of Louis J. Lekai, O. Cist.*, ed. Francis Swietek and John Sommerfeldt (Cistercian Studies Series 141), Kalamazoo, pp. 233–62

Littger, Klaus Walter (1975), *Studien zum Auftreten der Heiligennamen in Deutschland* (Münstersche Mittelalter-Schriften 20), Munich

Little, Lester K. (1978), *Religious Poverty and the Profit Economy in Medieval Europe*, Ithaca

Lodolo, Gabriella (1977), 'Il tema simbolico del paradiso nella tradizione monastica dell'occidente latino (secoli VI–XII). Lo spazio del simbolo', *Aevum* 51: 252–88

Lohrmann, Dietrich (1980), 'Le rétablissement du grand domaine à faire-valoir direct en Beauvaisis au XIIᵉ siècle', *Francia* 8: 105–26

(1983a), *Kirchengut im nördlichen Frankreich. Besitz, Verfassung und Wirtschaft im Spiegel der Papstprivilegien des 11.–12. Jahrhunderts* (Pariser historische Studien 20), Bonn

(1983b), 'Die Wirtschaftshöfe der Prämonstratenser im hohen und späten Mittel-alter', in *Die Grundherrschaft im späten Mittelalter*, ed. Hans Patze (Vorträge und Forschungen 27), Sigmaringen, pp. 205–40

Longère, Jean (1982), 'La prédication sur saint Benoît du Xᵉ au XIIIᵉ siècle', in *Sous la règle de saint Benoît. Structures monastiques et sociétés en France du Moyen Age à l'époque moderne. Abbaye bénédictine Sainte-Marie de Paris 23–25 octobre 1980*

(Ecole pratique des haute études IVe section 5: Hautes études médiévales et modernes 47), Geneva and Paris, pp. 433–60

Lot, Ferdinand (1913), *Etudes critiques sur l'abbaye de Saint-Wandrille* (Bibliothèque de l'Ecole des hautes études 204), Paris

Lottin, Odon (1942–60), *Psychologie et morale aux XIIe et XIIIe siècles*, Louvain and Gembloux

(1961), 'Le vœu de "conversatio morum" dans la règle de saint Benoît' (1957), repr. in his *Etudes de morale, histoire et doctrine*, Gembloux, pp. 309–28

Louis, René (1946–7), *De l'histoire à la légende. Girart, comte de Vienne (... 819–877) et ses fondations monastiques*, Auxerre

Lubac, Henri de (1959–64), *Exégèse médiévale. Les quatre sens de l'Ecriture* (Théologie. Etudes publiées sous la direction de la Faculté de théologie S.J. de Lyon-Fourvière 41–2 and 59), Paris

Lucet, Bernard (1954), 'Les ordinations chez les Cisterciens. Témoignage d'Eudes Rigaud (†1275) pour la Normandie', *Analecta sacri ordinis Cisterciensis* 10: 268–301

Luchaire, Achille (1890), *Louis VI le Gros*, Paris

(1899), *Etudes sur quelques manuscrits de Rome et de Paris* (Université de Paris. Bibliothèque de la Faculté des lettres 8), Paris

Lunardi, Giovanni (1970), *L'ideale monastico nelle polemiche del secolo XII sulla vita religiosa*, Noci

Luneau, Auguste (1964), *L'histoire du salut chez les Pères de l'Eglise. La doctrine des âges du monde* (Théologie historique 2), Paris

Luscombe, David S. (1962), 'Aldgate Priory and the Regular Canons in XIIth Century England', in *Vita comune* (1962), II, 86–9

(1988), 'From Paris to the Paraclete: The Correspondence of Abelard and Heloise', *Proceedings of the British Academy* 74: 247–83

(1991), 'Monasticism in the Lives and Sufferings of Heloise and Abelard', in *Monastic Studies II*, ed. Judith Loades, Bangor, pp. 1–11

Lynch, Joseph H. (1973), 'The Cistercians and Underage Novices', *Cîteaux* 24: 283–97

(1975), 'Monastic Recruitment in the Eleventh and Twelfth Centuries: Some Social and Economic Considerations', *American Benedictine Review* 26: 425–47

(1976), *Simoniacal Entry into Religious Life from 1000 to 1260: A Social, Economic, and Legal Study*, Columbus

MacDermot, Violet (1971), *The Cult of the Seer in the Ancient Middle East: A Contribution to Current Research on Hallucinations Drawn from Coptic and Other Texts*, London

MacDonald, Allen J. (1926), *Lanfranc*, Oxford

McDonnell, Ernest W. (1954), *The Beguines and Beghards in Medieval Culture*, New Brunswick

(1955), 'The "Vita apostolica": Diversity or Dissent', *Church History* 24: 15–31

Macfarlane, Alan (1979), *The Origins of English Individualism: The Family, Property and Social Transition*, New York

McGuire, Brian Patrick (1979), 'Written Sources and Cistercian Inspiration in Caesarius of Heisterbach', *Analecta cisterciensia* 35: 227–82

(1983a), 'The Cistercians and the Rise of the Exemplum in Early Thirteenth Century France: A Reevaluation of Paris B.N. MS lat. 15912', *Classica et mediaevalia* 34: 211–67

(1983b), 'A Lost Clairvaux Exemplum Collection Found: The "Liber visionum et miraculorum" Compiled under Prior John of Clairvaux (1171–79)', *Analecta cisterciensia* 39: 26–62

(1988), *Friendship and Community: The Monastic Experience 350–1250* (Cistercian Studies Series 95), Kalamazoo

(1994), *Brother and Lover: Aelred of Rievaulx*, New York

McLaughlin, Eleanor (1975), ' "Christ My Mother": Feminine Naming and Metaphor in Medieval Spirituality', *Nashotah Review* 15: 228–48

McNulty, Patricia, and Hamilton, Bernard (1963), 'Orientale lumen et magistra Latinitas: Greek Influences on Western Monasticism (900–1100)', in *Le millénaire du Mont Athos, 963–1963*, Chevetogne, I, 181–216

Magnou [-Nortier], Elisabeth (1958), *Introduction de la réforme grégorienne à Toulouse (fin XIᵉ – début XIIᵉ siècle)* (Cahiers de l'association Marc Bloch de Toulouse. Etudes d'histoire médiévale 3), Toulouse

(1964), 'Abbés séculiers ou avoués à Moissac au XIᵉ siècle?', in *Moissac et l'occident au XIᵉ siècle. Actes du colloque international de Moissac 3–5 mai 1963*, Toulouse, pp. 123–9

(1974), *La société laïque et l'église dans la province ecclésiastique de Narbonne (zone cispyrénéenne) de la fin du VIIIᵉ à la fin du XIᵉ siècle* (Publications de l'Université de Toulouse–Le Mirail A 20), Toulouse

Magrassi, Mariano (1959), *Teologia e storia nel pensiero di Ruperto di Deutz* (Studia Urbaniana 2), Rome

Mahn, Jean-Berthold (1945), *L'ordre cistercien et son gouvernement des origines au milieu du XIIIᵉ siècle (1098–1265)* (Bibliothèque des Ecoles françaises d'Athènes et de Rome 161), Paris

Maitland, Samuel R. (1890), *The Dark Ages*, 5th edn, ed. Frederick Stokes, London

Maleczek, Werner (1990), 'Abstimmungsarten. Wie kommt man zu einem vernünftigen Wahlergebnis?', in *Wahlen und wählen im Mittelalter*, ed. Reinhard Schneider and Harald Zimmermann (Vorträge und Forschungen 37), Sigmaringen, pp. 79–134

Manteuffel, Tadeucz (1970), *Naissance d'une hérésie. Les adeptes de la pauvreté volontaire au moyen âge*, tr. Anna Posner (Ecole pratique des hautes études, VIᵉ section: Sciences économiques et sociales. Civilisations et sociétés 6), Paris and The Hague

Marca, Pierre de (1708), *De concordia sacerdotii et imperii*, ed. Etienne Baluze, Frankfort

Margue, Michel (1988), 'Aspects politiques de la "Réforme" monastique en Lotharingie. Le cas des abbayes de Saint-Maximin de Trèves, de Stavelot-Malmédy et d'Echternach (934–973)', *Revue bénédictine* 98: 31–61

Marosszéki, Solutor (1952), 'Les origines du chant cistercien', *Analecta cisterciensia* 8: vii–xvi and 1–179

Martène, Edmond (1736–8), *De antiquis ecclesiae ritibus*, Antwerp (IV = *De antiquis monachorum ritibus*, which is cited here with its subdivisions)

Martin, Francis (1972), 'Monastic Community and the Summary Statements in Acts', in *Contemplative Community*, ed. M. Basil Pennington (Cistercian Studies Series 21), Washington, pp. 13–46

Martin, Gabriel (1893–4), 'La Haute-Marche au douzième siècle', *Mémoires de la Société des sciences naturelles et archéologiques de la Creuse* 8 N.S. 3: 47–127

Massini, Rudolf (1946), *Das Bistum Basel zur Zeit des Investiturstreites* (Basler Beiträge zur Rechtswissenschaft 24), Basel

Mattoso, José (1968), *Le monachisme ibérique et Cluny. Les monastères du diocèse de Porto de l'an mille à 1200* (Université de Louvain. Recueil de travaux d'histoire et de philologie 4 S. 39), Louvain

Mayer, Hans Eberhard (1963), 'Die Peterlinger Urkundenfälschungen und die Anfänge von Kloster und Stadt Peterlingen', *Deutsches Archiv* 19: 30–129

Mayer, Theodor (1950), *Fürsten und Staat. Studien zur Verfassungsgeschichte des deutschen Mittelalters*, Weimar

Mayr-Harting, Henry (1975), 'Functions of a Twelfth Century Recluse', *History* 60: 337–52

Medieval Women (1978) = *Medieval Women* (presented to Rosalind M.T. Hill), ed. Derek Baker (Studies in Church History: Subsidia 1), Oxford

Meersseman, Gilles Gerard (1952), 'Die Klerikervereine von Karl dem Grossen bis Innocenz III.', *Zeitschrift für schweizerische Kirchengeschichte* 46: 1–42 and 81–112 (1962), 'Disciplinati e penitenti nel Ducento', in *Il movimento dei disciplinati nel settimo centenario dal suo inizio* (Deputazione di storia patria per l'Umbria. Appendice al *Bollettino* 9), Perugia, pp. 43–72

Mehne, Joachim (1977), 'Cluniacenser-Bischöfe', *Frühmittelalterliche Studien* 11: 241–87

Meichelbeck, Karl (1724–9), *Historia Frisingensis*, Augsburg and Graz

Meiller, Andreas von (1866), *Regesten zur Geschichte des Salzburger Erzbischöfe*, Vienna

Melville, Gert (1978), 'Zur Abgrenzung zwischen "Vita canonica" und "Vita monastica". Das Übertrittsproblem in kanonistischer Behandlung von Gratian bis Hostiensis', in *Secundum Regulam vivere. Festschrift für P. Norbert Backmund, O. Praem.*, ed. Gert Melville, Windberg, pp. 205–43

Merk, C. Josef (1914), *Anschauungen über die Lehre und das Leben der Kirche im altfranzösischen Heldenepos* (Beiheft zur Zeitschrift für romanische Philologie 41), Halle

Metzger, Bruce M. (1991), 'The New Revised Standard Version of the Bible: Its Making and Character', *Proceedings of the American Philosophical Society* 135: 368–81

Meuthen, Erich (1959), *Kirche und Heilsgeschichte bei Gerhoh von Reichersberg* (Studien und Texte zur Geistesgeschichte des Mittelalters 6), Leiden and Cologne

Mews, Constant (1985), 'On Dating the Works of Peter Abelard', *Archives d'histoire doctrinale et littéraire du moyen âge* 60: 73–134

(1991), 'St Anselm and Roscelin: Some New Texts and their Implications, 1. The "De incarnatione verbi" and the "Disputatio inter christianum et gentilem"', *Archives d'histoire doctrinale et littéraire du moyen âge* 66: 55–98

Meyer, Otto (1956), 'Pro regularis ordinis correctione. Ein Saalfelder Äbte-Kapitel im benediktinischen Reformstreben', in *Coburg mitten im Reich*, ed. Friedrich Schilling, Coburg, pp. 238–48

Miccoli, Giovanni (1958), 'Per la storia della pataria milanese', *Bullettino dell'Istituto storico italiano per il medio evo* 70: 43–123 (repr. in Miccoli (1966a), pp. 101–60)

(1960), *Pietro Igneo. Studi sull'età gregoriana* (Istituto storico italiano per il medio evo: Studi storici 40–1), Rome

(1966a), *Chiesa gregoriana. Ricerche sulla riforma del secolo XI* (Storici antichi e moderni N.S. 17), Florence

(1966b), 'Ecclesiae primitivae forma' (1960), revised repr. in Miccoli (1966a), pp. 225–99

Michaud-Quantin, Pierre (1970a), *Universitas. Expressions du mouvement communautaire dans le moyen-âge latin* (L'église et l'état au moyen âge 13), Paris
(1970b), *Etudes sur le vocabulaire philosophique du moyen âge* (Lessico intellettuale Europeo 5), Rome
Miethke, Jürgen (1972), 'Abaelards Stellung zur Kirchenreform. Eine biographische Studie', *Francia* 1: 158–92
Mikkers, Edmond (1958), 'Neuere Literatur über Joachim von Fiore', *Cîteaux in de Nederlanden* 9: 286–97
(1962), 'L'idéal religieux des frères convers dans l'ordre de Cîteaux au 12ᵉ et 13ᵉ siècle', *Collectanea ordinis Cisterciensium reformatorum* 24: 113–29
(1963), 'De vita et operibus Gilberti de Hoylandia', *Cîteaux* 14: 33–43 and 265–79
Milis, Ludo[vicus] (1969), *L'ordre des chanoines réguliers d'Arrouaise. Son histoire et son organisation, de la fondation de l'abbaye-mère (vers 1090) à la fin des chapitres annuels (1471)* (Rijksuniversiteit te Gent. Werken uitgegeven door de faculteit van de letteren en wijsbegeerte 147–8), Bruges
(1979), 'Ermites et chanoines réguliers au XIIᵉ siècle', *Cahiers de civilisation médiévale* 22: 39–80
(1992), *Angelic Monks and Earthly Men: Monasticism and its Meaning to Medieval Society*, Woodbridge
Mohrmann, Christine (1962), 'Le rôle des moines dans la transmission du patrimoine latin', in *Mémorial de l'année martinienne M.DCCCC.LX–M.DCCCC.LXI. Seizième centenaire de l'abbaye de Ligugé. Centenaire de la découverte du tombeau de saint Martin à Tours* (Bibliothèque de la Société d'histoire ecclésiastique de la France = Revue d'histoire de l'église de France 47), Paris, pp. 185–98
Mois, Jakob (1953), *Das Stift Rottenbuch in der Kirchenreform des XI.–XII. Jahrhunderts. Ein Beitrag zur Ordens-Geschichte der Augustiner Chorherren* (Beiträge zur altbayerischen Kirchengeschichte 3 S. 19), Munich
Molinier, Auguste (1890), *Les obituaires français au moyen âge*, Paris
Mollat, Michel (1978), *Les pauvres au moyen âge*, Paris
Moller, Herbert (1971), 'The Social Causation of Affective Mysticism', *Journal of Social History* 4: 305–38
Moltmann, Jürgen (1965), 'Die Kategorie "Novum" in der christlichen Theologie', in *Ernst Bloch zu Ehren*, ed. S. Unseld, Frankfort, pp. 242–63
Monachesimo (1971) = *Il monachesimo e la riforma ecclesiastica (1049–1122). Atti della quarta settimane internazionale di studio, Mendola, 23–29 agosto 1968* (Pubblicazioni dell'Università cattolica del Sacro Cuore, Contributi 3 S.: Varia 7. Miscellanea del Centro di studi medioevali 6), Milan
Montagu, Ashley (1957), *Man: His First Million Years*, New York
Montalembert, Charles [Forbes René de Tryon, comte] de (1896), *The Monks of the West from St Benedict to St Bernard*, London and New York
Monti, Gennaro Maria (1927), *Le confraternite medievali dell'alta e media Italia*, Venice
Moore, Robert I. (1970), 'The Origins of Medieval Heresy', *History* 55: 21–36
(1980), 'Family, Community and Cult on the Eve of the Gregorian Reform', *Transactions of the Royal Historical Society* 5 S. 30: 49–69
(1986), 'New Sects and Secret Meetings: Association and Authority in the Eleventh and Twelfth Centuries', in *Voluntary Religion*, ed. W.J. Sheils and Diana Wood (Studies in Church History 23), Oxford, pp. 47–68

(1987), *The Formation of a Persecuting Society: Power and Deviance in Western Europe, 950–1250*, Oxford

Moos, Peter von (1965), *Hildebert von Lavardin, 1056–1133* (Pariser historischer Studien 3), Stuttgart

(1989a), 'Literatur- und bildungsgeschichtliche Aspekte der Dialogform im lateinischen Mittelalter', in *Tradition und Wertung. Festschrift für Franz Brunhölzl zum 65. Geburtstag*, ed. Günter Berndt, Fidel Rädle, and Gabriel Silagi, Sigmaringen, pp. 165–209

(1989b), 'Le dialogue latin au moyen âge. L'exemple d'Everard d'Ypres', *Annales* 44: 993–1028

Morard, Françoise-E. (1973), 'Monachos, Moine. Histoire du terme grec jusqu'au 4ᵉ siècle', *Freiburger Zeitschrift für Philosophie und Theologie* 20: 332–411

Mordek, Hubert (1983), 'Urban II., St. Blasien und die Anfänge des Basler Klosters St. Alban', *Zeitschrift für die Geschichte des Oberrheins* 131 (N.F. 92): 199–223

Moreau, Edouard de (1909), *L'abbaye de Villers-en-Brabant aux XIIᵉ et XIIIᵉ siècles*, Brussels

(1946–52), *Histoire de l'église en Belgique*, 2nd edn of I–II (Museum lessianum: Section historique 1–3, 11–12, and 15), Brussels

Morice, Hyacinthe (1742–6), *Mémoires pour servir de preuves à l'histoire ecclésiastique et civile de Bretagne*, Paris

Morin, Germain (1893), 'Un écrivain belge ignoré du XIIᵉ siècle. Geoffroi de Bath, ou Geoffroi Babion?', *Revue bénédictine* 10: 28–36

(1928), 'Rainaud l'ermite et Ives de Chartres. Un épisode de la crise du cénobitisme au XIᵉ–XIIᵉ siècle', *Revue bénédictine* 40: 99–115

Morlet, Marie-Thérèse (1967), *Études d'anthroponymie picarde. Les noms de personne en Haute Picardie aux XIIIᵉ, XIVᵉ, XVᵉ siècles* (Collection de la Société de linguistique picarde 6), Paris

Morris, Colin (1972), *The Discovery of the Individual, 1050–1200* (Church History Outlines 5), London

(1980), 'Individualism in Twelfth Century Religion: Some Further Reflections', *Journal of Ecclesiastical History* 31: 195–206

(1989), *The Papal Monarchy: The Western Church from 1050 to 1250*, Oxford

Morrison, Karl F. (1969), *Tradition and Authority in the Western Church, 300–1140*, Princeton

(1992a), *Understanding Conversion*, Charlottesville and London

(1992b), *Conversion and Text: The Cases of Augustine of Hippo, Herman-Judah, and Constantine Tsatsos*, Charlottesville and London

Mortimer, Richard (1978), 'Religious and Secular Motives for Some English Monastic Foundations', in *Religious Motivation: Biographical and Sociological Problems for the Church Historian*, ed. Derek Baker (Studies in Church History 15), Oxford, pp. 77–85

Motta, Giuseppe (1985), 'Monachesimo e società in un dibattito del secolo XII. La risposta dell'abbate di s. Marco al preposito di s. Eufemia di Piacenza', *Aevum* 59: 232–40

Moullet, Maurice (1938), *Die Galluspforte des Basler Münsters* (Ars docta 1), Basel and Leipzig

Mousnier, Roland (1953), 'Saint Bernard et Luther', in *Saint Bernard. Homme de l'église* (Témoignages. Cahiers de la Pierre-qui-Vire 38-9), Paris, pp. 152–69

Moyse, Gérard (1973), 'Les origines du monachisme dans le diocèse de Besançon (V^e– Xe siècles)', *Bibliothèque de l'Ecole des chartes* 131–2: 21–104 and 369–485

Mundy, John H. (1966), 'Charity and Social Work in Toulouse, 1100–1250', *Traditio* 22: 203–87

Munz, Peter (1972), 'The Problem of "Die soziologische Verortung des antiken Gnostizismus" ', *Numen* 19: 41–51

Murray, Alexander (1978), *Reason and Society in the Middle Ages*, Oxford

(1991), *Excommunication and Conscience in the Middle Ages* (John Coffin Memorial Lecture 1991), London

(1993), 'Confession before 1215', *Transactions of the Royal Historical Society* 6 S. 3: 51–81

Murray, A. Victor (1967), *Abelard and St Bernard: A Study in Twelfth Century 'Modernism'*, Manchester and New York

Musset, Lucien (1954), 'Le satiriste Garnier de Rouen et son milieu (début du XIe siècle)', *Revue du moyen âge latin* 10: 237–66

Müssigbrod, Axel (1988), 'Zur Necrologüberlieferung aus cluniacensischen Klostern', *Revue bénédictine* 98: 62–113

Nagel, Peter (1966), *Die Motivierung der Askese in der alten Kirche und der Ursprung des Mönchtums* (Texte und Untersuchungen zur Geschichte der altchristlichen Literatur 95 (5 S. 40)), Berlin

Nahmer, Dieter von der (1972), 'Die Klostergründung "in solitudine" – ein unbrauchbarer hagiographischer Topos?', *Hessisches Jahrbuch für Landesgeschichte* 22: 90–111

Nazet, Jacques (1983), 'Crises et réformes dans les abbayes hainuyères du IXe au début du XIIe siècle', in *Recueil d'études d'histoire hainuyère offertes à Maurice A. Arnould*, ed. Jean-Marie Cauchies and Jean-Marie Duvosquel (Analectes d'histoire de Hainault. Collection publiée par Hannonia sous la direction de Jean-Marie Cauchies et Jean-Marie Duvosquel 1–2), Mons, I, 461–96

Neale, John Mason (1856), *Medieval Preachers and Medieval Preaching*, London

Nelson, Janet L. (1972), 'Society, Theodicy and the Origins of Heresy: Towards a Reassessment of the Medieval Evidence', in *Schism, Heresy and Religious Protest*, ed. Derek Baker (Studies in Church History 9), Cambridge, pp. 65–77

(1992), *Charles the Bald*, London

Newman, William M. (1971), *Les seigneurs de Nesle en Picardie (XIIe–XIIIe siècles). Leurs chartes et leur histoire* (Bibliothèque de la Société d'histoire du droit des pays flamands, picards et wallons 27, and Memoirs of the American Philosophical Society 91.1), Paris and Philadelphia

Nicholl, Donald (1964), *Thurstan, Archbishop of York (1114–1140)*, York

Nobels, A. (1911), 'Le symbolisme liturgique dans les écrits du moyen âge', *Annuaire de l'Université catholique de Louvain* 75: 452–63

Nock, Arthur Darby (1972), *Essays on Religion and the Ancient World*, ed. Zeph Stewart, Oxford

Norton, Christopher, and Park, David (1986), *Cistercian Art and Architecture in the British Isles*, Cambridge

Nothdurft, Klaus-Dieter (1963), *Studien zum Einfluss Senecas auf die Philosophie und Theologie des zwölften Jahrhunderts* (Studien und Texte zur Geistesgeschichte des Mittelalters 7), Leiden and Cologne

Nussbaum, Otto (1961), *Kloster, Priestermönch und Privatmesse. Ihr Verhältnis im Westen von den Anfängen bis zum hohen Mittelalter* (Theophania 14), Bonn

Oberman, Heiko A. (1989), *Luther: Man between God and the Devil*, tr. Eileen Walliser-Schwarzbart, New Haven and London

Oediger, Friedrich Wilhelm (1960), 'Mönche und Pfarrseelsorge im Erzbistum Köln im 11. und 12. Jahrhundert', in *Zur Geschichte und Kunst im Erzbistum Köln. Festschrift für Wilhelm Neuss* (Studien zur Kölner Kirchengeschichte 5), Düsseldorf, pp. 40–7

Oexle, Otto (1978), *Forschungen zu monastischen und geistlichen Gemeinschaften im westfränkischen Bereich* (Münstersche Mittelalter-Schriften 31), Munich

Oliger, Paul Remy (1958), *Les évêques réguliers* (Museum lessianum. Section historique 18), Paris and Louvain

Olsen, Glenn (1969), 'The Idea of the "Ecclesia Primitiva" in the Writings of the Twelfth-Century Canonists', *Traditio* 25: 61–86

——— (1987), 'St Augustine and the Problem of the Medieval Discovery of the Individual', *Word and Spirit* 9: 129–56

Omont, Henri (1894), 'Satire de Garnier de Rouen contre le poète Moriuht (X^e–XIe siècle)', *Annuaire. Bulletin de la Société de l'histoire de France* 31: 193–210

Oppenheim, Philipp (1932), *Symbolik und religiöse Wertung des Mönchskleides im christlichen Altertum, vornehmlich nach Zeugnissen christlicher Schriftsteller der Ostkirche* (Theologie des christlichen Ostens. Texte und Untersuchungen 2), Münster i. W.

Osheim, Duane J. (1989), *A Tuscan Monastery and its Social World: San Michele of Guamo (1156–1348)* (Italia sacra 40), Rome

Ott, André G. (1899), *Etude sur les couleurs en vieux français*, Paris

Otto, Stephan (1963), *Die Funktion des Bildbegriffes in der Theologie des 12. Jahrhunderts* (Beiträge zur Geschichte der Philosophie und Theologie des Mittelalters 40.1), Münster i. W.

Oudart, Hervé (1988), 'L'érémitisme dans les actes de la pratique au diocèse de Bourges (XIe–XIIe siècles)', *Revue Mabillon* 61: 375–95

Oulmont, Charles (1911), *Les débats du clerc et du chevalier*, Paris

Oursel, Charles (1926), *La miniature du XIIe siècle à l'abbaye de Cîteaux d'après les manuscrits de la bibliothèque de Dijon*, Dijon

Oury, Guy-Marie (1975), 'La vie contemplative menée en communauté d'après Geoffroi Babion (†1158?)', in *Etudes ligériennes d'histoire et d'archéologie médiévales*, ed. René Louis, Auxerre, pp. 297–305

Pächt, Otto, Dodwell, Charles R., and Wormald, Francis (1960), *The St Albans Psalter* (Studies of the Warburg Institute 25), London

Panofsky, Erwin (1946), *Abbot Suger on the Abbey Church of St.-Denis and its Art Treasures*, Princeton

——— (1957), 'In Defense of the Ivory Tower', *Centennial Review of Arts and Science* 1: 111–22

Pantin, William A. (1976), 'Instructions for a Devout and Literate Layman', in *Medieval Learning and Literature: Essays Presented to Richard William Hunt*, ed. Jonathan J.G. Alexander and Margaret T. Gibson, Oxford, pp. 398–422

Parisse, Michel (1968), 'Les chanoines réguliers en Lorraine. Fondations, expansion (XIᵉ–XIIᵉ siècles)', *Annales de l'Est* 5 S. 20, 347–88

(1983), *Les nonnes au moyen âge*, Paris

(1989), 'Noblesse et monastères en Lotharingie du XIᵉ au XIIᵉ siècles', in *Monastische Reformen im 9. und 10. Jahrhundert*, ed. Raymund Kottje and Helmut Maurer (Vorträge und Forschungen 38), Sigmaringen, pp. 167–96

(1991), 'Les monastères de femmes en Saxe Xᵉ–XIIᵉ siècles', *Revue Mabillon* N.S. 2: 5–48

Passerini, Luigi (1876–7), 'Una monaca del duodecimo secolo', *Archivio storico italiano* 3 S. 23: 61–79, 205–17, 385–403, and 24: 3–4

Pauly, Ferdinand (1958), 'Die Consuetudines von Springiersbach', *Trierer theologische Zeitschrift* 67: 106–11

(1962), *Springiersbach. Geschichte des Kanonikerstifts und seiner Tochtergründungen im Erzbistum Trier, von den Anfängen bis zum Ende des 18. Jahrhunderts* (Trierer theologische Studien 13), Trier

Paxton, Frederick S. (1985), 'A Canonical Dossier on Monastic Rights in Leipzig Universitäts-Bibliothek MS 276', *Bulletin of Medieval Canon Law* N.S. 15: 1–17

Peltier, Henri (1946), 'Hugues de Fouilloy, chanoine régulier, prieur de Saint-Laurent-au-Bois', *Revue du moyen âge latin* 2: 25–44

Penco, Gregorio (1960), 'Monasterium – Carcer', *Studia monastica* 8: 133–43

(1963), 'Il ricordo dell'ascetismo orientale nella tradizione monastica del medio evo europeo', *Studi medievali* 3 S. 4: 571–87

(1969), 'Il senso della natura nell'agiografia monastica occidentale', *Studia monastica* 11: 327–34

(1985), 'L'eremitismo irregolare in Italia nei secoli XI–XII', *Benedictina* 32: 201–21

Perry, Ralph Barton (1935), *The Thought and Character of William James*, Boston

Peters, Edward (1986), 'Restoring the Church and Restoring Churches: Event and Image in Franciscan Biography', *Franziskanische Studien* 69: 215–36

Petit, François (1934), *Ad viros religiosos. Quatorze sermons d'Adam Scot*, Tongerloo

(1939), 'Les vêtements des Prémontrés au XIIᵉ siècle', *Analecta praemonstratensia* 15: 17–24

Petot, Pierre (1954), 'Servage et tonsure cléricale dans la pratique française au moyen âge', *Revue d'histoire de l'église de France* 40: 193–205

Petré, Hélène (1936), ' "Haeresis", "schisma", et leurs synonymes latins', *Revue des études latines* 14: 316–25

(1948), *Caritas. Etude sur le vocabulaire latin de la charité chrétienne* (Spicilegium sacrum Lovaniense. Etudes et documents 22), Louvain

Petrus Venerabilis (1956) = *Petrus Venerabilis 1156–1956: Studies and Texts Commemorating the Eighth Centenary of his Death*, ed. Giles Constable and James Kritzeck (Studia Anselmiana 40), Rome

Pfaff, Richard W. (1989), ' "De cella in seculum": The Liturgical Aspects', in *'De cella in seculum': Religious and Secular Life and Devotion in Late Medieval England (St Hugh of Avalon 8th Centenary Conference. Lincoln 1986)*, ed. Michael G. Sargent, Cambridge and Wolfeboro, pp. 17–27

Pflüger, Helmut (1958), 'Die Zisterzienser und die Vogteifrage', *Zeitschrift für württembergische Landesgeschichte* 17: 223–80

Pfurtscheller, Friedrich (1972), *Die Privilegierung des Zisterzienserorderns im Rahmen der allgemeinen Schutz- und Exemtionsgeschichte vom Anfang bis zur Bulle 'Parvus Fons' (1265). Ein Überblick unter besonderer Berücksichtigung von Schreibers 'Kurie und Kloster im 12. Jahrhundert'* (Europäische Hochschulschriften XXIII,13), Frankfurt

Piazzoni, Ambrogio M. (1988), *Guglielmo di Saint-Thierry. Il declino dell'ideale monastico nel secolo XII* (Istituto storico italiano per il medio evo: Studi storici 181–3), Rome

Picasso, Giorgio (1993), 'Ancora un florilegio patristico sulle prerogative dei monaci (Firenze, Riccardiana 3006, ff. 203^v – 205^v)', in *Nobiltà e chiese nel medioevo e altri saggi. Scritti in onore di Gerd G. Tellenbach*, ed. Cinzio Violante, Rome, pp. 223–32

Pierre Abélard – Pierre le Vénérable (1975) = *Pierre Abélard – Pierre le Vénérable. Les Courants philosophiques, littéraires et artistiques en occident au milieu du XIIe siècle. Abbaye de Cluny, 2 au 9 juillet 1972* (Colloques internationaux du Centre nationale de la recherche scientifique 546), Paris 1975

Pigeon, Emile Auber (1892–8), *Vies des saints du diocèse de Coutances et Avranches*, Avranches

Pinard de la Boullaye, Henri (1950), 'Aux sources des "Exercices". Guillaume de Saint-Thierry et Vincent Ferrer', *Revue d'ascétique et de mystique* 26: 327–46

Piolin, Paul-L. (1879–80), 'Note sur la réclusion religieuse', *Bulletin monumental* 45: 449–80 and 46: 518–50

Pivec, Karl (1939), 'Stil- und Sprachentwicklung in mittelalterlichen Briefen vom 8.–12. Jh.', *Mitteilungen des österreichischen Instituts für Geschichtsforschung: Ergänzungsband* 14: 33–51

Place, François de (1984), 'Bibliographie raisonnée des premiers documents cisterciens (1098–1200)', *Cîteaux* 35: 7–54

Plandé, Romain (1932), 'Géographie et monachisme. Sites et importance géographique de quelques abbayes de la région de l'Aude', in *Mélanges Albert Dufourcq*, Paris, pp. 21–35

Platt, Colin (1969), *The Monastic Grange in Medieval England*, London, Melbourne, and Toronto

Poeck, Dietrich (1981), 'Laienbegräbnisse in Cluny', *Frühmittelalterliche Studien* 15: 68–179

Poirier-Coutansais, Françoise (1974), *Les abbayes bénédictines du diocèse de Reims* (Gallia monastica, ed. Jean-François Lemarignier, 1), Paris

Pollock, Frederick, and Maitland, Frederic W. (1898), *The History of English Law before the Time of Edward I*, 2nd edn, Cambridge

Post, Regnerus R. (1968), *The Modern Devotion: Confrontation with Reformation and Humanism* (Studies in Medieval and Reformation Thought 3), Leiden

Postles, David (1993), 'The Austin Canons in English Towns, c. 1100–1350', *Historical Research* 66: 1–20

Potts, Timothy C. (1980), *Conscience in Medieval Philosophy*, Cambridge

Principe, Walter (1983), 'Toward Defining Spirituality', *Studies in Religion* 12: 127–41

Prinz, Friedrich (1965), *Frühes Mönchtum im Frankenreich. Kultur und Gesellschaft in Gallien, den Rheinlanden und Bayern am Beispiel der monastischen Entwicklung (4. bis 8. Jahrhundert)*, Munich and Vienna

(1974), 'Topos und Realität in hagiographischen Quellen', *Zeitschrift für bayerische Landesgeschichte* 37: 162–6

Proceedings (1963) = *Proceedings of the Conference on the Climate of the Eleventh and Sixteenth Centuries. Aspen, Colorado, June 16–24, 1962*, Boulder

Prosdocimi, Luigi (1965a), 'Chierici e laici nella società occidentale del secolo XII: A proposito di Decr. Grat. C.12 q.1 c.7: "Duo sunt genera Christianorum" ', in *Proceedings of the Second International Congress of Medieval Canon Law* (Monumenta iuris canonici C: Subsidia 1), Vatican City, pp. 105–22

(1965b), 'Unità e dualità del popolo cristiano in Stefano di Tournai e in Ugo di S. Vittore: "Duo populi" e "Duae vitae" ', in *Etudes d'histoire du droit canonique dédiées à Gabriel Le Bras*, Paris, I, 673–80

Quacquarelli, Antonio (1953), *Il triplice frutto della vita cristiana: 100, 60 e 30 (Matteo XIII–8, nelle diverse interpretazioni)*, Rome (repr. 1989)

Quilici, Brunetto (1941–2), 'Giovanni Gualberto e la sua riforma monastica', *Archivio storico italiano* (1) 378: 113–32, (2) 379–80: 27–62, and (3) 381–2: 45–99

Rambaud-Buhot, *see* Buhot

Redonet y López Dóriga, Luis (1919), *El trabajo manual en las reglas monásticas*, Madrid

Reeves, Marjorie (1958), 'Joachimist Expectations in the Order of Augustinian Hermits', *Recherches de théologie ancienne et médiévale* 25: 111–41

(1961), 'The Abbot Joachim and the Society of Jesus', *Medieval and Renaissance Studies* 5: 163–81 (repr. in West (1975), pp. 209–27)

Reimann, Norbert (1991), 'Die Konstitutionen des Abtes Wilhelm von Hirsau', in *Hirsau. St. Peter und Paul 1091–1991. Geschichte, Lebens- und Verfassungsformen eines Reformklosters*, ed. Klaus Schreiner (Landesdenkmalamt Baden-Württemberg. Forschungen und Berichte der Archäologie des Mittelalters in Baden-Württemberg 10.2), Stuttgart, pp. 101–8

Reinke, Arnold (1937), *Die Schuldialektik im Investiturstreit* (Forschungen zur Kirchen- und Geistesgeschichte 11), Stuttgart

Renaissance and Renewal (1982) = *Renaissance and Renewal in the Twelfth Century*, ed. Robert L. Benson and Giles Constable with Carol D. Lanham, Cambridge, Mass.

Renaudet, Augustin (1916), *Préréforme et humanisme à Paris pendant les premières guerres d'Italie (1494–1517)* (Bibliothèque de l'Institut français de Florence I,6), Paris

Resnick, Irven M. (1988a), 'Peter Damian on Cluny, Liturgy, and Penance', *Studia liturgica* 18: 170–87

(1988b), 'Odo of Tournai and Peter Damian: Poverty and Crisis in the Eleventh Century', *Revue bénédictine* 98: 114–40

Reuter, Timothy (1976), 'Das Edikt Friedrich Barbarossas gegen die Zisterzienser', *Mitteilungen des Instituts für österreichische Geschichtsforschung* 84: 328–36

Reynolds, Leighton D. (1965), *The Medieval Tradition of Seneca's Letters*, Oxford

Reynolds, Roger E. (1968), ' "Virgines subintroductae" in Celtic Christianity', *Harvard Theological Review* 61: 547–66

(1978), *The Ordinals of Christ from their Origins to the Twelfth Century* (Beiträge zur Geschichte und Quellenkunde des Mittelalters 7), Berlin and New York

(1984), 'Odilo and the "Treuga Dei" in Southern Italy: A Beneventan Manuscript Fragment', *Mediaeval Studies* 46: 450–62

Reynolds, Susan (1994), *Fiefs and Vassals: The Medieval Evidence Reinterpreted*, Oxford

Richard, Jean (1954), *Les ducs de Bourgogne et la formation du duché du XIe au XIVe siècle* (Publications de l'Université de Dijon 12), Paris (repr. 1986)

Riedlinger, Helmut (1958), *Die Makellosigkeit der Kirche in den lateinischen Hohelied-kommentaren des Mittelalters* (Beiträge zur Geschichte des Philosophie und Theo-logie des Mittelalters 38.3), Münster i. W.

Riesman, David (1964), *Abundance for What? and Other Essays*, Garden City

Robinson, Ian Stuart (1978), *Authority and Resistance in the Investiture Contest: The Polemical Literature of the Late Eleventh Century*, Manchester and New York

Roby, Douglass (1971), 'Stabilitas and Transitus' (Diss. Yale)

Rochais, Henri-Marie (1962), *Enquête sur les sermons divers et les sentences de saint Bernard* (Analecta sacri ordinis Cisterciensis 18.3–4), Rome

Rochais, Henri-Marie, and Binont, R.M. Irène (1964), 'La collection de textes divers du manuscrit Lincoln 201 et saint Bernard', *Sacris erudiri* 15: 15–219

Roisin, Simone (1943), 'L'efflorescence cistercienne et le courant féminin du piété au XIIIe siècle', *Revue d'histoire ecclésiastique* 39: 342–78

—— (1947), *L'hagiographie cistercienne dans le diocèse de Liège au XIIIe siècle* (Université de Louvain. Recueil de travaux d'histoire et de philologie 3 S. 27), Louvain and Brussels

Ronquist, Eyvind C. (1990), 'Learning and Teaching in Twelfth Century Dialogue', *Res publica litterarum* 13: 239–56

Rordorf, Willy (1995), 'The Gestures during Prayer according to Tertullian, "De ora-tione" 11–30, and Origen, "Perì euchês" 31–32', *Liturgy OCSO* 29: 87–99

Rouche, Michel (1979), 'Saint Anselme et la spiritualité érémitique de l'action', in *Saint Anthelme, chartreux et évêque de Belley*, ed. L. Trenard (N° spécial du *Bugey*), Belley, pp. 325–33

Rouse, Richard H., and Rouse, Mary A. (1979), *Preachers, Florilegia, and Sermons: Studies on the 'Manipulus florum' of Thomas of Ireland* ([Pontifical Institute of Mediaeval Studies] Studies and Texts 47), Toronto

Rousseau, Olivier (1957), *Monachisme et vie religieuse d'après l'ancienne tradition de l'Eg-lise* (Irénikon N.S. 7), Chevetogne

Rousselot, Pierre (1908), *Pour l'histoire du problème de l'amour au moyen âge* (Beiträge zur Geschichte der Philosophie des Mittelalters 6.6), Münster i. W.

Rousset, Paul (1961), 'L'homme en face de la nature à l'époque romane', in *Mélanges offerts à M. Paul-E. Martin* (Mémoires et documents publiés par la Société d'his-toire et d'archéologie de Genève 40), Geneva, pp. 39–48

Rudolph, Conrad (1990), *The 'Things of Greater Importance': Bernard of Clairvaux's 'Apologia' and the Medieval Attitude toward Art*, Philadelphia

Russell, Josiah C. (1944), 'The Clerical Population of Medieval England', *Traditio* 2: 177–212

Ruthven, Malise (1988), 'Rapture and the American Right', *Times Literary Supplement* 1988: 110 and 120

Ruyffelaere, Peter (1986), 'Les "historiae fundationum monasteriorum" et leurs sources orales au XIIe siècle', *Sacris erudiri* 29: 223–47

Ryan, Patrick (1974), 'The Influence of Seneca on William of St Thierry', *Cîteaux* 25: 24–32

Salmon, Pierre (1947), 'Le silence religieux. Pratique et théorie', in *Mélanges bénédic-tines publiés à l'occasion du XIVe centenaire de la mort de Saint Benoît par les moines de l'abbaye de Saint-Jérôme de Rome*, Abbaye S Wandrille, pp. 13–57

(1954), 'L'ascèse monastique et les origines de Cîteaux', in *Mélanges saint Bernard* (XXIVᵉ Congrès de l'Association bourguignonne des sociétés savantes), Dijon, pp. 268–83

(1955), *Etude sur les insignes du pontife dans le rite romain. Histoire et liturgie*, Rome

Saltman, Avrom (1988), 'Hermann's "Opusculum de conversione sua": Truth or Fiction?', *Revue des études juives* 147: 31–56

Sansterre, Jean-Marie (1983), *Les moines grecs et orientaux à Rome aux époques byzantine et carolingienne (milieu du VIᵉ s. – fin du IXᵉ s.)* (Académie royale de Belgique: Mémoires de la classe des lettres, Collection in-8° 2 S. 66.1), Brussels

Sauvel, Tony (1956), 'Les miracles de Saint-Martin. Recherches sur les peintures murales de Tours au Vᵉ et au VIᵉ siècle', *Bulletin monumental* 114: 153–79

Saxer, Victor (1959), *Le culte de Marie Madeleine en occident des origines à la fin du moyen âge* (Cahiers d'archéologie et d'histoire 3), Auxerre and Paris

Schaefer, Karl Heinrich (1903), *Pfarrkirche und Stift im deutschen Mittelalter* (Kirchenrechtliche Abhandlungen 3), Stuttgart

Schapiro, Meyer (1964), *The Parma Ildefonsus: A Romanesque Illuminated Manuscript from Cluny and Related Works* (Monographs on Archeology and Fine Arts 11), New York

(1977), 'On the Aesthetic Attitude in Romanesque Art' (1947), repr. in his *Selected Papers* [I]: *Romanesque Art*, New York, pp. 1–27

Schauwecker, Helga (1964), *Otloh von St Emmeram*, Munich

Schelb, Bernard (1941), 'Inklusen am Oberrhein', *Freiburger Diözesanarchiv* 68: 147–253

Schenk, David (1984), 'Couches culturelles du "Moniage Guillaume": "bellatores, oratores" ', in *Essor et fortune de la chanson de geste dans l'Europe et l'Orient latin. Actes du IXᵉ Congrès international de la Société Rencesvals pour l'étude des épopées romanes. Padoue-Venise, 29 août – 4 septembre 1982*, Modena, pp. 169–77

Schieffer, Rudolf (1988), 'Consuetudines monasticae und Reformforschung', *Deutsches Archiv* 44: 161–9

Schlesinger, Walter (1962), *Kirchengeschichte Sachsens im Mittelalter* (Mitteldeutsche Forschungen 27), Cologne and Graz

Schmale, Franz-Josef (1959), 'Kanonie, Seelsorge, Eigenkirche', *Historisches Jahrbuch* 78: 38–63

Schmeidler, Bernhard (1927), 'Anti-asketische Äusserungen aus Deutschland im 11. und beginnenden 12. Jahrhundert', in *Kultur und Universalgeschichte (Festschrift Walter Goetz)* Leipzig and Berlin, pp. 35–52

Schmid, Karl (1970), 'Die Mönchsgemeinschaft von Fulda als sozialgeschichtliches Problem', *Frühmittelalterliche Studien* 4: 173–200

Schmidt, Peter L. (1976), 'Zur Typologie und Literarisierung des frühchristlichen lateinischen Dialogs', in *Christianisme et formes littéraires de l'antiquité tardive en occident* (Entretiens sur l'antiquité classique, ed. Olivier Reverdin 23), Geneva, pp. 101–80

Schmitz, Philibert (1948–56), *Histoire de l'ordre de Saint-Benoît*, 2nd edn of I–II, Maredsous

Schneider, Bruno (1960–1), 'Cîteaux und die benediktinische Tradition', *Analecta cisterciensia* 16: 169–254 and 17: 73–114

(1965), 'Eine zeitgenössische Kritik zu Janauscheks "Originum Cisterciensium tomus I" ', *Analecta cisterciensia* 21: 259–83

Schneider, Rudolf (1928), *Der Mönch in der englischen Dichtung bis auf Lewis's 'Monk' 1795* (Palaestra 155), Leipzig

Schreiber, Georg (1910), *Kurie und Kloster im 12. Jahrhundert. Studien zur Privilegierung, Verfassung und besonders zum Eigenkirchenwesen des vorfranziskanischen Orden vornehmlich auf Grund der Papsturkunden von Paschalis II. bis auf Lucius III. (1099–1181)* (Kirchenrechtliche Abhandlungen 65–8), Stuttgart

(1940), 'Prämonstratensische Frömmigkeit und die Anfänge des Herz-Jesu-Gedankens', *Zeitschrift für katholische Theologie* 64: 181–201

(1940–1), 'Praemonstratenserkultur des 12. Jahrhunderts', *Analecta praemonstratensia* 16: 41–108 and 17: 5–33

(1941), 'Mittelalterliche Passionsmystik und Frömmigkeit. Der älteste Herz-Jesu Hymnus', *Theologische Quartalschrift* 122: 32–44 and 107–23

(1942), 'Studien über Anselm von Havelberg zur Geistesgeschichte des Hochmittelalters', *Analecta praemonstratensia* 18: 5–90

(1948a), *Gemeinschaften des Mittelalters. Recht und Verfassung. Kult und Frömmigkeit* (Gesammelte Abhandlungen 1), Münster i. W.

(1948b), 'Gregor VII., Cluny, Cîteaux, Prémontré zu Eigenkirche, Parochie, Seelsorge', in Schreiber (1948a), pp. 283–370

(1948c), 'Studien zur Exemtionsgeschichte der Zisterzienser' (1914), repr. in Schreiber (1948a), pp. 371–96

(1954–5), 'Christlicher Orient und mittelalterliches Abendland. Verbindungslinien und Forschungsaufgaben', *Oriens christianus* 38: 96–112 and 39: 66–78

Schreiner, Klaus (1964), *Sozial- und standesgeschichtliche Untersuchungen zu den Benediktinerkonventen im östlichen Schwarzwald* (Veröffentlichungen der Kommission für geschichtliche Landeskunde in Baden-Württemberg B 31), Stuttgart

(1966), 'Zum Wahrheitsverständnis im Heiligen- und Reliquienwesen des Mittelalters', *Saeculum* 17: 131–69

(1987), 'Hirsau, Urban II. und Johannes Trithemius. Ein gefälschtes Papstprivileg als Quelle für das Geschichts-, Reform- und Rechtsbewusstsein des Klosters Hirsau im 12. Jahrhundert', *Deutsches Archiv* 43: 469–530

(1992), 'Dauer, Niedergang und Erneuerung klösterlicher Observanz im hoch- und spätmittelalterlichen Mönchtum', in *Institutionen und Geschichte*, ed. Gert Melville (Norm und Struktur 1), Cologne, Weimar, and Vienna, pp. 295–341

Schroll, Mary Alfred (1941), *Benedictine Monasticism as Reflected in the Warnefrid–Hildemar Commentaries on the Rule*, New York

Schwarz, Marianne (1957), 'Heiligsprechungen im 12. Jahrhundert und die Beweggründe ihrer Urheber', *Archiv für Kulturgeschichte* 39: 43–62

Schwarzmaier, Hansmartin (1968), 'Der "Liber vitae" von Subiaco. Die Klöster Farfa und Subiaco in ihrer geistigen und politischen Umwelt während der letzten Jahrzehnte des 11. Jahrhunderts', *Quellen und Forschungen aus italienischen Archiven und Bibliotheken* 48: 80–147

Séguy, Jean (1971), 'Une sociologie des sociétés imaginées. Monachisme et utopie', *Annales* 26:328–54

Semmler, Josef (1956), 'Das Stift Frankenthal in der Kanonikerreform des 12. Jahrhunderts', *Blätter für pfälzische Kirchengeschichte und religiöse Volkskunde* 23: 101–13

(1959), *Die Klosterreform von Siegburg. Ihre Ausbreitung und ihr Reformprogramm im 11. und 12. Jahrhundert* (Rheinisches Archiv 53), Bonn

(1959–61), 'Klosterreform und gregorianische Reform. Die Chorherrenstifter Marbach und Hördt im Investiturstreit', *Studi gregoriani* 6: 165–72

Senn, Félix (1903), *L'institution des avoueries ecclésiastiques en France*, Paris

Serbat, Louis (1912), 'Inscriptions funéraires de recluses à l'abbaye de Saint-Amand (Nord)', *Mémoires de la Société nationale des antiquaires de France* 71 (8 S. 1): 193–224

Shorter, Edward (1973), 'Female Emancipation, Birth Control, and Fertility in European History', *American Historical Review* 78: 605–40

Siegwart, Josef (1965), *Die Consuetudines des Augustiner-Chorherrenstiftes Marbach im Elsass* (Spicilegium Friburgense 10), Fribourg

(1967) 'Der gallo-fränkische Kanonikerbegriff', *Zeitschrift für schweizerische Kirchengeschichte* 61: 193–244

Silvestre, Hubert (1968), 'Notes sur la controverse de Rupert de Saint-Laurent avec Anselme de Laon et Guillaume de Champeaux', in *Saint-Laurent-de-Liège*, ed. Rita Lejeune, Liège, pp. 63–80

(1985), 'L'idylle d'Abélard et Héloïse. La part du roman', *Académie royale de Belgique: Bulletin de la classe des lettres et des sciences morales et politiques* 5 S. 71: 157–200

Simonin, Servan (1961), 'Le culte eucharistique à Cluny de saint Odon à Pierre le Vénérable', *Centre international d'études romanes. Bulletin trimestriel*, 1961.1, pp. 3–13

Simons, Walter (1980), 'Deux témoins du mouvement canonial au XIIᵉ siècle. Les prieurés de Saint-Laurent-au-Bois et Saint-Nicolas de Regny et leurs démêlés avec l'abbaye de Corbie', *Sacris erudiri* 24: 203–44

(1989), 'The Beguine Movement in the Southern Low Countries: A Reassessment', *Bulletin de l'Institut historique belge de Rome* 59: 63–105

Smalley, Beryl (1952), *The Study of the Bible in the Middle Ages*, 2nd edn, Oxford and New York

(1966), 'A Pseudo-Sibylline Prophecy in the Early Twelfth Century in the "Life" of Altmann of Passau', in *Mélanges offerts à René Crozet*, ed. Pierre Gallais and Yves-Jean Riou, Poitier, I, 655–61

(1975), 'Ecclesiastical Attitudes to Novelty, c. 1100 – c. 1250', in *Church, Society and Politics*, ed. Derek Baker (Studies in Church History 12), Oxford, pp. 113–31

(1979), 'Peter Comestor on the Gospels and his Sources', *Recherches de théologie ancienne et médiévale* 46: 84–129

Smith, Constance (1969), 'Aelred's Immersion', *Harvard Theological Review* 62: 429

Smith, Jacqueline (1978), 'Robert of Arbrissel: "Procurator mulierum" ', in *Medieval Women* (1978), pp. 175–84

Smith, Julia M.H. (1985), 'Celtic Asceticism and Carolingian Authority in Early Medieval Brittany', in *Monks, Hermits and the Ascetic Tradition*, ed. W.J. Sheils (Studies in Church History 22), Oxford, pp. 53–63

Smith, Wilfred Cantwell (1979), *Faith and Belief*, Princeton

(1983), 'The Modern West in the History of Religion', *Journal of the American Academy of Religion* 52: 3–18

Sokolowski, Robert (1978–9), 'Making Distinctions', *Review of Metaphysics* 32: 639–76

Soldani, Fidele (1741), *Historia monasterii S. Michaelis de Passiniano*, I, Lucca

Somerville, Robert (1976), 'Pope Innocent II and the Study of Roman Law', *Revue des études islamiques* 46: 105–14

(1981–2) 'Luther, Erasmus, and the Thunderstorm of 1505', *Union Seminary Quarterly Review* 37: 77–90

Southern, Richard William (1963), *Saint Anselm and his Biographer: A Study of Monastic Life and Thought, 1059. – c. 1130*, Cambridge

(1970a), *Medieval Humanism and Other Studies*, Oxford

(1970b), *Western Society and the Church in the Middle Ages* (Pelican History of the Church 2), Harmondsworth

(1970–3), 'Aspects of the European Tradition of Historical Writing', *Transactions of the Royal Historical Society* 5 S. (1) 20: 173–90, (2) 21: 159–79, (3) 22: 159–180, and (4) 23: 243–63

(1986), *Robert Grosseteste: The Growth of an English Mind in Medieval Europe*, Oxford

(1995), *Scholastic Humanism and the Unification of Europe*, I. *Foundations*, Oxford

Spahr, Kolumban (1955), 'Die Anfänge von Cîteaux', in *Bernhard von Clairvaux, Mönch und Mystiker. Internationaler Bernhard-Kongress Mainz 1953*, ed. Joseph Lortz (Veröffentlichungen des Instituts für europäische Geschichte Mainz 6), Wiesbaden, pp. 215–24

(1966), 'Zum Freundschaftsbündnis zwischen Cisterciensern und Prämonstratensern', *Cistercienser Chronik* 73: 10–17

Spätling, Luchesius (1947), *De apostolicis, pseudoapostolicis, apostolinis* (Pontificium athenaeum Antonianum: Facultas theologica. Theses ad lauream 35), Munich

Spiritualità (1987) = *La spiritualità medievale: metodi, bilanci, prospettive* (= *Studi medievali* 3 S. 28.1), Spoleto

Spitzer, Alan B. (1973), 'The Historical Problem of Generations', *American Historical Review* 78: 1353–85

Sprandel, Rolf (1962), *Ivo von Chartres und seine Stellung in der Kirchengeschichte* (Pariser historische Studien 1), Stuttgart

Stange, Carl (1954), *Bernhard von Clairvaux* (Studien der Luther-Akademie N.F. 3), Berlin

Starn, Randolph (1971), 'Historians and "Crisis"', *Past and Present* 52: 3–22

Steidle, Basilius (1938), 'Die Tränen, ein mystisches Problem im alten Mönchtum', *Benediktinische Monatschrift* 20: 181–7

Stengel, Edmund Ernst (1910), *Die Immunität in Deutschland bis zum Ende des 11. Jahrhunderts*, I. *Diplomatik der deutschen Immunitäts-Privilegien vom 9. bis zum Ende des 11. Jahrhunderts*, Innsbruck

Stenton, Frank M. (1920), *Documents Illustrative of the Social and Economic History of the Danelaw* (British Academy: Records of the Social and Economic History of England and Wales 5), London

(1961), *The First Century of English Feudalism 1066–1166* (Ford Lectures 1929), 2nd edn, Oxford

Stiegman, Emero (1988), 'Analogues of the Cistercian Abbey Church', in *The Medieval Monastery*, ed. Andrew MacLeish (Medieval Studies at Minnesota 2), St Cloud

Stiennon, Jacques (1951), *Etude sur le chartrier et le domaine de l'abbaye de Saint-Jacques de Liège (1015–1209)* (Bibliothèque de la Faculté de philosophie et lettres de l'Université de Liège 124), Paris

(1955), 'Cluny et Saint Trond au XII⁰ s.', in *Anciens pays et assemblées d'états. Etudes publiées par la Section belge de la Commission internationale pour l'histoire des assemblées d'états*, VIII, Louvain, pp. 55–86

(1968), 'La Vierge de dom Rupert', in *Saint-Laurent de Liège*, ed. Rita Lejeune, Liège, pp. 81–92

Stock, Brian (1972), *Myth and Science in the Twelfth Century: A Study of Bernard Silvester*, Princeton

(1975), 'Experience, Praxis, Work and Planning in Bernard of Clairvaux: Observations on the "Sermones in Cantica"', in *The Cultural Context of Medieval Learning*, ed. John E. Murdoch and Edith D. Sylla, Dordrecht, pp. 219–62

(1983), *The Implications of Literacy*, Princeton

Storm, Joseph (1926), *Untersuchungen zum 'Dialogus duorum monachorum Cluniacensis et Cisterciensis'. Ein Beitrag zur Ordensgeschichte des 12. Jahrhunderts*, Bocholt

Störmer, Wilhelm (1973), *Früher Adel. Studien zur politischen Führungsschicht im fränkisch-deutschen Reich vom 8. bis 11. Jahrhundert* (Monographien zur Geschichte des Mittelalters 6.1–2), Stuttgart

Strachey, Lytton (1980), 'Militarism and Theology' (1918), repr. in *The Shorter Strachey*, ed. Michael Holroyd and Paul Levy, Oxford and New York, pp. 45–8

Stratford, Neil (1981), 'A Romanesque Marble Altar-Frontal in Beaune and Some Cîteaux Manuscripts', in *The Vanishing Past: Studies in Medieval Art, Liturgy, and Metrology, Presented to Christopher Hohler*, ed. Alan Borg and Andrew Martindale, Oxford, pp. 223–39

Strathern, Marilyn (1988), *The Gender of the Gift: Problems with Women and Problems with Society in Melanesia*, Berkeley, Los Angeles, and London

Stuckert, Howard (1923), *Corrodies in the English Monasteries: A Study in English Social History of the Middle Ages*, Philadelphia

Suttor, Marc (1985), 'Le "Triumphus sancti Lamberti de castro Bullonio" et le catharisme à Liège au milieu du XII⁰ siècle', *Le Moyen Age* 91 (4 S. 40): 227–64

Świechowski, Zygmunt, and Zachwatowicz, Jan (1958), 'L'architecture cistercienne en Pologne et ses liens avec la France', *Biuletyn Historii Sztuki* 20: 139–73

Swietek, Francis R., and Deneen, T.M. (1983), 'Pope Lucius II and Savigny', *Analecta cisterciensia* 39: 3–25

Symonds, John Addington (1875), *Renaissance in Italy: The Age of the Despots*, London

Szövérffy, Joseph (1979), ' "False" Use of "Unfitting" Hymns: Some Ideas Shared by Peter the Venerable, Peter Abelard and Héloïse', *Revue bénédictine* 89: 187–99

(1992–5), *Secular Latin Lyrics and Minor Poetic Forms of the Middle Ages*, Concord

Tabacco, Giovanni (1954), 'Privilegium amoris. Aspetti della spiritualità romualdina', *Il saggiatore* 4: 324–43

Tellenbach, Gerd (1928), *Die bischöflich passauischen Eigenklöster und ihre Vogteien* (Historische Studien 173), Berlin

(1963), 'Der Sturz des Abtes Pontius von Cluny und seine geschichtliche Bedeutung', *Quellen und Forschungen aus italienischen Archiven und Bibliotheken* 42–3: 13–55

(1993), *The Church in Western Europe from the Tenth to the Early Twelfth Century*, tr. Timothy Reuter, Cambridge

Temps (1984) = *Le temps chrétien de la fin de l'Antiquité au Moyen Age, III⁰–XIII⁰ siècles* (Colloques internationaux du Centre national de recherche scientifique 604), Paris

Tentler, Thomas (1983), 'Seventeen Authors in Search of Two Religious Cultures', *Catholic Historical Review* 71: 248–57

Théologie (1961) = *Théologie de la vie monastique. Etudes sur la tradition patristique* (Théologie. Etudes publiées sous la direction de la Faculté de théologie S.J. de Lyon-Fourvière 49), Paris

Thomas, Keith (1971), *Religion and the Decline of Magic: Studies in Popular Beliefs in Sixteenth and Seventeenth Century England*, New York

Thomas, Paul (1906), *Le droit de propriété des laïques sur les églises et le patronage laïque au moyen âge* (Bibliothèque de l'Ecole des hautes études. Sciences religieuses 19), Paris

Thomassin, Louis (1864–7), *Ancienne et nouvelle discipline de l'église*, ed. J.-F. André, Bar-le-Duc

Thompson, Alexander Hamilton (1919), 'Double Monasteries and the Male Element in Nunneries', in *The Ministry of Women: A Report by the Committee Appointed by his Grace the Lord Archbishop of Canterbury*, London, Appendix VIII, pp. 145–64

Thompson, Sally (1978), 'The Problem of the Cistercian Nuns in the Twelfth and Early Thirteenth Centuries', in *Medieval Women* (1978), pp. 227–52

Thoss, Dagmar (1972), *Studien zum 'locus amoenus' im Mittelalter* (Wiener romanistische Arbeiten 10), Vienna and Stuttgart

Tirot, Paul (1981), *Un 'Ordo missae' monastique: Cluny, Cîteaux, La Chartreuse* (Bibliotheca 'Ephemerides liturgicae'. Subsidia 21), Rome

Tönnies, Ferdinand (1909), *Die Sitte*, Frankfort

Toubert, Hélène (1983), 'Les fresques de la Trinité de Vendôme, un témoignage sur l'art de la réforme grégorienne', *Cahiers de civilisation médiévale* 26: 297–326

Toubert, Pierre (1973), *Les structures du Latium médiéval. Le Latium méridional et la Sabine du IXe siècle à la fin du XIIIe siècle* (Bibliothèque des Ecoles françaises d'Athènes et de Rome 221), Rome

(1977), 'Monachisme et encadrement religieux des campagnes en Italie aux Xe–XIIe siècles', in *Le istituzioni ecclesiastiche della 'Societas christiana' dei secoli XI–XII. Diocesi, pievi e parrocchie. Atti della sesta Settimana internazionale di studio Milano 1–7 settembre 1974* (Pubblicazioni dell'Università cattolica del Sacro Cuore: Miscellanea del Centro di studi medioevali 8), Milan, pp. 416–41

Trelcat, Emile (1924), *Histoire de l'abbaye de Crespin, ordre de saint Benoît*, Paris

Trinkaus, Charles E. (1970), *In Our Image and Likeness: Humanity and Divinity in Italian Humanist Thought*, London

Tüchle, Hermann (1950–4), *Kirchengeschichte Schwabens*, Stuttgart

Turk, Joseph (1948), *Cistercii statuta antiquissima* (Analecta sacri ordinis Cisterciensis 4.1–4), Vatican City

Turner, Victor (1972), 'Passages, Margins, and Poverty: Religious Symbols of Communities', *Worship* 40: 390–412 and 482–94

(1974a), *Dramas, Fields, and Metaphors: Symbolic Action in Human Society*, Ithaca and London

(1974b), 'Pilgrimages as Social Processes' (1973), repr. in Turner (1974a), pp. 166–230

(1974c), 'Social Dramas and Ritual Metaphors' (1971), repr. in Turner (1974a), pp. 23–59

Turner, Victor, and Turner, Edith (1978), *Image and Pilgrimage in Christian Culture: Anthropological Perspectives*, New York

Uhl, Bodo (1972), *Die Traditionen des Klosters Weihenstephan* (Quellen und Erörterungen zur bayerischen Geschichte N.F. 27.1), Munich

Uhlhorn, Gerhard (1894), 'Der Einfluss der wirtschaftlichen Verhältnisse auf die Entwicklung des Mönchtums im Mittelalter', *Zeitschrift für Kirchengeschichte* 14: 347–403

Valvekens, Jean-Baptiste (1961), 'Fratres et sorores "ad succurrendum" ', *Analecta praemonstratensia* 37: 323–8

Van Damme, Jean B. (1962), 'Formation de la constitution cistercienne', *Studia monastica* 4: 111–37

Van den Eynde, Damien (1950), 'On the Attribution of the "Tractatus de sacramento altaris" to Stephen of Baugé', *Franciscan Studies* 10: 33–45

(1960), *Essai sur la succession et la date des écrits de Hugues de Saint-Victor* (Spicilegium pontificii Athenaei Antoniani 13), Rome

(1962), 'Le recueil des sermons de Pierre Abélard', *Antonianum* 37: 17–54

Van Dijk, Stephen A. (1949), 'Historical Liturgy and Liturgical History', *Dominican Studies* 2: 161–82

(1950), 'Saint Bernard and the "Instituta patrum" of Saint Gall', *Musica disciplina* 4: 99–109

Van Engen, John H. (1980), 'Theophilus Presbyter and Rupert of Deutz: The Manual Arts and Benedictine Theology in the Early Twelfth Century', *Viator* 11: 147–63

(1983), *Rupert of Deutz* (Publications of the UCLA Center for Medieval and Renaissance Studies 18), Berkeley, Los Angeles, and London

(1986a), 'The Christian Middle Ages as an Historiographical Problem', *American Historical Review* 91: 519–52

(1986b), 'The "Crisis of Cenobitism" Reconsidered: Benedictine Monasticism in the Years 1050–1150', *Speculum* 61: 269–304

Van Gennep, Arnold (1935–6), *Le folklore de la Flandre et du Hainaut français* (Contributions au folklore des provinces de France 2), Paris

(1939), 'Patronages, chapelles et oratoires de la Haut-Maurienne', *Revue d'histoire de l'église de France* 25: 145–82

Van Haeften, Benedictus (1644), *S Benedictus illustratus sive disquisitionum monasticarum libri XII*, Antwerp

Van Moolenbroek, Jaap (1990), *Vital l'ermite, prédicateur itinérant, fondateur de l'abbaye normande de Savigny*, tr. Anne-Marie Nambot, Assen and Maastricht

Van Rijnberk, Gerard (1953), *Le langage par signes chez les moines*, Amsterdam

Vauchez, André (1975), *La spiritualité du moyen âge occidental, VIIIe–XIIe siècles* (Collection SUP. L'historien 19), Paris

Veissière, Michel (1961), *Un communauté canonicale au moyen âge. Saint-Quiriace de Provins (XIe–XIIe siècles)* (Société d'histoire et d'archéologie de l'arrondissement de Provins: Documents et travaux 1), Provins

Verheijen, Luc [Melchior] (1967), *La Règle de Saint Augustin*, Paris

Vexliard, Alexandre (1956), *Introduction à la sociologie du vagabondage* (Petite bibliothèque sociologique internationale), Paris

Vicaire, Marie-Humbert (1963), *L'imitation des apôtres. Moines, chanoines et mendiants, IVe–XIIIe siècles* (Tradition et spiritualité 2), Paris

Vidier, Alexandre (1906), 'Ermitages orléanais au XIIᵉ siècle. Le Gué de l'Orme et Chappes', *Le Moyen Age* 19 (2 S. 10): 57–96 and 134–56

Vignes, Bernard-Joseph-Marie (1928), 'Les doctrines économiques et morales de saint Bernard sur la richesse et le travail', *Revue d'histoire économique et social* 16: 547–85

Viller, Marcel, and Rahner, Karl (1939), *Aszese und Mystik in der Väterzeit*, Freiburg

Violante, Cinzio (1960), 'Il monachesimo cluniacense di fronte al mondo politico ed ecclesiastico (secoli X e XI)', in *Spiritualità cluniacense, 12–15 ottobre 1958* (Convegni del Centro di studi sulla spiritualità medievale 2), Todi, pp. 155–242

—— (1963), 'La chiesa bresciana nel medio evo', in *Storia di Brescia, I. Dalle origini alla caduta della signoria Viscontea (1426)*, Brescia, pp. 999–1124

—— (1968), 'Hérésies urbaines et hérésies rurales en Italie du 11ᵉ au 13ᵉ siècle', in *Hérésies et sociétés dans l'Europe pré-industrielle: 11ᵉ–18ᵉ siècles*, ed. Jacques Le Goff (Civilisations et sociétés 10), Paris and the Hague, pp. 171–97

—— (1977), 'Pieve e parrocchie nell'Italia centrosettentrionale durante i secoli XI e XII', in *Le istituzioni ecclesiastiche della 'Societas christiana' dei secoli XI–XII. Diocesi, pievi e parrocchie. Atti della sesta Settimana internazionale di studio, Milano 1–7 settembre 1974* (Pubblicazioni dell'Università cattolica del Sacro Cuore: Miscellanea del Centro di studi medioevali 8), Milan, pp. 643–799

—— (1979–81), 'Per una riconsiderazione della presenza cluniacense in Lombardia', in *Cluny in Lombardia* (1979–81), pp. 521–664

Vita comune (1962) = *La vita comune del clero nei secoli XI e XII. Atti della Settimana di studio, Mendola, settembre 1959* (Pubblicazioni dell'Università cattolica del Sacro Cuore, 3 S.: Scienze storiche 2–3. Miscellanea del Centro di studi medioevali 3), Milan

Vogüé, Adalbert de (1965), ' "Comment les moines dormiront". Commentaire d'un chapitre de la règle de saint Benoît', *Studia monastica* 7: 25–62

Vuillaume, Christophe (1991), 'La profession monastique, un second baptême', *Collectanea cisterciensia* 53: 275–92

Wada, Yoko (1994), *'Temptations' from the 'Ancrene Wisse'* (Kansai University. Institute of Oriental and Occidental Studies: Sources and Materials Series 18), Suita

Waddell, Chrysogonus (1971), 'The Early Cistercian Experience of Liturgy', in *Rule and Life: An Interdisciplinary Symposium*, ed. M. Basil Pennington (Cistercian Studies Series 12), Spencer, pp. 77–115

—— (1978), 'The "Exordium Cistercii" and the "Summa cartae caritatis" ', in *Cistercian Ideals and Realities*, ed. John R. Sommerfeldt (Cistercian Studies Series 60), Kalamazoo, pp. 30–61

—— (1983–5), *The Old French Paraclete Ordinary* (Cistercian Liturgy Series 3–4), Trappist

—— (1984), *The Twelfth-Century Cistercian Hymnal* (Cistercian Liturgy Series 1–2), Trappist

—— (1987), *The Paraclete Statutes: Institutiones nostrae* (Cistercian Liturgy Series 20), Trappist

—— (1992), 'The Clairvaux Saint Bernard Office: Ikon of a Saint', in *Bernardus Magister: Papers Presented at the Nonacentenary Celebration of the Birth of Saint Bernard of Clairvaux, Kalamazoo, Michigan*, ed. John R. Sommerfeldt (Cistercian Studies Series 135), Spencer and Cîteaux, pp. 381–427

(1993), 'Toward a New Provisional Edition of the Statutes of the Cistercian General Chapter c. 1119–1189', in *Studiosorum speculum: Studies in Honor of Louis J. Lekai, O.Cist*, ed. Francis Swietek and John Sommerfeldt (Cistercian Studies Series 141), Kalamazoo, pp. 381–419

(1994), 'The Cistercian Institutions and their Early Evolution', in *L'espace cistercien*, ed. Léon Pressouyre, Paris, pp. 27–38

Waha, Michel de (1978), 'Aux origines de Cîteaux. Rapports entre l'"Exordium Cistercii" et l'"Exordium parvum" ', in *Lettres latines du moyen âge et de la Renaissance*, ed. Guy Cambier, Carl Deroux, and Jean Préaux (Latomus 158), Brussels, pp. 152–82

Waites, Bryan (1961), 'The Monastic Grange as a Factor in the Settlement of North-East Yorkshire', *Yorkshire Archaeological Journal* 40: 627–56

(1967), *Moorland and Vale-Land Farming in North-East Yorkshire: The Monastic Contribution in the Thirteenth and Fourteenth Centuries* (University of York: Borthwick Institute of Historical Research, Borthwick Papers 32), York

Wakefield, Walter L., and Evans, Austin P. (1969), *Heresies of the High Middle Ages* (Records of Civilization 81), New York

Walter, Johannes von (1903–6), *Die ersten Wanderprediger Frankreichs*, I. *Robert von Arbrissel* (Studien zur Geschichte der Theologie und der Kirche 9.3), and II. *Bernhard von Thiron; Vitalis von Savigny; Girald von Salles; Bemerkungen zu Norbert von Xanten und Heinrich von Lausanne*, Leipzig

Walther, Hans (1920), *Das Streitgedicht in der lateinischen Literatur des Mittelalters* (Quellen und Untersuchungen zur lateinischen Philologie des Mittelalters 5.2), Munich

Ward, Benedicta (1976), 'The Desert Myth: Reflections on the Desert Ideal in Early Cistercian Monasticism', in *One Yet Two: Monastic Tradition East and West*, ed. M. Basil Pennington (Cistercian Studies Series 29), Kalamazoo, pp. 183–99

Ward, Herbert L.D., and Herbert, John A. (1883–1910), *Catalogue of Romances in the Department of Manuscripts in the British Museum*, London

Warichez, Joseph (1937), *Etienne de Tournai et son temps, 1128–1203*, Tournai and Paris

Warren, Ann K. (1985), *Anchorites and their Patrons in Medieval England*, Berkeley, Los Angeles, and London

Warren, Wilfred L. (1973), *Henry II*, Berkeley and Los Angeles

Wathen, Ambrose (1975), ' "Conversatio" and Stability in the Rule of Benedict', *Monastic Studies* 11: 1–44

Wattenbach, Wilhelm (1894), 'Magister Onulf von Speier', *Sitzungsberichte der königlich preussischen Akademie der Wissenschaften zu Berlin* 1894: 361–86

Weinfurter, Stefan (1977), 'Norbert von Xanten – Ordensstifter und "Eigenkirchenherr" ', *Archiv für Kirchengeschichte* 59: 66–98

(1980–1), 'Bemerkungen und Corrigenda zu Karl Bosls "Regularkanoniker und Seelsorge" ', *Archiv für Kirchengeschichte* 62–3: 381–95

Wenzel, Siegfried (1966), ' "Acedia" 700–1200', *Traditio* 22: 73–102

(1967), *The Sin of Sloth: Acedia in Medieval Thought and Literature*, Chapel Hill

Werner, Ernst (1953), *Die gesellschaftlichen Grundlagen der Klosterreform im 11. Jahrhundert*, Berlin

(1955), 'Zur Frauenfrage und zum Frauenkult im Mittelalter. Robert von Arbrissel und Fontevrault', *Forschungen und Fortschritte* 29: 269–76

(1956), *Pauperes Christi. Studien zu sozial-religiösen Bewegungen im Zeitalter des Reformpapsttums*, Leipzig

Wessley, Stephen E. (1990), *Joachim of Fiore and Monastic Reform* (American University Studies VII, 72), New York, Bern, Frankfurt, and Paris

West, Delno C. (1975), *Joachim of Fiore in Christian Thought*, New York

Wheaton, Robert (1975), 'Family and Kinship in Western Europe: The Problem of the Joint Family Household', *Journal of Interdisciplinary History* 5: 601–28

White, Hayden V. (1958), 'Pontius of Cluny, the "Curia Romana", and the End of Gregorianism in Rome', *Church History* 27: 195–219

(1960), 'The Gregorian Ideal and Saint Bernard of Clairvaux', *Journal of the History of Ideas* 21: 321–48

White, Lynn, Jr (1967), 'The Life of the Silent Majority', in *Life and Thought in the Early Middle Ages*, ed. Robert S. Hoyt, Minneapolis, pp. 85–100

White, Stephen D. (1988), *Custom, Kinship, and Gifts to Saints: The 'Laudatio Parentum' in Western France 1050–1150*, Chapel Hill and London

White, Stephen D., and Vann, Richard T. (1983), 'The Invention of English Individualism: Alan Macfarlane and the Modernization of Pre-Modern England', *Social History* 8: 345–63

Whitney, Marian P. (1923), 'Queen of Mediaeval Virtues: Largesse', in *Vassar Mediaeval Studies*, ed. Christabel F. Fiske, New Haven, pp. 183–215

Wichner, Jakob (1874–80), *Geschichte des Benediktiner-Stiftes Admont*, Admont

Wielers, Margret (1959), 'Zwischenstaatliche Beziehungsformen im frühen Mittelalter (Pax, Foedum, Amicitia, Fraternitas)' (Diss. Münster i. W.)

Wilkinson, Maire (1990), 'The "Vita Stephani Muretensis" and the Early Life of Stephen of Muret', in *Monastic Studies I*, ed. Judith Loades, Bangor, pp. 102–26

(1991), 'The "Vita Stephani Muretensis" and Papal Re-Constitution of the Order of Grandmont in 1186 and Thereafter', in *Monastic Studies II*, ed. Judith Loades, Bangor, pp. 133–55

Williams, David (1991), 'Layfolk within Cistercian Precincts', in *Monastic Studies II*, ed. Judith Loades, Bangor, pp. 87–117

Williams, George H. (1962), *Wilderness and Paradise in Christian Thought*, New York

Wilmart, André (1923), 'Les ordres du Christ', *Revue des sciences religieuses* 3: 305–27

(1928a), 'Une lettre inédite de S. Anselme à une moniale inconstante', *Revue bénédictine* 40: 319–32

(1928b), 'Le livre du chapitre de Saint'Ilario près Venise', *Revue bénédictine* 40: 235–42

(1932a), *Auteurs spirituels et textes dévots du moyen âge latin. Etudes d'histoire littéraire*, Paris

(1932b), 'Les ouvrages d'un moine de Bec. Un débat sur la profession monastique au XIIᵉ siècle', *Revue bénédictine* 44: 21–46

(1933a), 'La collection d'Ebrach', *Revue bénédictine* 45: 312–31

(1933b), 'L'appel à la vie cartusienne, suivant Guigues l'ancien', *Revue d'ascétique et de mystique* 14: 337–48

(1934 and 1938), 'Eve et Goscelin', *Revue bénédictine* 46: 414–38 and 50: 42–83

Winandy, Jacques (1960), 'Conversatio morum', *Collectanea ordinis Cisterciensium reformatorum* 22: 378–86

Wirges, Johannes (1928), *Die Anfänge der Augustiner-Chorherren und die Gründung des Augustiner-Chorherrenstiftes Ravengiersburg (Hunsrück) Diözese Trier*, Betzdorf

Wirth, Louis (1938), 'Urbanism as a Way of Life', *American Journal of Sociology* 44: 1–24

Wischermann, Else Marie (1986), *Marcigny-sur-Loire. Gründungs- und Frühgeschichte des ersten Cluniacenserinnenpriorates (1055–1150)* (Münstersche Mittelalter-Schriften 42), Munich

Wiswe, Hans (1953), 'Grangien niedersächsischer Zisterzienserklöster. Entstehung und Bewirtschaftung spätmittelalterlich-frühneuzeitlicher landwirtschaftlicher Grossbetriebe', *Braunschweigisches Jahrbuch* 34: 5–134

Wittmer-Butsch, Maria Elisabeth (1990), *Zur Bedeutung von Schlaf und Traum im Mittelalter* (Medium aevum quotidianum 1), Krems

Wolff, Robert Lee (1978), 'How the News was Brought from Byzantium to Angoulême; or, The pursuit of a Hare in an Ox Cart', in *Essays Presented to Sir Steven Runciman* (Byzantine and Modern Greek Studies 4), Oxford, pp. 139–89

Wollasch, Joachim (1961), 'Muri und St. Blasien. Perspektiven schwäbischen Mönchtums in der reform', *Deutsches Archiv* 17: 420–46

(1967), 'Ein cluniacensisches Totenbuch aus der Zeit Abt Hugos von Cluny', *Frühmittelalterliche Studien* 1: 406–43

(1973a), *Mönchtum des Mittelalters zwischen Kirche und Welt* (Münstersche Mittelalter-Schriften 7), Munich

(1973b), 'Reform und Adel in Burgund', in *Investiturstreit und Reichsverfassung* (Vorträge und Forschungen 17), Sigmaringen, pp. 277–93

(1973c), 'Neue Quellen zur Geschichte der Cistercienser', *Zeitschrift für Kirchengeschichte* 84: 188–232

(1979), 'Les obituaires, témoins de la vie clunisienne', *Cahiers de civilisation médiévale* 22: 139–71

(1980), 'Parenté noble et monachisme réformateur. Observations sur les "conversions" à la vie monastique aux XIᵉ et XIIᵉ siècles', *Revue historique* 264: 3–24

(1982), *Synopse der cluniacensischen Necrologien* (Münstersche Mittelalter-Schriften 39.1–2), Munich

(1985), 'Sulla presenza cluniacense in Germania', in *L'Italia nel quadro dell'espansione europea del monachesimo cluniacense. Atti del Convegno internazionale di storia medioevale. Pescia 26–28 novembre 1981* (Italia benedettina 8), Cesena, pp. 327–51

(1987), 'Markgraf Hermann und Bischof Gebhard III. von Konstanz. Die Zähringer und die Reform der Kirche', in *Die Zähringer in der Kirche des 11. und 12. Jahrhunderts*, ed. Karl Suso Frank, Munich and Zürich, pp. 27–53

(1992), 'Cluny und Deutschland', *Studien und Mitteilungen zur Geschichte des Benediktiner-Ordens und seiner Zweige* 103: 7–32

Wolpers, Theodor (1964), *Die englische Heiligenlegende des Mittelalters. Eine Formgeschichte des Legendenerzählens von der spätantiken lateinischen Tradition bis zur Mitte des 16. Jahrhunderts* (Anglia Buchreihe 10), Tübingen

Yeo, Richard (1982), *The Structure and Content of Monastic Profession* (Studia Anselmiana 83), Rome

Yver, Jean (1963–4), 'Autour de l'absence d'avouerie en Normandie. Notes sur le double thème du développement du pouvoir ducal et de l'application de la réforme grégorienne en Normandie', *Bulletin de la Société des antiquaires de Normandie* 57: 189–283

Zafarana, Zelina (1966), 'Ricerche sul "Liber de unitate ecclesiae conservanda" ', *Studi medievali* 3 S. 7: 617–700

Zarnecki, George (1954), 'The Chichester Reliefs', *Archaeological Journal* 110: 106–19

Zimmermann, Gerd (1958–9), 'Patrozinienwahl und Frömmigkeitswandel im Mittelalter dargestellt an Beispielen aus dem alten Bistum Würzburg', *Würzburger Diözesangeschichtsblätter* (1) 20: 24–126 and (2) 21: 5–124

(1973), *Ordensleben und Lebensstandard. Die 'Cura corporis' in den Ordensvorschriften des abendländischen Hochmittelalters* (Beiträge zur Geschichte des alten Mönchtums und des Benediktinerordens 32), Münster i. W.

Zorzi, Diego (1954), *Valori religiosi nella letteratura provenzale. La spiritualità trinitaria* (Pubblicazioni dell'Università cattolica del S. Cuore N.S. 44), Milan

INDEX OF PAPAL DOCUMENTS

References are to the numbers in Jaffé, *Regesta* (see Abbreviations).

BIBLICAL INDEX

All references are to the Vulgate and to the Douai translation of the Bible.

388

GENERAL INDEX

The following abbreviations are used: abp = archbishop, abt = abbot, bp = bishop, card.= cardinal, emp.= emperor. St (= Saint) is used only when there is no other identification. Some supplementary information has been added to assist in identification, but a few references to people and places cited primarily as examples have been omitted. For original sources, either the author or the subject, as for hagiographies, has as a rule been cited, but not both.

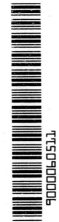